The Dutch Reformation

THE

DUTCH REFORMATION:

A HISTORY

OF THE STRUGGLE IN THE NETHERLANDS
FOR CIVIL AND RELIGIOUS LIBERTY,

IN

THE SIXTEENTH CENTURY.

BY W. CARLOS MARTYN,

AUTHOR OF "A HISTORY OF THE ENGLISH PURITANS," "A HISTORY
OF THE HUGUENOTS," ETC., ETC.

PUBLISHED BY THE
AMERICAN TRACT SOCIETY,
150 NASSAU-STREET, NEW YORK.

PREFACE.

THE Anglo-Saxons and the Dutch are cousins-
german. The records of their respective histories
are of mutual interest. To thoughtful Americans
the annals of the Netherlands are of special concern. It was in Holland that British Protestantism
found an asylum in the Marian epoch; it was in
Holland that New England was conceived; it was
in Holland that some of the stoutest of the colonial
immigrants were cradled; it was in Holland that
our statesmen of '76 sought the model of the Fed-
eral Republic.

Nor do these links, strong and sufficient in themselves, form the whole sympathetic chain. Regulated liberty comes to us as much from the Low
Countries as from England. In the sixteenth century the Dutch soil was the battle-ground of human
progress: when the Reformation was guaranteed
there, it was won for Christendom.

That struggle was a long conspiracy of king and
priest against religion and the masses. For a time
it was local. On the one side the empire of the
mediæval Cæsars, aggrandized by a multitude of
dependencies, cis and trans Atlantic, rich beyond
the dreams of Crœsus, puissant as the fabled Hercules; on the other side a group of cities governed
by merchants and advocates— "these regarding
profit, those standing upon vantage of quirks," as
Walsingham sneered; precariously planted on an un-

stable and meagre soil. Spain was strong in every
thing but justice; the Netherlands were weak in all
save right. In the end, weak right conquered
strong injustice. Spanish veterans, Italian *condot-
tieri*, German mercenaries, papal bulls, Mexican
gold mines—all were pressed into service against
the striving spirit of Dutch independence, only to
be transformed, one after another, into stepping-
stones to liberty and an empire world-embracing,
when the hand of the Spaniard was palsied in de-
crepitude. 'T is a lesson worthy the conning.

As the war went on it became of European importance. Distinctions of nationalities were lost.
Morally, there were but two nations in existence—
that of Protestantism and that of the popes; for it
was primarily a religious war. It took a sanction
from the much-prized burgher-charters, but the new
theology vivified the old dead forms. It is impossible to understand the Reformation era without a
familiarity with this, its grandest chapter; a fact
which gives the story an indisputable claim upon
the attention of all thoughtful men.

These pages undertake to photograph this agony
of the Netherlands—fighting and conquering not for
themselves alone, but for humanity. And as the
struggle was inspired by the gospel, this narrative
is written from the evangelical standpoint of the
actors in it—an *entente cordiale* which is never broken. The volume opens with a description of the
primitive condition of the provinces, analyzes the
causes of the revolt against Madrid and the Vatican, details somewhat minutely the events of the
first decade of the prolonged contest, and closes at

the Union of Utrecht: not that the interest ends
with that achievement, not that the war there furls
its banners, but because that act assured the Reformation, and because thereafter fierce internal strifes
began, sect raving against sect, each "swearing a
prayer or two" against the other, a quarrel neither
proper nor desirable for these sheets to depict;
therefore a few paragraphs summarize the later history of the republic.

It would be impossible conscientiously to write
a history of the Dutch Reformation without a thorough examination of the original records *pro* and
con. Accordingly all the leading contemporary
chronicles and pamphlets of Holland, Flanders,
Spain, France, Germany, and England have been
studied—at least all obtainable in this country, very
many more than any one not acquainted with the
facts would suspect. These have been supplemented by a liberal use of the works of the Netherland
archivists, and by citations from a multitude of
comparatively recent writers where these seemed
likely to enhance the interest or enlighten the doubts
of the narrative. ·For every statement of fact, authority, volume and page, is given. Possibly the
imputation of tediousness and pedantry may be
hereby incurred; but that has been esteemed as
nothing compared with the importance of an impregnable fortification of the text.

The many friends who have lent their personal
aid and their libraries to this work, are most cordially thanked.

Wherever it was possible, the actors in this
drama have been summoned to the witness-stand

and made to tell their own story in their own words; for what basis can compare with that afforded by the written correspondence of the parties themselves? "I have long believed," says Ruskin, "that *restored* history is of little more value than restored painting or architecture; that the only history worth reading is that written at the time of which it treats, the history of what was done, and seen, heard out of the mouths of men who did and saw· One fresh draught of such history is worth a thousand volumes of abstracts and reasonings and suppositions and theories." Without accepting this *dictum* in its fullest sense, it may be conceded to carry a modicum of truth. The facts of history may be chalked down by the chronicler; the hidden causes of great movements—at the best but indistinctly and uncertainly—may be traced by the philosophic historian; but the spirit, the aroma, even the outward form of a picturesque age, can only be caught from the vivid, impassioned, roughshod writers of the time.

Such a history of the Dutch Reformation—full, yet sufficiently compendious for general circulation, has long been a *desideratum*. Of course, this work falls sadly short of its aim; but it is at least an honest attempt to focus and to popularize a marvellous story; one of which the sages of the Porch and the Grove in the great days of Athens would have loved to speak to their disciples, had Christian hearts beaten within their breasts; one which requires the pencil of a lineal descendant of Livy or of Tacitus to do it justice.

New York, 1868.

CONTENTS.

CHAPTER I.

CHAPTER II.

CHAPTER III.

CHAPTER IV.

CHAPTER V.

CHAPTER VI.

CHAPTER VII.

CHAPTER VIII.

CHAPTER IX.

CHAPTER X.

CHAPTER XL

CHAPTER XII.

CHAPTER XIII.

CHAPTER XIV.

CHAPTER XV.

CHAPTER XVI.

CHAPTER XVII.

CHAPTER XVIII.

CHAPTER XIX.

CHAPTER XX.

CHAPTER XXI.

CHAPTER XXII.

CHAPTER XXIII.

CHAPTER XXIV.

CHAPTER XXV.

CHAPTER XXVI.

CHAPTER XXVII.

CHAPTER XXX.

CHAPTER XXXI.

CHAPTER XXXII.

CHAPTER XXXIII.

CHAPTER XXXIV.

CHAPTER XXXV.

CHAPTER XXXVI.

CHAPTER XXXVII.

CHAPTER XXXVIII.

CHAPTER XXXIX.

CHAPTER XL.

CHAPTER XLI.

CHAPTER XLII.

•

CHAPTER XLIII.

THE

DUTCH REFORMATION.

————————

CHAPTER I.

THE "DEBATABLE LAND."

THERE is a gore of land in the extreme north-western corner of Europe which juts out into the German ocean, and seems, like Venus, to have just risen fresh and blooming from the sea-foam. Indeed, it can hardly be said to have arisen from the waves, for it is all afloat. The land is full of lakes, or the lakes are full of land—you may phrase it which way you please. 'T is an amphibious country: its legs are water; its body is a spongy soil; its arms are ships; its veins are canals; its eyes are schools and churches; its crown is liberty—for though of late years it has had a king, he is but a name, and the state is in fact as free as Switzerland.

Holland is the modern sphinx; everything about it is unique and unprecedented. Nothing could be more prosaic than a sail along its long, low, sandy coast, which hugs the sea so closely that

you cannot see it until you are within a stone's toss.
But, once landed, nothing could be more bewilder-
ing, strange, and picturesque than the buoyant,
breathing, thrifty landscape which salutes you. You
seem to have entered an enchanted garden. Canals,
spanned by ten thousand bridges, creep with their
sluggish waters before and behind, to the right
and to the left, interlacing the whole scene. The
smooth, clean roads are embroidered with willows,
and gemmed with beautiful suburban villas. Teem-
ing cities and thriving villages—the wealthiest
towns of continental Europe—vivify and humanize
the landscape. The laughter of trade is heard.
The commerce of two hemispheres crowds the harbors. The land seems bursting with prosperity.
Here runs a river, floating a flock of boats to market; there a church-steeple peers and beckons;
yonder stands a group of happy citizens, chatting,
and motioning to a canal-boat captain to pause
and take them on board; and beyond looms a sentinel windmill, scooping up the ever-encroaching
water with its tireless fingers, waging its never-
ending combat with the complaining sea, spoiled of
its rights.

That plain which touches France on one side
and Prussia on the other, shelves towards the northwest, and ends in a marsh. Here sits Holland—a
made country, a land of art. It is simply an alluvial deposit, washed by the Rhine and its tributa-
ries from the Alpine regions of the interior—mud,
sinking to the bottom of the sea and rising with the

gradual accumulations of ages into arid sandbanks,
which the skill and grim persistence of the Hollander have transformed into fat and fertile pas-
tures. Much of the land lies lower than the ocean
level. At such points artificial dykes have been
constructed and laced with willows, to bar the outwitted sea.

The coast being thus secured, the Hollander
next begins to pump out his half-submerged country; and he realizes dry ground by raising low,
green mounds in all directions across the morass,
so as to enclose sections or fields, which may be
cleared by the individual proprietors. Each of
these leaky enclosures has wet ditches cut all
around it and through its centre; then, for the purpose of drawing off the water and keeping it in
subjection, windmills are stationed to work pumps;
and these, set in motion by the wind, drain the soil,
and send the reluctant water in channels along the
tops of the dykes to the main canals, which inter-
sect the country on a level with the sea; while the
Dutchman rests in peace, knowing that "Fatherland" is made safer by the passage of each breeze.
At times man has been momentarily beaten in this
terrific conflict between human intelligence and the
blind force of the elements; then, surging over these
frail barriers, the jubilant sea has roared and tum-
bled, swamping villages, and drowning in an hour
the toilsome acquisitions of long centuries.

The whole country is a dead level, broken only
by an occasional mound of sand; but it is so cun-

ningly filled up and variegated, so brimful of odd
sights, that it is impossible to call it monotonous.
From any point it is possible to command a picturesque *coup d'œil*. If we were in Amsterdam, by
ascending to the dome of the Stadt-house, we might
gaze upon a highly-finished and curious picture,
rich with the fragrancy of meadows and the beauty
of the abounding flower-gardens; or, if we stood in
Rotterdam, we might ascend a lofty tower, and look
down upon the buzzing city, and glance off to the
country beyond—a delightful background, cultivated like a continued garden, and stretching away
to the misty horizon.

Looking southward across the city, we should
perceive the river Maas winding majestically on-
wards to the sea, with the rich plains of Isselmonde
on the opposite side, and the towering dome of the
old church at Dort in the distance. Turning towards the northwest, we might see the sea-bordered
territory of Holland spread out as far as the human
eye could reach. The steeples of the towns of Schie-
dam and Delft would seem quite at hand; while the
spires of the Hague, more distant, might be discerned rising above the mass of trees which veil the
horizon. Gouda lies more in a southerly direction;
while innumerable little villages, sprinkled over the
scene, and hundreds of windmills revolving in every
direction, would serve to decorate and animate the
landscape. Everywhere we should see water; and
then the land, so singularly flat, yet so rich and
pastoral, would be flecked here and there with

straggling herds of those beautifully spotted cattle which Paul Potter loved so well to paint.*

But the most wonderful feature of this marvellous country is its history. Springing from a few fisher-boats on a dreary coast, it grew gradually stronger, in arms, in intelligence, in wealth, until it would brook no superior by land and could have none by sea. The Hollander first created his "Fatherland," and then, standing on piles, conjured modern commerce into being. With territory just wide enough to give him elbow-room, he monopolized for centuries the trade of the world, and annexed continents as coffers wherein to garner his wealth, patching out his little country with vast colonial possessions, until he held a principality greater than Christendom before had known. In the darkest ages he was the merchant, the trader, the manufacturer of Europe. His municipal system was the germ of republicanism. His cities struck the key-note of civilization, resuscitating the industrial arts, and bequeathing to mankind that idea of union which begets and assures liberty.

For a thousand years the Netherlands† were the camping ground of Europe; their whole existence was a fight; and nobles of every nationality sped thither to flesh their maiden swords and to win their spurs. "Mars," says Strada, "only trav-

* Many of the facts above cited, and some bits of description, are taken from W. Chambers' Tour in Holland in 1838; London, 1839; and from an old volume, entitled "A Tour in Holland, by an American;" Worcester, 1790.

† From the Dutch, *Neider land, under land,* or low country.

2*

els other countries, and carries about a running
war, but here he seats himself.   Beyond poetic
miracles, we have not only fought with man, but
with mighty rivers; and not alone with these, but,
breaking the cloister of the sea, we have challenged
the ocean itself.   We walk upon the water as if it
were firm ground; we let in the sea to make the
land navigable, fighting in both elements at once."*

But it was in the sixteenth century, which Schiller calls "the brightest of the world's epochs,"† that
the Netherlands played the sublimest part.   The
backbone of that struggle was religion.   When
France was rent by faction, when Germany cowered, when England stood lukewarm, when the rest
of Europe was actively hostile to reform, Holland
espoused it—struck the tocsin of resistance to civil
and religious tyranny.   The gallant little territory
collected its scattered energies, and flung its whole
being into the spasm of its effort.   It was humanity
agonizing for its noblest rights; and "the resources
of resolute despair" triumphed in this unequal contest with a king who was the Crœsus of modern
times; who coined his gold in "either Ind;" who
had Spain and Germany for his fulcrum; whose
anathema-maranatha was the awful malediction of
the church of Rome.

If we would understand effects, we must study
them through the medium of causes.   Events, like
Hebrew, are to be read backwards.   A cursory re-

---

* Strada, Hist. of the Low Country Wars.   London, 1650.
† Schiller, Hist. of the Revolt of the Netherlands.

view of the rise and progress of the Netherlands
before the dawn of the second birth in the sixteenth
century, will help us to solve the riddle of that age;
familiarize us with the mainsprings of Holland's
action, with the *rationale* of her development, with
the causes of her revolution; tell us why, though
Spain won battles and the Dutch Republic lost
them, every victory brought tyranny only nearer to
defeat; how Holland was snatched half drowned
from the Netherland morass, and girt with beneficent sovereignty; and we shall learn that the secret
of this Samson's strength was in the well-thumbed
Bible.

Our earliest glimpse of the Netherlands is gotten through Roman eyes. Half a century before
the Christian era, Rome, while pushing her triumphal car around the world, stumbled upon these
marshy meadows, and paused to gather the reluctant inhabitants into her heterogeneous retinue of
conquest, dragging them into history.

The Low Countries were then a huge bog—"a
wide morass, in which oozy islands and savage forests were interspersed among lagoons and shallows." This misshapen mudbank was born of three
rivers, the Rhine, the Meuse, and the Scheldt, which
had been for ages spitting their slimy deposit
among the dunes and sandbars heaved up by the
ocean about their mouths.

It is impossible to portray the geography of the
Low Countries at the period of the Roman invasion. The coasts were mere slime-banks; inland,

trees might be seen, but they were rooted in a soil so marshy, that an inundation or a tempest threw down whole forests; and these are still sometimes discovered imbedded ten feet below the surface of the earth.* The sea had no limits, the rivers no beds nor banks, the earth no solidity, and there was not a spot of ground which did not yield beneath human footsteps.†

Pliny the naturalist once visited the Netherlands, and he has left us a dreary portrait of their aspect. "There," he says, "the ocean pours in its flood twice every day, and produces a perpetual uncertainty whether the country may be considered as part of the continent or of the sea. The wretched inhabitants take refuge on sand-hills or in little huts, which they construct on the summits of lofty stakes, whose elevation is conformable to that of the highest tides. When the sea rises, they appear like navigators; when it retires, they seem as though they had been shipwrecked. They subsist on the fish left by the refluent waters, and which they catch in nets formed of rushes or seaweed. On the shore is neither tree nor shrub. The people drink rain-water; and their fuel is a kind of turf, which they gather and form with the hand."‡

In geography and ethnography the Netherlands belong partly to Gaul and partly to Germany. The Belgian provinces stretch out the right hand of fel-

---

* Grattan, Hist. of the Netherlands, p. 3.
† Eumenius, Paneg. Const. Cæs.
‡ Pliny, Hist. Nat., lib. 16.

lowship to the Gallic tribes; Holland is Saxon, and the Dutchman is the nearest blood relative of the Anglo-Saxon race.*   This difference of race was as marked eighteen centuries ago as it is to-day. Tacitus noted it; and it is a fact which has colored the whole history of Europe:

The Celt and the Saxon were alike physically; they were equally brave; and the Roman annalists bear the most glowing testimony to their valor.† But in their social customs they were dissimilar, and in their theology they did not agree.   The Gaul was superstitious and priest-ridden; he worshipped a thousand blood-stained deities.   The German held to a single supreme, almighty God—too sublime to be imaged, too infinite to be enclosed in earthly temples, visible always to the reverent eye of faith.   Such is the Roman's testimony to the lofty conception of the Saxon.‡ And such were the Netherlands in their physical aspect and in their native tribes, when Cæsar essayed to leash them to his car of conquest.

* Motley, Gibbon, Hume, Grattan.
† See Cæsar's Comm. de Bell. Gall. Annu. Marcel., 15, 12, 1. Tacitus.
‡ Motley, vol. 1, p. 9.

CHAPTER II.

THE NETHERLANDS IN EMBRYO.

WHEN, some twoscore years before Christ, imperial Cæsar, having subjugated Celtic Gaul, paused
to wipe the perspiration from his brow, he was told
that the warlike tribes to the northeast, who made
their lair in the tangled patches of the Ardennes
wood, had refused to accept his alliance or to
implore his protection.   At once the conqueror
pushed his legions into the Netherlands.   Here he
was met by a swarm of separate tribes, each of
which, however, was allied to one of three great
nations who then occupied the morass.

The district which stretches from the Scheldt
to the Rhine, embracing substantially the modern
territory of Belgium, was inhabited by a hardy race
of warriors—men who ranged the interminable forests without a fixed home, indebted to rude agriculture and the chase for their livelihood.*   These
were the Belgians.

Beyond the Belgic flats, on the old island of
Batavia,† was another people, the Batavi,‡ fierce
even beyond their savage neighbors, whose occupa-

---

* Div. Cass. lib. 4. Cæsar, Comm. de Bell. Gall.
† Tacitus, de Mar. Ger.   The name comes from *Bet-ana,*
"good meadow."
‡ Ibid. Grattan, Motley.

tion was also war—a race which aforetime had streamed from the German highlands.*

Still farther north, in what is now North Holland, dwelt yet another nation, the Frisians, a nation of fishermen—of nascent traders, uniting the distinctive qualities of merchants and navigators; moderate, sincere, slow but sure, and implacable in anger, when once aroused. Their more southern neighbors were more inflammable, quicker to strike, and fiercer, but they were less steady and more ambitious; for they were rovers, while the fishermen sat contented on their piles, made slow progress towards civilization, thought little of conquest, and gave their thoughts chiefly to the improvement of their country.†

Like the Germans, whose blood they shared, the Frisians lodged sovereignty in the people— built it upon the basis of individualism. At the full of the moon the popular assemblies met and legislated, electing their chiefs and deciding mooted points of policy.‡ Almost alone among barbarians, they were not addicted to polygamy;§ and among them there were no slaves but their prisoners of war, and a few unfortunates who had gambled away their liberty ‖—for gambling, one of the most deep-rooted and pernicious of the vices, was even then the curse of mankind, and as much in vogue

---

* Pliny, Berlier, Préc. de l'Ancienne Gaule.
† Grotius, de Antiquitate Reip. Batav.
‡ Ibid. Davies, Hist. of Holland.
§ Ibid. Motley, vol. 1, p. 10.   ‖ Ibid.

in the Netherland marshes as in the civilized haunts of the profligate Romans.*

The Belgians and the Batavians knew nothing of this primitive democracy. Their polity recognized three classes, nobles, priests, and pariahs; and Cæsar testifies that their commonalty were all slaves.† In war, the nobles led their retainers to battle; in peace, the Druids, the bloodiest of priesthoods, governed.‡

These were the races whom Cæsar had come to subdue. They defended their liberty with headlong valor; but discipline was invincible, and the hapless barbarians could only die sword in hand. Across these warm corpses stepped the grim Roman, and on he pushed, gaining now by his arms and now by his arts, until eventually he either conquered all opposition, or seduced it into his alliance.§ First, the Belgians were subdued;‖ then the Batavians submitted, and entering the Roman service, became the most renowned cavalrymen of the empire, often clutching victory from the jaws of defeat.¶ "Others," says Tacitus, "go to battle; these go to war;" and we are told how the Dacians were terrified by the wild courage of these untamed horsemen, as they saw them in full armor plunge into and swim across the Danube.**

○ See Davies, vol. 1, p. 13.
† Cæsar, de Bell. Gall.
‡ Motley, vol. 1, p. 8.   Grattan, Davies.
§ Cæsar, de Bell. Gall.   Tacitus, de Mar, etc., cap. 29.
‖ Ibid.   ¶ Tacitus, Hist.
** Schiller, Hist. of the Revolt of the Netherlands, p. 2.

The Frisians attracted attention later, and the bogs among which they dwelt enhanced the price of conquest.   But at last they too yielded, and their country was made the pedestal of farther conquest; for "the Roman Darsus, warring in these swamps, cut a canal from the Rhine into the Flevo— now merged in the Zuyder Zee—through which the imperial fleet penetrated into the German ocean, and thence, entering the mouths of the Ems and the Weser, found an easy passage into the interior of Germany."*

Now, for a time, the Netherlands were united in their servitude to Rome, and the old Belgic tumults were pacified in a gilded slavery.   At once a metamorphosis commenced.   The cunning conquerors began to eradicate all feelings of nationality in the victim races.   They dazzled their rude auxiliaries with the splendor of their capital, encouraged them to identify themselves with the world's masters, gave them Roman names, enervated them by initiating them into dissolute customs; and thus the young Netherland adventurers returned, after twenty years' service under the imperial eagles, and walked their native wilds with Roman hearts and tastes.   Gradually the forests of the Ardennes were pierced with highways and cleared for towns; and these innovations completed the amalgamation of the allies; nationality was obliterated, or merged in the all-devouring epithet, "Roman."   The Belgians began to borrow the

○ Schiller, Hist. of the Revolt of the Netherlands, p. 2.

usages and to ape the manners of Italy, and they finished by speaking Latin.*

The Batavians did indeed make one expiring effort to preserve their nationality as they saw it fading from history. Claudius Civilis, a Batavian soldier of fortune, who had studied war under the Roman eagles, is the phantom who flashes as the hero of this revolt. The confederacy was at first successful; the pillars of the prison-house began to totter; a commonwealth was well-nigh cemented by the courage and talent and eloquence of a single chieftain. But reverses followed; the frail confederacy fell apart like a rope of sand; the lowland mate of the German Arminius saw that his cause was shipwrecked, and held out only to coerce honorable terms; these were granted, and the Batavians once more became the allies of Rome in the latter half of the first Christian century†—an alliance which proved fatal to their existence. They became rapidly degenerate; and when, a hundred and fifty years later, the Franks overran their island, they said with a jeer: "The Batavians are not a nation; they are only a prey."‡

But this transformation was confined to the Belgic provinces—did not cross the Rhine. Isolated by their position, the Frisians were not corrupted by the Romans. They were of the Saxon race—a blood of unconquerable vitality, giving, not taking

---

° Grattan, Hist. of the Netherlands, p. 9. Des Roches, Hist. de la Belgique.

† Tacitus, Motley, etc.   ‡ Tacitus, lib. 4.

its color.   So the Frisian made an obeisance to
the victorious eagles of the empire, and there stop-
ped; he never intermarried with his conquerors;
he despised the super-refinement of the Sybarite
Italians, and

> "Left to the soft Campanian
> His baths and his perfumes;

he hugged the memory of his murdered liberty; he
clung with fidelity to his ancient customs; he adhered to his language with religious care; he stood
aloof from the Roman ranks; he rejected the titles
and distinctions for which others bartered independence; he asked no favors, and trusted solely
to industry for support, educating himself through
the stomach, by an incessant contest with famine
and the sea; and, spite of its original unattractive-
ness, as the Switzer loves his icy crags, so the Frisian adored his boggy "Fatherland."

The Frisians of the age of Tiberius and Vespasian differed little from their fathers, who,
perched on their high-built huts, fed on fish and
drank the water of the clouds.   Slow and successive
improvements had taught them to cultivate beans,
which grew wild among the marshes, and to tend
and feed a small, degenerate kind of horned cattle.
But if these first steps towards civilization were
slow, they were certain; and they were taken by a
race who never walked backward.*

The Menapians, as that portion of the Frisians
were called who occupied the west bank of the

* Grattan, Hist. of the Netherlands, p. 7.

Meuse, becoming at a later day the Flemings,* were a maritime people in the earliest ages, and had carried on a commercial intercourse with England from time immemorial. The staple article of this primitive traffic was salt, which they manufactured and exported in vast quantities.† They also understood the preparation of salted meat, which they did with such perfection that it became of high repute even in Italy; and Ptolemy tells us that they had planted a colony on the eastern coast of Ireland, in the twilight of the world.‡

So marked was the difference between the races who inhabited the Netherlands when Vespasian wore the purple. The southron was brave, impulsive, frank, but fickle; he was the shuttlecock of his time, and whoever held the battledore might buffet him which way he pleased. He took impressions easily, and any plastic hand might mould him.

The northener was cool, phlegmatic, calculating, self-dependent, untiring. He was able and determined to develop himself. The civilization of Italy he never accepted, for it suited neither his taste nor his genius. Like his country, he was self-made, and he grew his own civilization.

This hardy and intrepid race were mariners by instinct; and when once possessed of the coast-line, they did not seek to make the least progress

---

* Grattan, Hist. of the Neth., p. 7.   Motley, Davies, Grotius.
† Gibbon, Grattan, Grotius, Van Loon, Alande Hist.
‡ Des Roches, Hist. de la Belgique.

towards the interior. The element of their enterprise, the object of their ambition, was the ocean.
When they became too numerous for their narrow
limits, they sent off the redundant population to
colonize new regions.* When their veins became
too full, the blood spouted in expeditions.   Thus
Saxon warriors seated themselves at the mouth of
the Loire; thus Hengist and Horsa crossed the sea
into England, departing, as it has been conjectured,
from the Netherlands.†

The domination of the empire in the Netherlands continued upwards of five centuries.   Then
Rome, gouty with excess, dizzy with license, staggered to its grave. The empire lost its cohesive
power long before it crumbled.   "Stately, exter-
nally powerful, but undermined, putrescent at the
core, and death-stricken," nothing sustained it for
a century but the ghost of its former prowess.
Soon prying eyes detected this hidden weakness.
"I am a Roman citizen" ceased to be a passport
and a palladium; and at length jubilant barbarism
swooped to the sack of the Eternal City. "It was
the opening of the fountains of the frozen North;
and the waters prevailed, but the ark of Christianity floated upon the flood. As the deluge subsided,
the earth returned to chaos, the great pagan empire
was washed out of existence, but the dim, groping,
faltering, ignorant infancy of Christian Europe
began."‡

Then came what Schiller terms "the epoch of

* Grattan, p. 14.   † Ibid.   ‡ Motley, vol. 1, p. 19.

the immigration of nations "*—the nomadic age.
Europe was redivided. A confused horde of barbarous tribes quarreled over, and fought for the
possession of, the disjointed fragments of the
Roman empire. Gradually from these ruins rose a
new monarchy, that of the Franks.† Like their
Roman prototypes, they too aspired to universal
empire. In order to that, it was necessary to subjugate at the outset the adjacent territory. So the
Netherlands once again shook beneath hostile footsteps. The Belgians, already Romanized, were again
denationalized, and with the pliancy of old days,
they easily accommodated themselves to the new
régime, becoming as enthusiastically French, under
the pressure of necessity, as they had been Latin.‡

The Frisians—who had resumed their independence on the fall of Rome, erecting a nation whose
limits were nearly commensurate with those of the
Dutch Republic in after-days§—prepared for a desperate resistance. The death-tug continued through
the sixth and seventh centuries; nor did it terminate definitely until Charlemagne throttled Friesland.‖

Evil is the pioneer of good. War has been
finely called religion's "hewer of wood and drawer
of water." It is the clearer of choked channels,
the unknowing smiter of organized falsehood; in

○ Schiller, p. 364.
† Ibid., p. 364. Davies, Grattan, Grotius, Van Loon.
‡ Grattan, Hist. of the Netherlands, p. 14. Grotius.
§ Ibid. Motley, vol. 1, p. 20. Van Loon.
‖ Grotius, de Antiq. Reip. Batav.

twilight ages, the only light we see is the sabre's gleam.   And so now this epoch sowed gospel seed. The Franks, hewing their way to empire, opened a gap for the Bible.   Nominal Christianity was planted in the Netherlands—*nominal* Christianity, for it had been already emasculated and burdened with a host of idle ceremonies, and half-paganized by its adoption of the heathen dogmas of the Academicians.   Even thus early the bishopric of Rome had assumed dictatorial powers, and put the triple crown upon its brow.   The Eternal City, sighing for the sceptre of old days, said with the Greek, " The trophies of Miltiades will not let me sleep ;" and her ambitious prelates schemed—successfully, as the sequel proved—to cement a spiritual kingdom vaster and more world-embracing than the pagan empire of the Cæsars.

So, following in the wake of the Frankish armies, the popes sent their missionaries into the Low Countries.   Early in the seventh century, Dagobert, first king of Austrasia,* contended with the Frisians, and conquering Utrecht, he planted there the emblem of the cross: this was the first Christian church in Friesland.†   Nor did it long exist ; for in 692 Utrecht was again held by the Frisians, who were still stout unbelievers.‡   But in that same year, another of the Frankish monarchs, Pepin, vanquished Radbod, the Frisian chief, forcing him

* Afterwards the duchy of Lorraine.
† Davies, Hist. of Holland, vol. 1, p. 26.   Grotius, Motley, etc.
‡ Ibid.

to exchange a royal for a ducal title;* then, as the fierce pagan continued turbulent, the tremendous blows of Pepin's bastard, Charles the Hammer, pounded a large part of Friesland into Christianity.† Radbod himself was persuaded to allow himself to be baptized. But the imprudence of a monk spoiled all; for after Radbod had immersed one leg in the baptismal font, a thought struck him, and he paused. "Where are my dead forefathers?" queried he. "In hell," said the officiating priest. "Mighty well," retorted the pagan; "then I would rather feast with my ancestors in the halls of Woden, than shiver and starve alone in the heaven of the Christians;" and he declined the rite.‡

Radbod did not, however, actively oppose the conversion of his people. In 719, Gregory II. despatched Willibrod, an Anglo-Saxon monk, from England, into Friesland to preach the gospel§— selecting him because the languages of the English and the Frisians of that period were very similar.‖ This priest was created archbishop of Friesland by the pontiff;¶ and now, landing in the Netherlands,

---

○ Motley, vol. 1, p. 20.

† Ibid. Des Roches, Hist. de la Belgique. Van Loon, Alande Hist. ‡ Vita Sti. Bonifacii.

§ Brandt, Hist. of the Ref. in and about the Low Countries.

‖ "So late as the sixteenth century, the dialect of Friesland bore more resemblance to English than to any other tongue— Guicciardini, Des Belg., tom. 2, p. 288, duod.; and even now an acquaintance with the Dutch language is an excellent glossary to our old poets, for it has sustained little change in the lapse of time." Davies, Hist. of Holland, vol. 1, p. 18, note.

¶ Bede, Hist. Eccl., lib. 5, cap. 11.

he fixed the seat of his see at Utrecht, rebuilt the ruined church, supplemented it by a monastery, and gave a nucleus to the Christianity of the marshes.*

Thus England proselytized the Low Countries; and such was the origin of the famous bishopric of Utrecht. For many years it was piously fostered. Charles Martel granted the royal domains and privileges in the adjacent territories to the bishops of this see, enriching them besides by the cession of several other more distant estates.† Gradually they assumed to levy taxes and collect customs, until, in the lapse of ages, they vied in splendor and autocratic sovereignty with the Roman pontiffs.

From the date of the definitive establishment of the bishopric of Utrecht, the fight between Christianity and the national idols was spasmodic. Joining hands with the Saxons, the Frisians rebelled in the middle of the eighth century; but Charles Martel stamped down the rising;‡ and Charlemagne for ever laid the perturbed ghost of Woden—for the first time since the sack of Rome, uniting the Netherlands under one crown imperial.§   Once before, the lowland provinces had been united in their servitude to Cæsar. Eight hundred years had passed away, and now they were again made one in their subjection to Charlemagne—a conqueror of whom men might say, as Cassius said of Cæsar:

 ○ Hist. Wil. Hedæ in Willibrodo, p. 25 ; Bede, Hist. Eccles., lib. 5, cap. 11.
 † Davies, Hist. of Holland, vol. 1, p. 26, et seq.
 ‡ Grotius, Motley, Grattan.   § Motley, vol. 1, p. 22.

"He doth bestride the narrow world
Like a Colossus, and we petty men
Walk under his huge legs, and peep about
To find ourselves dishonorable graves."[o]

Through all these vicissitudes the Frisians and
the Menapians clung tenaciously to their nationality; of that nothing could rob them. "They agreed,
however, to obey the chiefs whom Charlemagne
should appoint to govern them, according to their
own laws—laws which were then collected, and are
still extant. The vernacular version of their Asega
book contains the Frisian customs, together with
the additions of the Franks. The general statutes
of Charlemagne were of course in force; but that
great legislator knew too well the importance attached by all mankind to local customs, to allow
his imperial capitulars to interfere unnecessarily
with the Frisian laws."[†] "The Frisians shall be
free as long as the wind blows out of the clouds and
the world stands;"[‡] so ran the text of their statute
book. It was the spirit as well as the letter of
their law, even in chains; it was the consolation
and the aspiration of their servitude.

From the recitals of the missionary monks who
went into the Netherlands to preach Christianity,
we may get an idea of their condition under Charlemagne. The old difference between the southern
provinces—some of which have since been incor-
porated with France—and those of the north, was

[o] Shakespeare, Julius Cæsar, act 1, sc. 2.
[†] Motley, vol. 1, p. 22.   [‡] Ibid.

as perceptible as ever. On the French border "the inhabitants had forgotten their former names; they were designated by the appellations of their rivers, woods, and towns, classified as accessories to inanimate objects; and having no monuments to remind them of their origin, they became without recollection or association—sank into a people without an ancestry."* The country was a desert. The monasteries, if we may credit the words of their charters, were established amid vast solitudes. The French nobles came into Brabant only for the sport of bear-hunting in its interminable forests.† A race of serfs now cultivated the domains of haughty lords and imperious priests. The clergy held immense estates in these wastes; a single abbey, that of Nivelle, owned fourteen thousand families of vassals.‡

The peoples to the north mounted one step higher with each age. A maritime race, they were more industrious, ingenious, prosperous, and happy than most others of that rude time; and the natural ferocity of their Saxon blood had been somewhat tempered by habits of labor. "They are handsome and well clothed," say the old chroniclers, "and their lands are well cultivated and abound in fruits, milk, honey."§ Friesland then swept from the Scheld to the Weser; and numbers of the Hanoverian and Westphalian Saxons, decimated by a barbarous edict which ordered every warrior of

* Grattan, p. 17. † Ibid., p. 14. ‡ Ibid., p. 18.
§ Acta Sanct. Belgii.

their tribes who exceeded the height of his own sword to be beheaded,* had adopted the Frisian name.†

The descendants of the Menapians began now to be called Flemings, and they had so greatly improved their provinces, that Pliny's shade would not have recognized the old morasses of his day. Already the turbulent waters had been gotten in hand—subdued to purposes of utility. Already dykes were built and canals were dug. The plains thus partially reconquered from the sea were distributed in portions, according to their labor, by those who had reclaimed them, except the parts reserved for the chieftain, the church, and the poor. This vital necessity for the construction of dykes had given to the Frisians and the Flemings a habit of union, good-will, and reciprocal justice; because it was necessary to make common cause in this good work of mutual preservation.‡   Indeed, at this very period the Flemings so well understood the principles of association, that they had formed political clubs as barriers to the despotic violence of their more barbarous conquerors; these they called *guilds*,§ and they comprised, besides their covenants for mutual protection, an obligation, which bound every member to succor every other in sickness, or shipwreck, or distress.‖   The guilds were the sure breeders of the free towns, and the

* Van Loon, Alande Hist.   † Ibid.   ‡ Grattan, p. 18.
§ *Gilden*, or in the Latin of those times, *gildonia*.
‖ Grattan, p. 20.

principle on which they were based originated the most ancient corporations.*   The increasing influence of these social compacts alarmed the quick-sighted despotism of Charlemagne, and he prohibited them.   But the imperial ban was powerless when opposed to the popular will; so the guilds stood their ground, and within a century after their prohibition they had cobwebbed Flanders with corporate towns.†   Already Bruges and Ghent, Antwerp and Courtray, Bergen-op-zoom and Thiel, were the seats of an ever-increasing trade; and Thiel contained in the tenth century fifty-five churches, from which, in the absence of other evidence, we may conjecture the extent of its population.‡

Contemporaneously with this social transformation in the Netherlands, a political revolution occurred in Europe.   The old Batavian and the later Roman forms faded away, and were succeeded by a new polity.   No great popular assembly asserted its sovereignty, as in the primitive epoch.   The elective power had been lost under the Romans, who had, after conquests, conferred the administrative power over their subject provinces upon officials appointed by the metropolis.   So did the Franks; and Charlemagne completed the revolution.   Popular assemblies, popular elections were ignored.   Military, civil, judicial officers were the creatures of the king.§   Counts, earls, dukes, were not then the hereditary heads of noble families;

---

* Grattan, p. 20.   † Ibid.
‡ Ibid.   § Motley, vol. 1, p. 25.

they were merely the officials of the empire, removable at will, possessing no hereditary rights.*

But Charlemagne did not live long enough to consolidate his revolution; and when he died, chaos came again. Europe had lost its old forms, and it had not yet acquired new ones. The great lawgiver reigned too soon. He was five centuries in advance of his epoch. Prodigious as was his genius, it was still too weak to remould society single-handed; and so, since he left no kindred soul sagacious enough to comprehend his plans, his clumsy, swollen, heterogeneous empire began to crumble. Cold masses up all things, sticks, stones, earth, and water, into dirty ice; heat first makes separation, then reunites elements of the same nature. Charlemagne was the cold, massing the empire; his dawdling descendants were the heat, severing the congealed lump, which, as it severed, reunited kindred particles; and thus Friesland found itself once more in its desolate corner, a cohesive unit. But it was not independent. The kings who had divided and subdivided Charlemagne's vast dominion, ceded the Netherlands now to the German, now to the Frenchman, until the country grew dizzy with changing masters; but the provinces were still parts of the loose, disjointed empire.† In this oscillation Friesland shared; and thus that narrow hook of land which was destined in future ages to be the cradle of a great republic, was for a time the oft-bartered victim of chaffering barbarians.

* Grattan, p. 19.   † Motley, *ut antea.*

CHAPTER III.

DEVELOPMENT.

THE Netherlands now trembled upon the threshold of those ages to which historians have fitly prefixed the epithet " dark." Mediæval life was subterranean. Europe at large groped in a fog-bank; saw " as through a glass, darkly"—"saw men as trees walking." Since Charlemagne there had been no central authority. Each local patch of territory was plundered, in the name of government, by whoever in the hurly-burly could usurp the rule; and though the continental provinces were nominally attached to one or the other of the several monarchies among which Europe was parcelled out, in fact each robber noble, each grasping prelate, swayed an absolute sceptre in whatever domain he had contrived to snatch. " Power, the more subdivided, became the more tyrannical. The sword was the only symbol of law; the cross was a weapon of offence; the bishop was a consecrated pirate; every petty baron was a burglar; while the people, alternately the prey of duke, prelate, and seignor, shorn and butchered, esteemed it happiness to sell themselves into slavery, hoping thereby to gain shelter beneath the eaves of a convent, or to huddle for protection under the castle walls of some little potentate."*

* Motley, Rise of the Dutch Rep., vol. 1, p. 26.

Besides this voluntary entrance into servitude, made by the timid or the weak, slavery was also compulsory. Criminals, vagrants, strangers, ship-wrecked sailors, prisoners-of-war, were commonly reduced to serfdom.[*]

There were three classes in this brotherhood of woe. Lowest grovelled the slaves of laymen—mere human cattle; brutes, with no claim to a fraction of their own labor, without rights, and with no mar-riage, except under infamous conditions.[†] One step higher stood the villeins, or villagers, only less for-lorn. But they had a beneficial interest in their own flesh and blood; for "they could commute the labor due their owner by a fixed sum of money, after annual payment of which they were graciously per-mitted to work for themselves."[‡] Then there were the serfs of the cloisters and the various ecclesi-astical establishments. With cunning policy, the churchmen made their slavery milder and more humane than that of the rude barons—as showing the superior clemency of their rule and the prefera-ble *status* of their serfs. And, indeed, Motley assures us that "the lot of a church-slave was freedom in comparison with that of his fellow-bondmen. To kill him was punishable by a heavy fine. He could give testimony in court: he might inherit, was able to make a will, and could plead before the law, if law could be found."[§] For these reasons most of the voluntary sales were made to ecclesiastics;

---

[*] Motley, Rise of the Dutch Rep., vol. 1, p. 26.
[†] Motley, vol. 1, p. 33.   [‡] Ibid., Grotius, Davies.   [§] Ibid.

and this gave the church an immense number of retainers; the number held by the bishopric of Utrecht is said to have been enormous.*

The picture is sickening. But there was another still darker: for

> "in the lowest deep, a lower deep
> Still threatening to devour men, opened wide,
> To which the hell they suffered seemed a heaven."

The Norsemen—as that pagan race was called which then inhabited Denmark and Sweden and Norway—began their ferocious raids. These fierce freebooters had long infested the northern seas, making desultory descents upon the coasts of Friesland, England, and France. Towards the close of the ninth century† they waged a wider, more determined war. Quitting their wild eyries in vast flocks, they swooped to batten on European civilization at large. The Netherlands were quickly overrun; Germany was harried; France was pillaged.‡ One province alone successfully resisted their first onset. Flanders, the patrimony of Baldwin *Bras-de-fer*—confirmed to him of the iron arm, with the title of count, by the king of France as the reluctant reward of his romantic and daring elopement with Judith, the monarch's daughter§— was preserved unplundered throughout the life of that doughty knight. But on his death, the Flem-

* Motley, Grattan.
† 882. Wheaton, Hist. of the Northmen.
‡ Michelét, Hist. of France; Grotius, Hume.
§ Van Loon, Alende Hist., Grotius.

ings, too, succumbed; and the whole Netherlands wore the terrible shackles of the sea-kings.*

But the domination of the Normans was not long. Their chief was assassinated by the command of Charles the Fat, the German emperor; and this left the nuisance to abate, just on the edge of the tenth century.† It was an alleviation; one link in the chain of the serfs was broken. The Crusades snapped another. Many knights, anxious to win barren laurels on the Syrian sands, were unable to command the money necessary for their outfit. Such always found a Shylock in the church. Ecclesiastics would dole out their hoarded gold to purchase the estates of the needy adventurers; and these were glad to sell or mortgage their serfs, if thereby they might get the means of fighting the Paynims.‡

Besides, any one might become a soldier of the cross—a service which took precedence of every other. The serf was invited to combat for the holy sepulchre equally with the noble; and he who did so returned a freeman:—liberty which many were adventurous enough to purchase at such an honorable price.§ Thus the Crusades—those Quixotic tilts against an Asiatic windmill—became at once educators and emancipators.

But throughout this period there were no longer laws—there were only forces, of which three were preëminently potent: feudalism, ecclesiasticism, and

---

* Grattan, p. 24.   Mallet, Northern Antiquities.   † Ibid.
‡ Michaud's Hist. of the Crusades.   § Motley, vol. 1, Introd.

the rising municipal power. Each of these extended an unwitting hand to civilization: in their grinding friction a light was struck.

The first force, and for a time the most powerful, was the feudal system — emblematic of the unsheathed sword. Even this brute power was a growth. It sprang from land; land, then as now, the pedestal of influence, almost of manhood. Estates were then of two kinds; proprietary, or *allodial*—a word synonymous with the *fee-simple* of our common law*—and *feudal*.† Besides the lands held in each kingdom by local owners, care was always taken, in those days, to reserve many estates to the crown, partly for the support of its dignity, partly for the exercise of its munificence.‡ These *desmense* lands, as the territory thus reserved was called,§ were the chief source of the royal revenue.‖ Often they were granted in trust to favored courtiers, to be held of and for the king, as *benefices*.¶ Though conferred originally during the royal pleasure, in the course of time benefices became hereditary ;** the claim of a son to succeed his father was frequently too plausible or too formidable to be rejected; and thus were laid the foundations of the half-independence of the great mediæval vassals.††

"A natural consequence of hereditary benefices,"

---

* Hallam, Hist. Middle Ages, p. 65.

† This word is probably the barbarous synonym of the Latin *beneficium*. See Du Cange v. *Freedom.*

‡ Hallam, p. 70.   § Montesquieu, *L'Esprit des Lois.*

‖ Ibid.   ¶ Ibid.   Maine, Ancient Law.

** Ibid.   Hallam.   †† Hallam, pp. 67 and 73.

remarks Hallam, "was that those who possessed them carved out portions to be held of themselves by a similar tenure of service and fealty."* Soon the law began to look upon allodial ownership with dislike, and to favor the more popular tenure, until eventually lands held in fee-simple were exceptional and rare.†

The same change occurred in the nature of the crown offices. The kingdom of Charlemagne, and of his predecessors, was divided into a number of districts called *counties*, each under the government of a *count*—a name long familiar to the Romans, and by which they rendered the *graf* of the Germans‡—whose duty it was to administer justice, preserve tranquillity, collect the public revenue, and lead his retainers into the field to the assistance of his monarch in time of war.§ The title of duke implied a still higher dignity, and commonly gave authority over several counties.‖

At the outset these offices, like the benefices, were awarded at pleasure; but like the others, they, too, gradually hardened into hereditaments, so that at last titled families came to regard the usurped duchies or counties which they governed as theirs *de jure* as well as *de facto*.¶

From this double usurpation nobility sprouted. In early times, all distinctions of rank were founded

○ Hallam, p. 72.
† Leg. Burgundy, tit. 26.   Hallam, Montesquieu.
‡ Hallam.   § Ibid.   ‖ See Hallam, p. 67, note.
¶ Montesquieu, L'Esprit des Lois.   Grotius.

on the possession of land and on civil employments.* When these became hereditary, and were
shut up to a few fortunate families, a patrician caste
was the inevitable result; " that landed aristocracy
arose which became the most striking feature in
the political system of Europe during many centuries, forming in fact its chief distinction both from
the despotism of Asia, and the equality of republican government."†

The customs of an epoch will always be moulded
by its habits. So now, what had begun through
ambition was at last dictated by necessity. " In
that dissolution of all law which ensued on the
death of Charlemagne, the turbulent nobles among
whom his empire was divided, constantly engaged
in internecine strife, placed their chief dependence
upon men whom they attached to their respective
banners by gratitude, and bound by strong conditions. The oath of fidelity which they had taken
on their accession to power, the homage which they
had paid to their sovereign, they exacted from their
vassals in turn. To render military service became
in that age, when war was a passion and a business,
the essential obligation which the tenant of a ben-
efice undertook; and out of those old royal grants,
now become for the most part hereditary, there
grew up in the tenth century both the name and
the reality of feudalism."‡

Such in its more salient aspects was the feudal
system. In many of the Netherland provinces, it

---

* Hallam, p. 69. † Ibid. Grotius. ‡ Hallam, p. 72.

took early and deep root ; in Friesland it was never
planted.* Under various pretexts, the sagacious traders contrived to retain their proprietary interest in
the soil.   Man and the land were linked together;
they were lawfully married for life or death; the
Frisian had wedded his bogs.   Thus it was that in
Friesland the lands were cultivated, not by laborers
or by serfs, as elsewhere, but by owners; and the
swamps yielded, some tenfold, some twenty-fold,
and some a hundred-fold, because they were loved.
It was one of the secrets of Frisian progress. Each
man was interested in the improvement of his country, and this fact nerved every arm, emboldened
every heart, to grapple with the sea, to erect dykes
and windmills ; as

> " Onward for aye, though diligently slow,
>   The firm, connected bulwark seems to grow ;
>   Spreads its long arms amidst the watery roar,
>   Scoops out an empire, and usurps the shore."†

But though feudalism did not ground itself in Friesland, it had an influence there.   Indeed, the essential principle of a fief, which Hallam defines to have
been " a mutual contract between suzerain and tenant of support and fidelity,"‡ was already exempli-
fied among the Frisians in the spirit of complete
concert which united them against the tyranny of
the ocean, and against the despotism of man; and
it might also be traced in the Flemish guilds.§

But the feudal polity was an advance, and made

---

* Motley, vol. 1, pp. 21 and 38.   Grattan, Grotius, Van Loon.
† Goldsmith, *Traveller*.   ‡ Hallam, p. 75.   § See chap. 2, p. 51.

for civil freedom chiefly in this, that at a time when the desolating hand of power seemed about to sweep individualism into the abyss, as it had done in Asia, it preserved the name, if not the essence, of right, and privilege, and honor ; and it cherished the idea of private justice, as we may learn from the consideration of the limitations of the services of vassalage, so cautiously marked out in those old lawbooks which record the customs of the past, and from the reciprocity of obligation between the lord and his tenant, from the consent required in every legislative measure, and from the security which every vassal found in the privilege of judgment by his peers.*

In its chivalric notions of the inviolability of faith, of the necessity for honor, and of the honesty of truth, the feudal system was an excellent school of moral discipline in an age drunk with excess, careless of treachery, vicious from habit, and riotous with power. In just these respects it was a help to civilization—the go-cart which held up its infant feet and strengthened them to walk.

By the side of feudalism, at one time inferior to it, but finally controlling it, stood another and a different force—the religion of the popes. With the *jus divinum* on its lips, every step it took was towards empire—temporal as well as spiritual. Dowered by the pious donations of the successors of Charlemagne, who chiefly signalized their authority

---

* See the very able *resumé* of the influence of feudalism, in Hallam, p. 123, *et seq.*

by lavishing territorial gifts on the church;* organized by the subtlest wit of man on an amalgamated
basis of truth and shrewd imposture; officered by
the most consummate genius of the age; engross-
ing the scholarship of the time: the Roman see
swept on conquering and to conquer. Europe was
cob-webbed with episcopal cities which gradually
became so many principalities, independent of the
civil law, taking orders from the popes alone; dic-
tating the political policy of the world; deposing
and setting up princes; consolidating their usurped
power, now by force, now by fraud; intriguing,
ubiquitous, all-powerful.

The clergy of that day were not merely churchmen, they were huntsmen and warriors; and so
"careering in helm and hauberk with other ruffians, they bandied blows in the thickest of the fight,
blasted their enemies with bell, book, and candle;
forced sovereigns at the head of armies to grovel
in the dust at their feet, and offer abject submission
for the kiss of peace; exercised the same conjury
over ignorant baron and cowardly hind, making
the fiction of apostolic authority to bind and loose
as prolific in acres as the other divine right to have
and hold; thus the force of cutivated intellect,
wielded by a chosen few, and sanctioned, as the
assumption went, by supernatural power, became
more potent than the sword"—directed its blows,
told it when and where to strike, and became the
guiding brain of feudalism.   'T is an instructive

* Grattan, p. 21.

picture, and it teaches the tremendous power of knowledge, the inevitable superiority of educated mind over brute violence. And this was why the holy see so carefully monopolized learning—knowing the secret of its authority, it could not but frown upon popular intelligence.

But God made the wrath of man to praise him; even priestcraft had its mission. It preserved and fostered art; it treasured up in crypts and convents the fossils of antique learning; it incarnated some of the Christian precepts; and at last its bold assumption and its corruptions provoked inquiry—forced honest men, spite of themselves, to investigate and to protest.

Cap in hand to feudalism and the Roman see knelt a third force—the rising municipalities of Europe. The constant tendency of mankind is towards aggregation. Even individualism gravitates towards population. And so now the clustering hovels of the villiens began to expand into towns. The nascent burghers built better houses, and threw up ramparts. Elbowing each other on the street, brought into daily contact, they commenced to combine and to trade. Little by little manufactures were started; the different trades were born, and each had its guild. Then money was made. Gold began to assert itself. Commerce was launched, and "plucking up half-drowned Holland by the locks, it poured wealth into her lap."

The nobles, scenting no danger, at first encouraged the towns, rewarded them with charters, erected

them into corporate bodies, and were bribed into
complacence by burgher gold.   The church, suspecting no heresy, spread out her arms in blessing
over the rising municipalities, and dictated the
recompense.   The cunning citizens long made no
claims, only asked leave to be.   But gradually they
grew in power and wealth.   "Fishermen and river
raftsmen became ocean adventurers and merchant
princes.   Needy Flemish weavers became mighty
manufacturers."   Like the imprisoned spirit in the
fabled casket, when the seal was broken, the little
towns lifted into colossal shape.   "Armies of workmen, fifty thousand strong, tramped through the
swarming streets.   Silk-makers, clothiers, brewers,
became the gossips of kings, lent their royal friends
vast sums, and burned the royal notes in fires of
cinnamon wood."

The opulence of the merchants of this period,
and their sumptuous style of living, quite shamed
the aristocracy, impoverished by war and frequent
spoliation.   On one occasion, it is related that the
count of Flanders invited a number of Flemish
magistrates to dine with him.   The chairs which
they were to occupy at table were unfurnished with
cushions.   The proud burghers, not satisfied with
bare seats, stripped off their valuable velvet cloaks,
and folding these, sat on them during the repast.
After the feast they were about to retire in apparent forgetfulness of those costly articles of dress.
A courtier ventured to remind them of their man-
tles: but the burgomaster of Bruges replied, "We

Flemings are not in the habit of carrying away the cushions after dinner"—and the cloaks were left in the count's dining-hall.* 'T is an illustrative anecdote; and though there was a spice of insolence in it, the action was high and authoritative.

But spite of the equivocal attitude in which they stood, the mediæval municipalities were the sole depositories of those rights which lay hid under the epithet "privileges." The logical sequence of their life was independence. Every dollar they coined meant emancipation. The keen competition of their trades opened men's eyes, and awakened intellect. The burghers were democratic by instinct; and this was why their cities were sure to become the cradles of republican and protestant ideas.

Indeed, the maritime spirit, wherever it showed itself, already bore the countenance of republicanism. In Italy the Lombard merchants were democrats.† Venice, then towering in her pride of place, with no sea-weed tarnishing her marble halls, the fresh, beautiful bride of the Adriatic, was an oligarchical republic. Avignon, and Arles, and Marseilles, commercial cities in the south of France, tottered to their feet and stood a moment as free commonwealths in the middle of the twelfth century.‡

The alliance of town with town for maritime purposes was common. Narbonne formed one with Geneva in 1166,§ and nearly a century later the fa-

○ Chambers' Tour in Holland, p. 9.
† Sismondi, Hist. des Rep. Ital.
‡ Velly, t. 14, p. 446.
§ Hallam, Middle Ages, p. 119.

mous Hanseatic* League was formed, and the chief
cities of Germany cemented a union whose purpose
it was to foster and protect commercial interests.†

But it was in the Netherlands that the municipal system was carried to the greatest perfection.
In Holland especially, the towns were not, as elsewhere, merely portions of the state; the state itself
was rather an aggregate of towns, each of which
formed a little commonwealth within itself, providing for its own defence, governed by its own laws,
holding separate courts of justice, administering its
own finances; the legislative sovereignty of the
whole being vested in the towns, forming in their
collective capacity the assembly of the states.‡

Each community elected its own municipal authorities; and thus inspired with the breath of life,
with plenty of blood in their veins, the miniature
republics made their gold weigh up the other forces
in the end, spite of the *jus divinum*.§

"Stability," says Schiller, "the security of life
and property, arising from mild laws and an equal
administration of justice—these are the parents of
activity and industry."‖ This advantage the Low
Country cities had. They became established marts.
Antwerp, Amsterdam, Dort, Ostend, and the rest,
were more or less affiliated with the Hanse-towns.¶
Their burghers, launching their ships, visited first

* From the German *Hansa*, a union.
† Appleton's Cyc., Art. Hanseatic League.
‡ Davies, vol. 1, p. 76, *et seq.*   § Motley.
‖ Schiller, Rev. of the Netherlands, p. 369.
¶ Appleton's Cyc., *in loco.*

the neighboring coasts of Denmark and England; and the wool which they brought back employed thousands of industrious hands in Bruges, Ghent, and Antwerp; while by the middle of the twelfth century the cloths of Flanders were extensively worn in France and Germany.*

Nor did the Netherland seamen pause here: with unprecedented daring, "they ventured, without a compass, to steer under the North pole, round to the most northern cape of Russia. And in this voyage they received from the Wendish towns a share of the Levant trade, which then passed from the Black sea, through the Russian territories, to the Baltic. When, in the thirteenth century, this trade began to decline, the crusades having opened a new passage through the Mediterranean for Indian merchandise, and after the Italian municipalities had usurped this lucrative branch of commerce, the Netherlands became the emporium between the Hanseatic League in the north and the Italian traders in the south.

The main current of this trade flowed through Bruges, in Flanders, for several centuries, and fattened that favored city. "Here," if we may credit Schiller, "a hundred and fifty vessels might often be counted at one time, entering the harbor of Sluys. Besides the rich factories of the Hanseatic League, here were seated fifteen trading companies, with warehouses, and merchants' families from every European country. This also was the market for

* Schiller.

all the northern products for the south, and for the
Levantine trade bound north."*   Bruges rolled in
prosperity.   The meanest citizen nursed his person
in velvet and silk.†

Such was the origin, such the varied influence,
of the three great mediæval forces, which "builded
better than they knew."

Meantime, the Netherlands remained divided
into numberless small provinces, whose rulers did
homage at one time to the German emperors, at
another to the kings of France.   To recite the
names and achievements of these "illustrious obscure" might well cause even the most patient gene-
alogist to shudder, and is foreign to the purpose of
these pages.   One of them, Count Baldwin of Flanders, was the father-in-law of William of Normandy;
and when the conqueror crossed the channel into
England, Netherland ships ferried him over, and
Netherland men-at-arms helped him subdue the
island‡—assistance which he recompensed by the
annual payment of three hundred silver marks into
the Flemish treasury;§ which proves that even in
the middle of the eleventh century, and in family
transactions, the Flemings looked sharply to the
main chance.   It was Mathilda, William's Flemish
wife, who worked with her own fair hands that celebrated tapestry of Bayeux, on which was deftly
embroidered the whole story of the conquest.||

Another of these petty sovereigns, and the last,

* Schiller, pp. 370, 371.   † Ibid.   Grattan, p. 29.
‡ Hume, Hist. of Eng., *in loco.*   § Grattan, p. 28. || Ibid.

was Jacqueline, the most lovely, intrepid, and talented woman of her times—the Helen of the Middle Ages. She was as unhappy as she was beautiful. Succeeding in her seventeenth year to an inheritance of three counties—Holland, Zealand, Hainault—she was mated successively with three greedy but titled adventurers, who persecuted her, tore her provinces by dissensions incessantly fomented, and drove her to implore the intervention of her cousin Philip of Burgundy; who, in his turn, despoiled her of her last possessions, and degraded her, on her marriage with Vrank Von Borselen, a gentleman of Zealand, whose gentle and knightly spirit consoled her for the cowardice and brutality of her former husbands, to be the lady-forester of her own dominions.* On the death of Jacqueline, in 1436, the uncourtly usurper took undisputed possession of her titles, drowning remorse in his thirst for aggrandizement.†

Thus began the rule of the Burgundian dukes in the Netherlands: that ambitious house, leaping into the saddle, was now to run its appointed race in pursuit of the illusive phantom of empire. By the various shifts of purchase, legacy, and bargain, Philip, surnamed "the Good," added territory after territory to the nucleus states which he had wrung from the reluctant hands of his fair cousin, until, finally, he united under his ducal coronet eleven of the richest provinces of Europe.‡ His court rivalled that

---

* Davies, vol. 1, p. 217, *et seq.* Motley, vol. 1, p. 40. Grattan. p. 47, *et seq.* † Ibid. Van Loon. ‡ Schiller, p. 365.

of the Vatican in ostentatious magnificence; and flushed with success, the smooth usurper proceeded to curtail the privileges of his burgher subjects. But he was so subtle and insidious in this spoliation, that the parchment liberties of the Netherlands were partially suppressed ere the cities awoke to protest. Besides, the citizens were so enervated by luxury, that they lacked heart to resist, and feared that they might lose every thing by claiming any thing. Meantime, their material prosperity increased, and they hoarded gold which their descendants were to melt into bullets and beat into swords.

Philip died in 1467; and his son Charles the Bold succeeded to the extensive and compact dukedom which he had so unscrupulously consolidated. Charles augmented his domains by the conquest of two additional provinces; then, casting an envious eye on the diadem of Louis XI., he aspired to expand his own coronet into a crown by carving out with his sword a kingdom which should surpass France in extent, as its present dukedom exceeded it in wealth.

The vaulting and restless spirit of this meteoric prince devised a scheme of conquest embracing the whole line of country from the Zuyder Zee and the old mouth of the Rhine away to Alsace, with the icy and granite battlements of Switzerland as the ramparts of his realm.* His execution was not equal to his conception. Narrow-minded, short-

* Schiller, p. 365. Motley, Grattan. Kirk, Life of Charles the Bold.

sighted, despotic, as a conqueror, he was as far removed as possible from Hannibal to whom he was fond of comparing himself; and as a politician, he could outwit no one but himself.*

Charles at once put his project afoot. Regarding the Netherlands only as an inexhaustible bank on which he had *carte blanche*, he confined his intercourse with his states to the extortion of vast sums of money with which to pamper his quixotism; and, since his military career was singularly unsuccessful, the frequency of these demands well-nigh drove the patient burghers to despair. By oaths and bravado he was nearly successful in establishing a central despotism on the ruins of the ancient provincial charter, when, in a happy moment for the Netherlands, he collected an army and dashed to the conquest of Switzerland—meeting, not the victory of which he felt assured, but an obscure death in the *mêlée* at Nancy; and this awful rout saved the republicanism of the Swiss, and partially restored the liberties of the Low Countries.†

For the Lady Mary of Burgundy, the daughter of the infatuated paladin, now became sole mistress of this magnificent dukedom—a woman as young, fair and unprotected as poor Jacqueline had been. Her strait was the opportunity of the burghers. Environed by difficulties, menaced by Louis XI., the most treacherous and subtle of kings, she appealed, as was usual in such cases, to the commons. Naturally, the citizens demanded a *quid pro quo.*

○ Motley, vol. 1, p. 48.   † Ibid. Kirk, Life of Charles.

Dutch Ref.   4

A convention was summoned to meet in Ghent, and the deliberations flowered in the "Great Privilege," an instrument which was the *Magna Charta* of the Dutch, and which, though it was afterwards rescinded, became the corner-stone of the Dutch republic.*

Thus a stroke of the pen restored the pristine Netherland charters; and Mary, besides, bound herself not to marry without the consent of the states.† The richest and most beautiful princess in Europe, she had many wooers; two were especially prominent. Louis XI. claimed Mary for the French dauphin; Frederick III., the German emperor, demanded her for his son, Maximilian of Austria; and to one of these suitors the choice soon narrowed itself. Then the states made an unfortunate choice. Dreading Louis XI., whose kingdom bordered on their territories, and aware that Mary's husband must become the most powerful prince in Christendom, they finally awarded the hand of their duchess to Maximilian, accelerating the very evil which they were striving to forestall.‡

A decade of squabbles succeeded; then Mary died, after giving birth to a son, Philip the Fair. This prince, young, handsome, engaging, was mated with Joanna, daughter of Ferdinand and Isabella of Castile and Aragon, a bride who brought Spain and the two Sicilies as her dower.§ From this

* Grotius, Motley, Van Loon, Grattan, Davies.
† Motley, vol. 1, p. 50. Schiller.
‡ Schiller, p. 366.   § Ibid.

union sprung Charles V. Born in 1501, he was destined to unite in his simple person this vast domain acquired partly by conquest, but chiefly by two fortunate marriages.

The reign of Philip the Fair was short and turbulent.* Dying in 1506, while on a visit to his brother-in-law, the king of Spain, he was speedily followed to the grave by Joanna, who became mad from grief at his loss, after nearly losing her senses from jealousy during the life of the handsome profligate.†

The regency of the Netherlands reverted to Maximilian, now become emperor of Germany, on this event; and he at once named his daughter Margaret governant of the states during the infancy of the second Charlemagne. And this brings the political history of the Low Countries into the dawn of the sixteenth century, when God said, "Let there be light."

---

* We must not omit to notice the existence of two factions which, for two centuries, divided and agitated the whole population of Holland and Zealand. One bore the title of *Hoeks*—fish-hooks; the other of *Kaabeljaus*—codfish. The origin of these grotesque names was a dispute between two parties at a feast, as to whether the codfish took the hook, or the hook the codfish. This apparently frivolous dispute was made the pretext for a serious quarrel: and the partisans of the nobles and those of the towns ranged themselves on either side, and assumed different badges of distinction. The *Hoeks* were partisans of the towns, and wore red caps; the *Kaabeljaus* were the friends of the nobles, and wore gray bonnets. These factions were finally extinguished in 1492. Grattan, p. 49, note. † Ibid., p. 65.

CHAPTER IV.

RUDIMENTS OF THE REFORMATION.

IT is an authoritative declaration of Michelét, that "whoever restricts himself to the present, the actual, will never comprehend the present and the actual. Whoever contents himself with seeing the exterior, and painting the form, does not even see it. To see it correctly, to paint it faithfully, we must know that which is within, the motor; no painting without anatomy."*

In obedience to this rule, we have traced the progress of the Netherlands towards civilization— seen men getting "first a house, and then a wife, and then an ox to plough," as Hesiod has phrased it,† and so slowly developing into society—a plural unit formed by daily exigency. It remains for us to retrace our steps a little, that we may thread the maze of the more distinctive rudiments of the Reformation by holding their clue.

And if we look back, we shall see that the Reformation itself was not an *émeute*, but a development, often most alive when it seemed most torpid;

* Michelét, The People, p. 15.
† Tremenheere, Political Experience of the Ancients, p. 2.

for every earnest opponent of ecclesiastical pride, of scandalous errors, of ill-morals in the early ages was a reformer. Luther in embryo lurked under the cowls, went girt by the cord, walked in the sandals of a hundred monks, preaching patches of truth, and uttering piecemeals of protest, centuries before the famous Wittemburger collected and moulded these *disjecta membra* into one body, armed by God with a flaming sword to smite the pretender who

> "Sat upon the Seven Hills,
> And from his throne of darkness ruled the world."

In the march of the Roman see to its supremacy, thoughtful men see less to marvel at than to deplore. When Christianity lost the democratic simplicity of the apostolic age, and began, like the Athenians, to "spend its time in nothing else but either to tell or to hear some new thing,"* the reign of bastard prelates—half fanatics and half mountebanks, dealers in terrible phantasmagoria, but unable to meet each other in the street without laughing, like the Roman augurs who were their prototypes—was insured.†

Though the Netherlands, with the rest of Europe, had been persuaded or coerced to break their idols and accept the pagan Mosaic, which the Italians called the gospel, they were always restless

---

* Acts 17:21.

† See Brandt's *rationale* in his History of the Reformation in the Low Countries, vol. 1, Introduction.

and fretful believers, prone to ask the reason of
their faith, "why this?" and "why that?"—terrible
questioners, in which undutiful and puzzling behavior they were long aided and abetted by their
native churchmen.   "Heresy," says Grotius, "was
the Hollander's immemorial inheritance."*

Indeed, the Low Country prelates, the bishops
of Utrecht especially, were more indebted to the
pious donations of kings and kaisers for their wealth
and influence, than to the good-will of the pontiffs;
therefore, as they were more independent of the
metropolitan see than most other churchmen, they
frequently, in the midnight ages, shouted "veto"
when the popes made extravagant demands or set
afloat new pretensions.

Thus, if you will have an illustration, in 860,
King Lotharius requested Nicholas I., who then
wore the purple, to decree his divorce from Tend-
berg his consort, as being too near of kin to him,†
or because of her scandalous life, as some say.‡
The pontiff said no; whereupon the monarch convened a synod at Aix la Chapelle, which Hunger,
bishop of Utrecht, attended; and this assembly
pronounced the divorce lawful and proper.§   The
enraged pontiff at once cited these ecclesiastics to
answer for their bold action at Rome, pretending
that his decision in such cases was final and unimpeachable.   The archbishops of Treves and of

* Grotius, de Antiq. Reip. Batav.
† Reginonis, chron. 11, p. 47.
‡ Blondel, de Papa poema, p. 136.   § Brandt, vol. 1, p. 5.

Cologne were delegated by the rest to answer at the bar of the Vatican.*

On reaching Rome, these high dignitaries were kept in waiting almost a month ere they were admitted to an interview with his holiness; and when they were at length conducted to his audience-room, they found themselves "surrounded by a company of ruffians, who treated them as robbers are accustomed to treat the entrapped," were insulted by the pope, and finally, without any attempt at confutation, they and theirs were bound by a scandalous sentence, "inconsistent with the Christian faith," which "bereaved them of all human assistance, and interdicted the use of every thing sacred or profane."†

On their return, the aggrieved bishops indited a letter to Pope Nicholas, which closes thus:

"God has made his queen and spouse the church a noble and everlasting provision for her family, with a dowry that is neither fading nor corruptible, and given her an eternal crown and sceptre; all which benefits, you, like a thief, intercept. You set up yourself in the temple as God; instead of a shepherd, you have become as a wolf to the sheep. You would have us believe you supreme bishop; you are rather a tyrant; under the mask of a pastor you hide your horns. Whereas you ought to be a servant of servants—as you call yourself, you intrigue to become lord of lords. What-

* Blondel, de Papa poema, p. 136.
† See their Letter, cited in Brandt, ut antea.

ever you desire, you think lawful; thus you have become a deceiver of Christians. For all these reasons, neither we nor our brethren and friends regard or submit to your commands—know not your voice, and fear not your bulls. You condemn all for irreligious and impious that do not obey your despotic precepts, forbidding them the use of the sacraments. We smite you with your own sword, because you bring the commands of God into contempt, dissolving the unity of spiritual assemblies, and violating peace, the badge of the Prince of heaven. The Holy Ghost is the builder of all churches as far as the earth extends. The city of our God, of which we are citizens, reaches to all parts of the heavens; and it is greater than the city, by the holy prophets named Babylon, which pretends to be divine, equals herself to heaven, and brags that her wisdom is immortal; and finally, though without reason, that she never did err, nor ever can."*

Such was the impeachment of a pontiff in the ninth century; and this tremendous indictment forcibly recalls Luther before the Cardinal-legate Cajetan eight hundred years later. The scenes are so much the same, that unless you knew the difference by the dates and names, you would fancy yourself present at the Augsburg interview. "For in human things," remarks Strada, "however times and persons die, still the same causes and events revive;"†

* Cited in Brandt, vol. 1, pp. 5, 6.
† Strada, Hist. of the Low Country Wars, p. 2.

and Schiller can tell us that "like conditions produce like phenomena."[*]

Leap now over a hundred and thirty years. In
992, that famous synod which deposed Pope John
XV. was convened at Rheims, and among the assembled bishops were several Netherlanders. Ar-
nulp, bishop of Orleans, presided. "This pontiff,"
said he, "is antichrist;" and he added, "In the
Low Countries and in Germany, both near us, there
may be found priests of God—men eminent in religion. Wherefore it seems to me much more expedient and proper, were it not for the godless obsti-
nacy of contending kings, that we should seek in
those parts for the judgment of bishops, than in
that city which is now set to sale, and whose determinations ponderate according to the weight of
gold."[†]

So also these early churchmen often sank their
esprit du corps in their patriotism; for whenever the
popes encroached upon the imperial crown, as they
constantly did in those days, the great part of the
Netherland bishops invariably sided with the emperor, and opposed mitre to mitre.[‡] When Hildebrand excommunicated Henry IV. in 1076, William,
bishop of Utrecht, responded by procuring an episcopal vote which excommunicated Gregory himself;
because "he had confounded profane and holy
things, by attempting to screw himself into the management of the popedom and the empire;" because

---

[*] Schiller, p. 361.
[†] Cited in Brandt, vol. 1, p. 6. [‡] Ibid.

" he deceived the common people with a hypocriti-
cal religion;" and " because he would make everybody believe that none were rightly consecrated
but such as bought the priestly office of his gold-
suckers."* The clergy of Liege espoused the imperial cause in this same spirit, were always the bitter
opponents of Hildebrand and his innovations—
stoutly Ghibelline and never Guelph.†

It was this same Hildebrand who in 1076 prescribed clerical celibacy, a manœuvre by which the
wily pope meant to insure the consolidation of
church spoils, and the ecclesiastical reversion to
each churchman's property; for if the priests were
deprived of marriage, they could have no legitimate children among whom to portion out either
their personal estates or the domain of the church
over which they might happen to preside.‡

This decree provoked a storm of indignation.
In the Netherlands the imprecations were loud and
deep. Sigebent, a monk of Gambloon in Brabant,
inveighed against the prohibition as " a rash sentence, contrary to the sentiments of the holy
fathers;"§ while the Hollanders compelled their
priests to marry, saying, " The man who has no
wife will naturally seek for the wife of another."‖

But with the dawn of the twelfth century these
plain, brave speakers, these reproving Nathans

---

* Cited in Brandt, vol. 1, p. 6.
† Brandt, vol. 1, pp. 8–10. Motley, vol. 1, p. 67.
‡ Ranke, Hist. of the Popes. Mosheim, etc.
§ Blondel de Pap. poema, p. 3. Chron. W. Heda.
‖ Grattan, p. 32.

among the clergy, began to die off. 'T is true indeed that when, in 1122, the canons of Middleburgh disgraced their cloth by lasciviousness, Godebald, bishop of Utrecht, drove them out of their cloister, and replaced them by other religionists.* It is the last instance of attempted reformation within the church for four centuries; and now we must seek for reformers elsewhere than upon archiepiscopal thrones and within monastery walls.

The chain of protest was not interrupted; but in the latter decades of the twelfth century a different class of dissidents appeared—reform changed front. The priests shut their eyes to the abounding and flagitious abuses, awed by the half-omnipotence of the holy see, and stripped of lay support by the *entente cordiale* patched up between the empire and the Vatican.

Just at this period, a sect which grounded its plea upon the Scriptures, holding doctrines which agreed in every vital point with the tenets of modern Protestantism, and haloed by unimpeachable antiquity, entered the Netherlands, and began to teach the primitive doctrines.† Their missionaries were known by a variety of appellations—names which originated either in their habits or in the localities in which they worked. They were indefatigable in prayer, and they were called "Beghards."‡ They were Puritans in religion, and they

* Chron. W. Heda, p. 147.
† Brandt. vol. 1, p. 12. Mosheim, Justin.
‡ Eccl. Hist., vol. 2, p. 224.

were styled "Cathari."* They were handicraftsmen by trade, and they were named "Weavers."†
They were humble, and they were nicknamed
"Humilists."‡ One of their chief seats was in
the French county of Alby, and they were styled
"Albigenses."§ Among their most famous teachers was Pierre Waldo, and they were called "Vaudois."‖ In Bohemia they proclaimed the brotherhood of Christianity, and they were named "Bohemian Brothers."¶ But whatever the *sobriquet* in
which they were clothed, their characteristics were
everywhere the same—zealous, untiring, patient in
suffering, constant in well-doing, sheathed in the
panoply of that charity which "beareth all things,
hopeth all things," and is "kind;" they were, if not
in fact, as some have claimed,** at least in spirit,
the lineal descendants of Peter and Paul and that
disciple whom Jesus loved, for they were the resur-
rectionists of Christianity.

* Sismondi, Hist. of Albig.   † Ibid.   Brandt.
‡ Brandt, *ut antea.*
§ Ibid.   Hist. of the Huguenots, Am. Tract Soc., 1866.
‖ Ibid.   Unless, as many hold, Vaudois and Waldonan were
older than Pierre Waldo, and meant simply a Valleyer, an inhab-
itant of the high *valleys* sloping from Mount Viso, early and long
the seats of a purer faith, which Rome branded as heresy.   ¶ Ibid.

** It is certain that the Vaudois themselves claimed a descent
from the apostles, and several of their writings do indeed bear
intrinsic evidence of such antiquity; but some authoritative scholars have denied their apostolic descent, though conceding great
antiquity to them.   The question has been much discussed *pro*
and *con;* nor is it probable that it will ever be definitely settled.
Consult and compare Vanema's Eccl. Hist. *in loco,* "The Noble
Lesson" in Blair, vol. 1, pp. 473, 484, Sismondi's History of the
Vaudois, Gibbon, Bossuet, Hist. des Variations, etc.

Some of these teachers rejected infant baptism;* and from these Baptists claim descent, tracing their genealogy through them up to apostolic times.† They won proselytes with almost inconceivable rapidity; and when Pope Innocent III. launched his crusaders once, twice, thrice against the French Vaudois, slaying a million of the most industrious artisans and pure citizens in Christendom,‡ the dazed and maimed survivors fled into Germany, into Bohemia, into the Netherlands, to swell the ranks of their brothers in the faith.§

The free fairs which the chief Low Country cities held once or twice every year for business purposes, and which attracted traders from all countries,‖ became the seed-ground of these reformers.¶ A word spoken, a convert won in the market towns of Holland, Flanders, and Brabant, was sure to spread the principles of dissent far and wide : and in the bustle, their first growth might easily escape notice, and be accelerated by concealment. Finally, the Beghards translated the Bible, which Waldo had previously turned into French, into Dutch rhymes, in imitation of the Teutons, who had long been accustomed to record their most memorable

---

* Brandt, vol. 1, p. 12.   Allix, chh., Pied., chap. 16, pp. 140–143.

† Orchard, Foreign Baptists, p. 324, *et seq.*

‡ Sismondi, Hist. of the Albig., *passim.*   Hist. of the Huguenots, *passim.*

§ Mosheim, Waddington, Clark, Martyn, p. 96, etc., Brandt.

‖ Schiller, p. 373.   ¶ Ibid., p. 381.

affairs in verse; because, said they, " there is great advantage in it; no jests, no fables, no trifles, no deceits, naught but words of truth. There is, indeed, here and there a hard crust, but even in this the marrow and sweetness of what is good and holy may easily be discovered."*

Then Rome awoke from the dog-nap into which she had fallen, weary with the Languedocian massacres. Incensed and alarmed at the wonderful growth and the increasing boldness of the reformers, the pontiffs—who had banned the Bible, published new decrees, and reinterpreted and glossed the early teachings—at once summoned the temporal sword to their assistance, and began the extirpation of the heresy which opposed what they assumed to be the church.

Previous to 1135, the punishment of death for heresy was unknown in the Netherlands.† In that year the bishop of Utrecht burned several victims before the doors of his archiepiscopal palace, because they were charged with holding with Berengarius, that the corporeal presence was a fable.‡

From this initial pyre the fire spread fast, until the whole horizon was red and fetid with burning bodies. Human bloodhounds were unleashed and put upon the scent. Hordes of idle priests were set to ferret out the heretics. Monks prowled in every city eager to clutch victims. Spies were bribed to become betrayers. A bounty-fund was raised for apostates. Suspicion was proof. Heavier and fiercer

---

* Brandt, vol. 1, p. 14.   ¶ Ibid., p. 11.   ‡ Ibid.

grew the persecutions; closer grew the scrutiny; severer grew the tests of orthodoxy. To doubt was heresy; to deny was death—not speedy death, but death by agonizing inches, by prolonged spasms. Human ingenuity racked itself to invent new tortures which should wring but not kill too soon.

In Flanders, the accused were stripped and bound to a stake, and then flayed from the neck to the navel; on this quivering, lacerated flesh, swarms of wasps or bees were let loose to fasten and sting to a death of exquisite torment.[*]

One of the bitterest of these persecutors was Monk Robert, surnamed Bulgarius. He was an apostate, and so when he assumed the Dominican hood he brought with him an acquaintance with the haunts, manners, signs, and hiding-places of the reformers, which made him the most successful of inquisitors. In his hands murder became a fine art. Butchery was his meat and drink: so much so that at last he even turned the strong stomach of the holy see, which vomited him into imprisonment.[†]

But spite of blazing fagots and torture-rooms dissidents increased in numbers and in knowledge. They held the Bible to be the sole infallible authority in religion:[‡] they proclaimed that "no man should be coerced to believe, but should be won by preaching;"[§] and they held to the democracy of

---

[*] Brandt, vol. 1, p. 14. Motley, vol. 1, p. 68.　　[†] Brandt.
[‡] Bossuet, Hist. des Variations. Motley, vol. 1, p. 68.
[§] Brandt, *ut antea.*

Christianity; for Voltaire himself confesses that they strove to implant in every breast the idea that all men are created equal.*

Truly a formidable list of heresies—an indictment on each of whose counts men might easily have been condemned in that bitter age. And we are to trace their story, as the Alpine hunters do the wounded chamois, by their bloody footsteps. Whenever, wherever discerned, Rome endeavored to stamp them out. She wounded them especially in their chief teachers. The famous Beghard, Walter Lollard, a Dutchman whose remarkable eloquence filled England with dissenters, and bathed the valley of the Rhine in light, was apprehended and burned in 1320.† Wickliff's long life was a miracle. Huss and Jerome vanished in the lurid fire of Constance early in the fifteenth century.‡ But the gaps thus made were always filled; and even in 1457, Germany, highland and lowland, was so full of Vaudois that in travelling from Cologne to Milan, from Antwerp to the Zuyder Zee, they could lodge nightly with their co-religionists; while it was their custom to affix private marks to their signs, to write cabalistic letters on their gates as an invitation and assurance to the Christian passer; and this Trithemius can substantiate.§ These were the "gap men" of the Middle Ages. Waldo, Lollard, Wickliff, Huss—these were the John the Baptists of the Reformation.

° Cited in Orchard, p. 336.   † Mosheim.
‡ Ibid.   § Danvers' Hist., p. 25.

Rome never succeeded in suppressing them, and though she drowned their voices by her thunders, often the very·means she took to crush them only increased their influence. For instance, when the Hussites rose in Bohemia to defend their faith, Rome preached a crusade. Many Netherlanders, tempted by the brave words and the indulgences of the pope, enlisted to share in the glory and to reap the reward. They got little of either, for Ziska, the illustrious Bohemian chieftain, always baffled the invaders of his country; and the Dutchmen, becoming familiar with the tenets and manners of the heretics in their campaigns, returned home with a greater aversion to the church for which they had fought than to the Hussites whom they had attacked.*

Meantime, the pride and the power, the extortion and the presumption ·of the priesthood, increased apace. They asserted their independence of the civil authority. They insinuated themselves into the management·of temporal affairs by holding the pens of princes, and cities, and towns—necessitated by the prevalent ignorance to seek their clerks among ecclesiastics. Then taking advantage of their position, they wrote in cloister-latin, a jargon understood by the monks alone, and often they got the civil magistrates to sign and seal instruments of bequest to the church—to sign and seal unwittingly; and these would be trumped up and used in after years.†

* Brandt, vol. 1, p. 19.　　　　　　† Ibid., p. 15.

Nor was their avarice less than their ambition. The bishops, not content with their old revenues, laid new burdens upon trade and land from time to time. In some places the husbandman was forced to pay so much wheat and oats for every plough he owned. The landless were charged a certain measure of corn as a fine for their poverty. Rapacious churchmen exhausted the laity by every species of extortion, establishing new orders of monks and friars, endowing abbeys, and enlarging and building countless monasteries with the spoils.*

Since the estates of the church might not be taxed, of course every acre of land which was added to the already enormous ecclesiastical domain increased by so much the burdens, and decreased in the same proportion the ability of both lord and burgher on whom alone the state expenses fell. Nor was this all. Numbers of the clergy became hucksters; and since they were shielded by their cloth from all taxation, they undersold the lay merchants. Common shopkeepers began to starve for want of custom, and deep were the curses which they muttered against priests who thus took bread out of the mouths of those who fed them. In this way it happened that monasteries were converted into shops, convents into warehouses, and the mansions of secular churchmen into inns and tap-houses—typifying exactly the prior change in the ethics of the church.†

Then the avarice of the clergy partially accom-

° Boxham, Ned. Hist., p. 179. Brandt.   † Ibid.

plished what their cruelty and paganism had been powerless to do. The people began to murmur at the burden thrown on their backs. Haughty nobles disputed the right of lazy priests to enjoy vast estates while refusing to be taxed or to draw the sword in the state's defence. Princes, piqued by the superior wealth of the churchmen, and aggrieved by their withholding of all rents, opened the law books and feed attorneys to hunt up or invent some statute which should salve this wound.*

Soon the Netherland sovereigns began to impose restrictions upon the right of the clergy to hold and acquire property—restrictions which grew sterner and more general in the lapse of time.†
And so the instinct of self-interest began to sharpen the eyes of all classes. Men's pockets were enlisted against Rome.

Then, too, the people of the Netherlands were slowly rising into intelligence. Their language was already one of the grandest as it was among the oldest of Europe. France had not yet begun to undermine the Belgic tongue, and Holland and Flanders still conversed in the same idiom:—an idiom which the nobles already began to hate as that of freedom and commerce, and which the clergy still more disliked as that of heresy and moral independence.‡
Still, the Low Dutch,§ as it was styled to distin-

---

* Boxham, Ned. Hist., p. 179.   Brandt, Motley.

† Brandt, vol. 1, p. 23, et seq.

‡ Bowring, Sketch of the Lang. and Literature of Holland. Amsterdam, 1829, p. 9.   § *Neder-duitsche.*

guish it from the High Dutch* or German language, was the Netherland tongue as the German
was that of the upper plains—and the coexistence
of these idioms has been historically proved since
the eighth century.†

In the beginning of the thirteenth century deeds
began to be drawn up in the national language;
and in that same century Van Maerlant and Uten-
hove gave a brilliant impulse to their native tongue
through their poetical writings.‡

Van Maerlant, born at Damme, in Flanders, in
1235, was a philosopher, an orator, and a poet whose
influence was singularly broad and marked.§ He
has been honored with the title of "Father of
Dutch literature;"‖ and what entitles him to especial distinction is, that he was a layman—a layman
renowned for taste and learning in an age when
reading was almost exclusively the prerogative of
the clergy.¶

Before him " poetry was a vagrant art, which, in
the long winter evenings, took refuge in the chimney corners of great feudal castles, where it served
to amuse and console maidens, who repaid the
efforts of the troubadour by a sympathetic tear of
compassion. Disdaining cities, the minstrel of that
period was to be seen wherever noble blood presided, and it was an exception when he occasionally
condescended to bestow a poem upon the most emi-

° *Hoch-deutsche.*
† Delepierre, Hist. of Flemish Literature, p. 5.   ‡ Ibid, p. 11.
§ Bowring, Batavian Anthology, p. 22.   ‖ Ibid.   ¶ Ibid.

nent among the plebeian classes.. At court he was ever welcome; the princes loaded him with favors, and sought to make him one of their retinue; for it was to the minstrel's art alone that they were indebted for their fame."[*]

The quality of the troubadour's muse corresponded with the vagrant character of his life, and with the habits of the time. They sang of love and war to the exclusion of higher themes; though even in the Middle Ages translations of the masterpieces of Athenian and Roman literature were not wholly unknown to the Germanic races. Translations of the *Odyssey* and the *Æneid* were rare, but they existed,[†] while the legend of King Arthur was familiar as a household tale throughout Europe.[‡]

Van Maerlant revolutionized early literature. He wrote in the vernacular, and for the people; and he gave the Dutch, which is peculiarly adapted to the expression of devout, dignified emotion, the high tone of religious feeling and sublimity which has ever since distinguished it, and which made it at one time the representative of Christian thought.[§]

Beginning life as a minnesinger, Van Maerlant soon gave up the composition of madrigals to devote himself to sacred and profane history. Henceforth his writings were didactic; and he taught his countrymen philosophy, and medicine, and the natural sciences, through the medium of his verse. He dealt the Romanists of his age a hard blow, and when

---

[*] Delepierre, p. 31.   [†] Ibid., p. 19.
[‡] Ibid., Bowring, Hallam.   [§] Bowring. Batav. Anth., pp. 13, 14.

he touched upon the duties of men, his pure and vigorous style enabled him to demonstrate that a title of nobility is something more than a sheet of parchment, and that the virtue of a priest does not lie in his tonsure.*

Inveighing against the vices of the church, he put the Bible into verse. "What," says he, "the reading of the Bible is forbidden to the people, and they listen to the adventures of *Tristan* and *Launcelot*, imaginary personages, while throughout the world love and war stories alone are read, and the Gospel is thought to be too grave because it teaches truth and justice."† And he exclaims again, "Is Antichrist already come into the world? If I dared, I would say, Yes. Let a cunning serf become a judge or a priest, and he will be listened to in the councils of princes. Does a fool become a grain the wiser by increasing the size of his tonsure even to his ears?"‡

This energetic and unwonted language gradually acted on the awakening minds of the Hollanders, and abandoning lighter reading, they opened books of history and science: the useful began to prevail over the merely entertaining. The classics began to be dug up. The best thoughts of the ancients were pondered and acted upon, so that Van Maerlant himself could sing with truth:

> "All these realities have we sought,
> And out of Latin to Dutch brought,
> From the books of Aristotle."§

* Delepierre, p. 38.   † Ibid.   ‡ Ibid., pp. 41, 42.
§ Bowring, Batav. Anth., p. 63.

This iconoclastic poet had many admirers and imitators: a race of nobler minnesingers was begotten by his stately verse. Then the stream of literature began to gather as it rolled a thousand contributing rivulets. In the fourteenth century the Chambers of Rhetoric were founded. Diest lays claim to the possession of a poetical society as early as 1302;* and ere long the "Rhetoricers" covered Flanders and Brabant. The object of these associations was the cultivation and exercise of letters; and though they introduced much exaggeration of expression, and many foreign idioms, their influence could not fail to make for progress at that time, by awakening thought and rewarding literary effort.

It is to the Greeks and Romans that we are indebted for the theatre in its modern sense; but the muse of Æschylus and of Terence had long been silent, and when the Chambers of Rhetoric resurrected the drama, it took a different form, became the repository of mediæval Christianity, and was surrendered to scenic representations of the life of Christ.† At a later day these religious plays became the engines of reform. Rhetoricers making the circuit of the provinces, satirized the abuses and immoralities of the clergy through the theatrical representations, and thus helped largely to break the charm of the Roman church:‡ for ridicule is the most potent of spell-breakers. But the crowning

* Delepierre, p. 63.   † Ibid.
‡ Bowring, Sketch of Lang. and Lit. of Hol., p. 28.   Schiller, p. 381.

achievement of the Middle Ages was the invention of the printing press. "At the very moment when Philip the Good, in the full blaze of his power and flushed with the triumphs of territorial aggrandizement, was instituting at Bruges the famous order of the Golden Fleece, 'to the glory of God, of the blessed Virgin, and of the holy St. Andrew, patron saint of the Burgundian family,' and enrolling the names of the kings and princes who were to be honored with its symbols, an obscure citizen of Haarlem, Lorenz Koster, succeeded in printing a little grammar by means of movable type.* The invention of printing was accomplished, but it was not ushered in with such a blaze of glory as heralded the contemporaneous erection of the Golden Fleece. The humble setter of type did not deem emperors and princes alone worthy of his companionship. This invention sent no thrill of admiration throughout Christendom; and yet what was Philip of Burgundy, with his knights of the Golden Fleece, and all their effulgent trumpery, in the eye of humanity and civilization, compared with this poor citizen and his wooden type?"†

From this time popular intelligence marched forward with vast strides and to assured triumph.

* The question of the invention of printing has long been a mooted one. Germany claims it for Faust, Holland for Koster. It will most probably never be satisfactorily settled. But all the Netherland historians give Koster the honor, fixing the time variously between the years 1423 and 1440. The first and faulty editions of Koster are still religiously preserved at Haarlem.

† Motley, vol. 1, p. 45.

Rome could no longer monopolize learning. Books soon became cheap and plenty; and whereas men before were shut up to the use of manuscripts, and for one copy of the Bible tolerably written upon vellum, were wont to pay five hundred crowns, now as the art of printing grew common they might buy one for four crowns. Thus the people who could not reach the price of the Scriptures in manuscript, found it easy to purchase and read them in Koster's prints.* Towards the close of the fifteenth century a Dutch translation of the Old Testament was made from the Vulgate, and this, first printed in 1477, is at once a monument of language and a remarkable specimen of primitive typography.†

Thus "all things worked together for good." The first protests of the monks; the worn voices of the Waldenses; the songs and plays of the minne-singers; and Koster's type—these were rudiments of reform, the creators of thought; and growing knowledge was the spear of Ithuriel, whose touch made masked impiety and hidden despotism start up and reveal themselves. The world, long agoni-zing to speak, now possessed the most potent of voices. Analysis began. Men of *nisi*—"I take an exception;" and of *distinguo*—"I draw a distinction," entered the long-closed temple to investigate and to dispute. Christendom was at last prepared to listen intelligently to the protest of the Reformation, stood ready to shout, "Welcome Luther, and all hail."

* Brandt, vol. 1, p. 23.
† Bowring, Sketch of the Lit. and Lang. of Hol., p. 27.

CHAPTER V.

THE GERMAN CÆSAR.

WHEN, in 1515, Charles V.,* a boy of fifteen, placed the crown upon his brow and grasped the sceptre, the Netherlands had reached the acme of material prosperity. The tamest portrait of their condition looks like exaggeration. Seventeen provinces,† huddled in an obscure morass, extending, when counted together, but three hundred Flemish miles, covering an area not a fifth part as large as Italy, had dug themselves out of the mud, and now stood bathed in the meridian sun of a splendor as unexampled as it was honorable.

Grouped within this narrow neck of land were three hundred and fifty cities, humming with trade, alive with industry, many of them fortified by their natural position, and secure without artificial barriers, six thousand three hundred market-towns of a large size, and scores of farming hamlets and picturesque castles, imparting to the landscape a singular aspect of unbroken, breathing life ; while

---

* Chap. 3, pp. 77, 78.

† The duchies of Brabant, Limburg, Luxembourg, and Guelders, the seven counties of Artois, Hainault, Flanders, Namur, Zütphen, Holland, and Zealand, the margravate of Antwerp, and the five lordships of Friesland, Mechlin, Utrecht, Overyssel, and Gröningen.

the whole was guarded by a belt of sixty fortresses
of maiden fame, hitherto uncaptured.*

Antwerp was at this time the commercial metrop-
lis of Europe, the *entrepôt* and the exchange of
nations. She scrawled "Antwerp" on her bills,
and they passed current from Peru to Pekin. Beautifully seated on a plain beside the river Scheldt,
shaped like a bent bow, with the water for its
string, the city had long been a bustling one ;
but it was indebted to a recent discovery for its
sudden importance. The Levant trade no longer
rolled overland to pour itself into Europe through
the Italian cities; it now took ship, and sailing
round the cape of Good Hope, landed in Portugal
for European distribution—a divergence which revolutionized the commerce of the Middle ages,† helped largely to wither the Hanseatic league, and sent
ruin into the counting-rooms of the Mediterranean;
robbed Genoa of her sails; and degraded the city
of the doges to sit a beggar amid the broken pillars and defaced frescoes of her choked and weedy
palaces—gave her nothing to do but bathe her feet
in the stagnant waters of her canals, and hug the
bitter memory of the past.

On this ruin the new metropolis fed and was
fattened; and while Verona, Venice, Nuremburg,
Augsburg, Bruges, were sinking, Antwerp, with its
deep and convenient river, stretched its arm to the
ocean and caught the golden prize as it fell from

* Schiller, p. 388. Motley, vol. 1, p. 91.
† Van Loon, Grotius.

its sister-cities' grasp.* The Portuguese established
the mart of their East India trade in Brabant, and
"the spices of Calicut were displayed for sale in
the markets of Antwerp."† Here, too, centred the
West Indian merchandise, with which the haughty
indolence of Spain repaid the industry of the Netherland burghers. Here the Hanse towns stored the
manufactures of the north.‡ Here the English had
a factory which employed thirty thousand hands.§
And here, on the new Rialto, the great mediæval
commercial houses, the Gaulteratti and Bouvisi of
Italy, the Velseus, the Ostetts, the Fuggers of Germany, established themselves and competed for
custom.‖

Hundreds of splendid buildings dignified the
city. Here was the cathedral of Nôtre Dame; here
the stately Exchange, thronged daily by five thousand merchants, prototype of all similar establishments throughout the world.¶

In its harbor between two and three hundred
ships might often be seen loading at one time; "no
day passed on which the boats casting or weighing
anchor did not exceed five hundred; on market-
days the number was swollen to eight or nine hundred. Daily more than two hundred carriages
drove through its gates; above two thousand heav-
ily-laden wagons arrived each week from Germany,

---

* Motley, vol. 1, p. 82.
† Schiller, p. 374. Van Meteren, Hist. der Nederlanden.
‡ Ibid.   § Camines, Preuves des Memoires.
‖ Van Meteren, Schiller, Motley.   ¶ Ibid.

THE GERMAN CÆSAR.   101

France, Lorraine, without reckoning the farmers' carts and corn-vans, seldom less than ten thousand in number."* Thus it was that, while the culture of grain, flax, the breeding of cattle, grazing, the chase, and fisheries enriched the peasant, arts, manufactures, and trade brought wealth to the burgher, sent Flemish and Brabantine manufactures to either India, and as far east as Araby and the Persian steppes, making this the distinctive characteristic of the Netherland seaman—that he made sail at all seasons, and never laid up for the winter.‡

Antwerp had a twin, Ghent; like itself one of the most important and influential cities in Europe. "Erasmus, who, as a Hollander and a courtier, was not likely to be partial to the turbulent Flemings, asserted," so Motley reports, "that there was no town in Christendom to be compared with it for size, power, political constitution, or the culture of its citizens. It was rather a country than a city. The activity and wealth of its burghers was proverbial. The bells were rung daily, and the drawbridges over the many arms of the river which intersected the streets were raised in order that business might be suspended while the armies of workmen were going to or returning from their labors. As early as the fourteenth century, the age of the Arteveldes, Froissart estimated that Ghent could bring eighty thousand men-at-arms into the field; and now, by its jurisdiction over many other

---

* Schiller, p. 375.   † Ibid., 374

large but subordinate towns, it could muster upwards of two hundred thousand.

"Placed in the midst of well-cultivated plains,
Ghent was surrounded by strong walls, the external
circuit of which measured nine miles. Its streets
and squares were spacious and elegant; its churches and public buildings were many and splendid.
The sumptuous church of St. John, where Charles
V. had been baptized, the ancient castle whither
Baldwin *Bras de Fer* had brought the stolen
daughter of Charles the Bald, the City Hall, with
its graceful Moorish front, the well-known belfry,
where for three centuries had perched the dragon
sent by the emperor Baldwin of Flanders from
Constantinople, and where swung the famous Roland, whose iron tongue had called the citizens,
generation after generation, to arms—all were conspicuous in the city and celebrated in the land.
Especially the great bell was the object of the
burghers' affection, and generally of the sovereign's hatred; while to all it seemed a living personage, endowed with the human powers and passions which it had so long inflamed and directed."*

Both Antwerp and Ghent were essential republics in miniature. Each guarded its charters—the
trophies of a dozen centuries of toil and struggle—
with jealous care. Each was scrupulously watchful of the personal and domiciliary rights of the
citizen. Ghent divided its population into fifty-two
guilds of manufacturers, and thirty-two tribes of

* Motley, vol. 1, pp. 59, 60.

weavers; each fraternity elected its own deans and subordinate officers annually or biennially. The city senate, composed óf twenty-six members, was the administrative and judicial power; but was subject to the supervision of the grand provincial council which sat at Mechlin.* Antwerp was governed by the sovereign—solemnly sworn as Marquis of Antwerp to rule under the charters—who shared his authority with the four municipal estates—the senate, the deans of the guilds, and two officers called respectfully the schout and the amman, who represented the king, one in criminal, the other in civil affairs.†

The condition of the people at large corresponded with the importance and wealth of their cities. Thrift had dowered them with plenty. "There were but few poor; and these did not seek, but were sought by the almoners. Schools were excellent and cheap. It was difficult to find a child of sufficient age who could not read, write, and speak at least two languages; and the sons of the wealthier citizens were sent to the universities of Louvain, Douay, Paris, or Padua, where education, though feeling the onward movement of the age, still preserved its monkish spirit, and now wrapped learning in the ancient cere-cloths, and the stiffening sarcophagus of a by-gone age which had once saved it from annihilation."‡

'Tis a high saying of Macaulay that "The man-

---

* Motley, vol. 1, pp. 83, 84. Van Meteren.   † Ibid.
‡ Ibid. Schiller, pp. 388, 389.

ner in which a nation treats its women is a correct criterion of its civilization." In the Netherlands, woman's influence was broad and healthful. There the harems of the East, the jealous surveillance of the Spaniard, the hothouse culture of the mediæval epoch, when woman was looked on as the toy of passion, as a drudge to be watched, were happily unknown. Treated as sentient beings, the Dutch girls mixed from infancy with all classes and sexes, travelled alone, and so became self-reliant, frank, courteous; while their morals were as pure as their decorum was undoubted.* Distinguished by beauty of feature and form, and glowing with health, they were fond of dress—a taste which their burgher husbands, fathers, lovers, were always eager to gratify. "Really," exclaimed a queen of France, with astonishment not unmixed with envy, when on a visit to Bruges she witnessed the splendor, the fine linen, silk, and velvet in which the common ladies were habited, "really, I thought myself the only queen here; but I see six hundred others who appear more so than I."†

No, the Dutchman did not think with that old Chinese sage whom Aristotle endorsed, "A wife should be a shadow and an echo in the house." He enthroned her in his heart and at his hearthstone, where she became the genius of economy and order; while each addition to her influence was a step in morality. Not only so, but as, in Italy, Vittoria Colonna and Veronia Gambara were the friends and

* Motley, vol. 1, p, 91. Comines.   † Grattan, p. 75.

equals of Michael Angelo, the women of the Netherlands became the counsellors of princes, the silent heroines of suffering, the inspiration of many thrilling dramas of the revolution, the jewelled setting of the picture of Low Country life.

It has been said that modern civilization gets its conscience from the Hebrew, its brains from the Greek, and its hands from the Roman. The Netherlander was heir to this inheritance—indeed, he was the Yankee of the middle ages. Never a niggard, he was yet an economist, and knew how to utilize. His cattle, grazing on the bottom of the sea, were the finest in Europe.* His agriculture was esteemed the wisest in Christendom.† That he could make money we know, as also that his liberality kept pace with his opulence. When John the Fearless was captured at the battle of Nicopolis, a single merchant of Bruges ransomed him at two hundred thousand ducats.‡ And once a provost of Valenciennes, visiting Paris during one of the great fairs periodically held there, purchased, on his own account, every article that was for sale.§

Nor was the Netherlander content to grub for wealth alone. Ranging above the splendid linens, woollens, silks, and tapestries which his looms wove, he became an inventor, an artist, a discoverer— work to which his genius, developed by commerce, and by intercourse with many nations, pushed him.‖ In the lap of abundance and liberty, all

* Motley, vol. 1, p. 90.   † Ibid.
‡ Grattan, p. 75.   Guicciardini.   § Ibid.   ‖ Schiller, p. 375.
5*

arts, all sciences, were cultivated and perfected. From Italy, to which Cosmo de' Medici had lately restored its golden age, painting, architecture, and the arts of carving and engraving on copper, were transplanted into the Netherlands, where, in a new soil, they flourished with fresh vigor.*

The Flemish artists were the brothers of Titian and the teachers of Angelo. One of their number, John Van Eyck, discovered the art of painting in oil, and thereby immortalized the vivid touches of the brush, the sweet blushes of the canvas.† The Dutch musicians were the first in Europe—the instructors of Italy, the amusers of France.‡ The weaving of tapestry, the art of painting on glass, of polishing diamonds, of making sun-dials and pocket watches—all these, so Guicciardini tells us, were the original inventions of Low Country workmen.§ Even the points of the compass were known by Flemish names; and when Koster perfected his type, the industrial pyramid of the Netherlands was capped, while the Dutch, seizing the new engine, recognized it from the outset as an emancipator. Where they did not originate, they perfected; for Schiller says, "The people of the Netherlands united with the most fertile inventive genius a happy talent for improving the discoveries of others; so that there are probably few of the mechanical arts and manufactures which they did not either produce or perfect."‖

* Schiller, p. 375.   † Grattan, p. 75. Guicciardini.
‡ Ibid.   § Guicciardini.   ‖ Schiller, p. 376.

While the Netherlands, as a whole, were thus felicitously circumstanced, Freisland had been temporarily wrenched from her connection with the sister provinces, partly by natural, partly by political causes. In the thirteenth century, the slender stream which alone separated East and West Freisland was swollen into the Zuyder Zee by a tremendous inundation. A watery chasm yawned between kindred people, destroying at once the political and geographical continuity of the land. West Freisland was ere long absorbed in Holland; the eastern section, isolated, left somewhat free, became a federation of self-governing maritime provinces. Each of its seven little states was subdivided into cantons, governed by their own laws and by *grietmen* of their own selection; while the whole confederacy was ruled by an annual congress, presided over by the *podesta*, an elective magistrate identical in name and functions with the chief officer of the Italian commonwealths.[*]

Here there were few towns, no magnificence. The people lived in patriarchal simplicity. Their fine instinct had led them to curb the clerical power; priests were not recognized as a political estate;[†] monasteries were not common, but they existed; and one of the old chroniclers relates that a convent of Benedictines was once terrified at the voracity of a Saxon sculptor, who had been employed to decorate the chapel. The monks implored him to go elsewhere for his meals, because he and

* Motley, vol. 1, p. 37, *et seq.* † Grattan, pp. 31, 32.

his sons consumed enough to eat out the entire brotherhood in a week.* The Frisians were sure to become civilized, for they had capacious stomachs.

In the last years of the fifteenth century, Maximilian had prevailed upon East Freisland to elect the duke of Saxony as podesta;† and when Charles V. succeeded to his paternal inheritance in the Low Countries, the Saxons held the nominal sovereignty of Freisland—a title which he purchased,‡ thereby reuniting a kindred race.

In 1516, the ambitious boy caused himself to be proclaimed king of Spain, in right of his mother, mad queen Joanna ;§ and a few years later his skilful intrigues won for him the imperial crown of Germany, which made him sovereign of the Netherlands, monarch of the twin kingdoms of Spain, lord of the two Sicilies, duke of Milan, emperor of Germany, dominator of Asia, Africa, America, autocrat of half the world :‖ and this combination of titles gained him also that other surname of the German Cæsar.

* Chron. Menconis Abb. in Weram.
† Motley, vol. 1, p. 55. Grotius, Van Meteren.
‡ Grattan, p. 67.
§ Robertson, Hist. of the Reign of Charles V., vol. 1, p. 189, *et seq.*   ‖ Ibid., *passim.*

CHAPTER VI.

THE NEW RÉGIME.

TIME is the finest of organizers, the greatest of reformers. It transforms impediments into instruments, and subdues the most formidable mischiefs of the past into the most useful slaves of the future. Growth itself is the fruit of time; and growth is but another name for progress. "The fossil strata," says Emerson, "show us that nature began with rudimental forms, and rose to the more complex as fast as the earth was fit for their dwelling-place; and that the lower perish as the higher appear."[*]

Civilization is a similar development, unfolding naturally from its causes. In the sixteenth century these causes flowered. Want with its scourge, war with its cannonade, trade with its money, art with its portfolios, had long tapped the tough chrysalis; but the vivifying power still lagged, until reformed Christianity came with its charity, with its spirituality, with its holiness, and broke the shell, set the dull nerves throbbing, and helped the new epoch to emerge erect and free.[†]

Thus out of the past there grew at last an age whose "mouth was to speak great things;" words which should liberate the human soul, long a prisoner in the Vatican;[‡] whose hands were to new-

[*] Emerson, Conduct of Life, p. 143.　　　　　　[†] Ibid.

[‡] "L'Anima nostra e sempre prigioniera nel Vaticano." De Boni, La Chiesa Romana e l' Italia, p. 19.

model the map of Europe. The dawning atmosphere of the sixteenth century was heavy with revolution. Widespread abuses necessitated change. Rome had touched the muddiest bottom, and like Jerrold's profligate, insisted with drunken gravity that all mankind should lie beside it in the gutter; to which decent men objected. In an age of rising intelligence and progressive tendency, the Holy See held to the maxims, preached the dogmas, and claimed the absurd, wornout prerogatives of the darkest epochs—set itself in resolute opposition to the spirit of the time. The pontiffs became a tribe of deplorers and copiers. They esteemed the virtues of the present vices, and the vices of the past virtues. They stoned the saints of their day, and canonized mediæval sinners. They endeavored to manufacture the antique, and strove to reënact the Innocents and Hildebrands.

In the meantime, Platonism, which the Medici had resurrected in Italy, the communal idea, which had grown from the German municipalities, the printing press, and the Waldense protests in the Netherlands, all combined to spread intelligence and to awaken inquiry. Then a new power arose—public opinion; for heretofore there had been but two kinds of opinion, the opinion clerical, and the opinion baronial. Enlightenment popularized thought; and thought was the pool of Siloam, in which blind Europe bathed its eyes and recovered sight. Suddenly men saw, and what they saw both shocked and amazed them. An ecclesiasticism which they had immemorially worshipped as an inspiration and a saviour, revealed itself as the most brazen of mountebanks, whose greed was insatiable, whose morals were licentious to a prov-erb, whose schemes looked only to self-aggrandizement, whose forged keys rattled only to lure men to destruction.

Such was the awakening of the human intellect; and the danger was that the force of the rebound would send Europe over into jeering infidelity. Then God commissioned a second band of apostles to arrest this fate, and to point out the true path—reformation, not abolition.

Rome banned the Bible; "it must be put into all hands, and diligently searched,"* said Luther. Rome promised Paradise as the reward of meritorious works; "it must be won by prayer, and faith, and a renewed spirit through Christ,"† said Zwingle. Rome made fine distinctions between the priesthood and the laity; "we are all sons of God and heirs of heaven, if we but accept the Saviour,"‡ said Melancthon. Rome talked loudly of the supererogatory merits of the saints, a fund which the popes administered, and labelled "indulgences;" "all a snare and a delusion,"§ said Bucer. Rome rattled the keys of St. Peter; "they are forged,"‖ said Luther. Rome claimed and held

---

* John 5 : 39. † Gal. 2 : 16 ; Rom. 5 : 1 ; Rom. 3 : 28.
‡ Gal. 3 : 26 ; 2 Cor. 6 : 18 ; Rom. 8 : 17.
§ Psa. 143 : 2 ; Augustine, Confess., ix. Luther, L. Opp. Lat.
1, 211. ‖ 2 Thess. 11 : 9.

the temporal sword; "Christ's kingdom is not of this world "* said Zwingle. Rome went clothed in purple and fine linen and "fared sumptuously every day;" "the Son of man had not where to lay his head,"† said Melancthon. Rome forbade the clergy to marry; "marriage is one of the most honorable of earthly estates,"‡ said Bucer.

These and kindred sayings spread throughout Christendom with amazing rapidity. The infant press groaned beneath the load of pamphlets which were printed for the "healing of the nations."§ The writings of the reformers were publicly hawked by the booksellers of the period, and by hundreds of monks who had been "born into the Spirit."‖ Everywhere the sheets were seized and scanned while yet wet with printer's ink.¶ In the castle of the noble, in the dwelling of the burgher, in the hovel of the peasant, nothing was talked of but the Reformation.

In the Netherlands especially, the new tenets received the most speedy, heartfelt, and unanimous welcome.** For this there were many reasons. Instinct is often keener than intellect; and the democratic instincts of the Netherlanders had long recognized an enemy in the Roman oligarchy. They were also more broadly educated than any other race. Thinkers from habit, they had always

---

° John 18 : 36.   † Luke 9. 58.   ‡ Matt. 19 : 4–6.
§ Seckendorf, Hist. Ref.   D'Aubigne, etc.   ‖ Ibid.
¶ Michelét, Life of M. Luther.
°° Schiller, Davies, Motley, Grotius, Van Loon, Van Meteren.

listened half incredulously to the fables of the priests. For them the charm of the papacy was broken. Their cities and their nobles had frequently united to curtail ecclesiastical estates. They had themselves questioned, and they had heard others question many of the assumed prerogatives of the Holy See. The burghers in the happy leisure of affluence, had forsaken the narrow circle of immediate wants, and pushed by the spirit of independence, which is wont to go hand in hand with abundance, learned to examine the authority of antiquated opinions.* Moreover, in a country where industry was the most lauded virtue, mendicancy the most abhorred vice, a slothful horde like the monks must have been objects of long and deep aversion.†

Thus Romanism, which was indigenous to Italy, was an exotic in the Netherlands. Rome was the antithesis of Holland. The Dutch were half-protestantized before the Reformation, and when Luther began to preach, they instinctively accepted the pure gospel. If Saxony bore and nursed the reform, Holland was the guardian and defender of its maturer growth.‡

A happy collocation of circumstances attended the inception of the Reformation. The elector Frederick of Saxony shielded Luther from the first onset of Rome, and enabled him to develop and organize the principles of his dissent. In 1519,

---

* Schiller, p. 352.   † Ibid., p. 381.
‡ Davies, History of Holland, vol. 1, p. 358.

Maximilian died. At once the succession had as many claimants as Christendom had kings, each of whom began to demonstrate his unquestionable right to wear the imperial purple—a right which each proved to be just as clear as his sword was long. In the interregnum caused by this squabble, the disputed dominions were without a definitive rule, and the gospel theology was thus left free to ground itself. Finally, Charles V. clutched his grandfather's sceptre;* and then God so occupied his time in politics, compelling him to defend himself now against home-bred mischief, now against the Saracen, that the environed emperor could never pause long enough to strangle heresy.

For there were political as well as moral giants in those days. A constellation of great princes gemmed the horizon. Leo X. wore the tiara, Henry VIII. ruled England, Francis I. was king of France; and while Charles V. was being crowned at Aix-la-Chapelle, one of the most accomplished, enterprising, and victorious of the Turkish sultans, Solyman the Magnificent, ascended the Ottoman throne.† Each of these sovereigns had his own ends to subserve, and a singular scrub-race for power ensued. Leo X. used all the arts of his protean see to cheat Europe into a new crusade against reform. Henry VIII. fomented discord, and then

---

* In 1520.

† Robertson, History of the Reign of Charles V., vol. 1, p. 234.

laughed at those he had entangled from the safe
distance of his island throne. Francis I. was
wrestling with Charles V., and Solyman, the constant and formidable rival of the rest, led his Moslem hordes into the heart of Christendom, planting
the Orient now here, now there; for in those days
the Porte was not the "sick man" of Europe, and
its continued existence had not become a mere
diplomatic juggle.

Still, spite of this dizzy and incessant rivalry,
Charles V. did make spasmodic efforts to curb the
prodigious progress of the innovating tenets. The
same astute instinct which had won the Netherlands to espouse the Reformation, made the emperor, a despot from temper and position, its implacable enemy, for he recognized in it the essence
of republicanism. As a papist and as a king, he
could not fail to despise its teachings, and to persecute its adherents.

Besides, there were other causes for the violence
with which he now began to hack the Low Country
reformers—causes which aggravated the more placid
dislike which he bore to the innovation generally
into a passion in the Netherlands. Since his accession to the Spanish throne, Charles had become
accustomed to the exercise of absolute power. In
Aragon and Castile he was an irresponsible despot,
vexed by no barriers, troubled by no questioners.
But when he entered the provinces all was changed.
There he was only the first citizen; multitudinous
checks, in the form of privileges and charters,

o Robertson, *ut antea.*

which the burghers defended and extended with
unsleeping vigilance, constantly fretted and thwarted his arbitrary will. Inflated with pride, staggering beneath titles, and habituated to the submission of the commons, Cæsar's stomach was turned by
the hardy independence of the haggling burghers.
"This talk of privileges I hate," said he.*

Moreover, it has been well said that, as the
whole government of the famous emperor was but
one tissue of plots and manœuvres to enhance his
authority, it was, of course, necessary from his
standpoint, that he should become absolute master of the various links of his mighty empire,
so that he might move all or any at will, effectually, suddenly; and this necessitated centrali-
zation—he must make himself the soul of his
dominions.†

In the execution of this scheme, Charles met
with little opposition outside of the Netherlands.
There the citizens, awakened to the distrust which
always accompanies comparative weakness, had
never before been so alive to their constitutional
rights, never before so jealous of the royal prerogative.‡ Violent outbreaks of the republican spirit
and ominous mutterings warned him of danger;
yet he persisted, and even made insidious progress.

He subjected the decrees of the national courts
of judicature to the revision of a royal council

* Robertson, Hist. of the Reign of Charles V.
† Schiller, p. 378.   ‡ Ibid., p. 377.

seated in Brussels, and his echo.* He ousted all doubtful natives from office, and intrusted the most vital functions of the provinces to his foreign creatures—men whose only tenure of office was his favor, and consequently certain to infringe privileges which they knew to be obnoxious to their master, but of which otherwise they knew nothing.†
He, like his predecessors, regarded the provinces as an inexhaustible bank, on which he might draw at will, and "the ever-increasing expenses of his warlike government pushed him as steadily to augment his resources; and in this, trampling on the most sacred guarantees, he imposed new and strange taxes. To preserve even the name of their liberties, the states were forced to grant what he had been so modest as not to extort; for the history of this emperor's government in the Netherlands is a continual list of imposts demanded, refused, and finally accorded. Contrary to the constitution, he introduced mercenary troops into these territories, directed the recruiting of his oft-decimated armies in the provinces, and involved his burgher subjects in wars which could not advance if they did not injure their interests, and to which, against all precedents, they had not been even so much as asked to assent."‡

But Charles V. was much too sagacious not to foster the business enterprise of the Netherlands— the exchequer of the empire; so much was essen-

---

* Davies, Hist. of Holland, vol. 1, p. 357. Grotius. Van Loon.
† Ibid. Van Meteren.   ‡ Schiller, pp, 382, 383.

tial to the success of his politics. Their commerce
was his strength; and since liberty was the creator
of commerce, he spared just so much of it as he
could work over into the sinews of war; which
explains why he did not strip the Low Countries of
all their hated privileges.*

But while the wily emperor did, in a certain
sense, protect and enlarge the business of the
states, he hit upon an ingenious plan for the gradual impoverishment of the most wealthy and dangerous families of the land. " He crippled the
great vassals of the crown "—it is Schiller who says
it—" by expensive embassies, under the specious
pretext of honorary distinctions. Thus, William of
Orange was despatched to Germany with the imperial crown; and Count Egmont was commissioned
to conclude the marriage contract between Philip
and Queen Mary. Both afterwards accompanied
the duke of Alva to France, to negotiate the new
alliance of their sovereign with Madame Elizabeth.
The expenses of these journeys amounted to three
hundred thousand florins, towards which the emperor did not contribute a single penny. The
Netherland nobles were also encouraged to keep
open table, and display a lavish magnificence. By
these and kindred arts, the nobles were soon bankrupt."†

But in this Charles outwitted himself. The
great vassals, reduced from affluence to poverty,
became needy adventurers, and finally midnight

* Guicciardini, Descriptio Belgii.   † Schiller, pp. 389, 390.

conspirators—plotters from necessity and from pique; for, already ruined, they had no motive to preserve the peace, and could not fail to gain from revolution.

When the emperor had thus bled the Netherlands, and, as he supposed, somewhat thinned the veins of their exuberant independence, his next step was to restrain their religious liberty.* At the Diet of Worms, in 1521, he formally anathematized the person and the teachings of Martin Luther.† This anathema was, a few weeks later, published in the Low Countries, and soon supported by an edict forbidding the composition or publication of lampoons on the church, or of any writings on matters of faith, under pain of "punishment according to temporal and spiritual justice;" terms which were afterwards construed to mean death by torture.‡

Spite of the imperial decree, the reformers continued to talk, write, publish, propagate. In 1522, Charles commissioned a special agent to weed out the heretical books, and fulminated a new edict; measures which proved futile.§ Then the emperor, enraged by this contemptuous disregard of his parchment *fiats*, and bent on convincing Pope Leo—who affected to doubt his zeal, and was then coquetting with Francis I.‖ —of the sincerity of his

* Davies, vol. 1, p. 357. Brandt.
† Ranke, Hist of Popes, Leo X. Mosheim. Michelét, etc.
‡ Davies, vol. 1, p. 358.
§ Brandt, Hist. of Ref. in Low Countries, vol. 1, book ii.
‖ Robertson, Hist. of Charles V., p. 280, *et seq.*

faith, rained a tempest of decrees upon the obstinate provinces.

By these, to open the evangelists was pronounced a crime; to attend any meeting, secret or public, to which religion lent its name, even by implication, was an indictable offence; to converse on the subject of reform, at home as abroad, was damnation.* Everywhere unheard-of courts were established to enforce these laws; and a conviction of holding, diffusing, or listening to heretical doctrines was death—if a man, by the sword; if a woman, by burial alive. Even apostacy was banned, for all recanters were ordered to be burned.†

Despotic politics and bastard religion now clasped in the raid on freedom. "The fiefs of the condemned were confiscated, contrary to the statute law, which permitted the heir to redeem them after payment of a trifling fine; and in defiance of an express and valuable privilege of the citizens of Holland, by which they were not to be tried out of their own province, culprits were forced beyond the limits of the native judicature, and condemned by foreign tribunals. Thus Romanism guided the faltering hand of despotism, to attack with its sacred

○ Brandt, Schiller, Van Meteren.

† Ibid. "The usual mode of executing the punishment of burial alive was to lay the victim in an open coffin, placed on the scaffold, of a length and breadth just sufficient to contain her; three iron bars were then placed, one on the neck, another on the stomach, and a third on the legs; through a hole at the upper end of the coffin was passed a rope, fastened round the neck, which the executioner drew tight from under the scaffold as the body was covered with earth." Davies, vol. 1, p. 383, note.

weapon, and without danger of opposition, liberties which were inviolable to the secular arm."*

But these appalling preparations could not affright the dauntless, and they made no converts, while the gospellers still prayed, and sang, and spoke of Christ.† Then Charles invoked the fire goblins. On the first of July, 1523, the initial *autos-da-fé* were kindled in the Netherlands. Two Augustine monks, convicted of heresy, were dragged through the streets of awe-struck Brussels, and publicly burned.‡ "Alas," sighed Erasmus, the "doubting Simon" of the age, the twin of Bunyan's "Mr. Facing-both-ways," "two heretics have been burned at Brussels, and that city now begins strenuously to favor Lutheranism."§

Some eight months previous to these executions, the papal throne, left vacant by the premature decease of Leo X., who died "as the poppy fades,"‖ was filled by the election of the venerable Cardinal Tortosa, who reigned under the title of Adrian VI.¶ This pontiff was a Netherlander by birth, the son of a boat-maker, educated at Louvain by charity, and by nature of an austere and monastic temper; but his genuine piety was sadly distorted by those prejudices which he had sucked out of the divinity of the schools.** By his attempts at the regeneration, in some sense, of his church,

---

* Schiller, p. 383.   † Brandt, vol. 1, book ii, *passim.*
‡ Ibid, p. 49. Motley.   § Erasmus, Epist.
‖ Ranke, Hist. of the Popes, p. 31.   ¶ Ibid.
** Brandt, vol. 1, p. 47.

and by his fierce denunciation of the reformers, he won the hatred of both parties in those passionate days, dying after a stormy rule of twenty months, profoundly convinced that the greatest misfortune of his life was to have worn the triple crown.[*]

Tortosa was in his turn succeeded by the crafty Giulio de' Medici, who took the name of Clement VII.;[†] and he, dying in 1534, was followed by a number of short-lived pontiffs, until, on the commencement of the Dutch Revolution in 1566, Pius V. was on the throne.[‡]

But while the history of the pontificate was marked by these vicissitudes, the march of mighty necessities which swayed the destiny of Christendom went on and on, fulfilling Goethe's maxim, "Without haste, without rest."

In 1529, the clash of arms ceased for a moment, and Europe was permitted to catch breath in the pause occasioned by the treaty of Cambray, sometimes styled the "Ladies' Peace," because it was negotiated by two statesmanlike women—Louise, queen-mother of France, and Margaret, the singularly able and astute governante of the Netherlands.[§]

---

[*] Ranke, Motley.   [†] Ranke, *ut antea.*   [‡] Ibid.

[§] Dumont, Corps Dip., tom. 4, p. 2, pa. 42. Margaret was the emperor's aunt. She had been twice married—to Charles VIII. of France, who had broken from the nuptial contract before its consummation; and to the Infant of Spain, who died immediately after the union. While on a voyage to Spain, to wed the heir apparent of that kingdom, the vessel in which she had sailed was

But Charles V. made a bad use of the pacification, for he employed the interval of leisure in renewing edicts against reform, and in sharpening the punishment and narrowing the tests of heresy.* He was a physician of the heroic school, and blood-letting was his panacea. Or, if you will have another figure, he was a schoolman of the mediæval pattern, and the scaffold was his favorite syllogism.

Worst of all, while the Reformation was thus excommunicated, and imperilled, and hacked from without, internal dissension commenced to tear its vitals, and it lost the fine moderation and the dignified unity which had characterized its inauguration. The good cause began to split into sects—a dangerous tendency in the face of the common enemy in hostile array, and moving to the storm of the camp. At such a crisis, division looked like suicide. "This is the true path," said Luther. "Nay, hither it runs," cried Zwingle. "Wrong," affirmed Menno Simon, the able and famous Netherland teacher who organized the Mennonites ;†

tempest-tossed, and all hope was given up ; whereupon the courageous princess wrote her own epitaph, as follows :

"Here gentle Margaret sleeps beneath the tide,
Who twice was wedded, yet a maiden died."

She was not shipwrecked after all. See Davies, vol. 1. p. 385.

* Brandt, vol. 1, book 2, *passim*.

† "The venerable Menno Simon was born at Witmorsam in Friesland, in 1496. His education was such as was generally adopted in that age with persons designed for the priesthood. He entered the church in the character of a priest in 1524, and had then no acquaintance with the Bible, nor would he touch it, lest he should be seduced by its doctrines. At the end of three years,

"wrong; 't is as clear as day that I am on the only road." All good men, and true; but at that critical moment, when the safety of the cause they loved dictated union against the foe of each, somewhat too heatedly wedded to subordinate phases of the grand movement for reform. The gospel phalanx was confused and embarrassed. The soldiers of the cross took sides. Some said, "I am of Paul;" some, "I am of Apollos;" others, "I am of Cephas." Did they forget those wise words of the apostle to the Gentiles: "Is Christ divided? was Paul crucified for you? or were ye baptized in the name of Paul?"*

But a blacker and still more portentous cloud dimmed the horizon. The Reformation was being compromised by the excesses of an insane gang robed in its colors and mouthing its watchwords. A horde of apocalyptic visionaries, in motion throughout Europe, were especially violent in the Netherlands. What have been called the "anabaptistical† atrocities" commenced. "A handful

he began to doubt the dogma of transubstantiation; but attributed the doubt to Satan. Dissipation could not put the cries of conscience to sleep, and he was won to search the Scriptures; and this, with the aid of Luther's writings, convinced him of the error of popery." In 1536, he became a gospel preacher. The plan of doctrine and practice, which he threw into the form of catechisms, did for the Low Country Baptists what Calvin's "Christian Institutes" did for nascent Protestantism at large. See Orchard, Foreign Baptists, p. 365, et seq. Also, Mosheim, vol. 3, p. 329.

* 1 Cor. 1 : 13.

† "It is but justice to observe, that the Baptists of Holland, England, and the United States are essentially distinct from the seditious and fanatical individuals who were called Anabaptists at

of madmen," says Mosheim, "who had got into
their heads the absurd notion of a new spiritual
kingdom, soon to be visibly established in an extraordinary manner, formed themselves into a society under the guidance of a few illiterate leaders
chosen out of the populace. And they persuaded,
not only the ignorant multitude, but even several
among the learned, that the city of Munster was to
be the seat of this new Jerusalem, whose ghostly
dominion was to be propagated thence to all the
ends of the earth. The ringleaders of this furious
tribe were John Matthison, a baker of Haarlem, John
Brockhold, a tailor of Leyden, one Gerhard, with
some others, whom the blind rage of enthusiasm, or
the still more culpable principles of sedition, had
embarked in this extravagant and desperate cause.
The band made themselves masters of Munster,
deposed the magistrates, and committed every crime
which perversity could suggest, every folly which an
infernal imagination could devise. Brockhold proclaimed himself King of Zion, and substantiated his
title by running naked through the streets and marrying eleven wives at one time. But his reign was
transitory and his end was awful; for Munster was

the Reformation. They do not consider the word applicable to
their sect." D'Aubigne, Pref. to Hist. of Ref., p. 10.

"The true origin of that sect which acquired the name of Anabaptists, by their administering the rite of baptism even to those
who came over to their communion, and derived that of Mennonites from that famous man, to whom they owe the greatest part
of their present felicity, is hid in the remote depths of antiquity,
and is consequently extremely difficult to be ascertained." Mosheim, vol. 3, pp. 318, 319. Ed. of 1826.

retaken in 1636, the New Jerusalem of the fanatics was destroyed, and the mock monarch, chained for a time in an iron cage, was finally put to a painful and ignominious death."*

This did not stay the plague. Scenes of tumult, license, blood, were every where exhibited. On one bitter winter night at Amsterdam, in 1535, the snug burghers were roused as the clock chimed twelve, by a hideous outcry in the street. Quitting their cosy couches, they ran shivering to their windows, and lo, they saw seven naked men and five nude women raving and bawling as they hurried over the cold pavement, "Woe, woe, woe to Babylon." When, after being seized and brought before the magistrates, clothes were proffered them, they refused them stoutly, crying, "We are the naked truth."† And when marshalled for execution they sang and danced upon the scaffold.‡

Romanists have often pointed to these, and to kindred wild outbreaks as the logical result of schism; and nonplussed Protestants have sometimes relieved themselves of the odium by saying, "'Thou canst not say I did it,' for these madmen did not belong to my sect." But no sect is to be judged by its exceptions; none is responsible for the acts of fanatics whom it disowns. Venner called himself a Puritan; were the Puritans Fifth Monarchy men and seditious because he was? In Germany every audacious varlet who broke into churches and cloisters and plundered altars, called himself a

---

* Mosheim, vol. 3, p. 328, *et seq.*   † Ibid., note.   ‡ Ibid.

Lutheran; were the Lutherans a horde of pilferers because one robber stole and stabbed under that name?

Perhaps you will say, Why, then, charge fraud, and ambition, and irreligion upon Rome because Hildebrand, and Innocent, and Loyola were churchmen? For this reason: these infamous churchmen were not the exceptions, they were the rule of the papacy—the type-men and the models of the holy see for ages; the logical, consummate fruit of that ecclesiasticism, never disowned, never even deprecated. When the Baptists canonize the Munster madmen, when the Puritans organize a propaganda under the name of St. Venner—then, and not till then, can they be asked to adopt the *enfants perdus* of the past, and defend their atrocities with complacent infamy. Many Protestants have been fanatics, and some have been intolerant and bloodthirsty; but on the shield of such warriors is the bar-sinister which marks them as the bastards of reform. Neither Protestantism as a whole, nor Protestantism in its sects, is to be impeached for their offences— offences alien to the spirit and to the letter of the faith.

Emeutes like that at Munster were sure to mark the Reformation. Such outbreaks are the inevitable concomitants of revolution. Intense social, moral, intellectual agitation is certain to fanaticize weak minds "whose zeal is without knowledge;" and demagogues and profligates will always saddle fanaticism and ride it booted and spurred to the goal of their ambition. What then, shall there be no reform? Reform must be; and the evil which accompanies it is to be charged, not to progress, but back upon the opposition which seeks to conserve the ignorance and the wrong of whose embrace fanaticism is begotten.

But this aside. These fanatical antics were unfortunate for the Reformation, for they armed the emperor with a pretext for fresh severities; stimulated him to redoubled exertions to extirpate a creed which policy and superstition united in his mind to condemn; and furnished him with a specious plea against the new doctrines on the ground of decency and outraged nature.

"In my opinion," wrote Mary, queen-dowager of Hungary, who had succeeded Margaret in the government of the Netherlands, to her brother the emperor, "In my opinion all heretics, whether repentant or not, should be persecuted with such severity as that error might at once be extinguished, care only being taken that the provinces be not wholly depopulated."* In this opinion Charles so fully concurred that he promised to introduce the Spanish Inquisition into the Netherlands.†

This bare threat paralyzed the nation. Antwerp was shocked, shut its shops, left its ships to rot, hushed the hum of its market-place, hid its gold, and dropped the prices and rents of its houses below zero; while the chief foreign merchants prepared to quit the ruined metropolis.‡ At once the

* Motley, vol. 1, p. 80.　　† Schiller, p. 383.　　‡ Ibid.

shrewd emperor abandoned this resolution in form, but he kept the fact, and established the tribunal by hiding the frightful name of inquisitor under the milder title of Spiritual Judge.* "Then," says Schiller, " this abhorrent court proceeded to rage with the inhuman despotism which has ever been peculiar to it. And we may get an idea of its success in slaughter by the fact that during the reign of Charles V. fifty thousand persons perished by the hand of the executioner for the sole crime of imputed heresy."†

In the midst of these orgies, the wailing, bleeding Netherlands learned that Charles V. had determined to abdicate—learned and marvelled with mankind.

° Schiller, p. 383.   † Ibid., p. 384.

CHAPTER VII.

EXEUNT.

ON the morning of the 25th of October, 1555, there was an unusual stir in the good old town of Brussels. It was not the bustle of traffic, for trade was at a stand-still, and the only marketable commodity was talk. The city had emptied itself into the streets. Thousands of promenaders, brave in their gala garb, blocked up the thoroughfares, and broke into eager, excited groups; here a dozen ranged about a shop-door, yonder a score under the windows of a mansion. The gay capital was draped for a *festa*. Flags and quaint devices, rare flowers and costly tapestries were lavishly displayed in each of the irregular, picturesque streets through which the town climbed, in the form of an amphitheatre, from the banks of the little river Senne up the steep hillside to the border of the forest of Soigniers, ending abruptly at its gates.

Brussels, unlike its lowland sisters, did not spring from the ocean mud; it nestled in the lap of a bluff, wrapping around it " a wide expanse of living verdure, cultivated gardens, shady groves, fertile cornfields," flowing like a mantle. " In the heart of the place rose the audacious and exquisitely embroidered tower of the Stadt-house, three hundred and sixty-six feet high, a miracle of needlework in stone, rivalling in its intricate carving the cobweb tracery of that lace which for centuries has been synonymous with the city, and rearing itself above a façade of profusely decorated and brocaded architecture. The crest of the elevation was crowned by the towers of the old ducal palace of Brabant, with its extensive and thickly wooded park on the left, and by the stately mansions of the Flemish grandees, of Orange, of Egmont, of Aremberg on the right. Just at hand lay the forest, dotted with monasteries and convents, swarming with every kind of game, whither the citizens made their summer pilgrimages, and where the nobles chased the wild boar and the stag."*

Such was Brussels, and such was now the scene within its walls. Why met the burghers? and why stirred the city? It was the day appointed by Charles V. for his abdication and for the coronation of his son†—an eventful day for Brussels, for the Netherlands, for Christendom; and the loyal town had draped itself and proclaimed a holiday that it might fitly say good-by to Cæsar, and cry welcome to King Philip.

The drama was enacted in the grand hall of the ducal palace. Kings were the actors; seven crowned heads, the foreign ambassadors, the knights of the Golden Fleece, the Netherland nobles, the Low Countries, present by delegates—these were the audience.‡ Charles was fond of ceremony, and he knew its

---

* Motley, vol. 1, p. 96.

† Van Meteren, Hist. der Nederlanden, vol. 1, p. 16. Badavaro, Relazione, MS.   ‡ Ibid.

effect; and, determined that this last public act should be a fit close to his stormy career, he lavished his gold and his skill to make it so.

He succeeded; Christendom looked on with open mouth, and the emperor not only sent his immediate auditors home weeping—stranger still, he wept himself.* Could men have foreseen the future, there had been greater cause for tears; facts would have been more pathetic than leave-taking Cæsar.

Two sentences will summarize the imperial address: "In a quarter of a century of successful war I have heaped up a mighty dominion, which is now menaced by religious heresy and by political assault—so fiercely threatened, that to defend its integrity youthful vigor must·enter the arena. At fifty-five I am an old man, with shattered health; but here is my son, I seat him on my throne as the defender of the faith, as the ruler of my realm."†

This was the spirit of the abdication, and it was the emperor's solution of the riddle. What says history? History acquiesces in this *dictum*, but finds additional motives. Charles was the greatest glutton of his day,‡ and after forty years of unexampled abuse, his long-patient physique revolted. Lame with gout, half choked with asthma, he was also a confirmed dyspeptic, and physiologists can tell what whims a disordered stomach puts into the

---

* Pontus Heuterus, 14, pp. 336–339.

† See the address *in extenso* in Gachard, Anal. Belg., pp. 81-102. It is also given in Pont. Heut. 14, p. 338, *et seq.*

‡ Godelærus, Motley, and others.

heads of men. Depression caused by dyspepsia—
this cropped out in abdication. Originally of an
athletic, well-proportioned frame, though always of
an ugly countenance,* the emperor was now a sad
wreck. "When physicians questioned his lower
limbs, Death-in-life answered, 'I am here;' when
their eyes, rising attentively by way of his hands
and arms, questioned upward to the muscles round
the protruding Burgundian jaw, Death-in-life answered, 'I am coming.'" Charles was keen enough
not to sit still and rot into the grave, sceptre in hand;
by a splendid affectation of unselfishness, he withdrew decorously from public view; withdrew because
he willed to do so, not because he was compelled—
and got the credit of unprecedented self-abnegation.

But racking disease was not the only ingredient
in the bitter cup of the emperor's last years. Political misfortune began to overtake him. The conqueror at Pavia had, on two recent occasions, been
humiliated, outwitted, defeated. Young Maurice of
Saxony, who had once sat at the feet of this Gama-
liel to verse himself in war and diplomacy, left his
master when he had learned the lesson, and, putting
himself at the head of menaced German Protestantism, dashed down upon the emperor while he was
seated in solemn conclave at Innspruck forging
thunderbolts with which to smite reform; drove him
to hasty and ignominious flight in a peasant's wag-
on; defeated his troops a little later at Füssen;
forced the sick and half-stunned monarch to an-

‡ Van Meteren, Gachard.

other headlong midnight flight through the difficult Alpine gorges in an awful storm; permitted his escape only because "for such a bird he had no convenient cage;" and, finally, anchored the Reformation in Germany by the advantageous treaty of Passau—a peace which he compelled the staggered emperor to sign.*

So, too, when Charles had attempted to retake the French town of Metz; of the hundred thousand men whom he brought to the siege, he returned balked and bloody with a loss of forty thousand†— returned to hear that the Protestant princes, that the Turkish sultan, that the Holy Father had formed a "triple alliance" against his tottering throne.‡ "For some days," says Strada, "he kept his chamber, and ever after his disease grew sharper. Nay, it was commonly believed that Cæsar's fortune, glutted and grown coy, began to retire, and that the happy genius of this long-unconquered emperor was fled to Henry the French king; Cæsar himself, not able to dissemble it, being heard to say, 'It seems fortune is the young man's mistress.' And therefore for his device of Hercules' pillar, and the motto *plus ultra*—'more beyond'—there was painted on his palace walls a crab, with the words *plus citra*—'more on this side'—a jeer agreeable to the times. 'The emperor,' said some, 'does like a wary gambler at dice, who, having drawn a great sum of money in many hours' play, holds his hand, and suffers not himself to be stripped of all his

* Robertson, vol. 2.   † Ibid., Strada,   ‡ Ibid., Motley.

victorious heap at one throw.'"* On the other hand, it has been contended that the abdication came from no soreness of defeat, but was the consummation of a purpose avowed many years before this lesson of the mutability of success, to Francis Borgia, when Charles confessed that "he was minded to divest himself of all the cares and baggage of this world," and seek peace in quietude; recalling the words of an old cavalry officer who had petitioned for a discharge from service, giving this reason: "I wish to put a space of religious contemplation betwixt my life and my tomb."†

However all this may be, it is certain that from one motive or another Charles did resign his dignities and retire, "like a nobody," to a private house in Brussels. His tarry was not long. One night a comet was discerned flaming athwart the sky, presaging—as was at that time thought—disaster, and the death of princes. *Me mea fata vocant*—"my fates call for me,"‡ he said; and at once embarking, the self-discrowned emperor sailed for Spain, and buried himself in the monastery of St. Juste,§ where he died in 1558,|| after a residence embittered by the memory of the world he had surrendered; after hours wasted in reading despatches, in whining over dishes, in making epigrams on his cook's inability to tickle his tanned palate."¶

So passed the last years of Charles V.—what

---

* Strada, pp. 8, 9.   † Ibid.   ‡ Godelærus, p. 645.
§ Robertson. || Sept. 21st.
¶ Stirling, Cloister Life of Charles V.

was he at his best? An able soldier, a shrewd, unscrupulous politician, a cool, determined despot. He had no convictions—only a purpose. He had no heart—only a muscle to circulate his blood. His most familiar weapons were trickery and brute force. Charles *qui triche*—such was the *sobriquet* which his frauds had won him.[*]

To aggrandize his house, this was his object; and to this he bent every thing, as one might twist a nose of wax. He persecuted from policy, not bigotry, and stabbed reform because he was keen enough to see that its talk of religious rights necessitated civil rights—meant political as well as moral heresy. He plucked the bud, that he might kill the flower. The glass of his history reflects no fanatic; every action of his life turned on the well-oiled hinge of imagined policy. Policy made him listen to Luther at Worms, and dismiss him in peace. Policy persuaded him to proclaim *The Interim*, that bastard juggle of a creed. Policy pushed him to permit his German troops to listen to the exhortations of their own chaplains, accompanying them from city to city. Policy led him at the same time to bury alive in the Low Countries any woman who should read her Bible. Policy urged him to sign the treaty of Passau, the Papal *coup de grâce* in Germany. Policy led him, first since Attila, to sack the "Eternal City." Policy decided him to fling an offending pontiff into the dungeons of the castle of St. Angelo.

[*] Brantôme, Art. Charles Quint.

Yet spite of his *finesse*, spite of the connivance with which he met connivance, spite of his triumphs, and his titles, and his power, greatest since Charlemagne, his career was a magnificent failure, a gilded cheat. He lived to see the Reformation which he had essayed to crush, triumphant in England, conqueror in Germany, and spreading in the Netherlands—men reading the interdicted evangelists in the lurid light of the very fire kindled to consume them.

So with the empire which he had massed. Already it was crumbling. The imperial crown went to his brother Ferdinand, the Roman throne passed also into his tenacious possession.* In what remained there was no cohesion—a mere congeries of victim states held under the lock and key of despotism, tending inevitably to dismemberment: like the rich mud of our Mississippi, shifting with every flood from one side to the other of the channel.† Vast and rich as was his realm, Philip's chief inheritance was the revolution.

* Robertson.
† Wendell Phillips, Letters and Speeches, p. 350.

CHAPTER VIII.

AFFINITIES.

UNDER Charles V., the Netherlands were decimated by ambition; under Philip II. they were decimated by fanaticism.   Standing on the threshold of his reign, let us pause a moment to analyze this king—for it is a safe rule of the ancients, "If you would comprehend events, understand men."

Philip II. was the Sphinx of his own day; he is the spelled riddle of our time.   The iron mask which, unlike the famous Bastile prisoner, he wore from choice, not necessity, has been torn off by the hand of time, and we may read his features—see him as a man of starch and buckram.   It was his constant effort to divorce himself from humanity. If he ever had a heart, he murdered it in boyhood, and he was more stoical than the stoics.

This icy temper—which caused his courtiers to shiver when they approached him, which made them hear a crash when he smiled—was exactly typical of his mind.   Narrow, incapable of generalization, tied down to *minutiæ*, sluggish, chained in forms, enamored of the letter of the law which kills, he yet had a remarkable memory, and when he once embraced a purpose, he moved to execution with tedious but pitiless certainty.

He was singularly patient. " Time and I," such

was his boast, "are a match for any two."* But it
has been well said that time was not always his
ally—sometimes refused to hunt in couple; for time
succors virtue and helps genius, tenders to the one
golden opportunities, which must be snatched with
ready grasp, and renders to the other tardy justice.
Philip's patience often balked him; for while he
advanced with measured, methodical step, success
was clutched by a more rapid hand. While the man
of system deliberated and shaped his plan, the man
of action, inspired by the moment, extemporized a
triumph. While Philip was writing a despatch, his
father would have conquered a kingdom.

Gloomy, sour, conceited, ascetic, Philip had not
the faculty, and he lacked the desire to please. He
would not compromise his pride by affecting to be
debonair. He studied solitude, stood apart from
choice. Surrounding himself with mystery and terror, he aped deity.

In this he was unlike Charles V. "When the
emperor returned to his palace escorted, as he usually was, by a train of nobles and princes of the
empire," observes Prescott, painting him on one
occasion at Augsburg, "he courteously took each
of them by the hand, and raised his hat on parting.
But Philip then, and always, walked directly to his
apartments, without so much as turning round, or
condescending in any way to notice the courtiers
who accompanied him. In fact, it was said of him,
that he considered himself greater than his father,

* Gayarré, Philip II. of Spain, p. 59.

inasmuch as the son of an emperor was greater than the son of a king."*

This sullen haughtiness was his by nature, but it was increased by untoward circumstances. He was born and educated in Spain. "Castile, Aragon, Leon," Grattan reminds us, "were in some degree excluded from European civilization. A contest of seven centuries between the Mohammedan tribes and the descendants of the Visigoths, cruel, like all civil wars, and, like those of religion, not merely a contest of rulers, but essentially a war of races, had given to the manners and feelings of the Spaniard a deep stamp of barbarity. The ferocity of military chieftains had become the basis of government and law. The Christian kings had adopted the perfidious and degrading etiquette of the despotic sultans whom they had displaced. Magnificence and tyranny, power and cruelty, sagacity and dissimulation, respect and fear, were inseparably associated with government in the minds of such a people. They could comprehend nothing in religion but a God armed with omnipotence and vengeance; nothing in politics but a king as terrible as the deity he represented."†

It was in such a school that Philip was cradled and taught. His earliest lesson was the omnipotence and irresponsibility of royalty. "The vassal who kills a man by his sovereign's order," so wrote his confessor at a later day, "is free from blame, because the king, being master of the lives of his sub-

* Prescott, Hist. of Ferdinand and Isabella.   † Grattan, p. 79.

jects, can dispose of them as he pleases, either with or without the formality of law."* This was the doctrine which the monarch was set to learn. Is it strange that the unquestionable despot of the south should become the usurping master of the north?

Besides this, Philip was isolated by ignorance. Two out of three of the Netherland burghers could speak several languages; their king was master of but one, and he never became sufficiently familiar with the modern languages to be able to do more than write a little French and Italian with painful slowness.† Of the Dutch he could not speak a word, and he was the most prejudiced of foreigners when he essayed to govern the Low Countries—dominated solely by a hatred of their liberties, which barred him from the absolutism to which he was habituated; and by a contempt for the hearty, familiar manners of the burgher populace, whose character was so fatally antipodal to his, whose loquacity was so constant a reproach upon his taciturnity, whose somewhat boisterous joy grated so harshly on his cynical ear, whose freedom was so perpetual a menace to his despotism.

Philip was a manikin, not a man. He had a low instinct of cunning, and flattered himself that he could read men. He mistook deceit for sagacity, and esteemed cruelty to be an imperial quality. He thought he had an aptitude for business, and was indefatigable in work. A passion for contemptible details was his most prominent intellectual trait;

* Cited in Gayarré, p. 163, et seq.   † Grotius, Motley, Grattan.

and his chief delight was to pen, despatch, receive, and scrawl silly comments on despatches, in which he was a glutton.* "He hated to converse; but he could write a letter eighteen pages long, when his correspondent was in the next room, and when the subject was, perhaps, one which a man of talent could have settled with six words of his tongue. The world, in his opinion, was to be moved upon protocols and *apostilles.* Events throughout his dominions had no right to be born without a preparatory course of his obstetrical pedantry; and he could never learn that the earth would not rest on its axis while he wrote out a programme of the way in which it was to turn."†

He was grossly licentious, as well as cruel and unscrupulous, yet he was as constant and regular at mass, at sermons, at vespers, as a monk.‡ He probably esteemed himself a model Christian, for it is Schiller who informs us that "egotism and fanaticism were the title-page and contents of his life."§

Philip was the contented jackal of Rome. "My mission," said he, "is the suppression of heresy."‖ The man was worthy of the mission, and the mission was worthy of the man. In the prosecution of this atrocious purpose, he embarked his diminutive soul, stuck at no oaths, balked at no barrier, scrupled at no crimes; for had he not read and pondered that papal canon which sanctifies the means if the

---

* Motley, vol. 1, p. 142.   Watson, Life of Philip II.
† Ibid.   ‡ Ibid., p. 145.   Gayarré.   § Schiller, p. 392.
‖ Gayarré, p. 30.   Grattan, Van Meteren, etc.

end be good? "Keep no faith with heretics"—it was the essence of his ethics; there was merit in the breach, sin in the observance.

Constitutionally and systematically Philip was the champion of immobility. Movement disturbed him. Progress of any kind smelt of heresy in his nostrils. "No innovation," cried he, when reform was broached. "We cannot but fancy," observes his biographer, "that if Philip had been gifted with omnipotence, he would have delighted in creating a world without motion. Creeping things might perhaps have been tolerated, but the wind would certainly have been excluded; and he would have said to the ocean, ' Peace, be still.' "*

Philip's person corresponded with his intellect— like that was narrow, angular, meagre, and awry. He had the air of an habitual invalid; and his timid, shrinking frame was surmounted by a small head and a pinched face, weighed down by the heavy, protruding Burgundian jaw.† In this human cage his tiger spirit crouched and growled.

Such in temper, mind, and body was Philip II. when, at the age of twenty-eight,‡ he entered the Netherlands to succeed the wornout and gouty emperor. Other traits he had, which time was to develop, and some which we have sketched were still in embryo; but if this was Philip in the green tree, what was to be expected of him in the dry?

---

* Gayarré, p. 302.
† Pont. Heut. 14, p. 346, *et seq.* Watson, Life of Philip II.
‡ He was born in May, 1527.

Now we may be sure that an outbreak will not be long in coming. Philip piqued himself on being a foreigner—widened the chasm which already yawned between the Netherlands and himself; dismissed his father's Dutch officers; would be attended by none but Spaniards, and brought in his retinue and cantoned on the Netherlanders a swarm of needy Castilian adventurers.*

The unnatural union into which Spain and the Low Countries were now forced was pregnant with ill. No two people could be more dissimilar. Each misunderstood the other.

There had always been ill-blood between the Spaniard and Netherlander; and now, when the burgher saw his old enemy quartered on his country in the guise of a conqueror; and under a monarch who took no pains to disguise his contempt for the time-honored customs and parchments which he so highly prized, the seeds of bitter discontent were sown in his heart prior to the commission of any overt act. This mutual jealousy was sharpened by the religious differences of the time. Spaniard and Romanist were synonymous words. Just as synonymous were Netherlander and Protestant. While the Spaniard saw in the Dutchman a heretic in religion, a Jew in trade, and a rebel in politics, the Dutchman saw in the Spaniard a fanatic in faith, a slothful mendicant in business, and an ignorant slave in civility.†

* Meteren, Grotius, Motley, etc.
† Grotii Annal. Belg. Latin., 1, 4, 5, *et seq.*

This feeling extended to all classes in the Low Countries. Even the nobles whom Charles V. had done so much to corrupt and impoverish, paused between their cups to hiccough curses upon Spain; while all whose chief demand, like the Roman savages under the empire, was for food and amusement—*panem et circenses*—echoed a deep amen. It was imperilled nationality rising to assert itself.

The manner of Philip and the insolent presence of his Spanish satellites awakened thought. A strong republican reaction set in. Men began to question the *jus divinum* of Madrid as they already had that of Rome. The absurdity of an hereditary monarchy which might lapse into absolutism at any moment, was almost as generally felt as that of the establishment which the Reformation had exploded, and to which Fletcher of Saltoun compares it—an hereditary professorship of divinity.

For the Reformation had created a people—taught men to think—educated men through responsibility. The religious conflict had been let down to common comprehension; it was seen to be no quarrel in the upper air between angry and loquacious priests, each afraid to soil his latinity by a popular appeal. And when the reformers "awoke all antiquity from the sleep of the libraries," and moved to their work, not

> "to the Dorian mood
> Of flutes and soft recorders,"

but with lips touched like Isaiah's, they planted—without intending to do so, for their sole purpose was religious reformation—they planted the rude idea of political democracy, and left it to unfold through Christian martyrdom and faith in God.

But all this was latent—in the minds, not yet in the acts of the people. The burghers still stood intrenched behind their parchment guaranties, and fought inside of constitutional forms. Hoping against hope, they applied a rule to Philip which Coleridge has put into an epigram: " When you cannot understand another's ignorance, account yourself ignorant of his understanding." But the rules of construction have their limits, and patience, if entertained too long, becomes a vice.

CHAPTER IX.

SCHEMES.

WHEN Philip II. placed his father's discarded crown upon his head, he grasped with it the sceptre of a limited monarch; for already the prerogative of the throne had gained a visible ascendency over the republican spirit.* Still, many of the ancient. franchises remained in nominal force, and these had acquired fresh importance, in the estimation of the provinces, by the wholesale oaths of office which the new king had not scrupled to take.

Seven years before the abdication, Philip had visited the Netherlands at the request of Charles; coming to receive their oaths of future fealty, and to swear in return to support the whole round of privileges which hedged in the sturdy burghers—indiscriminate concessions which king and emperor alike believed would be an opiate certain to make vigilance slumber, and which, as each knew, need not shackle an unscrupulous conscience.† By these oaths Philip assented to larger liberties than any of his ancestors had yielded since Mary of Burgundy signed the " Great Privilege "‡—assented all the more readily because he did not mean to hold himself bound by his amen.

* Schiller, p. 389. † Meteren, Davies, Motley.
† Chap. III., pp. 76, 77.

Thus it was that the wily monarch began his connection with the Low Countries, not as emperor, not as king, but as hereditary prince. This was the theory, the fact had a different face.

Philip and the burghers had hated each other at first sight—one reason why the citizens had bound their prince with so many and so unusual green withes of concession. For, this haughty, sullen, retiring, impassible foreigner, what confidence could he inspire in the hearts of one of the most lively, frank, energetic, and progressive of the European races? Vainly had they striven to make him smile by the warmth of their greeting. Brussels exhausted itself in festivities, Antwerp outdid itself in the magnificence of its celebrations, Ghent shouted itself hoarse in his honor; and yet the icy phlegm of Philip remained unthawed. The joyous roar of the populace grated on his ear, the frequent expression of popular rights he esteemed the voice of incipient rebellion, the magnificence of the display offended his jealous vanity.*

"Well, then," said the angered citizen, "if we cannot make this frigid señor smile at our greeting, we will see if we cannot make him wince by our demands." The good burghers were doubly piqued, for Philip subscribed concessions as imperturbably as he received addresses of welcome.

This was in 1548.† Now, in 1555, Philip was again on Netherland soil, this time not as heir but

* Wagenær, Varderlandsche Historie, vol. 4, p. 294, et seq. Meteren, 1, f. 13. Motley, vol. 1. Grattan, p. 81.   † Ibid.

as master. Both prince and citizens remembered
the former visit—both anticipated trouble. But
there was quiet in the land, that frightful calm
which precedes a storm. Philip began to dissemble; it was not safe yet to throw off the mask. As
for the Dutch, they put their fingers to the lips of
their foreboding suspicions, and waited.

Meantime the government was settled. The old
governant, Mary of Hungary, had resigned her office
on the abdication of the emperor, alleging that she
was "too old to recommence and learn a new
alphabet" under another reign.* Philip reluctantly
assented to her resignation,† and, convening an
assembly of the state, inducted into the governor-
generalship of the Netherlands his cousin Emanuel
Philibert, duke of Savoy—a brilliant and astute ad-
venturer, who had been spoiled of his estates, and
stripped of every thing but his title and his skill by
French usurpation.‡

The court—a herd of Spanish grandees, with
here and there a Netherland noble for appearance'
sake§—had been organized prior to the appointment of the pauper duke. At about the same time
Philip seated half a dozen Spaniards at his council-
board‖—among the rest the duke of Alva, destined
later to play an awful part in the opening drama of
the revolution ; and Ruy Gomez, the royal favorite,

* Papiers d'état du Cardinal Granville, vol. 4, p. 476.
† Gachard.
‡ Brantôme vol. 1. Badavaro, MS., cited in Motley, vol. 1, p.
150, et seq.   § Badavaro, ut antea.
‖ Apolog. d'Orange, p. 47, et seq.

valet, councillor, and finance minister, the king's right hand, the gate to his good-will, the power behind the throne.*

These preliminaries settled, Philip, with the mingled craft and caution of his nature, began to smooth the way towards the accomplishment of his lifework. It was the nature of this man to plot in secret, to stab in the dark, to act in enigmas. He would have been a midnight conspirator, if he had not been a despot. He never went straight towards an object—always chose the crooked path, and would naturally tell a lie unless he had a dozen different and distinct reasons for speaking the truth.

So now, resting with one hand on Alva's shoulder, and with the other upon that of Ruy Gomez, "the pillars of his power," as the shrewd Venetian envoy, Suriano, called them,† he did not command, he schemed. Philip was anxious to cement his authority before he strained it. Yet, like his father, he desired to regard the Netherlands as a whole, and not as a congeries of provinces, and he hated the antique liberties, the obstinate privileges, which interfered with his ideas of symmetry; and he, too, like the emperor, looked about him for some engine which should crush these irregular, heterogeneous rights into the uniformity of despotism.‡

Philip's first move was adroit. He reënacted his father's merciless edict of 1550, which made burning,

---

○ Brantôme, Art. Philip II.   Gayarré.

† Suriano, MS., cited in Motley, vol. 1, p. 147.

‡ Motley, vol. 1, p. 155.

hanging, drowning, and burial alive the punishment which awaited even a suspicion of heresy;* and then, skulking behind the emperor's ghost, he cried, "I do not innovate, I simply reënact. These punishments are a part of the national institutions which I find, do not bring, here. They have received Cæsar's sanction, and have been sustained by past generations."†

But though the act was subtle, though innumerable appeals were made to the conservative sentiment, and to the patriotism of the commons; though they were summoned to enforce the edict because it had been acquiesced in by their ancestors, and because Philip had made no change in it, but only essayed to stand in the old ways of the emperor, "of very laudable memory;" yet, spite of all, the people growled ominously. Antwerp refused to publish the placard;‡ other cities echoed this veto of the commercial metropolis;§ and these protests drove Philip to recede in their case, though in sections where the placards had been published it was ordered to be enforced—a strange anomaly, to subject some towns to the Inquisition and to excuse others; yet advantageous, because it made the resistance of Antwerp and the rest all the more conspicuous.‖

In the meanwhile the fire of persecution wanted no human fuel to feed on. At Mons, in Hainault, two men, suspected of heresy because they were diligent in their study of the Bible, were first im-

---

* See Chap. VI., pp. 126–128.   † Motley, *ut antea.* Meteren.
‡ Brandt, vol. 1, p. 110.   § Ibid.   ‖ Ibid.

prisoned, and then, without any very close scrutiny into their notions of religion, condemned to be beheaded. One Adrian Van Lappen, a citizen of Bruges, returning from a fair at Frankfort, halted for the night at Aste, in Hainault, and gave his satchel to the landlady of the inn : she being curious, opened it in his absence, and found it to be filled with heretical books. Some of these she showed to the village priest ; the hapless merchant was at once arrested, and after a brief space, burned to death in a slow fire.*

These are two instances out of hundreds. Philip would have kindled similar fires throughout the Low Countries had it not been for the protest of brave Antwerp ; which he heeded, because he was anxious to disarm suspicion, and by securing a subsidy, emancipate himself from the control of the popular deputies.† He had already demanded of the assembly which met to confirm Emanuel Philibert, that a tax be imposed on Flanders, Brabant, Holland, and the sister provinces, which should fill his exchequer without the intervention of the states. "No," said the provinces ; but they softened the refusal by granting Philip a generous commutation in gold.‡

In the midst of these intrigues, when partially balked in one direction and partially successful in another, Philip found himself suddenly compelled to suspend this congenial campaign of trickery and

---

* Brandt, vol. 1, p. 108.   † Meteren, Wagenær, Grattan.
‡ Ibid. Davies, vol. 1, p. 490, *et seq.*

murder, in order to defend himself against exterior assault: France menaced him on one side, the pope thundered on the other. The jackal of Rome had been forced into the false position of foeman to the Holy See.

This was how it happened. The emperor's half century of life had been an incessant battle. Now he smote Francis I.; now he caged a Protestant prince; now he buffeted the pope; now he pulled the beard of the paynim Solyman. But he was a lover of dramatic effect; and when he decided upon abdication he was anxious to improvise a peace, that a serene sky might lend lustre to the pageant. He began to intrigue. "Hush," said Cæsar; and he juggled up a truce, hollow, treacherous, made to be broken, but solid enough to bridge over the period of the imperial comedy.

A farce of a pacification was signed at Vaucelles early in 1556.* It was ostensibly an armistice for five years, and suspended hostilities throughout Europe. "Ah ha," cried Charles. "'Tis well," said Philip. "Good," exclaimed Henry. Complacent diplomacy rubbed its hands. "The science of government is fraud," says Machiavelli; and while the negotiators were assembled at Vaucelles, Henry II. and the pope had concluded an offensive and defensive alliance against Spain, whose object was the expulsion of the Spaniards from the Italian peninsula.† Henry was to aid the pontiff to emancipate

* Meteren, De Thou, Brantôme.
† Brantôme, Mémoires de Coligny.

7*

himself from neighbors whose influence reduced him to the position of head chaplain to the court of Madrid; and as a reward he was to be permitted "to carve thrones for his royal brood out of the confiscated realms of Philip—out of Naples and Milan. When was France ever slow to sweep upon Italy with such a hope? How could the ever-glowing rivalry of Valois and Hapsburg fail to burst into a general conflagration, while the venerable vicegerent of Christ stood beside them fan in hand?"*

The reigning pope, Paul IV., was the Faust of ecclesiasticism, the antithesis of Charles. While the emperor laid down a crown to become a monk, Paul Caraffa quitted his convent cell—whither he had betaken himself after abdicating the episcopal dignity—to assume at eighty the tiara, and then immerse himself in the vanities of earth, to stir up wars with his trembling fingers, to croak havoc with his aged voice, and to strut and totter in the purple in his second childhood.† Such was the game which was now afoot, and such was the pontiff who had launched it.

With a heavy sigh and a muttered curse, Philip postponed his Netherland schemes, and turned to the consideration of foreign affairs. He hated war— for he was not a soldier, he was only an assassin. He preferred *autos da fé* to battle-fields; the pleasure was greater, and the risk was less. Besides, he felt the anomaly of his position—he, the Romanist, the fanatic, the antagonist of the pope. It was his

* Motley, vol. 1, p. 153, *et seq.*   † Ranke, Brandt.

dream to consolidate a league of the papal powers, for the purpose of uprooting heresy. Evidently, then, this absurd crusade of mutual friends against each other must be ended; and how end it more fitly than by union against Protestantism, the common foe? To the consummation of that purpose, the royal plotter determined to demand every thing, or to sacrifice every thing, as circumstances might dictate; for whatever he might win, or whatever he might lose, all was gained if that was gained.*

Meantime this sluggish prince acted for once with strange energy, the vicious activity of his mind conquered even the stubborn slowness of his body. Convening a council of theologians, he asked, " Is it lawful for me to wage war against the Holy See?" " Yea, truly," responded the chorus, " so it be only in defence."†

With this decision in his pocket, Philip crossed into England to cajole Queen Mary, his wife—fit consort for such a king—and to browbeat the British parliament, exactly contrary to his marriage vows, into a participation in the pending contest— which concerned England just as much as it did the Arabs.‡ He succeeded. England declared war; and while arming, dropped from her girdle Calais, the key to France.§

* Watson, Life of Philip II. Apolog. d'Orange.
† Michele, *Relatione*, MS. Cited in Motley, vol. 1, p. 163. Gayarré.
‡ Motley, vol. 1, p. 169.
§ De Thou, Brantôme, Hume, *in loco*.

While the king was thus occupied, Ruy Gomez, absent in Spain, had raised a contingent and sent it to the seat of war ;* and Philip, on his return from England, wrung the money which paid for this strife, and two thirds of the soldiers who won barren laurels in it, from the Netherlands. Then followed siege and counter-siege, marching and counter-marching, mêlée, and rout, and death. Finally, Guise, who had passed the Alps into Piedmont, was worsted by Alva, who held Italy for Philip; Coligny, who had been ravaging Artois, was coopèd up in the fatal city of St. Quentin ; and France heard one day that her power had been broken in two awful routs, at St. Quentin and at Gravelines, and that her noblest children were either dead or prisoners—a double Pavia ;† while Pope Paul IV., also in extremity, craved peace for his old age.

Philip, elate and triumphant, then exhibited his true character. " I crave peace at any price," said he‡—why, we know. He granted the baffled occupant of St. Peter's chair terms which astonished no one more than Paul himself ; ordered the victorious Alva to make an abject submission for him to the pope, and to kiss the great toe of his holiness ; and crowned this pitiful surrender to the vanity of a peevish old dotard by a congenial act of perfidy— for he confirmed his grumbling captain's consent to the confiscation of the estates of those Italian

* Documentos Ineditos para la Hist. de España, vol. 9, p. 487.
† Brantôme, De Thou, Motley.
‡ Watson, Life of Philip II. Gayarré, p. 40.

princes who had espoused his cause.* "Sire," queried Alva, "Do we capitulate, or does the pope?"

Having thus placated the beaten pontiff by treating with him as the conqueror, Philip next cemented peace with France. In this treaty he compelled Henry II. to concede important advantages,† but he did not ask all that he might, because he gained all that he wished when he was assured that Henry would cordially unite with him in any scheme which looked to the extirpation of heresy.‡ The gloomy and victorious bigot was now at leisure to resume his interrupted game in the Netherlands—to resume it with fresh advantage, fortified on the right hand and on the left.

So bright was the out-look for despotism—so portentous were the prospects of reform—when, in April, 1559,§ the facile diplomats scrawled their signatures across the treaty of Chateau-Cambray.

* Grattan, p. 82, *et seq.* Gayarré, Motley.

† Meteren, Grotius, De Thou.

‡ Apolog. d'Orange. De Thou, lib. 22, cap. 6. Davies, vol. 1, p. 497.

§ De Thou, Meteren.

CHAPTER X.

THE MASK LIFTED.

THE pacification of Chateau-Cambray placed in Philip's hand the *bâton* of the dictator of Christendom—recognized in him a dreaded superiority which menaced the independence of Europe. His wealth seemed inexhaustible; deep as the unfathomed gold mines of Peru and Mexico, which formed his coffers in the West, untold as the glittering diamond heaps of Borneo and Golconda, which formed his dowry in the Orient. His captains were the ablest of the age. His soldiers were veterans hardened by war, accustomed to victory, habituated to obey the daring genius of their leaders with blind, unquestioning audacity—soldiers whose tread, like that of Cæsar's cohorts, shook Europe; soldiers who had scaled the pyramids, and planted the Spanish banners on the walls of Rome. Had he been Alexander, he would have ground the world under the heel of his military boot. Had he been Cæsar, he would have carved out an empire whose limits would have been the globe. But he was Philip II., and it was his ambition to become the assassin of Netherland reform. This was the pivotal point of his policy; upon it he brought all his terrible resources to bear. "I will succeed, or I will sink Europe," said he. Philip was narrow, dogmatic, fanatical; but he had a purpose, and he was in deadly earnest—the chief promoters of success in any sphere. But cunning and powerful as he was, this bold, bad man had one antagonist on whom he did not count, God; God, whose name is love, and whose other name is justice, which was before Philip, before Rome, and will be after it.

Still, Philip entered the arena with all the material forces on his side.

Peace is the essential condition of successful commerce, and the Netherlanders craved it. When they heard that a pacification had been signed, the jocund, excitable burghers were wild with delight. The holiday was nine days long. Bonfires blazed, bells pealed, cannon belched pacific flame. But thoughtful men looked on the jubilee with gloomy faces and foreboding hearts—what meant the conditions of the peace? Rumor had already bruited the alliance of crowned heads for the extirpation of heresy.* Across keen souls there fell the chilling shadow of the future.

Suspicion might well awaken thought. "Philip had not made peace with all the world that the Netherlanders might climb on poles, or ring bells, or strew flowers in his path for a joyous movement, and then return once more to their counting-rooms and looms." This treaty meant deadlier war, war bitter for its peaceful garb; and when the unthinking populace rose to hail it, they shouted over the initial step in a scheme which Philip meant to end in a national murder.

* Davies, vol. 1, p. 497. Thuanus, Meteren.

The king had long pined for the congenial atmosphere of Madrid;* in 1559 he determined to quit the Netherlands and return to Spain. He had a twofold motive: he thought that it would be safer for him to direct the movements of his satellites at a distance and by impersonality; he dearly loved to write voluminous despatches.† Evidently, Madrid was preferable to Brussels.

Possibly, two additional considerations may have influenced this decision. Charles V. had just breathed his last, bewailing his impious folly in permitting Luther to slip through his fingers at Worms,‡ and employing the last fevered spasms of his strength in writing these lines to his son, whose eager spirit did not need a spur: "Deal to all heretics the extremest rigor of the law, without respect of persons, and without regard to any favoring pleas."§ Philip could now return to Spain more really a king than he would have been while Cæsar lived, even though weakened and fanaticized by a rot of his faculties, and buried in a monastery.

The battle of St. Quentin, one of the most decisive of the recent war, had been fought and won on the festival of St. Laurence, to whose intervention Philip attributed the success of his arms. In grateful homage to the saint, and to commemorate the manner of his martyrdom, he vowed to erect a monument in the form of a gridiron, as a memorial—an idea which gradually expanded, in thirty-two years

* Watson, Gayarré.   † Ibid., Brantôme.
‡ Stirling. Cloister Life of Charles V.   § Ibid.

of incessant labor, into that gigantic architectural absurdity, the Escurial, at once a palace, monastery, and mausoleum.* Philip's anxiety to return to Spain may have been heightened by his pious ardor, for, soon after, he laid the foundation-stone of the marble anachronism.

But many things remained to be done before he could shake the Netherland dust from off his feet. "Let me see," thought the king: "some grave matters await adjustment; delicate and menacing questions must be answered; a programme for the future will have to be written out; the instruments· of my despotism must be selected, and so selected as not to provoke suspicion; and the government must be deputized and new modelled." To these several duties Philip at once addressed himself. It was work to his taste; for, as the petrel loves the storm, so his element was chicanery.

The Netherlands were ominously restless and fretful. Illegal robbery, under the name of taxation, fettered trade, and mortgaged the labor of the future.† A bureau of ubiquitous spies made all classes anxious and uneasy by their surveillance.‡ The merciless execution of the merciless edicts against heresy, stirred constant riot§ and insured rebellion; for what is it that the old saw says? "Persecution necessitates revolt." The most potent and eloquent of reformers was the Inquisition; for every *auto da fé* that it kindled illuminated a score of

* Watson, Gayarré.   † Meteren, Wagenær.
‡ Watson, Hoofd.   § Hoofd, Meteren.

darkened souls. The early victims begat the later soldiers of the Reformation. The gospel throve even amid devastation; and when a martyr died, the multitude saw liberty and virtue burning by his side.

Philip had taken care, on the conclusion of peace, to canton his Spanish men-at-arms on the large cities of the Netherlands, for the double purpose of overawing local mutiny and having them at hand in case of need.[*] At the same time he split the renownèd Low Country cavalry—but three thousand strong in time of peace, for the Netherlands had a sturdy republican distrust of standing armies, though still redoubtable to the fears of despotism—into infinitesimal squads, and scattered these in different sections under independent captains.[†]

These sinister movements increased the popular discontent, and were universally construed to be a menace to the nationality of the provinces.[‡] The conduct of the foreign soldiers added fuel to the fire. Their ribaldry and licentiousness were proverbial; and since their pay was kept habitually in arrears by Philip that he might have a pretext for their retention, they did not hesitate to indemnify themselves at the expense of the citizens.[§]

A trial of wits ensued. The burghers exhausted persuasion in their effort to win Philip's assent to the departure of his troops; the king was fertile in

[*] Grattan, Schiller, Motley, Wagenær.

[†] Grattan, p. 85. Motley, vol. 1, p. 210, *et seq.*

[‡] Van der Vynckt, vol. 1, p. 135.   [§] Schiller, p. 400.

excuses—now he dreaded a sudden invasion from France, although that kingdom, rent by the League and Huguenot wars, was too weak to send a trooper across her frontiers; now he said that they were to form the escort of his son, Don Carlos, whom he was careful to retain in Castile; again they were his creditors, and since the exchequer was empty, "quite exhausted, gentlemen, I assure you," he dared not bid them go unpaid lest they should mutiny—such were the expedients to which he had recourse.* These men-at-arms were a part of Philip's programme of usurpation, and necessary to his purpose; he never meant to say good-by to them. Despots love bayonets. Cannon were the props of this king's throne.

But the greater the desire which Philip showed to retain his docile Spaniards in the country, the more obstinately the states insisted upon their removal:† on that point all classes were a unit. The spirit showed itself in various ways—especially in the "Chambers of Rhetoric." The rhetoricians were the newspapers of that day—filled the exact place occupied by the modern press, and used their influence better than some editors use theirs in the middle of the nineteenth century. They were eminently liberal in their tendencies, and they made it their business to spin verses and street farces out of the raw material of public sentiment.‡ Civil and religious tyranny was their constant butt; and "sharing with the pulpit the only power which then

---

* Schiller, p. 401.   † Ibid.   ‡ Motley, vol. 1, p. 340.

existed capable of moving the passions and directing the opinions of the people," they used their
influence nobly. The best of their comedians was
not even cousin-german to Aristophanes; but if
they had less attic salt, they had equal heartiness
in their truculent, effective, homely satire, and they
made "the galled horse wince."

The court had long suspected and watched these
homely wits; and now, when they began to satirize
the king's men-at-arms, the bishop of Arras urged
that they be gagged under heavy pains, and a placard to that effect was issued early in 1559.* "At
this time," wrote Sir Richard Clough to a friend in
England some years later, "these plays are forbidden much more strictly than any of the works of
Martin Luther."† But it is easier to ban than to
suppress. Public opinion cannot be gagged by
statutes. So new comedies were still written and
enacted—"plays which first opened the word of
God in the Low Countries, and which, as they were
persisted in, cost many thousand lives."‡

At this same time, Philip, always anxious to
enlarge the boundaries of the ecclesiastical realm,
solicited from the pontiff permission to erect fourteen new bishoprics in the Netherlands—sending
the request to Rome on the two feet of a double
reason: the insufficiency of the existing seas to supply the spiritual wants of an increasing population;
and their weakness, unenlarged, as a barrier against

---

* Burgon, Life and Times, vol. 1, p. 377, et seq.
† Burgon, ut antea.   ‡ Ibid.

heresy.* The octogenarian pope, willing to pleasure a prince whose victorious viceroy had kissed his toe, and eager to smite reform, readily granted a bull decreeing the innovation.†

Perhaps this manœuvre was the most generally odious of Philip's acts thus far; the Netherland churchmen were incensed because the revenues of the new sees were to be created by alienating a portion of the funds of the existing bishoprics and abbeys—against which their fat pockets vehemently protested;‡ the nobles were angered because the prelates thus created were certain to be the subservient tools of the Spanish interest, eclipsing them by superior power and dignity;§ the people, largely converted to a purer faith, and detesting the very name of priest, were convinced by their keen instincts, and rightly convinced, spite of the king's declaration that the project was a century old, bequeathed from father to son and neglected till now, but now enforced by the emperor's dying admonitions,‖ that the "sole purpose for which the new bishops were instituted was to increase the efficiency of the Inquisition—a conviction substantiated by the fact that each prelate was empowered to appoint nine prebendaries in his cathedral to assist the agents of that abhorrent tribunal, while two of their own number were themselves inquisitors."¶

But the conflicting excuses from day to day put

---

* Strada, p. 17.   Miræi Dip., tom. 3, p. 523.
† Ibid. Davies, vol. 1, p. 497. Grattan.   ‡ Ibid.   § Ibid.
‖ Strada, p. 17.   Davies, vol. 1, p. 498.   ¶ Ibid.

forth for the retention of the Spanish troops, the placard against the comedians, the erection of the new sees, and the sullen temper of the provinces, did not disturb the icy serenity of Philip, nor make him hesitate; they only quickened his movements and pushed forward the reorganization of the government—necessitated by his approaching departure, and by Emanuel Philibert's resignation of the governor-generalship of the states, in consequence of the restoration to him by France of his long-lost duchy of Savoy, in compliance with a clause of the treaty of Chateau-Cambray.[*]

It was necessary to refill the deserted office at an early day, since Philip grew hourly more impatient to quit Brussels. Who should succeed the recusant duke? The court was perturbed, the citizens were anxious. The merits of those most likely to succeed Philibert were ardently canvassed. In this talk of the drawing-rooms and the sidewalk, three names were especially prominent—the duchess of Lorraine, Count Egmont, and the prince of Orange.[†] Who were they?

[*] De Thou, Brantôme.
[†] Meteren, Strada, Wagenær.

CHAPTER XI.

EGMONT AND ORANGE.

ONE of the three personages who seemed most certain to succeed Philibert in the Netherland regency, was Christierne, duchess of Lorraine, Cæsar's niece, and cousin-german to the king. A woman of rare political talent, she had been foremost in negotiating the recent treaty of peace; and this circumstance, added to her high rank and personal fitness, gave her claim no small authority.*

The suit of Lamoral, Count Egmont, prince of Gavere, was pressed by his own great achievements and by the popular voice. He was the most dashing and brilliant captain of his age; worthy to have filled the vacant seat among the Round Table knights. It was to him that Philip was indebted for the crushing victories of St. Quentin and Gravelines,† and the wars of the emperor had been the school of his genius. Though his brow was crownless, he could boast of as lofty a lineage as most anointed kings; for he traced his origin up to the Frisian Radbold, while many illustrious marriages had allied him to scores of the first European families, and centred in him some of the proudest titles and some of the richest estates of the Low Countries.‡ "Flemish pride, like a fond mother, exulted

---

° Strada, p. 19.   Meteren.   † Ibid., Brantôme.
‡ Motley, vol. 1, p. 171.

over this illustrious son, who had filled Christendom with admiration. His appearance on the street was a triumphal procession; every eye which was fastened upon him recounted his exploits; his deeds lived in the plaudits of his companions-in-arms; at the games of chivalry mothers pointed him out to their children as a model."*

Egmont was at this time thirty-eight years old† — in the noon of a life as yet sunny and unclouded. Happy and prosperous himself, he was inclined to underrate the dangers which menaced his country. Indeed, his temper led him to see every thing *couleur de rose;* for, light and buoyant, the cares which ploughed his heart at one moment, only insured a harvest of fresh hopes at the next.

The truth is, that he was volatile and vain—vain of his handsome person, of his magnificent costume, of his dark lovelocks, of his soft brown eye, of his smooth cheek, of his features, almost femininely delicate, but emboldened by a slight mustache ;‡ vain of his fame and of his popularity.§ For, though a Dutchman, Egmont resembled the fickle Walloons of the southern provinces, and fatally lacked the firmness of character, the tenacity of purpose which have placed the Saxon race in the van of modern civilization. He was easily cozened and easily led, and open to a fault. Carrying his unsuspecting soul on his brow, "his frankheartedness managed his secrets no better than his

---

* Schiller, p. 401.   † He was born in 1522.
‡ Motley, vol. 1, p. 100.   § Brantôme, Schiller, Davies.

lavish benevolence did his immense estate, and a thought was no sooner his than it was the property of all"—a dangerous trait in that age, and one unfitting him for diplomacy, which Machiavelli and the Medicis had reduced to a science of fraud.

Egmont had a conscience, but was without fixed principles. His religion was of the mildest Roman type, and not enlightened, because it derived its light from a code which he had learned by rote, not from the heart and the intellect.* In a word, though fascinating and pure-minded, he was a mere soldier; beyond that, he was a childish bungler—a human pipe played on by cunning fingers. He often fettered his patriotism by lower duties; was as timid in council as brave in the field; and was sure to bend when he should stand firm, and to stand firm when he should have bent. Thus he was at one time the puppet, at another the victim, of Spanish perfidy.

The prince of Orange was another of these candidates. From this moment Orange becomes the pivotal man of the Netherland drama—the brain and the right hand of the revolution; it is fit, therefore, for us to pause and make his acquaintance.

William of Nassau, prince of Orange, was born at the castle of Dillembergh, in the German county of Nassau, on the 25th of April, 1533.† God granted him to be the heir of a glorious past as well as the inaugurator and liberator of a grander future; for

---

* Schiller, p. 409.
† Lives of the Princes of the House of Orange, p. 2. London, 1734.

he, too, like Egmont, was the representative of an august and ancient family, able to boast, with the Venetian oligarchy, that it stood upon the basis of a thousand years, yet whose age had been from time to time reinvigorated by puissant alliances, until now its head was as wealthy and as influential as most kings.*

For many generations the house of Nassau was divided—a kind of double unit. One branch remained in Germany—tarried to wear the purple in the person of Adolph of Nassau, and to give, besides, countless captains, bishops, and electors to the Fatherland. The other branch, though retaining the sovereignty of the modest birthplace of their house, Nassau, emigrated to the Netherlands and at once attained influence and authority.† Just previous to the birth of the liberator, two brothers held the entire estates, Count Henry inheriting the Low Country properties, Count William succeeding to the German sovereignties.‡ It was Count Henry to whom Charles V. was indebted for his empire— he who cheated Francis I. out of the crown—he who placed that royal bauble on the head of Cæsar at Aix-la-Chapelle § spite of which, Francis, with singular generosity, married him to Claude de Chalons, whose dowry was the sovereignty of Chalons. From this union sprang René of Nassau, who, later,

<hr/>

* Lives of the Princes of the House of Orange, p. 2. London, 1734. Archives de la Maison d'Orange Nassau, tom. 1.

† Motley, vol. 1. p. 235.

‡ Lives of the Princes, etc. Archives, etc.   § Ibid.

acquired the little principality of Orange, in France, as heir to his mother's brother Philibert of Chalons, prince of Orange, who died childless.* Meantime, Count William also had married a noble lady, Juliana of Stalberg; and this couple, too, had a son— the first of a numerous progeny—whom they named William, and whose earliest breath was drawn in the ancient cradle of his race.†

Years sped, and little William was in his eleventh year, when news reached Dillembergh that Prince René had been killed at the emperor's feet in the trenches before St. Dizier, leaving to his cousin the whole magnificent inheritance of Nassau, Chalons, and Orange—a retinue of principalities stretching from Germany through Holland, Flanders, Brabant, and Luxemburgh, to the old kingdom of the popes.‡ So much for the genealogy of the Nassaus; let genealogists look closer if they will, we know enough for the purpose of these pages.

Of course, this accidental union in his person of the immense possessions of his house, broadened and elevated the young prince's destiny. "Yes, yes," muttered Charles, "this brave little monseigneur must be looked to; I'll have him here at court." This purpose was strengthened by the fact that William's parents were Lutherans, and had been among the first to embrace, and the most active to propagate, the principles of the Reformation.§

* Archives, etc., *ut antea*.   † Ibid.

‡ Ibid. Vandervynckt, Troubles des Pays Bas, tom. 1.

§ Ibid. Robertson, Hist. of Charles V.

Thus far the boy had been educated in the gospel faith.* The emperor saw this with alarm; and one of the chief objects of his proposed removal of the prince was to run him, like ductile metal, in the mould of Latin orthodoxy.†

William was brought to Brussels at the age of twelve, and placed in the family of Queen Mary of Hungary, then governant of the Netherlands, where he was bred in the Roman tenets.‡ He became and remained through his early manhood, a nominal papist; but the prayerful letters of his pious mother, and the good seed sown in his boyish heart in the old Dillembergh castle, flowered at last in ardent Protestantism, as we shall see.

At fifteen, the prince was transferred into the imperial household, and passed under Cæsar's eye as his special page.§ Charles prided himself on his ability to read and use men, and his discernment in this case proved that he possessed that crucial test of greatness; for he at once recognized the extraordinary character of his youthful attendant, and made him his intimate, confidential friend.‖ Here William resided for nine years; here he was initiated into the tortuous politics of his epoch; here he studied history with attention, and learned to speak and write Latin, French, German, Dutch, and Spanish with equal facility and elegance.¶

But chiefly the thoughtful boy studied men; *Le*

---

* Robertson, Hist. of Charles V. Lives of the Princes of the House of Orange.   † Ibid., p. 7.
‡ Ibid. Prescott, Schiller, etc.   § Ibid.   ‖ Ibid.   ¶ Ibid.

monde est un livre—the world is a book; and this
volume he mastered thoroughly. In the earliest
months of his residence at court, Charles was accustomed to retain him at his side even in interviews
with the highest diplomats, and on the gravest questions.* The secrets of the empire were intrusted
to his discretion; and Cæsar once declared that
William had often furnished him counsel, and extemporized for him expedients of which otherwise
he had never thought.† In such a school "the
perceptive and reflective faculties of the future
statesman, naturally of remarkable keenness and
depth, acquired a precocious and extraordinary
development. He was brought up behind the curtain—in the green-room of that great stage where
the world's dramas were daily enacted; therefore
the machinery and masks which produced the grand
delusions of history had no deception for him.
Carefully to observe men's actions, and silently to
ponder their motives—this was the favorite occupa-
tion of the prince during his apprenticeship at
court."‡

Charles loved to honor him; now employing his
dexterous wit, now invoking his military genius. It
was Orange, scarcely yet of age, whom he appointed
generalissimo in the place of Philibert, in the French
war which preceded his abdication—chose him, too,
in his absence, unsolicited, against the unanimous
advice of his council, and to the exclusion of his

* Prescott, Schiller, etc.   Motley, Davies, Vandervynckt.
† Vandervynckt, Meteren.   ‡ Motley, vol. 1, pp. 236, 237.

laurel-crowned band of heroes—Egmont, who was twelve years his senior, among the rest—and found no reason to repent his selection of the youthful "tyro" in arms, who grappled with Guise and baffled Coligny.* It was Orange on whose shoulder he rested during the delivery of his farewell address.† It was Orange whom he despatched with the imperial crown to his brother Ferdinand of Germany.‡ So ripe was the prince in honors even while so young in years.

The marks of confidence and friendship which the emperor had showered upon William, would alone have sufficed to bring him into disrepute with Philip; who seems to have laid it down for himself as a rule, to avenge the slights of the Spanish grandees, for the preference which his father had, on all important occasions, shown to the Low Country nobles, by a similar leaning toward the other side.§

Still, the prince had not been inactive since Philip's coronation. He bore an important part in the negotiations which resulted in the pacification of Chateau-Cambray; and he was one of the hostages left in the French king's hands for the fulfilment of the treaty.§ It was during his residence at Paris in this capacity that he earned his surname of the "silent." One day he was hunting

---

* Schiller, p. 405.   Prescott, Hist. of the Reign of Philip II.
† Ibid.   Lives of the Princes, etc.   Archives, etc.
‡ Ibid.   § Schiller, p. 405.
§ Motley, Vandervynckt, Meteren, Archives, etc.

beside Henry II. in the forest of Vincennes. Suddenly Valois paused, laid his hand on William's arm, and opened to him a budget of perfidy— imagining that Orange, like Alva, was in the plot. A general extirpation of Protestants was to be the cement of the pacification; Henry was to assist Philip in strangling heresy in the Netherlands, Philip was to aid them in assassinating the Huguenots of France; and in these massacres the Spanish regiments detailed in Flanders were to bear a central part: such was the revelation of the king. William heard him with horror; but suffered no trace of surprise or disgust to appear in his imperturbable countenance, and they called him later the "silent," because he knew when to hold his peace as well as when to speak.*

Henry's blunder enabled the keen prince to fathom the muddy policy of Philip, forewarned him, and did much to ripen him for his after work; and he it was who had evoked and organized the protest against the continuance of the Spanish troops on Netherland soil.†

The prince of Orange was at this time but twenty-six, though he had been married and was now a widower.‡ Like Egmont, he was a tall and stately man. His features were dark, well chiselled, and symmetrical; his head was well turned and finely placed upon his shoulders; his forehead was lofty, spacious, and already prematurely engraved with

* Meteren, Vandervynckt, Motley.   ‡ Ibid.
† Lives of the Princes, etc.

the lines of anxious thought; his eyes were brown, full, well opened, and expressive of profound reflection.*

His courtly bearing and charm of manner fascinated all who came within the sphere of his influence.† Graceful, familiar, caressing, yet dignified, Orange was king of hearts.‡ "Never did an arrogant or indiscreet word fall from his lips," remarks a chronicler who was his bitter foe; "nor did he upon any occasion manifest anger to his inferiors, however much they might be in fault, but contented himself with admonishing them graciously, without menace or insult. For he had a gentle and agreeable tongue with which he could turn all the gentlemen at court which way he liked."§

In some respects his *sobriquet* was a misnomer, for Motley tells us, what others have avouched, and what William's life proves, that "he was neither 'silent' nor 'taciturn' from habit; though these are the epithets which will be for ever associated with the name of a man, who, in private, was the most affable, cheerful, and delightful of companions, and who on a thousand public occasions was to prove himself, both by pen and by speech, to be the most eloquent man of the age."‖

He was ambitious, not with the vulgar purpose of self-aggrandizement, but to enrol himself

---

* Motley, vol. 1, p. 106.
† Ibid., p. 246.   Schiller, Strada.   ‡ Ibid.
§ Pontus Payen, MS., cited in Motley, *ut antea.*
‖ Motley, *ut antea.*

among the builders of states by liberating his country.

No one was ever more perfectly equipped to organize a revolution. Imperturbable, cautious yet decisive and irresistible, master of men, coolest and firmest in disaster, sound and commanding in body as in mind, sitting apart, as the heathen deities talked from peak to peak all round Olympus, yet easy himself and able to make others share his ease—persistent, kind, forbearing—Orange was all this, and more, even from the outset. In the Netherlands he had no mate in genius—was, like most great men, a unique. "The Scipioism of Scipio," says an epigrammatist, "was precisely that part of him which he could not borrow." The Orangeism of Orange was exactly that part of him which none other could imitate. And though Egmont, his friend and compeer, was fully his equal as a soldier, as a statesman he was not worthy to unloose the latchet of his shoes.

Such was the duchess of Lorraine, such was Count Egmont, such was the prince of Orange, when, in the spring of 1559, they competed with each other for the governor-generalship of the Netherlands. They were none of them to be successful. Philip had an instinctive dread of Orange. These two men, so unlike in most respects, had two points of contact. Both were gifted with intuition; and the king saw deeply enough into the character of the prince to know that, while he possessed the qualities as a politician which he highly prized, he

8*

yet bottomed his statesmanship upon a theory which was fatal to absolutism—human rights; and was therefore necessarily his foeman. Then, too, both had sat at the feet of the same master, only Philip had learned by rote and was an imitator; William had looked deep, and completely mastered the perilous arts by which thrones then rose and fell; and the king had an especial dread of him because he was aware that in him he had an antagonist who was armed against his policy by forecast, and who in a great cause, was able to command the science and resources of a bad one.*

Add to this instinctive hatred William's popularity and wealth; and we shall see that, notwithstanding the deep sea and fair wind on which he sailed, in Strada's figure, the bark of his chances was sure to founder.†

As for Egmont, his family had been, in times past, the bitter and successful foes of the house of Austria. He was a soldier; he was the popular idol. "If I intrust the supreme stadtholdership to him," thought Philip, "he may endeavor to revenge the oppression of his ancestors on the son of the oppressor; nay, but I'll none of him."‡

Thus it was that what seemed the clearest titles of Egmont and Orange to the succession, were really fatal to their success; while the king was supplied with an excellent pretext for passing both by on the ground that where merit was so equal it was impossible to decide.

○ Schiller, p. 407.   † Strada, p. 19.   * Schiller, p. 100.

William's sagacity speedily convinced him of the hopelessness of his success; and, therefore, he shrewdly withdrew his claims and pressed those of the duchess of Lorraine, to whose daughter he was paying suit, "with the intention," if we may credit Strada, "of giving his proposed mother-in-law the title, and taking to himself the power."*

The advocacy of Orange ruined the prospects of Christierne, for Philip made a point of always running against the current of the prince's will; and one morning Brussels was astonished to hear that Margaret of Parma had been appointed governant, and had already quitted Italy to take her seat. Philip the Taciturn had for once outmanœuvred William the Silent. The prince was soon to return the compliment.

* Strada, *ut antea.*

CHAPTER XII.

A CHECK.

WHILE Orange and Egmont were digesting the disappointment of their hopes, dashed by the announcement of the new governant's name, and while the burghers were still sulking over the rebuff of the national favorites, Philip, trailing after him a glittering cortége, sped towards the Netherland frontier to welcome Margaret of Parma.* It was in 1559, in the early days of June, pregnant with summer, that he met her, and, accompanying her to Brussels, inducted her into office, with a pomp which recalled the days of the abdication.†

Margaret's story was a romance. The natural daughter of Charles V. by a Flemish orphan of gentle blood, named Van Gheest, and born in 1522, she had been acknowledged by the emperor, and educated as became a princess.‡ For a time she was the ward of the emperor's aunt, then regent of the Netherlands; but the little waif was only in her eighth year when this lady died; whereupon the guardianship devolved upon her successor, Queen Mary of Hungary.§

According to the custom of that age, when hearts were the chattels of princes, and when marriage

* Strada, p. 24.   Meteren, Vandervynckt.   † Ibid.
‡ Strada, p. 20.   Prescott, Levensbusch, Nederl. Man. en Vroumen.   § Ibid.   Brantôme.

was a mere counter in diplomatic games, this child was wedded at twelve to the *passé* duke of Tuscany, Alexander de' Medici.[*] A dozen months elapsed, and this profligate was assassinated by a kinsman in the streets of Florence.[†] A widow at thirteen, the girl was once more in the matrimonial market, finding many bidders. But Charles was in no haste to find Margaret another husband, and it was not until she was a woman of twenty that she was again mated, this time to Ottavio Farnese, nephew of Pope Paul III., and a boy of thirteen—thus at the age of maturity being married to a child, as in her infancy she had been sold to a man.[‡]

To Farnese she brought the duchies of Parma and Piacenza as her dowry;[§] but the youth of the prince inspired her with such contempt for him that, as Strada remarks, "her indifference was only softened into a kindlier feeling when she had been long separated from him."[‖]

This, roughly outlined, was the history of the woman whom Philip had installed as governant of the Low Countries. As for her character, she did not lack ability; but qualities which might otherwise have raised her above mediocrity, were fatally biased by a monkish superstition learned at the feet of Ignatius Loyola, who had been her confessor while she tarried in Italy[¶]—the chiefest of her recommendations to Philip.

° Brantôme.   † Ibid.
‡ Schiller, p. 412.   § Ibid. Strada, p. 22.
‖ Ibid., p. 23.   ¶ Ibid. Prescott, Motley, Schiller.

In person, Margaret was tall and ungainly. Upon her upper lip a mustache had sprouted.* " Her gait itself was so devoid of grace," as Schiller paints her, " that one was far more tempted to take her for a disguised man than for a masculine woman; and nature, whom she had derided by thus transgressing the limits of her sex, revenged itself upon her by a disease peculiar to men—the gout."† Spite of the surprise it caused, the appointment of this odd woman to the regency was dictated by profound policy, and was, as rumor had it, the result of Alva's counsel and the bishop of Arras' advice.‡   For, while certain to be the puppet of the king, Margaret had four excellent recommendations : she was earnest for the faith ; she was Philip's sister ; she was a Netherlander by birth ; she had spent her youth in Brussels, where she had acquired a knowledge of the national manners, while the duchess Margaret and Queen Mary of Hungary, the two regents under whose eyes she had grown up, had gradually initiated her into the maxims by which they had governed in the past.§   It was, indeed, a formidable list of recommendatory circumstances, and justified the choice.   " Withal," observes Strada, " Philip hoped that the Low-Countrymen, for the reverence they bore the name of Charles V., would cheerfully obey his daughter, born among them, and bred up to their fashions, and be able the better to digest her government, because

---

* Strada, *ut antea.*   † Schiller, p. 412.
‡ Schiller, p. 413.   § Ibid., p. 412.

subjected people think themselves partly free if ruled by a native."* Besides, the Netherlands were habituated to female government; and the king thought that the innovations he had designed would be more popular coming from a lady—like an incision, that pains the less when made by a soft hand.†

With the prevision of a despot, Philip seldom trusted individuals—never, unless he had a curb in their mouths. So now he put a double check upon his sister by demanding her little son, Alexander Farnese—a name famous in the Low Countries at a later day—as a hostage, and by equipping three chambers to assist her in the administration of the government.‡

The organization of these chambers was a masterpiece of political skill. The idea was old, it was only the composition that was unique. There had been a council of finance, a privy council, and a state council under the emperor—all composed of Netherlanders.§ Now just so many citizens were seated at these council-boards as were deemed sufficient to deceive the nation with a show of representation—not enough to command a majority on any one important measure, the decision resting with the creatures of the court.‖ The royal juggler shouted, "Presto," and instantly a republican barrier was transformed into the citadel of despotism.

To the board of finance was intrusted whatever

---

* Strada, p. 24. † Ibid.
‡ Vandervynckt, vol. 1, p. 148. Meteren, Wagenær.
§ Hoofdt, vol. 1. p. 22. Meteren, 24. ‖ Ibid. Grattan, pp. 84, 85.

related to the royal exchequer in the states, and its president was Count Barlaiment.* To the privy council was given the general administration of justice, and its president was Viglius.† To the council of state was referred all matters of foreign intercourse, all inter-provincial affairs, and its president was the bishop of Arras :‡ of this board Orange, and Egmont, and Horn, and Aerschat were members,§ sharing in the responsibility of the government, but powerless to shape its policy. These three boards were quite independent of each other, with this important exception : while the members of the council of state had no voice in the other two chambers, the privy and finance councillors, together with the knights of the Golden Fleece, had access to their deliberations‖—an arrangement which lassoed that board to Philip's feet, and reduced the national nobles to titled nullities at Brussels.

But to make surety doubly sure, the wily monarch created another board behind the government, back of the councils, hidden, tireless, omnipresent, all-powerful—the *Consulta*. "It was a committee of three members of the state chamber, by whose deliberations the regent was secretly instructed to be guided at all critical moments. The three, Barlaiment, Viglius, and Arras, who composed this back-stair conclave, were in reality but one. The bishop of Arras was in all three, and the three together constituted only the bishop of Arras."¶

° Hoofd, Meteren, *ubi sup.*   † Ibid.   ‡ Ibid.   § Ibid.
‖ Schiller, Hoofd, Strada.   ¶ Motley, vol. 1, p. 209.

Barlaiment was an antique. He had the un-
qualifying, blind, audacious temper of the darkest
ages. He had been dug up from the crusades. The
simple lesson which his life was devoted to learning
and teaching was, submission to superiors, subor-
dination of inferiors. He had no brains—he had
scraped his skull clean on entering Philip's service,
and he stood asking, not, Is this right? but, What
shall I do? In war he was a soldier; in politics he
was an ultra absolutist; in religion he was a fanatic.*
Barlaiment was just honest enough to be a tool;
just wise enough to be an ultramontanist; just religious enough to be a bigot. Philip treated him as
a human bull-dog; Arras subdued him to be his
lackey.

Viglius was a pedant, but de did not lack talent.
Unlike Barliament, he was of "boor's degree,"† but
a round of studies at the Lorraine, Padua, and
Paris schools had kindled ambition in his heart,
and set him scheming, until now in the autumn of
his life, he had acquired fame, and wealth, and influence.‡ Infirm and overtasked, he still held on to
power and was singularly patient of work. Ambition has been defined to be satiety *with* desire.
Perhaps it was this which held Viglius still feeding
at the public trough.

A small, brisk man, round, timid, sleek, with
rosy cheeks, glittering green eyes, and a flowing
beard,§ Viglius was a jurist of extensive erudition;

* Hoofd, Meteren, Levensbusch.
† Levensbusch, vol. 4, p, 75. ‡ Ibid. § Motley, vol. 1, p. 101.

a monarchist by instinct, a papist from policy; able
to quibble with any one; adroit enough to baffle
most antagonists; plausible enough to cheat the
majority of hearers; eloquent enough to hide the
intentions of the court beneath a fluent stream of
common places; and unscrupulous enough to balk
at nothing.*   Politics is the hospital for broken
scoundrels; and this Bohemian, this political bri-
gand under the mask of a legal doctorate, had
drifted into it to end his days.

But the bishop of Arras was the soul of the
trio, as he was the Mephistophiles of the tragedy
whose prelude these days were.

· Anthony Perrenot of Granvelle, bishop of Arras,
was born in 1517, at Besançon, in Burgundy.†   His
father had risen, step by step, from the condition of
an humble country attorney to the chancellorship
of the empire under Charles V.‡   The secret of this
marvellous career was hidden in two words—sycophancy and industry.   By the one he gained the
heart of Cæsar; by the other he mastered the science of government, and deserved confidence.

In 1517, the elder Perrenot was the emperor's
favorite minister, successful, honored, courted.   Thus
he was able to secure for his son Anthony a sunny
opening to his career.   The boy was precocious.   He
learned as others play.   At twenty he had mastered
the civil and the canon law, and spoke seven lan-

* Prescott, Meteren, Motley.
† Levensbusch, Strada, Motley.
‡ Prescott, vol. 1, p. 405.   Meteren, Levensbusch.

guages without halting.* Three years later he was
chosen a canon of the Liege cathedral, through whose
massive door he entered, though under age, the rich
see of Arras.† In 1543, the youthful bishop, commissioned as plenipotentiary, entered the council of
Trent, where his dulcet eloquence so captivated
Charles that the dazzled emperor created him a
councillor of state.‡

From that time his rise was rapid. With consummate art he insinuated himself into the confidence of Cæsar, remembering the secret of his
father's success—sycophancy in winning, industry
in preserving confidence.

At the abdication, Charles recommended this
crafty, prévoyant chancellor to Philip's confidence,§
bidding him rely upon an intellect which had lifted
him out of many a "slough of despond," caged
for him numberless birds, sung for him countless syren songs. Such a recommendation would
have been as useless in his case as in that of
Orange, had not the keen priest known how to rec-
ommend himself. He vanquished Philip's doubt of
him by one master-stroke. It was he who put into the
treaty of Chateau-Cambray the secret clause which
was to cement peace in the blood of Protestantism,
and which Orange so strangely discovered in the
Vincennes wood.‖ This rascality was exactly in the
vein of the gloomy bigot whom the facile chancel-

* Prescott, Meteren, Levensbusch, Motley.   † Ibid.
‡ Ibid., Schiller.   § Ibid.
‖ Prescott, Motley, Schiller.

lor termed "the master." Henceforth, two such men were needful to each other.

This all-powerful prelate had the subtlest of intellects; he had also profound and varied learning.* To talent of a high order he wedded patience—a rare union. He was, too, a man of thoughtful, mechanical regularity. Always vigilant, always collected, nothing escaped him; and he weighed the most important and the most insignificant affairs with the same scrupulous attention.†

In a combat of *finesse*, a duel of intrigue, no one could outwit him. Cool, wary, imperturbable, hiding all concern under an easy *nonchalance*, masking inordinate ambition under an *insouciance* which never disclosed a feature of the real Perrenot, he walked calmly on—this serene, smiling priest—and with paternal benignity did Satan's work.

Arras was diplomacy personified: he had that fine quality which is colorless because inscrutable, and irresistible because far-seeing—acumen: acumen, which crowns genius and dethrones kings. And this silkiest, most dulcet of churchmen aimed at ubiquity, withal. Monsignore had his politic webs spun over Italy, over France, over Austria, over England, over Spain. Monsignore had his secret spies of the ablest. Monsignore was the lover of great ladies who played Iscariot for him in palaces. Monsignore never gave a *Benedicite* without some diplomatic touch. Monsignore never administered the *Viaticum* that the church was not

* Motley, vol. 1, p. 248.   † Schiller, p. 421.

the richer for a legacy. Monsignore never yet was compromised by a lie, and never yet was driven to the vulgarity of a truth.

But what would you have? Even Achilles could be shot in the heel; and Monsignore himself had his weaknesses. One of them was, that he disbelieved in any virtue that was proof against a bribe, or capable of preferring a creed to a sovereignty. He could not credit it, that any one should be so mad as not to exchange, if it were made worth his while, the Phrygian bonnet for a coronet. Another was, that, educated between the throne and the confessional, he knew of no other relation between man and man than that of rule and subjection.* This idea was the rock on which his bark was to be wrecked; for, in the Netherlands, half republican and two-thirds Protestant, the statesmanship which bottomed itself on absolutism, however adroit, was certain to be suicidal. The prescient wit, the exhaustless capacity which would have lifted this man into a statesman at Rome or in Spain, dwindled him into a mere politician at Brussels; for his *rationale* did not suit that atmosphere. He could weary half a dozen amanuenses at a sitting, but he could not tire out a people determined to be free.

So much shall suffice to depict the government, and so much to paint the persons who composed it, in that smiling June when Margaret of Parma entered Brussels. The initial ceremonies of the governant's reception once over, Philip pressed on to

* Schiller.

another arrangement. Some of the provinces were supplied with new executives; others had those local rulers whose credentials bore the imperial seal, confirmed.* In this distribution of offices, the prince of Orange was accredited as stadtholder of Holland, Zealand, Utrecht, and West Friesland.† To Egmont were awarded Flanders and Artois.‡ And among others of the national grandees, Aremberg, Bergen, Barliament, the remainder of the states were parcelled out;§ but Brabant was reserved to the regent, who was there executive *ex officio*.‖

This done, nothing remained but to say farewell—for on several recent occasions the king had exerted the whole weight of his personal influence to impress upon the country the paramount importance of the edicts against heresy; and once he had stammered out an address to the grand council at Mechlin, with his own lips emphasizing his demand for Protestant blood.¶

On the 7th of August, 1559, an assembly of the states was convoked at Ghent.** The court was gay and giddy with triumph. Diplomats smiled placidly. The bishop of Arras was as serene as the summer sky above him. Even Philip lost a little

---

° Vandervynckt, Meteren.   † Ibid.   ‡ Ibid.   § Ibid.
‖ Ibid.   ¶ Meteren, Ivach, Hopperus, Hoynckt.
°° To give *eclat* to his presence in Ghent, a chapter of the Golden Fleece was held just before the convocation of the states-general, and fourteen knights were admitted to the order. This chapter was the last ever held. After this date, knights were preferred to the honor of the Fleece by the king's nomination. Vandervynckt, Troubles des Pays-Bas, tom. 2, p. 21.

of his *hauteur*. On the eve of the convention all whirled in a thoughtless glitter. There were wines of the rarest. There were feastings of the daintiest. Turkish and Levantine fruits imported by the Antwerp merchants, with crystallized confections in silver baskets, which dainty statuettes of Odalisque slaves and Greek girls held up in a shower of flowers. Every palace was transformed into a chamber of revelry, and in the perfume and the lustre human rights were mocked at, and heresy was impaled on dainty skewers, with a light laugh, amid the whirl of the dance and the glitter of gold and azure, of silver and scarlet, while the air was drowsy with the odor of wines, and spices, and incense.

While the orgy was at its maddest, a stately but haggard man might have been seen to quit the supper-room and wend his way with quick, firm step past the stadthouse, past the tower where Roland had swung, on through the quaint, crooked streets, towards the quarters of the town where the deputies found shelter. It was William of Orange going at midnight to warn the delegates of the lurking danger, and to suggest a plan of action for the morrow.* How well his warning was heeded we shall see.

In the morning the states assembled. Here the king, the governant, Philibert of Savoy, and the courtiers, still drowsy with the night's excess; yonder in the body of the hall the deputies, cool, collected, determined. For the sturdy burghers took their seats in no friendly mood. For once, as-

* Grattan, p. 85. Archives of the House of Orange—Nassau.

tonished absolutism was to listen to republican truth.*

With a benignant smile, the bishop of Arras stepped forward to harangue the states as the mouthpiece of the king. Very smoothly, very plausibly he spoke, skipping, like a chamois, from topic to topic, touching lightly on obnoxious, dwelling largely upon popular subjects; insinuating, elaborating, always with a glacial smile upon his face, and with roguery at his heart. Not a word did he say about the Spanish troops; his only reference to the disordered state of the public finances was when, in calling attention to his majesty's "request," he asked the deputies to vote him an additional sum of three millions of gold florins;† but his allusion to reform was pregnant. "These beggars and vagabonds," smiled the suave orator, "who, under cover of religion, traverse the land for purposes of plunder and disturbance—as it regards them, his majesty desires to follow in the footsteps of his august father. Therefore he has commanded the regent, Margaret of Parma, for the sake of religion and the glory of God, accurately and exactly to enforce the edicts made by his imperial majesty and renewed by his present majesty, for the extirpation of all sects and heresies."‡

The complacent rhetorician sat down; the deputies, according to an ancient custom, adjourned to

---

○ Prescott, Schiller.

† Documentos Inédits, vol. 1, p. 326, *et seq.*   Vandervynckt.

‡ Bor., vol. 1, p. 19, *et seq.*

deliberate,* and the court awoke out of its dog-nap to dine. Philip, however, occupied himself in penning a last exhortation to the Mechlin council, the supreme court of the Low Countries, in which appendix to his recent speech he commanded them anew to be diligent above all things in " inquiring on all sides as to the execution of the placards, employing the utmost rigor not alone against transgressors, but equally against such judges as should dare to prove remiss in their prosecution of heretics, without respect of persons."† Some thought that the placards were fulminated against Anabaptists alone. The wily fanatic corrected the error. " All who reject Rome are heretics," said he ; " enforce the edicts against all sectaries, without any distinction or mercy, if they be merely spotted with Luther's errors."‡ This was Philip's dinner.

On the morning of the eighth of August the states again convened. They had voted their contingents to the " request;" but made the removal of the Spanish squadrons a condition precedent to the payment of their respective quotas.§

" Sire," demanded the blunt syndic of Ghent, addressing Philip in person, " why are foreign hands needed for our defence ? Is it that the world shall consider us too stupid or too cowardly to protect ourselves ? Why have we made peace, if the burdens of war are still to oppress us ? In war, neces-

* Pontus Payen, MS. Bentivoglio.
† Cited in Motley, vol. 1, p. 218.　　　　　　　‡ Ibid.
§ Motley, vol. 1, p. 216. Vandervynckt.

sity enforced endurance; in peace, our patience is exhausted by its burdens. Or shall we be able to restrain these licentious bands, which your presence is powerless to restrain? Here Cambray, there Antwerp, cry for redress. Here Thionville, there Marienburg, lie waste. Surely you have not bestowed upon us peace that our cities may become deserts? Perhaps you desire to guard us from exterior assault? 'Tis a wise precaution; but the report of our neighbors' preparations will long outrun their hostilities. Have you not still at your command the same brave Netherlanders to whom your father intrusted the republic in far more troublous times? Will not they be able to sustain themselves, when they held their country inviolate for so many centuries?"*

Each of these short, sharp interrogatories cut Philip to the heart; as for the courtiers, they gaped in wonder. The pithy sentences of the burgher orator, and the addresses of the separate states, all in the same strain, were followed by a remonstrance, drawn up in the name of the states-general, and signed by Orange, Egmont, and a long bead-roll of patricians.†

A gallant stand was also made that day for liberty of conscience. "Every people," it was so they argued, "ought to be treated according to their natural character, as every individual should be in accordance with his idiosyncrasies. Thus the south

* Schiller, pp. 401, 402.
† Meteren, vol. 1, p. 24. Bor., vol. 1, p. 22.

may be considered happy under a certain degree of constraint, which would press intolerably on the north. Different nations often require different laws. What suits the Spaniard would not for that reason suit the Netherlander. The Inquisition is ill-adapted to men accustomed from their cradles to freedom of action and of thought."[*]

Philip was dumb with anger. This tone, unheard of in Castilian legislative halls, and new to his haughty ears, made him gasp for breath. The shock was so great that it threw down the barriers of his self-possession. Rising from his seat and rushing from the hall, he flung back this query: "I, too, am a Spaniard and a papist; must I therefore quit the land and resign all authority over it?"[†]

The assembly adjourned in disorder. The wiseacres put their heads together. Philip closeted himself with the bishop of Arras. They decided to dissemble[‡]—a policy kindred to both their natures. They were driven to that last resource of baffled despotism, a compromise. On one point, however, the king was firm. The religious edicts must remain intact.[§] "It may lose you the provinces, sire," said the minister. "Well, then," responded the inexorable bigot, "better not reign at all than reign over heretics."[||]

A few days later, the king, who would not again face the deputies, sent to the assembly a response to their remonstrance—a wily, plausible paper,

---

[*] Schiller, Prescott.   [†] Wagenœr, Vaderl. Hist., vol. 6.
[‡] Ibid. Motley.   [§] Ibid.   [||] Vandervynckt, Schiller, Wagenœr.

which bore the imprint of Arras' brains. It was to this effect: "I desire not to place strangers in the government—as witness my selection of Margaret, your countrywoman, as governant. I regret not having learned your wishes sooner touching the removal of the troops. Their pay is in arrears, and I cannot order them away unpaid. Immediately on reaching Spain I will forward the moneys owed them, and within three months you shall be quit of their presence. Meantime, Orange and Egmont shall command them."*

Philip II. was a lie with a moral at the bottom of it. The moral was this: Trust him least when he promises most. Now, the king's three months stretched into eighteen; and at last the Spanish regiments were withdrawn, "rather hastily than willingly," because further delay meant insurrection, and because the exigencies of the state called for their presence in another quarter of the globe.†

But this was in the future when the king sent this word to the states, and the deputies were fain to be content.‡ With an undisturbed mien, but with the anger of humiliation gnawing at his heart, Philip now set out for the Netherland seaport of Flushing, whence he was to embark for Spain.§ He was accompanied by a throng of nobles, William of Orange among the rest. The irate despot suspected that it was the prince's hand that had upset his

---

* Response du Roy á la Remonstrance, cited in Documents Inédits, vol. 1, pp. 326–329.   † Schiller.

‡ Meteren, Suriano, *Relatione* MS.   § Motley, vol. 1, p. 219.

schemes and given this check to his tyranny. Just as he was about to quit the seashore for his fleet, he gave voice to this suspicion. Turning abruptly upon Orange, who stood close beside him, he bluntly accused him of having engineered the opposition which had partly wrecked his policy. "Sire," rejoined the imperturbable prince, "that is to be regarded not as the work of any individual, but as the act of the states." "No," hissed Philip, shaking his antagonist fiercely by the wrist, "No los Estados, mas vos, vos, vos"—not the states, but you, you, you!*

William was silent, and by his silence he admitted the glorious accusation—admitted that he had earned his title to the hatred of the king, and the gratitude of his country.†

The royal fleet at once set sail. Philip left the Netherlands never to see them more; left them agonizing to reach Spain, in which, so he was told, the Reformation had ventured to raise its voice.‡ A widower for the second time by the death of Mary Tudor in 1558, he was to celebrate his marriage with the beautiful Isabella de Valois, "discreet, witty, and good," as Brantôme paints her,§ on reaching Toledo.‖

After a stormy voyage, he landed at Laredo in

ᵃ "Vos" is an epithet of contempt in the Castilian, equivalent to "toi" in French. This anecdote rests on the authority of Aubéry, whom Vallaire terms a "well-informed writer." See Mémoirès de l'Aubéry du Maurier, p. 9. † Grattan, p. 88.

‡ Prescott, Hist. Reign of Philip II., vol. 1., chap. 3, *passim.*

‡ Brantôme, Œuvres, tom. 5, p 126. ‖ Prescott.

the early days of September, and found an *auto da
fé* awaiting him. Report had spoken truth. Spain
itself, where Romanism was at once a principle of
honor and a part of the national history, where for
eight centuries the Spaniard had been fighting the
battles of the church at home; where every inch of
the soil was won by arms from the infidel; where
life had always been a crusade for Rome; Spain
was infected with the distemper of heresy.* Philip
was half crazed. The Inquisition was invoked.
Human bonfires blazed merrily. At Valladolid the
king paused to witness one. "Sire," cried one
of the sufferers, young Carlos de Lessa, a noble of
talent and distinction, "how can you look on and
permit me to be burned?" "I would carry the
wood to burn my own son withal, were he like you,
a heretic," rejoined the royal brute.†

On reaching Seville, Philip had the happiness
to witness another *auto da fé* of fifty living heretics.
This scene so refreshed him in body and in soul,
that immediately afterwards he solemnized his marriage. "These human victims, chained and burning at the stake, were the blazing torches which
lighted the monarch to his nuptial couch."‡

* Prescott, *ut antea.* Hist. Crit. de l'Inqui., vol. 2, chap. 18.
† Cabrera, vol. 5, p. 236.   ‡ Motley, vol. 1, p. 223.

CHAPTER XIII.

UNDERCURRENTS.

To a casual observer, unfamiliar with the causes and effects of history, it would have seemed that the Netherlands were never more prosperous, never more snugly well-to-do, than on that day when Philip II. weighed anchor for Castile. The states were lapped in a luxury that recalled the Sybarites. "Not the most minute strip of the soil," says Guicciardini, "was without its production; even the sand-heaps afforded shelter to vast numbers of rabbits, esteemed for their delicate flavor; and on every creek of the sea were to be found incredible flocks of water-fowl and their eggs, both of which formed a reliable article of export."* It was indeed so : the shrewd Italian painted to the life.

Off the coasts of Holland, Zealand, and Friesland, two thousand boats found daily employment in the fisheries.† Flanders freighted fifty ships in a single year with household furniture and utensils for Spain and the colonial wants.‡ A single city—Bruges—sold annually stuffs of Spanish and English wool to the amount of eight millions of florins,§ and the least value of the florin then was quadruple its present worth.‖

* Guicciardini, Belg. Des., tom. 2, p. 95.
† Velius Hoorn, book 2.   ‡ Grattan, p. 88.   § Ibid.
‖ The florin was a coin originally made in Florence. The name

The English commerce of the provinces, less important than that with Spain, was valued yearly at twenty-four millions of florins.* Amsterdam was a rising town, but Antwerp was still the pivot of European trade.† Oftentimes the table service of her wealthy burghers consisted entirely of solid silver ;‡ and these merchant princes were the money-changers of Christendom. Germany, England, France, Italy, Spain, constantly fed their lean exchequers from the fat coffers of the burghers. Immense loans were asked and gotten, not in negotiable bills, or for unredeemable debentures; but in hard gold, and on a simple acknowledgment.§

But beneath the sunny surface of this material prosperity crouched death and chaos, soon to reveal themselves. The useful and inoffensive Netherlanders wished to add yet one thing more to their immense possessions—the gospel. Aghast Rome and angered despotism leagued to crush it out. From that fanatic effort sprang the revolution.

Many historians have run up and down, groping for the causes of the prodigious convulsion that now begins to rumble beneath our feet, for scenes of tremendous horror are just at hand. It needs no long search. The past sows the seed, which the

is given to different coins of gold and silver, of different value in different countries. The silver florin now varies in value from twenty-three to fifty-four cents. The gold florin of Hanover is now held at 6s. 11d. sterling.

° Grattan, p. 88. Vandervynckt.   † Ibid.
‡ Velius Hoorn, book 2, p. 142.   § Grattan, *ubi sup.*

present ripens, and the future reaps. In one sense, it was the reopened New Testament which brought the sword into the Netherlands; in another sense, it was an emasculated church, shod in ambitious worldliness, and clothed in fanaticism, that lighted the conflagration; a church prolific as Proteus in disguises, but, like him, ever the same under whatever mask it lurked. To restore to the provinces the uniformity of papistry, to break the coördinate power of the nobility and the states, and to exalt the royal authority on the ruins of the old republican rudiments—this was the purpose of King Philip II.* For that he plotted, and for that he dissembled; and that purpose was the germ which flowered in revolt. Margaret was commissioned, and so was the bishop of Arras, to compass that object;† and this fact at once reduced the so-called government of the regent to a colossal fraud, to a chartered hypocrisy, to a conspiracy against justice and honest men, to a junta of licensed stabbers.

The ship in which Philip sailed for Spain was hardly hull-down upon the ocean, before the governant and her crafty Mentor began to carry out the prescribed programme of despotism, heedless of the increasing excitement of the people—that "mischievous animal" which the bishop of Arras held in such supreme contempt.‡

Before opening the Medician volume of governmental acts, let us glance briefly at the *status* of the Netherlanders towards the close of the year

* Schiller, p. 426. † Ibid. ‡ Papiers d'Etat, vol. 7, p. 367.

1559, and familiarize ourselves with the mainsprings of the national action, with the affected indifference, but real bitterness of the patrician, with the sentiments of the burgher, with the inspiration of the boor.

As for the aristocracy, it was, like all others, rotten to the core; indeed it had sunk lower than kindred castes in other countries; for the lavish expenditure, the eager competition, the profligate habits into which Charles V. had lured the Lowland nobles, had, as he wished, steeped them to the lips in ruin, and left them bankrupt in character as well as purse.*

But, though stripped of their property, they retained their tastes, and hungered morbidly for the luxuries of the past. Many a seedy noble took to gambling as a panacea for his ills. The money thus gotten was lavished in riotous debauchery: they worshipped a carouse, and a banquet was their god. Those patricians who still retained their estates were doing their utmost to waste them in lavish display. "They spent twice as much as they were worth," remarks a contemporaneous critic, "on their palaces, furniture, troops of retainers, costly liveries, and sumptuous entertainments."† And another observer says, "Instead of one court at Brussels, you would have said that there were fifty."‡

* Pontus Payen, MS.
† Albertos de Flandes, MS., cited in Prescott, vol. 1, p. 477.
‡ Pontus Payen, MS.

As the nobles grew poorer, their orgies waxed madder. "*Dum vivimus, vivamus*" was the motto of every bacchanal. Drunkenness was a wide-spread vice. "When a Flemish gentleman finds himself sober, he thinks that he is ill," sneered the bitter Badovaro,* one of those keen Italians, half spy, half ambassador, whom the Venetian doges kept at the different European courts, that they might acquaint themselves with the most intricate phases of the social and political life of Christendom. The English Camden phrased it more naively when he said that, "in drinking others' health they impaired their own."†

Nor was this wild life confined to the gentlemen of the Lowland cities: the ladies of the higher ranks were every bit as fond of presiding at midnight orgies; and at the best, the distinction between the morals of what modern *feuilletonists* style the *monde* and the *demi-monde*, were very shadowy.‡

As a body, this aristocracy was without principle and without patriotism, but not without hate; and the more they became impoverished, the bitterer grew their hate of the Spaniard who had tricked them into ruin, the closer they drew towards the burgher class which held the wealth of Crœsus in its iron boxes, and the more they labored to stir up sedition; for an *émeute* meant, possibly, the repudiation of their debts, and mortgaged lands wrested

---

* Badovaro, Relatione MS.   † Camden, book 3, p. 263.
‡ Badovaro, Pontus Payen, etc.

from the maw of creditors; at the worst, beggared lords and mendicant gentlemen had naught to fear.

No question but the nobles joined the republican ranks and swelled the chorus for reform, more from pique than from conviction, and more from selfishness than from either. But while this is so, we should not therefore conclude with the Roman publicists, or believe, as the bishop of Arras pretended to believe, that the trouble now at hand was stirred by a few score of needy and ambitious patricians; for revolutions are not made, they grow, and this one was begotten of the collision of two radically antagonistic ideas—Christian liberty and Roman despotism. It was a popular, not an aristocratic movement. The patricians joined it, not from choice, but from necessity, and impelled by the hope of gain. "Those nobles so conspicuous in the surface at the outset, only drifted before a storm which they neither caused nor controlled," as Motley records. "Even the most powerful and sagacious were tossed to and fro by the surge of great events, which, as they rolled more and more tumultuously around them, seemed to become both irresisible and unfathomable."* If the Prince of Orange was an exception to all this, it was not because he was a patrician, but because he was a Christian patriot, earnest to serve God and to advance the common weal.

The movement for reform in the Netherlands

* Motley, vol. 1, p. 256.

had been democratic from the commencement, and
it grew constantly more and more popular. How
could it be otherwise? Had not the Reformation
called the people into being? Had it not crumbled
classes into men? Had it not dug out of the lowest, dirtiest boor the diamond of an immortal soul?
Truly, the pariah classes, the villains of the feudal
ages, might well love the gospel and die for it; for
it had enfranchized them. Who can marvel that
such a gospel, "the hidden might of Christ," had
ever a victorious power joined with it, like him in
the Apocalypse that went forth on the white horse,
with his bow and his crown, conquering and to conquer? Who can feign to wonder that it leaped the
Rhine, and clasped Germany to the bosom of its
faith? that it won Switzerland by a word, and enthroned its great apostle at Geneva? that it lisped
in England, and was buried in ten times ten thousand hearts? that it sighed in France, and awakened the Huguenots? that it pleaded in Holland, and
subdued the Netherlands? The lowermost classes
of all tribes and tongues could not choose but love
and adhere to the reform, which resurrected Christ
for the second time—Christ, who had promised to
reward all who loved him with "the glorious liberty
of the sons of God."

And still the reform spread. The Sclavonian
races hailed it with rapture. Scandinavia entered
the gospel fold with eager alacrity. Bugenhagen,
the founder of Lutheranism in Denmark, could find
no words to describe the zeal with which the Danes

listened to his preaching, "even on work-days, even before daylight, on holidays, and all day long."* The evangelical pastors had traversed the ice-fields of Lapland in company with the Swedish governors.† On the south shores of the Baltic Protestantism was predominant.‡ Already the great cities of Polish Prussia had confirmed the ritual of Luther by express charter.§ And in Poland itself it was a common saying, "A Polish nobleman is not subject to the king; is he to be the vassal of the pope?"‖ Hungary swarmed with reformers; the mountains of Franconia echoed to their exhortations.¶ In Vienna, twenty years had elapsed since a single student of the university had taken priests' orders.** Scotland was as Protestant as Knox could make it.†† In England, an alliance between the Reformation and the throne had moulded the ecclesiasticism of the island into the peculiar form which it still wears from the south of the Thames to the Tweed.‡‡ As for France, the Venetian ambassador at Paris, Micheli, gave this testimony to the doge: "Your highness, with some few exceptions, this nation has quite fallen away from the Latin faith, especially the nobles and the young men under forty almost to a man; and though many still go to mass, they do so for appearance sake, and out of

---

º Narrative of D. Pomerani, 1539.
† Ranke, Hist. of the Popes, p. 130. ‡ Ibid.
§ Ibid. ‖ Ibid. ¶ Ibid.
ºº Ranke, *ubi sup.*
†† Chambers, Rebellions in Scotland, 1638–1660.
‡‡ Hist. Eng. Puritans, Am. Tract Soc., 1867.

fear; when they think themselves unobserved, they turn their backs on both mass and church.*

Protestantism everywhere triumphant; Romanism everywhere subdued and despoiled—such was the jubilant European fact in the middle decades of the sixteenth century. Why was it that the reformed faith did not extend its sway over the whole of Christendom at this auspicious moment, when, conqueror in the east, in the north, in the west, it had insinuated itself into that holy of holies of the popes, the Spanish peninsula, and stood knocking at the gates of the Vatican itself? Why? Balmes, an eminent Romanist pamphleteer, shall answer: "Philip II., a prince devoted with his whole soul to the interest of the Latin church, and at the head of the most powerful empire in the world, by his energy and determination afforded a counterpoise to the Protestant cause, which prevented it from making itself complete master of Europe."† It was, indeed, Philip's dogged fanaticism which assisted the holy see to organize and launch its counter movement.

Of course, while the atmosphere of Europe was in this highly electric state, the Netherlands could not fail to inhale heresy. Their very position made them the reservoir of opinion. Among them, at least, it was impossible to put an effectual embargo on thought, for the great majority of the people could read. Seated "in the heart of Europe, the blood of a world-wide traffic was daily coursing

---

* Micheli, Relatione delle cose di Francia, l'anno 1561.

† Balmes, Protestantism and Catholicity compared, p. 215.

through the veins of their water-inwoven territory. There was a mutual exchange between the Low Countries and all the world, and ideas were as liberally interchanged as goods. Truth was imported as freely as less precious merchandise. The psalms of Marot were as current as the drugs of Malacca or the diamonds of Borneo. The strict prohibitory measures of a despotic government could not annihilate this intellectual trade; nor could bigotry devise an efficient quarantine to exclude the religious pest, which lurked in every bale of merchandise, and was wafted in every breeze from east and west."*

Besides, the history and the habits of this people tended to alienate them from Rome. The old bishops of Utrecht, the mediæval Waldenses, had bitterly opposed the holy see. The precious parchments which guaranteed their liberties had been clutched from ecclesiastic as well as from feudal lords. Then, too, the republican virtues of thrift and intelligence had taught them to loathe the priests—a horde of lazy epecureans, telling beads, and pampering themselves in luxurious vice on the earnings of others.† Added to all this, the burghers were men accustomed to think and act for themselves. This independent spirit they brought to the discussion of the new doctrines. Read in this way, the gospel tenets looked reasonable and true, the papal dogmas seemed absurd and atrocious. They began to love the one and to doubt the other. The authority on which the gospel rested was the

* Motley, vol. 1, p. 258.   † Ibid.

Bible. The authority on which popery depended was the haughty *ipse dixit* of a priest. The shrewd burghers remembered that the Greeks believed the legends in Herodotus—that the Romans credited the figments in Livy. "Are not the Italians as credulous and as nationally vain as the Greeks of the Athenian forum, as the Romans of the heathen empire?" queried they; and they demanded better sponsors for their creed.

For a time the Netherlands held to Protestantism as an intellectual conviction; but when the fiery field-preachers of the south of France entered the states, they speedily kindled this cold adhesion of the brain into a blazing faith in the heart, ready to cry with Paul: "I am persuaded that neither death, nor life, nor angels, nor principalities, nor powers, nor things present, nor things to come, nor height, nor depth, nor any other creature, shall be able to separate us from the love of God, which is in Christ Jesus our Lord."* For Protestantism entered the provinces, not by the Hapsburg, but the Huguenot gate.†

It was the Netherland people, thus enlightened by their memories of the past, thus inspired by the grace of Christ aglow in their hearts, that now entered the arena, armed like David with a simple pebble, the gospel, to contend with the two Goliaths of Spain and of the Vatican. The nobles? they were but the gilded hands on the outside of the dial; the hour to strike was determined by the

* Rom. 8:38, 39.   † Motley, vol. 1, p. 259.

people, the obscure but weighty movements hid within.*

A bitter baptism of suffering, trying the faith of the Netherland disciples "so as by fire," had ripened them for heroic deeds, for martyrdom is the grandest developer of revolutions. For years the pitiless edicts of Charles V. had hacked them; of late the yet more merciless placards of Philip II. meted and peeled them; and though content to

"Wait beneath the furnace-blast the pangs of transformation,"

quivering lips could not at all times choke the wail, "How long, O Lord, how long?"

Singularly enough, the Reformation, hypocritically acquiesced in for a space in Germany, peacefully settled in England by the recent accession of Elizabeth to the throne, armed and militant in France, was still banned and burned in the Netherlands, and all the more fiercely persecuted, because the general pacification left Philip nothing else to do. From the east and from the west the clouds rolled away, leaving a comparatively bright and peaceful atmosphere, only that they might concentrate themselves with portentous blackness over the devoted soil of the Netherlands.†

Philip did indeed lend his assistance to the ultramontane party in France, and scheme to set on foot another "Sicilian vespers." But the splintered lance which pierced the brain of Henry II. in the dismal tournament of 1559, postponed the Huguenot massacre for a dozen years, and seated a wom-

* Motley.   † Ibid.

an in the regency whose tenure of power depended upon the division of the kingdom into hostile factions. The power of Catharine de' Medici grew from her policy of balancing Coligny against Guise, Huguenot against Romanist; therefore "the persuasions of Philip and the arts of Alva were powerless to induce her to carry out the scheme which Henry had revealed to Orange in the forest of Vincennes." Eventually the queen-mother thought that she might say "yes" to the project without being the suicide of her own influence; but "when the crime came, it was as blundering as it was bloody; at once premeditated, and accidental; the isolated execution of an integral conspiracy, existing for half a generation, yet exploding without concert; a wholesale massacre, but a piecemeal plot."*

But St. Bartholomew was still in the future, and we have to do with the Netherlands in the year 1559. We know now what their *status* was, and what their sentiments. What remains then but to open the governmental book?

* Motley.

CHAPTER XIV.

QUICKSANDS.

HAD Philip II. been Aurelius, or had he risen to the level of the old philosophers of Academus, he would have known that a system of toleration in the domain of faith, and of liberality in the realm of politics, would be best suited to the genius of the Netherlands; but he was a fanatic, and it was his grim ambition either to desolate the country—sweep it clean as the palm of his hand, or to Romanize it.

Some say the king was mad. Gayarré bids us remember that "his royal line sprang from insanity in the person of his mother, Joanna of Castile, and ended as it began, in the idiotic madness of Charles II., the last Hapsburg on the throne of Spain."[*] 'T is an ingenious argument; but if it be indeed so, we cannot fail to think that Philip had "method in his madness."

Still, his departure from the Netherlands on the eve of the battle between absolutism and conscience, was a capital error. He should have remained, to give his innovations the advantage of the personal presence of royalty. Delegated power is at best but weak; and when, as now, the government was known to be but the shadow of a shadow—for Mar-

[*] Gayarré, Hist. of Philip II., p. 83.

garet was seen to be but the puppet of Arras—the people were still less disposed to brook insulting changes and to pocket wrongs.

Besides, their lingering loyalty forbade them to connect the king with their grievances: they strapped the load upon the shoulders of his minister; and borrowing the tactics of their ancestors, who, while *pretending*, were really *shaking off* obedience to Tiberius and Vespasian, they pelted the usurpations of the regency as treason against the throne,* which had been an impossible *ruse*, with Philip at Brussels.

As for the minister, he had a wit that could easily new-cast itself into any mould. He endeavored to veil his influence from vulgar eyes; for which purpose he revived a custom which draws its date from the times of Augustus and Tiberius, and transacted his business with the government through the medium of notes, even though they were both dwelling under a common roof—a practice which Arras esteemed to have this further advantage, of more deeply imprinting his counsel upon Margaret's mind, and affording him *data* to fall back on in case of need.† "But 'tis hard to deceive the keen eyes of the court," says Strada; "and now no man doubted but that Arras inspired every move; and as often happens in such cases, even matters in which he really had no hand, when once his name was up for a favorite and a do-all, were held

* Vandervynckt, Troubles des Pays-Bas, tom. 2.

† Strada, *ubi sup*.

to be his doings."* It was an early and striking application of that graceful fiction of modern parliamentary law in England, which shields the sovereign beneath ministerial responsibility.

In January, 1560, the administration opened its campaign against the people by the publication of the papal bull creating those new bishoprics which Philip had solicited while yet at Brussels.†

The object of the innovation was palpable, for it sought to destroy the equilibrium and to corrupt the independence of the three orders, the clergy, the nobility, and the cities, whose delegates formed the states-general of the Netherlands. For many years the clergy had been a free and powerful order in the state, governed and represented by four bishops, chosen by the chapters of the towns, or elected by the suffrages of the monks of the abbeys.‡ Possessing an independent territorial revenue, and not directly subject to the influence of the crown, these churchmen had to some extent interests and feelings in common with the nation; while bishops and abbots occupied the upper benches of the states-general, side by side with their good friends the barons.§ Thus circumstanced, and immensely wealthy, these recluses were lazy to a proverb. Like Erasmus, they were optimists, so long as their ease and purse were left them. Philip saw that he could never spur these epicurean monks into preaching a crusade against heresy, in which they

* Strada, *ubi sup.*   † Chap. X., p. 160.
‡ Vandervynckt, Grattan.   § Ibid.

were certain to gain nothing, and exposed to lose much.*

Besides, he could not reach them, for they were within the spiritual jurisdiction of the two archiepiscopal sees of Cologne and Rheims in France— an extra-provincial allegiance which had long been a stumbling-block to the Low Country sovereigns.†

Presto! and now look. The bull authorized Philip to increase the number of the Netherland bishops from four to eighteen, he to have the nomination, the pope to retain the confirmation. Three archiepiscopates were established, one at Cambray, one at Utrecht, one at Mechlin, which snatched the prerogative from the alien archbishops; and to crown all, Perrenot was made archbishop of Mechlin, and promoted from the see of Arras to the primacy of the Netherlands.‡

A trick was to insure the subserviency of the abbeys. From a pretended motive of economy, the new prelates were endowed with the title of abbots of the chief monasteries of their respective dioceses, which not only insured them a reversion in the gold chests of these establishments; but, better still for despotism, made them the legal heirs of the political rights of the abbots, after the death of those then living; secured the dominance of the ecclesiastical order to the creatures of the court; and gave

---

* Motley, vol. 1, p. 265.
† Schiller, p. 428. Meteren, Vandervynckt.
‡ Strada, p. 40.

Philip the control of that estate in the national assembly.*

When the papal *fiat* announced this programme, the Netherlands were filled with consternation, for the negotiations with the holy see which resulted in the decretal had been kept secret, and were known to but few.† For once, priest, noble, and citizen united to execrate this fatal usurpation. "It is impious, for it confiscates our houses, perverts to selfish objects riches which a devout charity has placed in our chests for the relief of the unfortunate, and usurps for the plunderers of the poor the places of superiors elected by and among ourselves from time immemorial," cried the abbots. " 'T is a trick, by means of which we are to be out-voted in the states-general by lackey churchmen bound to enact what the king shall be pleased to dictate," said the barons. "It is the entering wedge of the Inquisition—part of the merciless machinery of persecution," exclaimed the citizens.‡ With one accord the innovation was hooted as a fraud, and scouted as unconstitutional — fatally against the ancient charters of the states; and so it was.

For the constitution of Brabant contained these three provisions among others: "The prince of the land shall not elevate the clerical estate higher than of old has been customary and by former princes settled, unless by consent of the other two estates,

---

* Grattan, p. 92.

† Papiers d'Etat, tom. 5. Cor. de Philippe II., tom. 1.

‡ Schiller, p. 430. Motley, vol. 1, p. 271, *et seq.*

namely, the nobility and the cities." "The prince shall appoint no foreigners to office in Brabant." "Should the prince, by force or otherwise, violate any of these privileges, the inhabitants of Brabant, after regular protest entered, are discharged of their oaths of allegiance, and as free, independent, and unbound people, may conduct themselves as seems to them best."*

So spoke the charter of Brabant, to which Philip II. had sworn and set his seal; and so that of Holland, its twin brother; and so the rest.† To these brave old parchments the Netherlanders now had recourse, and a combat of words, a battle of pens, a war of letters at once commenced. The humblest citizen could quibble, when liberty was in peril from a misconstruction of statute law, as glibly as the primate himself, and closely and widely were the constitutions studied. The people were keen to see and quick to note. It was quite impossible to cheat their instincts, for the Reformation had been their teacher, and the Reformation was a schoolmaster that carried its pupils up from room to room in the university of the mind.

However, the masses did err in attributing the inception of this assault upon their privileges, as everybody did, to the new metropolitan. They mistook when they thought Perrenot had spun his honors out of his own brain, as spiders spin their houses out of their own bowels. For once the churchman

* Meteren, vol. 1, p. 28. Bor, vol. 1, p. 19.   † Ibid.
† Papiers d'Etat, tom. 6, p. 554.
Dutch Ref.   10

was innocent. Until the bull came, he knew nothing
of the project;* but when it came, by adopting and
attempting to enforce it he made the offence his own.

When it was bruited on the streets that Perrenot
had accepted the see of Mechlin, the rage of the
people was portentous. Even the minister's matchless serenity was a trifle disturbed. When Holiness
strangled Error, in Spenser's immortal poem,

"Her vomit full of books and papers was."

When report made Perrenot the originator of this
innovation, his alarm was full of despatches. Once,
twice, thrice he hurried couriers off to Madrid,
freighted with letters to this effect: "They say that
the episcopates were devised to gratify my ambition; as your majesty did not consult me in the
matter, I pray you contradict these ill reports."†
And the docile monarch sent back the denial as
repeatedly as it was asked for.‡ But it was useless; denials subscribed "Philip, Rex," and piled
as high as the dome of St. Peter's, would not have
absolved him in the minds of the people. He was
the friend of Spain; Spain had the Inquisition;
therefore he wished to plant it in the Netherlands;
and the syllogism seemed without a flaw. "Bah!"
cried they, with a bitter, incredulous smile; "is not
Perrenot the lion of this fable? Who is it that is
striving to settle the new order?" No epigram was
made that did not blister him; not one after-dinner speech but took him for its text. At last the

---

* Papiers d'Etat, tom. 6, p. 554.   † Ibid., pp. 552–562.
‡ Cor. de Phil. II., tom. 1, p. 207.

complacent prelate, who had patted the new arrangement on the head and styled it "a holy work," warmly pledging fortune, blood, and life to its success, wailed this prayer in the ears of the Spanish ambassador at Rome : "Would to God that the erection of these new sees had never been thought of. Amen ; amen."*

The excitement of the people, already finding voice in a menacing chorus, was tuned to a still higher pitch by the continued retention of the Spanish soldiers in the Netherlands. Three months, six months, nine months, twelve months passed, and yet they lingered, in the teeth of the royal promise that they should be speedily removed.† "Whatever else is left undone, retain the men-at arms," said the royal liar to the minister, at their parting interview.‡ Perrenot strained every nerve to obey the mandate. Setting his imagination at work, he invented evils which the presence of the soldiers could alone avert. Trading on credulity, he based their tarry on events which he knew would never take place. Thus, by elevating fables into realities, he illustrated the old saying, that "there is nothing so false as figures but facts."

But the platitudes of the prelate were unheeded. It was an open secret that the men-at-arms were part and parcel of the conspiracy against the states.§ Fiercer and louder grew the clamor. The Zealand-

---

* Papiers d'Etat, tom. 6, p. 341. Cited in Motley, vol. 1, p. 275, and in Prescott, vol. 1, p. 501. † Chap. XII., p. 212.
‡ Vandervynckt, Meteren. § Apologie d'Orange.

ers, among whom the mercenaries were quartered for a time, were so exasperated at their presence that they refused to go near the dykes, then in need of the annual repairs, and indeed threatened to swamp the province, unless speedily ridden of the pest.*

Some time before Margaret learned of the feeling in Zealand, she had cajoled the Low Country merchants into advancing the pay of these soldiers, on pretext of the necessity of settling their arrears before removing them, pledging the royal treasury to refund the debt.† Now, disgusted with the treaty of Philip, and convinced that there was no intention to send off the troops, they too lent their voices to swell the chorus of dissatisfaction, and even went so far as to refuse to pay their taxes to the government collectors.‡

At last the court was alarmed. In October, 1560, a session of the council of state was held, on which occasion Orange threw up the command of his legion, and affirmed, supported by Viglius and by the primate himself, that the longer retention of the Spanish regiments would inevitably provoke a revolt. The governant begged that action might be deferred until the return of Egmont, then absent on an embassy to Spain, but expecting ere long to return to Brussels; but this proposition was negatived without dissent.§

---

* Vandervynckt, Troubles des Pays-Bas.
† Meteren, Grotius.   ‡ Strada, p. 51.
§ Documents Inedits, tom. 1, pp. 330, 331.

Nothing remained but to succumb. Accordingly, the regent wrote to acquaint the king with the result of the council; but since this missive was to be read at the open board before being despatched to Madrid, she touched slightly and perfunctorily on the causes which had influenced the decision, lest she might be thought to act from fear.[*]

In a private note, written in cipher and sent by the same post, she opened the cause more fully to Philip's eye: "The provinces are resolved, sire, that so long as they are overawed by the foreign soldiers, they will not give a penny to the collectors by way of subsidy. The bankers complain that the cities which borrowed of them great sums wherewith to pay the Spaniards when they seemed about to quit the land, when they saw them delayed, grew angry, and refused to pay interest on the money. Our sky is overcast; mischief impends; I pray you, sire, release our fears by ordering these regiments hence."[†]

At the same time the primate wrote these lines to "the master:" "It cuts me to the heart to see the troops leave us; but go they must. Would to God that we could devise some pretext for their stay, as your majesty desires! We have tried all means humanly possible; but I see no way to retain them without incurring the risk of a sudden revolt, which, just now, would be a blunder."[‡]

Upon the receipt of these letters, Philip was

[*] Strada, *ubi sup.*   [†] Cited in Strada, pp. 51, 52.
[‡] Papiers d'Etat, tome 5.

plunged into doubt; but happily for the Netherlands, just at this moment he received news of a reverse to his arms on the coast of Barbary—a reverse which necessitated reinforcements. Taking up his pen, he scrawled these lines to Margaret: "You may, if you see fit, send away the Spanish soldiers, who will be a seasonable supply in Africa. As for the money-masters, I will look· to their engagement with the cities."*

This permit was decisive. Early in 1561, the hated mercenaries embarked for the Mediterranean amid the execrations of the seventeen provinces.† Over their departure, Margaret and the primate alone grieved. The Netherlands gave that day at least to *vivas*.

---

* Strada, *ubi sup.*   † Ibid., Schiller, Motley.

CHAPTER XV.

AGITATION.

WHEN the ships which bore the mercenaries to Africa lifted anchor, the court said with a sigh, "Alack, 't is a sad necessity; but there is one good thing, we shall see the flood-tide of popular rage begin to ebb, which will leave us to new-model the abbeys without danger of catching cold from wet feet." It was an error into which Margaret fell, because she was more skilful as a hawker than as a governant; and into which the primate stumbled because his politics were precisely those which least qualified him for the control, or even comprehension of a republican movement, not to be barred by artful dodging, suave lies, and occult cruelty.

The Netherlanders hooted the embarking Spaniards, but refused to hush their suspicions to sleep when they were gone. The Inquisition impended, and nothing was done while any thing remained undone. The agitation gathered to a focus, and was increased by concentration. The talk of the sidewalks crystallized into organized resistance. Brabant expended thirty thousand florins in the defence of her charter, paid for the opinions of the most eminent of the European jurists, and accred ited an agent to Rome to appeal from the pope ill-informed to his holiness better-informed.* Utrecht, Guelders, Deventer, Raremond, and Leuwarden slammed their gates in the faces of the prelates for whose benefit they had been erected into dioceses.† Brave Antwerp absolutely refused to install her bishop, and despatched a commission to Spain to represent to Philip the ruin that such an innovation would send along her wharves. For a twelvemonth the remonstrance which was thus carried to his throne, was suffered by the king to lie, unanswered and neglected, in the pigeon-holes of his royal cabinet; and at the last, he would render no defin-ite decision, though consenting to defer the installa-tion of that individual prelate until his personal arrival at Brussels, which he seems at that time to have contemplated. This was more than Antwerp had expected, and her burghers regarded themselves as indefinitely reprieved.‡

In some towns no open resistance was made to the new bishops, though they were everywhere received with the most marked and bitter con-tempt.§ When the primate himself entered the capital of his see, Mechlin contained no voice to cheer him, and no tongue to shout a welcome :‖ "he seemed more like a thief stealthily climbing into the

---

° Vandervynckt, Troubles des Pays-Bas, tom. 2, p. 71.

† Ibid., Cor. de Philippe II., tom 1. Meteren.

‡ Papiers d'Etat de Granvelle, tom. 6, p. 612. Meteren. Hist. des Pays-Bas, folio 31.

§ Ibid., Cor. de Philippe II., tom. 1.

‖ Vandervynckt, tom. 2, p. 77.

fold, than a good shepherd who had come to guard it."*

In February, 1561, Margaret secured for Arras a cardinal's hat. From this time, Anthony Perrenot, the notary's son, vanishes; he is transformed into Cardinal Granvelle, and by that name we must know him, if we wish to be in the fashion. This unexpected honor—his good friend the duchess had obtained the red hat from his holiness unknown to the bishop—did not tend to abate the rigor or to lower the autocratic tone of the upstart minister.

The evident rulership, the careless impudence of Granvelle could not fail to madden a body of nobles as haughty as himself, and who despised him as a mushroom favorite who had been cradled in the dingy office of a country lawyer. When he cracked his whip, they refused to cower.

On his part, the cardinal repaid contempt with contempt, and regarded the bulk of his antagonists as a horde of titled blockheads. He treated them as if they had been a parcel of foolish children; and never consulted those lords who were nominally associated with him in the government, except upon the most trivial questions: every matter of importance being decided by the *consulta,* whose irresponsible and unknown acts, meanwhile, were done in the name of all the members of the council of state.†

Against this absolutism of the minister the fiery Egmont rebelled, nor was Orange the man to acknowledge its legitimacy. Neither fancied respon-

* Prescott, vol. 1, p, 500.   † Meteren, Schiller, Motley.

sibility without participation. Between Egmont and Granvelle there was bitter feud. They were antipodal characters. The count was a rude soldier, ignorant, impetuous, blunt, and proud. The cardinal was a Machiaevellian politician, deeply read, shrewd, self-controlled, and unscrupulous. Such men could not but despise each other.

Not only so, but on several occasions Granvelle had taken pains to thwart Egmont: once when the count had requested the governorship of Hesdin for a friend, whereupon the minister awarded it to a gentleman who had no claim to the office; and once again when the count asked that the abbey of Trulle might be given to a relative, on which the greedy cardinal appropriated it to himself.* By similar acts he had angered others of the Netherland seignors—Horn and Berghen and Brederode.

One day there was a scene in the council-chamber, which came near having a tragic close. Egmont, exasperated by the bland insolence of the cardinal, drew his sword, and was about to sheath it in the body of his foe, when Orange with others seized and disarmed him; and all this occurred before the eyes of the duchess regent.†

The relations between Orange and Granvelle had once been very intimate; and now, though the

* Dom l'Eresque Mémoires, tom. 1, p. 231. Cited in Motley, vol. 1, p. 283.

† Pontus Payen, MS. Some say Egmont cuffed Granvelle's ears. See Van der Haer, tom. 1, p. 180, et seq.

cardinal plotted for absolutism while the prince planned for the opposition, both were a trifle timid about precipitating an open rupture of the old-time friendship. Granvelle knew how to dissemble, and Orange had learned to piece out the lion's skin with the fox's;* therefore the forms of amity were carefully preserved long after the reality was dead.† But in this play of diamond cut diamond neither was foolish enough to depreciate the other. The prince knew that Granvelle was Machiavelli resurrected. The cardinal, not even affecting to underrate Orange, wrote Philip soon after his departure for Spain: "'T is a man of profound genius, vast ambition—dangerous, acute, politic."‡

With all their caution it was impossible that two men so widely at variance in motive and purpose should long be able to mask their feelings behind a decayed intimacy; and indeed it was not many weeks after Egmont's escapade at the council-board that these "good friends" announced their enmity.

Orange was hereditary burgrave of Antwerp, a connection which entitled him to a potential voice in the municipality. The selection of the magistrates was at this moment an important matter, as the city was in hot opposition to the bishopric's usurpation. At such an hour, Granvelle, riding rough-shod over the rights of the prince, presumed to nominate the political foes of the burgrave; and

* "Si leonina pellis non satis est, vulpina addenda."
† Motley, vol. 1, p. 285.　　　　　　‡ Ibid., p. 284.

then, without consultation, coolly confirmed them in the magistracy by a fiat of the *consulta*. Not pausing here, the minister carried his impudence still farther by selecting Orange as one of the commissioners who were to see that the decree was carried into effect. This audacity exhausted the patience of the prince. "Tell the duchess," sneered he with a cold smile, on being handed the commission, which he returned unopened, "that I am not her lackey; she may send some other on her errands."*

Then, repairing to the council, Orange bitterly resented Granvelle's insolence, stabbing the smooth churchman with such cutting words that he too lost temper, and rushing from the chamber with unprelatical imprecations on his lips, vowed henceforth to drop all communication with these grand seignors.†

Concealment was at an end, and Orange, with his accustomed promptitude, acted. On the 23d of July, 1561, he addressed an epistle to Philip, which was also signed by Egmont. Complaining of Granvelle's impudence, and of his bold usurpation of authority—to the complete disfranchisement of the other counsellors, who were held responsible for the secret decisions of the *consulta*—the missive closed by requesting the king either to curb the cardinal by forcing him to admit all to the deliberations and decisions of the council of state, or to

---

° Bakh, v. d. Brink. Cited in Motley, vol. 1, p. 286.
† Ibid.

accept the resignation of his servants Orange and Egmont.*

Philip received these lines in the secrecy of his cabinet at Madrid, and cursed the writers. But he replied blandly enough that he thanked the nobles for their zeal: "I will answer more at large," said he, "on the return of Count Horn."† Horn was admiral of the Netherlands, and had escorted Philip to Spain.‡ A man of haughty and somewhat sullen temper, brave and honest, but overbearing and quarrelsome,§ Horn had incurred the enmity of the cardinal by contemptuously rejecting the suit of a brother of the prelate, who aspired to the hand of the admiral's sister.‖ His own hatred for Horn the wily favorite succeeded in planting in Philip's breast, and we shall ere long see what bloody fruit it bore.

The voluminous minister took care to despatch a dozen manuscript quartos of news to Madrid every twenty-four hours; and thus the royal scribe was kept freshly familiar with events at Brussels, always, however, from Granvelle's stand-point. Of course the opposition which was made to the new bishoprics received a copious recital. "Your majesty," wrote he in one of his tri-daily epistles, "there is the same kind of talk now about the bishoprics which brought about the recall of the Span-

---

* Correspondance de Philippe II., tom. 1, pp. 195, 196.
† Ibid., p. 197.   ‡ Meteren, Hist. des Pays-Bas.
§ Motley, vol. 1, p. 100.
‖ La deduction de l'innocence du Comte de Horn.

ish troops."* On another occasion Granvelle charged and primed "the master" with an answer to a letter which was about to be sent him in opposition to the new-modelled abbeys. "When they say the scheme is contrary to the charters of the states, tell them, sire"—it was so he wrote—"that you have consulted those learned in the laws, and have convinced yourself that the project is perfectly constitutional; wherefore command Orange and the rest to use their influence to promote the success of the good work."† Happily for Philip this letter reached him just before the arrival at Madrid of the deputation sent out by the estates of Brabant to solicit his abandonment of the innovation. The king listened patiently, and then rejoined by reciting to them with great accuracy the lesson which he had privately received from the ubiquitous cardinal.‡

But while dissembling in public, Philip opened his heart to Granvelle in his correspondence. "'T is no time to temporize," said he; "we must chastise with rigor, with severity. These rascals can only be made to do right through fear, and not always even by that means."§

Even thus early nothing kept Philip from sending an army into the Netherlands to enforce his wishes with the iron hand, save the exhausted state of the royal finances. The home exchequer was dismal enough—looked blue as indigo.

* Papiers d'Etat, tom. 6, p. 261.
† Ibid., pp. 463, 464.   ‡ Motley, vol. 1, p. 291.
§ Papiers d'Etat de Granvelle, tom. 6, p. 421.

Nor was the financial horizon brighter in the Netherlands. The cardinal was constantly hampered and cramped by the constitutional opposition of the states, who very naturally grudged money which was to be forged into fetters for their limbs. This " meddling " provoked Granvelle's ire. " Sire," wrote he to Philip, " we are often in such embarrassment as not to know where to look for ten ducats. These are very vile things, this authority which the deputies assume, this audacity with which they say whatever they think proper, these impudent conditions which they affix to any proposition for supplies."* The cardinal protested that he had in vain attempted to convince them of their error; but they remained perverse.†

It was while the royal exchequer was thus disordered that the keen Venetian ambassador, Suriano, discovered that the Spanish court had a plan for debasing the coin. He hastened to communicate the news to the doge: " Your highness, a skilful chemist named Malen has discovered a certain powder, of which one ounce, mixed with six ounces of quicksilver, will make six ounces of silver. 'T is a source of revenue hitherto kept secret, on account of the opposition of the states and the theological scruples of the king. In an exigency it may be used."‡

Now need we marvel that the royal counterfeiter, with bankruptcy before him and a chaos of debts

* Papiers d'Etat, tom. 6, pp. 178-180.
† Motley, *ubi sup.*   ‡ Suriano, MS.

behind, resolved to exhaust the resources of his chicanery before launching an army upon the Netherlands?

Philip loved to manœuvre and deceive, and in
this crisis he forbore to press the installation of the
new bishops upon those sees which manifested an
invincible repugnance to their reception, muttering,
"All in time; all in good time;" but he confirmed
those prelates who had gotten possession of their
dioceses.* Meanwhile, the resistance which the
abbeys made to the royal innovation compelled a
compromise, by which it was arranged that the
prelates were to receive an annual stipend from the
revenues of the abbots, who were to retain the
remainder of the ecclesiastical funds, and to be
elected, as before, by and from among the monks
of the religious houses.†   In the very face of advancing despotism, the voice of the people had cried,
"Halt."

* Brandt, vol. 1, p. 134.   Davies, vol. 1, p. 510.
† Hoofd, Nederl. Hist., book 1. Hooper, Rec. et Mem., chap. 8.

CHAPTER XVI.

THE INQUISITION.

VARIOUS voices have united to assure us that the Inquisition was the chief agent of that Pharisaical tyranny which frenzied the Netherlands. No question but that it was an occasion of the brooding revolt. Strada, himself a loyalist and a Jesuit, affirms it in these words: "One thing most of all troubled and exasperated, and opened a door of war in the Low Countries; at first a suspicion, and then an endeavor of setting up an Inquisition against heresy."*

What wast the Inquisition? what its motive? what its origin? what its methods? what its instruments? what its influence? An analysis shall answer. It can only be limned in the sternest colors; but we must not forget that nature's sternest painter has been crowned the best.

---

* Strada, Hist. of the Low Country Wars, p. 32.

† It were more fit to inquire what is the Inquisition? since that abhorrent paganism is to-day as active and as vicious as ever; still plotting to resurrect the blackest dogmas of the dark ages; still the most dangerous, implacable, and ubiquitous enemy of civil and religious Protestantism, and only so far changed by the lapse of ages as to cloak its purpose yet more closely in deceit and fraud than it was wont before, if that be possible. But Satan is Satan still, whether towering in the clouds or "squat like a toad." All who would study this subject are referred especially to the able work of Michelét and Quenet, "The Jesuits," and to Achilli's "Dealings with the Jesuits."

Christianity was instituted as a means to an end.
The end was the salvation of souls; the means,
what else could they be but the propagation of the
gospel?*   Christ proclaimed it by the sea of Gali-
lee; St. Peter was fettered for it in the Roman
dungeons; St. Paul pleaded for it from the summit
of Mars' hill, in the face of assembled and incredulous Athens; and the precious seed they scattered
took such deep root, that no heathen madness of
Tiberius, no pagan rage of Caligula, no ferocity of
Nero, no Coliseum fights under the declining empire, could destroy the harvest.

But success is a harder test than misfortune,
and prosperity is more corrupting than adversity.
The church of Christ, long scourged and scorned,
at length assumed the purple, and ascended the
throne of the Cæsars. Dizzy and debauched by
the transformation, the whilom disciples of the cat-
acombs put on paganism with the mantle of the
emperors, and the prediction of the apostle was fulfilled: "Some shall depart from the faith, giving
heed to seducing spirits and doctrines of devils;
speaking lies in hypocrisy, having their conscience
seared with a hot iron."†

Heedless of faith and forgetful of charity, churchmen began to arrogate to themselves unwarranted
and impious powers, distorting the Scriptures into
sanctioning their selfish ends, and foisting sacrile-

---

* Matt. 4 : 23 ; 9 : 35 ; Mark 1 : 14 ; 11 : 5 ; 14 : 9 ; 16 : 15 ; Luke
4 : 18 ; 9 : 6 ; Acts 16 : 10 ; Rom. 10 : 15, etc.

† 1 Tim. 4 : 1, 2.

gious dogmas into the blameless text of the apostles. Christ became an alien; was replaced by saints; faith was smothered by a code of works; and images and relics, canvas daubs, and filthy rags, and pieces of thumb-nails, were worshipped as very God. Good men still lived and labored— Tertullian, and Origen, and Justin the martyr. The Greek and Latin churches were yet united, and clasped hands in the persons of Ambrosius and Athanasius, of Augustine and Chrysostom of the golden lips, as they are made to do under the magnificent altar of St. Peter's cathedral; where four colossal bronze statues, each twenty-four palms high, and labelled with their names, sustain lightly, and as if in triumph, the pulpit of the papacy, splendid with gilded metal and matchless sculpture. But these fathers were powerless to stem the torrent of abuse. Some of them, indeed, shared the grossest errors of their times. Often Christians were stayed from inveighing against acknowledged usurpations by a dread of exciting scandal: as in that terrific scene which Beckford has drawn for us in his "Hall of Eblis," where the crowd runs round, each man with an incurable wound in his bosom, and agrees not to speak of it; they went about keeping their hands pressed on the secret sore, with an understood agreement that it should never be mentioned, lest the church should come to pieces at the talismanic word.

In the East and in the West flaunted unrebuked corruption. Nothing was proscribed but virtue.

When Christianity became paganized, naturally it did not scruple to use heathen weapons. And here mark, that the rise of Christian persecution was contemporaneous with the fatal divergence of Christianity from that path of humility and faith and charity in which Jesus had appointed it to walk, with its assumption of worldly prerogatives, and with its ambitious and unscriptural arrogance.

It was the Nicene council, convoked by Constantine in the fourth century, which first pronounced formal and extra-ecclesiastical judgment upon all who refused to subscribe to its decrees, sentencing such "heretics" to banishment.* In support of this usurpation, the emperor himself issued an edict ordaining death to " every one who should conceal any of Arius' books, and not commit them to the flames ;"† and a little later he fulminated another decree, by which the Arians were deprived of their churches, and prohibited from assembling even in private houses.‡

Punishments still more severe were afterwards inflicted on those whose opinions the council had been pleased to condemn; and from pecuniary mulcts they proceeded to the forfeiture of goods, to banishment, and to slaughter. It was a policy actively pursued under the early Christian emperors—by Theodosius II., by Valentinian III., by

* Guerin, Hist. des .Conciles.   Landon, Councils of Holy Catholic Church.
† Guerin, Hist. des Conciles.
‡ Ibid. Gibbon, Decline and Fall of Roman Empire.

Marcian, and by Justinian.* And upon the accession of Galens, an emperor of the Arian school, these long-tortured schismatics took in their turn a terrible revenge upon the orthodox.† The entire century which passed between the reign of Constantine and the division of the empire among the children of Theodosius, was spent in the proscription of opinion. Arianism, Manichæism, Paganism, Romanism, but never Christianity, became successively the religion of the court, according to the opinion adopted by the reigning prince; and in this rage of sect against sect the interests of this world and the next were alike forgotten; the decay of the empire was accelerated; and before the close of the fifth century God moved a barbarian horde to wash out in blood the robber band at Rome which murdered and poisoned in his holy name.‡

Out of the chaos which succeeded the downfall of the empire, Rome evoked a new order—forced Europe to kneel before a hierarchy as absolute as the priest-caste of ancient Egypt, as arrogant as the Druids of Gaul. As captive Greece is said to have subdued her Roman conqueror, so Rome, in her own turn of servitude, cast the fetters of a moral captivity upon the fierce invaders of the north.§

Almost as far back as ecclesiastical testimonies can carry us, the bishops of Rome had been ven-

---

° Guerin, Hist. des Conciles. † Ibid.

‡ Hist. of the Inquisition. Published by J. Stockdale, London, 1810. Hallam, Hist. Middle Ages, in loco.

§ Hallam, Hist. of Middle Ages, vol. 2, p. 217.

erated as high in rank among the rulers of the
church. The nature of this distinction is doubtless
a very controverted subject; but it is reduced by
some moderate Romanists to little more at the outset than an honorary precedency attached to the
see of Rome in consequence of its apostolic foundation and its imperial dignity.*   It was the Western
complement of the patriarchates of Antioch, Alexandria, and afterwards of Constantinople in the
East.   A difference of rituals and discipline, together with the bickerings born of mutual ambition,
begat the schism which definitively separated the
Latin and the Greek churches in the ninth century.†
But Rome, foiled in the Orient, only redoubled her
exertions to cement an Occidental empire.

Starting with a kind of general ecclesiastical
supervision, admitted as an attribute of their primacy,‡ the Latin bishops eventually broadened their
see into the popedom—that Sinai of the middle ages
which shot rays of flame from the brow of Hildebrand into the hearts of prostrate peoples.   But the
papacy was a growth, not a creation.   When the
bishops were merged in the popes, retaining nothing of Christianity but the name with which to conjure, they busied themselves wholly, tirelessly, in the
usurpation of temporal and spiritual power.   When
they could not bully, they wheedled.   Step by step
they walked to dominion.   The infallibility of the

* Hallam, Hist. of the Middle Ages, vol. 2, p. 225.   Cyprian,
De Unitate Ecclesiæ.   † Neal, Eastern Church.
    ‡ Hallam, *ubi sup.*

holy see was claimed and acknowledged. The confessional was set up and submitted to. The church councils, creatures of the popes, composed a grand ecclesiastical code, under the title of canons, which should bind all true believers; and Christendom consented to be bound. Claims long disputed, or half preferred, began gradually to assume a definite shape; and nations too ignorant to compare precedents, too credulous to discriminate principles, yielded to assertions confidently made by the authority which they most respected—which explains how it was that Gregory I. succeeded in establishing the appellant jurisdiction of the see of Rome.[*]

So much and such uninterrupted success made the holy see audacious. Not satisfied with these spiritual usurpations, the pontiffs began to foray on the border lands of the ecclesiastical and civil realms. Little by little they acquired political rights, until, in the end, the pope snatched the children of the church from the civil jurisdiction, and assumed to set up or depose kings by virtue of the *jus divinum* of the church.[†] In a rude and ignorant age, the holy see was irresistible through the intellectual superiority of its children, who monopolized learning and were the only schoolmasters. In a turbulent and chaotic time, the popes were half omnipotent through unity of purpose and a clear design. In this paralysis of society, any knight-errant of truth who might venture to draw

[*] Gregorii Opera, tom. 2, p. 783. Edit. Benedict.
[†] See Hallam, Middle Ages, Art. Eccl. Power, *passim.*

up a catalogue of grievances and to clamor for redress, was certain to be silenced.

The appetite of Rome for riches was as insatiable as her appetite for supremacy; for she knew that wealth was the guarantee of power. "Many of the peculiar and prominent characteristics of mediæval faith and discipline," as Hallam tells us, "were either introduced or sedulously promoted for purposes of fraud. To such an end conspired the veneration of relics, the worship of images, the idolatry of saints, the canonization of martyrs, the religious inviolability of sanctuaries, the consecration of cemeteries, the sale of indulgences, and the twin absurdities of purgatory and of masses for the relief of the dead. A creed thus contrived, operating upon the minds of ignorant races, lavish though rapacious, devout though dissolute, naturally caused a flood of opulence to pour in upon the church."*

To these sources of revenue were added the fee simple of the territory which bordered upon Rome, which the popes partly purchased and partly stole when the barbarians new-modelled the map of Europe: pious donations from superstitious deathbeds, moneys paid from time to time by warring monarchs to secure the friendship of the successors of St. Peter, and a score of ecclesiastical imposts collected on the various pretexts of aiding the poor and propagating the gospel.†

Such, in rude outline, was the rise of the papacy, by ambitious worldliness, by sordid fraud; and this

---

* Hallam, *ut antea*.   † Hist. of the Inquisition, p. 38.

unscrupulous system of aggrandizement was cunningly, unremittingly, uniformly pursued for upwards of eleven centuries by the holy see, until cajoled or overawed Christendom made obeisance to the pontiff as the arbiter of this life and of the life to come.

Authority gained by violence and fraud can only be sustained by violence and fraud. "Do men gather grapes of thorns, or figs of thistles? Even so every good tree bringeth forth good fruit; but a corrupt tree bringeth forth evil fruit. Wherefore by their fruits ye shall know them."* It was to preserve a power which was the evil fruit of a series of usurpations eleven hundred years long, that Rome had recourse to the Inquisition. The holy see had commenced in its infant days to ban "heresy"—meaning by that epithet not to stigmatize scriptural error, but to brand opposition to the arrogance of clerical government. Such "heresy" the papacy was eager to stamp out by remorseless persecution. The Inquisition was merely persecution systematized—reduced to rules and supplied with a code; therefore the Inquisition was a fact, before it had a recognized existence; and we may see its spirit in the resolutions of the Nicene council, in the edicts of the Christian Cæsars, in the canons of the church, and in the decretals of the popes ages before it had "a local habitation and a name."

The Inquisition has had three phases, each a

* Matt. 7:16, 17, 20.

development—the episcopal, the papal, the Spanish. The episcopal was the embryonic phase.

A variety of concurrent circumstances, the command of Christ, and the necessities of an insular and persecuted society,* gave the primitive Christian pastors an arbitrative authority in church affairs; and even after Christianity became the religion of the empire, Christians continued to feel a strong aversion to appeals to the imperial tribunals for the settlement of their mutual differences. This trait was among the first to mirror the corruption which entered ecclesiasticism when the apostles were laid asleep. Selfishness and ambition led the early bishops to stretch this arbitrative jurisdiction to unwonted lengths; in which design Constantine powerfully assisted them by issuing an edict which directed the civil magistrate to enforce the execution of episcopal sentences.†

A little later, another decree was trumped up, annexed to the Theodosian code, and ascribed to Constantine, which went farther, and extended the jurisdiction of the bishops to all causes, ecclesiastical or lay, which the parties in litigation, or either of them, chose to refer to their tribunal, even when suit had been already commenced in a secular court.‡

This gross forgery§ was palmed off upon Charlemagne as a legitimate institute, and he legalized by amion.

° Discourse of Fleury.   Institutions du Droit Ecclesiastique.

° Hallam, vol. 2, pp. 213.   § Ibid.

it by repeating all its absurd and enormous provisions in one of his capitularies.* For a time this bastard prerogative, thus legitimatized by fraud, was permitted to sleep; but at last it was awakened to give countenance to the coercive control which the holy see began to claim over the clergy in civil as in criminal suits; to sanction the complete withdrawal of ecclesiastics from the secular jurisdiction, and to cloak the ceaseless efforts which were being made to subject the temporal power to the spiritual sovereignty of the pontiffs.†

From these claims to an assumption of the right to punish all offences against religion was but a step, and it was soon taken. Such offences were tried before the metropolitan of the diocese in which they occurred, and the secular arm was invoked to enforce the sentence of the prelate-judge.‡

This was the earliest form of procedure against ecclesiastical offenders—the form of the Episcopal Inquisition. It was this germ which eventually expanded into the Papal Inquisition.

Innocent III., whose thunders stunned Philip Augustus and John, surnamed Lackland, the inglorious usurper of the English crown; whose audacious pride had laid France under an interdict, because Philip repudiated his wife Ingelburge, and absolved England from the oath of fidelity because John did not, as he thought, pay sufficient respect

---

* Hallam, vol. 2, p. 213. Baluzzi, Capitularia, tom. 1, p. 985.
† Hallam, Middle Ages, Art. Eccl. Power, *passim.*
‡ Limbock, Hist. Inq., liber 1, chap. 16

to the rights of the clergy; this pope, whose intrigues and whose arms had seized upon the sovereignty of Umbria, of La Marcha, of Ancona, of Orbitello, of Viterbo, and of the entire Romagna; whose despotism had robbed the Roman senate of its ancient rights, and made it a subservient herd of slaves; whose enterprising rashness had ravished from the German emperors the honorary prerogatives which they held in the capital of the Christian world, the remains of the power of Charlemagne, that benefactor of the holy see, so outraged in the persons of his successors—Innocent III. it was, whose pontificate, fatal to the human race, witnessed the establishment and enforced the recognition of the Papal Inquisition; and gave birth to the Dominicans, the kindlers of so many persecuting fires, and to the Franciscans, those lazy blood-suckers who fattened on the wealth of states and on the toils of the unfortunate.*

In the beginning of the thirteenth century, the southern slopes of France were inhabited by the Provençals, a race pacific, learned, wealthy, astute.† Wedded to the Vaudois tenets, which bore the impress of the apostolic teachings, the Provençals scouted the pretensions of Rome, refuted the papal missionaries from their open Bibles, and offered prayer to God without the mediation of saints and priests. Criminals buying Paradise for money; monks spending the revenues thus gotten in gaming-

---

° Hist. of the Inquisition, pp. 42, 43.

† *Vide* Hist. of the Huguenots, chap. 2, Am. T. Soc., 1866.

houses, in taverns, in brothels; and popes lavishing
the funds of the church on their wines and stables
and hawks and mistresses—all this seemed to their
unsophisticated minds to be a gross violation of
the Divine law, and they searched in vain to find a
warrant for it in the Scriptures.*

Pope Innocent undertook to enlighten them by
the fagot and the stake. An inquisitorial commission, headed by a Spanish monk called Dominic,
whose name was afterwards enrolled among the
Roman saints, advanced into the heretical provinces armed with authority to convert the erring,
ascertain their numbers, spy out the disposition of
the Provençals, spur the lagging magistrates to the
performance of their penal duties, and sound the
views of the local prelates to see if haply they
might not be infected with Vaudoisism.† This, at
the outset, was the extent of their power; they
were only a kind of peripatetic inquisition on the
old Episcopal pattern.

A very short sojourn in Languedoc convinced
these inquisitors of the hopelessness of their mission. The heresy was deeply rooted and wide-
spread. The Vaudois overmatched them at con-
troversy. When they appealed to the bishops, and
urged the sentence of the incorrigible, lukewarm
prelates often hesitated to pronounce a verdict;
when they did, sympathizing magistrates defeated
its execution by legal quibbling.‡

° Limbock, Hist. Inq. Hist. Huguenots, ut antea.　† Ibid.
‡ Sismondi, Hist. of the Albigenses. Limbock, Hist. Inq.

This resistance angered Innocent; and breathing fire and slaughter, he launched a crusade upon the sunny Provençal plains, and at once erected the ancient ecclesiastical superintendence into a separate, independent, irresponsible tribunal, which he called the Inquisition.* Then, to make sure that no human sensibility, no natural tenderness, should thwart the frightful severity of this horrid court, whose jurisdiction covered all offences against religion, he took it out of the hands of the bishops, who, by the ties of civil life, were still too much attached to humanity for his purpose; and consigned it to the monks, a half-denaturalized horde, who had abjured the feelings of men, and sworn themselves into unquestioning subserviency to the holy see.†

Years passed, and this court, which had reduced murder to a fine art, having completed the butchery of the Vaudois, passed into Germany, into Italy, into France, into Spain; finding few states bold enough to bar its entrance, marking its pathway with ghastly heaps of dead men's bones.

But frightful as it was, the papal inquisition was only the half-way house of fanaticism—only a milestone, showing how far persecution had travelled; the Spanish type was the end of the journey—necessarily the end, for weary bigotry could take no farther step.

In the eighth century, the Saracens, attracted

---

* Sismondi, Hist. of the Albigenses. Limbock, Hist. Inq.
† Schiller.

by the smiling and fertile soil of the ancient Iberia, crossed from Arabia and tore Spain from the barbarian hands of the Visigoths, to whom Honorius had surrendered it.* Bringing with them the Orient splendor of the Ottoman empire, the Moors gradually changed the rudeness of the forests into the polish of the Arabian courts; and the African cloak and the Tunisian albornos, the Koran and the Moslem cimetar, heralded a civilization as romantic as it was unique.† The land itself was transformed, wrought up to wonderful prosperity, embroidered with gardens, sheeted with grainfields, clothed with orchards and vineyards from sterile mountain-top to verdant valley.‡ Letters too were ardently cultivated, philosophy had its schools, poetry had its disciples, and the Morisco universities of Cordova and Seville were thronged by Occidental as well as by Eastern students, anxious to acquaint themselves with the Magian and Chaldean lore.§ Christian Spain, entrenched in the northern mountains, grew a degree less barbarous by imitation; until at last the polished infidels insensibly imparted their burning civilization to the primitive tribes—gave them every thing except their altars.

But the Spaniards, while animated by the example of the Moors, bitterly resented their intrusion

---

* Flavian, Hist. of the Moors of Spain. Murphy, Mahometan Empire in Spain.

† Irving, Conquest of Grenada. Prescott, Ferdinand and Isabella.　　　　　　　　　　　　　　　　　‡ Ibid.

§ Ibid. Sismondi, Literature of the South of Europe.

into the peninsula; and an incessant conflict was the result, a conflict which became a chronic crusade, and which culminated, towards the close of the fifteenth century, in the total overthrow of the alien domination in the reign of Ferdinand and Isabella.*

The Moriscoes were given their choice between exile and conversion to the Roman faith; and it was to enforce this decree that the Inquisition was invoked.† Thousands of faithful Mahometans repassed the straits of Gibraltar into Africa; but other thousands, detained by a passionate attachment to their homes—for the Moors had been seated in Spain eight hundred years, a period longer than that which has elapsed since the Norman conquest of Great Britain—purchased remission from the dreadful necessity of expatriation by a show of conversion, and continued to serve Mahomet at Christian altars.

But "so long as prayers were offered towards Mecca, Granada was not subdued; so long as the dusky proselyte was a Christian only in public, and became again a Moslem in the retirement of his own dwelling, he was secured neither to the throne nor to the Roman see. It was no longer deemed sufficient to compel a perverse people to adopt the exterior forms of a new faith, or to wed them to the victorious church by the weak bands of ceremonials; the object was to extirpate the roots of the old creed, and to subdue the obstinate bias which, by

° Prescott, *ubi supra*.   † Limbock, Hist. Inq.

the slow operation of centuries, had been planted in the Moriscoe manners and language and laws, and by the enduring influence of dear, familiar objects was still maintained in its pristine vigor."*

The Papal Inquisition was found unequal to this task; therefore the old forms were new-modelled and wrought up to perfection, and the Spanish Inquisition was the result—an institution invested with the most complete apparatus for inflicting human misery and for appalling the human imagination.

It owed its existence to two monks—Torquemada, a Dominican, and Ximenes, a Cordelier, each in turn the confessor of Queen Isabella, the first in her childhood, the other after her ascension of the throne.† Singularly enough, the motive of this "couple" in the hunt for heresy was not fanaticism.

Torquemada was inspired by a malignant hate of the Moors begotten of an amour at Cordova, where his *inamorita* was snatched away from him by a fascinating Moslem and carried off in triumph to Granada.‡ The revenge for which he agonized was reinforced by ambition. Desirous of drawing to himself the favors of the pope, and of securing an office independent of the oscillating favor of the king, he used his influence with Isabella so well

* Schiller, p. 395.
† Llorente, Hist. of the Inq. Prescott, Ferd. and Isabella.
‡ Hist. of the Inquisition, published by J. J. Stockdale, London, 1810.

11*

that, "squat like a toad" at her ear, he persuaded
her into the adoption of the most horrid features
of the new inquisition by alarming her for her salvation, and was himself the first Moloch to be
placed upon this pedestal of blood.*

Ximenes had a somewhat similar motive for his
support of the Spanish inquisition. A prelate of
imperious, sordid, and cruel temper, he had aspired
to become prime-minister of Spain, and he attained
the dignity—a success which made him detested by
the nobles whose pomp he eclipsed, hated by the
people whom he oppressed, and bitterly reviled by
the monks whose manners he had attempted to
reform. So circumstanced, he saw safety alone in
countenancing the Inquisition; in doing which his
great object was, not to extirpate heresy, not to
burn Jews—heretical opinions were of small importance to him, and he would have preferred to let
the Shylocks live that he might plunder them when
they were rich—but to secure a weapon which he
could silently, unexpectedly plunge into the hearts
of his foes, and to have at his beck a tribunal whose
authority might assail the throne itself, if need
were—a court possessing the power, in the name of
God, to penetrate into every corner of Spain, and
ferret out those victims whom he had resolved to
sacrifice to his security.† Torquemada regarded the
Inquisition merely as a ladder up which he could
climb to vengeance, and the highest honors of the

---

* Hist. of the Inquisition, published by J. J. Stockdale, London, 1810.   † Hist. of the Inquisition, p. 113, et seq.

church; Ximenes used it as a rampart to guard those dignities which he had already grasped.

Thus it was that the spiteful ambition of a Dominican, and the selfish pride of a Cordelier, begot and nourished the most frightful and the latest form of the Inquisition. The pious caprice of a woman, the spite of a licentious monk, the venomous wiles of a cardinal, the speculations of a priest—such were the wheels on which rolled the destiny of Christendom in those "good old times" of which poets sing.

So much shall suffice to show the triple origin of the Inquisition. But no acquaintance with its motive and its origin can paint it to our minds; if we would know what it was, we must see it at work.

The Inquisition was a machine for inquiring into men's thoughts, and a court of punishment when that examination proved unsatisfactory. Naturally it affected mystery, like the cuckoo in the fable, delivered its oracular decrees from its hole in the rock; for Rome was perfect master of the art of dramatic effect, and the popes knew well that a secret, mysterious, always impending danger is the most freezing of horrors.

This hell, invented by priests, had its head-quarters at Rome, in what was blasphemously styled the "Holy Office," an office holy only by that classical figure of speech which names a thing from something which it lacks, as the dreadful fates were said to be merciful because they were without mercy; or like that kindred extravagance which that remarkable traveller in China, the Abbé Huc, relates of a gloomy hole in which he was lodged, pestered by mosquitoes and exhaling noisome vapors, where light and air entered only through a single narrow aperture, but called by Chinese pride, "The Hotel of the Beatitudes."

The Inquisition was, as we have seen, a tribunal owning allegiance to no temporal authority, superior to all other courts—a bench of monks without appeal, having its familiars in every house, diving into the secrets of every fireside, judging and executing without responsibility, condemning not deeds, but thoughts, and affecting to descend into the individual conscience for the purpose of inquiry and punishment.*

It professed to believe that the end sanctifies the means; and it was built upon one principle—mutual *surveillance*, mutual denunciation, perfect contempt for human nature. Society was reduced to a vast and terrible *espionage*. Comrades were compelled to spy upon each other, observe every action, note every unguarded expression of familiar conversation. Every priest was an informer, and the confessor was spied upon by his penitent—police and counter-police. A woman often served as a spy upon two different men by turns, men mad with jealousy of each other—hell beneath hell. Where is the Dante who would have found that out?†

Worse still: with regard to these denunciations,

---

* Motley, vol. 1, p. 323.
† Michelét and Quinet, The Jesuits, p. 50.

the Inquisition declared that it was the positive, bounden duty of every one to become an accuser in matters of offence against religion. Children were bidden to denounce their parents, wives their husbands, servants their masters; and there are multitudes of well-authenticated instances of such frightful domestic treachery — treason robed as pious duty, and performed under penalty of excommunication;* for the law was, according to the decrees of numbers of the popes, that whoever became acquainted with an offence against the faith, whether from personal knowledge or from hearsay, was bound, within fifteen days, to bring forward an accusation before an inquisitor, or the vicar of the holy office; or, where these were not present, before a bishop;† otherwise the crime, whatever it might be, attached not only to the principal and his accomplices, but also to all who knew it and did not reveal it.‡

And in order to facilitate denunciation, the Inquisition withheld the names of the accusers from the accused, and practiced the most careful secrecy in that vital matter—a procedure which often sunk the holy office into the mere vehicle on which private vengeance rode to secure triumph; for it was a bounty on denunciation, and men might safely gratify their personal grudges where they were not brought face to face with their victims.§

* Achilli, Dealings with the Inquisition, p. 84. New York, 1851.
† Ibid. Llorente, Hist. of the Inquisition.   ‡ Ibid.
§ Hist. of the Inq. Achilli, a converted Romanist, formerly

Moreover, since society was an incarnate spy, and since to know of an offence and not to denounce it was to be guilty of it, awful fear transformed thousands into accusers that they might themselves escape denunciation; for even inanimate objects seemed endowed with prescience—every wall, every building, every tree was a head and face hearing and seeing, for ever hidden, sealed, immovable.

What the inquisitors could not learn by terror, they wormed out of men and women by complacence. Assuming the *rôle* of everybody's friend, they invited all who desired office, all who wished for help, to apply to them. Masters were supplied with *valets*, families were supplied with servants, all without charge; and when the courteous, zealous gentlemen, who asked nothing for their services, and who chatted so pleasantly, desired to know the news, was it possible to resist the inclination to detail the transactions and to recite the gossip of society?*

Sworn to the degradation of the understanding and the murder of the intellect, the agents employed by the Inquisition were terror and infamy. Every evil passion was in its pay; its snare was set in every joy of life. It prostrated all the instincts of humanity before it; it yielded all the ties which men held most sacred. A heretic forfeited all claims

high in office at Rome, and cognizant of the facts, gives instances of this kind, as also of the denunciation of husbands by their wives—facts which came within his own observation. See pp. 85, 86, *et seq.*

  ° Achilli, *ut antea.*

upon the race; the most trivial infidelity to Rome divested him of the rights of human nature. A modest doubt of the infallibility of the pope met with the punishment of parricide and the infamy of sodomy: its sentences resembled the frightful corruption of the plague, which turns the most healthy body into rapid putrefaction. Even the inanimate things belonging to a heretic were accursed; its decrees were enforced against pictures and against corpses, so that the grave itself was no asylum from its tremendous arm.*

The code of the Inquisition, with all the punishments for every supposed crime, together with the mode of conducting the trial so as to elicit the guilt of the accused—all this is contained in a large manuscript volume, in folio, carefully preserved by the head of the holy office, and styled *Praxis Sacræ Romanæ Inquisitionis*, and sometimes *Libro Negro*, the Black Book, because it has a cover of that color; or, as an inquisitor once said, *Libro Necro*, "the book of the dead."†

Let us open this horrid volume and acquaint ourselves with what Tacitus called "the secrets of the kingdom"—*arcana imperii*. Concerning the method of conducting a process, we read these words in the Black Book:

* Schiller.

† In the revolution of 1848, when the holy office was entered and rifled by the mob, this book was discovered, and Achilli actually held it in his hands. The explanation given in the text is the one made to him by one of the inquisitors on that occasion. *Vide,* "Dealings with the Inquisition," pp. 12–81.

" With respect to the examination and the duty of the examiners, either the prisoner confesses and is proved guilty by his own confession, or he does not confess and is equally guilty on the evidence of witnesses. If a prisoner confesses the whole of what he is accused of, he is unquestionably guilty of the whole ; but if he confesses only a part, he ought still to be regarded as guilty of the whole, since what he has confessed proves him to be capable of guilt as to the other points of the accusation. And here the precept is to be kept in view : 'no one is obliged to condemn himself'—*nemo tenetur se ipsum prodere.* Nevertheless, the judge should do all in his power to induce the culprit to confess, since confession tends to the glory of God. And as the respect due to the glory of God requires that no one particular should be omitted, the judge is bound to put in force not only the ordinary means which the Inquisition affords, but whatever may enter his thoughts as fitting to lead to confession. Bodily torture has ever been found the most salutary and efficient means of leading to spiritual repentance. Therefore the choice of the most befitting mode of torture is left to the judge of the Inquisition, who determines according to the age, sex, and constitution of the prisoner. He will be prudent in its use, always being mindful at the same time to procure what is required—the confession of the delinquent. If, notwithstanding all the means employed, the unfortunate wretch denies his guilt, he is to be con-

sidered as a victim of the devil, and as such, deserves no compassion from the servants of God, nor
the pity or indulgence of holy mother church: he is
a son of perdition. Let him perish, then, among
the damned, and let his place be no longer found
among the living."*

This astounding page is followed by another, in
which the mode of attaining a conviction is given
in sickening detail. "The rack was the court of
justice; the criminal's only advocate was his fortitude; for the nominal counsellor, who was permitted
no communication with the prisoner, and was furnished neither with documents nor with power to
procure rebutting evidence, was a puppet, aggra-
vating the lawlessness of the proceedings by the
mockery of legal forms. The unhappy victim,
arrested on suspicion, accused perhaps by his son
or father or wife; consigned to a cell, and broken
by famine and misery and confinement; knowing
that one unknown witness could send him to the
rack, and two could consign him to the fire, was
summoned at last to confess. If he was innocent,
he had nothing to confess; yet the law held him
guilty, and refused to give him an opportunity to
prove his innocence, an avowal of which was an
invocation of the rack. The torture took place at
midnight, in a gloomy dungeon dimly lighted by
torches. The victim—whether man, matron, or
tender virgin—was stripped naked, and stretched
on the wooden bench. Water, weights, fires, pulleys,

* Cited in Achilli, pp. 82, 83.

screws—all the infernal apparatus by which the sinews could be strained without cracking, the bones crushed without breaking, and the body racked exquisitely without giving up its ghost, was there put in operation. The executioners, enveloped in black robes from head to foot, with eyes glaring through holes cut in the hoods which muffled their faces, practiced successively all the forms of torture which the devilish ingenuity of the monks had invented."*

If from the quivering lips of the mangled victim no confession could be wrung, he was sentenced to be burned alive. The presumptuous arrogance of this decree could only be surpassed by the inhumanity with which it was executed. By coupling the ludicrous with the terrible, and by amusing the eye with the strangeness of the spectacle, it weakened compassion by the gratification of another feeling; it drowned sympathy in derision and contempt.†

Usually "the number of condemned prisoners was allowed to accumulate, that a multitude of victims might grace each gala-day. The act of faith—*auto da fé*—was a noted festival. The monarch, the high functionaries of the land, the reverend clergy, the populace, regarded it as an inspiring and delightful recreation. When the appointed morning arrived, the victims were taken from their dungeons. Each one was attired in a yellow robe without sleeves, like a herald's coat, covered with

* Motley, vol. 1. p. 323. † Schiller.

figures of black devils. A large conical paper mitre was placed upon each head, surmounted by a human figure, around which played lambent flames, and ghastly demons flitted. Each mouth was painfully gagged, so that it could neither be opened nor shut. Thus accoutred, and just as .the prisoners left their cells, a breakfast, consisting of every delicacy, was placed before them, and they were urged with ironical politeness to satisfy their hunger. All were then led forth into the public square. The procession was formed with pomp. It was headed by little school-children, who were immediately followed by the band of prisoners, attired horribly yet ludicrously. Then came the magistracy and the nobles, the prelates, and the dignitaries of the church. The holy inquisitors, with their officials and familiars, followed on horseback, with the blood-red flag of the holy office waving above them, blazoned on either side with the portraits of Pope Alexander and King Ferdinand, the pair of brothers who had established the new form of the Inquisition. After the procession came the rabble.

"When all had reached the scaffold, a sermon was preached to the assembled multitude. It was filled with laudations of the holy tribunal, and with blasphemous revilings of the condemned heretics. Then the sentences were read to the individual victims; after which the clergy chanted the fifty-first psalm, the whole vast throng joining in one tremendous *miserere*. If a priest was among the culprits, he was stripped of the canonicals which he had hitherto worn, while his hands, lips, and shaven crown were scraped with a bit of glass, by which process the oil of his consecration was supposed to be removed. He was then thrust into the common herd. Then all mounted the scaffold, where the executioner stood ready to conduct them to the fire blazing just at hand; and into his hands the inquisitors delivered their charge, with an ironical request that he would deal with them tenderly and without blood-letting or injury. Then those who remained steadfast to the last were burned at the stake; and they who in the last extremity renounced their 'errors,' were strangled before being cast into the flames."*

On these occasions the king was often present; he sat with uncovered head, in a lower chair than that of the grand-inquisitor, to whom he yielded precedence. Who, then, would not tremble before a tribunal at which even majesty must humble itself?† These scenes were repeated again and again and again. In the eighteen years of Torquemada's administration, ten thousand two hundred and twenty individuals were burned alive, ninety-seven thousand three hundred and twenty-one were punished with infamy, confiscation of property, and perpetual imprisonment; making a grand total of one hundred and fourteen thousand four hundred and one families destroyed by this single friar.‡

---

* Motley, vol. 1, pp. 322, 323.   † Schiller. p. 397.
‡ Llorente, Hist. Span. Inq., tom. 1, p. 280.

The tremendous horror of the Inquisition is deepened by a consideration of its instruments. The whole tribe of the *inquisitori* were base and sordid and cruel and licentious to a proverb.* Rome took no notice of the scandal which their conduct provoked, but winked at personal immorality to obtain that which constitutes her moral code—wealth and dominion; for dealing in immoral acts, immoral agents are necessary. Would an honest man do for an inquisitor? Would a follower of Christ, who said, in speaking of man and wife, "Whom God hath joined let not man put asunder"—would such a one sow discord between them, and demoralize the wife to make her betray her own husband? To be an inquisitor, it was essential that the heart should be hardened to humanity, deadened to every social feeling by long monastic discipline, and that the conscience should be fatally debauched.†

The Inquisition recruited its ranks by bribery, that patent opiate for scruples. 'T is related of the Jesuit cardinal Palavicini that, being chosen by the holy see to write the history of the council of Trent, in opposition to the account penned by Paolo Sarpi, and promised a red hat as his reward, the churchman grieved over the many lies he would have to invent; but comforted himself by sending for the insignia of his future dignity, which he shook in his hand with a sigh, exclaiming, "Ah, how much I endure on your account"—*oh, quantum per te patior.*

* Achilli. † Achilli, p. 101.

Precisely so, though possibly with fewer sighs, did the *inquisitori* fill their ranks.

But when the "Society of Jesus" was organized, the children of Loyola did from love what others had done from hope of gain or from ambition. Created expressly to combat heresy, nullities when not fighting, the Jesuits—whom Michelét terms "the counter-revolution"*—were spies by nature, infamous from habit, and inquisitors by choice. The Dominicans did indeed retain the ostensible control of the holy office, but the sons of Dominic were merely its automatons—the Jesuits were its soul.

Loyola's book of Spiritual Exercises, that physiology of ecstasy, that formula of sanctity, was the new school of discipline. Do you know what distinguished Loyola from the ascetics of the past? This, that he was able coldly, logically to observe himself, to analyze his feelings when in that state of ravishment which ordinarily excludes the very idea of reflection. Imposing upon his disciples as operations acts which with him had been spontaneous, he asked but thirty days—"triginta dies"—to break the will and to subdue the reason, as Rarey conquered an unruly horse. Jesuitism developed itself as the inquisitor's counterpart; one dislolated the body, the other dislocated thought and racked the soul.†

The *marseillaise* of the counter-revolution was

* Michelét, The Jesuits, p. 8.
† Quinet, The Jesuits.

the rosary.* Chanting this the Jesuits wriggled everywhere, reducing souls after their master's method, planting convents of the Sacred Heart as auxiliary societies, and seducing lovely and brilliant women to repeat their lies, and to twist society into their toils. They will show you in Venice a picture in which, upon a rich, sombre carpet, a beautiful rose lies withering near a skull, and in the skull moves at pleasure a graceful viper. Does it typify the Jesuits, those vipers of the mind?

If now we look at the influence of the Inquisition, we shall find it as deadly as the poisoned bowl which its agents so frequently employed. It blighted all virtues; it stabbed civilization; for it tore away mutual confidence and disorganized society. The scourge of those states which had the weakness to adopt it, it was also the corrupter of provinces which had attempted to resist its entrance. Thus, Germany, always opposed to it, yet experienced the curse of this secret tribunal; whose seat always concealed, whose emissaries ever unknown, caused the monarch to tremble on his throne, the peasant to shiver in his cot. This terrible court, always felt, never unveiled, saddened the lives of all who lived within its vortex.†

---

* Christ said, "When ye pray, use not vain repetitions. After this manner therefore pray ye: Our Father," etc. Matt. 6 : 7–13. But this rosary is a repetition of fifteen *Pater Nosters*, with one hundred and fifty *Ave Marias;* and it is said that the Virgin herself taught this stupid form of devotion to Domenico di' Gusman. This is certain, he was the promoter of it, and left it as a heritage to his order. † Hist. of the Inq., Stockdale's ed., p. 89.

This terror extended even to the civil authorities, whose members were not exempt from the inquisitorial censure; the base apprehension stifled the high spirit of the magistrates.   Uncertain whether a courageous resistance to the arbitrary will of the monks would be favorably interpreted by the princes from whom they derived their powers; fearful of being sacrificed either to some political interest which they were unable to foresee, or to that abject dependence in which Rome habitually kept the European sovereigns, they suffered their fellow-citizens to be racked and burned; and looked on serenely, preferring their own security to the sacred obligation of protecting the innocent, and to that generous courage which might have ruined but must have immortalized them.*   They did not heed L'Hôpital's exclamation, "To lose liberty! good God, what remains there to lose after that is gone?"

It was in Spain that the Inquisition was most active and untrammelled; and it is there that its malignant desolation is most perceptible.   The isolation of society—death in life, the sterility of genius, the ignorance, the sombre mood, the hideous morals, the furtive suspicion—these are the fruits of the Spanish Inquisition.

Such, in its motive, in its origin, in its methods, in its instruments, and in its influence was the Inquisition.   It was the Spanish form which had crossed the ocean with Pizarro and Cortez, and taught the

* Hist. of the Inq., Stockdale's ed., p. 89.

Incas of Peru and the Montezumas of Mexico to shudder at the name of Christianity.* It was the Spanish form which the holy see had invoked when the reformers said, "the church meddles with the world, and teaches us our business. Very well; we will teach it God."† It was the Spanish form which Philip II. had determined to plant in the Nether- lands as an antidote for heresy.‡

* Hist. of the Inq., Stock. ed., chap. 7, *passim.*
† Michelet, Schiller. ‡ Meteren, Vandervynckt.

CHAPTER XVII.

THE EDICTS.

IN one form or another the Inquisition had been long seated in the Netherlands, existing not as a tentative but as a permanent institution. The earlier persecutions were acts of episcopal inquisition, performed by the various diocesan inquisitors.[*]

In the beginning of the sixteenth century, the Rhine from Germany and the Meuse from France flooded the Low Countries with the pamphlets of Luther and the tracts of Calvin; and the Emperor Charles found the existing Romish dykes insufficient to bar out the heretical inundation. Cæsar applied to Adrian VI., who then wore the tiara, for aid. It was granted; and in 1522 an inquisitor, commissioned from Rome and aided by a band of priestly coadjutors, entered Brabant.[†] A little later, Clement VII. sent two additional pontifician censors of the faith into the states, basing the Inquisition upon this triumvirate; but his successor, Paul III., reduced the number to two, and these were in office when Philip put on his father's crown.[‡]

This brace of censors proved viciously active. Not satisfied with domestic cruelty, they had burned

---

[*] Strada, p. 33. Renom de Francia MS.
[†] Ibid. Schiller, Motley, Meteren.   [‡] Schiller, p. 398.

William Tyndale with his English Bibles at Vilvarde, in 1536; and a decade later, their emissaries tortured that army of exiles, thirty thousand strong,* whom Mary Tudor's rasping fanaticism had driven to seek an asylum in Holland and Brabant, into which they smuggled their Protestant books in their bales of merchandise.†

The provincial inquisition, like Janus, had two faces. It was papal, because the censors bore the pontifical *imprimatur;* it was episcopal, because its sentences might only be enforced by the civil authorities.‡ Thus far it had been always administered by natives; and it was a degree less barbarous, and many degrees less obnoxious than the Spanish tribunal, because the imperial edicts, issued from time to time, and known to every one, served as the rules of its decisions.§

A variety of reasons made Philip anxious to replace this form of the holy office with the Spanish tribunal. Severe as it was, it did not affright the states into orthodoxy. Its publicity robbed terror of its worst stings. Its connection with the civil courts half paralyzed its arm. Celerity, certainty, lack of pity, mysterious secresy—these were the characteristics of that awful tribunal which had cramped Spain and cursed Portugal and cowered Italy and frenzied France and wracked pagans into churchmen at Goa in the Indies. It alone was esteemed by Philip to be fit and able to dragoon

---

* Strada, p. 36. Brandt, vol. 1, p. 70.   † Ibid.
‡ Van der Haer, p. 175. Brandt, vol. 1.   § Schiller, p. 398.

the Netherlands into the dual despotism which was his goal.*

The new bishoprics scheme was a vast stride towards the consummation of this purpose; hence Philip's earnestness in pressing its adoption; hence the popular determination to defeat it. The text of the edict which decreed this innovation had used the word "inquisitor." Granvelle, with habitual slyness, wished to have it expunged. If the Inquisition could be planted, why startle people by the use of unpopular phrases? "People are afraid of the new bishoprics," it was so that he wrote to Perez, Philip's secretary, "on account of that clause providing that of nine canons one shall be an inquisitor. I suggest instead that the canons shall be obliged to assist the bishop as he may command, which would suffice, because a bishop is an ordinary inquisitor. 'T is best to expunge words that give offence."† But Philip stickled for the letter of the law, and the cardinal's rose-water was not sprinkled over the text.

The half-defeat of the king's attempt to inaugurate his bishops, gave the reform fresh impetus. The number of its proselytes increased in proportion as the popular fear abated, and many avowed themselves Protestants before they well understood what they professed.‡ The zeal of such disciples was not always tempered by discretion nor in accordance with knowledge, and their wild antics

* Schiller, p. 398.   † Cited in Motley, vol. 1, p. 276.
‡ Brandt, vol. 1, p. 134.

stirred constant tumults, the opprobrium of which good men, better grounded in the faith, were compelled to bear. One of these charlatan reformers set himself up in Tournay as a worker of miracles; others appeared in Lille and in Valenciennes.*

Nevertheless, there were many earnest and honest and able Christians in the states, whose faith was immovably grounded on the Bible, and these seized every opportunity to propagate their opinions. And now tracts were everywhere distributed and everywhere read; preachers openly addressed conventicles; the people by tens of thousands assembled in broad daylight, and marching in procession to and from their churches, chanted the psalms of David in the translation of Marot.†

This open defiance of the edicts, at length provoked the vengeance of the government. "Philip himself, ever occupied with details, from his palace in Spain," as Motley tells us, "sent frequent informations against the humblest individuals in the Netherlands. It is curious to observe the minute

---

* Schiller, Meteren, Vandervynckt.

† Meteren, Strada, Renom. de Francia.

Clément Marot, a French poet of celebrity in his day, was born in Cohors in 1495. For some time valet-de-chambre to Francis I., he followed that knight-errant king in his Italian campaign, was captured with him at Pavia, and shared his imprisonment at Madrid. Released earlier than Francis, he returned to France, where he was imprisoned on a charge of heresy preferred by Diana de Poictiers, whom he had offended. The king released him, but he was again imprisoned, and again released. He died very miserably in Turin, in September, 1544. Marot's most famous composition was a translation in French of the Psalms of David, which was very popular with the reformers. *Vide* Am. Cyc.

reticulations of tyranny which he had begun already
to spin about a whole people, while cold, venomous,
and patient, he watched his victims from the centre
of his web. He forwarded particulars to the regent
and to the cardinal concerning a variety of men and
women, sending their names, ages, personal appearance, occupations, and residence, together with directions for their immediate immolation. Even the
inquisitors of Seville were set to work to increase,
by means of their branches in the provinces, the
royal information on this all-important subject.
'There are but few of us left in the world'—it was
so that he moralized in a letter to Granvelle—'who
care for religion. 'T is necessary, therefore, for us
to take the greater heed for Christianity. We must
lose all, if need be, in order to do our duty; in fine,'
he added, with his usual tautology, 'it is right that
a man should do his duty.'"*

Granvelle at once responded, bewailing the cold-
ness and lack of heart which the Netherland judici-
ary exhibited in the service of the cannibal church.
"I find that the civil officers go into the matter of
executing the edicts with reluctance, which, I believe, is caused by their fear of displeasing the populace," he said: adding, "when they do act, they
do it but lukewarmly; and when these matters are
not taken in hand with the necessary liveliness, the
fruit desired is not gathered. We do not fail to
exhort and to command them to do their work.
Viglius and Barlaiment display laudable zeal; but

* Motley, vol. 1, p. 279.

as for the councillors of Brabant, they are for ever prating of the constitutional rights of their province, and deserve much less commendation."*

The governant was at her wits' end. Philip sent her lists of heretics, and said, "Burn me these." The people persistently interposed; the magistrates would not stir; the nobility were either timidly neutral or actively hostile, assuring her that "it was no good time to move this stone again, at which they had so often stumbled."† The states that had slipped the Romish bridle under Charles V., and would not suffer Philip himself, when he was at Brussels, to put it on again—should they now halter themselves, called by a woman's voice?

Margaret determined to use coercive measures. An inquisitorial campaign was organized, and one of the pontifical censors, named Peter Titelmann, was selected to head it. This wretch was represented by his contemporaries as a grotesque, yet terrible goblin, careering through the country by night and by day; alone, on horseback; smiting the trembling peasants on the head with a great club; spreading dismay far and wide; dragging suspected persons from their firesides or their beds; thrusting them into dungeons; and torturing, strangling, and burning men for idle words or suspected thoughts—for, by his own confession, he never waited for deeds.‡

On one occasion, three reformers, Christian de

* Papiers d'Etat de Granvelle, tom. 6, p. 208, *et seq.*
† Strada, p. 34.   ‡ Motley, vol. 1, pp. 332, 333.

Queker, Jacob Dieussant, and Joan Koniags, who had formerly taken shelter in England under Elizabeth's throne, where they had connected themselves with the Dutch congregation in London, were apprehended by Titelmann in the Low Countries, whither they had come to trade. On being interrogated, they confessed their heresy and gloried in it; which procured their speedy sentence to be burned alive.

Another of Master Titelmann's exploits was to hack an Anabaptist to death with seven blows of a rusty sword, in the presence of his wife, who was so horror-stricken that she died on the spot before her hapless husband.*

The secular sheriff, familiarly called Red-Rod, from the color of his wand of office, met Titelmann upon the highway one day, and thus addressed him: "Master Inquisitor, how can you risk your precious bones in this way alone, or at most with an attendant or two, arresting people on every side, while I dare not attempt to execute my office, except at the head of a strong force, armed in proof; and then only at peril of my life?" "Alack, Red-Rod," was the jocose reply, "you deal with bad people. I have nothing to fear, for I seize only the innocent and virtuous, who make no resistance, and let themselves be taken like lambs." "Mighty well," retorted the sheriff; "but if you arrest all the good people and I all the bad, 't is difficult to say who in the world is to escape chastisement." The censor's reply has not been recorded; but there is no reason

* Brandt, vol. 1, p. 167.

to doubt that he proceeded, like a strong man, to run his course.*

When Philip heard of Titelmann's activity and success, he wrote back blithely, "After all, wherefore introduce the Spanish Inquisition? The Netherland tribunal is much more pitiless than that of Spain."†

Granvelle himself has borne unintentional witness to the courage of the Netherland Christians. "'T is quite a laughable matter," wrote he, "that the king should send us information from Spain by which we are to hunt up heretics here, as if we did not know of thousands already. Would that I had as many doubloons of annual income as there are public and avowed heretics in the provinces."‡

Titelmann had boasted to Red-Rod of the pacific temper of his victims; the people were not always equally calm and non-resistant. At Valenciennes, in 1562, two preachers were arrested as teachers of heresy. After a summary trial they were sentenced to be burned alive. It was necessary, however, before executing them, to obtain the stadtholder's signature. The marquis of Berghen, one of the patriot nobles, was governor of the Walloon provinces, and he constantly absented himself from his post, because he liked not to be the right hand of the inquisition.

The administration was specially anxious to shed

⊙ Motley, vol. 1. Brandt, vol. 1.
† Cor. de Philippe II., tom. 1, p. 207.
‡ Ibid., p. 240. Papiers d'Etat.

12*

the blood of the Valenciennes ministers; consequently, after the lapse of seven months, the governant wrote to remonstrate with Berghen on his
prolonged absence from his provinces. "Madam,"
was the fine retort, "it suits neither my station nor
my character to play the part of an executioner."*

For this Granvelle denounced him to the king.
"The marquis says openly," wrote he, "that 't is
not right to shed blood for matters of faith. With
such men to aid us, your majesty can judge how
much progress we are like to make in rooting out
this heresy."†

Meantime, determined not to be balked of an
auto da fé, the cardinal despatched letter after letter
to the magistrates of Valenciennes, to proceed with
the execution without awaiting the return of the
truant stadtholder.‡

This they were reluctant to do. Finally, however, the convicted preachers were taken from jail
and conveyed to the market-place to be burned.
Attended by an excited crowd, chanting the psalms
of David under the very noses of the inquisitors, the
victims passed on. Just as they were being strapped
to the stake a rush was made, at a signal given by an
old woman who threw her shoe towards the fagots,
and nothing but the adroitness of the guard prevented the prisoners from an immediate rescue. As it
was, they were huddled up and hustled back to jail.

---

* Mémoires de Granvelle, tom. 1, p. 304.
† Papiers d'Etat, tom. 7, p. 75.
‡ Dom l'Erosque, tom. 1, p. 302, *et seq.*

The magistrates were dismayed; the inquisitors were frightened; the people were at white-heat. At last the vast throng surged towards the prison. "You should have seen this vile populace," wrote an unfriendly eye-witness, "moving, pausing, recoiling, sweeping forward, swaying to and fro like the waves of the sea when it is agitated by contending winds."* There was no long indecision. With a wild shout the people stormed the jail, rescued the ministers, and hurried them away into safe retreats; then the crowd melted away into individual fragments and dribbled homeward. And this went into history as "the day of the ill-burning."†

When this news reached Brussels, the court was furious. An army was despatched to avenge the outraged majesty of the laws, and the governant demanded a propitiatory offering in the shape of the heads of the ringleaders of the Valenciennes *émeute*, which she obtained.‡

It was noticeable that after this event, Titelmann fell to imitating Red-Rod, for he increased his body-guard, and armed his familiars *cap-à-pie*.

The northern provinces, Holland, Zealand, Utrecht, Friesland, were almost unanimously Protestant,§ and this circumstance caused an immigration thitherward. It is impossible for despotism to gag public opinion. The most biting statute is not executive against the popular pulse-beat, unless its

---

* Valenciennes MS. Cited in Motley, vol. 1, p. 345.
† Ibid.   ‡ Renom. de Francia, Strada.
§ Velius Hoorn, book 3.

fingers are swords and its feet are cannon. So here
the feeling of the people and the bias of the magistracy constantly united to oppose the Inquisition—
not a town whose burgher government did not find
or create opportunities to nullify the penal edicts.*

As an antidote to this disease, the administration, on the 29th of March, 1562, issued a new placard commanding "that none of the inhabitants of
the Low Countries should be allowed to come and
settle in any of the towns or villages of the heretical provinces, unless they brought with them a certificate signed by the parish priest and the civil
magistrate of their former habitation, attesting that
they had been reported good papists, and were not
tainted nor suspected of heresy."† The punishment for forging or using such a certificate unlaw-
fully was death.‡ Moreover, it was decreed that
"censors and magistrates were strictly to inquire
not only into the character of those who for the
future should come and dwell in any of these towns
and villages, but also of such as had settled there
at any time during the preceding four years, in case
there should be just cause of suspecting them; and
all persons were obliged to prove that their children had been baptized according to the rites of
the Romish church."§

Hand in hand with this edict went a letter, written by Margaret herself, requiring its publication,
together with the former decrees, and bidding the

* Davies, vol. 1, p. 515.   † Brandt, vol. 1, p. 143.
‡ Ibid.   § Ibid.

people to go to mass on Sundays and holidays as the rules of holy mother church prescribed*—all absentees to be punished at the discretion of the inquisitors.†

The efforts of the magistrates to shield their Protestant fellow-citizens from the effects of these decrees were various and unceasing. On one occasion the municipality of Hoorn was accused by one Dirk, a hot-headed, meddlesome priest, of remissness in the punishment of heretics, and worse still, of inducing them to attend mass once or twice for appearance' sake, and then appealing to that fact as evidence of their orthodoxy; while often, when it was known that certain Protestants had been denounced to the holy office, these were snatched from punishment by a timely warning, and provided with a place of safe concealment.‡

A commissioner was at once despatched to Hoorn by the council of state, with authority to investigate this charge. On his arrival, the burgomasters received him with great courtesy, and took him by turns to their homes, where he was entertained so effectually, that the only movement he was able to make was, "from bed to table, and from table to bed." Having spent a week in this way, during which he had heard no accusation—for all who came to give him information were repulsed either on pretext of the commissioner's being at table or in bed—he returned to the council lauding the reli-

* Brandt, vol. 1, p. 143. † Ibid.
‡ Velius Hoorn, book 3, bl. 155.

gious disposition of the good citizens of Hoorn to the skies: "Not one lisp of heresy have I heard during my whole tarry," said he.*

Just previous to the publication of Margaret's edict, several of the Netherland Protestants got together and drew up a treatise in French, under the title of, "A Confession of the Faith generally maintained by Believers dispersed throughout the Low Countries, who desire to live according to the Purity of the holy Gospel of our Lord Jesus Christ."† It was sent to Geneva for Calvin's approval, which it received; whereupon it was compressed a little, and then printed in Dutch and German.

This confession, consisting of thirty-seven articles, was the antithesis of popery. It differed from that of Augsburg chiefly in its reading of the Lord's Supper; from that of the Anabaptists, in the doctrines of baptism, the incarnation, and the religious authority of the civil magistrate; and from others, in the point of predestination. Since it was in substantial agreement with the confession of the reformed French churches, those who adopted it styled themselves, in imitation of the Huguenots, "The Dutch Reformed church."‡ Before this, the reformed of the Low Countries had adopted the London longer and shorter catechisms as standards in matters of faith, regulating their morals by the rules of the Scriptures; now they rallied under the banner of their own confession.§

---

* Velius Hoorn, book 3, bl. 155.
† Brandt, vol. 1, p. 142.   ‡ Ibid.   § Ibid.

CHAPTER XVIII.

MINES AND COUNTER-MINES.

It was a patent fact that a crisis impended in the Netherlands. As a man in the midst of avalanches, by a loud word, may bring one thundering down upon him, so now all saw that an exclamation might precipitate revolt. The wrath of a nation is never impersonal; it must vent itself upon some individual. In the Low Countries this individual was Granvelle. To the people he seemed to be, as he was, the incarnation of all they hated. This feeling added tenfold to the bitterness with which he was assailed by the nationality he had come to stab.

In spite of his pride, and notwithstanding his courage—qualities in which no one excelled him—the cardinal bent at times beneath the crushing weight of popular odium. He pressed Philip to return to Brussels. "It is a common notion here," he wrote to the royal secretary, Perez, "that they are anxious in Spain to sacrifice the Low Countries. The lords talk so freely, that any moment I fear an insurrection. For God's sake, persuade the king to come, or it will lie heavy on his conscience."* No reply was vouchsafed. A little later, Granvelle wrote again: "It is three months since I have received a line from Madrid. We know as little of

* Cor. de Philippe II., tom. 1, p. 213.

Spain here as of the Indies.   Such silence is dangerous, and may cost the master dear."*

Granvelle, however much he might fret at "the master's" course in his Spanish letters, bated no jot of his hauteur in public; and carried it with as high a hand as ever at the council board, disdaining to make an effort to placate resentment.   He owned a villa just outside the gates of Brussels, which the populace nicknamed "The Smithy," in derision of his attributed ancestry.†   There, surrounded by all that was beautiful in art and luxurious in wealth, the hated politician dwelt, occupying himself in transacting the public business, corresponding constantly with the Spanish court, and giving dinners to the lesser gentry—a class he had patronized since his breach with the nobles, and urgently recommended to the king, hinting that high military and civil offices bestowed upon these would lower the pride of the grandees.‡   "It makes me laugh," wrote he to Philip, "to see the great seigneurs absenting themselves from my dinners; nevertheless, I can always get plenty of guests at my table, gentlemen and counsellors.   I sometimes even invite citizens, in order to gain their goodwill."§

While the cardinal was making merry over the absence of the seigneurs from his table, the disaffect-

---

° Correspondance de Philippe II., tom. 1, p. 199.
† Vandervynckt, tom. 1, p. 164.
‡ Dom l'Eresque, tom. 2, p. 53.
§ Papiers d'Etat, tom. 6, p. 552.

ed lords were busied in consolidating a league, whose avowed object was the expulsion of Granvelle from the Netherlands.* The greater, and most of the lesser nobles, bottoming their measures upon the patriotism of the masses, commenced, early in 1562, an able and open constitutional opposition to the minister and his absolute policy. There was nothing underhand in this, because, as Motley has reminded us, "the Netherlands did not constitute an absolute monarchy—did not even constitute a monarchy. The provinces knew no king. Philip was king of Spain, Naples, Jerusalem; but he was only duke of Brabant, count of Flanders, lord of Freisland: hereditary chief, under various titles, of seventeen states, each one of which, although not republican, possessed a constitution as sacred as, and much more ancient than, the prerogatives of the crown; charters, too, whose infraction, by Philip's own oath, absolved his subjects from all allegiance, left them absolutely independent of his sceptre. Resistance, therefore, to the bold absolutism of the Spanish court was logical, loyal, constitutional; not a cabal, no secret league, as Granvelle had the effrontery to term it; but a legitimate exercise of powers which belonged of old to those who wielded them, and which only an unrighteous innovation could destroy."†

At the head of the opposition, by right of pre-eminent genius and the tacit assent of the nation,

* Prescott, Hist. of Philip II., vol. 1, p. 524. Papiers d Etat.
† Motley, vol. 1, p. 363.

stood the great statesman whom God had commissioned to lead that Israel out of the house of bondage through the Red sea of war, the Prince of Orange. Imperturbable, wary, subtle, prescient, it was hopeless to outwit him—it was impossible to administer an opiate to his vigilance. Men were the pawns, knights, bishops, and castles of William's chess—Europe was his board.

The fanatic king, not content with being deaf to the admonitions of justice, amused himself by applying fresh irritants to the galled back of the people, forgetful of the fact that, if maddened, the "vile animal" might balk and throw him from the saddle. When Philip espoused Isabella of France, he promised the queen-mother, Catharine de' Medici, to assist her against the Huguenots, whenever she might solicit aid.* In 1562, France had another attack of her chronic disease, civil war. The Huguenots, officered by Condé and Coligny, once again sounded to saddle in defence of edicts which granted them liberty of worship, but which the French court, issuing such permits only under the pressure of compulsion, always hastened to recall upon regaining confidence.† It was not long ere the queen-mother was driven to the wall, and reduced to extremity—seeming about to expire, as a poisoned rat dies of rage in its hole. Her shriek for aid reminded Philip of his promise; he commanded Margaret of Parma to despatch the native

---

* Prescott, vol. 1. Strada.
† Hist. of the Huguenots, Am. Tract Soc., 1866.

bands of the Netherlands to the camp of Catharine de' Medici with all speed.*

The governant received this order with amazement. Its ludicrous audacity paralyzed Granvelle himself. "Why," cried Viglius, startled out of his eloquent commonplaces, "obedience would be suicide;" and Barliament rounded the sentence with his "Amen."† The Protestants of that age constituted a kind of federative republic—formed a species of secret association ramifying throughout Europe, yet so closely united that a blow struck at it in any member instantly vibrated to every other.‡ The relationship between the Huguenots and the reformed of the Low Countries was especially intimate and cordial. Any attempt to wheel the national cavalry into line against Condé and Coligny would, as the *consulta* knew, cause an outbreak in Brussels itself. When the royal mandate was read at the council-board, there was not a voice which did not urge delay until the king could be apprized of the danger of his move.§ Margaret was in a dilemma. She dared not act, for she feared the people; she dreaded delay, for she feared "the master." Doubt tied her hands. While still undecided, a sudden express came from Madrid, in which Philip chided the delay, and bade the governant send off the auxiliaries without further pause.‖ Margaret summoned Granvelle to her side and showed him the missive. "What shall I do?" queried she.

° Strada, p. 60.   † Ibid.   ‡ Prescott, Schiller.
§ Strada, *ubi sup.*   ‖ Ibid.   Cor. de Philippe II.

The facile minister blandly answered, " 'T is impossible to send the horsemen into France. Change the name and keep the substance of his majesty's desires by substituting money for men."*

The advice was followed; and after a heated debate in the council-chamber, the compromise was assented to, and the money was voted. Philip sent fifteen hundred troopers from Spain to Catharine's assistance on being told of this transaction by the cardinal, drawing upon the states to pay the cost.† Thus the industry of the Protestant Netherlands was taxed that the Huguenots might be persecuted by the court of France.

Taking this manœuvre as an index that affairs were rapidly drifting from bad to worse, the people clamored for the convocation of the states-general. Orange and Egmont pressed Margaret to heed this request—pressed it so earnestly that she was obliged to confess that Philip had expressly charged her not to call an assembly of the states-general in his absence.‡

"Well, then," was the reply, "we pray your highness to convene the knights of the Golden Fleece, and take counsel with them." The governant assented, and the order assembled at Brussels, in May, 1562.§ Viglius addressed them in a long and eloquent speech, in which he discussed the troubled condition of the provinces, alluded to some of the causes, and suggested various remedies.

* Strada, pp. 60, 61. Prescott, Motley.   † Ibid.
‡ Strada, p. 69. Vandervynckt.   § Ibid.

On the adjournment of the order for the day, each knight was handed an invitation from the Prince of Orange to attend a caucus in the evening at Nassau-house.* Just after nightfall the motley gathering was called to order, and a furious debate ensued. Motives were aspersed, epithets were bandied, and a fierce verbal assault upon the cardinal was as furiously repelled. Towards midnight the heated knights separated, having decided upon no programme.†

Some days later the adjourned meeting of the order was held. The passionate discussions of the caucus were revived, but finally it was decreed that two things should be done: an application should be made to the individual states for a subsidy, of which the governant stood in sad need; a special envoy should be despatched to Spain.‡ Then the knights dissolved.

The monetary request was preferred to the provinces *seriatim*, and rejected by each;§ so there was an end of one half of the advice of the knights of the Golden Fleece. The other half was acted upon; Margaret selected the seigneur de Montigny, a gentleman of talent and patriotism, for the Spanish mission.‖ "He will make an excellent decoy-duck," thought she.

It was certain that Montigny would recite the story of the disaffected; he was not trusted to tell

* Hoofd, tom. 1, p. 40. Hopper, Rec. and Mem., tom. 4, p. 25.
† Ibid.   ‡ Vita Viglii, p. 36.
§ Ibid. Vandervynckt, Meteren.
‖ Strada, p. 69. Vandervynckt.

that of the administration. While he was packing his bag, a budget was secretly prepared between Margaret and Granvelle, and despatched to Philip by a special courier, to prepare him for his coming interview with the envoy.*

Let us seat ourselves beside the king in the royal cabinet, and read a line of the correspondence. "Your majesty," wrote the cardinal, "this talk about the Inquisition is all a pretext. 'T is only to throw dust into the eyes of the vulgar, and to persuade them into tumultuous demonstrations, while the real cause of this breeze is that the nobles choose that your majesty should do nothing without their permission and through their hands."†

Philip faithfully conned these words, and then awaited the arrival of Montigny with complacent tranquillity. The seigneur reached Madrid in the summer of 1562. He was received graciously, given two audiences, and bidden to speak freely. "What is the cause of this disturbance? what the origin of these complaints?" asked the king. "Sire," was the frank reply, "the discontent arises partly from the clandestine manner in which the new episcopates were brought in without the knowledge, advice, and consent of the states, bringing in their train an inquisition alien to our tastes and habits; and partly from the universal hatred in which the cardinal is held—hatred so implacable that yet greater tumults are to be apprehended."‡

---

* Strada, *ubi sup.*   † Papiers d'Etat, tom. 4, pp. 569, 570.
‡ Strada, p. 71. Brandt, vol. 1, p. 143.

Philip, who was as really the plenipotentiary of Granvelle as Montigny was of Margaret, retorted by repeating the instructions of his ministerial mentor, and closed with an expression of his fraternal sentiments towards the Netherlands.*   Nothing definite, nothing satisfactory was said; and when the envoy, after being petted and *fêted*, was sent home in the winter of 1562, he carried back with him nothing but a dreary package of *equivoques*— words without meaning; the mere bait for gudgeons.†

The nobles felt aggrieved, but they were not surprised; for Orange was in constant receipt of intelligence, through secret channels, of what passed in Madrid.‡   But so far were they from being disheartened by this failure, that they only drew the bands of their confederacy against Granvelle more closely; binding themselves either to remove the cardinal from office or to absent themselves from the council board, where they sat as stupid nullities.§

It was the pet purpose of the court to dissolve this league; and for that, what means so fit as to sow distrust and to awaken jealousy among the confederates?   Ere Montigny had reached Madrid, Philip had sent urgent and profuse directions to Margaret and the cardinal to consummate this good work.   "By no means suffer private assemblies among the nobles," he wrote, "but find out some

* Schiller, p. 439.   † Ibid., Motley, Meteren.
‡ Schiller. p. 440.   § Ibid., Prescott, Motley.

expedient whereby the union of these men, packed together to disquiet the state, may be handsomely dissolved. Above all, set spies upon the prince of Orange and his counsels; yet continue to keep him at court, and under your eyes."*

It was deemed especially necessary to estrange Egmont and Orange, the twin pillars of the league. Equal in fame and in popularity, though fatally dissimilar in character and intellect, one was the Ajax, the other the Ulysses of the patriot cause. What better augury of the success of their party could be asked than that afforded by the union of wisdom in council with audacious skill in execution?

Their alienation was not esteemed difficult to compass. The hot-headed, frank, imprudent soldier had always felt a lingering jealousy of Orange's influence and superior acumen. "We will play upon that string," said Granvelle; "we will say that the prince leads him by the nose." And the cardinal, who entertained a profound contempt for Egmont's political talent, as well he might, wrote Philip: "The count is weak and vain—a wreath of smoke. He means honestly, but abler men pervert him."† Then he essayed to wean Egmont from Orange by cajolery and judicious flattery. He mentioned him to the king in terms of vague commendation. He strove to humiliate Orange and to placate Egmont at the same time, by paying the count

* Cited in Strada, p. 70.
† Papiers d'Etat, tom. 7, p. 115.

a large instalment of his back salary, while awarding the prince an insignificant sum.*   Then looking wider, he moved the governant to send the
duke of Aerschot, an avowed enemy of the prince,
as extraordinary ambassador to Frankfort, to be
present at the election of a Roman emperor, though
it was known that Orange was entitled to, and
expected and desired that honor; thus attempting
to suborn patriotism by showing what a splendid
reward hatred to the prince might win.†

But these pitiful manœuvres failed.   Orange
went to Frankfort in his private capacity, saying,
"We shall be stronger one day "—an enigmatic
phrase which puzzled the court, but with which
Granvelle hastened to acquaint the king.‡   As for
the relations between Egmont and the prince, they
remained undisturbed.   Each knew that he was
now indispensable to the other; a common peril
and a common purpose united them by a bond of
fellowship which their hearts would never have furnished.§   Across this Medician campaign of the
court was written one word—"Defeat."

* Dom l'Eresque, tom. 2, pp. 41–45.
† Schiller, p. 439.
‡ Correspondance de Philippe II., tóm. 1, pp. 241, 242.
§ Schiller, *ubi sup.*

CHAPTER XIX.

GRANVELLE'S WITHDRAWAL.

In the beginning of 1563, the Netherlands seemed on the high road to ruin. Bankruptcy was in the vice-regal exchequer. Trade was at a halt. Swarms of inquisitors were scouring the provinces, and burning heretics from the Meuse to the Zuyder Zee. A vague fear chilled all hearts. Twenty thousand religious refugees had crossed from the states into England.*

Grieved and alarmed, the grandees determined to make another effort to persuade Philip to redress these evils; and though all were at this time Romanists, they were a unit in branding the Inquisition as an infamous tribunal, impatiently endured, but never accepted by the people.†

On the eleventh of March, 1563, Orange, Egmont, and Horn signed a letter to the king, which consisted of a fact and a deduction. The fact was, that the cardinal was odious to all classes of the nation: the deduction was, that the government could no longer be carried on by him without imminent danger of ruinous convulsions.‡

Most of the nobles assented to this epistle; but

* Cor. de Philippe II., tom. 1, p. 247.
† Vandervynckt, Meteren.   ‡ Motley, vol. 1, p. 380.

few dared affix their signatures to it. Granvelle
was the Mentor of the king—powerful, unscrupulous; Philip was known to be treacherous and
unforgiving. "It may end badly," said Berghen
and Montigny. Egmont and Horn, men of reckless
daring, dashed down their names without counting
or caring for the cost—signed as one would have
led his fleet into action, and as the other would
have charged a hostile squadron on the battle-plain.
It is probable that Orange alone fully appreciated
the abyss on whose edge this open and recorded
opposition to the cardinal placed the triumvirate.*

The letter had been written secretly, and it was
sent ostensibly to Charles de Tisnacq, a Belgian
and Philip's procurator at Madrid for the business
of the Low Countries, who was requested to hand
it to the king.† Spite of this precaution, the secret
leaked out—perhaps through the lips of Count
Aremberg, who had been solicited to sign it and
had refused, and who was openly charged by Egmont with betraying it.‡ Granvelle hastened to
"The Smithy," and dashed off a few lines to the
king, informing him of this last move of Orange,
bidding him expect the missive at an early day, and
as usual, directing him how to reply to it. He
repeated, for the hundredth time, his opinion that
the nobles were inspired, not by patriotism, but by
mere lust of authority; and he pretended to fear
lest power should be concentrated in the nation,
instead of being safely diffused throughout the

* Motley, vol. 1, p. 380.   † Strada, p. 73.   ‡ Ibid.

hands of one man—Philip.* A special messenger placed these lines in the king's hands before the March letter of the grandees reached him, and he was on his guard.†

Nearly three months elapsed ere Philip deigned to notice the note of the triumvirs. When at last he did reply, it was briefly and to this effect: "I thank you for your zeal and affection to the state and me; but you send me no specifications against Granvelle. 'T is not my custom to remove my ministers from office without proof against them. Some of you, then, come over to Spain and acquaint me with the facts."‡

"'Will you walk into my parlor?' said the spider to the fly." The flies begged to be excused. And though Philip, in a private note to Margaret, indicated that Egmont, as being the most tractable, was the fly whom he should be glad to see, informing her at the same time that his only object was to deride the nobles and to gain time,§ Egmont politely declined the invitation.‖

Naturally, Philip's meagre response embittered the grandees by its very adroitness. "'T is a cold and bad reply to send after such long delay," wrote Louis of Nassau, the prince's brother; "'t is easy to see that the letter came from the cardinal's smithy. In truth, it is a vile business, if we are to be gov-

* Papiers d'Etat, tom. 7.
† His letter was dated April 6, 1563.
‡ Cor. de Philippe II., tom. 1, p. 251.   § Ibid.
‖ Ibid., pp. 255–259.

erned by one person.   Nevertheless, the gentlemen
are wide awake, for they trust the red fellow not a
bit more than he deserves."*

After some consultation, Orange, Egmont, and
Horn resolved to address Philip again.   "We are
surprised," wrote they, "that your majesty has
thought our representations so unworthy of attention.   'T is not as accusers of the minister, but as
councillors of your majesty that we speak.   As to
our omission of specifications against Granvelle,
we had imagined that our fidelity and past services
would witness to the truth of what we charged.
The present state of the provinces would not permit us to leave home on so long a journey as is that
to Spain, even did not honor hold us from consenting to travel so far merely to lodge a complaint
against such a man as Granvelle.   In case your
majesty does not see fit to comply with our request
for the cardinal's dismission from office, we pray
you to excuse us from farther attendance at the
council-board, where we are powerless to serve your
interests, and only appear contemptible in our own
sight."†   To this same effect were two private letters to the king, written by Counts Egmont and
Horn, which went out about the same time.‡

This done, the grandees waited upon the governant, and handing her a formal protest against the
prevailing policy, predicted inevitable ruin to the

---

* Cited in Motley, vol. 1, p. 383.

† Cor. de Guillaume le Tacit., tom. 2, p. 42, *et seq.*

‡ Cor. de Philippe II., tom. 1.

common weal, unless Granvelle was removed; and while expressing a determination to serve in their respective governments to the best of their abilities, avowed their purpose to withdraw from the council of state.* Orange, Egmont, and Horn were as good as their word; they disappeared from the council, and left it to the minister and his two shadows, Viglius and Barliament.†

"We will consider your representations; meanwhile, do you attend at the council as before," wrote the king after long delay to the seigneurs in answer to their last budget. But the triumvirs paid no heed to the mandate.‡

It seems that Philip had transmitted his correspondence with the grandees to the duke of Alva, with a request for his opinion. This was that brute's reply: "Every time that I see the despatches of these three Flemish seigneurs, my rage is so excited, that if I did not exert myself to the utmost to repress it, I should express the sentiments of a madman."§ After this wild exordium, he gave this advice: "If you cannot take off their heads, dissemble. I prescribe this treatment not as a remedy, but as a palliative, because just now only weak medicines can be employed; one day we can proceed to vigorous chastisement.‖

This was counsel after the king's own heart. It was destined to bear bloody fruit at no distant day.

° Hoofd, tom. 2, p. 43.   † Motley.   ‡ Schiller, p. 442.
§ Cited in Prescott, vol. 1, pp. 537, 538; and in Motley, vol. 1, p. 387.   ‖ Prescott, Motley, *ut antea*.

This long skirmish of pens was succeeded in the Netherlands by a war of wit. A tremendous assault was made upon Granvelle through the medium of caricatures and petty comedies. The provinces teemed with lampoons and pasquinades.* History has preserved a number of these witticisms, which add color to the picture of the times, as the value of amber is enhanced by the insect it preserves.

The general respect for the cardinal had sunk so low, that on one occasion a caricature was publicly placed in his hand by a pretended petitioner, which represented a hen with Granvelle's face, seated upon a pile of eggs, out of which she was hatching a brood of bishops. Some of these were chipping the shell, some thrusting forth an arm, some a leg, while others were running about with mitres on their heads—all bearing a ludicrous resemblance to various prelates recently installed. Above the cardinal's head loomed Satan, in the act of saying: "This is my dear son, listen to him."†

The comedians, too, ridiculed the minister in the public plays. The tyranny which was able to drown a nation in blood and tears was powerless to prevent the people from laughing bitterly at their oppressors.‡ Indeed, spite of the king's command that the authors of these satires should be punished, Margaret feared to stir a step in the business, so hazardous did she esteem it to gag the guffaw.§

Nor did the comedy seem to tire the actors; the

---

* Hoofd, book 1. Strada. † Hoofd, tom. 2, p. 42.
‡ Motley, vol. 1, p. 349. § Hoofd, Strada.

nobles themselves began to share in the sport. Two
of them especially, Brederode, " a madman, if there
ever was one," as a contemporary calls him,* and
" Robert de la Marck, a descendant of the famous
'Wild Boar of Ardennes,' a man brave to temerity,
but sanguinary and depraved, were most untiring
in their efforts to make Granvelle ridiculous."

Granvelle's red hat was a new crime in the eyes
of Brussels; consequently most of the wits seized
upon that hated badge as a target. One evening
the lord of Grobbendonck, Philip's receiver of customs, gave a supper to a number of the Flemish
nobles. After a while the conversation drifted upon
the expensive habits of the aristocracy, particularly
as exhibited in the liveries of the nobility. These
were showy and costly, intimating by colors the
families to which they belonged—a fashion inaugurated by Granvelle, and a radical departure from
the simpler German custom.

At this feast it was proposed, by Berghen perhaps, or possibly by Montigny, that all should agree
to adopt a more modest and a uniform apparel.
The idea was well received. " Who shall select a
pattern?" demanded one. " Let us cast the dice
for it," said another. This was done, and the lot
fell upon Egmont.

The next morning Brussels was surprised to see
the count's retainers clothed in a new livery of a
dark gray color, and very coarse, as a contrast to
the fineness of Granvelle's dress. Upon each sleeve

* Pontus Payen, MS.

was embroidered the figure of a head and a fool's
cap. The head was marvellously like that of the
cardinal, and the cap, being red, was thought to
resemble a cardinal's hat. Some, indeed, imagined
that the fool's cap was intended to remind Granvelle, who had often styled the nobles zanies and
lunatics, that now, as of old, a Brutus might be
found lurking under the costume of a fool.

This "fool's cap livery," as it was called, was
received with acclamation. Everybody adopted it;
not a tailor in Brussels whose stock of frieze-cloth
was not exhausted. The governant herself laughed
at the joke, and sent Philip some specimens of the
coats; but eventually she intervened, and persuaded
Egmont to invent another emblem less obnoxious
to the court. The count acceded, and that device
was succeeded by a bundle of arrows similarly embroidered; and this was afterwards adopted as the
device of the seven united provinces.*

Granvelle bore up bravely under these assaults;
yet they galled him. He wrote Perez: "My hair
has turned so white, you would not recognize me."†
He was then but forty-six. Like a pestilential va-
por, the infamy of universal reprobation hung over
him. Philosophy itself could afford him no refuge.
A stranger in the land; alone among millions of
enemies; uncertain of his tools; supported only by
the arm of distant royalty; what wonder that his
hair turned gray?

* Vita Viglii, tom. 2, p. 35. Strada, p. 78. Vander Haer.
† Cor. de Philippe II., tom. 1, p. 268.

13*

"If his majesty comes not soon to Brussels, I must withdraw," wrote he to Perez, in whose sympathetic ear he was wont to pour his complaints.[*] And now the governant herself, heretofore the cardinal's fast friend, began to desire his withdrawal. The repeated complaints against the extent of the minister's power must have convinced her at last that she was a cipher; perhaps, too, she began to fear that the abhorrence which attached to him would soon include herself, and that his longer tarry would indeed provoke a revolt. Possibly she may have felt cramped by Granvelle's superior acumen, and esteemed herself competent, schooled by his long tuition, to control in person.[†]

Be all this as it may, it is certain that a coolness had grown up between these two, and that the duchess of Parma had commenced to coquette with the patriot nobles, with Egmont especially.[‡] At last, Margaret concluded to send her secretary and confidant, Thomas Armenteros, a man of fine address, but of low origin and deceitful character,[§] on a special mission to Madrid, for the purpose of procuring the cardinal's recall.[||]

Quitting Brussels in the autumn of 1563, he reached Madrid, and presented the voluminous letters of Margaret to the king; and then cunningly pronounced a vague eulogium upon Granvelle's tal-

---

[*] Cor. de Philippe II., tom. 1, p. 274.
[†] Schiller, Prescott, Vander Haer.
[‡] Mémoires de Granvelle, tom. 2.   Strada.
[§] Motley.   [||] Ibid., Prescott, Meteren.

ents and services, into which he interwove the real
facts which called for his retirement.*

Philip was nonplused. Policy demanded Granvelle's dismissal; pride called for his retention. He
had recourse to his usual tactics—he postponed a
decision, trusting that time might help him at the
crucial moment. Armenteros was detained on one
pretext or another until January, 1564; then, since
there seemed no help for it, Philip sent him back
loaded with letters and instructions, and in this
mail-bag was a note to Granvelle. "On consideration," he wrote, "I deem it best that you should
leave the Low Countries for some days, and go to
Burgundy to see your mother, with the consent of
the duchess of Parma. In this way, both my authority and your reputation will be preserved."†

This letter was concealed from every one but
Margaret, and Granvelle continued to appear and
to act as always for some weeks after its receipt.‡
Privately, however, the cardinal began to prepare
for exile; because, though he knew that "the master" intended to retain him at Brussels, and so
would not dismiss him, he was keen enough to see
that his rule was over in the Netherlands.

One day, according to arrangement, he asked
permission of the governant to visit his aged mother, whom he had not seen for fourteen years. "Certainly," said Margaret. On the 13th of March,
1564, the minister quitted Brussels ostensibly upon

* Schiller.　　　† Mem. de Granvelle, tom. 2, p. 55.
‡ Motley, Prescott, Meteren.

this visit, promising gayly to be back shortly. "Not good-by, but *au revoir*," cried he.*

This was exile; but the facile cardinal, unconquered even in his fall, over-awed the shouts which, as he well knew, quivered on the lips of the hostile city, by giving to his exit the air of a brief pleasure jaunt.†

* Archives de la Maison d'Orange, Nassau, tom. 1, p. 266. This date has been disputed. 'T is probable, however, that the chronology of the Prince of Orange is correct.

† For a time Granvelle resided in Burgundy, on his patrimonial estate at Besançon. "After the death of Pius IV. he went to Rome, to be present at the election of a new pope, and at the same time to discharge some commissions of his master, whose confidence in him remained unbroken. Soon after, Philip made him viceroy of Naples, where he succumbed to the seductions of the climate; and the spirit which no vicissitudes could bend, voluptuousness overcame. He was sixty-two years old when the king allowed him to visit Spain, where he continued with unlimited powers to administer the affairs of Spanish-Italy. A gloomy old age and the self-satisfied pride of sexagenarian administration made him a harsh and rigid judge of the opinions of others, a slave of custom, and a tedious panegyrist of past times. But the policy of the closing century had ceased to be the policy of the opening one. A new and younger ministry was soon weary of so imperious a superintendent, and Philip himself began to shun the aged councillor, who found nothing worthy of praise but the deeds of his father. Nevertheless, when the conquest of Portugal called Philip to Lisbon, he confided to the cardinal the care of his Spanish territories. Finally, in the year 1589, on an Italian tour in the town of Mantua, in the seventy-third year of his life, Granvelle terminated his long existence in the full enjoyment of his glory, and after possessing for forty years the uninterrupted confidence of his king." Schiller, p. 449.

For an interesting account of Granvelle's state papers, see Prescott, vol. 1, pp. 550, 551. Motley says Granvelle died in 1586, at the age of seventy, vol. 1, p. 421.

CHAPTER XX.

JUGGLING.

As the waves of a tempest-lashed sea swell and toss long after the subsidence of the storm, so the Netherlands, passion-lashed by Granvelle, surged and seethed long after his quiet disappearance. "Is it really true?" was the query on all lips; "has Monsieur Red Hat gone for good?"

That was the very riddle. Some held that the cardinal's departure for Besançon was a mere *rûse*, a temporary withdrawal, which, rightly read, meant an armed return. This view Granvelle was careful to countenance, and his frequent letters to Viglius and Barlaiment and Aerschot were filled with artful allusions to his speedy reappearance at Brussels.*

This fear bridled joy. "They say," wrote Brederode, "that the red fellow is to be back, and that Barlaiment is to meet him at Namur. The devil after the two would be a good chase."† Orange felt convinced that the minister's retirement was practical exile; but with the caution which was his second nature, he had his wily foeman closely watched. "'T is a sly and cunning bird that we deal with," said he; "one that sleeps neither day

---

* Papiers d'Etat, tom. 8. Vita Viglii, Vandervynckt.
† Groen v. Prinst. Arch., tom. 1, p. 305.

nor night when prey is to be gotten. We must be on our guard."*

However, days, weeks, months passed, and the cardinal did not come; at last men said, "Good; he is a thing of the past. He lay heavy on the stomach of the nation, and we vomited him up."

Simultaneously with Granvelle's exit, the grandees reëntered the council of state, wrote to assure the king of their loyalty, received gracious letters over the royal autograph in reply; and then, easing Margaret of the burden of business under which she staggered, sat tied to their desks by emulous industry all day and every day into the "wee sma' hours ayant the twal'."†

As for the governant, she seemed born into a new world. All paid devoted court to her: the nobles were full of zeal and submission; the peo- were obliging in temper.‡ For the first time, Margaret knew what it was to reign; and in proportion as she was enamored of this new power, she cursed the priestly task-master who had so long withheld her from it. "The duchess cannot hear your name mentioned without an indignant blush," wrote Morillon to Granvelle, his friend and patron; "'T is easy to tell what's o'clock."§ One day Margaret was heard to exclaim, "Thank heaven, I have but one son; since, if I had a second, he must have

* Groen v. Prinst. Arch., tom. 1, pp. 226, 259.
† Vita Viglii, Meteren, Schiller.
‡ Schiller, p. 450. Motley.
§ Papiers d'Etat, tom. 8, pp. 92, 94, 131.

been an ecclesiastic, and as vile as priests always are."*

Surely Peter Titelmann ought to have expostulated with the duchess.

At the same time Margaret endeavored to undermine the cardinalists in Philip's esteem. "They are a vile set, Granvelle, Viglius, and the rest," so she wrote in effect; "they loved to fish in troubled waters, and aimed at anarchy that they might control. They opposed the convocation of the states-general for fear their accounts might be scrutinized, and their frauds, injustice, simony, and rapine, ooze out."†

The Prince of Orange had at this hour a three-fold purpose—the convocation of the states-general, the abolition of the religious edicts, and the merging of the councils of justice and finance in the council of state.‡ "This achieved," said William, "and I defeat the absolute policy of the Spaniard, and lift the council of state into supreme control—make it dispenser of justice, holder of the public purse, and agent for foreign affairs."§

It was a statesmanlike programme, but it was certain that Philip would never assent to its first and second points, since they robbed him of his most esteemed prerogatives—the power to persecute and the power to domineer; and as for the last item, the whole cardinalist party, led by Viglius

* Papiers d'Etat, tom. 8, p. 132.
† Correspondance de Philippe II., tom. 1, p. 295.
‡ Ibid., p. 329. Motley, Prescott.
§ Correspondance de Guillaume le Taciturne, tom. 2.

and Barlaiment and Aerschot and Mansfield and Aremberg—natives of the Netherlands all, and men of wide influence, though just now eclipsed in the governant's saloons—denounced it as an attempt to concentrate revolutionary authority in an irresponsible, uncontrollable senate, fashioned after the Venetian Council of Ten, dwarfing the monarch into a mere doge.*

Notwithstanding the much-lauded probity of Barlaiment, and the "honor" of Viglius, the finance and privy councils over which they respectively presided were sinks of corruption.† Indeed the most barefaced depravity existed in every branch of the administration. Justice was sunk into the trade of hucksters—law was an article of merchandise.‡ Nothing could be obtained without, every thing could be had for, money. Life, liberty, and religion were insured at certain rates; for gold, murderers went unhung and malefactors were set free; the government itself plundered the nation by a public lottery.§ Ten per cent. a year was the Sermon on the Mount to Brussels.

Of course this frightful malversation gave rise to mutual accusations of venality and fraud. Some said, "It is the cardinalists;" some, "It is the nobles;" others, "It is the governant." Sooth to say, all were guilty. The grandees, impoverished by habits of luxury into which they had been persist-

---

* Motley, vol. 1, p. 441. Papiers d'Etat, de Granvelle, tom. 7, p. 136.   † Motley, *ubi sup.*   ‡ Ibid.
§ Schiller, p. 455.

ently lured, and thus relaxed in their morals, were thankful for a chance to thrust their itching fingers into the pockets of the nation.* Those who had just been ousted were no whit more conscientious about reaping a florin harvest, and Viglius had taken priests' orders in his old age that he might become provost of the church of St. Basan at Ghent.†

Most flagitious of all was Margaret herself. Her secretary, Armenteros — whose intimacy with his mistress procured for him the name of "Madame's barber," in allusion to the governant's famous moustache, and to the historical influence enjoyed by the barbers of the duke of Savoy and of Louis XI.‡—carried on a shameless traffic in benefices, honors, offices, patents, privileges, reducing bribery to an art, simony to a science, and roguery to a school ; and he divided the spoils of this disgraceful commerce with the regent.§ "The duchess has gone into the business of vending places to the highest bidders, with the bit between her teeth," reported Morillon to his exiled patron.‖ When the governant was auctioneer, is it to be wondered at that the bidding was brisk?

The bravest stemmers of this torrent of corruption were almost swamped by it—Orange himself opposed it in vain. "It soon became evident,"

* Schiller, p. 455.
† Papiers d'Etat de Granvelle, tom. 8, p. 320.
‡ Motley, vol. 1, p. 443.
§ Ibid. Groen v. Prinst., Arch. et Corresp., tom. 1, p. 405.
‖ Papiers d'Etat de Granvelle, tom. 7, p. 635.

remarks Motley, "that as desperate a struggle was to be made with this many-headed monster of iniquity, as with the cardinal by whom it had been so long fed and pampered."[*]

Not many months elapsed ere the effects of this venality and rapine were seen and felt in the disorganization of society. Margaret was aroused from her delicious trance by the clamors of a mutinous army, eager for the payment of its long arrears,[†] by the boisterous petitions of the burghers demanding justice,[‡] and by the daily receipt of letters from the king, complaining of the growth of heresy, and commanding that renewed recourse be had to the fagot and the stake.[§]

The reformed, "instant in season and out of season" in God's service, had indeed availed themselves of the opportunity afforded by the unsettled state of the provinces to proclaim the gospel. The Calvinists in the territories which bordered upon France, the Anabaptists in the north, the Lutherans on the German frontier—all were busy, all ubiquitous.[||] Even the Jews, outlawed and surrendered to persecution by all mediæval sects, now swarmed in the cities of the Netherlands unracked, unburned.[¶] Granvelle, before his fall, had written to Philip, "'Tis more than a year since a single arrest on a charge of heresy has been made in

[*] Motley, vol. 1, p. 441.

[†] Schiller, p. 458. Meteren, Vandervynckt.

[‡] Ibid.   § Ibid.   Strada, p. 83.

[||] Prescott, vol. 1, p. 556.   ¶ Ibid.

Brussels;"* and since the exit of the cardinal, public opinion had quite drawn the sting from the venomous edicts. The Inquisition was an object of contempt as well as of hatred;† and the *inquisitori* were compelled to memorialize the king for protection and support.‡ The burgomasters of Bruges flung a number of their own officers into prison, and kept them on bread and water for several weeks, as a punishment for an attempt to lay hands upon a heretic.§

Philip's anger was fanned to white-heat. Scores of letters, brimful of minute descriptions of suspected individuals, were forwarded from Madrid to Brussels by special couriers;‖ and spurred forward by the absolute command of the king, the reluctant governant once more unleashed the hounds of persecution.¶

In the summer of 1564, an effort was made to burn a reformer in the market-place of Antwerp. One Fabricius, a converted Carmelite friar, who had quitted the cloister, married, and settled in Antwerp as pastor of a reformed congregation, was arrested, racked by the inquisitors, that an accusation of his secret associates might be wrung from his tortured lips; and at last, when it was found

---

* Correspondance de Philippe II., tom. 1, p. 240.

† Vita Viglii, Vandervynckt.

‡ Correspondance de Philippe II., tom. 1, p. 353.

§ Strada, p. 84.

‖ Ibid., p. 83. Correspondance de Philippe II., tom. 1, p. 327, *et alibi.*

¶ Brandt, vol. 1, p. 146. Strada, *ubi sup.*

that no "confession" could be extorted from him, sentenced to the stake.*

As he was led out to die, a multitude of excited spectators surged round the executioners; and from the sidewalk, the doorways, the balconies on his route, sympathizing voices shouted, "Take courage, Fabricius, and endure manfully to the last."† When the stake was reached, and the victim was lashed to it, a shower of stones, cast from unseen hands, fell upon the pile, driving the executioner from his post just as the fire was kindled. Determined, however, not to be deprived of his prey, he stabbed the martyr to the heart ere he fled, so that when the crowd rushed to release Fabricius from the flames he was already dead.‡

Antwerp was mutinous throughout the night, and in the gray of the next morning the city was found to be placarded with verses written in blood, which announced that Fabricius' death would be avenged. Indeed, that same day a woman, who was accused of having betrayed the martyr to the Inquisition, was publicly stoned, and would have been killed, had she not taken refuge in a neighbor's house, where she was hidden from the mob.§

When the news of this riot reached Madrid, Philip was enraged. "S'death, madame," wrote he to Margaret, "unearth these vermin, and move heaven and earth to punish them."‖ The governant

---

* Brandt, *ubi sup.*
† Brandt, vol. 1, p. 146, *et seq.* Strada, p. 84.
‡ Ibid.   § Ibid.   ‖ Strada, Prescott.

heard, but stood powerless. To have punished all
the guilty would have been to flay Antwerp, for the
whole city was the rioter. One of the stone-casters
was hung; the rest it was impossible to identify.[*]

Scenes of outrage which went off more smoothly
than this at Antwerp, were now enacted throughout the Netherlands. The people cursed; the states
protested. Flanders solemnly memorialized the
king against Peter Titelmann, and forwarded to
Madrid a vivid list of his enormities.[†] The seign-
iors were conjured to intervene; Margaret was
beseeched to curb this wretch. Neither the nobles
nor the governant dared move. "May I perish,"
wrote Marillon to Granvelle, "if the duchess does
not stand in exceeding awe of Titelmann."[‡] Egmont himself, the hero of Gravellines and St. Quentin, was more than suspected of trembling before
this blood-smeared butcher of the Inquisition.[§]

As for Philip, instead of reproof, he bestowed
the royal benediction upon Titelmann; they were
congenial souls. So far was he from mitigating the
horrors of the new crusade against reform, that he
instructed the governant to publish throughout the
Netherlands, and to enforce, the decrees of the
Council of Trent.[‖]

This memorable synod, first called by Paul III.

---

[*] Strada, Prescott.

[†] Brandt, vol. 1. Corresp. de Philippe II., tom. 1. Papiers
d'Etat.   [‡] Papiers d'Etat, tom. 8, p. 425.

[§] Motley, vol. 1, p. 434.

[‖] Strada, p. 84. *et seq.* Hopper, Rec. et Mem. Corresp. de
Philippe II.

in 1537, and continued through twenty-one twad-
dling years, had finally effected a *sine die* adjournment in December, 1563.* Its avowed purpose was
the settlement of disputed points of orthodoxy. The
tedious labors of these doctors, instead of purifying
the Romish church from its corruptions, had only
reduced its errors to greater definiteness and precision, and invested them with the sanction of authority. All the subtleties of its teachings, all the
arts and usurpations on which the see of St. Peter
was based, and which had rested hitherto largely
upon arbitrary usage, were now enacted into laws,
and framed as a system.

The decrees of the Council of Trent contained
many provisions which were deadly to the prerogatives of the European sovereigns, and which were
meant to restore the temporal supremacy of Rome,†
Against several of these Philip had earnestly protested, while the decision was pending; but he was
defeated, and on this account Europe expected that
he would follow the example of France, and reject
the decrees.‡ This belief became a certainty in
most minds when Pius V. settled a question of precedence between the Castilian and the French ambassadors at the papal court, in favor of France.§

But Philip could not remain at feud with Rome.
"In matters of faith," wrote he to the duchess of
Parma, "I am always ready to sacrifice my private

---

* Fra Paolo Sarpi, Hist. du Concile de Trente.
† Ibid.   ‡ Prescott, vol. 1, p. 570.   Strada, p. 85.
§ Strada, *ubi supra.*

feelings to the common weal.''* Early in 1564, he had ordered the decrees to be received as law in Spain;† now he assured the governant that they must be obeyed in the Netherlands. "No exceptions are permissible,'' added he. "What is law in Madrid must be law in Brussels.''‡

The announcement of Philip's determination surprised Christendom, and provoked a storm of indignation in the Netherlands. Now again, as in the days when the new bishoprics won the anathema of the states, all classes united in denouncing these abhorrent decrees. "They contravene our charters,'' said the provinces. "They conflict with our immunities,'' cried the clergy. "They murder conscience,'' affirmed the reformers.§

Margaret convened her council in dismay. "What shall I do?'' queried she. "Proclaim the canons,'' said Viglius.‖ "Send an envoy to Madrid to lay the grievances of the nation before the king, and to submit what we think the most effectual remedy,'' advised Orange.¶ The prince carried the day, and Egmont was selected for the mission.** "I will go,'' said the handsome soldier—all the more readily because he had a list of personal favors to crave of Philip.††

Viglius drew up Egmont's instructions.‡‡ The

* Strada, *ubi supra*.   † Ibid.
‡ Correspondance de Philippe II., tom. 1, p. 328.
§ Meteren, Prescott.   ‖ Groen v. Prinst, Arch., etc., tom. 1.
¶ Prescott, vol. 1, p. 571.   Strada.
** Strada.   Papiers d'Etat. tom. 8.   †† Prescott, *ubi sup*.
‡‡ Ibid.   Motley.

prince esteemed them timid and pointless. When the rough draught was presented for the action of the council, he rose and rolled out one of the most massive and impassioned speeches of his life.*

As William poured out his eloquence, he bore conviction on the tide of his rapid invective; and as he closed his address at seven in the evening, with the affirmation that he "could not look on with pleasure while princes strove to govern the souls of men, and to take away their liberty of conscience," the council adjourned.†

Viglius was astounded. He piqued himself on his rhetoric, and he feared for his laurels. It was necessary to surpass the declamation of Orange, if he wished to obliterate the impression of the patriot orator. Perplexed and despairing, he tossed in his bed till dawn without closing his eyes; then, on rising to dress, he was stretched senseless by a stroke of apoplexy.‡

It was some weeks ere Viglius was able to resume his place at the council-board. His smooth tongue was paralyzed, his limbs were rigid. Meantime his seat was filled by his friend and fellow-countryman Joachim Hopper, like himself, a Frisian doctor of ancient blood and extensive acquirements.§ Motley tells us that Hopper was "the projector of that ultra-Romanist university, which, at Philip's desire, was successfully organized at

---

* Summarized in Motley, vol. 1, pp. 455, 456.
† Motley, vol. 1, p. 456.   ‡ Vita Viglii.
§ Motley, *ubi sup.*

Douay in 1556, in order that a French university might be furnished for Walloon students, as a substitute for the seductive and poisonous Paris. For the rest, Hopper was a man of mere routine—often employed by Philip in weighty affairs, but never entrusted with the secret at the bottom of them. His mind was a confused one, and his style was inexpressibly involved and tedious. 'Poor Master Hopper,' said Granvelle, 'did not write the best French in the world; and though learned in letters, he knew little of statesmanship.' His manners were as cringing as his intellect was narrow. He never opposed Margaret, so that his colleagues called him 'Councillor Yes Madame;' and he did his best to be friends with all the world."*

Hopper new-modelled Egmont's instructions, so that they echoed the sentiments of the prince's speech.† The governant gave them to the envoy, saying, "I pray you impress upon his majesty the importance of what is herein writ, the impossibility of enforcing the edicts in their present severity, the refractory spirit of the people, the exhaustion of the exchequer, and the necessity which should seem to dictate the abrogation of the Tridentine canons, as also the necessity of sending me precise instructions how to act."‡

"Rely upon me, madame," responded Egmont. On the thirtieth of January, 1565, the gallant envoy embarked for Spain;§ a few days later he entered

---

* Motley, vol. 1, p. 457.   † Vita Viglii, p. 41.
‡ Ibid.   § Papiers d'Etat, tom. 9.

the lion's den. This time the beast's mouth was
closed. Philip understood the giddy, open-hearted,
vain soldier whom the states had deputed to wait
upon him. "I shall receive Egmont graciously,"
wrote he to the duchess.* He knew that the ego-
tistic envoy could be easily cozened; and he determined to juggle, not to growl.

Accordingly, Egmont received the most cordial
and royal of welcomes. His tarry was one prolonged *fête*. Never before in Castilian halls had
subject been so received by king. The courtiers
of Madrid seemed to have conquered their ancient
grudge against the Flemings; and they too buried
the envoy in their hearts—feasted him, courted him,
and deferred to him.†

Philip took his guest to see the foundation-
stones of the Escurial—the memorial of that battle
of St. Quentin of which Egmont was the hero; and
though it was February, he insisted upon showing
him the beauties of his summer retreat in the Segovian forest.‡ Nor did the crafty monarch neglect
to confer upon his "good cousin" more solid favors. Egmont was something of a spendthrift, and
his estates were mortgaged. "I will remit all royal
dues," said the debonnaire and liberal monarch.§
Fifty thousand golden florins were handed him;
altogether his journey was worth a hundred thousand crowns.‖

---

* Prescott, vol. 1, p. 576.
† Cor. de Philippe II., tom. 1, p. 349.   Papiers d'Etat, tom. 9.
‡ Ibid.   § Ibid.   ‖ Papiers d'Etat, tom. 9, p. 385.

So much kindness, such judicious flattery, quite
won Egmont's heart, and completely vanquished his
acumen. Business was scarcely thought of; and
when it was referred to, a few plausible, non-com-
mittal, double-meaning words easily satisfied the
tyro diplomat; or, if he seemed inclined to press
any disagreeable question, a well-turned compliment, an invitation to dine out, or a request for an
opinion upon a new cut for a collar, could always
lure the volatile count into pleasanter discourse.*

Back of this royal courtesy lay deadly earnestness. Philip had considered deeply the despatches
of the governant, and he had decided not to swerve
a hand's breadth from his former policy. To reinforce and to sanctify this purpose, he summoned a
council of the most eminent theologians in Madrid;
and after explaining the condition of the Netherlands to them, put this question: "Am I justified
in granting religious toleration to the provinces?"

From the form of the query, the conclave imagined that Philip desired an affirmative decision; and
thinking to please him, their easy virtue led them
to respond, "Yes, sire, considering the critical situation of the Netherlands and the imminent danger
of revolt, if care and prudence be not used, we think
you might be justified in decreeing liberty of worship." "S' death," cried Philip, in a rage; "I did
not call you to learn what I *might* do, but what I
ought to do." The sycophantic churchmen, finding
that they had mistaken the cue, promptly faced

* Schiller, Van der Haer, Meteren, Strada.

about, and indignantly vetoed the idea of toleration.[*]

Then followed a notable instance of fanaticism, or of hypocrisy. Prostrating himself before a crucifix, the king exclaimed, "I implore thy divine majesty, Ruler of all things, that thou keep me determined as I am now never to become nor to be called the lord of those who reject thee for their Lord."[†]

All these determinations were carefully concealed from Egmont; and when, after a delightful sojourn at the Spanish court, he prepared to return to Brussels, he really thought that he had been completely successful in his mission, avowed himself the most contented man in the world, and construed Philip's gracious phrases to mean that nothing had been denied to his brilliant diplomacy.[‡]

"Here, my dear count," said the monarch at their parting interview, "here is a packet of sealed instructions for the governant. You will hand it to her, when you reach Brussels."[§] The cozened envoy took it with a smile, nothing doubting that it tallied with the verbal assurances which the royal juggler had given him.

Early in April, 1565, the count rode gayly into Brussels,[||] received a warm welcome home, announced his success at Madrid, handed the royal despatches to the duchess, and kissed his countess with the consciousness of having done a good deed brilliantly.

　° Strada, p. 89.　　† Ibid.　　‡ Schiller, Motley, Prescott.
　§ Hopper, Rec. et Mem.　　|| Hoofd, Hopper, Van der Haer.

A few days after his return, Egmont was summoned to attend a session of the council of state. The sealed instructions were opened and read. This was their substance: "I have reached no decision as it regards the proposed change in the councils. Concerning the edicts, there must be no change in them. I would rather lose a hundred thousand lives, if I had so many, than allow a single alteration in religion. This, however, you may do: appoint a commission, consisting of three bishops and a number of jurists, to advise with the members of the council of state as to the best means of instructing the people in their spiritual concerns. Moreover, since public executions of heretics do but afford them an opportunity of boastfully displaying a foolhardy courage, and of deluding the common herd by an affectation of the glory of martyrdom, I urge you to devise means for putting in force the final sentence of the Inquisition with secret despatch, thereby depriving the condemned of the honor of their obduracy."*

Egmont was astounded. "These specious favors, then, which were lavished upon me," exclaimed he loudly and bitterly, "were nothing but an artifice to expose me to the ridicule of my fellow-citizens, and to destroy my good name. If this is the fashion after which his majesty keeps the promises which he made me in Spain, let who will take my offices; for my part, I will prove, by my retirement from public affairs, that I have no share in this breach of faith."†

* Cor. de Phil. II., tom. 1, p. 347, et seq.   † Schiller, p. 467.

Orange was indignant, but not surprised. He had suspected that Egmont would be outwitted, and now he accused his friend of neglecting the public business in the pursuit of private ends and pleasures. "Count," said he, "you have been deluded by Spanish cunning. Self-love and vanity have blinded your penetration. You have forgotten the general welfare for your own advantage."*

The rebuke was sharp, but it was merited.

Worst of all in Egmont's eyes, he lost *caste* with the people. They too echoed the charge of the prince of Orange, and cursed the king's instructions as establishing a more bitter code than the existing one.† Philip could have adopted no surer method of breaking Egmont's popular credit than by gibbeting him at the cross-road of public opinion as a traitor or a dupe.

It has been said that "Prudence is only fear with a wise cloak on." On this occasion Prudence caught cold without her cloak.

* Schiller, p. 467. Papiers d'Etat, tom. 9, p. 345.
† Prescott. vol. 1, pp. 583, 584.

CHAPTER XXI.

THE DRAGON'S TEETH.

As the year 1565 sped on, absolutism became more pronounced; protestation grew more emphatic. The country at large was feverishly excited. Special couriers hastened hither and thither freighted with weighty mail-bags, covering every high-road with dust flung from the heels of their flying horses. Margaret was in daily communication with the king. The patriot nobles interchanged incessant letters. Granvelle, from his quiet retreat at Besançon, maintained a busy correspondence with his partisans in Flanders and Brabant, forwarding vivid summaries of his epistolary gleanings—and sometimes the original notes themselves—to Madrid.*

In July,† 1565, a mixed conclave of ecclesiastics and civilians was convened at Brussels, pursuant to the royal mandate, to deliberate upon the fittest "mode of instructing the people in their spiritual concerns."‡ It was composed of six divines and three gentlemen of the long robe from the courts of justice, reinforced by Barliament and Viglius,§ who had so far recovered from his recent apoplexy as to be able to resume his duties. The governant asked,

---

* Prescott, vol. 1, p. 588.
† Brandt says on the 25th of May. See vol. 1, p. 154.
‡ Chapter XX., p. 313.   § Brandt, *ubi sup.*

"Gentlemen, ought any change to be made in the punishment of heresy?" The lawyers, those professional fishers in troubled waters, those thrivers on discord, responded: "Madame, we favor the repeal of the death penalty for heretical offences." The clergy, those preachers of peace, those pleaders for charity, snarled angrily, "Your highness, we stoutly maintain the contrary opinion."* Viglius was especially vehement in his eulogy upon the *auto da fé* principle. "I can find no words sufficiently harsh," cried he, "in which to characterize those who would abolish such a vital safeguard."†

Of course, the prelates carried their point. It was decided that no change was permissible, save perhaps some mitigation of the punishment of those who, without being heretics or sectaries, might bring themselves within the provisions of the edicts "through curiosity, nonchalance, or otherwise." Such offenders, it was hinted, might be "whipped with rods, fined, banished, or subjected to similar penalties of a lighter nature."‡ From which it should seem that those theologians were disposed to pardon curiosity and nonchalance in the reformed proselytes; while they had nothing for the just and conscience-tied but the rack and the stake. Rome could forgive every thing except—honesty. It is a pregnant page of history.

* Papiers d'Etat, tom. 9. Cited in Motley, vol. 1, p. 471.
† Ibid., tom. 9, p. 408.
‡ Hopper, Rec. et Mem., pp. 48, 49. Cited in Motley, vol. 1, p. 472.

The conclave put this decision in writing on the eve of adjournment. Margaret presented it to the council of state. "What shall I do with it?" queried she. "'T is no affair of ours," replied the cautious councillors; "his majesty has not demanded our opinion."* The sentiments of the patriot seigneurs were well known, but they did not deem it necessary to volunteer a statement of views which they knew were asked only to commit them. "Fabius was a wise general," said Orange; "he knew how to wait and watch."†

Early in July, the governant forwarded the proceedings of the commission to Madrid for the king's inspection, and to him she repeated the question which she had put to the council of state, "What shall I do with this decision?" The interrogator had no better success in the royal cabinet than in the council chamber at Brussels. Philip had taken refuge in taciturnity.

Meantime, public opinion, less cautious than the nobles, less taciturn than the king, made its comments on the deliberations of the conclave. The doctors were pelted with opprobrious epithets. Free-spoken Brederode expressed the universal feeling, when he said, "As for those blackguards of bishops, I would the race were extinct, like that of green dogs."‡

* Hopper, Rec. et Mem., pp. 48, 49. Cited in Motley, vol. 1, p. 472.

† Lives of the Princes of the House of Orange, William the Silent. ‡ Groen v. Prinst., Archives, etc., tom. 1, p. 382.

Viglius was agitated, but he still plumed himself on the result of the conclave's labors. "Many here seek to abolish the chastisement of heresy," so he wrote to Granvelle. "If they gain their point, *actum est de religione Catholicâ;* for as most of the people are ignorant fools, the heretics will soon be the great majority, if they are not kept in the true path by fear of punishment."* It is a notable admission; but is it not fair to inquire, What must men think of a church which confesses that it can only bind its disciples to its faith by fettering their bodies in brute fear? What must be the nature of a faith which permits its exponents to esteem such a course permissible?

As for the ignorance of the heretics, that was even then a point on which doctors disagreed. At a feast, Montigny once asked a strange cavalier, "Prithee, friend, are there not many Huguenots in Burgundy?" "Nay," was the reply; "nor should we permit them there." "Is 't so?" was the retort; "then there can be but very few people of intelligence in that province, for those who have any wit are mostly Huguenots."†

There was at this time something ominous in the temper of the provinces. The wildest rumors were afoot. "The king is recruiting an army for our subjugation," said some.‡ "Bands already hang on the German border," affirmed others.§

* Groen v. Prinst, Archives, etc., tom. 1, p. 370.
† Papiers d'Etat de Granvelle, tom. 7, pp. 187, 188.
‡ Arch. de la Maison d'Orange-Nassau, tom. 2, p. 33.   § Ibid.

Gaunt famine, frequent forerunner of revolution, stalked through the land.* "Bread! bread!" shouted the rabble.   Bread was doled out, and Margaret vehemently proclaimed that the reports of her royal brother's belligerent intentions were false.† Apprizing Philip of them, she requested him to brand them as the lies of the seditious.

The king was silent.

In June, 1565, an event occurred which stirred new tumults.   Isabella of Spain, journeying with the duke of Alva as her chaperon, met at Bayonne the queen-mother of France, Catharine de' Medici.‡ Ostensibly, it was the visit of a long-absent daughter to her mother; really, it was an interview to concoct an international massacre of the French and Low Country heretics.§   Spite of the tact of Isabella and the adroitness of the duke, this object was not attained, as we may learn from Alva's report to Philip; because Catharine, true to her policy of governing through the division of her foes, would not destroy the balance of the hostile factions in France by exterminating the Huguenots.‖   St. Bartholomew was only possible when the reformers ceased to promote the ambition of the wily dowager—and that time was still seven years off.

Wrong in their estimate of the result, the Neth-

° Corresp. de Philippe II., tom. 1, p. 378.

† Archives etc., *ubi supra*.

‡ Davila, Guerre Civili di Francia, tom. 1, p. 348.   Milano, 1807.

§ Ibid., Brantôme, Œuvres, tom. 5, p. 58, *et seq.*

‖ Alva's letters are cited in Papiers d'Etat de Granvelle, tom. 9, p. 281, *et seq.*

erlanders were right in their opinion of the object
of this sinister interview; all held it to be a plot
against the liberties of their country.* The governant was more than ever alarmed. "I implore
you, sire, bestir yourself, and contradict this rumor," wrote she to Philip, in a letter filled with an
account of the popular apprehension of the meaning of the mutiny at Bayonne.

Philip made no response.

Every day the gloom grew deeper around Margaret's throne. There were incessant conflicts between the inquisitors, bent on executing the edicts,
and the magistrates, who exhausted the armory of
the law in their efforts to defeat persecution.† The
people were crazed with rage. Nothing was thought
of but the edicts. "And he terms this a mitigation," said they, "this new order that heretics shall
be executed, not by public burning, as heretofore,
but secretly, at midnight, in their dungeons, while
the inquisitors hold the heads of their victims
between their knees and slowly suffocate them in
tubs of water."‡ "Can there be viler slavery,"
demanded some, "than to lead a trembling life in
the midst of spies and informers, who register every
word we speak, note every look, and put the worst
construction upon every action?"§

"Well, then," said a magistrate of Amsterdam
when asked on one occasion to coöperate with the

* Hopper, Rec. et Mem.   Hoofd, Meteren.
† Corresp. de Philippe II., tom. 1, p. 353.
‡ Motley, vol. 1, p. 475.   § Brandt, vol. 1, p. 154.

inquisitors in the execution of the edicts, "when I appear before the tribunal of God, I shall do well to have one of your placards in my hand, to observe how far it will bear me out in the persecutions."[*]

In the streets, in the shops, in the taverns, in the fields; at market, at church, at funerals, at weddings; in the noble's castle, at the farmer's fireside, in the mechanic's garret, upon the merchant's exchange—everywhere the Inquisition was the one perpetual subject of shuddering conversation.[†]

The press, too, was invoked. Never since Koster formed his type had printing been pressed into such relentless, unceasing service.[‡] Tracts were thrown off which treated of the reciprocal obligations of the king and the states;[§] pamphlets were widely circulated which boldly pointed out the perfidy of Philip;[‖] the Netherlands were placarded with satirical verses—lampoons on the bishops, on the inquisitors, on the governant, on the king himself;[¶] notes were affixed to the palace gates of Orange and of Egmont which summoned them to enter the lists against the tyrant—"Rome awaits her Brutus," such was their tenor;[**] wild insurrectionary songs wailed through the streets,[††] the *ça iras* of an earlier and grander struggle than that of revolutionary France in 1791; for this did not commit moral suicide by attempting to depose God.

° Brandt, vol. 1, p. 154.   † Motley, vol. 1, p. 473.
‡ Arch. de la Maison d'Orange-Nassau. Hoofd, Prescott.
§ Vandervynckt, Troubles des Pays-Bas, tom. 1, p. 97.
‖ Ibid. Meteren.   ¶ Ibid. Hoofd.
°° Archives, etc., Supplément, p. 22.   †† Hoofd, Meteren.

Pale, sleepless, affrighted, Margaret reported these things to her royal brother, and again prayed him to intervene.

Philip was heedless.

At last, the inquisitors themselves were cowed. They united their prayers to those of Margaret. "Sire," wrote one of them, Michael de Bay, "be merciful, and dismiss us, or else come to our support."*

This despairing cry touched Philip's heart. "The Inquisition in danger!" exclaimed he; "this must be seen to." On the 17th of October, 1565, he who had been deaf to the prayers of Margaret of Parma, indifferent to the wail of an agonized people, yielded to the entreaties of an inquisitor, and addressed that memorable letter to the duchess, from the Segovian forest, which determined the fate of the Netherlands.†

The royal rescript was to this effect:

"I am surprised at the tumult which you report as rife in the Low Countries—surprised at the course of the people—indignant at the conduct of the nobles. Whatever interpretation Count Egmont may have given to my verbal communications, it never entered my mind to think of altering in any, the slightest degree, the penal statutes which the emperor my father published in the provinces thirty-five years agone. Those edicts I hereby order to be henceforth rigidly enforced. The In-

---

* Corresp. de Philippe II., tom. 1, p, 353.

† Hopper, Rec. et Mem. Strada, Prescott.

quisition must receive active support from the secular arm. The decrees of the council of Trent must be at once, and irrevocably and unconditionally acknowledged throughout the Netherlands. I acquiesce fully in the opinion of the conclave of bishops and canonists, as to the sufficiency of the Tridentine decrees as guides in all points of reformation and instruction; but I do not concur with them touching the mitigation of punishment which they propose in consideration of the age, sex, and character of offenders; I esteem my edicts quite merciful enough as they stand."*

Here at last was something frank, decisive, unmistakeable. For once Philip had spoken his mind, the oracle had uttered its message without recourse to subterfuge. Surprised and agitated, Margaret opened a private note addressed to herself, hoping to find some loophole through which to escape from the necessity of immediate obedience to this stern mandate. It was useless. Never before had the king expressed his meaning so clearly. So with the whole budget; a few lines to Egmont, and responsive epistles to the inquisitors, left no doubt as to the monarch's determination "to frame mischief by a law."

The council of state was instantly convened. The despatches from Spain were read. "God knows what wry faces were made by us on learning this absolute will of his majesty," affirmed Viglius.† But even Viglius feared to obey the royal mandate.

* Summarized in Schiller, p. 471.
† Arch. de la Maison d'Orange-Nassau, tom. 1, p. 442.

Rising gravely from his seat, he said, "Your highness, it would be the height of folly in us to think
of promulgating the royal edict at this perilous
juncture. Let us apprize his majesty of the situation, and meantime suspend all action."*

All were astonished at such advice from such a
person. But the sensation was yet greater when
Orange rose to oppose delay. "The royal will,"
said he, "is much too clearly and precisely stated;
't is too plainly the result of long and mature delib-
eration for us to venture to delay its proclamation."
"I take the risk; I assume all; I oppose myself to
the king's displeasure," interposed Viglius. "What,"
continued the prince—"what have the many representations already made effected? Of what avail
was the embassy so recently despatched? And
what, then, do we wait for? Shall we bring upon
ourselves the whole weight of the king's displeasure, by determining at our own peril to render him
an unasked service—a service for which it is certain
he will never thank us?"†

These short, sharp interrogations frightened the
duchess into obedience to the royal mandate. "His
majesty's decision must be proclaimed,"‡ faltered
she, certain that she walked over a precipice whichever path she followed, but dreading Philip even
more than the mob. The die was cast; and as the
council adjourned, Orange tapped Horn upon the

---

* Cited in Schiller, *ubi sup.*
† Meteren, tom. 2. Bor, tom. 1. Schiller.
‡ Ibid. Vita Viglii.

shoulder, and whispered, "Now we shall soon see a national tragedy."*

On this occasion Viglius and the prince seemingly changed *rôles;* the spur became the check, the check became the spur. But really there was no inconsistency; each was true to his faith. Viglius demanded delay in the interest of absolutism, imperilled by action; Orange urged action in the interest of liberty, jeoparded by delay. "All may yet be gained," thought Viglius, "if we can suspend, perhaps mitigate the rigor of the law, till this tempest be stilled." "Now," thought Orange, "the provinces are shut up to resistance by despair. Delay will enable the tyrant by secret negotiation and intrigue to win stealthly what would be denied to force. The same purpose will inspire Spanish politics, only the method of action will become more subtle and occult. We are prepared now— no postponement; extremity alone can combine great masses in unity of purpose, and move a nation to bold action."

It should seem, therefore, that the adroit absolutist and the sagacious patriot chief merely changed their language, not their principles, their tactics, nor their purpose.

When it was proclaimed that the canons of Trent, the existing edicts, and the Inquisition were to be received and obeyed throughout the provinces, the decree was answered by a howl of execration.† The people were ready for any method of resistance, as

* Vita Viglii, p. 45.　　† Motley, vol. 1, p. 482. Vita Viglii.

William knew they would be. "The Netherlands are not so stupid," many were heard to say, "as not to know right well what is due from the subject to the sovereign, and from the king to the people. Perhaps means may yet be found to repel force with force."* Pamphlets, handbills, pasquils "snowed in the streets."† The justice and the policy of armed resistance to tyranny were openly inculcated.‡ Every honest soul, every patriotic heart was compelled to assume the Phrygian cap.

The Brabantine cities solemnly denounced the royal proclamation as a bold usurpation.§ "We entrench ourselves behind our constitution," cried Antwerp and Brussels and Louvain and Herzogenbusch; we appeal to the law." Margaret ordered the council of Brabant to search the archives of the province for precedents. The lawyers looked. "Well," queried the governant, "what do you find?" The canonists hesitated and equivocated. "Answer me distinctly," said the duchess. "We can find no precedent for the Inquisition," was the reply.‖ Brabant was jubilant. "Then we will have none of it," shouted the sturdy burghers. Margaret acquiesced, and that province was declared free of the holy office.¶

Other states followed this example. Eminent lawyers counselled disobedience to the edicts.** Montigny, Berghen, Mansfeld flatly refused to en-

---

° Schiller, p. 474.   † Motley, *ubi sup.*
‡ Hoofd, Meteren.   § Hopper, Rec. et Mem., p. 63, *et seq.*
‖ Ibid., p. 64.   Hoofd, tom. 2, p. 69.   ¶ Ibid.
°° Vita Viglii.   Bor.

force the decrees within their stadtholderates. Orange retired to his town of Breda in Holland, where, in observant repose, he watched the drift of events.[*] "Without kindling a war," wrote he to the duchess, "it is absolutely impossible to comply with his majesty's orders within my government. If obedience is insisted upon, I must beg that my place may be supplied by some other, fitter to meet the royal expectations. As the case now stands, I have no alternative but either to disobey the king, or to betray my country and disgrace myself."[†]

Of all the patriot seigneurs, Egmont alone remained in Brussels—Egmont, ever vacillating between the republic and the throne, ever wearying himself in the vain attempt to unite the good citizen with the obedient subject.[‡] Margaret, fearful of displeasing the king by declaring for either faction, now turned for sympathy and support to Egmont, who belonged to both and to neither of the conflicting parties.[§]

So ended the memorable year 1565. "It was the last of peace and happiness," sighs Strada.[||] Yes, the last of a peace which had subserviency for its father and fanaticism for its mother; the last of a happiness in which *inquisitori* were the sole participants—which was builded upon murder, and cemented in the blood of martyrs.

---

[*] Schiller, p. 476.   Meteren.   [†] Ibid.   [‡] Ibid.
[§] Schiller.   [||] Strada, p. 97.

CHAPTER XXII.

"THE BEGGARS."

In the afternoon of a day in the early spring of 1566, Margaret of Parma, lounging in her council-chamber, was listening half-inattentively to a drowsy discussion of routine affairs. The meeting was informal. Egmont was seated at the board; and among the councillors towered the stately form of the prince of Orange, who had been called to town for a day or two by business. "Well," said the duchess with a light laugh, in response to some inquiry, "I think—"

The sentence was checked in the utterance by the precipitate appearance of Count Meghen, an ultramontanist with liberal proclivities, who burst into the apartment pale, nervous, breathless. "Pardon me," said he, replying to the mute look of interrogation turned upon him by the councillors; "but I beg you to postpone what matters are before the board; I have an important announcement to make." Then addressing the governant, he continued: "Madame, I have just received information from one whom I trust, and who is, moreover, an affectionate servant of the king—though, tongue-tied by promise, I may not give his name—that a very extensive conspiracy of heretics has been formed both within and without the Netherlands; that the leaguers have a force of thirty-five thousand men, horse and foot, now ready for action; and that they are about to take arms, unless they are assured of an immediate and formal concession of entire liberty of conscience. Within a week, fifteen hundred cavaliers will appear, to demand so much, here in Brussels, before your highness."*

This startling announcement was confirmed by Egmont. "So also speaks my information; but with this addition, that these men are leagued to revolutionize the government," said he. "Here, madame," he continued, "are the precise words of the new-fledged cabal."†

Margaret was speechless with astonishment. "Your highness," drily interposed the prince, "there is a modicum of truth in what you hear, but dame Rumor has absurdly exaggerated the story. 'T is not an armed league against the throne, though certes it may grow to that, but an organized protest against the Inquisition."‡

A stormy and indecisive debate ensued. "I shall order an immediate assembly of the notables," said the duchess; whereupon she retired to her cabinet, to report this new danger to Philip. "Sire," she wrote, "the time has come for you to take up arms, or to make large concessions."§

What did this rumor mean? What were the facts which spawned it?

Some months previous to this scene in the coun-

* Hoofd, tom. 2, pp. 71, 72. Hopper, Rec. et Mem., p. 69, et seq.   † Hopper, Rec. et Mem., p. 70.
    ‡ Ibid.   § Motley, vol. 1, p. 509.

cil-chamber, in the feverish November of 1565, a double wedding was celebrated at Brussels with lavish magnificence. The fated Montigny espoused a princess of the noble house of d'Espinay, and was to be called ere long to leave his bridal-chamber for an imprisonment which ended in a bloody death; and Margaret's son, Alexander of Parma, who had come back with Egmont from Spain, where he had been educated, married the young and beautiful Donna Maria of Portugal.*

All the world crowded up to Brussels to witness the *fêtes*. The ancient halls of the old dukes of Brabant, in whose palace the regent resided, were thronged by the loveliest women and the courtliest nobles of the age—soldiers, poets, artists, giddy with gayety. Smiles which cost a diamond each, wit which was paid a handful of gold a *mot*, abounded. Jousts and feastings made ultramontanism oblivious for an hour of the brooding revolt; the peal of merry marriage-bells drowned for an instant the wail of national despair.

In the midst of this mad revelry, while the courtiers and the triflers of the clubs floated themselves in dinner-stories and the gossip of the town, a sober company of twenty gentlemen were listening to a sermon in the palace of Count Culemberg.† The preacher was Francis Junius, a dissenting minister then settled in Antwerp, and now in Brussels by invitation. Young, eloquent, scholarly, Junius had

---

* Strada, p. 92, *et seq.*
† Brandt, vol. 1, p. 162. Vita Junii, p. 14, *et seq.*

studied divinity sitting at the feet of Calvin at Geneva, and he had proved his faith after the apostolic pattern, "in much patience, in afflictions, in necessities, in distresses;"[*] on one occasion advocating the doctrines of the Reformation with serenity in a room overlooking the Antwerp market-place, where at that very moment several of his parishioners were being martyred, while the light of the flames in which their bodies were sheeted flickered up through the glass windows of the conventicle.[†]

Now in Culemberg-house, Junius preached with his accustomed power. A grave conversation followed his sermon, and it was decided that a league should be formed against the Inquisition.[‡]

A little later this purpose was matured by a secret gathering at the baths of Spa. A paper call the "Compromise" was drawn up, by which its signers bound themselves to oppose the holy office, and to defend each other against all the consequences of this resistance.[§]

The original copy of this covenant bore but three names, those of Brederode, Charles Mansfeld, and Louis of Nassau;[‖] but it was speedily translated into half a dozen different tongues, and distributed throughout the provinces by scores of deft hands. Within sixty days, two thousand names

[*] 2 Cor. 6:4.   [†] Brandt, ubi sup.
[‡] Brandt, Vita Junii, ut antea.
[§] Motley, vol. 1, p. 494.
[‖] Ibid. Archives et Correspondance, tom. 2, p. 2, et seq.

were appended to the muster-roll of patriotism.*
The signatures represented all classes—nobles,
burghers, merchants, reformers, Romanists, priests,
men of all creeds and of none, various lives flooded
into one by common anxieties.   Ostensibly, it was
a league against the Inquisition ; the motives were
not the same with all, but the pretext was similar.
The papists desired to compass by it a mere mitigation of the too cruel edicts ; the Protestants aimed
through it at toleration ; traders esteemed it a good
business investment ; the needy and turbulent hailed
it as synonymous with anarchy ; a few keen souls
recognized it as a step towards revolution.†   This
was the strength and the weakness of the union ;
the strength, for it gave it numbers ; the weakness,
because it rested on an abnormal, heterogeneous
basis, sure to crumble in a crucial hour.   But these
were its halcyon days.   To sign the "Compromise"
became the rage.   It received the *imprimatur* of
fashion, one of the most potent of forces ; and this
blind Samson gave it the highest and the subtlest
of social distinctions.

At this time the movement was officered by
three individuals, Brederode, Louis of Nassau, and
Sainte Aldegonde,‡ men variously able and eminent.
Sainte Aldegonde especially, was one of the most
beautiful characters of his time ; and his motto,

---

* Correspondance de Philippe II., tom. 1, p. 400.   Strada.
† Schiller, p. 384,
‡ Strada, Meteren, Vandervynckt, Van der Haer.

"*Repos ailleurs*," seemed to indicate that the Sidney of the Netherlands, content with "rest hereafter," lent his earthly career to the stormy service of mankind.

Below Brederode and Nassau and Sainte Aldegonde stood Van Hammes, or "Golden Fleece," as he was styled from his connection with that order, whose king-at-arms he was, bluff, honest, tireless, and Count Culemburg, and Charles Mansfeld, who soon fell off, and a host of others inferior in position, but not in activity, to the chiefs of the league.*

The grandees were not among the signers of the "Compromise."† Orange would not identify his name with a movement officered by such a blundering swaggerer as Brederode; he reserved himself for a higher hour. Besides, he was still in the nominal confidence of the king, in whose name he held his stadtholderates. Horn followed the prince's lead. Egmont feared to compromise his relations with the court. But though the seigneurs thus held themselves aloof, the leaguers well knew that their protest against the subjection of the ancient liberties of the Netherlands to the fanatical whims of a junta of foreigners sitting at Madrid awoke an echo in the hearts of the patriot lords; while they gained fresh confidence from the refusal of the stadtholders to enforce the execution of the inquisitorial laws, and to countenance a human bon-

---

* Correspondance de Philippe II., tom. 1.
† Ibid., Strada, Prescott.

fire of sixty thousand victims ;* and from the accession to their ranks of the relatives, friends, and
retainers of the great families. If Orange was not
a leaguer, Nassau was; if Egmont stood aside, his
secretary was deep in the plot.†

Nor was the prince averse to using the league
as a counter in his game. He was aware that statesmanship wastes no strength—utilizes all elements.
He also knew, none better, that Philip was inflexi-
bly bent upon the establishment of the Inquisition.
The tortuous politics of Madrid were an open book
to him. The real views, the secret purposes, the
minutiæ of the plans of the king were regularly forwarded to William by spies—the eyes and ears of
princes—in his pay and in Philip's service.‡ Thus
it was that Machiavelli the patriot outwitted Machiavelli the tyrant.

With the heart of Philip in his hand, Orange
knew that to defeat his wily opponent's plots, it was
necessary to make the most of all the elements of
opposition in the Netherlands ; therefore he watched
the league.

Early in March, 1566, he was informed that the
leaguers were about to assemble at Breda for the

* Corresp. de Philippe II.

† Schiller, Procès Criminels des Comtes d'Egmont.

‡ There was one man especially who was very useful to Orange
in this capacity, a certain John of Castile, clerk to Andreas de las
Layas, the king's secretary; he, for a pension of three hundred
crowns, betrayed to the prince all the secrets of his master; and
as nearly all the affairs of the Netherlands were entrusted to the
hands of his master, the spy had ample means of acquiring the
fullest, most valuable information. Bor., book 16, bl. 288.

purpose of drawing up a petition to the regent against the holy office.* Under pretence of an invitation to a grand dinner —for it was a peculiarity of the Netherlands that there the most elaborate schemes were either hidden under a platter or cradled at banquets—the prince summoned a number of the seigneurs to meet him at the same time and place.† At his table, Horn, Egmont, Berghen, Montigny, and the rest, met Brederode and a deputation of the league. A conference ensued, which was soon adjourned to the town of Hoogstraaten.

Orange had a twofold object in this meeting; he wished to persuade the magnates to demand the convocation of the states-general, and he desired to win the leaguers to moderate the tone of their forthcoming petition.‡ He failed to compass his first purpose; the seigneurs, alarmed at the league, would not coöperate with it, even to the extent of asking for the states-general.§ He was more successful with the Covenanters; in obedience to his request, they softened the tone, but adhered to the object, of their petition.‖

So much for the inception of the "compromise;" and this was the situation when Margaret was apprized of its existence by Count Meghen.

True to her promise, the governant published a call for a convention of the notables; and letters were sent to Orange and Horn urgently requesting

* Motley, vol. 1, p. 506. Strada. † Ibid.
‡ Ibid. § Motley, vol. 1, p. 507.
‖ Ibid.

them to resume their seats in the council of state.*
Other portents besides the league made the duchess
tremble. The Netherlands seemed on the eve of
depopulation. Thirty thousand refugees had quitted the provinces and taken shelter under the
throne of Elizabeth.† Trade itself was an emigrant.
From time immemorial, silk and woollen stuffs had
formed the staple of an immense export trade from
the Low Countries to England. Now the current
was turned. The wise policy of Britain encouraged
the immigration of the Netherlands handicraftsmen.
Norwich and Sandwich were especially assigned to
them ; and the cunning islanders soon acquired the
secret of their craft. "The Low Countries," wrote
Assonleville to Granvelle, "are the Indies of the
English, who make war upon our purses as the
French, some years ago, made war upon our
towns."‡ This was sad ; but it was natural that
commerce and manufactures should hasten to escape from a doomed land.§

On the 28th of March, 1566, the notables assembled at Brussels.‖ "Gentlemen," said Margaret,
"I have summoned you that you may prevent, by
your counsels and endeavors, the impending evils.
And the first question which I have to ask is, Shall
this petition be received ?"¶

Barlaiment opposed its reception. "What need,"

---

* Brandt, vol. 1, p. 163 ; Strada, Schiller.
† Assonleville to Granvelle, in Cor. de Philippe II., tom. 1,
p. 392.   ‡ Ibid.   § Motley.
‖ Cor. de Philippe II., tom. 1, p. 403, et seq.
¶ Strada, p. 103.

queried he, "that so many people should deliver one petition? Let us either close the ports—which I favor; or else admit but one man with this paper, and if he carry himself contumaciously, let him be forthwith punished."[*]

Orange rose and rebuked this truculent language. "Let the petitioners be admitted to an audience," said he. "Treat them with respect. Many of them are my friends—some of them my relations; and there is no reason for refusing to gentlemen of their rank a right which belongs to the poorest plebeian in the land."[†]

The ultramontanists supported Barlaiment; the patriots sided with the prince. Finally, it was decided to receive the petitioners, who were to come unarmed; and at nightfall the assembly adjourned till the morrow.[‡]

On the following morning, the notables reassembled. The governant again opened the session with a speech, in which she apologized for the edicts, affirmed that the seigneurs had approved them, but asserted that she had no wish to influence the suffrage of the lieges. "And now," concluded she, "the question is, What answer shall be made to the petition?"[§]

Opinions were divided. The courtiers favored war; the patriots urged concession; Margaret inclined to temporize until the royal will could be

---

[*] Strada, p. 103.
[†] Ibid., Van der Haer, Pontus Payen MS.
[‡] Strada, *ubi sup.*   [§] Ibid.

ascertained. But an appeal to arms was absurd, since the leaguers were prepared for it, while the court exchequer was empty, and it was suspected that the few troops in the king's pay had been suborned. As for delay, it was suggested that the confederates would hardly permit themselves to be amused instead of answered. Orange pleaded boldly, convincingly, unanswerably for concession. Rising gravely, he said:

"Would to heaven I had been so happy as to have gained credence at the outset, when I foretold what has now come to pass. Then the last measures would not have been first invoked, nor would errorists have been made desperate by the extremest expedients. Would not that physician be thought out of his wits, who, instead of using gentle medicines in the commencement of disease, should begin by burning or cutting off the infected part?

"Now, on one point we are unanimous: we all wish to secure religion—but we differ as to the means. The Inquisition is one way. There are two kinds of Inquisition: the one is exercised in the name of the pope, and the other has been long practised by the bishops. To this last, men are in some measure reconciled by the force of custom; and considering how well we are now provided with bishops in these states, it would seem that this sort should alone suffice. As to the other, the repugnance of the people is manifest. This must be appeased, if we would not have it burst into rebellion. With the recent death of Pius IV., the full powers of the papal inquisitors have expired; the new pontiff has, as yet, sent no ratification of their authority. Now, therefore, is the time when it can be suspended without wrong to any party.

"So, too, with the edicts: the exigency which evoked them has passed. Heed not me, but listen to experience; and does not that teach that persecution increases error? and that the severity of the punishment is a temptation to the sin? The Netherlands have, of late years, been a school, in which, if we have not been extremely inattentive, we might have learned the folly of persecution. Have not many been drawn from the church by the contemplation of the heroism and serenity of those who have received the death-sentence as an invitation to a wedding, running with joy to the fiery trial? Such spectacles work on popular compassion, excite universal sympathy, and create a suspicion that the truth must certainly be found where so much constancy and fortitude are found.

"Now, these are the bitter pills which have been administered to patients in England and in France, and now here with us; but with what success? Let the incredible progress which the new religion has made respond. Well might it be said by the Christians of old that 'the blood of the martyrs is the seed of the church.' The emperor Julian, the most formidable enemy whom Christianity ever saw, was sensible of this truth. He had recourse, therefore, to the weapons of ridicule and contempt; and these he found far more effective than the

use of force. Force makes no impression on the
conscience—serves, in sooth, but to awaken zeal;
which liberty, ease, and idleness soon lay asleep.

"The Greek empire was, at different periods,
infected with various heresies. Arius taught errors
in the reign of Constantine; Hetius, in that of Constance; and Nestorius under Theodosius. No such
punishments were inflicted, either on the heresiarchs
themselves, or on their disciples, as are now practised in the Netherlands. Banishment was the
penalty; and though there were blood-edicts, they
were only *in terrorem*. Yet where are all those
false opinions now? Heresy is like iron in its nature: if it rests, it rusts; but he who rubs it, whets
it. If it is neglected, it loses its novelty, and with
that its attractiveness. Why have not we contented ourselves with similar measures? Surely example is the best and safest of guides.

"But what need to go to pagan antiquity for
guidance and example? A precedent is at hand:
Charles V., the greatest of kings, himself taught by
experience, for some years before his abdication
abandoned the blood-path of persecution and adopted milder curbs for heresy. The king of Spain,
our prince, seemed inclined, at one time, to walk in
the steps of the great emperor, his father, and to
make trial of gentler expedients. Through the influence of ecclesiastics, he has changed his views:
let these men answer for their conduct, if they can.
For my own part, I am satisfied that it is impossible to root out the new creed in these provinces

without also plucking up the foundations of the state.

"I conclude with reminding your highness, and you, seigneurs, of the connection which subsists between the French reformers and the Flemish Protestants. Beware, lest in acting the part of the French Romanists towards them, they be driven to play the Huguenots with us. Then, adieu prosperity, farewell peace; for our country would be plunged into the horrors of a civil war."*

This massive plea beat down all opposition : it was decided in advance that concessions should be made.†

On the 3d of April, 1566, in the gray of the evening, the petitioners entered Brussels. At the head of two hundred cavaliers rode Brederode ; and as the horsemen wheeled slowly through the streets, they were wildly cheered by the sympathetic populace.‡ Twelve hours later, Culemberg and Van den Berg came into town, bringing with them a hundred more cavaliers to swell the retinue of the league.§

Two days afterwards, the confederates, three hundred strong, met at Culemberg House, and there forming in procession, marched two abreast up the straight, handsome street to the summit of the hill where stood the ancient palace of the Bra-

---

* Bergundias, Hist. Belg., lib. 2.   *Vide* Brandt, vol. 1, p. 164.
† Strada, p. 106. Hopper.
‡ Bor., tom. 2, p. 58. Cor. de Philippe II.
§ Ibid.

bantine dukes, and where Margaret was to give them audience.* And now again, as the petitioners, young, titled, and splendidly attired, pressed forward, the thronging masses greeted those whom they esteemed the deliverers of the land with deafening shouts of welcome and Godspeed.†

The palace was soon reached; and there, seated on her throne of state and surrounded by the Netherland grandees, was the governant, waiting to receive her unwelcome visitors. Brederode, always unabashed, opened the interview with a low obeisance and a few commonplaces. Then the petition was read. It made two demands. The duchess was requested to send an envoy to Madrid humbly to implore the king to abolish the edicts; meantime, she was asked to suspend the Inquisition until Philip's pleasure should be known, and until new ordinances, made by the king with the advice and consent of the states-general duly assembled, should be established.‡

Margaret listened with emotion, and promised to return an answer after consultation with her councillors.§ The petitioners withdrew.

An excited debate ensued. Orange defended the confederates against the charge of being seditious rebels. Egmont, on being asked his opinion, shrugged his shoulders, and said, "It will be necessary for me to leave court for a space, as I wish to visit

* Motley, vol. 1, p. 512.   † Ibid.
‡ See the petition in Brandt, vol. 1, pp. 164, 165.
§ Hopper, Rec. et Mem. Motley.

the baths of Aix for an inflammation which I have in the leg."* Barlaiment was in a passion; and it was now that he uttered that taunt which gave a name to the patriot party, destined to become as immortal as that given to the French reformers when they were stigmatized as "Huguenots." "Madame," said he, "is it possible that you can entertain fears of these *gueux*†—beggars? Is it not obvious that they are broken spendthrifts plotting for gain in anarchy? They have not wisdom enough to manage their own estates; how, then, shall they teach your highness how to govern the country? By the living God, if my advice were taken, they should have a cudgel for a commentary. I would send them down the steps of the palace much faster than they mounted them."‡ This advice was congenial to Margaret, but she dared not follow it.

On the morning of the 6th of April, the confederates came before the regent for an answer to their request. It was written on the margin of the petition, and was to this effect: "Her highness has no authority to suspend the edicts; but she will despatch envoys to acquaint his majesty with your demands. Meantime she will order all inquisitors to proceed modestly and discreetly in their office."§

The petitioners took the paper, and retired to

* Pontus Payen MS. Cited in Motley, vol. 1, p. 515.

† The word *gueux* means not only a beggar, but a *sturdy* beggar. *Vide* Brandt, *ubi sup.*

‡ Pontus Payen MS. Cited in Motley, vol. 1, p. 515.

§ Groen v. Prinst., tom. 2, p. 84, *et seq.* Bor. Strada.

consult. They were not satisfied with the reply.[*] It was characterized as a quibble—as an evasion. On the 8th of April, Brederode and his comrades once more craved audience of the duchess. They were admitted. "Madame," asked Brederode, "is this all that you can say?" "It is," was the curt reply; "I will send envoys to the king; and here before me are instructions already drawn up, ready to be transmitted to the *inquisitori*. I can do no more." "At least permit our request to be printed," said Brederode. "It shall be so," replied the duchess. "Will you not also declare that we have done nothing inconsistent with loyalty to the king?" queried the pertinacious spokesman. Margaret's lip curled. "Of that I cannot judge," said she; "time must determine."[†]

Forced to rest content with these assurances, the leaguers chose four directors for the management of their affairs, who were to remain in Brussels; and at the same time, local committees were appointed to see that the peace was kept in the provinces, and to insure that the governant should keep her promises:[‡] then they prepared to separate.

Before the separation, however, Brederode, who thought that an object was never consummated until it was crowned by a dinner, invited the three hundred to a banquet at Culemburg House.[§] As

[*] Hopper, Bor.   [†] Ibid. Strada, p. 108.
[‡] Brandt, vol. 1, p. 166. Bor. Hopper.
[§] Strada. Bentivoglio, tom. 2. Hopper.

was usual when Brederode was host, there was a wild carouse. After the most sumptuous of dinners, the wine began to flow, and the noble bacchanals never wearied of drinking the health of the cause, of Brederode, of Egmont, of Orange.

Drunk with wine and hot with patriotic fervor, the company began to canvass the prospects of the league, when some one asked, " What shall be the name of our union?" With drunken gravity Brederode rose. "I am prepared to answer that question," hiccoughed he. "'Tis said that good Barlaiment styled us *gueux* in open council. Beggars for our rights we are: let us accept the name. We will contend with the Inquisition, but remain loyal to the king, even till compelled to wear the beggar's sack. Gentlemen, pledge me the beggars—*Vivent les gueux!*"

The mad-brained company sprang to their feet and drained their goblets in honor of the toast with boisterous excitement. Then, for the first time, and on the tipsy lips of reckless nobles, was heard the famous cry which was to ring over land and sea, amid blazing cities, on blood-stained decks, through the smoke and carnage of many a stricken field.

Brederode's humor was not yet exhausted. Seizing a leathern wallet and a wooden bowl, the regular appurtenances of the mendicants of the time, he slung the first about his neck, and again drained the bowl to the cry of "*Vivent les gueux!*" Each guest in turn donned the beggar's knapsack and took the bowl; and when the circuit of the table had been made, wallet and bowl were suspended to a pillar of the hall. The rites by which the league received its name were completed by the repetition of an impromptu distich, which was solemnly chanted by all, as each in succession threw salt into his goblet, and placed himself under the suspended symbol of the brotherhood:

" By this salt, by this bread, by this wallet we swear,
These beggars ne'er will change, though the world should stare."

The wassail was at its wildest when Orange and Horn and Egmont entered the apartment in search of Hoogstraaten, whom they wished to carry away with them. They were at once surrounded and compelled to drink to the health of the beggars—which they did, not knowing what the pledge meant. Their presence brought the festivities to a premature close, and the riotous cavaliers staggered off to bed.*

What they had resolved upon while drunk, the confederates prepared to perform when sober. They knew the value of a striking and original name. In the epithet *gueux* their opponents had given them precisely what they wanted. The word "beggars," while it cloaked their enterprise in humility, was at the same time appropriate to them as petitioners. What, then, could be better than to adopt this

---

* This scene is narrated in full by most contemporaneous chroniclers. An account of it is also given by Motley—vol. 1, pp. 519-523—and by Prescott.

name of *gueux*, and to borrow from it the tokens of the association?

"In a few days," says Schiller, "the town of Brussels swarmed with ash-gray garments, cut in the true mendicant fashion. Every leaguer clothed his family and put his retainers in this dress. Some carried wooden bowls thinly overlaid with plates of silver, cups of the same pattern, and wooden knives; in short, the whole paraphernalia of the beggar tribe, which they either fixed about their hats or wore suspended from their girdles. Round the neck the titled 'beggars' hung a golden or silver coin afterwards called the 'Guesen penny,' on one side of which was the effigy of the king, with the inscription, 'True to the king;' and on the reverse were seen two hands folded, holding a wallet, with the words, 'Even to the beggar's scrip.'"*

It was a jest which hid a growl.

* Schiller, p. 496.

CHAPTER XXIII.

FIELD-PREACHING.

WHILE the leaguers were still streaming home from the Brussels rendezvous, Margaret, seated in her cabinet, was sketching a pen-picture of all that had occurred for Philip's eye. With pre-Raphael-ite precision, she omitted nothing; the most trivial gossip was daubed upon the canvas, even to a rep-resentation of Brederode eating capons at Antwerp on Good Friday; the accuracy of which, by-the-by, "the great beggar," as he was called, stoutly denied. "They who say so," said he, "lie miserably and wickedly, twenty-four feet down in their throats."*

When this budget of facts and scandal was safely off, the duchess assembled her most confidential councillors to consult with her upon a plan which she had hatched for the mitigation of the edicts, in such shape as to keep the mean between the royal wishes and the popular demands.† Viglius—who had recently received Philip's permission to resign his seat at the council-board, though ordered to discharge the duties of his office pending the arri-val of his successor, Charles de Tisnacq, then in

* Groen v. Prinst., Archives, etc., tom. 2, pp. 98, 99.
† Bor., tom. 1. Strada. Vita Viglii.

Spain*—was requested by the governant to draw
up the form. The pedantic doctor willingly complied. Fearful lest his labor should, like the homilies of the fictitious bishop of Granada, smack of
the apoplexy which had laid him senseless, and
anxious that this last service should be his *chef-
d'œuvre*, he painfully elaborated fifty-three articles,
which were run into a legal mould by Chancellor
d'Assonleville, and named "The Moderation."†

In reality, this misnamed "moderation" was a
mere substitution of the halter for the stake.‡ When
a rumor of its preparation and purport leaked into
the ears of the people, as it did while it was still
under discussion in the council-chamber, they killed
it ere it was born, by a witticism. "This 'moderation'" said they, with a play upon words, the same
in Dutch as in English, "is a 'murderation.'"§

Unaware or heedless of this sarcasm, the duchess
continued to occupy herself with her project. "The
question is," said Margaret, "whether it is best to
promulgate the 'moderation' at once, or first to
submit it to the king for his approval." The councillors held that it would be presumptuous to publish
it without the royal sanction, but they advised her
highness to submit it to the states for their approval,
and when this was granted to send it to Madrid.‖

Of course, the proposed "moderation" should

---

* Vita Viglii, p. 45.
† Bor., tom. 1. Meteren, tom. 2. Hoofd, tom. 3.
‡ Motley, vol. 1, p. 527.
§ Meteren, tom. 2, p. 38. Hoofd, Brandt.
‖ Hoofd, Schiller.

have been submitted to the states-general; but Philip had vetoed the convocation of the national assembly, therefore the governant had recourse to a stratagem. She laid it secretly before the individual provinces, commencing with those which were smallest, and whose franchises were least liberal—Artois, Namur, Luxemburg—and when these assented, Flanders and Brabant were cozened into subserviency.* As for the northern states, Holland, Utrecht, Zealand, and the rest, where the spirit of independence was high and vigilant, they were not consulted;† it was forwarded to Philip without their assent.

Margaret had promised the petitioners to accredit an envoy to Madrid, armed with authority to demand the abolition of the Inquisition in the name of the nation. She selected Berghen, who, on account of the delicacy of the embassage, begged for a coadjutor. Montigny was chosen, and he at last gave a reluctant assent to act.‡ The instructions of these ambassadors were made out in accordance with the "moderation" scheme,§ and Montigny set out for Spain on the 29th of May. Berghen was detained for some weeks by a bruised thigh, hurt by a tennis-ball; but he too eventually quitted Brussels for the Segovian forest, where Philip spent his summers.‖

This mission, undertaken with reluctance and

* Hoofd, Schiller.   † Ibid., Brandt, Meteren.
‡ Hoofd, tom. 3.   Strada, p. 113.   Schiller.   § Ibid.
‖ Corresp. de Philippe II., tom. 1, p. 426.

half-stayed by accident, was destined to end in a
double tragedy; the hapless seigneurs went forward,
one to be murdered the other to die on a foreign
shore.   But the shadow of this doom did not immediately fall upon them.   Philip knew how to wait;
and he received the envoys graciously,* though at
the same time contriving to delay them in Spain until
he was ready to throw off the mask—playing with
his victims as a spider dallies with the fly he has
entangled in his web, and ending all by the fatal
pounce.

While the victim ambassadors were journeying
to their graves, the march of events in the country
they were to see no more went forward with a steady
step.   The summer of 1566 marked a new epoch.
Up to this time the record had been one of fanatical tyranny on the part of the court, of patient
endurance on the part of the reformed, of constitutional opposition on the part of the middle classes,
of petulant, spasmodic resistance on the part of the
lesser nobles, of persistent protest on the part of the
grandees.   Now the reformed no longer demanded
their rights; they took them.   Hitherto they had
met stealthily at midnight, rendezvoused in the
depths of the Netherland forests, skulked into upper
chambers to worship God.   At last, despairing of
governmental recognition, and emboldened by the
outspoken sympathy of the leaguers and by the
covert protection of the seigneurs, they threw off
disguise and began to meet publicly.   "If we are

---

* Corresp. de Philippe II., tom. 1, p. 426.   Hopper.

to be murdered," said they, "we will show the Inquisition how many it will have to burn and hang and banish."[*]

The confidence of the reformed was yet more increased by a declaration, forged by a party of reckless *gueux*, which guaranteed that no one should be molested on account of religion, pending the answer of the king to the recent demands of the confederates, and which purported to have been signed by the knights of the Golden Fleece.[†]   The knights themselves promptly branded this paper as spurious, and the duchess made every effort to expose the fraud.   It was useless; the report had served its purpose, and, to borrow Strada's quaint metaphor, "Wool that had been dipped in ink was incapable of another dye."[‡]

Forbidden to assemble in chapels and banned in the haunts of men, the Netherland Protestants were compelled, when they decided to convene openly, to stream forth from the gates of their cities into the adjacent meadows to erect their altars.   "Space," said Newton, "is the sensorium of the Deity."   The Low Country reformers recognized this truth long before the great Englishman put it into words, and the intuition begat field-preaching.

These out-of-door conventicles were first held in Western Flanders; thence the custom passed into Brabant, and from there it spread into all the other provinces with such rapidity that, by the middle of

---

[*] Davies, vol. 1, p. 526.

[†] Strada, p. 112, *et seq.*   [‡] Ibid.

July, 1566, there was not a lowland city which did
not have its camp-meetings as regularly attended as
the popish masses; while the audiences, small at
the outset, soon swelled to tens of thousands.*   The
devotion of the faithful, the curiosity of the careless, the novelty of the spectacle, every motive conspired to recruit a multitude of auditors; and while
the devout were strengthened and comforted, many
a roysterer who had slipped into the throng only to
laugh or to scoff at a comedy richer than the play-
house could present, returned with conviction hidden in his heart: for the human mind cannot be
isolated on a glass cricket; the lightning of thought
strikes when least expected.   Here in these open-
air cathedrals, grander than St. Peter's, vaster than
a score of Nôtre Dames, whose vaulted roof was the
empyrean, whose blazing tapers were the unquench-
ed stars, whose cushioned auditorium was God's own
green-sward—here thousands of weary, sinful hearts
found rest in Jesus; here hundreds of couples were
united in marriage; here multitudes were hallowed
to God's service.

The field-preachers were men eminently deserving of respect. Though outlawed and hunted
down, walking always in "the valley of the shadow
of death," and in constant danger of the halter and
the stake, they had cast fear from out their hearts,
and they proclaimed the gospel with an ardor as
fiery as that of Peter, with a faith as rapt as that of
the seer of the apocalyptic vision. Some among

* Brandt, vol. 1, p. 171. Vita Junii.

them there were, indeed, whose zeal was little tempered with discretion. and some too who were un-
lettered and of lowly station—dyers, curriers, hat-
ters—disciples who, thinking they had a call to
preach, carried the rude and boisterous manners of
their trades into the pulpit, and incurred the disdainful contempt of the learned by their extravagance and occasional license. But to men who,
girt by duty, dare and suffer greatly, much may be
pardoned.

Besides, these humble laborers were not the
only workers in the vineyard ; nor, indeed, were
they the majority. In the ranks of the reformed
clergy there were men of the finest æsthetic culture,
of the most graceful accomplishments, and of the
grandest eloquence—converted monks, like Luther,
and ripe scholars, graduated at Geneva.* These,
to the widow's mite of the homely preachers, added the splendid dower of their dedicated genius.
There was Peter Dathenus, who preached night and
day with prodigious effect at various places in
Western Flanders ;† there was Hermann Strycker,
another monk who had renounced his vows to become a successful preacher of the Reformation—a
man of stormy eloquence, who stately addressed
eight thousand auditors in the neighborhood of
Ghent ;‡ and there were the accomplished Ambrose
Wille, and Marnier, Guy de Bray, and Francis
Junius—whom Scaliger called "the greatest of all

---

* Brandt, vol. 1, p. 170, et seq., passim.   Vita Junii.   Hoofd.
† Ibid. Motley, vol. 1, p. 533.   ‡ Ibid.

theologians since apostolic days;"* and Peregrine de la Grange, scion of a noble Provençal family, with the fiery blood of southern France in his veins, brave as his nation, a troubadour and a Vaudois by right of inheritance, learned, eloquent, enthusiastic; who galloped to his field, preaching on horseback, and fired a pistol-shot as a signal for his congregation to give attention :† these and many more there were, who lent lustre and dignity to the cause they had espoused.

The assemblies which these men addressed grew vaster every day. On Sundays and holidays there was always preaching in the environs of the large towns.‡ The authorities gazed on these gatherings with open-mouthed amazement. The boldness of the heretics stupefied them. At length, however, they essayed to disperse the meetings. On one occasion, a magistrate of Ghent undertook to disturb a great assembly convened almost within sound of the iron tongue of Roland. Mounting a horse and seizing a naked sword and a pistol, he rode in among the multitude and made an effort to arrest the preacher. The people were unarmed, but their zeal soon furnished them with extemporized weapons. A storm of stones fell upon the interloper; and sorely bruised, he put spurs to his courser and sped back to the protection of the city walls.§

After this rencontre, the reformed went to their

* Cited in Motley, *ubi sup.* † Motley, *ut antea.*
‡ Hoofd, Strada, Vita Junii, Cor. de Philippe II., tom. 1.
§ Brandt, vol. 1, pp. 171, 172.

conventicles armed.   Pikes, staves, hatchets, guns,
the most motley weapons were impressed; sentinels
were stationed at the different avenues of approach;
bands of horsemen scoured the plains between the
rendezvous and the city; and a kind of camp was
formed and rudely intrenched behind carts.   When
these precautions were taken, a rough staging was
erected in the centre of the ground, and covered
with an awning.   The preacher mounted this pulpit; and the hearers, grouping themselves about
it—the women and children in front, the men behind, the patrol in the outer circle—sermons were
listened to, prayers were offered, and psalms were
sung by ten thousand voices in the mother-tongue,
until the welkin rang with the rude harmony.*
Either the sermons were better in those days than
in ours, or the listeners were more easily satisfied;
for it was common for an audience to sit four uninterrupted hours in rapt, unflagging attention to a
favorite minister.†   Nor were the pastors fierce
inveighers against law and order; often they
breathed the most Christian spirit, and even while
groaning under the cross, they prayed for all conditions of men—for themselves, for their friends,
for the government which hunted and bound them,
for the king whose face was turned on them in
fanatical anger.‡

But these men were resolute to maintain their
rights.   Before the services commenced, hawkers

* Brandt, vol. 1, p. 172.   Hoofd.
† Ibid., *et seq.*, *passim*.   ‡ Ibid.

sold the prohibited books; and when sometimes a cry was raised that the militia were approaching, the stern reply was, as each man grasped his weapon, "Let them come; we are ready to receive them."* When the exercises were concluded, the camp was broken up, and the multitude quietly dispersed at the city gates.†

Such was field-preaching in the Netherlands in the year 1566. This scene was everywhere reproduced—at Valenciennes, at Ghent, at Amsterdam, at Haarlem, at the Hague; it was the locality alone that shifted.‡

But Antwerp was the great centre of these demonstrations.§ Here there were three dominant sects: the Lutherans, who were the wealthiest; the Anabaptists, who were the most quiet; the Calvinists, who were the most numerous and active.‖ Widely at variance on minor points of faith, they were a unit against persecution; and though they sometimes assailed each other with rancor, an allusion to the common foe melted all differences into cordial union.

The Calvinists were especially identified with the field-preaching. Ambrose Wille and Peregrine de la Grange often assembled twenty thousand people to listen to them at the bridge of Eronville, just without Antwerp gates.¶ After the sermon,

* Brandt, vol. p. 172. Hoofd.   † Ibid.
‡ Cor. de Philippe II.
§ Bor., tom. 2. Strada, p. 117.
‖ Schiller, p. 505. Motley, vol. 1, pp. 537, 538.
¶ Renom de Francia, MS. Cited in Prescott, vol. 2, p. 31.

the reformers openly escorted their preachers back to town, and gave them hospitable entertainment, defying interference.*

The *gueux* witnessed this outburst with secret pleasure. "There will soon be a hard nut to crack," said Louis of Nassau. "The king will never permit the preaching; the people will never give it up, if it costs them their necks. There's a hard puff coming upon the country before long."† The court beheld the movement with mingled awe and anger. Margaret smeared the provinces with placards reciting the freezing penalties which awaited heresy; put a price upon the heads of the prominent preachers; offered a reward of six hundred florins to whoever should bring an offender to punishment; and sent message after message to the municipalities, whom she ordered to disperse the mass-meetings by calling out the citizen train-bands.‡ But this war of proclamations was futile; men who had not feared to brave the Inquisition, were not to be frightened by parchment *fiats*. With other weapons the duchess could not fight. Without money and without troops, she could only rave—though she did, indeed, attempt to exorcise the spirit which was abroad by "public prayers, processions, fasts, sermons, and exhortations;"§ all, however, without effect, as she afterwards assured the king.‖

* Ibid. Strada, *ubi sup.*
† Groen v. Prinst., Archives, etc., tom. 2, p. 208.
‡ Strada, p. 117. Brandt, vol. 1, p. 173.
§ Cor. de Marguerite d'Autriche, p. 84.
‖ Cor. de Philippe II., tom. 1, p. 432.

As for the magistrates, they received these orders with many· expressions of zeal; but they were as powerless as the governant. How could the guild militia of the cities, the crossbowmen of St. Maurice, the archers of St. Sebastian, the sword-players of St. Christopher, be ordered out to suppress the preaching, when they had themselves gone to the preaching? Often, indeed, these very magistrates were the pillars of the temple they were bidden to pull down—might be seen listening approvingly to the preachers they had received orders to arrest.*

Meantime, grown bolder from impunity, the reformed began to clamor for legal recognition. At Antwerp, they waited upon the magistrates and formally demanded the appropriation of some chapel to their worship within the gates of the city.† The authorities were in a dilemma: they dared not say yes, and they feared to say no. The town was feverishly excited. Trade, proverbially timid, was at a stand-still. Merchants, fearful of a riot, locked and double-barred their shops. The streets were ominously crowded. Margaret was informed of the sinister situation of the commercial capital of Europe. "Hasten to our relief," cried the vested interests of Antwerp. "I fear to stir," was the laconic response. "At least send the prince of Orange," said frightened conservatism. The prince was reluctant to go: he preferred watch-

* Motley, vol. 1, p. 535.   Prescott, vol. 2, p. 27.
† Brandt, *ubi sup.*

fulness to action at this crisis. The governant disliked to send him; already over-powerful, she feared
that he might win new laurels. But the danger was
imminent; the burghers were clamorous; Orange
was hereditary burgrave of the imperilled city, and
he seemed the only person able to subdue sedition:
so the reluctance of the prince and the jealousy of
the duchess were alike overborne, and William set
out for Antwerp.*

On entering the perturbed town, he at once addressed himself to business. Consultations were
held with every department of the municipality; no
one was neglected, no one was wronged. Orange
worked to restore quiet with restless energy and
profound tact. His task was no easy one; animos-
ities were kindled, fears were rife, rumors of the
coming of a mercenary garrison were on every lip.
But eventually he prevailed; mutual confidence was
restored, and the reformed consented to waive their
right of worship within the corporation limits, out
of the especial respect they bore the prince, on condition that they were protected in the fields.† It
was evident that there was to be no outbreak in
Antwerp while Orange remained.

This brilliant success won the cap-in-hand congratulations of the court. "This seigneur is very
skilful in the management of great affairs," said
Assonleville.‡ Margaret was profusely complimen-

---

* Hoofd, tom. 2, p. 87. Strada, p. 118. Brandt.
† Meteren, folio 42. Brandt, vol. 1, pp. 173–176. Strada.
‡ Cited in Motley, vol. 1, p. 542.

tary.* Philip himself wrote to assure William of his grateful satisfaction and of his undiminished confidence;† a message which the shrewd prince valued at its exact worth. At this very time the duchess was avenging herself upon the saviour of Antwerp, by assuring the king that Orange was a traitor at heart. "I am thoroughly aware," wrote she, "that this 'good friend' aims at self-aggrandizement through these tumults."‡

While the prince was thus busied at Antwerp, the governant received a fresh shock. She was told that the *gueux* had published a call for a convention at the town of St. Trond, in the bishopric of Liege. In the middle of July, the leaguers, to the number of two thousand, assembled in stormy conclave.§ Scenting danger in the reticence of Philip, who had as yet returned no reply to their petition, and undecided how to shape their future course, they now met for mutual counsel.‖ Two questions were especially debated: whether they were safe in case the king should resent their action, and whether they ought to ask for ampler liberty than was demanded in the petition against the Inquisition.¶ Touching the first point, the conventionalists voted to require the regent to insure their security.** As regards the second question, opinions differed, and no defi-

---

* Cited in Motley, vol. 1, p. 542.

† Corresp. de Guillaume le Tacit., tom. 2, pp. 170, 171.

‡ Vide Strada, p. 121.

§ Ibid. Archives de la Maison d'Orange-Nassau, tom. 2, p. 171.

‖ Ibid. Schiller, Prescott.

¶ Strada, p. 119. Vandervynckt.   ** Ibid.

nite decision was reached.* Those who were Romanists said: "We can go no farther; the Inquisition is bad, but toleration is infinitely worse." Those who were Protestants replied: "You mistake the halfway-house for the end of the journey." This discussion revealed the weakness of the *gueux*, laid bare the substratum of radical disagreement; showed each party the purpose of the other. The stancher papists, led by Charles Manfeld, at once renounced the league.†

No whit discouraged by this bolt, the confederates continued their deliberations. The longer they talked and the oftener they shouted, *Vivent les gueux*, the more radical they grew, until at last they decided upon two things: in answer to memorials presented to them by the reformed, they formally granted the protection of the league to all religionists pending the decision of the states-general‡—an act which openly identified the *gueux* with the sectaries; and they subsidized a force of German men-at-arms, consisting of four thousand horse and forty companies of foot, to be at their disposal in case of need.§

Apprized by her spies of these doings at St. Trond, Margaret summoned Egmont from his stadtholderate in Flanders, and called Orange from his post at Antwerp, to meet and remonstrate with the *gueux* leaders.‖ A conference was held at the village

---

* Strada, p. 119. Vandervynckt. Groen v. Prinst., Archives, etc. † Ibid.

‡ Groen, Archives de la Maison d'Orange-Nassau, tom. 2, p. 159. § Ibid., p. 167.

‖ Strada, p. 119, *et seq.* Groen v. Prinst., Archives, etc., tom. 2.

of Duffel, in the vicinage of Antwerp.* "Wherefore this new move?" demanded the governant through the lips of the two seigneurs—upon whom, by-the-by, she always fell back at critical moments.

Brederode, Culemburg, and the rest of the deputation replied in a strain of rare boldness: "Know then, messieurs envoys, that the pledges of her highness were a clever farce; that she has played us false; that the 'moderation' was a mockery; that the letters to the *Inquisition* were waste-paper; that a price has been set upon the heads of preachers, as if they were wild beasts; that the ambassadors are still unanswered; that the states-general are still unconvened; and that the government has driven the people to despair, not the *gueux*."†

This crimination and recrimination could have but one result; the seigneurs returned to Brussels to report their failure.‡ But the leaguers did not rest here; a paper was drawn up in solemn vindication of their conduct; and this, Louis of Nassau, accompanied by a dozen friends who were irreverently styled "Count Louis' twelve disciples,"§ set out to deliver to the governant.‖ Nassau laid the document before her highness in council. In it the

---

* Strada, p. 120.
† Motley, vol. 1, p. 548. Vandervynckt.
‡ Groen v. Prinst., Arch., etc. Meteren.
§ Strada, p. 120.
‖ Ibid. Vandervynckt, Bentivoglio.

gueux disclaimed all desire for pardon; what they had done deserved only honor; they demanded security, because that was a guaranty of their right of petition. As for the rest, two things would satisfy them—the convocation of the states-general, and an agreement on the part of her highness to take no important step without the guidance of Orange, Egmont, and Horn.*

The tone of this memorial is much more haughty than that of the petition. It marks the progress of opinion in the Netherlands, and shows that in revolutions, concessions which would be deemed amply satisfactory at the outset, if too long withheld, but serve to whet the appetite of demand.

To this audacious paper Margaret returned an evasive reply. "Madame," said the leaguers, "do not drive us to violence; if you do, you will find that we are not without assured friends, both here and abroad."† With this sinister threat on their lips, the *gueux* deputies quitted Brussels. The governant at once wrote Philip to implore him to come to some speedy decision. " The sectaries go armed, and the league is with them," so ran her letter; "nothing remains but for the two to band together and sack towns and churches."‡

Cornered by obstinate necessity, Philip was again compelled to act. Summoning his councillors to consult with him at the grove of Segovia, he

---

* Hoofd, tom. 2, p. 98.   Hopper, p. 94, *et seq.*
† Groen v. Prinst., Archives, etc., tom. 2, p. 167.
‡ Corresp. de Marguerite d'Autriche, p. 121.

laid the situation of the Netherlands before them, and solicited their opinion of the fittest means to stifle the smoking embers of mutiny. Many and protracted were the sittings of the council, incredible was the number of the notes which the royal clerk made, fatally slow was the haste of all.*

The councillors agreed in thinking that the Low Country grandees were plotting to secure the independence of the provinces. They read this fact in the legible writing of four events: the pressure for Granvelle's recall; the mission of Egmont to Madrid to urge the mitigation of the penal statutes; the league of the *gueux;* and the present embassy of Burghen and Montigny to demand the abolition of the Inquisition, the adoption of the "Moderation," and the proclamation of an amnesty for the past. Nevertheless the royal advisers counselled Philip to bend to the storm until he was ready to breast it, and, meantime, to depart at once for Brussels.†

The king pleaded that the stormy season of the year was approaching, and suggested that the *gueux* might oppose his landing in the Netherlands, unless he should be accompanied by an armed force; and for these reasons he esteemed it best to postpone his visit to Brussels until the spring of 1567.‡ As for the rest, he accepted the advice of his council-

---

* Hopper, then in Spain, was a member of this council, and he has reported its doings in his Recueil et Mémorial, pp. 81, 87.

† Hopper, Rec. et Mem., *ubi sup.*

‡ Corresp. de Marg. d'Autriche, p. 100, *et seq.*

lors in the most literal sense.   Retiring to his cabinet, he addressed a letter to Margaret, under date
of July 31, 1566, to this effect: "I consent to the
abolition of the papal Inquisition in the Netherlands; substitute for it the episcopal form.   The
plan of 'moderation' is far too mild.   'T is equivalent to a concession of toleration within the domi-
ciles of individuals.   Veto!   Draw up some new
form more careful of the faith, and send it here to
be weighed and considered ere it becomes a law.
In respect to a general pardon, as I abhor rigor, I
am content that it should be extended to whomsoever you choose, always excepting those already
condemned; and under a solemn pledge, moreover,
that the nobles at once abandon their league, and
henceforth heartily support the government."*

This was the mouse which the long-laboring
mountain had brought forth—this was the panacea
esteemed fit and able to cure the national complaint.

But even these meagre and absurd "concessions" were not sincerely granted; they were a
mere jumble of unmeaning words, meant to cheat
the public mind.   Four days afterwards, Philip
wrote privately to the duchess, peremptorily and
absolutely forbidding her to consent to a meeting
of the states-general; yet he commanded her on no
account to make this mandate known, but to lead
all to imagine that the national assembly would
soon be convened.†   At the same time he bade

* Corresp. de Marg. d'Autriche, p. 100, *et seq.*   † Ibid.

Margaret prepare secretly for war; and he transmitted to her three hundred thousand gold florins
with which to recruit an army of ten thousand foot
and three thousand horse.*   By the same carrier,
the most gracious and seductive letters were sent
to the ultramontane nobles of the provinces.†

But the masterpiece of kingcraft remained behind. While the ink was hardly dry on the parchment which recited the royal concessions, Philip
enacted a characteristic comedy.   "Call a notary,"
said he; and one soon appeared.   "Now summon
Alva and two legists;" they entered the apartment.
"Gentlemen," said the king, "I hereby solemnly
protest that the amnesty which I have proclaimed
in the Low Countries was not made of my own free
will; therefore I do not feel bound by it, but reserve
to myself the right to punish the authors and abet-
tors of sedition in the provinces."   A document to
this effect was drawn up and signed by the king
and by the three witnesses whom he had summoned.‡

Nor was this all. Making a confessor of the
pope, he explained to his holiness, through the
mouth of Requesens, the Spanish ambassador at
Rome, that the recent royal decisions would not
have been made without consultation with the Vatican, had not time pressed. "Assure his holiness,"
wrote Philip to the envoy, "that as for the aboli-

* Corresp. de Marg. d'Autriche, p. 100, *et seq.*
† Ibid., pp. 106–114.
‡ Cor. de Philippe II., tom. 1, p. 443.

tion of the Inquisition, it cannot be abolished without the consent of the pope, by whose authority it was established. This, however, must be said in confidence. As to the edicts, bid the pontiff to believe that I never will approve any scheme which shall favor the guilty by diminishing in the slightest degree the penalties of their crimes. Let this also be considered as secret. Concerning the grant of pardon, assure the holy father that it will never be extended to offenders against religion. Briefly, say that the pope may be sure that I will consent to nothing that can prejudice religion; that I deprecate force, as it would involve the ruin of the Netherlands; spite of which, however, I will march in person, without regard to my own peril and though it should cost me the provinces, but I will bring my vassals to submission; for I would rather lose a hundred lives than reign a lord over heretics."*

Doubtless Pius V. listened and approved as Philip thus unburdened his bosom in the confessional of the Vatican; nor was the shrift likely to bring down a heavy penance from one who held sternly to the orthodox maxim of "No faith is to be kept with heretics."†

Philip II., dissembling and treacherous everywhere else, was plain and sincere at Rome. Yet even on this occasion he told a lie—which deceived nobody. He had said, "I will march in person to

---

* Corresp. de Philippe II., tom. 1, p. 445, et seq.
† Prescott, vol. 2, p. 49.

subdue revolt;" but it was an open secret that he had no intention of going to the Netherlands. "I feel it in my bones," said Granvelle, divining public opinion as rheumatics foretell a change of weather, "that nobody in Rome believes in his majesty's journey to the provinces."* This much-talked-of visit was the standing joke of the Madrid wits. Philip's graceless son, Don Carlos, scribbled one day this title on the cover of a blank book: "The Great and Admirable Voyages of King Philip II.;" and within, for the contents, he wrote: "From Madrid to the Pardo, from the Pardo to the Escurial, from the Escurial to Aranjuez."†

Of course, this trickery of the king was hidden from its destined victims. The royal concessions professed to be *bonâ fide*. But they reached Brussels too late. While Philip had been walking in leaden shoes, the reform had assumed a new phase, and one which necessitated war. Men may be overreached, but it is impossible to outwit ideas. This was not a case at law; it was revolution.

---

* Corresp. de Philippe II., *ubi sup.* † Prescott, *ubi sup.*

CHAPTER XXIV.

THE IMAGE-BREAKERS.

THE field conventicles of 1566 were to the Netherlands, in fact, though not in motive, what the Whig clubs were to our fathers in '76, what the Jacobin clubs were to the French revolutionists, what the secret societies are to the Republicans of modern Europe—the forums of the disaffected. Under the bitterest of legal bans, ostracized in the towns, anathematized in the churches of the dominant faith, the reformers were forced to listen to the gospel message in the open air; and they occupied the intervals before, between, and after the sermons in conversation upon the injustice of a rule which sentenced them to herd for worship in moorland or forest, like bands of outlaws, and condemned them to live as exiles under the shadow of their homes. Often the preachers themselves contrasted these stealthy gatherings of the disciples with the pompous and law-protected ceremonials of the bigots who adhered to Rome; and, wandering off from spiritual themes, they commented on the towering cathedrals where the papists swung their censers and told their beads in the haughty ease of a magnificent but intolerant devotion, and inveighed against the legalized impiety which knelt to adore marble effigies and pictured saints. As they listened to descriptions of such blasphemy, fiery and ill-regulated spirits chafed and shivered with impatient horror. When they returned from the field meetings, and saw the gay processions and the authorized temples of their persecutors, these seemed to cast contempt on their proscribed belief. Every image which they met, every cross set up upon the highway, appeared to be a trophy erected over the humiliation of their faith, and put on the aspect of an abiding insult to God, who had proclaimed from the awful summit of Mount Sinai: "Thou shalt not make unto thee any graven image, or any likeness of any thing that is in heaven above, or that is in the earth beneath, or that is in the water under the earth: thou shalt not bow down thyself to them, nor serve them: for I the Lord thy God am a jealous God."* To the untutored minds of some, the papal image-worship seemed a constant and flagitious transgression of this commandment, and forgetful of that other mandate of the Most High: "Vengeance is mine, I will repay,"† zealots cried, "Come, then, let us break these idols."

The Low Countries were crowded with churches and chapels and monasteries and convents. Some of these were the creations of days which antedated Charlemagne—huge Gothic piles where daylight melted into poetic gloom, fitted with storied windows glowing in brilliant and forgotten colors, over which bereaved art still weeps, and where the effulgent robes of priests chanting the mass in a

* Exod. 20 : 4. 5.   † Rom. 12 : 19.

language as dead as their piety, the breathing of choral music unearthly sweet, and the suffocating odors of myrrh and spikenard suggestive of the oriental scenery and imagery of Holy Writ, combined to bewilder and bewitch the senses; others were born of the *Renaissance:* all were profusely adorned by the gifts of wealthy penitence, which had thus purchased absolution for crime; all were flushed with paintings from a school which in time and merit had precedence of its sister nurseries of art in Germany; and all were peopled with statues.*

When the image-breakers looked about them, they said, "Lo, here is no lack of religious houses to despoil, of paintings to rend, of idols to behead."

Upon Assumption eve, on the 14th of August, 1566, while the papists were busied in completing the arrangements for the processions and the grand salaams with which they celebrated the ascension of the madonna, rites peculiarly offensive to the Protestants, the wild work began. Suddenly, without concert, without warning, a frantic band of three hundred iconoclasts, rudely armed with staves, hatchets, hammers, and ropes—weapons fitter for spoliation than for fight—threw themselves upon the blasphemous relics and marbles and paintings in the districts of lower Flanders between the river Lys and the West sea.† Their purpose was not

---

* Motley, vol. 1, p. 552.

† Strada, p. 121. Hoofd, tom. 3. Bor, tom. 2. Hopper, Rec. et Mem.

plunder, but demolition; though, as in all similar outbreaks, the zealots were reinforced by an abandoned mob of thieves and prostitutes and impish boys without principle in the onset, eager only for what they could pick up.

First, the highway crosses and the roadside images were assailed;* then, gaining courage as they increased in number, the destroyers broke into the hamlets and towns about St. Omer, ransacking churches, rifling chapels, sacking convents, defacing pictures, overturning images, demolishing shrines, burning monastic libraries, trampling with unsandalled feet upon the sacred treasures of the Roman crypts. On, on, on they rushed, swift as the wind, destructive as the tempest, meeting with no resistance, for the law was surprised and dazed; molesting no human being, for they warred alone upon artistic sacrilege—upon pictures, and images, and buildings associated in their minds with the remorseless persecution of half a century, and which had thus grown human and hateful.†

Through the frightened gates of St. Omer they sped to Ypres. There again they spoiled the religious houses; and entering the cathedral, they mounted on ladders to the pictured walls, and hammered them to pieces, hewed the altars and pews to bits with axes, stripped the pulpits of their ornaments, and carried off the holy vessels of silver and

* Brandt, vol. 1. p. 191.   Meteren, tom. 2.

† Schiller, Revolt of the Neth., vol. 2, p. 3., Bohn's edition. Motley, vol. 1.

gold and precious stones.* From Ypres, the madness quickly spread to Menin, to Comines, to Lille, to Oudenarde; in the space of seventy summer hours four hundred churches were gutted in the single province of Flanders.† Drunk with success, crazy with license, the iconoclasts now passed the Lys, and dividing into two bands, some hastened on to Douay, others sped towards Secklyn. Before the gates of Secklyn their march was for the first time contested. A few resolute knights charged the motley and undisciplined invaders and routed the whole force, driving many into the neighboring bogs, drowning some in the river, and carrying others into the town in triumph.‡ 'T is a signal illustration of what composed determination can achieve.

Reports of this unique insurrection against marble saints and painted effigies soon travelled to Antwerp. "It is frightful sacrilege," said the papist burghers, crossing themselves. "Idols ought to be removed from our sight as well as from our hearts; but this should be a voluntary act, not the work of mobs," commented the vast majority of the reformers. "Riot will soon sweep through our streets, torch in hand: 't is time to bar our shop-doors," stammered startled traders, trembling for their coffers. "Ah, if it only would, it would be

---

º Schiller, Revolt of the Neth., vol. 2, p. 3., Bohn's edition. Motley, vol. 1. Strada, p. 122.

† Strada, p. 127. Cor. de Marguerite d'Autriche, p. 183.

‡ Strada, p. 122. Brandt, vol. 1, p. 192.

a capital diversion," drawled careless idlers, weary of all common forms of amusements. There were some hot-heads who panted to imitate the image-breakers of the provinces. "These idol-smiters," said they, "ought to have twins in Antwerp. The town cannot sweep the dirt out of itself: let us wash its face."

The orderly classes of all sects feared a tumult, but no measures were taken to prevent one.* Happily, the prince of Orange was in the city—a fact which went far to preserve the peace.† As was usual in the gala days of Assumption week, Antwerp was thronged with strangers‡—merchants with an eye to business, roysterers intent on pleasure, rustics with bewildered mien, all of whom had come up ostensibly to witness the *fêtes;* but it was suspected that unquiet spirits with another purpose lurked under the tunics of the traders, under the slashed doublets of the rakes, under the modest russet of the peasants.

The grand procession which was annually formed to conduct a colossal image of the Virgin Mary around the city, paraded now as aforetime, spite of the fact that, at such a moment, the pageant was exactly fitted to increase the irritation of the people.§ However no riot occurred, though the populace, grown weary of antiquated mummery, hissed, and hooted, and jeered as Our Lady passed. "Lit-

---

* Brandt, *ubi sup.* Hoofd, tom. 3. † Bor., tom. 2, p. 81.
‡ Brandt, vol. 1, p. 192. Hopper, Rec. et Mem., p. 96.
§ Motley, vol. 1, p. 357.

tle Mary, little Mary, your hour has come. 'T is
your last promenade: the city is tired of you"*—
such was the ribald salute which greeted the bediz-
zened and effulgent madonna. It was evident that
insurrection was at hand; its *avant-courier* had
already arrived, for the masses had begun to jest.
The spectacle ended somewhat abruptly; and when
Antwerp went to bed that night, it congratulated
itself that the day had ended without a riot.†

In the morning, Orange left the city for Brussels, whither he had been summoned to attend an
extraordinary session of the council of state.‡ He
departed much against his will. "Madame," wrote
he to Margaret, "it will be dangerous for me to
quit my post at this juncture."§ "It is necessary,"
was the reply.‖ William had not been gone many
hours when a noisy assemblage gathered in front of
the far-famed cathedral—next to St. Peter's at
Rome the most magnificent church in Christendom. It was customary to deposit the effigy of the
Virgin in the centre of this edifice after the procession of the Assumption, that it might, in that
conspicuous station, receive the adoration of the
faithful. Now, as a measure of precaution, Our
Lady was huddled into the choir, half out of sight;
so that when the throng entered the cathedral they

* Bor., tom. 2, p. 81. Strada, p. 123. Meteren, tom. 2.

† Motley, *ubi sup.*

‡ Hoofd, tom. 3, p. 99. Bor., *ubi sup.*

§ Cor. de Guillaume le Taciturne, tom. 2, p. 188.

‖ Cor. de Marguerite d'Autriche. Groen v. Prinst., Archives,
etc., tom. 2, p. 236.

at once missed the image, until, peering about, they discovered it in its new station.* Derisive laughter greeted this bo-peep concealment. "Little Mary, little Mary," shouted the jokers, "art thou terrified so early? Hast thou flown to thy nest so soon? Dost think thyself beyond the reach of harm? Beware, little Mary; thine hour is fast approaching." The sub-base of this chorus of light raillery was the incessant shout of "*Vivent les gueux*," while innumerable voices hoarsely commanded the image to join in the beggars' cry.†

Presently there was a scuffle. An elfish lad, having ascended the pulpit, commenced to mimic the tones and gestures of the monkish preachers, a proceeding in exact harmony with the feelings of the riotous audience; but which so exasperated a papist waterman, who was present as an indignant spectator, that he rushed up to the altar, and collaring the interloper, flung him headlong to the marble floor of the cathedral. "*Vivent les gueux*," shouted the crowd; and angered by this rude interruption of their amusement, they surged forward, and began lustily to belabor the courageous mariner. The waterman did not lack adherents, and blows were interchanged with a vim and science worthy of the gladiators of the pagan coliseum. In the midst of this heady brawl the rabble rout were driven from the church by the cry of "The officers are coming, the officers are coming." Ere long

---

* Hoofd, tom. 3, p. 99. Strada, p. 124. Hopper, Rec. et Mem.
† Ibid. Motley, vol. 1, p. 557, *et seq.*

silence reigned in the profaned cathedral, and the
sacristans closed the gates for the night.*

In the midst of this tumult, the city magistrates
were seated in solemn conclave in the great hall
of the Hotel de Ville.†   Left without a helms-
man by the departure of the prince, they were
rocked rudderless in the wind of doubt.   Without
practical authority, accustomed to lean in stormy
crises upon sturdier arms, and fearful of making
bad worse by premature action, they knew not
what to do.   They were aware that a proclamation
would be waste paper without men-at-arms to enforce it; but they feared to appeal to the guild
militia, lest these should fraternize with the mob;
while to call in the aid of mercenaries, even had
this been possible, they esteemed sure to add fresh
fuel to the fire.   Thus circumstanced, the city
fathers contented themselves with sending a courier to apprize Orange that the danger he had foreseen had come.   This done, they retired to their
homes and put on their night-caps, in the futile
hope that the storm they knew not how to lay
would blow over by the morrow.‡

But it did not; for on the afternoon of the following day§ the crowd gathered again about the
doors of the cathedral, and became more clamorous
than ever.   The church itself was filled with a bois-

---

* Hoofd, *ubi sup.* Meteren, fol. xc. Bor., tom. 2, p. 83. Strada,
ubi sup.

† Hoofd, tom. 3, p. 99.   Bor., tom. 2, p. 83, *et seq.*

‡ Ibid.   § August 21st. Strada, p. 124.

terous multitude. The air was heavy with laughter, and jests, and shouts of "*Vivent les gueux.*" About one old woman, especially, who was seated as usual beneath the choir to sell wax tapers and to receive oblations, a flock of boys were grouped, teasing and baiting her to the top of their bent. "Madame," said they, "your consecrated wares are out of date; your idolatrous traffic must end in your starvation." Provoked by this reckless chaffer, the hucksteress began to pelt her tormentors with whatever missiles she could lay hands on, and the hubbub increased apace.* The sacristans, scenting mischief, essayed to clear the church; but their efforts were vain.† They called in the magistrates, who endeavored in their turn to evoke order out of chaos. "Retire, retire," shouted they, flourishing their staves of office. "Nay," was the reply; "we have a mind to stay and hear the hymn of *Salve Regina.*" "There will be no vespers to-day," said the officials. "Indeed," was the retort; "then we will stay and sing Our Lady's lullaby ourselves:" and one of Marot's psalms was struck up.‡

Foiled here, the magistrates had recourse to stratagem. Pretending to retire, they shut all the doors of the cathedral save one, through which they hoped that the rioters would follow them into the street.§ A few did so, but the mass remained. Beaten again, they once more entered the edifice,

---

* Brandt, vol. 1, p. 192.
† Meteren, folio 2, p. 40. Brandt, vol. 1, p. 192, *et seq.*
‡ Ibid. § Brandt, *ubi sup.*

and fell to expostulation.*   But the multitude were
crazed with license, and they hustled the alarmed
dignitaries through the single open door, while a
new crowd burst through the closed portals into the
cathedral.†   Once more the officials approached the
church; but terrified by the wild, insurrectionary
choruses which echoed from within, and convinced
of the folly of unarmed intervention, they concluded to leave the fated cathedral; and retiring
to the stadthouse, they barricaded that against
assault.‡

These few trifles, drifting before the event, were
the heralds of the outbreak.§   When night had fairly
fallen, the image-breakers commenced their carnival.   As the great clock in the belfry tolled the hour
of eight, they chanted a German psalm; and then,
as if the weird music were the formal opening of
their raid, they sprang upon the long-menaced image
of the Virgin, tore off her embroidered robes, and
rolled the dumb idol in the dust amid frantic shouts
of *"Vivent les gueux!"*‖   This served but to whet
the fury of the image-breakers.   Snatching the wax
tapers from the altars, they struck a flickering light,
which served but to make the darkness visible, causing the vast arena of the dusky church, painted with
shapes of terror, of gloom, and of weird grandeur, to
glint fitfully out in the solemn shadow.   Nimbly, inde-

---

* Brandt, *ubi sup.*   Strada, p. 124.   † Ibid.

‡ Brandt, *ubi sup.*   Bor., tom. 2, pp. 83, 84.

§ Motley, vol. 1, p. 560.

‖ Strada, *ubi sup.*   Hoofd, tom. 3, p. 100.

fatigably, audaciously the destroyers worked, bringing into requisition axes, bludgeons, sledge-hammers, ladders, pulleys, ropes, and levers, all of which
they had carried concealed under their clothes.*
Huge statues of saints, which stood in niches in the
walls, were unfastened, hurled from their pedestals,
and hacked in pieces; the marvellously-painted windows were shattered; the walls were defaced; scores
of pictures, the choicest specimens of the Flemish
pencil, were cut into shreds; the seventy altars were
hewn to bits, and rifled of the sacred plate; the
famous organ, the finest then extant, was demolished, while the air resounded with choruses wilder
than any its keyboard had ever sounded. Above
the choir there was one matchless group, Christ
nailed upon a massive crucifix, with the two thieves
hanging on either hand; the whole rested upon a
single column, but rose arch upon arch, pillar upon
pillar, to the sheer height of three hundred feet,
until the head of Christ was lost in the cloudy
vault.[†] This dizzy masterpiece was scaled, and
the image of the Redeemer was thrown down, but
the two thieves were left to hang, as if they alone
were fit subjects for the human chisel.[‡] In this
sacrilege there was so much concord and forecast,
that it seemed as if each rifler had been allotted his
separate task;[§] and so swiftly and cunningly did all
labor, that ere midnight struck the wreck was com-

---

* Hoofd, tom. 3, p. 100, *et seq.*   Strada, p. 124.

† Motley, vol. 1, p. 563.

‡ Strada, *ubi sup.*   § Ibid.

plete—the richest temple in the world had been reduced to a mere empty shell.*

Although the cathedral was crowded throughout these orgies, the majority were there as passive, though sympathetic spectators; the spoliation was accomplished by a band of men, women, and children, numbering at the most but a hundred individuals.† We may well marvel at the utterness of the desecration which they wrought in those few brief hours of the midsummer night; nor is it the least remarkable fact of the congeries of wonders, that though they toiled in a darkness feebly dispelled by tapers, no one of the whole vast throng was injured by the random blows of the iconoclasts or by the falling masses of timber, metal, and stone.‡

When all was over, the image-breakers regaled themselves by draining the wine prepared for the altar from the pyxes and chalices, and by greasing their shoes with the holy oil, to show their contempt for the chrism.§ Then, snatching fresh tapers from the vestry storehouse, they poured out into the streets, and startled the drowsy city from its slumber by the flaming light of their torches, and by resounding shouts of " *Vivent les gueux !*"‖ On they swept, smiting every image of the Virgin, every

---

° Bor., tom. 2, p. 84. Bentivoglio, tom. 2, p. 36.

† Strada, p. 125. Corresp. de Marg. d'Autriche, p. 183.

‡ Strada, *ubi sup.* Strada thinks this "no light argument that, with God's permission, the work was done under the immediate direction of demons from hell." Strada, p. 125.

§ Ibid. Brandt, vol. 1, p. 193.

‖ Ibid. Hoofd, tom. 3, p. 103. Bor., tom. 2, p. 85.

sculptured saint, every cross which they passed.
Reinforced by some scores of "lewd fellows of the
baser sort," intent on plunder, they broke into the
other religious houses of Antwerp. When morning
dawned, thirty churches had been sacked within
the city walls.* Entering the monasteries, they
routed the monks out of bed, tore up their ecclesiastical robes, trampled the mass-wafers and the
sacrament-bread under foot, daubed the books of
the monkish libraries with butter to make them
blaze merrily, and then threw them into the fire;
and finally, descending into the cellars, and broach-
ing every cask which they could find, they drank
their fill from the consecrated chalices, and then
poured out in one grand flood all the old ale and
wine with which these holy men had been wont to
solace their retirement from generation to generation.† The convents also were invaded; and while
the hapless nuns huddled on their dresses and flut-
tered out into the midnight streets in quest of an
asylum unmolested—for they had come to destroy,
not to insult—the iconoclasts wreaked their vengeance on the ecclesiastical paraphernalia.‡

While this mischief was afoot, the trembling
citizens of Antwerp remained close shut up in their
dwellings, or ventured, at the most, but to peer timidly out upon the street from their barred windows.
Ignorant of the strength of the rioters, whose num-

---

* Motley, vol. 1, p. 564.
† Brandt, vol. 1, p. 193. Strada, p. 126. Motley, *ut antea.*
‡ Strada, *ubi sup.*

ber their imagination stretched portentously, without leaders, furnished with no rallying-spots, and surprised at midnight, the last thing which the honest burghers thought of was, to sally out and resist the spoilers. The papists suspected that it was a Protestant plot for their slaughter, and so dared not stir; the reformers feared to move abroad, lest they should be confounded with the image-breakers.* Thus tied by terror, the city stood still, while a hundred zealots, aided by as many more thieves and prostitutes, grown bold from impunity, raged up and down unmolested through three days and nights.†

But eventually the citizens, apprized of the insignificant number of the rioters, and fearful that the sack might be diverted from the religious houses to private mansions, degenerating from fanaticism to a raid for plunder, sallied forth; and, as if they meant to revenge the commonwealth, shut all the city gates save one, through which the image-breakers scampered to pour out their fury upon the adjacent towns, where they reënacted the scenes of their sacrilegious free-boot in Antwerp.‡ Presently a few ventured to return. Entering the cathedral, they saw that they had neglected to erase the royal arms and the escutcheons of the Knights of the Golden Fleece emblazoned on the walls. While busied in completing their vandalism, they were charged by several knights who had hastily collected a handful of

---

∘ Bor., tom. 2, p. 89. Strada, p. 125. Hopper, p. 97.

† Ibid. Hoofd, tom. 3, p. 101.   ‡ Strada, p. 126.

their followers for that purpose. Resolution easily dispersed the band; ten or twelve of them were arrested; while a gallows, erected on a rise of ground, admonished Antwerp that the riot was suppressed.[*] A homœopathic dose of this stern physic stayed the distemper.

What the sun is to the solar system, that was Antwerp to the Lowland cities—the vivifying and the fructifying centre. Whatever word was spoken there, was certain to awaken an answering echo in the provinces; it struck the key-note in every march. So now the iconomachy spread out from the streets of the metropolis east, west, north, south, convulsing the country from the banks of the Scheldt to the Zuyder Zee, as well surprising religion as the land. The image-breakers travelled with the swiftness of the wind, appearing almost simultaneously in widely distant places, shattering the consecrated trophies of Amsterdam, and Leyden, and Gravenhage at the same time that their comrades were sacking Breda, and Bois-le-Duc, and Bergen-op-Zoom.[†] The ubiquitous destroyers were rarely resisted; the audacity of their onslaught paralyzed the arm of opposition. At Mechlin, less than a hundred persons destroyed the ecclesiastical treasures of the town in the very teeth of the grand council, under the eyes of the astonished magistrates.[‡]

[*] Prescott, vol. 2, p. 60. Strada, *ubi sup.*
[†] Hoofd, tom. 3. Bor., tom. 2. Hopper.
[‡] Pontus Payen, MS., cited in Motley, vol. 1. p. 565.

In some towns, the magistrates themselves demolished the obnoxious ornaments, to prevent the mob from doing so; and when they plumed themselves upon their foresight, Viglius shrugged his shoulders and said, "They have been wisely mad—*insaniebant cum ratione.*"[*]

At Ghent, the iconoclasts had the assurance to send delegates to the city senate with this message: "We have been ordered to take the images out of the churches, as has been done elsewhere. If we are not opposed, all shall be done quietly and with as little injury as possible; otherwise we shall storm the churches. It would be wise in you to take the initiative in this work, by ordering the officers of the law to break the idols. In that case, we shall look on with folded arms."[†] The *naiveté* of this demand astounded the magistrates; but upon reflection they concluded to comply with it, thinking thus to restrain excess. Accordingly, a band of city messengers marched from church to church, from monastery to monastery, toppling over images, tearing books and paintings, and breaking organs to pieces. Throughout Ghent, and for six miles about it, this lawful spoliation took place; and when it was finished, the city fell quietly to its employments again.[‡] Haarlem, Dort, and Rotterdam, averted the storm by a kindred procedure.[§]

The Valenciennes magistrates were less complacent; so the image-breakers assumed the task.

* Brandt, vol. 1, p. 191.   † Ibid., Schiller.
‡ Brandt, *ubi sup.*   § Brandt, vol. 1, p. 201.

" ' The tragedy,' as an eye-witness calls it, was performed upon St. Bartholomew's day. It was, however, only a tragedy of statues. Hardly as many senseless stones were victims as there were to be living Huguenots sacrificed in a single city on a St. Bartholomew's day which was fast approaching; for in the Valenciennes 'tragedy' not a human being was injured."*

The scene at Tournay was the counterpart of that at Antwerp. Ecclesiasticism was completely gutted of its treasures—nothing was spared, nothing was overlooked; even the bowels of the earth, in which the churchmen had concealed the most valuable badges of their creed, were ripped open by the shrewd spoilers, keen to discover the hidden idols.†

While burrowing in the vaults of the cathedral, they turned up an embalmed body in a state of perfect preservation. It was dragged from the coffin, and recognized as the corpse of Duke Adolphus of Guelderland, who had been dead for nigh a century. His career had been stormy and criminal: one of his deeds especially, something unnatural in its wickedness, had been preserved by tradition; and now, after the lapse of a hundred years, was as fresh in men's minds as his undecayed remains were in the opened vault. Ambitious and turbulent, Duke Adolphus had essayed to extort from the grasp of his aged father, Duke Arnol-

* Motley, vol. 1, p. 569.
† Brandt, vol. 1, pp, 198, 199.

dus, a crown which must soon, in the course of
nature, have fallen to him.   One night he laid violent hands upon the old patrician, and dragging
him from his bed, forced him, clad only in his
night-dress and barefooted, to walk in the bitter
winter cold twenty-five miles, from Grave to Buren,
while he rode by his father's side on horseback.
There he flung the venerable victim into a dungeon,
where he was left to rot to death.   For this abhorrent crime, Charles the Bold disinherited the brute,
flinging him, in his turn, into prison.   After some
years, he was released by the seditious citizens of
Ghent, who forced him to lead them in a raid upon
Tournay.   In a *melée* beneath the walls of that
city, Duke Adolphus was slain, and there interred.
Now, after the passage of so many years, fanaticism
desecrated the grave in order to expose once more
to execration the features of a parricide.   "He who
has offered violence to one who brought him into
the world, is not worthy to rest in the earth," said
the stern avengers; and they sported with the dead
duke's bones, laid out in mockery on the floor of
the cathedral.*   It has been well called a startling
act of posthumous justice.

It is not necessary to detail farther the deeds
of the iconomachy—no need to mention all the
churches spoiled, all the idols demolished, all the
nunneries set open, all the abbeys sacked, all the
libraries burned: enough is here for truth, and
there is sufficient to deplore.   The image-breakers

* Brandt, vol. 1, p. 199.   Schiller.

were abroad less than a fortnight; yet such was their celerity, and such their discipline, that of the seventeen provinces but four—Limburg, Namur, Luxemburg, and a part of Hainault—came out of the storm unharmed.* In all the rest the destruction was so utter, that Strada compares it to the ruin caused by that historic earthquake, which, in the reign of Tiberius Cæsar, swallowed up twelve of the Roman cities.†

And indeed, much of the injury inflicted was irremediable. The silver, the gold, the precious stones which were lost, might be replaced. Four hundred thousand ducats might go far towards the restoration of the rifled splendor of Antwerp cathedral, which was considered to have been damaged to that amount.‡ But what wealth could re-collect the yellow and time-worn parchments of the consumed library of Vicoque? What hand could block out anew the desecrated marbles of Angelo's chisel? What pencil could retrace the tattered beauties of the antique masters? Surely Art has a right to weep for her lost children.

But art alone may be permitted to moan—humanity deplores no victims. None but ecclesiastical property was wrecked—not a private house was touched, not a public building was sacked; and it is a singular fact that throughout the tumult, the iconoclasts outraged no woman, and slew no opponent. It was a massacre of images—vandalism,

* Hoofd, tom. 3, p. 103.   + Strada, p. 126.
‡ Strada, *ubi sup.*

but not bloodthirstiness. Who, then, shall venture
to compare this havoc among stocks and marbles
and canvas to the human ravages of the Inquisition? 'Tis an instructive illustration of the radical
difference between Rome and the Reformation.
Protestantism in its most frantic mood beheaded
images; the Inquisition in its most placid temper
slew men.

Nor were the image-breakers a profligate rabble—" the lowest dregs of an abandoned populace,"
as many chroniclers of their acts have asserted. It
is indeed true that their camp-followers, to borrow
a military figure, were thieves and prostitutes, struggling merely for what they could filch, taking advantage of the tumult to plunder; but the chief
actors in the drama were honest, though mistaken
zealots. The guiding helm of the iconomachy was
conscience—conscience awry and fanaticised; but
still conscience. A thoughtful writer has reminded
us that while " an educated nation without religion
is like a skeleton bearing a lamp with light but no
force; a people with the religious instinct strongly
developed is like a giant smitten blind, who rushes
wildly on, impelled by a resistless motor, but towards no noble goal."* This was the hapless pre-
dicament of these spoilers; ignorant and frenzied,
they " saw as through a glass, darkly."

But that the iconoclasts were honest there is
abundant evidence. Their moderation in every
thing save the ecclesiastical spoliation, proves it.

* Bayne, Christian Life, p. 527.

"Everywhere," observes Motley, "they left heaps of costly embroidery, of gold and silver plate, of glittering jewels, lying unheeded on the floor; feeling instinctively that a great passion would be contaminated by admixture with paltry motives. In Flanders, a company of them hanged one of their own number for stealing articles to the value of five shillings. In Valenciennes they were offered a round sum if they would refrain from demolishing the churches—a proposal which they rejected with disdain. At Tournay, the floor of the cathedral was strewn with 'pearls and precious stones, with chalices and rich reliquaries;' but the ministers of the reformed religion, in company with the city magistrates, came to the spot and found no difficulty, though utterly powerless to curb the tumult, in taking quiet possession of the wreck. 'We had every thing of value,' says Procureur-Général De la Barre, 'carefully inventoried, weighed, locked in chests, and placed under a strict guard in the prison of Halle, to which one set of keys were given to the ministers and another to the magistrates.' "*

In many instances, the image-breakers voluntarily restored to the municipal authorities rich collections of plate;† and when any of the valuables were appropriated, these were gathered into heaps and delivered to their preachers, who caused them to be melted down and distributed among the

* Motley, vol. 1, pp. 571, 572.

† Meteren, book 2, folio 43. Hoofd, tom. 3, pp. 98, 99. Brandt, vol. 1, p. 195.

most needy of the sectaries.* The destruction itself was discriminating. At Bois-le-Duc every marble saint was martyred, but two brazen statues of
Moses and David were left untouched—these were
not idolatrous.† In the *melée* at Antwerp, a Carmelite monk who had lain for twelve weary years
in the dungeon of the Barefoot monastery, on a
charge of heresy, was liberated.‡

But even had all this been otherwise, the iconoclasts were an insignificant faction—here a hundred,
and there a score ;§ and the odium of their pranks
ought not to fall upon the Netherland Protestants.
The reformed preachers—Wille, Strycker, Junius,
and the rest—labored indefatigably to quell the
riots.‖ The *gueux* pronounced the outbreak insen-
sate and flagitious.¶ The whole body of the reformers formally disavowed it.** "I do not think
it strange," says the famous Dutch historian Hoofd,
"since there are good and bad men in all sects,
that the vilest of the reformed showed their temper
by these extravagances; nor that others fed their
eyes with a sport that grew up to a plague, which
they thought the papal clergy had justly deserved
by the rage of their persecutions. 'T is probable
that many did not trouble themselves overmuch

---

* Renom. de Francia. Cited in Prescott, vol. 2, p. 64.
† Brandt, vol. 1, p. 197.   ‡ Ibid., p. 193.
§ Strada, p. 125. Renom. de Francia, MS., tom. 1, chap. 20.
Pontus Payen, MS.
‖ Brandt, vol. 1, pp. 194–221, *passim.* De la Barre, MS.
¶ Groen v. Prinst., Archives, etc., tom. 2, pp. 261, 265, 483.
** Brandt, *ubi sup.* Hoofd, tom. 3, p. 102.

about the matter, hoping that one madness might cure the other, and thus order come from confusion. But the generality of the reformed certainly behaved nobly, by censuring results which they esteemed good and proper, because these were brought about by improper methods."*

Some one has said that fools and wise men are not two separate nations, with a sea rolling between them, but neighbors on a common border land, where many dwell whose nationality it is difficult to decide on. The image-breakers seemed to prove it, for, as Viglius said, they were wisely mad. A church which believed that it could chain the future under the past, deified images; the iconomachy was the scoffing answer of a faction half awake to the truth. Thus it is that fanaticism breeds fanaticism.

After all, there was a profound philosophy at the bottom of the image-breaking. It has been customary to bewail the fact that the first steps of the Reformation were taken on the ruins of art, and that the reforming so readily degenerated into the destructive principle; though eminent historians have found a compensation in the good done by breaking the fetters of the intellect, and opening a free range in those domains of science to which access hitherto had been denied.† Doubtless, this was the fact; nevertheless, destruction has its part in God's law of progress, as countless analogies in nature avouch.

* Cited in Brandt, vol. 1, p. 194.
† See Prescott, vol. 2, p. 64 ; and Motley, vol. 1, p. 552.

But, rightly read, the iconomachy was not a crusade against *art as art*. The image-breakers had no quarrel with the breathing canvas of the master artists—with the life-like statues of the antique sculptors, considered as mere artistic trophies: it was their idea; it was that subtle something which these represented; it was the madonna and the saints who had entered into and made them instinct with idolatrous life, and the uses to which they were put, that awakened their ire and provoked their assault.

In assailing the art of that epoch, the iconoclasts struck at what it stood for—smote the jailer who had imprisoned the spirit of beauty; for it is Ruskin, the most fascinating writer on the ethics of art in our English letters, who assures us that " art is always the expression of natural life and character; that every nation's vice or virtue is written in it— the soldiership of early Greece, the sensuality of late Italy, the visionary religion of Tuscany, the splendid but human beauty of Venice."*

The image-breakers were the contemporaries of the Revivalists, and they recognized the covert atheism of their art by intuition. Nor must the argument which educes this be esteemed metaphysical. What we can see is but the bone and muscle of wonder; what we think is its soul. The eye of imagination sweeps a wider horizon than the glasses of astronomy.†

* Ruskin, Crown of Wild Olive, Lecture on Traffic, p. 55.
† Hunt, Men, Women, and Books, vol. 1, p. 9.

Now ignorance never stops to reason; it divines and acts. "Thought widens, but lames; action narrows, but animates," is a profound apothegm of Goethe. The iconomachy was no murder of art; it was blind Samson dragging down the temple on the heads of the Philistines; it was Baconian induction and Platonic ardor.

We have looked upon the bloodless "massacre of the innocents" in the provinces; how was the report of this catastrophe without a victim received by the court at Brussels? With tears and imprecations. The government oscillated between resentment and dismay. When the first tidings came, most of the grandees were in town, summoned thither by the duchess to attend an important meeting of the state council.* Margaret at once convened them. "Seigneurs," said she, "'tis commonly reported that these villanies are committed, some of you not only not resisting, but being also privy and assistant in the plot. What is fit to be done by men of honor, look you to that; for what concerns myself, I religiously profess that no man's menaces shall persuade me to mix the new figments of these heretics with the ancient and orthodox religion. Nay, if the king himself, upon whose grace and pleasure I depend, should grant the Low Countrymen to be of what religion they list—which how far it is from his majesty's intention none can be ignorant—I would instantly quit the land, because I would not be the agent or interpreter of such indul-

* Strada, p. 127. Vita Viglii, Hoofd.

gence. Look not, then, to fright me with great names, and so enforce my consent to unjust demands."*

Evidently the duchess was in a bellicose mood; events soon "tamed the shrew."

Orange opposed harsh measures, and advised conciliation. His practical statesmanship never mistook the look of an argument for the proof of it. "Look, madame," said he, "the reformed number upwards of two hundred thousand armed men; their temper is now sullen; but grant them to meet safely and peaceably in those places where they have been wont to assemble, and they are instantly transformed into loyal citizens. Disarm them by such a *coup d'état*. What else can we do? Here are no mercenaries; and for the guild militia-men, they will not enforce the placards against their co-religionists."†

"It would ring the death-knell of our holy faith," replied the duchess.‡ "Your highness," chimed in Egmont, "first let us save the state; when that is done, it will be time enough to think of religion."§ "Nay," cried the regent heatedly, "faith demands our first care; for the ruin of religion would be a greater evil than the loss of the provinces."‖ "Those who have any thing in them to lose will probably think otherwise," was Egmont's dry retort.¶

° Given in Strada, p. 128. † Brandt, vol. 1, p. 204.

‡ Cor. de Marg. d'Autriche, p. 188. § Prescott, vol. 2, p. 67.

‖ Ibid. Cor. de Philippe II., tom. 1, p. 449. ¶ Ibid.

But the seigneurs argued in vain; for several days the governant remained inflexible. Meantime, the riot broadened portentously. Gossips told of the wild deeds done in Flanders; news came of the sack of Antwerp cathedral; the city grew pale as it listened to accounts, somewhat exaggerated, as is dame Rumor's wont, of the outbreaks at Amsterdam, at Valenciennes, at Tournay. The whole country seemed ablaze; every breeze that swept over Brussels wafted the frantic choruses of the image-breakers into Margaret's ears. The doubt and anxiety of the unhappy duchess brought on a fever; she tossed on her couch in a delirium of anguish.* But when she was told that Brussels stood next on the red list of the iconoclasts, fear conquered disease, and she determined to forsake the capital.†

She selected Mons, a strongly fortified town in Hainault, whose citizens were sturdy papists, as an asylum;‡ and when this choice was made, ordered the preparations for her flight to be pushed forward with the utmost secrecy and celerity. At three o'clock in the morning of the 22d of August, Orange, Egmont, Hoogstraaten, Horn, and Mansfeld were aroused from their slumbers by a summons to repair at once to the governant's residence.§ When the drowsy seigneurs reached the palace, they were surprised to find that Margaret, attended by Barlaiment, Aerschot, and Noircarmes, was equipped

° Corresp. de Marg. d'Autriche, p. 194.
† Strada, p. 129. Vita Viglii, pp. 47, 48. ‡ Ibid.
§ Motley, vol. 1, p. 573.

for flight, while her waiting-women and lacqueys with mules and hackneys already harnessed stood waiting in the court-yard for the order to set out.[*]

" Yes," said the duchess, in response to the mute looks of inquiry which her guests directed upon her, " his grace of Aerschot has offered me the protection of the stout walls of Mons. I shall there abide the subsidence of the rebellion."[†]

The enormous blunder of such a step as the regent's flight before the threats of a few score of rioters, was perceived by all. " Madame," said Orange, " if you thus abandon the government, it will be necessary at once to summon the states-general, that measures may be taken to preserve the country."[‡] " If you quit Brussels for Mons," cried the fiery Egmont, " I will muster forty thousand men and besiege Mons in person."[§] " Your highness, tarry here," pleaded Horn ; " nowhere else can you be so safe. I pledge my word that, if necessity occurs, I will escort you in safety from the city, or lose my life in the attempt."[||]

But so great was Margaret's trepidation, that she was deaf to reason, until Viglius entered the apartment and told her that the burghers had learned of her intended departure and defeated the plan by closing and guarding the gates.[¶] Thus a prisoner in the capital, the duchess was compelled to relin-

---

[*] Motley, vol. 1, p. 573. Corresp. de Marg. d'Autriche, p. 188.   [†] Ibid.

[‡] Prescott, vol. 2, p. 69. Corresp. de Philippe II., tom. 1, p. 454.   [§] Ibid.

[||] Motley, *ubi sup.* Strada, p. 129.   [¶] Vita Viglii, p. 48.

quish her madcap jaunt; and at length, somewhat calmed by the promises of protection which the grandees uttered, she consented to retire to her apartment; while Orange, Egmont, and the rest went to the stadthouse to convene the citizens and concert measures for the security of Brussels.*

Mansfeld was appointed captain-general of the city; the seigneurs agreed to serve under him, and there was not the ghost of a disturbance.† Nevertheless, Margaret suffered a relapse. At seven o'clock in the evening of this same day, she once more summoned the nobles to her palace, and informed them that she had certain information that the churches would be sacked that night; that Viglius, Barliament, and Aremberg would be slain; and that she herself with Egmont would be taken prisoners.‡ Then turning fiercely upon Horn, she reproached him for hindering her flight, and bade him redeem his promise by cutting his way through the burgher guard at the Brussels posterns.§ Finally, the regent was again calmed; and the night passed without disturbance.‖

It was evident, however, that something must be done beyond soothing the silly fears of a fevered woman. Margaret herself at length recognized the necessity of action. On the 25th of August, notwithstanding her oath never to be the agent of in-

---

* Vita Vigli, p. 48.   Prescott, Motley.   † Ibid.
‡ Bor., tom. 2, p. 85.   Hoofd, tom. 3, p. 107.
§ Letter of Horn to Montigny.   Cited in Motley, vol. 1, p. 575.
‖ Hoofd.   Bor., *ubi sup.*   Cor. de Marg. d'Autriche, p. 196.

dulgence to heretics, she signed a paper which buried the past in oblivion; guaranteed the right of the reformers to assemble for worship in places already dedicated as altars, pending the decision of Philip and the states-general; and exacted in return a promise of peaceable behavior on the part of the Protestants, and on the part of the *gueux* a renunciation of their league so long as the accord was faithfully observed by the government.*

To this agreement all parties appended their signatures; and while the ink on the parchment was still wet, couriers sped with it in all directions to proclaim it law.†

This was, thus far, the high-water mark of concession. The governant shed tears of shame and resentment as she scrawled her name at its bottom. On retiring to her cabinet, she at once wrote to Philip an account of what she had been obliged to do. "Alas, sire "—it was so that the letter ran— "believe not that the execrable deed is mine. I beseech and conjure you not to make it good."‡

Thus deliberately did the duchess perjure herself, thus without a scruple did she counsel dishonor. Such meanness was in her blood. Her father, the emperor, had once and again pawned his word only to break it. Her brother, the king, had called in a notary to bear solemn witness that he repudiated

---

* Meteren, folio 45.   Corresp. de Philippe II., tom. 1, p. 144. Brandt, vol. 1, p. 204.   Strada, p. 130.   † Ibid.

‡ Cor. de Philippe II., tom. 1, p. 453.   Strada gives a transcript of this letter at p. 130.

an absurd list of concessions, because events had wrung them from him against his will. In the sixteenth century this was diplomacy; in the nineteenth century it would be swindling. The bastard duchess had learned morality from the lips of Ignatius Loyola. This is not the only incident in her career which proves that the lessons of the Jesuit were not barren labor.

It would be idle to speculate as to the effect of the accord had it been honest; that consideration must be remitted to what mediæval Scotchmen called the *media scientia*—the science which treats of how affairs would have fallen out, had it not been for the happening of certain other things.

However, as they separated, each to return to his post, most of the seigneurs pocketed the paper complacently; they esteemed it certain to cure the diseased land. "Presto!" cried they; "we are well." But, alas, the patient was not convalescent; this was the hectic flush of fever, not the roseate hue of health.

CHAPTER XXV.

THE REACTION.

THE accord, though wrung from the reluctant hand of the frightened governant, was one of the most popular state papers ever published in the Netherlands; for the masses, always credulous, ever charitable in the construction of doubtful acts, believed it to be at once the death-warrant of the Inquisition and the guaranty of plenary toleration. Consequently, the grudged concessions, more potent than the exhortatory chatter of the bewildered magistrates, more efficacious than the mandatory letters of Margaret, went far to restore tranquillity.

But the cessation of image-breaking, though general, was not universal. Local outbreaks occurred here and there—isolated evidences of the subsiding convulsion. To complete the pacification, the grandees cut short their conferences at Brussels and instantly set out for their respective stadtholderates, following hard upon the couriers who sped before to announce the accord. Orange reëntered Antwerp; Hoogstraaten repaired to Mechlin; Megen returned to Guelders; Egmont went to Flanders; Horn, in the absence of his brother-in-law Montigny, entangled in the Spanish web at Madrid, hastened to Tournay, the seat of that hapless seigneur's government.[*]

At Antwerp, wearied insurrection had sobbed

---

[*] Bor., tom. 2, p. 84, et seq. Pontus Payen, MS.

itself to sleep; therefore the duty of the prince was not repression, but conservation. Soon after his arrival, the burgomasters, emboldened by his presence, and to display their zeal, hung three of the rioters whom they had captured.* To prevent further bloodshed, William hastily arranged terms of agreement between all parties on the basis of the accord, and labored with tireless energy to exorcise the spirit of discord that still lingered in the city. After protracted negotiations, the reformers, who had possessed themselves of the despoiled churches, were persuaded to surrender them to the Romanists; but, in return, each of the Protestant sects received permission to erect a chapel in a specified quarter of the town. At the same time, armed attendance upon sermons was prohibited; and preachers of all creeds were forbidden to assail their adversaries from the pulpit, or to enter upon controverted points—at least beyond what ethics and the doctrine inculcated made unavoidable. Into this convention, which was to hold good until the king, with the consent of the states-general, determined otherwise, the well-satisfied citizens of Antwerp entered; with the proviso that if the final decision of the government should nullify this settlement, its ratifiers might submit, or be free to quit the provinces, with their families and properties, at their option: meantime, all the well-disposed were taken under the protection of the city.†

---

* Hoofd, tom. 3, p. 102. Groen v. Prinst., Arch., etc.
† Bor., tom. 2, p. 98, *et seq.* Hoofd, tom. 3, p. 111.

The clause of this plan which permitted the
reformed to meet for worship within Antwerp gates,
displeased the regent.   To her letter of remonstrance, Orange replied by offering to resign.*

Nothing was farther from Margaret's intention
than to permit the prince to retire; he was not to
be spared at this crisis.   Accordingly, the politic
princess made haste to mollify the offended seigneur, by verbally approving a measure which had
awakened her secret resentment.†

But Orange was not deceived; he was aware
that this whole chapter of events would be offensive reading to Philip.   While the concessions which
quieted Antwerp still awaited the endorsement of
the burghers, he gave a dinner to Sir Thomas Gre-
sham, the English ambassador resident in the metropolis.   "In all his talk," reported the Englishman, "the prince said to me, 'I know that this will
nothing content the king.'"‡

Still, William relaxed no effort to restore order,
nobly true to himself and to his promise to the
regent, made on the ratification of the accord.   In
pursuance of this purpose, now that Antwerp was
"sitting clothed and in its right mind," he started
for the north, to placate Utrecht and Holland.   His
presence was required; for the Dutch, though less
easy to excite than the Flemings and Brabanters,

* Hoofd, *ubi sup.*   Brandt, vol. 1, p. 206.

† Prescott, vol. 2, p. 72.   Strada, pp. 130, 131.

‡ Burgon, tom. 2, page 161.   Cited in Motley, volume 2, page
18.

were, when aroused, much more difficult to appease. Even as he journeyed, reports of their wild doings reached his ears.

The bruited approach of Orange appeased these unseemly tumults; and when the statesman-prince reached the insurgent districts, his wise and pacific measures disarmed riot. In Amsterdam, in Leyden, in Utrecht, at the Hague, law and order were reëstablished on the basis of the liberal Antwerp agreement.* The genius of Peace seemed to clasp hands with William as he sped through the country to the borders of the Zuyder Zee.

Equally active was Hoogstraaten at Mechlin. The young and fiery seigneur construed the concessions of the prince into precedents, and he employed the same means to conciliate and tranquillize the turbulent citizens of Granvelle's former see.† His success was added evidence of the policy of justice. From the enjoyment of these peaceful triumphs, he was called by Margaret to take charge of Antwerp in the absence of Orange.‡

Guelders, less happy than Holland and Brabant, was dragooned into submission by weapons forged in a ruder armory than that of justice. The bigoted Count Megen was stadtholder of that province, and he suppressed the conventicles of the reformed, banished the evangelical preachers, and hacked right and left without stint or mercy, in

* Bor., tom. 2, p. 101, *et seq.* Hoofd, tom. 3.
† Brandt, vol. 1, p. 206. Prescott, vol. 2, p. 74.
‡ Motley, vol. 1, p. 58.

the exploits of Bakkerzeel, a gentleman in Count Egmont's service. On one occasion he hanged twenty-nine heretics at a single heat."[*] Doubtless the true explanation of Egmont's conduct is, that he was a volatile, vain, enthusiastic blunderer in politics, whose zeal was wont to run away with his discretion, making him to-day a champion of the people, to-morrow a contender for autocracy.

However this may be, it is certain that Egmont speedily filled Flanders and Artois with the tearful wives and moaning children of men whose heads had fallen beneath the axe of the executioner, or who had crossed the sea to escape the devouring wrath of the "lost leader."[†] The sight of these things moved Louis of Nassau to expostulate with Egmont; but it does not appear that the honest words of this "reproving Nathan" were effectual in curbing his merciless rigor.[‡]

Tournay, one of the first of the cities to gird up its loins in the iconomachy, was one of the last to disarm. Count Horn met with manifold discouragements in his efforts to restore order. Entering the town at great personal risk, he found six thousand citizens in armed possession of the streets; while the governor, Maulbais, with a few sullen and sulky retainers, were cooped up in the citadel.[§]

Instead of taking up his residence in the half-

[*] Renom. de Francia, MS. Cited in Motley, vol. 2, p. 13.

[†] Groen v. Prinst., Archives, etc., tom. 2, p. 296, *et seq.* Hoofd, tom. 3.   [‡] Groen v. Prinst., *ubi sup.*

[§] Brandt, vol. 1, p. 207.

starved castle, Horn lodged with a Protestant merchant in the city—a shrewd, but generous confidence, which won the good will of the people at the
outset, though the papists complained bitterly of the
condescension.[*] Then, like Hoogstraaten, taking
Orange as his model, he strove to quiet Tournay
by dealing justly with all sects.   But the reformed
were suspicious, Maulbais was crabbed, and the
governant constantly intervened to thwart a · fair
accommodation.   Horn—an honest, blunt, above-
board kind of man, with no special gifts as a diplomat—was infinitely fretted by the quibbling, the
contradiction, the counter-orders which met him at
every step.   Towards his goal, however, he still
walked, though he went by hitches.

When the vacation of the usurped churches was
demanded of the reformed, they acceded; but,
speaking through the lips of Councillor Tassin, they
requested permission to build chapels without the
city walls at the town's expense, since at the most
moderate computation, two thirds of the citizens were
dissenters; notwithstanding which, all the churches
erected for the use of the people were to be surrendered to the exclusive use of the minority.[†]

On this point there was a compromise; the
reformed were permitted to build meeting-houses
in three spots beyond Tournay gates; but their
demand upon the city treasury was somewhat heatedly refused, on the ground that " Romanists could

not be expected to contribute towards the maintenance of heresy, especially since they had just been
so exasperated by the image-breaking."[*]

After much wrangling, this agreement was assented to, and the duchess put upon it the seal of
her acceptance.

And now, for a few short days, the Netherlands
reposed in the lap of Toleration—a compulsory and
grudging nurse. Everywhere rude but substantial chapels were run up with incredible rapidity.
Young and old, gentle and simple assisted in this
pious labor; even women carried stones, and sometimes sacrificed their jewels to accelerate the work.[†]
In many of the cities, the reformed did not scruple
to impress into the service of their buildings the
shattered images and broken crucifixes and monumental tablets of the desecrated cathedrals of
Rome.[‡] Great was the scandal which this unwise
procedure occasioned among the papists, doubly
angered at the demolition of their shrines and at
the heretical use to which the consecrated fragments were put.

While the grandees, assisted by the *gueux*, were
thus actively successful in tranquillizing the provinces, what was the course of Margaret? Two
words paint it—treachery and dissimulation. For
a space, the frightened duchess seemed bent upon
the honest enforcement of the accord; but as the

---

[*] Motley, vol. 2, p. 21.
[†] Schiller, p. 19. Prescott, vol. 2, p. 74.
[‡] De la Barre, MS., p. 44, *et seq.* Cited in Motley, vol. 2, p. 21.

colossus of revolt dwarfed back into peaceful stature, her courage rose, and she began to meddle and to prevaricate, to question and to undo.

The fact was, that the image-breaking had completely severed the connection, feeble at best, between the governant and the popular party. From that moment the duchess ceased to coquette with the patriot nobles whom she had pretended to favor since the exile of Granvelle. But she was cautious; for she knew that tranquillity was the *desideratum*, and she was aware that that could only be secured by a seeming deference to the opinions and the acts of the popular leaders. This for a time she yielded, though she let no opportunity slip that could enable her to balk their purposes or to embarrass their plans.

At the same time, the wily duchess began to court the long-neglected partisans of the king— Aremberg, Megen, Noircarmes, and the rest. One morning she sent for Viglius. "Mr. President," said she, when that octogenarian doctor stood before her, "we have been too long estranged; I acknowledge my mistake. Prithee, give me thy counsel once more." Viglius was surprised; but he responded, "Madame, are you prepared to carry out the well-known wishes of the king?" "Aye, with all my heart," was the reply. "Well then," said Viglius, "put the same question to each member of your cabinet." The governant obeyed, and this touchstone revealed the unalloyed loyalty of three seigneurs—Mansfeld, Barlaiment, and Aerschot.

With these an alliance was extemporized, and the duchess again found herself at the head of a party composed of congenial souls.*

Another thing helped to raise Margaret's long-drooping courage; she had received those letters from Philip which placed money in her hands, and empowered her to recruit an army.† As usual, the royal concession had come *post factum;* but the three hundred thousand florins were welcome, even at the eleventh hour.

The pupil of Loyola began to intrigue. By shrewd management, she obtained from Charles IX. of France a proclamation which forbade his subjects to assist the Low Country heretics; and this was meant as a menace to the Huguenots, whose sympathy with their provincial brothers in the faith was notorious.‡ Flushed with this success, the elated duchess turned to Germany, at that time the recruiting-ground of Europe, and importuned the emperor for armed aid, while she essayed to unlock the hearts of the lesser Germanic potentates with a golden key. The Romanists among them readily yielded, and agreed to belt on their swords; the electors of Triers and Mentz offering free passage through their territories to the mercenary troopers.§ But there were some locks which were not to be picked; the landgrave of Hesse was one; the duke of Wurtemberg was another; and the count Palatin was a third; all of whom refused

---

* This conversation is detailed in the Vita Viglii, p. 47.
† Ante, pp. 370, 371.   ‡ Strada, p. 134.   § Ibid.

to move, on account of their Protestantism.* The emperor himself attempted to dissuade Margaret from these levies, offering to mediate between the late insurgents and the throne.† "No," said Margaret, "we will make no terms with an armed faction without arms ourselves." The emperor gave way, and the royal recruiting-masters plied their trade without interference.‡

Against Horn, Margaret was especially incensed. That seigneur had recently ventured to comply with the demand of the Tournay reformers for permission to meet within the walls of their city, since winter was at hand and their field-chapels could not be completed before spring, while the frequent storms made camp-meetings impossible.§ Horn reluctantly set aside the Clothiers' Hall for their use until their temples were finished; coupling the grant, however, with a proviso that it should be subject to the regent's revocation.‖

When her assent to this arrangement was asked, the duchess was beside herself with rage. "Never," exclaimed she, "shall the interior of Tournay be profaned by these heretical rites."¶ In the middle of October, 1566, Horn was recalled to Brussels.**

As her confidence increased, the governant made greater efforts to retrace the humiliating path up which circumstances had led her. She did not ven-

* Strada, p. 134.   † Ibid., p. 133.
‡ Ibid. Hopper, Rec. et Mem.
§ Motley, vol. 2, p. 21. De la Barre, MS.
‖ Ibid., Frappen's Supplément, tom. 2, p. 406.
¶ Frappen, *ubi sup.*, p. 499, *et seq.*   ** Ibid.

ture to revoke the accord; but she defined it so narrowly that it became that "letter of the law which killeth." For instance, the essence of the compact of the 25th of August was, that the preaching of the reformed religion should be tolerated wherever it had been established previously to that date. Yet now this was construed not to cover the performance of such rites as baptism, marriage, and burial—the necessary concomitants of preaching.[*] In this same autumn of 1566, she fulminated an edict, reciting the terrible penalties of the law against all offenders in this way; and this unscrupulous paper she formally commanded the authorities to enforce.[†]

Orange was indignant at this juggling, and he loudly complained of it, as also of the efforts of the regent to undermine his character at Madrid.[‡] The duchess endeavored to mollify him. She specially commissioned Assonleville to assure her "cousin of Orange" that "she had always loved and honored him as her good son;" and at the same time she wrote Hoogstraaten in a similar siren strain.[§] But the long-headed prince was not to be hoodwinked. "Madame," retorted he, "I am not so frivolous as to believe in your having used language to my discredit, without being certain of the fact—as I shall shortly prove by evidence."[||]

* Prescott, vol. 2, p. 96. Strada. †Strada.
‡ Motley, vol. 2, p. 54.
§ La Défense du Comte de Hocstrate, p. 94.
|| Cor. de Guillaume le Taciturne, tom. 2, p. 233, *et seq.*

At bottom, Orange cared little for the estrangement of the duchess; he expected it, for he knew the radical differences which divided them. Still he would not permit Margaret to believe that she could cheat him. . Horn also viewed this coolness with sullen indifference. It was Egmont, who could only live in the sunshine of the court, that took this exclusion from the royal confidence most to heart. "They tell me," wrote Morillon to Granvelle, "that it is quite incredible how old and gray Egmont has become."*

Of course, this whole momentous chapter of events had been closely read by Philip. Accounts of the image-breaking had reached Madrid with the usual expedition of evil news—that fastest of all travellers. The tidings found the king stretched upon a tertian-fever bed at his Segovian retreat; but, if we may credit Morillon, rage proved stronger than disease, and losing for once his habitual self-command, he leaped from his couch, and tearing his beard in a paroxysm of frenzy, cried, "It shall cost them dear: by the soul of my father I swear it—it shall cost them dear."†

Soon, however, regaining the reins of his temper, he curbed its expression, determined to let deeds speak for him. Never again was his serenity disturbed, though his eyes devoured letter after letter full of the details of the iconomachy. Indeed, more potent than the royal leeches, the news seem-

---

* Archives de la Maison d'Orange-Nassau, Supplément, p. 36.
† Gachard, Analectes Belgiques, p. 254.

ed to shock him into health; and though enfeebled by the sickness, he at once summoned his councillors to convene, attending personally upon their discussions: so superior is the spirit to the weaknesses of the body.*

Prejudice is the most plausible of special pleaders. The Castilian ministers assembled at Segovia imagining that the image-breaking was a national act; and in their investigations they scanned the facts from the standpoint of that belief, twisted the evidence into that meaning. They held the iconoclasts to have been the mere tools of abler rogues: they were moved by the sectaries; the sectaries were inspired by the *gueux;* the *gueux* were the creatures of the leading seigneurs—Orange, Egmont, Horn.† Thus all were branded as guilty, while the chief responsibility was strapped upon the shoulders of the men who had been most instrumental in evoking order out of chaos.

In this the advisers of the king were agreed; but when they came to discuss the policy to be adopted, there were two opinions at the councilboard. There were still, as at Philip's accession,‡ two rivals in the royal favor—Ruy Gomez prince of Eboli, and the duke of Alva. No two characters could be more antipodal in disposition, habit, interest. Eboli was a man of peace; Alva was a man of war. Eboli was pacific and temporizing, and these were the arts by which he had acquired influ-

* Hopper, Rec. et Mem., p. 104.
† Ibid.   ‡ Ante, p. 149.

ence; Alva was ferocious and uncompromising, and these were the means by which he had become a power in the state. Eboli, true to his character and also to his policy—for commotion was his rival's element, and in it he was ruler—was ever the advocate of mildness and delay. Alva, true to his character and also to his policy—for in a calm his rival was supreme—always counselled vengeance and expedition. " Thus it is," philosophizes Strada, " that most men form their opinions; and the vote which nature extorts, we think is given to the cause, when indeed we give it to our humor."*

These councillors of opposite ideas were now wrangling in Philip's presence. Eboli urged his master to set out in person for the Netherlands, not in warlike panoply, but accompanied only by such a retinue as should look down opposition and befit the royal dignity. Alva made no objection to the king's departure, but clamored for the equipment of an army which should be empowered to chastise the states.

Evidently Alva was a surgeon of the heroic school.†

Usually, the procrastinating and tortuous policy of Eboli was that most congenial to the kindred soul of Philip; but now his dark and sullen temper was in arms, and he panted for revenge. Therefore Alva's advice was taken; the king decided to

* Strada, vol. 2, p. 23.
† Ibid., et seq. Brandt, vol. 1, pp. 260, 261.

equip an army for the subjugation of the provinces,
and the iron duke was himself selected to head the
crusade.*

However, he infused into this policy something
of his own spirit, for he insisted upon keeping the
decision secret.† He preferred to advance by crooked ways, even when straight ones were the best.
He mistook dissimulation for diplomacy. The
throat of the provinces was to be cut, but the politic assassin meant to steal in on tiptoe and creep
round behind. In pursuance of this plan, the accepted advice of Alva was hidden behind the scenes,
while before the footlights Philip played the part
of a benignant pacificator. Not before the spring
of 1567 could the arrangements for the invasion of
the Netherlands be completed; it was necessary to
bridge over six months with treachery.

Accordingly, Alva was sent to Paris, ostensibly
as the Spanish ambassador, but really for the purpose of persuading Catharine de' Medici to open
a path through France for Philip's avengers of the
faith.‡ The king himself began to make noisy preparations for his supposititious voyage to the states—
long promised, much derided, never credited. But
now the laughers were cheated into the belief that
this time his majesty was in earnest, so formal was
his haste, so profuse were his arrangements for a
speedy departure. Nevertheless, the biographer of
the Farneses avers that this was but a cleverly

° Strada, vol. 2, p. 23. Brandt, vol. 1, pp. 260, 261.
† Strada, *ubi sup.*   ·   ‡ Strada.

enacted comedy, not serious at the bottom.* Certain it is that the voyage of the royal actor must be set down in continuation of D'Israeli's chapter of "Events that never took Place."

While his cozened lacqueys were busied in packing trunks which they were for ever destined, on one pretext or another, to unpack again, Philip was in active correspondence with madame of Parma. She also was his dupe, for she devoutly believed in the certainty of the king's speedy arrival at Brussels, and constantly proclaimed it.†

In the autumn of 1566, Philip addressed two letters to Margaret. In the first of these, which was meant to be made public, he announced his own restoration to health and the birth of an infanta, closing with the affirmation of his purpose to set out for the states at an early day, and with the assertion of "his intention to treat his subjects like a good and clement prince, not to ruin them by reducing them into servitude." "I shall exercise only humanity, sweetness, and grace, avoiding all harshness,"‡ said his Machiavellian majesty King Philip II., who had already proscribed the whole nation. In the other note, which was private, he urged the governant to strain every nerve in the enrolment of the German levies, and to let slip no opportunity to effect the dissolution of the *gueux;* and for this purpose he sent her a batch of letters, overflowing with kind expressions and artful flattery, to distri-

○ Strada.   † Ibid.
‡ Corresp. de Marg. d'Autriche, p. 206.

bute among the leaguers as she deemed best.* Not
one allusion did he make to the accord; he dared
not, at present, annul it; and he was still less disposed to acknowledge its validity; so he obeyed the
English statesman's rule, and when he had nothing
to say, he said nothing.†

Margaret received these despatches but to credit
and obey them. She was already doing her utmost
to recruit an army; she was determined to break up
the union of *les gueux.* In this work, circumstances
were her allies. The country had outgrown the
league. Internal dissensions had enfeebled it. At
St. Trond many of the Romanists had shaken off
the dust from their feet against it. The iconomachy had wholly robbed it of ultramontanist support.
The conduct of the leaguers in siding with the court
against the image-breakers had deprived it also of
the confidence of the sectaries.‡ Thus undermined
with both parties, it was sure to fall an easy prey to
the snares of the governant.

And it must be confessed that Margaret played
her game shrewdly. She made brave use of the
royal letters. They were directed with an appearance of profound secrecy to a variety of individuals,
and then made to miscarry, so as to fall into the
wrong hands. In this way the seeds of distrust
were quickly sown. Many of the confederates began to doubt the honesty of those of their brothers

* Cor. de Marg. d'Autriche, p. 206.   Schiller, p. 18.
† Schiller, *ubi sup.*
‡ *Vide* Relatione di M. H. Tiepalo, MS., 1567.

to whom such brilliant offers were made; and those who had received no such promises commenced to importune the duchess for pardon. A scrub-race for court favor ensued. A general rumor of the impending visit of the king made those who knew that his presence would augur no good to them all the more eager to accept what conditions they could get. A brief campaign completely discomfited the league, and madame rested on her laurels, confident that it was definitively broken as a nucleus of political offence.* A few of its members, like Brederode, and Louis of Nassau, and St. Aldegonde, were still untamed; but these were powerless, for they were robbed of *prestige*.

Margaret next essayed to lasso the seigneurs to her feet. Egmont was brought to the ground; but Hoogstraaten and Horn and Orange were too wary to be caught.

The prince was perfectly familiar with the whole programme which had been decided on at Madrid; his eyes had scanned the book which Philip thought that he had sealed. By a system of espionage singularly perfect, he held all Europe under *surveillance*, and could fix his eye at pleasure on the most distant courts, or so place his ear that it should catch the faintest whispered secrets of the Spanish despot.† Doubtless, there was no high morality in the employment of these Protean pryers into the most secret consultations and resolutions of crowned

---

* Groen v. Prinst., Archives, etc., tom. 2, p. 282. Tiepalo, *ut antea.* † Prescott, vol. 2, p. 84. Strada.

heads—eaves-droppers and disguises, the sum of
whose life was to know and not to be known; but
the use of spies was a part of the machinery of
diplomacy in the sixteenth century. William had
acquired the art in the school of Machiavelli. It
was the intelligence thus gained which enabled him
to fathom the dark depths of the policy of the most
tortuous of kings. Without this intelligence he
would have groped in the gloom—there would have
been no equality in his struggle with the royal inquisitor. And this may be said for him, that while
Philip spied for despotism, *he* spied to secure the
liberation of his country.

Just now William's spies were unusually busy.
These ubiquitous agents of his secret service constantly forwarded to him copies, and sometimes the
originals of Margaret's private letters to the king,
together with extracts from the minutes of the royal
cabinet. From time to time, the pilfered papers
were made public; the governant was astounded to
learn that manuscripts weighty with state secrets,
which she imagined safely buried in the hidden
recesses of the king's *escritoire*, were passed from
hand to hand by the gaping burghers of her own
capital. "Sire," complained she to Philip, "the
contents of my despatches are known in Flanders
almost as soon as at Madrid; and not only copies,
but the original autographs circulate in Brussels.
Be pleased to burn my letters after reading them, if
you cannot keep them without danger."*

* Corresp. de Philippe II., tom. 1, p. 474.

The *naiveté* of the king's reply is laughable. "This of which you complain is impossible. I always keep my papers locked, and the key lies in my pocket."[*] The idea seemed not to occur to this man, who was rather the chief of a bureau of secret police than a monarch, that the arts which he practised upon others, might possibly by others be practised upon him. But they were. "Men of leisure," affirmed Orange, "may occupy themselves in philosophical pursuits, and with the secrets of nature; as for me, it is my business to study the hearts of kings."[†]

Made aware by this "study" of what was in Philip's heart, and conscious of the imminent peril in which the Netherlands stood, Orange was anxious to concert some plan of resistance. Feeling that the hour for action had dawned, he sent a private courier to acquaint Egmont with the impending danger, proposing, with his coöperation and with that of Horn, to convene the states-general, and if the national representatives proved propitious, to risk preparations against Alva's coming raid.[‡]

On the 3d of October, 1566, before an answer to this proposal could be received, Orange, Egmont, Horn, Louis of Nassau, and Hoogstraaten met at Dendermonde in Flanders, to chat over what had best be done, in person.[§] Here two important let-

[*] Corresp. de Philippe II., tom. 1, p. 491.
[†] Strada. Cited in Motley, vol. 2, p. 41.
[‡] Groen v. Prinst., Archives, etc., tom. 2, p. 326.
[§] Strada, tom. 2, p. 134. Cor. de Guillaume le Tacit., tom. 2.

ters were read and considered. One was from Montigny, the Netherland envoy, held in duress at Madrid. Addressing his brother-in-law, Count Horn, he wrote: "Nothing can be in worse odor than are our affairs at the court of Castile. The great lords in particular are considered the source of all the mischief. Violent counsels are altogether in the ascendant, and the storm may burst upon you sooner than you think. Nothing remains but to fly from it prudently, or to face it bravely."* The other was an intercepted letter from Alva, then in France, to the duchess of Parma. The duke gave a circumstantial account of the approaching invasion of the provinces, for which purpose the king was busily levying an army, asserted that the seigneurs were marked out for heavy punishment, and cautioned Margaret in the meantime so to regulate her deportment as to persuade all that the past had been forgiven and forgotten.†

"Now, gentlemen," queried Orange, "with these facts before us, what ought we to do?"

"I counsel an immediate appeal to arms," cried Louis of Nassau. "At all risks, the king should never be permitted to dragoon the country into servitude." "I say amen to that," said Hoogstraaten. Horn was silent. Egmont repudiated the idea of revolt, and his emphatic protest broke up the conference. Orange did not pronounce himself, for he knew that Egmont's popularity and military *prestige* made his coöperation essential to the success of any

* Bentivoglio, p. 118.   † Cor. de Phil. II, tom. 1, p. 485.

scheme of armed resistance. A feast closed this interview; after which the seigneurs mounted horse and separated—separated in both senses, for the old community of interest was lost.*

Had the Dendermonde meeting resulted, as Orange meant it should, in a firm coalition against Philip, the history of a decade would have been differently written. That it did not so eventuate, was the fault of Egmont.† The count was a brilliant cavalry officer—the Murat of the sixteenth century—but he utterly lacked prevision, while his vanity was so great that he would not credit those whose sight was keener. Besides, he was a courtier by nature, and he felt the incongruity of his recent position as a liberal leader—a position into which circumstances, acting upon an impulsive and sympathetic nature, had drifted him. His conscience acquitted him of any purpose to wrong the king; and judging Philip by himself, he felt sure of having won the royal forgiveness for what venial sins he had committed, by his honest conduct in restoring order. He was not the stuff of which revolutionists are made, for he was terrified by words, and he was turned from his purpose by a glance at his family. He had feelings, not principles. He was unduly anxious about appearances; belonged to that class of whom Wendell Phillips has said,

---

* Bentivoglio, pp. 123–128. Bor., tom. 2, p. 108. Hoofd, tom. 3, p. 114.

† Horn, in his "Justification," refers the failure to Egmont. Vide Procés de Horne, Frappen's Supplément.

"they creep 'prudently' into nameless graves, while higher spirits forget themselves into immortality." He had none of the unconsciousness of greatness which will not let the heart turn to examine the crimson of its own currents. So Egmont shook hands with Orange, meaning henceforth to "smother his prejudices," and like the jockeys at Epsom, to sweat down the truth till it could ride equal weight with any rascal. Still, with all his credulity, Alva's letter somewhat disturbed him, and on reaching Brussels he showed a copy of it to the governant. Margaret was surprised, but Egmont did not fright her confidence into a blush; she pronounced the epistle to be a forgery.* The count was not convinced of her sincerity. "This is a woman educated at Rome," said he; "there is no faith to be given her."† Happy would it have been for Egmont had he held to that belief.

Horn did not commit himself at Dendermonde;‡ but it is probable that, had Egmont pronounced for war, no objections would have come from him. However, as affairs had turned out, his hands were left clean of any thing which smelt of treason—if any attempt to protect the ancient, well-understood, and chartered privileges of the Netherlands against a forsworn foreign despot may be so designated. But Horn was sour and moody. Of a proud and ambitious temper, his pride had been outraged, and his ambition had been thwarted with pertinacious

---

* Archives de la Maison d'Orange-Nassau, tom. 2, p. 400, *et seq.*
† Ibid.   ‡ Procés de Horne, in Frappen's Supplément.

malignity by a court in whose service he had grown gray. He had spent four hundred thousand florins in the royal service without recompense, although it was well known that this expenditure had obliged him to pawn his massive family-plate, and had covered his estates ten feet deep with mortgages.* This was but one of many griefs; and recently, to the sum total of his discontent, the shabby treatment, the unscrupulous calumniation with which Margaret rewarded efforts which averted the "Sicilian vespers" from Tournay had been added.†

Wrathful and ruined, Horn determined no longer to serve a perfidious court. In a letter which he now wrote to Philip, he resigned his honors, and after reciting the indignities which had driven him to take this step, added: "It is not the regent, but your majesty, of whom I complain; for it is you, sire, who have compelled me to dance attendance at the court of Brussels. Henceforth I shall not discuss my conduct with the duchess, for it is not my way to treat of affairs of honor with ladies."‡

Having unwittingly dug his grave with these plain-dealing words—for to-morrow is a fog into which no one can see—Horn retired to his mortgaged "growlery" at Weert, severed his connection with all parties, and like Diogenes, asked only a fee simple of the sunshine.§ "Well," said he, "I

---

* Renom. de Francia, MS. Cited in Motley, vol. 2, p. 37.
† Ibid.
‡ Frappen's Supplément, tom. 2, p. 501, *et seq.*
§ Ibid. Vide Procés de Horne.

can turn hermit for the rest of my days, as well as the emperor Charles."*

The obstinate credulity of Egmont and the sullen retirement of Horn left Orange isolated at this critical hour—robbed him of his most prominent supporters; for though Hoogstraaten and Louis of Nassau and St. Aldegonde were devoted, they had not the influence in the land which the recusant seigneurs possessed. Nothing remained but to wait and watch. Retiring into the north, he paused at Utrecht. Here he addressed a pamphlet to the authorities of the province, in which he urged the necessity of religious toleration, as demanded by Christian charity, by the spirit of the age, and by the policy of cosmopolite states, inhabited by sects of all denominations; and he concluded by recommending that a petition of this tenor be laid before the throne; not probably from any belief that it would be heeded by Philip, but from the effect it would have in strengthening the principles of ecclesiastical freedom in the minds of his fellow-countrymen.†

This paper, which was ably and strikingly argued, marked an epoch in William's life, for it was his first written offering to the spirit of Christianity since his conversion to the religious tenets of the Reformation. In a letter to the landgrave of Hesse, in November, 1566, he announced this momentous

---

* Frappen, *ubi sup.*, p. 506.

† Prescott, vol. 2, p. 73. Archives et Correspondance, tom. 2, pp. 430, 431.

change in his creed.*   Doubtless the principles
planted in his infant heart by his pious parents at
the old Dillenberg castle, and the seeds of doubt
sown by recent events in the Netherlands, combined
to flower into Protestantism in his mind.   The impressions of childhood are proverbially lasting; and
the ashes of the countless innocents, martyred for
no crime but that of dissent from Rome, spoke
trumpet-toned to thoughtful and enlightened souls.
William saw the ligament which united the Siamese
twins of Rome and Spain—the *Chang* of the Vatican to the *Eng* of Madrid.   Then too his family—
his aged mother, still alive, his brothers, his sisters,
his wife, were of the reformed faith.   Thus the ties
of kindred, every pulsation of his patriotic heart,
the manifold influences of the time, moved the truant prince to face Zionward.   Now that he had
done so, another link was forged in the chain which
wedded him to the liberal party of the provinces.

The reformed had taken advantage of the interval of quiet which succeeded the iconomachy, to
methodize the formulas of their worship, hitherto
somewhat loose and unsettled.   In many of the cities consistories—a kind of sacred parliament, composed of ecclesiastical senators and magistrates—
were instituted; and these were subordinated to a
controlling assembly, which sat at Antwerp.†   Thus
the republic of religion was reduced to order, in

* Prescott, vol. 2, p. 93.   Dumont, Corps Diplomatique, tom.
5, part 1, p. 392.
† Strada, p. 138.   Brandt.

obedience to heaven's first law, and provided with
a mouth-piece through which its wishes might find
utterance.

But, unhappily, the Protestants of that day did
not comprehend the golden rule of modern Christian fellowship—fraternization in the fundamental
principles of the gospel, charity in all besides. In
the Low Countries, sects at absolute agreement on
vital tenets waged bitter war on minor points of
faith; a fact prophetical of ruin when the common
enemy was in the field.* In Germany, the princes
were Lutherans; in the provinces, the Calvinists
were the dominant denomination. They were at
open feud. From time to time good men essayed
to bring about a truce, but in the main, their efforts
were without success.†

Under these circumstances, each sect was left to
shift for itself, sole guardian of its interests. At
Antwerp, the reformed endeavored to buy toleration.
Through Hoogstraaten, they sent a petition to Margaret, offering to pay three hundred thousand florins into the royal treasury, if only they might be
guaranteed immunity of worship. But now at Brussels, as always at Madrid, there was one passion
yet stronger than avarice, and that was bigotry.
The disdainful court would vouchsafe no answer to
the memorial.‡

Margaret was now occupied day and night in the

* Prescott, vol. 2, p. 94. Hoofd, tom. 3.
† Strada, p. 138. Archives de la Maison d'Orange-Nassau,
tom. 2, p. 455.   ‡ Strada, p. 140.

"study of revenge."[*] Feeling that her star was once more in the ascendant, she lost the humility that had characterized her actions while the image-breakers were abroad. The divisions of the foes, the jingling of Philip's gold, the sight of her recruits, all combined to elate her. "Now," said she, "I am strong enough to work my will;" and immediately this woman, who already knew all the points in the compass of deceit, began to add to that knowledge the maxims of a bolder roguery. She sent Duke Eric, of Brunswick, into Holland at the head of an armed force.[†] She formally revoked the accord.[‡] She kept Egmont busy in forcing the cities of Flanders and Artois to receive her mercenary garrisons.[§] Not under the imperial sceptre of Charles V. had such bold stretches of arbitrary power been hazarded.

Great was the excitement which this conduct caused, and it provoked an ill-regulated, spasmodic, fragmentary resistance: foredoomed to an unhappy end by the apostacy of Egmont, who was viciously active against his old companions; by the neutrality of Horn, who could not be coaxed to leave his lair; and by the prudence of Orange, who stood aloof because he saw that the Netherlands, paralyzed by division, were not yet ready for a national rising, the only one which could be efficient. The

[*] Corresp. de Philippe II., tom. 2, p. 496.
[†] Groen v. Prinst., Archives, etc., tom. 2, pp. 322–326.
[‡] Corresp. de Guillaume le Tacit., tom. 2, p. 351, et seq.
[§] Motley, vol. 2, p. 44.

cities were the first to protest; those of Hainault
were especially out-spoken in their determination
not to open their gates for the reception of the
hated mercenaries.* Horn had been succeeded in
the stadtholderate of that province by Philip de
Noircarmes, a courtier by profession and a butcher
from instinct.† This personage had a peculiar
aptitude for making bad matters worse, as he
soon made manifest. Abandoning the policy of
justice, which his honest predecessor had inaugurated, he embraced the more congenial methods
of trickery and violence in his dealings with the
reformed.

Noircarmes, in common with Aremberg, Aerschot, Megen, and Egmont, had been ordered to
hunt up or invent pretexts for the introduction of
garrisons into all places suspected of favoring the
new doctrines.‡ It was work to his taste. On the
21st of November, 1566, he galloped across the
country to Valenciennes at the head of an unusually strong cavalcade, and pausing before the city
gates, summoned the citizens to receive a garrison
as a punishment for their flagitious conduct in cele-
brating the Lord's Supper within the corporate
limits.§ The cautious burghers asked time for consideration; whereupon Noircarmes fired a volley of
oaths into their faces, and rode off, protesting that

---

* Prescott, vol. 2, p. 97. Brandt, vol. 1, p. 207.

† Motley, vol. 2, p. 73.

‡ Prescott, *ubi sup.* Renom. de Francia, MS. Hoofd, tom. 3.

§ Brandt, *ubi sup.*

they would have themselves to blame for whatever mischief might befall them.*

The townsfolk at once met at the stadthouse in anxious consultation. The magistrates urged compliance with the regent's requisition; but "the people, whose ears were chained to the tongues of their preachers," on being informed by those eminent divines, Guy de Bray and Peregrine de la Grange, then resident at Valenciennes, that the result of acquiescence would be the suppression of their worship, voted to bar out the conscience-chaining soldiers.† One of the city councillors said to La Grange: "If you fear for your life we will guarantee you a safe conduct from our walls. Exert your all-powerful eloquence to win an assent to the demand of her highness." "Nay, friend," was the stout reply, "I care not unduly for myself—I am in God's hands; but may I grow mute as a fish, may the tongue cleave to the roof of my mouth before I persuade my people to accept a garrison of cruel mercenaries, by whom their rights of conscience are to be trampled on."‡ It was evident that if the foreign spearmen entered Valenciennes, it must be through breaches in the walls. La Grange was not a Jesuit, doing wrong that good might come. Two negatives make an affirmative; but he knew that two vices do not make a virtue. And if he gave counsel which brought the city to ruin, it was precisely the crime which Æschines charged upon

---

* Brandt, *ut antea*.   † Ibid. Valenciennes, MS.
‡ Corresp. de Philippe II., tom. 1, p. 561, note.

Demosthenes in the Athenian forum, and over which posterity has written the word "repudiation."

On the 17th* of December, 1566, Valenciennes—so named from its Roman founder, the emperor Valentinian†—was declared by Margaret to be rebellious and in a state of siege.‡ The city had long been considered by the court as "a hotbed of heresy," and though it had been originally founded as a city of refuge, it was thought wofully to have abused its privileges in affording an asylum to dissenters.§ For this high crime the duchess ached to scourge it, and accordingly Noircarmes was now sent with a strong force to administer the chastisement.‖ At the same time, its nearness to the French border and the Huguenot character of its inhabitants had impelled Philip to give the governant an order to proceed with circumspection—to exhaust artifice before resorting to violence.¶

While Noircarmes was digging his trenches, Valenciennes was busy in strengthening its naturally fine fortifications, and in issuing appeals for aid. The few remaining members of the *gueux*, heeding the appeal, at once set themselves in motion. Count Louis of Nassau passed into Germany to recruit an army.** Brederode drew up a remon-

---

° Brandt says on the 14th inst.—vol. 1, p. 207.

† Guicciardini, Belg. Des., p. 458, *et seq.*

‡ Valenciennes, MS. Brandt, vol. 1, p. 207. Hoofd. Pontus Payen, MS.   § Motley, vol. 2, p. 45.

‖ Bor., tom. 3, p. 136. Brandt, *ut antea.*

¶ Strada, vol. 2, pp. 8, 9.

°° Groen v. Prinst., Archives, etc., tom. 3.

strance which he intended to present to the governant in person, at the head of four hundred knights.*
Margaret, who was tired of petitions, on being told
of this determination, sent him this message: "If
you come to Brussels on such an errand, I shall
shut the city gates in your face."† But Brederode
could not be beaten at the game of bluff, and spite
of all, he succeeded in laying his memorial at the
regent's feet.‡ Her reply was blunt and haughty
enough—fit twin to her message: "I wonder what
kind of nobles these are who, after requesting, only
a twelvemonth back, to be saved merely from the
Inquisition, now presume to clamor for liberty to
preach in the cities. Know, then, that the *gueux*
are disbanded, and that the accord is cancelled.
As for you and your companions, sir count, you
will do well to go to your homes at once. Meddle
less with public affairs and attend more to your
own. Disobey at your peril."§

Thus with disdainful hauteur and sinister threats
did the duchess respond to a paper which ventured
to remind her of her straits and her pledges.

Meantime, Brederode's seed had sprouted. A raff
of fugitives, under the command of young Marnix
of Thoulouse, a brother of St. Aldegonde, fresh from
college, with no title but his courage to leadership,
made a descent on the island of Walcheren, a place
of strategic importance. Repelled by the vigilance
of the islanders, Marnix reëmbarked, and sailing

---

* Bor., tom. 3, p. 148. Strada, vol. 1, p. 142.
† *Vide* Prescott, vol. 2, p. 99.
‡ Ibid., p. 100. Strada, *ubi sup.* Cor. de Philippe II.
§ Strada, p. 143. Meteren, vol. 2, folio 47.

up the Scheldt, again left his boats at the hamlet of
Austruweel, under the shadow of Antwerp walls.*
The unhappy boy landed only to meet his death;
for on the 12th of March, 1567, his undisciplined
levies were surprised and literally butchered by
Beauvoir, commander of the regent's body-guard.†
This slaughter—for it was not a battle—stirred a
three days' tumult in Antwerp, which was finally
appeased without bloodshed by the courageous energy and tact of the Prince of Orange.‡

Some months before the tragedy of Austruweel,
Noircarmes was told that several straggling bands
of the *gueux*, mustering in the aggregate upwards
of three thousand men, had appeared in the vicinity of Tournay with the twofold object of protecting that city, which had refused a garrison, and
creating a diversion in favor of Valenciennes. The
ferocious soldier, among whose faults slothfulness
was not numbered, at once withdrew a moiety of
his troops from the Valenciennes trenches, and
speeding to meet the foe, assailed the unsuspecting
camp of the confederates with exceeding fury.
The *gueux* made a gallant effort to breast the onset;
mechanics, rustics, students, fought like brave men,
long and well; but the contest was too unequal,
and in the end the battle became a massacre.§
Pausing but to complete the rout, Noircarmes

° Strada, vol. 2, pp. 3, 4. Bor., tom. 3, p. 157.

† Ibid. Meteren, tom. 2, folio 45.

‡ Ibid. Hoofd, tom. 4, p. 127, *et seq.*

§ Groen v. Prinst., Archives, etc., tom. 3, pp. 7, 8. Hoofd.
Strada.

thundered up to the gates of Tournay, and compelled the town, no longer capable of resistance, to throw open its posterns and shout him a welcome. He garrisoned the citadel, suppressed the reformed worship, broke up the consistory, banished the preachers, reëstablished Romanism, and then hastened back to Valenciennes to press the siege with redoubled vigor.*

This victory made Brussels sweat with joyful wine and jubilant gluttony; multitudinous were the feasts, countless were the drunken orgies with which the courtiers celebrated it. "I saw Barlaiment just go by my window," wrote Schwartz to William; "he was coming from Aerschot's dinner with a face as red as the cardinal's new hat."†

Noircarmes left banqueting to the carpet-knights; and, freed from all danger of hostile interference by the recent crushing victories, concentrated his whole mind upon the reduction of Valenciennes. The rough soldier's pluck had been supplemented by the rare military skill of Egmont, a new-comer in the camp;‡ and now, under their united supervision, the hapless town was girt closer and yet closer by the grim cordon of mercenary spearmen. The beleaguered citizens fought with the energy of desperation;§ but on what field was untutored devotion ever known to conquer science? At length a terrific cannonade laid half the place in

* Strada, pp. 7, 8.
† Archives et Correspondance.   Cited in Motley, vol. 2, p. 49.
‡ Valenciennes, MS.   § Ibid.   Strada, vol. 2, p. 7, *et seq.*

ruins, and battered a dozen fatal breaches in the walls. Noircarmes, sword in hand, was about to lead his men-at-arms in a wild assault, when, to escape the horrors of a sack, the gallant city struck its flag, surrendering at discretion.*

On the 2d of April, 1567, exactly four months after the commencement of the siege, the victorious cohorts of the king trooped through the blood-stained and shattered streets of what had been the most prosperous commercial town on the whole French border.† Now fallen from its high estate, Valenciennes was deprived of its ancient immunities, sentenced to defray the expenses of its subjugation, and compelled to provide quarters for a permanent garrison of eight battalions of imperious soldiers.‡

Nor did Noircarmes rest satisfied with this humiliation. He tore down the chapels and abolished the worship of the reformed religion, decreed that henceforth none but the Roman service should be celebrated within or without the city gates; and to give emphasis to his decree, led out a host of victims to die.§ Among the sufferers were La Grange, and De Bray. "Citizens," cried La Grange, as he stood upon the ladder of the gibbet, "I am slain for having preached the pure word of God to a Christian people in a Christian land." "Friends," ech-

---

° Strada, vol. 2, p. 10. Bor., tom. 3, p. 142.
† Valenciennes, MS.
‡ Strada, *ubi sup.* Hoofd, tom. 4, p. 129.
§ Bor., tom. 3, p. 142. Hoofd, tom. 4, p. 129. Valenciennes, MS.

oed De Bray, "this also is my sole offence." Ere they had finished speaking, the eager executioner launched both into eternity.[*]

The keys of Valenciennes opened the gates of every city in the Netherlands. Oudenarde, Ghent, Ypres, Tornhut, became servilely submissive.[†] Megen dropped garrisons into the towns of Guelders.[‡] Aremberg cantoned his soldiers on the inhabitants of Gröningen and Friesland.[§] Soon throughout the provinces there was neither the power nor the purpose of resistance.

Emboldened by the success which had thus far attended her diplomacy and by the triumphant progress of her arms, Margaret determined to demand of the whole round of governmental functionaries the taking of a new and sweeping oath of allegiance—extra-judicial, unprecedented. This measure had been uppermost in her mind since the early weeks of 1566, when it was formally discussed and approved at the council-board.[‖] The test-oath itself, while binding all who took it to uphold the Roman church, to punish sacrilege, to extirpate heresy, to yield ready, unquestioning, unqualified obedience to the king's commands, of whatever nature they might be, decreed deprivation of office as the penalty of non-subscription.[¶]

This pledge, a kind of verbal inquisition, was

---

[*] Brandt, Hist. des Martyrs, folios 661, 662.
[†] Meteren, tom. 2, folio 45.   Strada, vol. 2, pp. 13-23.
[‡] Ibid.   [§] Ibid.
[‖] Strada, vol. 2, p. 11.   Bor., Meteren.   [¶] Ibid.

exacted by the governant, not as a test of temper, for she could well distinguish between the king's friends and foes; not as a bond for the insincere, for she knew that these could not be tied; but as a decent pretext for the dismissal from power of the disaffected who might refuse to sully their lips by a false vow, and as an excuse for the execution of whoever should take and then break the oath.* And she was especially induced to cast this prudent anchor to windward at this time, by the late arrival of an express from Madrid, which apprized her that the duke of Alva was about to embark for the Netherlands as the *avant-courier* of Philip.†

The oath was taken, with more or less willingness, by Aerschot, and Barlaimont, and Megen, and Egmont, and by Count Mansfeld, the new "factotum at Brussels," whose name led this bead-roll of court saints.‡ Four seigneurs—Brederode, Horn, Hoogstraaten, and Orange—spurned it with indignation. Brederode, who held an insignificant military command, threw up his commission in disgust. Horn, who had already resigned his honors, sent word from Weert that the demand on him was useless. Hoogstraaten asked Margaret to relieve him of the lieutenant-generalship of Antwerp. Orange promptly tendered the resignation of his many dignities.§

As for Brederode, and Horn, and Hoogstraaten, their pleas were answered with laconic disdain; but Orange was still too influential to alienate; so the

---

° Strada, vol. 2, p. 11.   † Ibid.   ‡ Ibid.   § Ibid.

duchess coaxed, wheedled, and bullied by turns, with a resolute purpose of persuading the prince to lay his head in the lap of Delilah; but all in vain.*

Berti, Margaret's private secretary, ventured to expostulate, and referred to the prince's honor, which would be impugned, and to his motives, which would be misconstrued. "Say no more," interrupted Orange; "I am determined to quit the provinces; I will await better days in another land. Leave me to care for my honor; and as for my motives, I leave their vindication to posterity."†

The wily secretary was at his wit's end; but as he was about to bow himself out of William's presence, he made one last effort. "I pray you, sir," said he, "ere you leave the Netherlands, talk this business over with Egmont and such others of the seigneurs as you may select." To this the prince readily assented; and the village of Willebrock, on the Rapel, between Brussels and Antwerp, was named as the place of conference.‡

Here, on the first of April, 1567, Egmont, accompanied by Count Mansfeld and Berti, met his highness of Nassau.§ Notwithstanding their dissimilarity of character and position, Egmont and Orange were warm personal friends, and each now exerted himself to the utmost to win over the other to his way of thinking. The prince knew that the leading

---

* Renom. de Francia. Corresp. de Guillaume le Tacit., tom. 2. Groen v. Prinst., Archives, etc., tom. 3, pp. 43, 48.

† Strada, vol. 2, p. 13. Corresp. de Guillaume le Tacit., pp. 354–417. Hoofd, tom. 4, p. 130.

‡ Ibid., p. 14. Cor. de Guil. le Tac., tom. 2, p. 416. § Ibid.

seigneurs had been proscribed at Madrid—that Alva's coming meant death to all. Had he not read the programme in black and white? "Count," said he, "fly before the coming storm; bide it out with me in Germany."

But Egmont was deaf to his friend's arguments. To him the prophetic warning of Orange seemed to come from a sad and dispirited heart. Above his head the sky still smiled. Never before had he been so courted by the duchess; and popularity is the best prism to see fancies by. Besides, for him, exile was pecuniary ruin. A Fleming, all his estates lay in the provinces; nor was he the man to accept beggary for a principle. Then, too, he was a sincere Romanist, and his creed tied him to the throne. Orange, on the contrary, was a Protestant. A moiety of his heritage was without the confines of the states. If he passed into Germany, he went not into exile, but to the home of his ancestors—to the warm greeting of leal kinsmen and devoted co-religionists. Every motive urged William to depart for a season; most motives persuaded Egmont to remain. Therefore neither could shake the determination of the other.

"It will cost you your provincial estates, Orange, if you persist in your purpose," said the count, as he led the prince aside into the embrasure of a window. "And you your life, Egmont, if you change not yours," was the grave reply. Orange added: "To me it will at least be some consolation in my misfortunes, that I desired in deed, as well as in word, to help my country and my friends in the hour of need; but you, my friend, you are dragging friends and country with you to destruction."

"Nay," said Egmont, "you will never persuade me to see things in the gloomy light in which they appear to your mournful prudence. The king is good and just; if I have erred, I will retrieve the past, and then throw myself on the royal clemency."

"Well, then," cried Orange, "trust if you will to Philip's gratitude; but my soul presages—may God grant that I be deceived—that you, Egmont, will be the bridge across which the Spaniards will pass to the destruction of our country." Then, clasping Egmont to his heart, while tears dimmed his eyes, he gazed at him long, as if the sight were to serve for the remainder of his life; and so they parted, one to go hoodwinked to the scaffold in a few brief months, the other to reserve himself for the glorious duties of the future.*

While Egmont hastened back to Brussels, to dispel the light cloud which the interview at Wille-

---

○ Strada, vol. 2, p. 14. Bentivoglio, tom. 3, p. 55. Hoofd, tom. 4, p. 130.

"Hoofd alludes to a rumor, according to which Egmont said to Orange at parting: 'Adieu, landless prince!' being answered by his friend, 'Adieu, headless count!' The story has been often repeated, yet nothing could well be more insipid than such an invention. Hoofd observes that the whole conversation was reported by a person whom the Calvinists had concealed in the chimney of the apartment where the interview took place. It would have been difficult to credit such epigrams even had the historian himself been in the chimney." Motley, vol. 2, pp. 88, 89, note.

brock had cast upon the horizon of his mind, by
sunning himself with fresh *abandon* in Margaret's
favor, the wiser prince occupied himself in pushing
the preparations for his expatriation. Time pressed.
The minutes now were full of scaffolds. Already
William had been warned by his wife's kinsman,
the landgrave of Hesse, to "beware of Alva." "I
know him well," added the acute old man; "let
him not smear your mouth with honey."* It was a
blunder which Orange was not likely to fall into.
A few days after the abortive conference with Egmont, he set out for Breda.† There he paused for
a space to settle his private affairs and to indite
farewell letters to Philip, to the governant, to Horn,
to Egmont. As if aware of the monumental importance which these missives were to assume for posterity, William drew them up in Latin.‡ In that to
the king, he once more resigned his offices—the governant had refused to accept the tender—announced
his intention of repairing to Germany, explained
the reasons on which he based this action, and concluded thus: " I shall always be ready to place myself and my property at your majesty's orders in
every thing which I believe conducive to your true
service."§ In that to Margaret, he wrote a few
polite commonplaces, and subscribed himself " her
highness' most faithful servant."‖ In that to Horn,

---

* Archives de la Maison d'Orange-Nassau, tom. 3, p. 42.
† April 11.   ‡ Motley, vol. 2, p. 89.
§ Archives et Correspondance, tom. 3, p. 64, *et seq.*
‖ Strada, vol. 2, p. 14.

he said: "I am unable longer to connive at the
sins daily committed against my country and my
conscience. Believe me, the government has been
accustoming us to panniers, only that we may accept more patiently the saddle and bridle. My back
is not strong enough to bear the weight already
imposed. I prefer exile to slavery."* In that to
Egmont, he again affirmed that he was acting, not
from caprice, but deliberately, conscientiously, and
in pursuance of a long-settled plan. "For yourself,
Egmont," he added, "I beg you to believe that you
have no more sincere friend than I am. My love
for you has struck such deep root into my heart,
that it can be lessened by no distance of time and
place; and I pray you in return to maintain the old
feeling towards me."†

On the 22d of April, 1567, the prince bade farewell to the Netherlands for a season, and, accompanied by his whole family—with the exception of
his eldest son, the count of Buren, who was left to
pursue his studies at the University of Louvaine,
sheltered, as his father thought, by the privileges of
Brabant‡—departed for the ancestral seat of the
Nassaus at Dillenburg.§

While Orange was leaving Breda, Sound-and-
fury Brederode was preparing to quit Amsterdam.
For the last two months he had spent his time be-

* Archives, etc., *ubi sup.*
† Archives de la Maison d'Orange-Nassau, tom. 3, p. 70.
‡ Strada, vol. 2, p. 14.
§ Ibid. Archives et Correspondance, tom. 3, p. 73.

tween that city and his town of Viana, causing riot
and debauchery to rave and leer wherever he appeared. An annoyance to all parties, he was shunned by all. Wealthy Protestants were especially
wary of him, for they had no confidence in his capacity to do any thing but demand contributions to
the patriot cause, and then distil their money into
drink.* He made much mischief, but did little
good. Indeed, what could be expected of a man
whose pot companions were outlaws and vagabonds—swaggering nobles disguised as sailors, and
bankrupt tradesmen?† Not from these shriekers
of "*Vivent les gueux !*"—these haunters of taverns
and frequenters of bagnios, was emancipation to
come.

Alarmed by the tone which affairs were taking,
Brederode had requested Egmont to intercede for
him with the duchess. "Offer her *carte blanche* as
to terms," wrote "the great beggar."‡ This late
submission was rejected by Margaret with disdain;
so that there was nothing left for it but flight. But
this historic Mark Tapley was never so happy as
when he was miserable. On the 25th of April,
1567, he summoned his adherents to meet him at
his Amsterdam hotel to say good-by; and at midnight, after a wild carouse, he, too, embarked for
Germany, being escorted to the water's edge by a

* Bor., tom. 3, p. 161. Hoofd, tom. 5, p. 127.

† Ibid. Motley, vol. 2, p. 92.

‡ MS. letter of Granvelle to Alva. Bibl. de Bourg. Cited in
Motley, vol. 2, p. 93. Strada, vol. 2, p. 19.

body-guard of tipsy followers bearing lighted torches and chanting bacchanalian songs.* Such was "the great beggar's" exit. Within a twelvemonth afterwards, Brederode drank himself to death while busied in Westphalia in recruiting an army of invasion—"dying as the fool dieth."†

The departure of Orange and the flight of Brederode were the signal for a general exodus. Hoogstraaten, Count Louis of Nassau, and Culemburg, with a host of others, followed William into Germany,‡ grouping themselves about their self-exiled chief by a law kindred to that which marshals the heavenly bodies around the sun—attraction. Those of the seigneurs who remained, made haste to imitate Egmont's example; even Horn succumbed and took the oath.§

Everywhere the reformed were cowed and panic-struck; everywhere the papists were jubilant and aggressive. Egmont, Noircarmes, Aerschot, Megen, were constantly in the saddle scouring the provinces, and hanging, burning, drowning such of the sectaries as had not already sought safety in flight.‖ The fickle masses, whose sympathies are ever with success, became as hotly Roman as they had been Protestant. The cities volunteered to suppress heresy. Mobs took it upon themselves, without awaiting the verdict of the civil tribunals, to punish the

---

* Vita Viglii, p. 51. Hoofd, tom. 4, p. 135.
† Strada, vol. 2, p. 20. Bor., Hoofd.
‡ Prescott, vol. 2, p. 128. Meteren, Bor.
§ Cor. de Marg. d'Autriche, p. 238. ‖ Ibid., p. 235.

iconoclasts and to uproot their monuments; accordingly, up and down they roamed, from Valenciennes to Amsterdam, assailing, gutting, demolishing the newly erected chapels of the Reformation, and decorating every cross-road with a gibbet shaped from the ruins of their sack, on which they hung "heretics" with scoffs and jeers.*

While these licensed spoilers were thus amusing themselves, Margaret, the chief mobocrat, was making a formal entry into Antwerp at the head of sixteen companies of men-at-arms.† The long unbroken metropolis had taken the bit and was now pulling in the traces of the court. The sectaries had been ousted; the city was swept clean of them; and now the duchess herself was come to secure this new prize for the king.‡

In the midst of her triumphs—while heretics were being hung and the Roman churches were being swept and garnished for the reception of seven other devils worse than the first—a deputation from the Lutheran princes of Germany waited upon her, and entreated her to grant liberty of worship to their provincial brothers of the Confession of Augsburg; but the masculine duchess whistled them down the wind with little ceremony§—as they deserved, for their narrowness in pleading merely for the toleration of their sect while Protestantism at large was in the valley of humiliation.

⚬ Brandt, vol. 1, pp. 208–260.   Hoofd, tom. 4.   Strada, *ut antea.*
† Strada, vol. 2, pp. 17, 18.   Brandt, vol. 1, p. 254.
‡ Ibid.   § Strada, *ubi sup.*

So far was Margaret from any idea of relaxing her severity, that on the 24th of May, 1567, she issued an edict which revived the code of the days of Granvelle, and smelt of blood in every letter. It was an ordinance of such searching cruelty, that it was quite impossible for any Protestant who had committed an overt act to escape its penalties;* and Margaret hastened to despatch a copy to Madrid for the king's inspection. Imagine her surprise on receiving, a little later, these lines from Philip: "This act is indecorous, illegal, and altogether repugnant to the true spirit of Christianity; it must be instantly revoked."† "What!" thought her highness, "have I gone too far?" But on reading the king's missive through, she found that his objections were not based on the *severity*, but upon the *over-leniency* of her frightful edict. "Not only those who have obtruded their heresy upon the public, but those who have been heretics in their secret thoughts, must be hunted out and executed,"‡ wrote his majesty. Margaret had not yet completed her education in the school of persecution, and Philip would not give her a diploma.

Nevertheless, "feeble" as the king declared it, the edict had half-depopulated the states—driven men from the country "in great heaps," in the homely phrase of an old chronicler.§ And the emigration became so frightful, that both foreigners

---

* *Vide* the edict given in full in Bor., tom. 3, p, 170, *et seq.*
† Cor. de Philippe II., tom. 1, p. 551. ‡ Ibid.
§ Bor., tom. 3, p. 171.

and natives were forbidden even to travel, by a proclamation which decreed death as the penalty of disobedience.*

"Thus," says Strada, with gratulatory emphasis, "the fire kindled by the people's discontent, blown to a flame by the bellows in the reformed pulpits, fed by the emulation of the lords, and scattered by the faction of the *gueux*, was so damped and extinguished by the governant, that religion and obedience were everywhere restored; the heretics being fitly punished, while the leaguers became *gueux* indeed, whose emblem was in fact and not in jest, poverty and an empty wallet."† The court had a right to felicitate itself; but its creatures were mistaken in supposing that the revolution was suppressed—it was but postponed.

The image-breaking had produced reaction; and reform, demoralized by excess, needed a fresh baptism of blood and suffering ere God would permit it to set its seal upon the future.

° Bor., tom. 3, p. 175.   † Strada, vol. 2, pp. 20, 21.

CHAPTER XXVI.

ALVA.

In the spring of 1567, the duchess of Parma was able to forward to Madrid tidings of the full success of her *coups d'état*. The abrogation of the tolerant edicts, the dissolution of the *gueux*, the subjugation of the insurgent cities, the flight of the chief innovators, beggars for their bread at foreign courts, the suppression of the Protestant worship, the restoration of the Roman church to its pristine authority—these were the spoils of her victory.

The future of reform did, indeed, look black. Betrayed by the excesses of fanatics, stabbed by the selfishness and inconstancy of the nobles, liberty lay at the last gasp—a fact which shows the absurdity of that charge of the Romanist historians, that the revolution was stirred by the uneasy ambition of the grandees; a class who, in the outset, obeyed, instead of exciting, the popular movement, and who later, by their vacillation and dissensions, brought the cause they had espoused to temporary ruin.

After acquainting the king with the pacification of the states, Margaret folded her hands and awaited the royal guerdon with complacent patience. But Philip "remembered to forget" her claims. In the quiet councils of the imperial will, it had

been decided to shift the government of the provinces into sterner hands. The definitive nature of
the regent's restored order was doubted at Madrid.
The gain was thought to be but transient; for the
causes of the recent outbreaks yet existed. The
ancient charters had been overridden, but they
were still unannulled. The tenets of the Reformation had been smeared with blood, but they still
commanded reverence. Both were sure to breed
new tumults.

Philip called to mind how his pious ancestors
had acted under somewhat similar circumstances.
The Moors, professing to acquiesce in the conquest
and to receive the faith of their foemen, nevertheless continued to adore Mahomet in their secret
hearts, praying towards Mecca when alone; whereupon the ministry of the Spanish Inquisition was
invoked. Evidently the monarch esteemed this an
act worthy of imitation.

Accordingly, the pacification which the governant vaunted did not alter the purpose of Philip to
despatch Alva into the Low Countries booted and
spurred for conquest; on the contrary, persuaded
that Margaret was treading upon hot ashes, he was
urged by the news to fresh exertions in the raising
and equipping of an army of invasion. All the
while, however, the king, mayhap for reasons similar to those ascribed by Tacitus to Tiberius under
somewhat analogous circumstances,* continued to

---

* Cœterùm, ut jam jamque iterus, legit comites, conquisivit
impedimenta, adornavit naves : mox hiemem, aut negotia varia

give out that Alva was to act merely as the herald of his own approach.*

In Spain the din of warlike preparation recalled the stirring days of the paladin emperor. The contagious epidemic infected all classes. Even those who had pleaded against a resort to arms at first, now, seeing that Philip had decided upon hostilities, with the ready tact of courtiers hailed that policy with louder *vivas* than its original advocates. Ruy Gomez perceived that the expedition would at least remove his rival from court, and engage him in difficulties which might haply prove ruinous to his fame; while Alva was content to leave his competitor behind, in whatsoever degree of place and favor, because, as it troubled him to see the king value his merits less than the other's person, so he was ambitious of some employment where war and the field might put a difference between those whom peace and the court had equalled.†

Thus from one motive or another opposition had hushed its voice, and the levies went briskly on. The viceroys of Sardinia, Sicily, Naples, and Lombardy were ordered to despatch the veteran troops, rusty from inaction in the garrisons of their respective territories, to the rendezvous in Piedmont, where Alva was to meet them, and supply their places with the raw Castilian recruits whom he brought out.‡ Money was sent to the Netherlands,

---

cansatus primò prudentes, dein vulgum, diutissimè provincias fefellit." Taciti Annales, tom. 1, cap. 47.

* Strada, tom. 2, p. 25.   † Ibid.   § Ibid.

that the regent might hold in readiness those men-at-arms who had just dragooned the provinces into submission.* And "since the invasion resembled both a crusade against the infidel and a treasure-hunting foray into the golden Indies, achievements by which Spanish chivalry had so often illustrated itself; since the banner of the cross was to be re-planted upon the conquered battlements of three hundred heretical cities, and a torrent of wealth richer than ever flowed from Mexican or Peruvian mines was to pour into the royal and ecclesiastical exchequers from the perennial fountains of confis-cation," it was fitting that the Spanish clergy, and especially the monks of the Inquisition, should con-tribute richly towards the expenses of this holy war.†

Alva was the Pizarro of the new crusade—a fact which exhibited alike the *animus* and the purpose of the king.

Fernando Alvarez de Toledo, duke of Alva, was the heir of an ancient Castilian house which claimed descent from the Byzantine emperors.‡ Born in 1508, and orphaned in his fifth year by the death of his father, slain by the African Moors at the siege of Gelves, he was adopted by his paternal grandfa-ther, famous as the conqueror of Navarre, and nursed on the breast of two ideas: a passion for war and a hatred of whatever bore the countenance of heresy.§

---

* Schiller, Revolt of the Netherlands.
† Prescott, vol. 2, p. 149. Meteren, Hist. des Pays-Bas, fol. 52.
‡ Hist. de Ferdinand-Alvarez, Duc d'Albe, p. 3 ; Paris, 1699.
§ Ibid. Conde de la Roca's Life, etc., of Alva.

Donning his armor at an early age, the skilful gallantry of young Alvarez speedily attracted the attention of the long-headed, though still boyish emperor. These two soon became sworn companions-in-arms, and for a quarter of a century the soldier was the strong right hand of Charles V. Always in harness, and studying war as a science in the camp of Cæsar, the nascent captain rose rapidly in his profession until, at the siege of Metz, in 1552, he held the *bâton* of generalissimo.*

Before this, in 1527, he had succeeded to the titles and the large patrimonial estates of the house of Toledo; and though his duchy yielded a comparatively small revenue, the rigid economy of the thrifty financier, which bordered upon niggardliness, together with what booty he could pick up in his campaigns—no inconsiderable source of gain—mated him with the wealthiest of the European nobles.†

As a soldier, Alva was singularly successful. He was scientific, he was adroit, and he was cautious to a proverb.‡ Like his Roman prototype, his delays had often saved the monarchy. Perhaps the success of his military career was owing more to the fact that he knew as well how to wait as how to strike—that, in an age when war was practised as

* Hist. de Ferdinand-Alvarez, Duc d'Albe, p. 3; Paris, 1699. Conde de la Roca's Life, etc., of Alva. Brantôme, Horn, Illust., etc.

† Ibid.

‡ "Caution was his most prominent trait; in which, even as a boy, he was a match for any graybeard in the army." Prescott, vol. 1, p. 163.

a street-fight is now waged, on rough-and-tumble principles, he was a thorough master of the *science* of offence and defence—than to his intuitive military genius. Indeed, Alva was not a genius, he was merely a consummate pedant. He was a hard student of war, but he originated nothing. Some one has said that most people's ideas are adopted children; few brains can raise a family of their own. Alva was Fabius Cunctator resurrected.

The soldierly qualities of this vivified copy of the dead were well known and appreciated throughout Europe. His cunning, his caution, his stealth, his discipline, his venom, made him the least desirable of antagonists, and won for him a reputation so sinister that his very name caused men to shudder; for his military qualities were but the outcome of his personal character. Hard, uncompromising, miserly, ferocious, patiently vindictive—such was his temper; and his manner, stern and overbearing from the practice of the camp, was the exact reflex of his mind.

As a politician, Alva possessed neither experience nor talent. Yet because he had expunged from his vocabulary the word mercy, because he was a bigot in religion, because he was an absolutist in politics—good qualities which counterbalanced all defects in his master's mind—Philip had selected him as the fittest of his satellites to organize murder in the Netherlands.

The famous captain was at this time in his sixtieth year, but hale and hearty as in middle life.* His tall, lean person, hardened by exposure and preserved by habitual temperance, seemed good yet for many a warlike bout, and gave him a striking martial air—though dark and sinister eyes, a yellow complexion, black hair which resembled the "quills on the back of a fretful porcupine," and a mottled beard which flowed, cascade-like, over the breast in a double stream,† did not impart to him the aspect of an Alcibiades or an Apollo.

On the 15th of April, 1567, Alva had a last interview with Philip at Aranjuez, receiving instructions so copious and minute, that he complained of them as hampering his actions beyond any programme of procedure which the emperor himself had ever marked out for his guidance.‡ A few days later,§ he embarked at Carthagena, where a fleet of thirty-six galleys, commanded by the Genoese admiral, Andrew Doria, had awaited him, and set sail for Italy, whence he was to cross the Alps into the Low Countries—a path rendered necessary by the refusal of Charles IX. to give him passage through France, under pretext that the Huguenots would misconstrue the courtesy.‖

Landing at Genoa, after a somewhat protracted voyage, Alva was pinched by the gout, brought on by the sea air, and this in its turn was aggravated

---

* Badavaro, MS. Cited in Motley, vol. 2, p. 119.

† Ibid. ‡ Documentos Inéditos, tom. 4, p. 354.

§ Prescott says on the 27th of April. Vol. 2, p. 153. Schiller says on the 5th of May. Vol. 2, p. 66. Bohn's ed. Motley says on the 10th of May. Vol. 2, p. 110. Strada gives no data.

‖ Strada, tom. 2, p. 26.

by an attack of tertian ague, which laid him on a sick-bed for a week.*

Upon being apprized of the duke's illness, Margaret of Parma made a desperate effort to bar out the invaders by a direct appeal to the king, ere the hostile trumpets should resound from beyond the Alps. Perfectly well acquainted with the imperious temper of Alva, thoroughly familiar with his arrogance, she was convinced that his mere presence at Brussels with the king's commission in his pocket, whatever might be its ostensible tenor, really meant that she was to be practically superseded, however high-sounding might be the titles which she retained. At the best, she was to have a yoke-fellow in authority—one, too, whose hauteur made Granvelle's arrogance seem tame in comparison; and even this seemed a grievance, accustomed as she had been to sipping the sweets of autocratic power.

Moreover, the governant felt especially sore at the duke's warlike incoming at this moment, because now, after years of toil and mortification and

---

° Analogous to the conflict of authorities just cited, is the disagreement regarding the *place* at which Alva was laid up by this sickness. Strada says it was at Milan. Tom. 2, p. 27. Motley tells us that it was at Nice. Vol. 2, p. 110. Davies affirms that it was at Genoa. Vol. 1, p. 546. Prescott leads us to suppose that it was at Asti. Vol. 2, p. 154. When such doctors disagree, who shall decide? So, too, in the matter of the Genoese galleys in which Alva sailed. Prescott says these were thirty-six in number. Vol. 2, p. 153. Motley says thirty-seven. Vol. 2, p. 110. Not very important matters, but worth stating correctly, if given at all.

patient intrigue, she had at length pacified the states, only to see another reap the glory and eat the ripe fruit of her weary planting. Her indignation was very natural; nor did she scruple to remonstrate with the king. Repeated and angry were the letters with which she had freighted the Spanish mail-bags ever since she had learned of Alva's invasive preparations. Now, once more, notwithstanding previous snubbings, she seized this opportunity of the duke's sickness to despatch another earnest protest against the crusade as at once a personal indignity and an injury to the state. "I am surprised, sire," it was so she wrote, "that you should have decided on so important a measure, one likely to be attended with such fatal results, without consulting me and against my uniform advice. But since you have withdrawn your confidence from me, and seeing that things are in such a good state— the royal authority more firmly established than in the time of Charles V.—and because you seem willing to permit another to reap the credit of my fatigue and danger, I pray you to accept my resignation."[*]

On the same day the duchess wrote to Alva, imploring him to await the farther orders of the king in Italy;[†] but it was the gout, more potent than Margaret's flurried letters, that held the soldier at Milan and at Asti. As for Philip, he sent the seigneur de Billy, Margaret's envoy, back to

[*] Cor. de Philippe II., tom. 1, pp. 523, 532.
[†] Motley, vol. 2, p. 112. Strada, tom. 2, p. 29.

Brussels with this message : "Do you think no more
of resignation. My army comes into the Low Countries for no other end but to establish peace."* At
this same time Ruy Gomez acquainted the regent
with the recent death of the Marquis of Berghen,
Montigny's colleague in the hapless embassy to
Spain.† Contemporaneous Europe believed that
his life was abridged by the poisoner's bowl.‡

In the meantime, Alva, now convalescent, mustered and reviewed his veterans at Alexandria de
Palla, and thence marched with them to San Am-
brosio, a rendezvous just at the chilly foot of the
Italian Alps.§   Here there was another and a final
review; after which the men-at-arms were divided
into three corps—the first, led by Alva himself,
started at once across the frozen heights of Mount
Cenis to wind down through Burgundy and Lorraine into the Netherlands, an Alpine path trodden
sixteen centuries before, according to tradition, by
Hannibal; the second advanced a day later, with
orders to bivouac nightly in the camp occupied
twenty-four hours earlier by the vanguard; and the
third in its turn was to put an equal space of time
between its march and that of its predecessor;‖ a
treble advance cunningly devised to jeopard but one
division at a time in the icy fastnesses of the moun-

     ° Strada, tom. 2, p. 27.   † Ibid.

    ‡ Ibid. Prescott does not seem to credit this rumor ; but Stra-
da refers to it, saying : "I mean not to affirm it otherwise than as
a conjecture." Tom. 2, p. 28.

    § B. de Mendoza. Guerras de los Payses baxos, folio 30.

    ‖ B. de Mendoza, ut antea.

tain, where a few sturdy chamois hunters might
have easily surprised and slaughtered an armed
host. "What could not the lion do if he were the
monkey also?" queries the Chinese proverb. Alva
was both—a lion in prowess, a monkey in *finesse*.

The invading force was small, numbering but fifty
men over ten thousand*—an army in miniature, but
it was absolutely perfect in equipment and discipline. Composed of picked soldiers, men trained
under the eye of Alva, and inured to victory beneath
the banner of Charles V., no more compact and vet-
eran-like array had answered to the roll-call since
the days of the old Macedonian phalanx.† Hardy,
practised, confident, each man was a host, and each
carried himself with the air of a prince. Each company of foot was flanked by a body of musketeers,
armed with a weapon now for the first time brought
into field service. Each of these was attended by
a servant, who bore his musket for him on the march,
and they were so richly habited and so gracefully
arrogant, that all yielded them the deference usually paid to officers alone.‡

But the oddest sight of all was a corps of two
thousand women—Italian prostitutes, as regularly
enrolled and drilled as the men-at-arms, whose ap-
pointments and discipline received the enthusiastic
commendation of Brantôme.§ "For their presence," said Alva, "I have the authority of the Athe-

* Documentos Inéditos, tom. 4, p. 382.
† Brantôme, Grandes Capitaines étrangers, etc.—Duc d'Albe.
‡ Ibid.　　　　　　　　　§ Brantôme, *ut antea*.

20*

nian general Iphicrates, who awarded the prize of valor to the pleasure-loving and rapacious soldier."[*] A Greek precedent always sufficed for him, and though driven by the necessity of expedition to dispense with artillery, and by the high price of provisions in the Alps to reduce his force to the smallest possible number, he preferred to count a few regiments less rather than leave behind the wantons who gave to the army the aspect of a bacchanalian procession, contrasting strangely with the gloomy seriousness and pretended sanctity of its aim.[†]

However, the presence of the courtesans did not relax the iron discipline of the troops; and it is certainly a remarkable illustration of the repressive skill of Alva, that, throughout his march, and in an age when soldier and license were synonyms, no woman was insulted, no peasant was plundered, no untoward accident occurred.[‡]

Thus, in the pleasant month of June, and by short marches, Alva scaled the Alps, trod over Savoy, crossed the Spanish corner of Burgundy, passed through Lorraine, and in the early days of August, entered the Low Countries, molesting none and himself unopposed—though the allied army of Geneva, called to arms by the prayer of Pius V. that Alva should destroy their city as a "nest of devils and apostates,"[§] and a French army of obser-

---

[*] Cited in Schiller, vol. 2, p. 67, Bohn's ed.   [†] Ibid.
[‡] Strada, tom. 2, p. 31.
[§] Leti, Vita di Filippe II., tom. 1, p. 489.

vation, hung on his skirts, carefully abstaining from all hostile acts, and aiming only to cover their respective frontiers.*

At Thionville, the duke, who was accompanied by a glittering *cortége* of distinguished officers—by Paciotti, by Vitelli, by Mandragone, by his sons Frederick and Ferdinand de Toledo,† was met by Noircames and Barlaiment, who gave him a cordial welcome for themselves, and a formal one for Margaret.‡ Advancing thence towards the capital, he was greeted from time to time by numbers of the Flemish grandees. Among the rest came Egmont, as anxious as the common herd to conciliate·the new viceroy by a show of friendship.

"Behold the arch-heretic !" exclaimed Alva in a stage whisper to one of his staff officers, as Egmont came into his presence. The Fleming paused, changed color, and seemed quite thrown off his balance. Alva, however, quickly resumed his mask, and embracing his illustrious dupe, he laughed away his insolent greeting as an excellent jest.§ But with all his caution, he found it impossible not to coin his thoughts into words and put them in circulation. To the welcoming congratulations of the sycophantic grandees, he responded brusquely: "Well, welcome or not, 't is all one; here I am."‖

This impudent reception should have opened

* De Thou, Hist. du Duc d'Albe. Meteren.
† Documentos Inéditos, tom. 4. B. de Mendoza.
‡ Strada, tom. 2, p. 31. Hoofd, tom. 4.
§ Meteren, Hist. des Pays-Bas, folio 53. Bor., tom. 4, p. 182
‖ Meteren, *ubi sup.*

Egmont's eyes to the precipice on whose brink he
tottered; and it would, had he not been determined
to be blind.   Like an infatuated gamester, he had
decided to sit out the unequal and tricky game—to
await the hazardous casting of the die.   Accordingly, he affected to regard the insults of the Spanish
captain as the most sportive of *bon mots*, presented
him with a couple of beautiful horses, the finest of
his stud and accompanied him on the route to Brussels.*   Thus it was that William's prophecy was fulfilled, and Egmont was the "bridge over which the
Spaniards passed into the Netherlands to destroy
them."   The hero of St. Quentin sank to be the cozened tool of his own future executioner.   "Scrape a
Russian, and you will find a Tartar," said Napoleon.
Strip Egmont of his gilding, and you see an idiot.

On the 22d of August, 1567, Alva entered Brussels.   The streets were deserted, not a *viva* was
shouted.†   Not the plague itself had ever hushed
the city to such frightful stillness.   Nor was it in
the capital alone that silence reigned : everywhere
trade was suspended.   The exodus, enormous before,
was now ruinous.   "Upon the very rumor of a foreign army," wrote Margaret to the king, "diverse
tradesmen and merchants at once departed from
us; and now, since Alva has entered the states, the
highways are choked with fugitives—trade flying
because no money can be made here now, while
there must be assessments and great taxes; popu-

* Hoofd, tom. 4, p. 150.   Meteren, *ut antea*
† Prescott, vol. 2, p. 163.

lation going out because men think these forces are come to be their executioners."*

Alva was serenely indifferent to the hatred which his name evoked. Like most military men, especially in that age, he despised a mercantile community; and this led him to underrate the race whom he had come to peel and butcher. "I have tamed men of iron in my day," said he with a sneer; "shall I not easily crush these men of butter?"† He saw in the Low-Countrymen not an enemy but a prey; and it was with a confident smile that he had said to Philip, "I will make treasure flow from the Netherlands into Spain in a stream a yard deep."‡ The speech was characteristic of the man. But has not some wit said that dogmatism is puppyism come to maturity?

Without pausing to rearrange his dress, dusty and travel-stained, Alva hastened to wait upon the governant. At the gates of her palace an unseemly *melée* occurred, caused by the refusal of Margaret's body-guard of archers to permit the duke's halberdiers to enter the court.§ At length, however, Alva was admitted to the audience-chamber. His reception was freezing. Quite in the centre of the apartment, with Barlaiment and Aerschot and Egmont grouped about her, stood the regent; nor would she break the statuesque rigidity of her *pose* by taking a single step forward to meet the unwel-

* Strada, tom. 2, p. 27.   † Hoofd, tom. 4, p. 148.
‡ Cited in Motley, vol. 2, p. 103.
§ Cor. de Philippe II., tom. 2, p. 631.

come duke.* Alva was more complaisant. Doffing
his steel bonnet, he begged, "with Castilian but
empty courtesy," to be permitted to lay his army
and himself at the feet of the sister of his king.†
Margaret, in recognition of Alva's right as a Spanish grandee to remain covered even in the presence of royalty, insisted upon his resuming his bonnet; after which a stiff and formal conversation of
half an hour's duration took place, marked on the
governant's side by an affectation of imperial hauteur; on the duke's, by an assumed deference which
ill disguised a contemptuous sense of his supreme
importance.‡ Throughout the interview, all remained standing.§

"May I ask, my lord duke," queried the regent,
"what may be the nature and extent of your powers?" "Really," was the cool response, "I do not
exactly recollect. I will look over my papers, and
let you know at my earliest convenience."‖ Apparently, Margaret was unmoved by these words, for
she said, "I commend his majesty's intention; all
may be well in case peace, newly restored to the
states, be not, like a tender plant, spoiled by digging too deep about it."¶ With this, icy adieux
were passed, and Alva retired to his headquarters
at Culemberg House**—the mansion in whose din-

* Mendivil's Acct. in Documentos Inéditos, tom. 4, p. 398.
† Ibid.   ‡ Vandervynckt, tom. 2, p. 53.
§ Ibid. Cor. de Philippe II., *ubi sup.*
‖ Vandervynckt, *ut antea.*
¶ Strada, tom. 2, p. 32.
** Cor. de Philippe II., tom. 1.

ing-hall the *gueux* had received their name at Brederode's mad revel.

The day after this interchange of empty congratulations, Alva had an official interview with the governant and the council of state, at which he exhibited his commissions. By one of these he was appointed captain-general of the Netherlands, with supreme power in all military spheres.* By another, these duties were enlarged and so defined as to lodge in the hands of the captain-general full authority to displace and replace magistrates and governors, and to examine into the causes of the late tumults, and to punish the participants—a commission which raised Alva to the level of an autocrat.†

These instruments were produced and inspected by the regent in council; but the wily duke kept a third and yet more important commission, which expressly invested him with the supreme authority in civil as well as in military affairs, and enjoined all persons, Margaret included, to obey the viceroy as the king himself,‡ in abeyance; replying to the regent's question, " Have you any farther instructions?" " Yes, more than can be opened at one meeting; but which, according to future exigencies, I shall impart to your highness."§

Although these instructions were careful to

° Ibid., tom. 2. Appendix, No. 88. This was dated December 1, 1566.

† Documentos Inéditos, tom. 4, pp. 388–396. This was dated January 31, 1567.

‡ Cor. de Philippe II., tom. 2. Appendix No. 102. This was dated on the 1st of March, 1567. § Strada, tom. 2, p. 32.

state that Margaret's authority was to remain unimpaired—that Alva was merely placed " in correspondence with his majesty's dear sister of Parma "*—the governant well knew that she had been superseded, and she felt especially humiliated by this juggling method of depriving her of the sceptre. Many and bitter were her complaints of the affront put on her by the king; nor was she at all careful into whose ears she poured the story of her wrongs: least of all was she reticent with Philip. "I disclaim all jealousy of the extraordinary powers conferred upon the captain-general," wrote she to her royal brother; "but I think, sire, that you should have dismissed me before depriving me of honor."†

After the exhibition of his credentials, Alva proceeded to canton his troops. The Milanese brigade was quartered in the suburbs of Brussels.‡ The cavalry, upwards of eighteen hundred strong,§ was encamped at a convenient point, ten leagues from the capital.‖ The other divisions of the army were saddled upon the larger cities of the provinces—Antwerp, Ghent, and the rest—whose authorities were at the same time required to transfer the keys of their respective municipalities to the hands of the captain-general.¶

These preliminary acts revealed the spirit of the duke, as the careless prattle of a petulant child

* Bor., tom. 4, p. 182.
† Strada, *ubi sup.*   ‡ Meteren, Bor., Prescott.
§ Documentos Inéditos, tom. 4, p. 382.
‖ Hist. du Duc d'Albe. Meteren.
¶ Hoofd, tom. 4, p. 150. Bor., tom. 4, p. 184.

reveals family secrets. Aside from his deeds, the mere presence of the man was ominous of evil. Was it not Alva who had advised the armed invasion of the Netherlands? Was it not Alva who had urged Philip to seize the pretext of the iconomachy to break the seals of the provincial charters—those badges of the weakness of his ancestors, those disgraceful chains upon the prince, those safeguards of heresy? Was it not Alva who had advocated the placing a sharp curb in the bridled mouth of the conquered states? And lo! this wild beast in armor had arrived with his veteran cohorts. Surely there was room for dismal apprehension.

CHAPTER XXVII.

THE COUNCIL OF BLOOD.

It required no acumen to understand the motives which had pushed the new captain-general into Brussels, and the purpose of his coming; both were palpable to the most stupid of dullards. The rooting out of heresy, the rigid enforcement of the Inquisition, the abrogation of the trophied privileges of the people, the degradation of the Netherlands into satrapies, chained to the feet of an alien and absolute monarch, and governed by a junta of foreigners sitting at the other end of Europe, with no voice in their own affairs, after the pattern of Sicily and the wretched Italian states*—such was the well-known programme.

To facilitate the work, Philip had clothed Alva with autocratic powers; the Spanish Inquisition had banned the provinces at large, Romanists as well as Protestants, these as guilty of treason by supineness, those as traitors by the commission of overt acts,† and the pontiff had absolved the king from his coronation oath‡—sanctifying usurpation and blasphemy and perjury by a *benedicite* muttered from the mock chair of St. Peter.

Denounced by the king, the Low-Countrymen

* Confessions of Counsellor Louis del Rio. Cited in Motley, vol. 2, p. 118, note. † Schiller, vol. 2, p. 77, Bohn's ed.
‡ Bor., Hutthen, Stuk., tom. 1, bl. 6.

were held to have forfeited all civil rights; condemned by the Inquisition, they were esteemed to
possess no religious privileges; sentenced by the
pope, they were thought to have parted with all
hope, with every claim to mercy here and hereafter.
Very naturally, Alva considered that this threefold
reprobation denaturalized his victims, and afforded
him

> "Ample space and verge enough
> The characters of hell to trace."

In all the backstair whisperings at Madrid, it
had been regarded as essential to the execution of
the royal plot, that the leading seigneurs of the
Netherlands, those of them at least who had espoused the liberal cause, whether now repentant or not,
should be brought at the earliest possible moment
to trial, and through that door to confiscation and
the block, in order that at one fell blow opposition
to the king's will might be punished, and the citizens be robbed of their natural leaders.* On the
black list were the names of Orange, Egmont, Horn,
Hoogstraaten, St. Aldegonde, and a host of lesser
luminaries in the Low Country constellation. To a
critical observer, nothing is superficial. "In what
part of that letter did you discover irresolution?"
demanded a king of the wisest of living diplomats. .
"In the *us* and *gs*," was the reply. So the keener
of the grandees had discovered the symptoms of a
bloody disease from their diagnosis of the days
which ante-dated Alva's march, and gone out in

* Confessions of Del Ryo, *ut antea.*

time; but many remained, against the counsel of the wiser ones, and these were now to pay the penalty of their thrice-sodden folly.

No sooner had the duke made known so much of his commission as sufficed to give him the supreme control; replaced the doubtful Walloon troops with his own trusty veterans; strung the keys of the larger cities to his girdle, and set Paciotti, the most eminent of the mediæval engineers, to work in constructing new fortresses, than he proceeded to arrange for the arrest of the doomed nobles, all of whom he wished to cage by a *coup de main*. It was this consideration which had inspired his courtesy to Egmont—this which had thus far shielded that blinded courtier from imprisonment. Alva had determined to make a decoy-duck of his infatuated dupe.

In the pursuance of this plan, the captain-general, assisted by his sons and by Chiappin Vitelli, Gabriel de Terbelloni, with others of his officers, kept Egmont occupied by an incessant round of *fêtes* and masquerades and plays, that the headsman's hour might have time to ripen.* The count wearied himself in this treacherous pleasure; while, according to Alva's calculation, scores of nobles who had quitted the capital to watch the actions of the duke at a safe distance, were completely gulled by the courtesy extended to Egmont, and began to straggle back to Brussels.†

It was some time before Horn could be per-

* Schiller, vol. 2, p. 74, Bohn's ed.   † Ibid.

suaded to trust his person in the enemy's camp; but at length the numberless flattering and urgent invitations of Alva, supported by the assurances of Egmont, who undertook that his friend should be no worse used than he himself,* overcame his stubborn scruples, and he quitted Weert for the capital.† Even Hoogstraaten set out for Brussels; but Alva mournfully informed the king that he "could not flatter himself with the hope of William's return."‡

Meantime, the city remained sullen and gloomy. Over its proverbial gayety a "blanket of the dark" seemed to have been thrown. The public haunts were deserted; the places of amusement were closed; only foreign faces were seen upon the streets. The awful shadow of impending calamity rested over the metropolis.§ It was in vain that Alva strove to amuse the burghers and to dissipate the gloom. At such a moment only fools could be won to laugh; but among the laughers were the cozened grandees and the foreign courtiers who buzzed in the treacherous sunshine of Culemberg-house.

At length the hour struck. Alva, convinced that further delay could give him no more victims but might snatch from his hands some of those already in his power, sprang the trap. On the 9th of September, 1567, Egmont and Horn were invited to wait upon the captain-general for the purpose of chatting over a plan for the erection of a citadel at

---

* Strada, tom. 2, p. 32.

† Cor. de Philippe II., tom. 1, p. 563, 564. Meteren, Hoofd.

‡ Cor. de Philippe II., tom. 1, p. 578.   § Schiller, *ubi sup.*

Antwerp.* Quitting the dinner-table of Fernando de Toledo, the seigneurs walked to the duke's residence in company. Alva received them graciously, and at once engaged them in a discussion with the engineer Paciotti, which occupied them until evening had fallen.† Then, as they were about to separate, Egmont was requested by Sanchio d'Avila, captain of the duke's halberdiers, to step for an instant into an adjoining apartment. Upon entering the room he was asked to surrender his sword. Astounded by the demand, the count could only gaze upon the officer with open mouth; but upon a repetition of the order, he recovered his composure, and tendering the blade, said, "Take it, sir captain; it has rendered the king some service in times past."‡ The illustrious prisoner was at once surrounded by a company of Spanish musketeers, who hurried him into the upper story of the building, where, in a chamber hung with black, barricaded, with daylight excluded, and dimly lighted by candles,§ he was left isolated to await transportation to a sterner dungeon.

A few moments after the arrest of Egmont, Horn, too, was captured just as he was emerging from Alva's court-yard into the street.‖ Satisfied of the futility of resistance, he calmly yielded, merely asking if Egmont had met the same fate. "Yes," was the reply. "'Tis well," responded

* Pontus Payen, MS.   † Motley, vol. 2, p. 124.
‡ Strada, tom. 2, p. 33.   § Motley, ubi sup.
‖ Strada, ubi sup.

Horn; "I have suffered myself to be guided by him, and 't is but fair that I should share his destiny."*

Just previous to the enactment of this drama, Backerzeel, Egmont's secretary, and Antony Van Straalen, burgomaster of Antwerp, a friend and correspondent of Orange, and one of the most popular, as he was one of the wealthiest citizens of the metropolis,† fell into a somewhat similar ambuscade, and were brought prisoners into Brussels.‡ Soon afterwards, Alva had the residences of these gentlemen searched from turret to foundation stone. All the papers found were seized, inventoried, and placed in his hands.§ "Thus," says Motley, "if amid their most secret communications, or that of their correspondents, a single treasonable thought should be lurking, it was to go hard but it might be twisted into a cord strong enough to strangle them all."‖ To be sure, these prisoners, together with most of their fellow-citizens who were still at large, had received the double pardon of the regent and of the king for whatever offences they might have committed. But had not Philip called a notary to bear formal witness that this pardon was wrung from him while under moral duress? And had not the sovereign pontiff solemnly absolved him from all oaths? The king considered swindling to be

* Vandervynckt, tom. 2, p. 223. Documentos Inéditos, tom. 4, p. 418.   † Strada, tom. 2, p. 33.
‡ Hoofd, tom. 4, p. 150. Strada, tom. 2, p. 33. Bor., tom. 4, p. 184.   § Cor. de Philippe II., tom. 1, p. 638.
‖ Motley, vol. 2, p. 126.

statesmanship ; the holy father named perjury religion.

A fortnight after the arrest, Egmont and Horn were conducted to Ghent by an escort of three thousand Spanish infantry, where they were held in rigorous confinement to await the farce which their captor called a trial.* Happily for himself, Hoogstraaten, already on the road to Brussels, had been momentarily detained by an accident at a wayside inn. There he learned the fate of those who had "put their trust in princes." As he had no craving for martyrdom, he at once faced about and crossed the border into Germany,† whence he ought not to have ventured.

Alva was extraordinarily elated by his success, and he at once wrote out a gloating account of his scientific manœuvres for Philip's eye.‡ The king shared in the viceroy's joy, and sent him back the warmest of congratulatory letters.§ Cardinal Granvelle, who was at this time in Rome, seemed less delighted. "Has the duke taken *Monsieur le Taciturne?*" queried he, referring to Orange by the nickname which he had come to bear. "Not so," answered his informant. The churchman shrugged his shoulders. "If that one fish has escaped the net, the duke's draught is nothing worth," quoth he.‖

Peter Titelmann, the once famous inquisitor, who

---

* Meteren, Schiller, Hoofd.
† Strada, tom. 2, pp. 32, 33. Bor., tom. 4, p. 185.
‡ Cor. de Philippe II., tom. 1, p. 637.   § Ibid., p. 666.
‖ Strada, tom. 2, p. 33. Meteren, folio. 50.

now, grown old and infirm, was living on the memory of his pious past and on the blood-money which had repaid his devotion, shared in Granvelle's opinion. "Is wise William a prisoner?" asked he on hearing of Alva's haul. On being told that he was not, he said mournfully: "Then will our joy be brief. Woe unto us for the wrath to come from Germany!"[*]

The duchess of Parma bitterly resented the flagrant contempt of her authority manifested by these arrests, made without consultation with her—nay, without a suspicion on her part that they were to occur.[†] But from the fact that she made no effort to secure the release of the prisoners, nor spoke one good word in their favor, it is safe to conclude that she quarrelled less with the deed than with the manner of its accomplishment. However, so great was her indignation that, heedless of Alva's explanation that he concealed his purpose at the king's command, in order to save her from the odium which it might reflect on her,[‡] she at one despatched an envoy to Madrid to solicit her dismissal from an office whose title alone she possessed, while another had usurped the sceptre.[§] While awaiting Philip's response, Margaret absented herself as much as possible from the council-board, and passed the days in hawking and the chase—sports of which the masculine governant was passionately fond.[||]

---

[*] Cited in Motley, vol. 2, p. 130.　　[†] Strada, tom. 2, p. 34.
[‡] Ibid. Bor., tom. 4, p. 185.　　[§] Strada, *ubi sup.*
[||] Documentos Inéditos. tom. 4, p. 399.

The consternation caused by Alva's act was unprecedented. Men of all parties were alarmed. "If Egmont and Horn, preëminent by position, active in suppressing the tumults, and Romanists withal, are not secure, who can be safe?" This was the question which each white-lipped Netherlander put to his neighbor; and as no one could give a satisfactory answer, emigration again rose to floodtide; to the one hundred thousand refugees who had left the states on learning of the duke's armed invasion, twenty thousand more were now added by the panic caused by the imprisonment of these seigneurs.[*] Alva stirred the regent to renew her edict against emigration;[†] but though this was formally proclaimed, though death was the well-known penalty for an unsuccessful attempt to pass the ports, and notwithstanding the fact that ten of the richest merchants of Tournay had been seized as they were about to cross the water into England, and punished by the confiscation of their estates,[‡] hundreds still continued to slip away, contented to lose their property, if only they might save their lives.[§]

Among these later refugees was an honest churchman named Thomas Tillius. Convinced of the errors of Rome and spurred by conscience, he forsook his rich abbey of St. Bernard, near Antwerp, with a revenue of seventy thousand guilders[||] *per*

---

[*] Watson, Life of Philip II., p. 116.   Meteren, Schiller, Brandt, vol. 1, p. 260.   [†] Strada, *ubi sup.*   Doc. Inéd., *ubi sup.*

[‡] Strada, *ubi sup.*   [§] Ibid.

[||] Guilder, a Dutch coin of the value of twenty stivers, about thirty-eight cents of our money.

annum, and fled into the duchy of Cleves, taking with him, to defray the expenses of the way, but four hundred guilders in coin. Having gained an asylum, he threw off his frock, married, and became a minister of the emancipated gospel; first at Haarlem, then at Delft, where he died.*

Alva affected to care little for this exodus, which impoverished the Low Countries, and enriched France and Great Britain. "They say many are leaving the provinces," wrote he to Philip. "'Tis hardly worth while to arrest them. The repose of the nation is not to be assured by beheading those who are led astray by others."† So much for the philosophy. The fact was, that prodigious exertions were made to hold back would-be outgoers. The people were transformed into a police force to catch emigrants. If any passed the sea, all were held guilty of that neglect which the law brands as fraud.

But the Aaron's serpent among the captain-general's designs, was a settled determination to enslave the Netherlands. He meant to metamorphose Philip from a mere duke of Brabant, from a simple count of Flanders—the only titles by which he had a right to reign in the Low Countries—into an irresponsible despot, absolute without the assent of the states, minus even the *Dei gratiâ.* He labored to inoculate the provinces with Spain. This was the hidden loadstone which always operated on the needle of his compass.

* Brandt, vol. 1, p. 260.
† Corresp. de Philippe II., tom. 1, p. 576.

Regarding the charters as the mischievous source
of independence in the Netherlands, and convinced
that an observance on his part of the forms and customs of the land would minister to the popular respect for these fundamental laws, the duke had from
the outset studiously treated the honored parchments as invalidated by sedition, and given the
established methods of procedure a contemptuous
go-by. He had already snared his titled prey, and
was now ready to make a quarry of the nation.
But though prepared to investigate the causes of
the recent troubles, and to execute the vengeance
of his king upon the actors in that scene, he would
not invoke the aid of the existing tribunals, whose
forms were too dilatory, whose checks were too
numerous, whose judges might prove over-honest:
against all precedent, in the teeth of the statutes
"in such case made and provided," he erected a
tribunal of his own, unique, unheard-of, which he
called the "Council of Troubles," and to which he
gave cognizance of all judicial offences originating
in the tumults.*

This abhorrent court, which was speedily nicknamed the "Council of Blood" by the citizens, was
a mere board of registry for the formal recording of
Alva's edicts; it was a bench, not of judges, but of
special pleaders, met to make out a case, not to sum
up the testimony. So profound was the captain-
general's contempt for law, that he did not even

* Corresp. de Philippe II., tom. 1, p. 637. Brandt, vol. 1, p.
261. Bor., tom. 4, p. 185. Strada, tom. 2, p. 41.

deign to give this brood of jackals a legal cloak by procuring for them letters patent from the king, or by himself granting them commissions; so that the blood-council was in fact merely an informal club, exercising the most tremendous functions at the verbal bidding of a satrap.[*]

This monstrous tribunal was composed of twelve judges—"the most learned, upright men, and of the purest lives, to be found in the states," as Alva informed his royal master.[†] Who were these mediæval Solomons? These immaculate blood-suckers, what were their names? Juan de Vargas, a Spanish legist, an outlaw over whom two criminal suits were hanging in Castile,[‡] was one. Louis del Rio, one of those clever, serviceable knaves whom troublous times are sure to vomit up, was another. Aremberg, an unscrupulous fanatic, was a third. Noircarmes, smeared with Valenciennes gore, was a fourth. Barlaiment, who, unlike the French philosopher's idea of an educated man, "was satisfied to survey the universe from his parish belfry," was a fifth. Sweep in half a dozen absolutist lawyers, men accustomed to running with volunteer haste to do the dirty work of "lewd fellows of the baser sort"—jurists after whose health thieves asked before they began to steal—and we have analyzed the new chamber of inquisitors.[§]

○ Notice sur le Cons. des Troubles, par M. Gachard, p. 7. Cited by Motley, vol. 2, p. 137.

† Corresp. de Philippe II., tom. 1, p. 576.

‡ Prescott, vol. 2, p. 189.

§ The names of the board were: Count Aremberg, Noircarmes,

This precious and highly honorable list of names was suggested by Viglius—who had wit enough, however, to keep his own from the number.* The vicious activity of this octogenarian, the wide scope of his influence, always baneful, ever exerted to defeat the right, recalls the criticism upon Lord Eldon: "No one ever *did* his race so much good as Eldon *prevented*."†

The duke's junta was armed with tremendous powers; but he had managed so shrewdly as not to cede a single element of his autocracy. For, as the council was his creature in its institution, so its sentences were stillborn unless vivified by his revision and assent.‡ Indeed, at the outset the sittings were held at his residence, and he presided in person.§

On the 20th of September, 1567, the council met for the first time.‖ The members were sworn to secrecy, pledged to denounce any of their number who should violate that oath, made to affirm their solemn adherence to Rome, and requested always to decide according to their convictions.¶ This ceremony perfected the machinery of slaughter. Nothing remained but to collect the victims.

Barlaiment, Hadrian Nicolai, chancellor of Guelders, Jacob Mertens and Peter Asset, presidents of Artois and Flanders, Jacob Hassels and John de la Porte, counsellors of Ghent, Louis del Rio, doctor of theology, John du Bois, king's advocate, and De la Torre, court secretary. Schiller, vol. 2, p. 79, Bohn's ed.

 * Vigl. ad Happ., epist. 27 et 28.

 † W. Phillips, Letters, Speeches, etc.

 ‡ Gachard, Notice, etc, Cited in Motley, vol. 2, p. 137.

 § Prescott, vol. 2, p. 195. Brandt, vol. 1, p. 260.

 ‖ Gachard, *ubi sup.*   ¶ Ibid.

CHAPTER XXVIII.

AT WORK.

AND now commenced the most iniquitous and wholesale persecution which history records, the wildest and most indiscriminate massacre known among men. Not the brutal proscriptions of Sylla; not Cinna's reckless waste of human life; not Marius' violation of the rights of property, can mate it; for these men fought their way into Rome after a hard struggle as incensed victors, while Alva in a time of peace sauntered unopposed into the Low Countries, to butcher in cold blood. They were hot-headed, ruthless citizens with cruel wrongs to be as cruelly avenged; he was a cool, methodical slaughterer, whose heart was soured by no private griefs. The pencil which essays to paint the picture of his deeds should be dipped in the blood he spilled.

Of course, the instrument of the captain-general in this work was the new tribunal; taking from his shoulders a load of details, yet vital only through the point of his pen. The blood-judges, as indifferent as their master to the forms of law, hedged themselves in with no set of subtle rules. Since their sole duty was proscription, they adopted only such brief, rough regulations as were essential to that end. It was certain that a court whose jurisdiction was as broad as the provinces must have an immense pressure of business; and to prevent disorder, this was distributed into several departments, over which specified judges were installed. Thus two of the twelve were instructed to devote themselves to the collection of evidence against the grandees then in exile—Orange, Culemberg, Brederode; while two others had charge of the causes which arose within the states; and so on.*

The labors of the junta were lightened and simplified by another arrangement. Provincial committees were appointed and empowered to try all minor causes, and even to pronounce sentence— taking care always to forward to headquarters minutes of their action.† These processes were then revised by the twelve, and submitted to the examination of Vargas and Del Rio, who alone were empowered to vote.‡ Even their decision was invalid until endorsed by Alva.§ When the duke's signature was obtained, the judgment of the court was executed. Alva reserved the final decision to himself, because, as he frankly told Philip, "Lawyers are unwilling to decide any case except upon the evidence, while measures of state policy are not to be regulated by the laws."‖ It is very probable that this consideration had a tendency to persuade him to erect this illegal, exceptional council on the ruins of the regular tribunals.

* Bulletins de l'Académie Royale de Belgique, tom. 16, part 2, p. 58. Cited in Prescott, vol. 2, p. 191.

† Prescott, vol. 2, p. 192.   ‡ Brandt. vol. 1, p. 260. Gachard.

§ Bulletins de l'Académie Royale de Belgique, tom. 16, par. 2, p. 52, note.   ‖ Ibid.

As showing how little respect was paid by these judges to the barest requirements of justice, it may be stated that a single document as often lodged information against a hundred men as against one; and if these denunciations—which were seldom read, so numerous were they—resulted in an adverse verdict, as they usually did, the whole hundred or the one, as the case might be, suffered death within forty-eight hours after conviction.* Such was the method of procedure of the Council of Blood; felt to be especially severe by the Netherlanders, used to the fair and open and above-board code prescribed by their charters: "No citizen shall be tried outside of his own province;" "no foreigner shall sit on the judicial bench."† This was the voice of the constitutions of the states. Alva's bench, on his mere *ipse dixit*, not only summoned men and women from every province before its bar; but was composed of members, all of whom were either Spaniards by birth, or Spaniards by the yet stronger nativity of the soul. It was a copy of the Inquisition in lay binding. If it be possible to weigh and adjudge demerit, Alva, inquisitor-general of the Low Countries, was a blacker character than Espinosa, inquisitor-general of Spain.

The initial measure of the blood-judges was the issuing a declaration, in which treason was so defined as to make it a moral certainty that all were

* Motley, vol. 2, p. 143.
† Compare Bor., tom. 1, p. 19; Meteren, tom. 1, p. 28, *et seq.*

21*

traitors. To have subscribed or presented any petition against the new bishops, the edicts, and the Inquisition; to have suffered or been privy to the exercise of the reformed religion; to have neglected to oppose heresy from the start; to have countenanced the petitions of the *gueux*, whether from fear or favor; to have submitted to the spoliation of the iconoclasts; to have said or thought that the Council of Troubles was obliged to conform with the charters, the cause of all the evils that had befallen the nation; to have asserted or insinuated that the king had no right to cancel the privileges of the states if he thought fit, or that he was not relieved from all his oaths and promises of pardon—was held to be conspiracy against the divine and human majesties.*

It was upon this occasion that Vargas pronounced his famous decision: "*Hæretici faxerunt templa, boni nihil faxerunt contra; ergo debent omnes patibulare*"†—language which is an equal crime against syntax and humanity. For the benefit of Vargas, who was ignorant of the vernacular tongue, the proceedings of the court were conducted in Latin, then the common language of learned Europe. Yet even in the Latin he used expressions " that would have made Quintilian stare and gasp," and, as in the instance cited, frequently got intoxicated on

---

* Brandt, vol. 1, p. 260.

† The heretics have broken open the churches ; the orthodox did nothing to hinder: therefore they ought all to be hung together. *Vide* Brandt, *ubi sup.*

paragraphs of his own brewing; at which the witty citizens laughed, feeling half avenged of their wrongs by the opportunity of ridicule afforded them by the shockingly bad taste of their persecutor in the tongue of the old Romans.

Under this ruling of Vargas, the inquisitors and the commissioners—the "couple" in this hunt—at once went to work. All who were known to have participated in the tumults were seized à l'outrance.* Then, with terrible industry, the less well-defined offenders were ferreted out. Suspicion was considered to be a synonym for proof. Circumstances the most innocent were twisted awry until they disclosed unthought-of guilt. Had this man been thought to favor reform? waste no time in the farther investigation of his case, but proceed to sentence the atrocious wretch. Had this woman's cousin been connected with the gueux? let the rack be her cross-examiner. Worst of all, secret denunciations abounded, informations from all sources being invited, nay commanded; so that the woes of the wretched victims were inflamed to frenzy by a suspicion that their undoing might have been worked by the deposition of parents, wives, husbands, children.†

With thrifty prevision, the captain-general had covered the land with multitudinous prisons against this day of wrath ;‡ but notwithstanding this, and in spite of the frightful draughts of the executioner,

---

* Hoofd, tom. 4, p. 157, et seq. Meteren. Gachard.
† Ibid. Prescott, vol. 2, p. 192. ‡ Schiller, v. 2, p. 81, Bohn's ed.

the gates of death were kept full of sufferers. No distinctions of age, sex, and condition were made. Maidens in the May of youth; boys not yet freed from parental control; men in middle age; women in the autumn of life; patriarchs hoary with three score years and ten—none were spared.*

Nimbly worked the deft fingers of the local magistrates, assorting and filing informations. Swiftly and incessantly rode the couriers who bore this freight of death to be inspected by the junta at Brussels. Busy were the rack of the inquisitor and the axe of the wearied headsman.

The sittings of the blood-judges often lasted seven hours in a day,† so indefatigable were these honorable men. During the first three months, Alva presided in person; but afterwards, being pressed by other business, and feeling that his confidence would not be abused, he inducted Vargas into his seat at the board, retaining, however, his revisory powers.‡ As a matter of fact, this reservation amounted to nothing, for Vargas understood the wishes of the duke so well, and was so energetic, unwearied, and unscrupulous that his sentences were always confirmed.§ "This man at least is youthfully active in your service, sire," wrote the delighted captain-general to Philip of this congenial spirit.‖

* Brandt, vol. 1. p. 261.   Hoofd, tom. 4.   Watson, p. 118.
† Bulletins de l'Académie Royale de Belgique, tom. 16, par. 2, p. 57.   ‡ Ibid.   Prescott, vol. 2, p. 195.
§ Brandt, vol. 1, p. 260.   ‖ Cor. de Philippe II., tom. 1, p. 583.

To be sure, men of all parties united to hoot the iniquitous character of this "wise and upright judge."* Unquestionably, he was an escaped criminal under Spanish law.† There was no denying that he had violated an orphan girl whose guardian he was.‡ But what then? "Because thou art virtuous shall there be no more cakes and ale?" In Alva's estimation, these peccadilloes were condoned by his present usefulness. To cut away the gangrene of heresy, it was necessary to have a knife like Vargas.§ The captain-general was not the man to sacrifice a serviceable tool to a sentiment.

But though the duke patronized Vargas on account of his acquaintance with that code of by-laws which constitutes a useful rogue, several of his brother judges were embittered by his arrogant behavior; not that they deprecated his cruelties, but because his prominence belittled their importance. Accordingly, seven or eight of them, in imitation of Alva, habitually absented themselves from the sittings of the court—a procedure the sole effect of which was to enhance the influence of Vargas, Del Rio, Blasere, and Hassels, the four who remained.‖ "They made," as one of the discontented judges complained to Granvelle, "but one head under a single cap."¶

As illustrating the careless ferocity of this quar-

---

* Schiller, vol. 2, p. 79.
† Hoofd, tom. 4, p. 152. Meteren, folio 54.
‡ Ibid.   § Brandt, *ubi sup*. Davies, vol. 1, p. 550.
‖ Levesque, Mémoires de Granvelle, tom. 2, pp. 91.   ¶ Ibid.

tette, it is related of Hassels, who had been attorney-general of Ghent under Charles V., that he was in the habit of dozing away his hours at the council-table, paying no attention whatever to the cause on trial, and ignorant often of the name of the prisoner. Nevertheless, when his opinion was demanded, he would start from his dog-nap and shout with great fervor: "To the gallows with him! to the gallows with him!"* so much a matter of course was conviction.

Vargas was equally careless. On one occasion a· case was called up for trial after the execution of the prisoner. A cursory review of the papers showed him to have been innocent. "Never mind," said Vargas with a cheerful smile, "it will be all the better for him when he takes his trial in the other world."†

Before these brutes, "half monkey and half tiger," as Voltaire said of the judges of Calais, the citizens of the states continued to be dragged in crowds. There was no cessation in the slaughter. There was no gradation of offences. Confiscation of estates succeeded by the death of the culprit— this was the common form.‡ Hanging, beheading, quartering, and burning human beings were the

---

* "Ad patibulum, ad patibulum!" Hoofd, tom. 14, p. 594. Brandt, Aubéri. In the year 1578, this wretch himself met the fate he had been so ready to award to others, being hung to a tree in that year by the people of Ghent, then in insurrection. *Vide* Meteren, folio 161.

† Hoofd, tom. 5, p. 191. Brandt, vol. 1.

‡ Meteren, folio 49, *passim.* Hoofd, tom. 4, *passim.* Schiller.

ordinary occupations of a thousand laborers.* Every day produced fresh objects of pity and mourning. The noise of the bloody passing-bell was continually heard, telling as it tolled of the martyrdom of this one's cousin and of that one's wife, and ringing dismal peals in the hearts of the survivors.† The land was crowded with gibbets; the trees by the wayside were loaded with corpses. Statues in the streets of towns, private door-posts, fences in the fields, all had their quota of mutilated carcasses.‡ The very atmosphere was impregnated with the awful odor of the grave. The living walked among the dead as in a charnel-house.§ Humanity seemed to have suffered shipwreck, the hulk being abandoned to those frightful underwriters, the worms.

While the blood-judges were thus torturing the Netherlands, France, almost equally unhappy, was torn by civil war‖—one half of the nation striving to cut the throats of the other half in the name of religion. The Romanists led by the Guises, the Huguenots officered by Condé and Coligny—these were the disputants; and the question was whether there were such things as rights of conscience. The Guises said No; the Protestant chiefs said Yes. As very many of those Low-Countrymen who had been driven into exile by the events which succeeded the

○ Schiller, vol. 2, p. 81, Bohn's edit.

† Brandt, vol. 1, p. 261. Hoofd, tom. 4, p. 153. •

‡ Ibid. Histoire des Martyrs, p. 449. § Ibid.

‖ De Thou. Hist. of the Huguenots, Am. Tract Soc., 1866

iconomachy, or had become fugitives under Alva's
rule, said Yes, too, they volunteered to aid Condé
and Coligny in maintaining that belief, doing yeomanly service in innumerable warlike bouts.

One day the French ambassador at Brussels
waited upon the duchess of Parma to complain of
these campaigners.* Her highness promptly issued
an edict denouncing as outlaws and punishing with
confiscation of their goods all absentees without
permission.† A little later, this act was supplemented by another which forbade any communication to be held with the exiles under the same penalty.‡ Nevertheless, the fugitives neither deserted
Condé nor returned to their homes. Whereupon
Catharine de' Medici, hard pressed by the Huguenots, urged Alva to send some of his veterans to
prop her falling cause. "If you do not," added
she, "I must succumb; and I disculpate myself in
advance before God and Christian princes for the
peace I shall be forced to make."§

Alva wrote this reply, finely illustrative of the
nature of the man: "Make no concessions; concessions must be either spiritual or temporal. If spiritual, they would be opposed to God's prerogatives;
if temporal, to the rights of the king. Better to
reign over a ruined land, which is true to the divine
and human majesties, than over one left unharmed
for the benefit of the devil and his followers, the
heretics."‖

* Strada, tom. 2, p. 34.   † Ibid.   Davies, vol. 1, p. 554.
‡ Ibid.   § Cor. de Phil. II., tom. 1, p. 694.   ‖ Ibid., p. 609.

Having spoken, the captain-general proceeded to act. In the last days of November, 1567, after innumerable masses chanted through three days,* Count Aremberg left Cambray at the head of thirty-five hundred men-at-arms to reinforce the Guises. His expedition was successful; the Romanists won the fight. But the queen-mother of France signed a treaty with Condé which angered Alva, and Aremberg was soon ordered to report at Brussels for home service.†

In the meantime, the duchess of Parma, more and more nettled by her position at Brussels, which was "a remarkable combination of the fiction of power with the reality of political nonentity," as Grote says of the state of modern British sovereigns, never ceased importuning Philip for permission to resign the apocryphal honors of the regency. At length, the royal procrastinator, persuaded that Margaret had served out her usefulness and was now an obstacle in the pathway of the captain-general, condescended to heed her prayer. Early in November, 1567, despatches were received from Spain, in which Ruy Gomez, *factotum* at Madrid, assured her highness that the king consented, though reluctantly, to her retirement.‡ A few days later, Philip himself penned half a dozen cold, formal lines to his sister, acknowledging his obligations in set phrase, and promising to increase her pension from eight thousand florins a

---

* Strada, *ubi sup.* † Ibid., p. 35. Prescott, vol. 2, p. 206.
‡ Documentos Inéditos, tom. 4, p. 481.

year, the present amount, to fourteen thousand florins.*

Margaret at once prepared to quit the Netherlands. She had requested the king to permit her to convene the states-general for the purpose of delivering in their presence a farewell address, in unconscious imitation of the emperor's abdication; but Philip, whom the sternest necessity had not sufficed to compel to convoke that detested body, returned a prompt, curt veto.† Her highness was consequently obliged to announce the dissolution of her official connection with the provinces in a public letter.‡ The duke of Alva was at the same time proclaimed as her successor in the regency.§

The states listened to this news in trembling dismay. Time was when the duchess had been regarded as the personification of severity; but since Alva's butcheries commenced, the masses had learned to look back upon her rule as quite mild and pacific. Now she was considered to be the sole breakwater between *terra firma* and the devouring flood of the captain-general. This feeling cropped out in multitudinous expressions of regret for her departure, in a hearty request that she might soon return to resume her robes of office, and in the yet more touching form of silver-sorrow—Brabant voting her highness the snug sum of twenty-five thou-

---

° Cor. de Philippe II., tom. 2, Appendix, No. 119.

† Prescott, vol. 2, p. 210. Schiller, vol. 2, p. 84, Bohn's ed.

‡ Strada, tom. 2, p. 36.

§ Ibid., p. 35. Cor. de Philippe II., tom. 2, p. 680.

sand florins, Flanders evincing its esteem by a vote of the still more comfortable sum of thirty thousand florins.*

Having nothing now to lose by frankness, cheered by these tokens of the national good-will, and perhaps touched by the sufferings of the citizens—for, after all, she was a woman—Margaret, on the eve of her departure, addressed Philip in these words, showing that, when not biased by self-interest, she could comprehend the principles of statesmanship: "Sire, the subjects of these provinces cannot be terrified into obedience. They who so advise you, do it—I wish I may be in error—to the ruin of your name and of the states, and will occasion fresh commotions and final desolation. Wherefore, as mercy is a divine attribute, so, too, be you merciful, desiring rather the repentance than the punishment of those who err."†

The advice was good; but a king like Philip was little likely to be much affected by it.

In the latter days of December, 1567, after a reign of eight years,‡ her highness bade the Netherlands farewell. Escorted by Alva to the borders of Brabant, she was accompanied thence by Count Mansfeld and a suite of Flemish gentlemen into the heart of Germany.§ Margaret made a much better figure in these closing days, than she had in the opening months of her residence at Brussels. Her

---

* Corresp. de Philippe II., tom. 2, p. 6.

† Strada, tom. 2, pp. 36, 37.   ‡ From 1559 to 1567.

§ Prescott, vol. 2, p. 212.

exit was touching; for she left leal and mourning
hearts behind her. On the dismal background of
Alva, she went out robed in light—almost angelic,
in the estimation of her contemporaries. But the
standpoint of Alva is not a proper one from which
to view the merits of the governant's politics. Posterity, uninfluenced by the proximity of her successor, sees with clearer eyes; and the verdict which
the muse of history pronounces is, that the bastard
daughter of Charles V. was a woman weak, treacherous, and cruel—qualities, perhaps, which might
be looked for in a pupil of Ignatius Loyola.

Possessed now of the title as well as the authority of governor, and freed from the presence of
Margaret, who might criticise, even though she
were powerless to curb his actions, Alva assumed
the tone and exercised the authority of an irresponsible despot. He assumed his honors, and commenced the new year with a procedure against
Orange. On the 19th of January, 1568, William,
Louis of Nassau, Count Culemberg, and the rest of
the grandees were cited by the blood-judges to appear before their bar within twenty-eight days after
the date of the citation, to answer to an indictment
for treason, under pain of the confiscation of their
estates with perpetual banishment.*

Of course, neither Orange nor his friends were
besotted enough to make their appearance before
the illustrious Vargas, skilful Del Rio, and sleepy

---

* Archives de la Maison d'Orange-Nassau, tom. 3, p. 119.
Documentos Inéditos, tom. 4, p. 428, *et seq.*

Hassels. But the prince, addressing the procurator-general in reply to the summons, pleaded to the jurisdiction of the Council of Troubles, claiming that, as a knight of the Golden Fleece, he could only be tried by his peers, the knights, solemnly convened, with the sanction of at least six of the brothers, and under the superintendence of Philip, sitting as grand-master.* The retort was cautious; for William had no desire to precipitate events, sure that Alva would do that; and it was technical—that the summons was illegal and an outrage.

Alva did put himself as indisputably in the wrong as the prince had foreseen he would; for, galled by the contemptuous tone of his antagonist, and hounded on by Granvelle,† he seized William's eldest son, Philip, count of Buren, a lad of thirteen, who was a student at Louvain, and in violation of time-honored franchises which exempted undergraduates from arrest, no matter upon what pretext, sent him a prisoner into Spain,‡ thinking to keep a hold upon the father through his anxiety for the safety of his heir.

* Bor., tom. 4, p. 222, et seq. Aubéri, Hist. de Hollande, p. 25.

† Corresp. de Philippe II., tom. 1, p. 701.

‡ Strada, tom. 2, p. 42. Vandervynckt, tom. 2, p. 261. The boy was detained in Spain twenty-eight years, and trained up in the strictest school of Romanism. When at length, in 1595, he visited the Netherlands, he was a complete Spaniard—gloomy. Jesuitical, denationalized. Dying in 1615, at Brussels, his brother Maurice succeeded to his titles, and inherited the Orange-Nassau estates, as he had from infancy possessed the heroic qualities of their great blood. Vide Lives of the Princes of Orange—Philip, William of Nassau.

This kidnapping stirred wide-spread reprobation. William formally protested against it as in palpable conflict with the charter-law of the states.* A deputation of the college dons went up to Brussels to remonstrate with Vargas on this insult to their privileges. That eminent jurisconsult dismissed them with contempt. " *Non curamus vestros privilegios*,"† exclaimed he; and the sentence has been admired for its Latinity for three hundred years. What cared Alva for the franchises of the provinces? Was not the nation a mass of convicts? Were not the states a vast prison-house, of which he was the keeper and his sword the key?

While the kidnapping of the count of Buren was the topic of common but whispered conversation, news came from Spain which fanned the excitement to a redder flame; it was rumored that Philip had imprisoned his son and the heir to his throne, Don Carlos; and it was asserted that Montigny had been arrested for high treason.‡ For once Dame Rumor hawked the truth. Don Carlos and Montigny were upon the king's red list. Don Carlos had excited the jealousy, Montigny had provoked the wrath, of a monarch who could not pronounce the word forgiveness; therefore, one was soon to fall, as some say, beneath the dagger of his own father ;§ the other by the hand of a secret executioner‖—making a double

* Prescott, vol. 2, p. 202.   † Vandervynckt, *ubi sup.*

‡ Strada, tom. 2, p. 42. Documentos Inéditos, tom. 4, p. 526.

§ Lloronte, Hist. de l'Inquisition, p. 171, *et seq.* Cabrera, Filipo Segundo, lib. 7, cap. 22.

‖ Documentos Inéditos, tom. 4, p. 560, *et seq.*

tragedy, wilder than any of which romancists ever dreamed.

But the Netherlands needed not to await the opening of the foreign budget to "sup full of horrors." Through all these months the frightful cruelties of the blood-judges were continued. Every day the executions took a wider sweep. "I would have every man feel that any day his house may fall about his ears,"* wrote Alva to the king. Of this benevolent wish he made a fact. Men of all creeds and of none felt equally insecure. The Romanists themselves, the most sturdy and devoted of them, shuddered and rubbed their necks, to be sure that their heads still rested upon their shoulders as they glanced towards Egmont's prison at Ghent. "The fury of the persecution spreads such horror throughout the nation," said Orange at the time, "that thousands, and among them some of the principal papists, have fled the country where tyranny is directed against all."†

The blood-judges flooded the land with citations; but so certainly did conviction follow an appearance at their bar, that few responded, while such as did not were condemned to exile and to suffer the confiscation of their estates for contumacy; or if caught, they were beheaded without trial.‡ Those who, strong in innocence, ventured to brave an examination, were inevitably doomed.§ In

* Corresp. de Philippe II., tom. 2, p. 4.
† Corresp. de Guillaume le Taciturne, tom. 3, p. 14.
‡ Davies, vol. 1, p. 552. Schiller. § Ibid.

batches of forty, fifty, and even a hundred, men women and children were led out to indiscriminate death. On one occasion ninety-five miscellaneous individuals, collected from various parts of Flanders, were butchered in company.* At another time forty-six of the citizens of Malines were decapitated.† On the 4th of January, 1568, eighty-four persons, charged with participating in the tumults, were executed together in the public square at Valenciennes.‡

Or, if you will have some individual instances, take these, culled at haphazard from the mass: William Bardes, an old man of seventy, and an ex-magistrate of Amsterdam, was accused upon uncertain evidence based on inuendoes, of having encouraged the *gueux*. He was arrested, racked, and whipped with rods for this atrocious offence—of which it seems he was not guilty, for he was acquitted after a punishment which was so severe that he became an idiot.§

One of this man's fellow-townsmen, Peter de Witt, was beheaded because, during a commotion at Amsterdam, he had persuaded a rioter not to shoot one of the magistrates—which was regarded as proof that he had influence with the rebels.‖

In 1566, in the heat of the iconomachy, a certain woman named Madame Juriaen had smitten a wood-

---

* Meteren, folio 45. Hoofd, tom. 4, p. 157.   † Ibid.

‡ Bulletins de l'Académie Royale de Belgique, tom. 16, par. 2, p. 62.   § Brandt, vol. 1, p. 263.

‖ Hoofd, tom. 5, p. 183.

image of the Madonna with her slipper—an action which her maid, who witnessed it, did not denounce. For this crime both were drowned by the hangman in a hogshead of water placed upon the scaffold.*

These are simple instances. Multiply this individual agony by three millions, and that into all the relations of husband and wife, of father and child, and that again by the continuance of months; then count, if possible, the pulse-beat of this feverish horror.

Innumerable as were the victims, Alva was always striving to invent more rapid processes of destruction. At the close of the carnival of 1568, he made a notable haul. As that was a season of wine-bibbing and jollity, he calculated on arresting an immense number of persons overcome by the wassail. Happily the scheme leaked out, and many of the doomed ones fled; but upwards of five hundred burghers were dragged from their beds to the block.†

The vast majority of all these sufferers were Protestant preachers and laymen—men easily apprehended, because they were too honest to deny their faith. For offenders of this class no punishment was sufficiently dreadful—the gibbet, the rack, drowning, the stake, all were invoked.‡ These martyrs, obscure men, who "built not fame, but godlike souls," endured their pangs with indomitable

* Brandt; cited in Motley, vol. 2, p. 145.

† Brandt, *ubi sup.* Corresp. de Philippe II., tom. 2. Appendix, p. 660. ‡ Reidanus, Annales, p. 6.

courage.* They lifted up their eyes to heaven, and cared little for what persecution could do unto them, paying scant attention to the jeers of the vile mob and to the denunciation of the blood-judges as law-breakers; for they were solaced by conscience, which makes the weakest strong, and they heard in their souls the approving echo of the law of laws. On the hearts of such men cruelty itself breaks all its teeth.

When it was seen with what constancy and alacrity these victims suffered, never ceasing to pray for their tormentors, and to give God the glory, confessing their faith in the midst of the flames, Alva had a machine invented for the purpose of silencing such dangerous preachers. The tip of each sufferer's tongue was seared with a red-hot iron, and then while thus swollen compressed between two pieces of flat metal screwed fast together. Thus secured, the tongue would wriggle about with the pain of burning, yielding a hollow sound much like the tyrant of Sicily's brazen bell, the contrivance of Perillus, and which was first experienced by the inventor himself.[†]

Once, at an *auto da fé* of these tongue-tied martyrs, a friar in the crowd exclaimed: "Hark how they sing! should they not be made to dance also?"[‡]

Alva had promised the king to make treasure flow from the Netherlands into Spain in a stream a yard wide. With an eye to the fulfilment of this

* Reidanus, Annales, p. 6. Brant, vol. 1, p. 260, *et seq.*
† Brandt, vol. 1, p. 275.   ‡ Ibid.

promise, he especially directed the blood-judges to
ascertain the wealth of the suspected.* The hint
was acted on. As poverty was no protection, so
'wealth was an unpardonable crime. Many a rich
citizen, convicted of a hundred thousand florins,
found himself tied to a horse's tail, and so dragged
without trial to the gallows.† The estates of absentees without leave had long since been declared to
have escheated to the crown. From these snap-
judgments there was no appeal, though the mischief worked was incalculable, since it affected a
host of others besides those directly interested—
such as innocent creditors, to satisfy whose claims
no allotment was made, hospitals, eleemosynary
institutions, widows, and orphans, who were by
knavish evasions deprived of the sources of their
income—the purses of the rich.‡

Moreover, though these wholesale proscriptions
sufficed to ruin trade and to depopulate the towns—
in Ghent half the houses are said to have stood
empty§—they did not even pay the expenses of
Alva's administration, to say nothing of that stream
of treasure which was to have flowed into Spain.‖
The duke was constantly embarrassed. More than
once he was obliged to beg a loan from Philip.¶
By the most shame-faced extortion, by the most

 * Prescott, vol. 2, p. 221.
 † Meteren, folio 50. Cited in Motley, vol. 2, p. 159.
 ‡ Brandt, vol. 1, p. 261.
 § Vandervynckt, tom. 2, p. 247.
 ‖ Prescott, *ubi sup.*, p. 230, *et seq.*
 ¶ Cor. de Philippe II., tom 1, p. 590.

open robbery, despotism could not pay its way,
even with the coffers of the Indies of Europe at its
command. Yet aforetime fair taxation, with the
sums voted, as occasion called, by the states-general, had kept the sovereign in funds. Surely honesty is the best policy.

However, this blunderer in finance mistook
bloodthirstiness for statesmanship, and he was too
thick-skulled to be convinced even by the teachings
of experience. Accordingly, he went on assailing
the most sacred rights of individuals, enforcing his
arbitrary will even in the circle of domestic life.
Hitherto the reformers had strengthened their party
by intermarriages with the most influential families
in the states. " I will scoop out the spring which
feeds that stream," said the duke; and he issued an
edict forbidding all Netherlanders, of whatever
rank or office, to marry without his prior permission, under penalty of death and the confiscation of
property*—an act of grievous and unheard-of tyranny. A little later, the hated decrees of the
Council of Trent were imposed upon the Low
Countries by the " I say so" of this enterprising
satrap,† whose strength, however, consisted in the
fact that he always represented his master's will.

Such searching despotism was certain to engen-
der evil. It had already transformed the naturally
jovial, boisterous, and out-spoken Netherlander into
a sullen, moody, and dispirited conspirator, brood-

* Schiller, vol. 2, p. 80, Bohn's ed.
† Brandt, vol. 1, p. 266.

ing over the memory of his violated charters. Indeed, at this very time the extensive and tangled forests of West Flanders were filled with outlaws bereaved of kindred and of country and fanaticized by their wrongs, who were banded together for the purpose of waging an unsparing guerilla war upon the oppressor.* Sallying from their untamed coverts at unexpected moments, these "wild beggars"—*gueux sauvages*, as they were named—carried dismay and death into all habitations known to be unfriendly to their mystic brotherhood. They esteemed the monasteries and ecclesiastics to be the primal causes of their woes; consequently they let slip no opportunity to sack the religious houses, and never passed by a chance to rob, maltreat, and maim the Roman clergy. Many were the convents whose plate and wine and game they confiscated; many were the priests whose ears they cropped and whose noses they slit. Sometimes, borrowing Alva's tactics, they dragged monks to forest scaffolds at the tails of their horses—pleading in justification of these deeds the *lex talionis*. The duke attempted to bridle the excesses of the freebooters by making each parish responsible for the safety of its clergy; but under this arrangement the highways became unsafe for any priest to tread. Whereupon Alva sent some men-at-arms to hunt them out; and by these veterans the wild beggars were for a time suppressed.†

* Vandervynckt. Brandt. *ubi sup.* Grotius.
† Vandervynckt, tom. 2, p. 450. Bor., tom. 4, p. 225.

While this tragical comedy was being enacted in the forests of West Flanders, the Netherland masses were calling upon the prince of Orange, since the imprisonment of Egmont the acknowledged chieftain of the states, to intervene in their behalf with the armed hand.*   William was willing

> " to take
> Occasion by the hand, and make
> The bounds of freedom wider yet."

He only doubted the success of an immediate rising, fearing that the time was not quite ripe. However, the people clamored and the exiles argued until he professed his willingness to take the field; and in his case it was known that the paper currency of profession would be redeemed by the minted gold of practice. With Orange, to resolve was to act, and he began to enroll volunteers. The tap of liberty's recruiting-drum was heard. The hour was at hand when the senseless mediæval cannon were to think, when the newly-invented muskets were to be loaded with ideas. War itself seemed to "smooth its wrinkled front" as it took the championship of such a cause.

* Archives de la Maison d'Orange-Nassau, Supplément, p. 87.

CHAPTER XXIX.

LIBERTY'S DRUM-TAP.

SOME one has said that it is as good for men as for beasts to be turned out to grass occasionally. Rest is a honey to be sipped—not gluttonously, but for refreshment. Apparently, William of Orange thought that he had earned a title to this recreative beatitude; for though he had now been a refugee above a twelvemonth, he continued to reside at Dillenberg Castle, and seemed engrossed by the enjoyment of the charming ruralities of Nassau.

However, exile is not conducive to peace of mind. Although the self-centred and reticent prince made few confidants, content to elaborate his plans in the quiet council-chamber of his own soul, it was more than suspected that neither he nor his illustrious following had passed into Germany to enjoy a life of indolence. Simulated acquiescence might be the policy of these men: it was well known that it could not be their intention to submit to outlawry without a struggle for the retention of their rights.

Those observers who held these views were correct. Orange especially, behind that imperturbability which masked his purpose, was restless and unhappy. At home though he was in Nassau, surrounded by kith and kin, and lapped in luxury, the great-hearted statesman could not feel at ease while every Netherland breeze that swept over the ancient stronghold of his race was heavy with the shrieks of the tortured, and with the death-cries of martyrs. That placid selfishness, that covert infidelity called optimism was not numbered among the tenets of his creed; and he was aware that Alva's rule ought not to claim submission. But he also knew—none better—that unless prefaced by all just concessions, by the trial of every fair means to keep the peace, a sanguinary appeal to the God of battles was a crime against humanity—that war, a confession that culture and religion were in some sort a failure, needed the most momentous and solemn justification.

Conscience is virtue's forum. To satisfy his conscience, William, though hopeless of success, determined to exhaust all peaceful methods of redressing the wrongs of the provinces before invoking the stern arbitrament of the sword. Accordingly, he moved the magistrates of Antwerp, whose manner from the moment of Alva's arrival at Brussels had been excessively obsequious, to interpose in favor of several of their fellow-townsmen who had been illegally imprisoned. This they did "with bated breath and whispered humbleness." "Well, well," retorted the governor-general in a tone which made the burghers shiver, "I am amazed that there should still be men in Antwerp so bold and impudent as to dare to plead with me for mercy to heretics. Have a care for the future, else I will hang you all for an example. Know this, that his majesty will speedily sweep these territories as clean as the palm of my hand, if that be necessary to extirpate heresy."[*]

Rebuffed through the magistrates, Orange next employed the august intercession of the German emperor, Maximilian. Early in March, 1568, Maximilian addressed a letter to Philip, in the name of the electors of the empire, in which, after intimating that the Netherlands had a right, as members of the Germanic body, to demand justice in the spirit of their charters, he warned his royal cousin that, without a cessation of the cruelties enacted by Alva, it would be impossible to restrain the Protestant princes of Germany from a combination which might deprive him of every acre of land in the Low Countries.[†]

Philip's purpose was not to be shaken; but he condescended to vindicate his conduct. "What I have done," wrote he in reply to Maximilian, "has been for the welfare of the provinces and for the defence of the holy faith. Nor would I do otherwise, though I should risk the sovereignty of the Netherlands—no, though the world should fall in ruins around me."[‡]

This was decisive. Before such a declaration, diplomacy stood disarmed. An incentive to war, this double failure was also William's justification for it. The prince felt that now duty as well as

[*] Brandt, vol. 1, p. 265. Watson, Life of Philip II., p. 119.
[†] Cor. de Philippe II., tom. 2, p. 15.
[‡] Corresp. de Philippe II., tom. 2, p. 27.

inclination bade him "storm the house of fame," that religion and liberty might

> "Sit on no precarious throne,
> Nor borrow leave to be."

Orange knew the frightful risk which war necessitated. Yet it was with the calm conviction of a statesman, not with the reckless desperation of a political gamester, that he prepared to stake wealth, reputation, family, life itself, upon the hazardous die of battle.

When the prince sat down to count up the chances of his success, he could not fail to acknowledge that the odds were greatly against him. Alva was the most experienced captain in Europe. Both the Indies were his treasure-house. He was already entrenched in the Netherlands. Behind him stood the king, clothed in a "divine right" which the mediæval masses were not sufficiently enlightened to ridicule. The engineering skill of Paciotti had already strongly fortified the frontier towns. If the Spanish army was small, it was composed of veterans, completely equipped, and formed to be the nucleus of a larger force, which might be recruited in a week.

Orange, on his part, was a tyro in war when compared with Alva. The private contributions of half-ruined refugees must form his exchequer. It was his part to assail. No "divine right" was supposed to hallow his Quixotism; no skilful engineers were in his pay; no veterans were to assemble beneath his banner; and yet the statesman-soldier did not hesitate. Evidently the captain of revolutionary France did not inherit the idea that "God sides with the strongest battalions" from the liberator of Holland.

But after all, William was not so weak as he seemed on the first look. All generous minds were sure to be his allies; all Protestant purses were his in such a cause. Christian Europe was his recruiting ground. The fanaticism of the persecutor worked in his behalf. All whom the Reformation had emancipated, all whom the Inquisition had menaced, were his from sympathy. The Netherlands themselves, if he could reach them, would yield him both men and means; for states like these act and endure with gigantic energy whenever pressing emergencies call forth their powers, and a skilful and provident administration elicits their resources—when conscience arms and genius shows the way.

Strengthened by some such reflections as these, and imploring God's aid, the heroic refugee began to weave the web of his policy. Not Philip himself could mate him in industrious subtlety; while to that he added the higher qualities of prescience and tact and management—a genius for all work. Never before had he labored as he labored now. Swift, secret, incapable of fatigue, this powerful and patient intellect sped to and fro, disentangling the perplexed skein where all seemed so hopelessly confused, and gradually unfolding broad schemes of a symmetrical and regenerated polity.*

° Motley. vol. 2, p. 182.

William's chief anxiety at this hour was the obtaining foreign countenance; for he saw that, scattered and peeled as the refugees were, it would be impossible for them to take the initial steps towards success without the active good-will and support of outside powers. Assistance and recognition—these were what the good cause required; and his painstaking statesmanship had conciliated widespread respect for the spirit and the prospects of the Netherland opposition to Philip II. At the English court no foreigner stood as well with the maiden queen as did the nascent liberator.* Among the Huguenots, no name was more frequently upon all lips than that of the sworn friend of Coligny.†. In Germany, the prince was peerless.‡

So wisely had Orange managed that, ere any overt act was committed, Protestant England, Huguenot France, and reformed Germany had all, more or less openly, promised to support their brothers in the Low Countries.§ England was prompted to do this, because William had persuaded Elizabeth that Great Britain was bound to act to the Reformation the part which Philip played towards the Romanist reaction. The Huguenots were incited, by the ties of a common creed and a kindred interest, to cripple Spain. The German princes were kindled by the reflection that Alva's

* Motley, *ut antea*.   † De Thou, tom. 6, p. 36.
‡ Meteren, folio 57. Motley, *ubi sup*.
§ Bor., tom. 4, p. 227. Hoofd, tom. 5, p. 162, *et seq*. Watson, p. 123.

rule would ruin the lowland cities, with whose trade
the prosperity of their towns was inseparably connected; by the fact that the Netherlanders were
their co-religionists; and by a fear that when King
Philip had completed the subjection of the lower
provinces, he would employ his veterans against the
liberties of Upper Germany—an adjacent and most
inviting field.* The diplomat who could play so
cunningly on all these chords, awakening such various responses, might safely be considered a dangerous opponent even by the Machiavellis of the Spanish cabinet in the sixteenth century.

Unwittingly, Philip himself had aided Orange
by his haughty refusal of Maximilian's proffered
mediation. So bitter was the anger of the smaller
Germanic potentates, that they did not deign to
conceal their sympathy for the Netherlands; while
the count palatine of the Rhine, the duke of Wir-
temberg, and the landgrave of Hesse announced
their purpose to support William in the field†—to
all which breaches of neutrality the emperor was
deaf, dumb, and blind from pique.

In these days the brother of Orange, Count
Louis of Nassau, was the most active and serviceable of his supporters. As William was styled the
brain, so Louis was called the stout right arm of
the revolt.‡ This knight-errant had long fretted at
his enforced inactivity. Now that the hour had

° Watson, *ubi sup.* Prescott, vol. 2, p. 237.
† Watson, p. 123. Meteren, Hoofd. Prescott, vol. 2, p. 237.
‡ Motley, vol. 2, p. 183.

struck for resistance to religious tyranny, he remembered his Genevan training and was happy. Every word he spoke smelt of gunpowder.

On the 6th of April, 1568, the prince of Orange invested Count Louis with authority to enroll and equip an army for service against Alva. He based the right to do this upon somewhat peculiar ground—fidelity to the king. The fiction of loyalty, the idea that the monarch could do no wrong, but that it was his counsellors who were to be chastised for whatever ills occurred; all this was craftily maintained, for William knew the value of having the old forms upon his side. This explains the phraseology of the commission, which ran thus: "To show our love for the king and his hereditary provinces; to prevent the desolation which hangs over the states by the ferocity of the Spaniards; to maintain the privileges sworn to by his present majesty and by his predecessors; to prevent the extirpation of the pure word and service of God by the edicts; to save the sons and daughters of the land from abject slavery—we have requested our dearly beloved brother Louis Nassau to recruit as many men-at-arms as he may deem fit."[*]

Under this commission—and duplicates of it had been granted to Hoogstraaten, Van der Berg, and the rest[†]—Count Louis and his friends began at once to solicit volunteers and to enroll mercenaries. But now, as always in such undertakings, the patriots were sadly hampered by want of money.

[*] Bor., tom. 4, p. 233, et seq.   [†] Ibid., p. 234.

Two hundred thousand florins, at the very least, were necessary to the getting an army on its feet;* much more would be required to fight out a campaign. Where was the Mexico, where the Peru to supply this sum?

The precious personal effects of the prince of Orange were the Golconda whence much of it was extracted. William pawned his jewels, sent his plate to the mint, sold his tapestry, parted with his furniture,† and still had not enough; for "the ornaments of a palace" as an old chronicler reminds us, "yield but little for the necessities of war."‡ But this princely generosity provoked emulation. Count John of Nassau mortgaged his estates in aid of the good cause.§ Count Louis threw his quota into the general fund. Culemberg, Hoogstraaten, Van der Berg, and the rest contributed their share, until one hundred thousand florins were raised from the donations of these refugee seigneurs, all of whom were half-bankrupted by outlawry.‖

Nor were the grandees the sole donors. The Protestants of Antwerp, of Haarlem, of Leyden, and of others of the Low Country cities, contributed towards the achievement of their emancipation; and the refugee merchants in England laid their

---

* Archives de la Maison d'Orange-Nassau. Supplément, p. 88.
† Hoofd, tom. 5, p. 163. Reidanus, Annales, p. 6.
‡ Reidanus, *ubi sup.*   § Hoofd, *ubi sup.*
‖ William contributed 50,000 florins, Culemberg 30,000, Van der Berg 30,000, Hoogstraaten 30,000, the dowager countess of Horn 10,000, Louis Nassau 10,000, and others in less proportion. *Vide* Villar's confession in Corresp. de Philippe II., tom. 2, p. 757.

gifts upon the altar.* In this way another hundred thousand florins were poured into the lean exchequer of revolt.†

With these moneys, the outcome of much generous self-sacrifice, an irregular and incongruous army was levied—free lances, enthusiasts, veterans, and raw recruits ranged side by side in the grotesque ranks.‡ These sudden levies of peaceful husbandmen and careless mercenaries, how were they to withstand the terrible onset of Alva's machine-like cohorts? To human eyes, the matching of those against these, was like bombarding Gibraltar with lumps of trembling jelly. Yet it was with these, and such as these, that the patriots were obliged to fight.

By the middle of April, 1568, this preliminary work of raising money and enrolling soldiers was done,§ and as well done as might be, if the circumstances are considered. It only remained to enter the Netherlands sword in hand. Orange had decided upon a tripartite invasion, with the twofold purpose of distracting the attention of the governor-general and of inviting a general rising in the states.‖ Louis Nassau at the head of a force, partly Flemish but chiefly German, was to plant the standard of revolt in the northern provinces of Groningen and Friesland—the immemorial home of the

---

* Hoofd, tom. 5, p. 164. Villar's Confession, *ubi sup.*
† Ibid. Prescott, vol. 2, p. 237.
‡ Prescott, *ubi sup.*   § Meteren, Hoofd, Bor.
‖ Strada, tom. 2, p. 46.

spirit of independence.* Hoogstraaten, accompanied by numbers of the banished seigneurs, was to enter the provinces through the gates of Maestricht and scour the land between the rivers Meuse and Rhine.† A corps of Huguenots, under the seigneur de Cocqueville, was to master Artois, and thence to beat up Alva's southern quarters.‡ Orange held himself in reserve in the duchy of Cleves, that he might complete the organization of his force, not yet ready for action, and that he might be prepared to support whatever division should call for aid.§

Such was the plan of campaign adopted by the patriot chiefs—a comprehensive scheme which bears unmistakably the impress of William's astute intellect.

Towards the latter part of April, the seigneur de Villars, who had replaced Hoogstraaten, crossed the frontiers of Juliers with a following of three thousand men. Alva, who was never to be caught napping, promptly despatched Don Sancho d'Avila with sixteen hundred veterans to parry the assault. Forty-eight hours later, De Villars was a prisoner, his troops either stiff in death or scattered in wild rout.‖

De Cocqueville fared no better. Taking the field a month later than De Villars, he crossed the

---

* Mendoza, Comment., folio 39. Bor., tom. 4, p. 233, *et seq.*
† Hoofd, tom. 5, p. 164. Mendoza and Bor., *ut antea.*
‡ Ibid.   § Ibid.
‖ De Thou, Hist. Universelle, tom. 5, p. 443. Mendoza, *ubi sup.*

French border into the bailiwick of Hesdin, in Artois, with a muster twenty-five hundred strong. Here, the count de Roeulx met him, and buffeted him back over the frontier. On the 18th of July, Maréschal de Cossé, governor of Picardy, came upon the rabble rout at the village of St. Valery, and dealt De Cocqueville the finishing blow.*

Those who were captured in these abortive expeditions neither expected nor received mercy. De Cocqueville was carried to Paris and beheaded by Charles IX., in requital of the assistance recently rendered him by Aremberg.† Whatever Netherlanders were taken with that hapless gentleman were handed over to the Spanish headsman at Brussels.‡ De Villars' head had fallen ere the effort of De Cocqueville was made.§

In the meantime, Louis Nassau had entered Gröningen. The Frenchman in league with Alva, and triumphant on the southern border; the Spaniard flushed with success in the middle provinces; the patriots in arms and advancing in the north— such was the political situation on the 1st of May, 1568.

Crossing Gröningen at his leisure, Count Louis paused from time to time, to set up his standard and to invite the coöperation of the sympathetic masses. Upon one side of his banner the words

---

* De Thou, Hist. Universelle, tom. 5, p. 443. Mendoza, *ubi sup.* Bor., tom. 4, p. 234. Strada, tom. 2, pp. 46, 47.

† Strada, tom. 2, pp. 46, 47.   ‡ Bor., tom. 4, p. 238.

§ De Cocqueville took the field near the end of June. Villars was executed on the 2d of June.

"Now or Never" were emblazoned, and on the
other the device was, "Freedom for Fatherland
and Liberty of Conscience"*—mottoes which
awakened the enthusiasm of the hardy Dutchmen,
and attracted hundreds of valiant but ill-armed and
undisciplined rustics to the liberal army.

On the western wolds of Frisia, the stronghold
of Wedde, a residence of Count Aremberg, stadtholder of the province, was surprised.† Thence
Nassau pushed on to Appingedam, on the tide-
waters of the Dollart, a bay created by an inundation which had swallowed thirty-three villages at a
gulp.‡ Resting here for a space, the patriot captain improved that opportunity to lay the neighboring city of Gröningen under contribution. The
prudent burghers, anxious to please Nassau and
not to anger Alva, refused to admit the count's
men-at-arms, but bought off for a time the menaced
assault by a present of good Dutch guilders;§
which came timely, for Nassau's mercenaries were
already mutinous.‖ Ere Count Louis resumed his
march, Adolphus Nassau, a younger brother of his
devoted house, rode into camp at the head of three
hundred cavaliers, a much-needed and very welcome reinforcement.¶

While rebellion was thus making headway, Alva,
who had been apprized of the new peril by lieuten-

---

* Brandt, vol. 1, p. 267.   † Motley, vol. 2, p. 186.
‡ Strada, *ubi sup.*   § Bor., tom. 4, p. 235.
‖ Prescott, vol. 2, p, 242.
¶ Mendoza, Comentarios, folio 46.   Bor., *ubi sup.*

ant-governor Groesbeck of Friesland, was preparing to cope with it. "Be you not taken napping, seigneur stadtholder," wrote he to Groesbeck on the 30th of April; "but keep your eyes well open until the arrival of succor, which is on the way."[*]

This done, Aremberg, who had just returned from France, was ordered to set out for the north without pause. "Your own regiment, some squadrons of cavalry, and Braccamonte's Sardinian legion shall follow you with all speed," said the governor-general.[†] At the same time, Alva had an interview with Count Megen, stadtholder of Guelders. To Megen he intrusted a park of artillery, three companies of light horse, and five vauderas[‡] of infantry—fifteen hundred men in all—bidding him coöperate with Aremberg.[§]   The wary old soldier cautioned both to beware of undervaluing the foe; and "above all," added he, "do nothing except in concert. Together, you have four thousand picked veterans—enough to disperse this peasant gang: but be not over-confident."[‖]

Worn by anxiety and lame with gout, Aremberg was fitter for an invalid's couch than for the saddle. Nevertheless, obedient to orders, he mounted horse and galloped with all speed towards the front. At Harlingen, on the 18th of May, he was joined by his entire division—upwards of three thousand sea-

---

[*] Cor. de Duc d'Albe. Cited in Motley, vol. 2, p. 187.

[†] Ibid.

[‡] One of Alva's vauderas counted one hundred and seventy men on an average.

[§] Mendoza, *ubi sup.*   [‖] Ibid.

soned campaigners.* Count Megen, delayed by
the untimely insubordination of his corps, clamorous for back pay, was a day's march in the rear.†

For the purpose of ascertaining the whereabouts
of Nassau, though with no desire to precipitate a
battle until his coadjutor should come up, Aremberg at once struck his tents at Harlingen, pushed
quickly through the streets of Gröningen, and on
the 22d of May, came upon Count Louis' vanguard
at Appingedam.‡ The Spanish advance, too fiery
to be controlled, charged the patriot pickets and
drove them in pell-mell. Then, as night was nigh,
farther fighting was postponed by mutual consent,
and both armies bivouacked.

Louis Nassau was dissatisfied with his position
at Appingedam. He knew his raw and mutinous
following to be inferior to the foe in all save numbers. Equity required that what his men lacked in
morale, they should counterbalance by position.
Accordingly, his camp-master was commanded to
keep the watch-fires brightly ablaze till midnight;
but at that time the patriot army retreated three
leagues to the south of the twilight bivouac, along
the Wold-weg,· forest-road, a narrow causeway
through a swamp. On a wooded knoll, hard by
the abbey of Heiliger-lee—the "Holy Lion," which
gave its name to the ensuing battle—Count Louis
halted and prepared to fight.§

* Bor., tom. 4, p. 235. Mendoza.   † Ibid.
‡ Strada, tom. 2, p. 47. Bor., *ubi sup*.
§ Ibid. Motley, vol. 2, p. 189.

This position was more to Nassau's mind, for it was one of extraordinary strength. In his rear loomed the abbey, girt by a dense wood; on his left stood a scraggy hill; on his right, and sweeping round to the front, there was a swamp, divided into squares by impassable ditches whence peat had been taken for fuel, leaving a fallacious and grasslike scum afloat upon the pools to simulate the turf that had been removed.*   On the knoll, high and dry, Count Louis' men-at-arms were drawn up in two squares, rather deep than wide, to defend the only approach to their position, the causeway, which crept serpent-like through the circumjacent bogs.†

On the morning of the 23d of May, Aremberg awoke to find that his opponent had given him the slip. He at once sounded the advance, though still, recalling Alva's orders, determined not to join battle until reinforced by Megen. When he discovered Nassau posted before the Heiliger-lee, the astute soldier was confirmed in his purpose to await the arrival of his colleague.‡ Did he not know the admirable strength of the enemy's position? Was he not well acquainted with the treacherous nature of the ground—one great sweep of traps and pitfalls?

But the Spanish veterans, vain from a hundred successful battle-fields, filled with contempt for the

---

* Motley, vol. 2, p. 191.   Prescott, vol. 2, p. 242.   Mendoza.
† Ibid.   De Thou, tom. 5, p. 445, *et seq.*
‡ Strada, tom. 2, p. 47.   Mendoza, folio 52.

disorderly levies of Count Louis, already in full retreat as they thought, and heated by the pursuit,
were clamorous for an immediate action. "No,"
said their prudent leader, "I shall not fight until
Count Megen is by my side."* This peremptory
refusal caused intense excitement in his camp; officers and soldiers were alike indignant. Why should
a halt be made merely to allow Megen's loitering
and mutinous troops, arriving at the eleventh hour,
to share in the triumph and the spoil?† "This
Aremberg is a disloyal coward," said some. "He
is inclined to play the traitor," cried others. "He
is a Netherlander himself, and therefore a heretic,"
shouted another chorus.‡ Aremberg was a brave
and prudent and skilful captain; but, unhappily
for himself, he lacked moral courage —he could
not stand fire under a battery of taunting tongues.
In this he was unlike Alva, unlike the foremost soldiers of all ages. "Recollect that the first foes
with whom one has to contend are one's own
troops"—it was so that Alva instructed Don John of
Austria—"with their clamors for an engagement at
this moment, and with their murmurs about results
at another; with their 'I thought that the battle
should be fought,' or 'It was my opinion that the
occasion ought not to be lost.' Your highness will
have ample opportunity to display valor, and will
never be weak enough to be conquered by the

* Strada, tom. 2, p. 47. Mendoza, fol. 52.
† Motley, *ubi sup.*
‡ Brantôme, Œuvres, tom. 1, p.382. Strada, tom. 2, p. 47.

babble of soldiers."*   'T is a useful lesson, this of
the responsibility and independence of a general in
the field, and one necessary to be learned by all
military men.

Aremberg had not learned it, though upon this
occasion the ancient jealousy between Netherlander
and Spaniard extenuated his fault.   "Come, then,"
cried he, "let us see whether a Netherlander dare
not lead where a Spaniard dare follow;" and with
a wild huzza, both captain and soldiers flung themselves upon the foe.†

The result was precisely that which Aremberg
had feared.   The Spaniards charged, not Nassau's
rustics, but the mud and water of the morass which
fronted the abbey of Heiliger-lee.   Scores were
entombed alive in the verdant pools.‡   Hundreds
were slaughtered by Count Louis' pikemen, as
they essayed to crawl up the oozy banks from out
the ditches.§   Dry-shod and unassailed, the patriot
men-at-arms were busied only in slaying the entangled and helpless veterans of Spain.∥   While Aremberg's main body was thus struggling in the mud,
Count Louis' cavalry, led by Adolphus Nassau,
made a detour around the base of the hill which
had thus far sheltered them from the enemy's fire,
and falling upon the Spanish rear-guard ere these
could advance to aid their perishing comrades, rode
them down, trampled them out of existence, and

* Documentos Inéditos, tom. 3, p. 273, *et seq.*
† Brantôme, *ubi sup.*   Mendoza, folios 49, 50.   Hoofd.
‡ Ibid.   Strada, *ubi sup.*   § Ibid.   ∥ Ibid., *ut antea.*

won the battle by a *coup de main*.* But, alas, the gallant young cavalry-man—he was but twenty-seven—crossed the path of Aremberg in this wild gallop; who, determined not to survive defeat, rushed with chivalrous ardor to meet his conqueror. Each fell by the other's hand†—Aremberg among the earliest killed on the side of Spain in this grim war; Adolphus the first slain of a house destined thereafter to lay so many of its children in untimely graves.

Nassau's laurels were dappled with the blood of his beloved brother; but nevertheless, great were the spoils of his victory. His loss was small, while five hundred‡ of his foemen strewed the battle-plain stiff in death. His booty—Aremberg's rich service of plate, a sum of money, military stores—was a welcome item in his list of captures;§ as were also six cannon brought by the Spaniards from Gröningen, and which had been baptized by the lovers of such harmony with the notes of the gamut, *ut, re, mi, fa, sol, la.*‖ But it had been ordained that when these musical pieces piped, the Spaniards were not to dance.¶

In the very midst of the rout, Count Megen came up, but not soon enough to succor Aremberg.**

* Motley, vol. 2, p. 193.

† Strada, tom. 2, p. 47. Mendoza, *et al.*

‡ Some accounts say 1,600. *Vide* Meteren, folio 52. Hoofd, tom. 5, p. 166. Compare Corresp. du Duc d'Albe, p. 3. Mendoza, p. 50.

§ Archives de la Maison d'Orange-Nassau, tom. 3, p. 221.

‖ Strada, *ubi sup.*   ¶ Motley, *ubi sup.*

** Corresp. du Duc d'Albe, pp. 90, 98.

Without striving to do so, he gathered what strag-
glers he could pick up into his train, and by a dex-
terous movement threw his division into Gröningen; whither Nassau followed him after a few days,
encamping before the town.*

* Bor., 4, p. 236.

CHAPTER XXX.

TRAGEDIES.

ALTHOUGH in the year of grace 1568 there were no steam-engines to rush from town to town, sneeze out the news, and dash into the horizon; and although the lightning had not been tamed as yet into an errand-boy, the report of Aremberg's defeat and death sped over Europe with a fleetness almost telegraphic. Men viewed the news through the eyes of their politics. Orange rejoiced; not on account of the material results of Count Louis' success, these were not many, but because of the moral effect of a victory won by raw, ill-paid, and half-mutinous troops over veterans esteemed invincible.

Alva was enraged for the same reason; not because of the loss sustained in men and munitions of war—though this was felt at such a crisis, and the governor-general, like Augustus, called vainly on the dead commander for his legions—but on account of the prestige acquired by the insurgents, certain to animate their allies to fresh exertions, sure to inspire the forces of William, nearly ready to march to the assistance of the invaders, and likely to stir the provinces themselves to widespread revolt. " *Cospetto!*" exclaimed Alva, "I must take the field in person against these insolent beggars."*

* Mendoza, Comentarios.

But before the enactment of that drama, there was a prelude to be played. An antidote was to be provided for domestic sedition. The hot blood of the governor-general was to be cooled by the precipitate execution of a long list of titled victims. The battle of Heiliger-lee had been fought on the 23d of May. On the 28th of May sentence by default was passed upon the prince of Orange, Louis Nassau, Culemberg, and the rest—perpetual exile and the confiscation of their estates to the use of the crown.* At the same time Culemberg-house, the cradle of Brederode's confederacy, where Alva had at first pitched his headquarters—he had moved thence to the castle of Brabant upon Margaret's retirement—was levelled to the earth. Above the ruins a marble column was reared, upon the pedestal of which were engraved these words in four languages: "In this area stood the palace of Florence Pallant, count of Culemberg, now razed to execrate the damnable conspiracy plotted therein against religion, the Roman church, the king's majesty, and the country."†

After witnessing this pageant, the blood-judges returned to their meal of vengeance with sharpened appetites, sentencing to death, ere they adjourned for the day, nineteen prisoners of high rank, guilty of having signed the papers of the league.‡ On the

---

* Sententien van Alba, p. 70.   Viglii Epist. ad Hop., p 481.

† Strada, tom. 2, p. 42.   Bor., tom. 4, p. 248.

‡ Meteren, folio 57.   Hoofd, tom. 5, p. 167, *et seq.*   Strada, tom. 2, p. 48.

1st of June these covenanters were beheaded in the horse-market at Brussels. Eight of them died Romanists, and their uncoffined remains were interred in unconsecrated ground. The others were heretics; their bodies were tied to stakes, their heads were set upon poles, and so left to rot back to dust.[*]

On the following morning, aghast Brussels again assembled to behold the execution of another batch of victims, a dozen in number,[†] among whom was Villars, the leader of that division of the invaders who were routed on the frontier of Juliers.[‡] On the 3d of June, Casembrot of Backerzeel, Egmont's confidential secretary, condemned as a whilom member of the beggars' union, was put to the torture— he had been racked before—in the hope that some confession which should implicate his master might be wrung from his tormented lips.[§] He made no disclosures; and when it became evident that he would say nothing to the prejudice of Egmont, Alva was so enraged that he bade the executioner tear him asunder with wild horses.[‖]

Twenty-four hours later, almost before poor Backerzeel's muscles had ceased to quiver, two close carriages, escorted by ten companies of pikemen and arquebusiers and a detachment of lancers, entered the capital. It was dusk as the cortége,

---

[*] Strada, *ubi sup.* Archives de la Maison d'Orange-Nassau, tom. 3, p. 241.　　[†] Bor., Hoofd, *ubi sup.*　　[‡] Ibid.

[§] Bentivoglio, Guerra de Fiandra, p. 200.

[‖] Bentivoglio, *ut antea.* This circumstance finds no place in the accounts of Backerzeel's execution given by the other contemporaneous historians. Compare Strada, Meteren, Hoofd, *et al.*

defiling through the streets to the music of a dead march, halted before the Bread-house—now the *Maison du Roi*, a picturesque old pile opposite the Town-hall, on the great square of Brussels. Here, two figures, muffled and carefully attended, alighted, one from either vehicle, passed quickly up the steps, and entered the building; whereupon, the men-at-arms broke ranks and prepared to bivouac in the square. Rapid as the transit had been, the gaping burghers recognized the features of Count Horn and the stately form of Egmont in the fading twilight of the summer day—recognized them, and instantly surmised that they were now in Brussels, after an absence of nine months, as guests of the headsman.[*]

How had these months been passed? Let us ascertain by looking back, for a moment, over the shoulder of this history.

Two facts are to be borne in mind: first, the cases of Egmont and Horn had been judged at Madrid, while they were at large and unsuspicious in the states, and the sentence, signed by Philip in blank, had been brought from Spain in Alva's portfolio;[†] second, the seigneurs would have been shot at sight by the decree of a drum-head court-martial, had it not been deemed safest, on account of their high rank and influential position, to pretend to base the imported judgment on the fraudulent developments of a mock trial. Hence

---

[*] Hoofd, tom. 5, p. 168. Mondaucet, op. Brantôme, Œuvres, tom. 1, p. 363.   [†] Hoofd, *ubi sup.*

the arrest; hence a formal impeachment. But since the verdict was in the pocket of the governor-general, the prosecution did not esteem it necessary to observe more than the flimsiest forms of what might look like law in the eyes of the ignorant—law itself being ignored at the very outset by holding the prisoners to answer at the bar of the blood-judges, an abnormal and unknown tribunal. Every step taken in such a trial necessarily became a cumulative illegality.

The betrayed grandees were hardly lodged in the dungeon-keep at Ghent, when Alva, as greedy for gold as for blood, sequestrated their estates, by a stroke of the pen reducing them from affluence to beggary.* As a consequence, their imprisonment was rigorous and necessitous.† Hardest of all, they were not allowed to look upon the dear faces of their friends and relatives.‡

On the 12th of November, 1567, Vargas, Del Rio, and Mr. Secretary Pratz visited the prison-house. Where the carcass is, there will the vultures be. The trio had been empowered by Alva to examine and cross-examine Egmont and Horn, for the purpose of entrapping them, if possible, into an admission of guilt.§ Through five days, the wily lawyers questioned and hinted and verbally writhed, until the interrogatories filled fifty octavo pages, and covered the entire ground of the recent

---

* Bor. Cited in Prescott, vol. 2, p. 253.   † Ibid.

‡ *Vide* letter of Countess Egmont to Philip in Cor. de Philippe II., tom. 2, p. 5.   § Bor., tom. 4, p. 190.

tumults.* Each prisoner was examined separately, and, unacquainted with the law, each was at first reluctant to answer; nor would either do so until informed that, in default of the required replies, each was to be proceeded against for contempt of court.†

With these records, obtained by bullying the captives, the inquisitorial attorneys withdrew; and from their report, which each swore to and signed, the procurator-general made out the processes against the illustrious condemned.‡

Two months passed ere the counts were again disturbed. But on the 10th of January, 1568, each was handed a copy of the accusations filed against him by the king's attorney.§ Upon scanning his indictment, Egmont found that it contained ninety counts; Horn discovered that his was composed of sixty-three counts.‖

As the indictments were substantially alike, they may be considered as one document. The general charge against both seigneurs was, "that they had plotted with the prince of Orange to dispossess the king of the Low Countries, and to divide the provinces among themselves."¶ The specifications in proof were masterpieces of impudent knavery. The most frivolous gossip, the most irrelevant circumstances were jumbled together with matters of real

* *Interrogations.* Prescott, *ubi sup.*
† La Déduction de l'Innocence du Comte de Horne, pp. 36, 37.
‡ La Déduction, etc., *ut antea.*
§ Procés du Comte d'Egmont, Bor., tom. 4, p. 190.
‖ Ibid. La Déduction, etc., *ubi sup.*
¶ Ibid. Strada, tom. 2, p. 49.

moment. The origination of the fool's cap livery was placed side by side with the meeting at Dendremond; the banquet of the *gueux* at Culemberg-house was collocated with the iconomachy; the unwilling answers of the prisoners were perverted into an acknowledgment of their open adhesion to the petitioners against the Inquisition; and from this muddled mass of fact and fiction, an inference of treasonable intent was drawn with subtle skill.*

The procurator-general had been given four months in which to elaborate these processes.† The counts, ignorant of law, deprived of the assistance of advocates, forbidden to consult with their friends, stripped of their papers, forced to rely on their unassisted memory of the events of a passionate crisis, were summoned to plead in writing to these labored and purposely mixed charges within five days, from the solitude of their dungeons, under penalty of condemnation by default.‡

Thus menaced, and under protest, Egmont and Horn consented to plead. Both excepted to the tribunal, "saving to themselves all advantages in law which excused them from accounting for their actions to any save the king, who, sitting as grand-master of the brotherhood, was the sole judge of the knights of the Golden Fleece."§ Then, in separate papers—they were not permitted to con-

---

º *Vide* La Déduction, etc., and Procés du Comte d'Egmont, *passim.* † Strada, *ubi sup.*

‡ La Déduction de l'Innocence du Comte de Horne, p. 39. Bor., tom 4, p. 195.

§ Strada, tom. 2, p. 50. Procés du Comte d'Egmont.

sult even with each other—both proceeded to a
critical analysis of the specifications, denying some,
explaining away the damaging purport of others,
and indignantly repelling the whole treasonable
inference.*

In the meantime, the families of the imprisoned
counts were indefatigable in their exertions to succor the imperilled loved ones. Horn's wife, a
German lady of high rank, aided by her husband's
step-mother, the countess-dowager, wrote to the
knights of the Golden Fleece, in whatever country
residing, and obtained their written testimony to
the inalienable right of the accused to be tried by
their companions of the order†—evidence of the
first importance, since a trial by the blood-judges
was known to be equivalent to a condemnation. |

Nor was the countess of Egmont less active.
By birth a duchess of Bavaria, interesting by the
double claim of beauty and misfortune, the mother
of eleven beggared children, she, the chiefest orna-
ment of the court of Brussels in happier hours, was
momentarily dazed by this calamity. But, passionately devoted to the count, every pulsation of
her heart soon became an effort for the liberation
of her husband. Upon Egmont's arrest, she had
taken refuge in a convent. From this retreat her
incessant appeals moved all Europe to sympathetic
action in her behalf. Friend and foe alike were

---

* Strada, tom. 2, p. 50. Procés du Comte d'Egmont.

† Supplément á Strada, tom. 1, p. 244. Latin, La Déduction,
etc., *ubi sup*

importuned, and what many would not have given to save Egmont personally from the block, was yielded to the clamorous tears of a mother pleading for the father of her children.

The countess of Egmont had retained Nicholas de Landas, himself a Fleece knight, and one of the most eminent of the mediæval jurists.* At the instigation and in the name of his fair client, this honest advocate sent letters by the cart-load to the emperor Maximilian, to the German princes, to Alva, to Philip himself†—"letters," says Strada, "which cannot well be read by any one without commiseration."‡ In these epistles the countess solicited, not Egmont's release, but the removal of his cause from the Council of Blood to the legitimate tribunal of the Golden Fleece.§

The result was that Christendom at large began to intercede. The princes of the Roman empire, the duchess of Parma, Count Mansfeld, Barlaimont, even Granvelle, to whose portrait-painting Egmont was largely indebted for his misfortunes, and Maximilian, who "remembered to forget" his recent snubbing in such a cause—all addressed Philip advising mercy, if they felt it not.‖ So infectious was the courage of this woman, resolute from despair, that the timid estates of Brabant plucked up the heart to petition Alva to transfer these causes

---

* Prescott, vol. 2, p. 256. † Ibid. Strada, tom. 2, p. 49.
‡ Strada, *ubi sup.* § Prescott, *ubi sup.*
‖ Cor. de Philippe II., tom. 1, pp. 588, 599, 614. Strada, *ubi sup.* La Déduction de l'Innocence, etc.. p. 605.

to the provincial courts, that the seigneurs might enjoy the protection of privileges which were the ægis of the meanest citizen.*

In response to these manifold appeals, Philip, so prolific on common occasions, would not deign to speak. Alva was quite as reticent, though he did grudgingly concede to the counts the right of employing counsel.† Each of them retained five of the foremost advocates of the day; and, to the credit of the Netherland bar be it said, these lawyers labored honestly, tirelessly, skilfully to save their clients, though such efforts, if not actually dangerous, were at least well understood not to lie in the path to preferment. But there have been attorneys who regarded a quiet conscience more than a tyrant's smile. When the emperor Caracalla murdered his own brother, and ordered Papinian to defend the deed, he went cheerfully to death rather than sully his lips with the atrocious plea. It was in the self-same spirit that these Dutch lawyers undertook to do their duty.

Their first step was to file a plea against the jurisdiction. They claimed that there were but three tribunals competent to try the prisoners. As knights of the Golden Fleece, they were privileged to be tried by the statutes of that order‡—statutes, indeed, which conferred on the brotherhood exclusive jurisdiction over all crimes committed by the

* Bor., tom. 4, p. 189.

† La Déduction de l'Innocence, etc., p. 42, et seq.

‡ Bor., tom. 4, p. 195. Procés du Comte d'Egmont.

knights.* Horn, a chief part of whose estates lay
in Germany, might justly claim to be a subject of
the Roman empire, impeachable alone by his peers,
the electors and princes of that realm.† Egmont,
the possessor of lands in Brabant, was properly
amenable to the supreme court of that duchy.‡
Here were three legal fountains of power, each sufficient; the three together, three times sufficient;
each exuberant, the three together three times exuberant.

The government began to feel embarrassed.
It had been thought best to murder Egmont and
Horn legally; but these masterly pleas against
the jurisdiction, these skilful invocations of time-
honored safeguards, had not been counted on.
Despotism blundered in its maintenance even of
the show of legality. Alva was tired of the farce.
"Sire," wrote he to Philip, "pray put a stop to the
harangues of these excepters by making known
your decision."§

The king complied, though he was careful to
have his decision confirmed by "men of authority
and learning;"‖ for, while regardless of the cancelled charters of the states, the statutes of the
Order of the Fleece, a miniature republic whose
citizens were emperors and kings and princes, were
not so rudely to be overridden. Nevertheless, he
was not to be balked of vengeance by parchment

---

* *Vide* chapters 11, 13, 14, 15 of the Order of the Fleece.
† Bor., *ubi sup.* ‡ Ibid.
§ Cor. de Philippe II., tom. 1, p. 582. ‖ Ibid., p. 612.

prohibitions. In the teeth of the statutes of the order, he declared that the immunities of the Fleece did not extend to treasonable practices; and letters-patent, antedated eight months, were despatched to Alva, which empowered him to try all persons charged with treason.[*]

Of course these credentials overruled all demurrers to the jurisdiction. The next step of the wary advocates was to delay the trial. Suspicious that the case had been prejudged, they thought that every day the decision was postponed was an opportunity won by their clients for escape.[†] On the 6th of May, the procurator-general remonstrated against these dilatory proceedings. "Eight months have elapsed," said he, "yet the defence have neglected to support their case by bringing forward their witness. I pray that a day may be named for the close of the processes."[‡] "Yes," was the reply, "we have abundant testimony at hand, but 't is customary for the prosecution to take precedence. Where are your witnesses?"

Alva, conveniently deaf to this retort, named the 8th of May as the day on which the cases should terminate.[§] On the morning of the 2d of June, 1568, a parcel of *ex-parte* papers were laid before the Council of Blood; and Vargas and Del Rio, *judges* who had acted as *prosecuting attorneys* at the out-

* Corresp. de Philippe II., tom. 1, p. 612.
† Prescott, vol. 2, pp. 267, 268.
‡ Supplément à Strada, tom. 1, p. 90.
§ La Déduction, etc., p. 43.

set, pronounced the prisoners—forbidden to adduce
the testimony in their favor, ignorant of that which
had been used against them—guilty of treason
and of connivance at heresy, and condemned them
to the block.* On the evening of the 4th of May,
the governor-general went in person to a meeting
of the blood-judges and joyfully approved this finding, scrawling "Alva" upon the back of it.†

To apply the word *trial* to these proceedings
would be an insult to its honest meaning. The tribunal was incompetent; the prisoners were long
without advocates, during which time wily lawyers
attempted to entrap them into fatal admissions;
the testimony for the defence was excluded; the
government evidence was concealed; and the causes
were finally decided before a thousandth part of
their merits had been placed under the eyes of the
judges who gave the sentence.‡

Viglius, an encyclopedical toady, did indeed
vouch for the legitimacy of the Council of Blood,
and testify to the honesty of the trial.§ But the
law maxim is that a witness should be trusted only
in matters he understands; his evidence therefore
goes for nothing.

The accusation and the defence are still extant.
On the facts, any impartial tribunal would have
acquitted the counts. It was plain that they had
not approved of the policy of the king at one time;

---

* Bor., tom. 4, p. 239. Strada, tom. 2, p. 51. Meteren, folios
52, 53. † Ibid. ‡ Motley, vol. 2, p. 177.
§ Cor. de Philippe II., tom. 2, p. 4.

it was evident that they had esteemed several of
Philip's measures to be impracticable; but there
was no evidence of a design to depose the tyrant.
On the contrary, it appeared that both had opposed
projects which squinted towards that end, earning
the thanks of her highness of Parma for their loyal
activity in a crucial hour.* Indeed, had Egmont
and Horn been guilty, it would have been better
for their posthumous fame. But how could men
foredoomed hope to prove their innocence in a land
where there was no law but the court-martial, no
justice but the sergeant's guard; where usurpation
was styled legitimacy, and right was nicknamed
brigandage?

More and more alarmed by the progress which
Louis Nassau was making in the north, anxious to
take the field at once, yet determined not to do so
until Brussels had been scoured with the blood of
Egmont and Horn, Alva named the day succeeding
the sentence for the execution of the seigneurs. On
the 4th of June he summoned the bishop of Ypres
to the capital to shrive the prisoners. At dusk the
prelate waited upon the governor-general. Falling
upon his knees and bursting into tears, he falter-
ingly entreated that Egmont might be spared, at
least that his execution might be deferred. "Rise,
sir bishop," answered Alva fiercely; "I did not

---

* "This was so evident, that Pierre Arsens, president of Artois,
himself a member of the blood-council, addressed an elaborate
memoir to Alva, criticising the case by the rules of law, and maintaining that Egmont, instead of deserving punishment, was entitled to a signal reward." Motley, vol. 2, p. 179.

bring you from Ypres to change or defer the sentence, but to confess the criminals."*

Towards midnight the churchman entered Egmont's chamber. Arousing the count from a heavy sleep, for he had been fatigued by the ride from Ghent, the bishop placed a parchment, on which the sentence was engrossed, in his hands. He thought at first that it was an order for his release, having been led to hope that the conclusion of his trial would result in an acquittal—a delusion in which Horn is said to have shared.† Soon discovering his mistake, he yet read the paper through without flinching, though he turned deadly pale.‡ "Father," said he, "'t is a terrible sentence. Little did I imagine that any offence I had committed against God or the king could merit such a punishment. It is not death that I fear—that is the common lot of all. But I shrink from dishonor." Then, after a pause, he asked, "Is there indeed no hope?" "None," replied the prelate with tearful accent. Again Egmont pronounced the sentence cruel and unjust; adding, "But since it is the will of God and his majesty, I will try to meet it with patience. I venture to hope that my sufferings may so far expiate my offences that my innocent family be not involved in ruin by the confiscation of my estates."§ He was told that his property had already escheated

<hr />

* Supplément à Strada, tom. 1, p. 259. Bor., Hoofd.
† Relacion de la Justitia, MS., cited in Prescott, vol. 2, p. 278.
‡ Supplément à Strada, tom. 1. p. 259.
§ Ibid. Meteren, folio 56. Bor., tom. 4, p. 239.

to the crown. "Then I will write his majesty," was the response; and seating himself, he penned a few lines to Philip, in which, after an affirmation of his innocence, he implored the king to take compassion upon his wife and children.*

"Here, father," said he, handing the letter to the bishop, "I charge you, as you value your soul, to forward this to his majesty. Send him this ring also"—and he drew one of great value from his finger—"'t was his own gift to me in happier times."† Egmont then remarked with exquisite courtesy, "I render thanks both to God and the duke that my last moments are to be consoled by such an excellent father confessor. Teach me how to meet my end."‡

He then confessed himself, and afterwards spent some time in prayer. Suddenly a thousand tender recollections trooped through his mind, almost unmanning him—his unhappy countess, his suffering children, his own full enjoyment of an existence now about to be cut untimely short. "Alas, alas," exclaimed he, "how miserable and frail is our nature, that, when we should think of God alone, we are unable to shut out the images of wife and children."§

After a little, he regained his self-possession. "What language shall I hold from the scaffold to

* Supplément à Strada, tom. 1, p. 259. Meteren, folio 56. Bor., tom. 4, p. 239.

† Supplément à Strada, *ubi sup.* Corres. de Philippe II., tom. 2, p. 764.

‡ Hoofd, tom. 5, p. 169. § Ibid.

the assembled multitude?" queried he. "I should advise you to say nothing," replied the prelate. "Those at a distance will not hear you; the Spaniards will not understand you. Silence would be more dignified." The count acquiesced.* "What prayer would be most fitting for my lips at the last moment?" was the next question. "None could be fitter," said the bishop, "than that which Christ taught the disciples: 'Our Father, which art in heaven.'"† Egmont spent the rest of the night in prayer, meditation, and the arming of his mind to suffer.‡

In Horn's apartment there was a similar scene. He was quite as much surprised as Egmont by the announcement of the verdict, and quite as calm. He too passed the hours in the exercises of devotion.§

In the mean time, the presence of so many men-at-arms in the market-place, and the sight of workmen busy in constructing a scaffold, gave rise to a rumor of the execution of the counts on the morrow.‖ The countess of Egmont heard of the report while on a visit of condolence to the newly-made widow of Aremberg. She did not credit it, for she had in her pocket at that very moment a kind letter from Maximilian, in which he said, "Be of good cheer; you have naught to fear on your husband's

---

* Hoofd, tom. 5, p. 170.   Bor., tom. 4, p. 240.
† Motley, vol. 2, p. 201.   ‡ Strada, tom. 2, p. 52.
§ Corresp. de Marguerite d'Autriche, p. 252.
‖ Meteren, folio 57.

account."* Nevertheless, she waited upon Alva at once. "Madame," said the duke with a brutal jest, "be not disheartened; your husband will leave his prison in the morning."† Reassured, the countess wept her thanks, and withdrew.

On the morrow, Whitsunday, the 5th of June, 1568,‡ the prisoners were led out to die. Egmont came first. He wore a robe of red damask, and over that a black Spanish cloak trimmed with gold lace. He had himself cut off the collar of his doublet to facilitate the executioner's duty.§ His hands were untied, and in one of them he carried a white handkerchief. His hat was of black silk garnished with white and sable plumes. As the stately soldier emerged from the Bread-house, with the bishop of Ypres and Julian Romero, camp-master, on either hand, a silence as of death fell upon the vast assembly of the citizens—ten thousand hearts could be heard to beat.

As he crossed the square, Egmont repeated portions of the fifty-first psalm: "Have mercy on me, O God." In a moment the scaffold was reached. Over its rough surface a black cloth was spread. Upon this rested two velvet cushions placed before a silver crucifix. At one side stood a small table, flanked by two iron spikes. The provost-marshal sat below on horseback, with his red rod of office

---

* Supplément à Strada, tom. 1, p. 252.
† Hoofd, tom. 5, p. 109. Hoofd is the sole authority for this anecdote. ‡ Strada, tom. 2, p. 52.
§ Schiller, Execution of Egmont and Horn.

in his grasp. The headsman—who was said to have been Egmont's footman*—kept out of sight. About the scaffold three thousand Spanish soldiers were drawn up, no needless precaution; while two vauderas of infantry were left to guard the palace of the duke, and one went the rounds of the city while the tragedy was being enacted.†

On ascending the scaffold, Egmont turned to Romero: "Is there no hope?" said he. The camp-master shrugged his shoulders.‡ Egmont clenched his teeth; then with a look of unutterable sadness he knelt, pulled the black cap over his eyes, cried with a steady voice, "Into thy hands, O Lord, I commend my spirit," and calmly awaited the death-stroke.§ Loud sobs of anguish alone broke the appalling silence; and for an instant these were hushed as the headsman leaped upon the scaffold and at a single blow severed the victim's head from his shoulders. Before the crowd had recovered from its stupor, the love-locks of Egmont dangled from one of the iron spikes.||

Then Horn appeared. With erect form and steady step he too mounted the scaffold, saluting his acquaintances as he went. Glancing at the bloody shroud which had been thrown over the remains of his poor friend, he said, "Is it the body of the count?" On receiving an affirmative answer, he muttered something in Castilian which was not

---

* Strada, tom. 2, p. 52.   † Hoofd, tom. 5, p. 170.
‡ Bor., tom. 4, p. 240.   Meteren, folio 58.
§ Ibid. || Ibid.

understood. Without farther delay, he knelt, repeated the words, "Into thy hands, O Lord," and
was beheaded.* As he received the fatal blow, a
half-smothered shriek rang out from twice ten thousand voices. His bloody head was set up opposite
that of his fellow-sufferer. Then ensued a scene
which baffles description. The enraged populace,
breaking through the serried ranks of the men-at-
arms, dipped their handkerchiefs in the blood of
the martyrs, and carefully laid them aside as monuments of love, or incitements to revenge. Many,
heedless of the presence of informers, openly threatened to avenge the counts.†

As Egmont died, the French ambassador, a
spectator of the scene, exclaimed, "I have seen his
head struck off whose valor has twice caused France
to tremble."‡ Even Alva, looking out from a window of the Bread-house, is said to have wept.§ But
blushes are not always virtue's signals of distress;
nor were Alva's tears the children of his sorrow—
rather they were the progeny of gratified malignity.

For three hours the heads of the seigneurs
remained upon the spikes exposed to the gaze of
the lamenting multitude.‖ Then they were taken
down, and Alva, as it is supposed, despatched the
ghastly trophies to Madrid for the delectation of
the king.¶ The mutilated trunks were huddled into

○ Meteren, *ubi sup.* Mondaucet, op. Brantôme. Œuvres, tom.
1, p. 367.   † Strada, tom. 2, pp. 52, 53.   ‡ Ibid.
§ Archives de la Maison d'Orange-Nassau. Supplément, p. 81.
‖ Bor., tom. 4, p. 241. Meteren, folio 57.
¶ Ibid. Hoofd, tom. 5, p. 171.

coffins and surrendered to their respective families, who laid them in their ancestral vaults.*

Such was the tragic end of Egmont and Horn. Living, they had defrauded not only their country, but their own genius. Dead, they were more useful to humanity, for they became a sentiment.

○ The countess of Egmont lived ten years after the death of her husband. For a time Alva paid her a small annuity. Her children were eventually reinstated in their rights by Philip, but not until after her death. Vide Prescott, vol. 2, pp. 300, 304.

CHAPTER XXXI.

DISASTROUS CAMPAIGNING.

A FEW days after the taking off of Egmont and Horn, the governor-general set out for the north to chastise Count Louis of Nassau. He would not delegate the duty; when the rent came, he meant to be present at the darning.

Every available veteran in the Spanish pay had been ordered to report for active service at the town of Deventer, on the southern frontier of Overyssel.* By the 10th of July, 1568, when Alva himself reached the rendezvous,† seventéen thousand pikemen and arquebusiers and three thousand light-cavalrymen and dragoons were in the camp, and two-thirds of the whole number were experienced sons of Mars.‡

As the duke was about to leave Deventer for the front, several of his scouts galloped into town and reported the patriots just at hand. "We have heard their drums and seen their colors," said they. Alva was astonished; but with his usual caution he drew up his legions in battle array, and at the same time sent out a squadron of lancers to reconnoitre. These were no sooner in the field than they too saw four

---

* Corresp. du Duc d'Albe, p. 154.   † Mendoza, p. 56.

‡ Bor., tom. 4, p. 243, et seq. Hoofd, tom. 5, p. 174. Compare Mendoza, pp. 53, 55, and Strada, tom. 2, p. 54. The last two writers reduce Alva's force to about 15,000 men.

banners gallantly displayed; but on riding closer, they discovered that the "patriots" consisted of four wagons covered with canvas and green boughs, in one of which a bride, married that morning, and not dreaming of war—at least with any one save her husband—was riding towards an adjacent village with a retinue of merry-making peasants.

When the Spanish men-at-arms were informed of the nature of their enemy, discipline was momentarily forgotten in mirth, and a volley of musket-shot was fired in honor of the bride. From this circumstance a military proverb arose. Thereafter, if any Low Country scout showed fear, he was asked, "Have you seen the bride?"[*]

The ascetic nature of Alva—in whose constitution that portion of the human anatomy popularly supposed to be synonymous with feeling, and which is situated in the left side of the breast-bone, seems to have been left out—was ill-fitted to enjoy such an interruption. Sharply rebuking those whose carelessness had occasioned the delay, he sounded an advance.[†] On the 15th of July he halted in the streets of Gröningen.[‡] After entrenching his troops in the suburbs, he himself, without dismounting, and with but few attendants, rode out to reconnoitre.

Since his victory at Heiliger-lee, Louis Nassau had been languidly besieging Gröningen. In his military chest there was a vacuum abhorred alike

<hr>

[*] Strada, tom. 2, p. 54.　　　　　　　　[†] Ibid.

[‡] Ibid. Bor., tom. 4, p. 235. Mendoza.

by nature and all treasury departments. Various
measures hit on to coerce a levy from the inhabitants of the adjacent towns had been substantial
failures.* The peasantry, friendly at heart, were
lukewarm from policy. At times actual starvation
stared the invaders in the face. Of course the mercenaries became clamorous and turbulent. As a
consequence, they were inactive. Nevertheless,
Count Louis, by liberal distributions of promises,
contrived to hold his soldiers—ten or twelve thousand men, such as they were†—together, and to
maintain some show of discipline.‡ His position
under the walls of Gröningen was good—on the
immediate front a deep ditch; an arrow's flight
beyond the ditch the river Hunse, spanned by two
wooden bridges, which pickets were prepared to
burn at need, thus isolating the patriot camp.§

Alva's keen eye could detect no flaw in Nassau's
position. Still, on rejoining his troops, he ordered
out five hundred musketeers to skirmish with the
gueux—less with the hope of beating them from
their entrenchments than for the purpose of testing
their strength and holding them in play until the
Spanish cannon could be unlimbered.‖

To the duke's surprise, before his skirmishers
had fired a dozen volleys, Count Louis' soldiers,

○ Corresp. du Duc d'Albe, p. 124, *et seq.*

† Groen van Prinsterer says they numbered between 7,000 and
8,000. Cited in Motley, vol. 2, p. 216, note.

‡ Hoofd, tom. 5, p. 174. Bor., *et al.*

§ Ibid. Strada, *ubi sup.*

‖ Strada, tom. 2, p. 54. Mendoza, Comentarios, p. 59.

conquered by their fears, burned the bridges and began precipitately to retreat. The base example had been set by the German mercenaries, who, believing that Nassau was wilfully withholding their arrears, refused to fight at this inauspicious moment, unless paid in full. Nassau pleaded and scolded and argued by turns; all to no purpose; nothing could stay the ebb-tide of the mutineers.*

Meantime the Spaniards, heated by the skirmish and fired by the retirement of the foe, could no longer be restrained. Crossing the blazing bridges, swimming the rapid river, floundering through the ditch, they fiercely assailed the flank of the coward invaders. Night alone, now just at hand, prevented the retreat from becoming a wild rout. As it was, three hundred were slain, while as many more were smothered in the abounding bogs—the king losing but nine men.†

On the edge of evening, Alva recalled his pursuing squadrons. "Lest," said he, "they be entrapped in the blind, cozening holes and pits of which this land is full."‡ That very night he sent off a courier to Brussels to announce that Nassau's forces were hopelessly dispersed; adding, "I shall complete my victory on the morrow."§

The duke was mistaken; by masterly generalship, Count Louis managed to regather his scat-

---

* Strada, tom. 2, p. 54. Mendoza, Comentarios, p. 59. Hoofd, tom. 5, p. 174.   † Strada, *ubi sup.* Mendoza, p. 62.

‡ Strada, *ubi sup.*

§ Corresp. du Duc d'Albe, pp. 154, 155.

tered cohorts. With these, still about ten thousand strong, he continued the retreat; halting finally, at the village of Jemmingen, on the border of West Friesland, between the Dollart and the river Ems.* The new camp was admirably chosen and guarded. At their back, the patriots had Embden, a friendly city; whence, by the Ems, they might expect provisions and reinforcements from the prince of Orange. About them were many marshes, always half-submerged, and impassable save by a single road on the top of the narrow dyke which overlooked the swelling billows, and ran directly into the camp and village—an avenue now defended by redoubts and ten cannon planted in its mouth.† Held by determined men, this position would have been impregnable; but fear can never be sufficiently entrenched.

On the 21st of July, Alva, who never slept out an opportunity, appeared before Jemmingen.‡ Nassau, suspicious of his troops, and anxious to make nature his ally, ordered out a corps of pioneers to open the sluices—a manœuvre which would have laid the whole adjacent territory under water;§ for in that artificial country dykes interlace the entire landscape, and these are furnished with floodgates, by means of which the waters are controlled.

The wily duke perceived this movement, and surmised its purpose. A company of mounted car-

---

* Strada, *ut antea.*   † Ibid.
‡ Ibid. Mendoza, p. 66. Cor. du Duc d'Albe, p. 156.
§ Meteren, folio 54. Hoofd, tom. 5, p. 175.

bineers were at once thrown forward to reclose the half-opened sluices; which they did, after a stubborn contest.* At this critical moment the German mercenaries again mutinied. When they should have been in line of battle, they stood clamoring for their arrears round Count Louis' tent.† Apprized of this unseasonable insubordination by deserters, Alva pushed his whole army up the one road to the village, cut down the few faithful soldiers who attempted to dispute the passage, scrambled over the redoubts, and was victorious without a struggle.‡ Count Louis' cannon were fired but once, and then by his own hand.§ A frightful slaughter instantly commenced. Turning their own artillery against them, the remorseless duke swept down his foemen in platoons. Hundreds of the coward mercenaries were cut to pieces offering their backs to the sword, as slaves do theirs to the master's whip. The river too was choked with the flying, most of whom were drowned by the weight of their armor; while those who contrived to swim were made targets of, and shot like so many ducks by the laughing Spaniards.‖ The citizens of Embden learned the issue of the fight long before Alva's couriers came into town, by the multitudes of patriot hats which floated down the stream;¶ as, many centuries

---

* Meteren, folio 54. Hoofd, tom. 5, p. 175. Mendoza.

† Strada, tom. 2, p. 55.

‡ Mendoza, Comentarios, pp. 67, 68. Strada, tom. 2, pp. 55, 56. Meteren, folio 54.

§ Hoofd, tom. 5, p. 176.   ‖ Strada, *ubi sup.*

¶ Ibid.

before, when the Romans battled with the Sabines on the banks of the Arno, they at Rome, seeing the arms of the Sabines floating upon the Tiber, into which the Arno empties, forestalled the messengers by their pre-knowledge of the joyful tidings.

The victory was complete. The Spanish loss was not above seventy; that of the invaders was between six and seven thousand men.* The whole camp was Alva's spoil—baggage, provisions, cannon; among the rest the six musical pieces captured at Heiliger-lee, fell into his greedy maw.† Thus terribly was Aremberg avenged.

For a time it was supposed that Nassau had perished in the rout, his clothes having been found among the spoils of the conflict.‡ His hour had not come. Though fighting to the last, death had shunned him. When all hope had fled, he stripped off his dress, swam the Ems, crossed into Germany, and with a handful of travel and blood-stained attendants, rejoined the prince of Orange.§

That very night, ere leaving the battle-ground, the fanatic conqueror despatched a messenger to acquaint the pontiff with the news; and upon its reception the holy father commanded three successive days of thanksgiving to be kept in as many of the chiefest churches; while bonfires, chimes of bells, and salvos of artillery betokened, and rang

---

* Strada, *ubi sup.* Meteren, folio 55. Bor., tom. 4, p. 245, *et seq.* Campana, Guer. di Fiand., lib. 2, p. 54. † Ibid.

‡ Strada, tom. 2, p. 56.

§ Meteren, folio 55. Hoofd, tom. 5, p. 176.

out, and thundered forth the pious joy of Rome.*
At the same time, the provinces were ordered to
celebrate the victory with processions and joy-bells
and *Te Deums*.† Justice had just had its throat
cut : it was natural that Rome should celebrate the
murder with the meretricious mummeries of a spec-
tacular religion.

Having thus routed and rejoiced over the invaders, Alva bethought him of still farther vengeance.
Had not thousands of the Frieslanders sympathized
with Nassau ? Had not many of their towns adhered to him ? Momentarily relaxing his iron discipline, the governor-general permitted his men-at-
arms to spread the wings of their desolation and
sweep the whole frontier. Jemmingen was fired,
after the inhabitants, of all ages, of both sexes, had
been slain, Hermes Bakkereel, the reformed minister, being stabbed to the heart in the arms of his
daughter.‡ Speeding thence, the pitiless victors
carried death and dishonor in all directions. Maids
and matrons were ravished before the eyes of
fathers and husbands.§ The water in the ditches
ran thick with blood. The very earth seemed
changed to ashes.‖

In this guise Alva marched to Gröningen, where
he forced the unwilling citizens to receive John
Kniffius, designated bishop of the town in Gran-

* Strada, *ubi sup.*, p. 57.
† Davies, vol. 1, p. 563. Mendoza.
‡ Campana, Guer. di Fiand, lib. 2, p. 55. Brandt, vol. 1, p. 268.
§ Mendoza and Bor. Cited in Motley, vol. 2, p. 222.
‖ Motley, *ut antea.*

velle's day.* From Gröningen, he took his way
through Amsterdam to Utrecht, proceeding thence
to Bois-le-Duc.† In all these towns havoc and the
headsman waited on his footsteps. The iconoclasts
had been rampant in this whole section, and here it
was that Brederode had received aid and comfort:
worst of all, in Alva's eyes, Amsterdam and Utrecht
and Bois-le-Duc were strongholds of heresy. Against
all these classes of offenders his anger was inexo-
rable. Woe betide the man or woman, child or
adult, upon whom even the shadow of a suspicion
fell. Any one whom the most searching inquiries
could connect with the opponents of the Inquisition, with the image-breakers, with the *gueux*, was
lost beyond a peradventure. At Haarlem, on the
29th of July, three peasants—one a former soldier
of Brederode, one a suspected breaker of images,
one a writer of verses against the pope—were hung.‡
At Utrecht, a little later, an aged gentlewoman, the
Vrow van Diemen, was convicted of having permitted her son to entertain a reformed preacher
over night, without denouncing him to the holy
office. She was herself a Romanist; but her income of four thousand guilders per annum was an
unpardonable crime. On being conducted to the
scaffold, she did not flinch. "Is your sword sharp?"
asked she, as the executioner prepared to deal her
the fatal blow; "because my poor old neck is very
tough."§ In this same city of Utrecht, another

* Brandt, vol. 1, p. 270. Strada, tom. 2, p. 58.
† Brandt, *ubi sup.* Mendoza. ‡ Brandt, *ubi sup.* § Ibid.

lady, a widow, was beheaded a month after the Vrow van Diemen, because she had encouraged her boy to frequent the conventicles of the reformed; though rumor had it at the time that the prosecuting attorney, to whom she had made heavy loans, had taken this " new way to pay old debts."*

Thus precarious was the hold which the wretched Netherlanders had upon existence; thus strong was their inducement so to live that they might inherit mansions inalienable, eternal, when death foreclosed its mortgage on their fleshly habitations.

For Philip, he was fanatically impressed with his mission: it was his enthusiasm to personify the wrath of God against heretics. For Alva, it was his enthusiasm to personify the wrath of Philip.†

" These were two wits ; one born so, and the other bred ;
This by the heart, the other by the head."

From this inquisitorial campaign against unarmed men and feeble women, with which he was supplementing his victory in the field, Alva was soon summoned by other duties. Couriers, constantly arriving, informed him that revolt, routed in the north, was afoot on the borders of the middle provinces; that this time Orange in person was at the head of large levies, armed for the liberation of the states.‡

Impressed by the gravity of this news, the governor-general delegated the farther punishment of the heretics to the blood-judges and their satellites,

* Brandt, vol. 1, p. 270.   † Motley, vol. 2, p. 178.
‡ Strada, tom. 2, p. 58. Mendoza, Bor., Hoofd.
24*

and prepared to cope with this new antagonist. At Utrecht, his son, Don Frederic de Toledo, had met him with a large instalment of Spanish doubloons and a reinforcement of twenty-five hundred veterans fresh from Castile.* The money he threw into his strong box, the men-at-arms he ordered into rank; and on reviewing his army, was gratified to learn that he had thirty thousand foot and seven thousand horse in camp.† With this chivalrous following, the duke, taking Brussels in his way, pushed towards the menaced frontiers of Juliers and Limburg in good heart and hope. Finally, he halted and intrenched himself at Kaisers-lager, where, before the Christian era, Julius Cæsar's camp-fires had been lighted.‡ Here, with Maestricht on the river Meuse sufficiently near to be defended by his presence, and convenient as a *dépôt* of supplies, Alva decided to await the incoming of the prince, as to whose position he was in doubt.§

Meantime, William of Orange, victorious over manifold discouragements, was in the field. He knew that he was stirring at the eleventh hour, that the time was "rotten ripe;" that he should have coöperated with Count Louis by entering the middle provinces while Alva was absent in the north, and before the trophies won at Heiliger-lee were reclutched at Jemmingen; but alas, the want

---

* Strada, *ubi sup.*

† De Thou, tom. 5, p. 462.   Other authorities reduce this force materially.   *Vide* Strada, tom. 2, p. 61.   Mendoza, pp. 76, 77.

‡ Meteren, folio 56.   § Ibid., Campana, Hoofd, *et alii.*

of money, felt equally in recruiting troops and in enforcing discipline after they were enrolled, fatally retarded the formation of his corps; while Nassau, similarly straitened, and therefore unable to retreat and stand idle, was forced prematurely into action; with what result we know.

William's pleadings for funds were pathetic. "If you have any love for me," wrote he to his friend the landgrave of Hesse, "I beseech you to aid me privately with a sum sufficient to meet the demands of the army for the first month. Without this I shall be in danger of failing in my engagements—to me worse than death, to say nothing of the ruin which such a failure would bring upon our credit and on the cause."[*]

The response was not ready. The disasters of the patriots had still farther chilled the always lukewarm hearts of the prince's allies. The German potentates began to counsel delay.[†] Maximilian forbade the preparations to go on—discovering the neutrality laws in the light of Alva's success.[‡]

A victim of that "hope deferred" which "maketh the heart sick," William nevertheless persisted. Doubt is the foe by whose subjection the young knight of truth wins his spurs. The statesman prince had conquered doubt. He knew that God reigned; therefore he felt certain of success in

---

[*] Archives de la Maison d'Orange-Nassau, Supplément, p. 89.
[†] Cor. de Guillaume le Taciturne, tom. 3, pp. 1–19.
[‡] Ibid.

heaven's good time—he could afford to be patient.
A firm, honest, enlightened Christian, he had already openly announced his adherence to the Reformation.* Steadfast faith—faith which grew serener as the prospect darkened, was his most marked trait at this period. Even Count Louis' overthrow did not appall him. On learning of the rout, he thus wrote his brother: "You may be well assured that I have never felt any thing more keenly than the pitiable misfortune which has overtaken you, for many reasons which you know. Moreover, it hinders us much in the levy which we are making, and has greatly chilled the hearts of those who otherwise would have been ready to assist us. Nevertheless, since it is God's will, it is necessary to have patience, and not to lose courage; conforming ourselves to his divine pleasure, as, for my part, I have prayed for strength to do in all things, still proceeding with his work with his almighty aid."†

Not a reproachful, not a grumbling word; naught but the most Christian resignation. What could long resist such a spirit?

The execution of Egmont and Horn was of material assistance to Orange. Upper Germany was as indignant as the Netherlands. "Sire," said the imperial ambassador at Madrid to Philip, "Alva's axe is William's best ally."‡ And so it proved; for the elector of Bavaria, Augustus of Saxony, landgrave William, and the rest, threw the

---

* Motley, vol. 2, p. 243.   † Archives, etc., tom. 3, p. 276.
‡ Correspondance de Philippe II., tom. 2, p. 37.

whole weight of their influence into the patriot scale;* though their enthusiasm was evanescent, much of their sorrowful anger venting itself in tears of ink.

Such as it was, however, the prince hastened to take advantage of it. Recruiting was pushed with increased energy, and with gratifying success. Near the end of September, 1568, upwards of twenty-eight thousand well-armed men responded to their names, as William's camp-master called the roll under the eaves of the monastery of Romersdorf, in the province of Treves, the patriot rendezvous.† To the German pikemen and arquebusiers—sixteen thousand strong—the count palatine, the duke of Wurtemberg, and the city of Strasburg had promised four months' pay.‡ The maintenance of the horse—eight thousand riders§—had been undertaken by the prince, assisted by Count Louis, Hoogstraaten, and some others, whose promises were fuller than their purses.‖ Marcus Perez, too, a wealthy and patriotic merchant of Antwerp—unawed by the recent execution of his fellow-townsman, the burgher Crœsus, Antony Van Straalen¶—had engaged to pour three hundred thousand crowns into the exchequer of the cause, as the contingent of the nobles and traders of the states.**

On the 31st of August, just before completing

* Strada, tom. 2, p. 58.
† Ibid. Hoofd, tom. 5, p. 183.   ‡ Strada, *ubi sup.*
§ Ibid. But compare Meteren, folio 55. Hoofd, *ubi sup.*, Campana, Bentivoglio, *et alii.*   ‖ Strada, *ubi sup.*
¶ *Vide* Bor., tom. 4, p. 247, *et seq.*   ** Strada, tom. 2. p. 58.

his levies, Orange, at the suggestion of the land-grave of Hesse, published the "Justification"—a famous document, in which he vindicated himself and his cause from the charges of Granvelle, Alva, and the king.*

A few days later, William issued two additional state papers—one, a declaration of war against the duke of Alva; the other a proclamation to the people of the Netherlands. In the declaration, after adverting to the reintroduction of the Inquisition, to the subversion of the charters, to the intolerable wrongs of the Low-Countrymen, boors, peasants, burghers, and grandees, he said: "We summon all honest men to come and help us. Pray God that you may take to heart the uttermost need of your country, the danger of personal slavery for your-selves and your children, and of the overthrow of the evangelical religion. Only with Alva's downfall can the states recover their privileges and their faith."† In the proclamation, he announced his intention to expel the Spaniards from the provinces, and solemnly invoked the aid of the oppressed against the tyrant.‡

Late in September, Orange crossed the Rhine, swept along the banks of the Meuse, and tempora-rily encamped opposite Alva's entrenchments near Maestricht.§ The duke, doubly defended by his redoubts and by the river, which he considered

---

* Arch. de la Maison d'Orange-Nassau, tom. 3, p. 183, *et seq.*
† Bor., tom. 4, p. 253, *et seq.* Cited in Motley, vol. 2, p. 249.
‡ Ibid.   § Strada, *ubi sup.*

unfordable, smoothed his beard and smiled derisively. But "where there's a will there's a way."
On the night and morning of the 4th and 5th of
October, the prince, in imitation of Cæsar's passage
of the Ligeris and Cicoris, placed some companies
of dragoons just above the shallowest of the fords,
to break the force of the current; then, aided by
this human dam, commanded his infantry to wade
silently across the Meuse.*   It was safely done,
though the water came up to the necks of the soldiers;† and Orange stood once more on Netherland
soil, coming not as a revolutionist, but as a champion of law. "*Pro Lege, Rege, Grege,*" this was the
motto inscribed upon one side of his banners; and
on the reverse was the painting of a pelican feeding
her young with her own life-blood.‡

Upon being told that the prince had crossed the
Meuse, Alva was incredulous. "Is the traitor army
a flock of birds, that it can fly over rivers like the
Meuse?" queried he.§   And a citizen of Amsterdam was scourged at the whipping-post for having
mentioned the passage as a rumor.‖ However,
the duke's own eyes soon convinced him; for,
marching within cannon-shot of Alva's camp, William formally challenged a battle by beat of drum
and blare of trumpet and the waving of defiant
ensigns.¶   With him, a stricken field was an actual
necessity. His means were slender; his soldiers

---

* Strada, tom. 2, p. 59.   Meteren, folio 56.   † Ibid.
‡ Hoofd, tom. 5, p. 184.   § Strada, *ubi sup.*
‖ Hoofd, *ubi sup.*   ¶ Strada, *ubi sup.*

were enlisted for short terms; upon his arms there
was the stigma of defeat; the masses were overawed by the spell of Alva's invincibility; a victory
here in the heart of Brabant would be ruinous to
the governor-general, as greatly hated as feared;
and if himself beaten, there at least was Germany,
whence he had come.

But Alva was too wary to pick up the gauntlet.
Every motive which prompted Orange to make the
campaign short and incisive, impelled him to adopt
his favorite policy of delusion and delay. He knew
that the result of a battle was doubtful, at best;
that defeat would rob him of the provinces; that the
narrowness of William's finances would not long
support an army; that winter was hard by; that
poverty and the frost would fight for him; that the
rebel ranks would speedily be thinned by desertion; that a rout could no more than anticipate the
already inevitable dissolution of the invasion: and
he would rather have the victory slow and secure
than dubious and bloody.* The duke's plan was
twofold; he meant to weary his antagonist by fruitless marches and countermarches; and he intended
to compel the patriots to shiver in the open country, by protecting all those cities in which they
might winter and find plunder;† but jeopard any-
thing he would not.

Vainly, therefore, did Orange offer battle. Vainly did the fiery spirits of the Spaniards chafe at the
insults showered on them by a foe whom they de-

* Strada, tom. 2, p. 61.   † Ibid., p. 60.

spised. Alva was as indifferent to the one as to the other—an unfeeling automaton.* Twenty-nine times did the prince change his encampment. Twenty-nine times also did the duke remove, keeping always behind, in front of, or beside his foe. Equal was the vigilance of the opposing commanders, equal the skill with which each chose his ground. It was Fabius Cunctator against Hannibal.†

. Though Alva was careful to avoid a general engagement, the outposts of the two armies, moving thus side by side, and especially their respective foragers, came incessantly in contact. Success inclined sometimes to one side, sometimes to the other, in this partisan warfare. On one occasion, at the river Geta, Alva's advance under Don Frederic de Toledo and the fiery Italian Chiappino Vitelli, assailed and routed the rear guard of the prince.‡ In the fight, Hoogstraaten received his death-wound.§ A faithful friend, a gallant soldier, he was greatly mourned. A few days afterwards, at Le Quesnay, and again at Chateau Cambray, William retaliated, achieving two unimportant but inspiriting victories.‖

In the meantime, cold weather came on, and the necessities of Orange advanced with the season, as Alva had foreseen. Of the three hundred thousand crowns promised by Marcus Perez, but ten thou-

---

° Strada, tom. 2, pp. 62, 63.
† Ibid. Mendoza, p. 88, et seq.   ‡ Ibid.
§ Strada, ut antea. Mendoza, Bor., Campana.   ‖ Ibid.

sand were sent.* Without money, without clothes, without provisions, denied admission into the chief towns, in the midst of a population secretly friendly but afraid to show it, letting "I dare not" wait upon "I would," constantly harassed by an unsleeping enemy—the condition and prospects of the patriot forces became desperate. A small reinforcement of Huguenot volunteers, led into camp by the count De Genlis, served but to increase the suffering by the addition of so many unfed mouths and empty pockets.† The troops began to murmur, then to mutiny; and in one outbreak William's sword was shot from his side.‡

Of course, with such a following it was impossible to keep the field. The prince made an effort to persuade his army to follow him to the assistance of Condé; in vain: they had enlisted to fight Alva, not to war in France.§ Sad, but not dismayed, he recrossed into Germany, and in November, 1568, disbanded his troops at Strasburg.‖ Money he lacked, therefore the arrears of the men-at-arms could not be paid at once; but he mortgaged his lordship of Montfort and the principality of Orange as security for the debt¶—upright and generous to the last. This done, and accompanied by Count Louis and twelve hundred devoted cavaliers, he

* Hoofd, tom. 5, p. 183. Bor., tom. 4, p. 251, et seq.
† Meteren, folio 56. Mendoza, pp. 87, 88.
‡ Strada, tom. 2, p. 61.
§ De Thou. Motley, vol. 2, p. 263.
‖ Hoofd, tom. 5, p. 188. Strada, tom. 2, p. 63.
¶ Arch. de la Maison d'Orange-Nassau, tom. 3, p. 334, et seq.

passed into France to assist the Huguenots, and to concert new measures for the liberation of his country.*

* Archives et Correspondance, tom. 3, p. 316.   Campana, lib. ℈ pp. 59, 61.   De Thou, lib. 43, cap. 19.

CHAPTER XXXII.

ALVA'S MILLENNIUM.

CONTEMPORANEOUSLY with the campaign in the Netherlands, and for some months after its disastrous end, the German emperor and Philip II. were engaged in a diplomatic game which it will interest us to observe.

On the 22d of September, 1568, the six electors of the empire, fierce Protestants, and anxious to succor the Low Country evangelicals, addressed a solemn memorial to Maximilian, in which, after thanking him for his previous interposition, they vividly outlined the abhorrent cruelties of the governor-general, and besought their sovereign to resume his mediation.*

The suave emperor, persuaded that he had nothing to lose thereby, and willing to pleasure the princes, acceded. " We will despatch our brother the archduke Charles on a special mission to Madrid," said he, "and he shall represent our wishes."†

Within thirty days after the date of the electorial request, the archduke started to perform this duty. In his portmanteau there was an ample letter of instructions, which a sentence shall summarize : the negotiator was told to refer to the following of Orange as evidence of his hold on the sym-

* Cor. de Philippe II., tom. 2, p. 791.   † Ibid., p. 793.

pathy of the empire, and as proof of the impossibility of banning him, as Alva had demanded; to request the substitution of clemency for severity in the government of the provinces; and to ask for the recall of the foreign mercenaries.* Then, having seen his brother off, the emperor sent envoys to the rival camps of Alva and the prince to request them to await the result of the intervention ere proceeding with their scientific duel—a proposition which each, convinced of the futility of the embassage, refused to accept.†

On the journey to Madrid the archduke Charles was told of the sudden death of Queen Isabella—poisoned in a fit of jealousy by her royal husband, if we may credit the light pages of contemporaneous diarists, often indeed mere *chroniques scandaleuses.*‡

Upon learning this news, Maximilian began to think the mediation a mistake. He was the father of sixteen children, several of whom were marriageable daughters.§ Unawed by the phantom which arose from Isabella's grave—the supply being so much in excess of the demand in the matrimonial market, he could not afford to be particular—he at once reflected that the king of Spain would make a most desirable son-in-law.

* Corresp. de Philippe II., tom. 2, p. 797. *Vide* Brandt's Summary, vol. 1, p. 276.

† Instructions of the Archduke Charles, in Correspondance de Philippe II., *ut antea.*

‡ *Vide* the very interesting chapter on Isabella's death in Prescott's Philip II., vol. 2, p. 588, *et seq.*

§ Motley, vol. 2, p. 268.

Accordingly, on the 17th of January, 1569, before his plenipotentiary had opened his letter of instructions in Philip's presence, the emperor wrote an autograph note to his "beloved cousin," in which he averred that he had no wish to vex such a model Christian and monarch, and made but a nominal intervention. " Whichever way it goes," quoth he, " I shall be satisfied."* Had there been any doubt, as there was not, "which way it would go," of course this disclaimer would have been decisive.

Upon going again to the archduke's portmanteau, we find the key to this complacent letter— Maximilian had empowered the ambassador to make to the widowed monarch an offer of the consolatory hand of his daughter, the archduchess Anne.† To be sure, the emperor had married Philip's sister, so that the proposed bride was her husband's niece ;‡ but then there was the pope—a dispensation from him would set aside the laws of nature and make all right.

The result was that Philip, after snubbing the electors for their interference,§ and soundly rating the emperor for his toleration of heresy,‖ gloomily accepted the hand of the archduchess Anne, "not for his personal gratification, but because the death of Don Carlos had left him without a son."¶   Perhaps also there was another and an unspoken rea-

* Corresp. de Philippe II., tom. 2, p. 817.
† Ibid., p. 835.   ‡ Brandt, vol. 1, p. 289.
§ Cabreza, Vita de Filipe Segunde, p. 578, et seq.
‖ Cor. de Philippe II., tom. 2, p. 835.   ¶ Ibid.

son. After this marriage, the king may have thought that the prince of Orange would hardly venture to make Maximilian's territories his recruiting-ground.

While the warp and the woof of the future were thus forming in Spain and at the imperial court, Alva was entering Brussels with the insolent port of an Alexander who could find no fresh worlds to conquer. Successful in the north, in the east, in the south, in the west; triumphant over the chosen champion of liberty, who, bankrupt alike in purse and fame, was now a broken fugitive, is it strange that the governor-general should have believed implicitly in the impregnability of the vice-regal throne in all time to come? Even Granvelle, a close observer of the campaign from the dome of St. Peter's, was exultant. "I felt sure of the result," wrote he to Philip; "the duke of Alva is a man upon whose administrative prudence and military skill you may rely. There is no one in the rebel ranks, least of all Orange, who has sufficient brains to organize an efficient insurrection. And as for this same beggar prince, he will now be much embarrassed to satisfy his creditors."*

Alva celebrated his victory with magnificent *fêtes*. Not the triumphs of the haughtiest of the Roman conquerors had ever surpassed the victorious pomp which this inflated soldier led down his " *Via Sacra.*" True, one half of Brussels was sad, while the other half was sullen; those sorrowing

* Corresp. de Philippe II., tom. 2, pp. 792, 795, 812.

for William's defeat, these wishing that some other
had achieved a success in itself desirable.* Nevertheless, though the whole city was "contracted in
one brow of woe," all were forced to smile, to sing
hosannas, to ring joy-bells, to deck out the capital
in *gala* flowers—even houses whence funeral hatch-
ments for murdered inmates were suspended†—to
witness the joustings in the market-place; for the
very square in which Egmont and Horn and a thousand more had been decapitated was transformed
into a tilt-yard;‡ and to listen to *Te Deums* chanted
in the churches of a spurious Christianity—of "a
religion," to borrow Sydney Smith's definition of
Puseyism, "of posture and imposture, of circum-
flection and genuflection, of bowing to the east and
courtesyings to the west, with such like absurdities."

Yet even these demonstrations did not satisfy
the governor-general. He felt that, as the inaugurator of this varnished millennium, he was deserving of some personal recognition, distinct, peculiar. What could be fitter to immortalize his actions
than a statue built of his trophies?

Accordingly, he caused the cannon taken at
Jemmingen to be melted, shaped into a colossal
effigy of himself, and set up in the citadel at Antwerp.§ This "brazen image" represented Alva
armed *cap-à-pie*,‖ with right arm uplifted, trampling

---

* Strada, tom. 4, p. 64.   † Bor., tom. 4, p. 257.

‡ Strada, *ubi sup.*   § Ibid. Bor., *ubi sup.*

‖ Strada says the head was bare; 'tis best to be correct in a
matter of such moment.

upon a prostrate hybrid with two heads, four arms, and one body—signifying two of the three estates of the Low Countries; the lords and commons, as some said, or Egmont and Horn, according to another interpretation.* On the pedestal was carved this inscription: "To the duke of Alva, the most faithful minister of the best of kings, Philip II. of Spain, because, extinguishing combustions, chastising rebellion, restoring religion, executing justice, he settled peace in these provinces, this statue is erected."†

Many centuries before the rout at Jemmingen, a similar event occurred. In the same province of Friesland, Germanicus Cæsar conquered Arminius by the banks of the Visargus. The Romans too took for their sport the slaying of the swimmers in the river. Arminius, like Nassau, fled disguised. The field was strewn with corpses. And on the return, the Roman erected his monument of spoils for posterity to gaze at. But here the parallel stops. When the Roman set up his trophy, his modesty led him to omit his name; the arrogant Spaniard chiselled in his title. Fame, therefore, in that inscription inserted the word *Germanicus;* but envy in this soon blotted out the name of *Alva.*‡

° Meteren, folio 61. Bor., *ubi sup.* Strada, *ubi sup.*

† Strada, *ut antea.* Meteren, folio 61, *et alii.*

‡ "It was wonderful to see with what a general hatred and envy this statue was looked upon. The Low-Countrymen inwardly fretting, as if they were daily conquered in that monument, and the nation daily triumphed over. The very Spaniards

The duke's festivities were soon interrupted by an untoward event. Notwithstanding the filchings from the confiscated hoards of the heretic traitors, Alva had found plunder an uncertain paymaster. Improvidence and peculation ate up all he could steal. As a consequence, constant draughts were made upon the Spanish treasury. Recently the mercenaries, whose pay was many months in arrear, had been grumbling—the mercenaries, who were the main prop, the palladium, of the usurpation. Of course the duke had recourse to Philip, who, in his turn, almost as necessitous as the governor-general, had been obliged to borrow half a million of dollars from two banking-houses at Genoa, in order to meet the demand.* The bankers had contracted to deliver the loan in silver at Antwerp. It

themselves were angry at the duke, that chose rather to sing his own praises than to hear them spoken by others. Nor was there any subject more frequent at the court of Spain, the prince of Eboli deriding his old rival for styling himself most faithful minister, because he inverted the honor due to his prince and transferred it to himself. Nay, the structure was not very pleasing to Philip, by whose command, four years after, it was removed. Perhaps the king did it to take away the nation's distaste; or, rather, his own, offended that another should have a monument raised out of a victory which his armies had won and his purse paid for. It was conjectured that Alva had knowledge of the king's displeasure, because the other statue—for he had two cast of the same model by the same workman—was not sent into Spain, as he at first intended." Strada, tom. 2, pp. 64, 65.

De Thou, who saw the statue after it was cast down, was "as much struck by the beauty of the workmanship, as by the insane pride of him who ordered it made." Hist. Univ., pp. 471–473.

° MS., Simancas, cited by Froude in Hist. of England, vol. 9, p. 366.

was accordingly packed into several chests, divided among a number of ships, and despatched from Italy by sea.*

In the British Channel the precious fleet "fell among thieves" in the shape of Huguenot privateers, commissioned by Condé to prey upon Romanist merchantmen of whatever nationality,† was scattered and driven into English ports. The captains of the treasure-ships complained to the Spanish ambassador at the court of St. James of the breach of neutrality committed by the corsairs in chasing the vessels of a friendly power in English waters; and the ambassador laid the accusation before Elizabeth.‡ The maiden queen listened graciously, and offered to send a British man-of-war to convoy the fleet to Antwerp—an offer which was accepted with many thanks.§

But at that time, though Elizabeth was in place, Cecil—Lord Burghley—was in power. Cecil was a statesman in whose brain there were only deep soundings—no shoals. A man of weighty intellect, of profound tact, of unrivaled acumen, as Dryden said of Shakespeare, "he needed not the spectacles of books to read nature, but looked inward and found her there." Cecil was a sturdy Protestant withal, nor were his sympathies bounded by his native island. He had long used his influence with his royal mistress in favor of Coligny and of Orange, both as a statesman and as a Christian; for

---

* MS., Simancas, cited by Froude in Hist. of England, vol. 9, p. 866. † Ibid. ‡ Ibid. § Ibid.

he was as much opposed as a politician to the house of Austria, as he was as a Protestant to the exegesis of the Roman theologians.

In these Spanish vessels now at anchor in British harbors he saw an opportunity at a critical moment to aid Orange, to cripple Alva, to provoke Philip, and to end the coquette dance of Elizabeth on the brink of a precipice. Accordingly, he persuaded the queen to seize and appropriate Alva's expected treasure-chests to her own use.*

Philip's ambassador was astonished. Waiting upon Elizabeth, he demanded an explanation. She gave him two. "I understand that 't is the property of the Genoese, and as I have occasion for a loan, I have borrowed it." "I have taken the money in my possession, in order to secure its safe delivery at Antwerp." These were her paradoxical answers.† The envoy was at liberty to accept either or both; like Luther's priest, who, when the Romanists told him to pray in one way and the Protestants in another, ended by repeating the alphabet, and begging each to frame a prayer to their taste.

The ambassador hastened to apprize Alva of the seizure;‡ and then, remembering that a main source of the wealth of the London merchants was the Netherland trade, he went on 'Change and told the news, in the hope that the impending breach might stir a riot that should force the queen to make res-

---

* Froude, Hist. of England, vol. 9, p. 371, *et seq.* Meteren, folios 57, 58. † Ibid. Bor., tom. 5, p. 272, *et seq.* ‡ Ibid.

titution.* He informed Philip that the indignity originated in the determination of Cecil to support the prince of Orange, adding: "Half the money goes to him to enable him to equip a new army; the other half is to be spent in doubling the English fleet."†

When Alva, who was impatiently awaiting the money, learned of its seizure, he was furious. Once, twice did he despatch envoys across the channel to wheedle and to bully the court of St. James. The queen snubbed the committees and rebuked the duke for venturing to treat with a crowned head. "Tell the governor-general that I will discuss this question with his master;" such was the message which the remonstrants bore back to Brussels.‡

This rebuke, which his arrogance merited, tuned Alva's indignation to the highest pitch. By a formal proclamation he instituted immediate reprisals. Every English resident in the Netherlands was arrested, and every British ship was seized and gutted of its cargo, which was sold.§ Elizabeth retaliated by swooping upon the persons and estates of all Low-Countrymen living or trading in the island.‖ Whereupon the duke, on the 31st of March, 1569, proclaimed a strict non-intercourse with Great Britain.¶

Antwerp grumbled and London was sulky: it

* Froude, *ubi sup.*, p. 373.
† Gueran de Espes to Philip, Dec. 27 and Jan. 1. MS., Simancas.   ‡ Meteren, *ut antea.* Froude.
§ Ibid. Froude, vol. 9, p. 373.   ‖ Froude, Hume. Bor.
¶ Bor., vol. 5, p. 277, *et seq.* Motley, vol. 2, p. 279.

was a quarrel in the upper air, about which they knew nothing and cared less. But Alva terrified the burghers into silence; and as the immediate advantage was largely on the side of the queen, Lombard-street became acquiescent. The iron grasp of this embargo was not unclenched until the spring of 1573,* four years after the seizure of the money-chests; within which time this quarrel made England the ally of Orange, as was Cecil's intention when he played the trick.

Interested as the governor-general was in the imbroglio with Elizabeth, he did not permit it to divert his attention from what he knew to be the main end of his presence in the states—the extirpation of heresy. In March, 1569, his past piety was honored by the arrival of an ambassador from Rome, who presented him with a helmet and a sword, both richly set, and inchased with gold and precious stones, solemnly consecrated by his holiness, and sent to the duke of Alva as the champion of holy church.†

Elated by this extraordinary present, and anxious to prove his right to the title conferred upon him by Pius V., the duke now redoubled, if that were possible, the fury of a persecution which had never lagged. The stadtholders of the provinces were instructed to see that, "when either the host or the holy oil for extreme unction, was carried to

---

* Bor., vol. 5, p. 277, *et seq.* Motley, vol. 2, p. 279. Camden, Annals of the Reign of Elizabeth, book 1, p. 126, ed. 1675.

† Strada, tom. 2, p. 64. Mendoza, Comentarios, p. 100.

the sick, strict notice should be taken of the behavior of all, in order that those in whom any signs of irreverence were discovered might be punished; that all dead bodies denied Christian burial by the clergy should be dumped in the gallows-field; and that all midwives should be Romanists, obliged under oath to give an account within twenty-four hours after birth of every child, to the end that the curate might proceed to baptism."* This order was followed up by a placard, signed by Philip on the 19th of May, 1569, repealing all declarations and agreements inconsistent with the inquisitorial edict of Charles V. in 1550, across which *esto perpetua* was now written.† The decrees of the Council of Trent were rigidly enforced,‡ especially those of them in which the Tridentine fathers enjoined the extirpation of heresy; and the evil army of priests thundered the accursed message from every altar, and breathed it with yet more fatal potency in the confessional.§

The police of persecution, in greater numbers than ever, were set at every street-corner to observe and report the behavior of the masses.‖ These spies were nicknamed "sevenpenny men," because the wages of their odious work was paid them in coin of that value.¶

From such seed a crop of murder was sure to

---

* Brandt, vol. 1, p. 280. † Ibid.
‡ Davies, Hist. of Holland, vol. 1, p. 566. Brandt, vol. 1, p. 288.
§ Froude, Hist. of England, vol. 10, p. 392.
‖ Brandt, vol. 1, p. 280. ¶ Ibid.

spring. The local records of that era reek with
perennial barbarities, performed not perfunctorily,
but *con amore*. Now, a batch of Protestant tradesmen were hung at Bois le Duc; and now, a parcel
of heretical husbandmen were beheaded at the
Hague.* Amsterdam, Leyden, Antwerp, Brussels,
Valenciennes—in each, and at the same time, there
were dreadful tragedies.†

As usual, those stigmatized as Anabaptists were
hunted with peculiar vindictiveness. On one occasion, an order was issued for the apprehension of a
burgher of Asperen named Richard Willemson, of
that persuasion. Knowing that an arrest was the
unfailing herald of death, he fled upon the ice, which
was yet thin, for it was early winter. After much
difficulty, he got over it; but an officer who was
pursuing him was not so successful, for he slipped
in. "Help! help!" shouted the drowning, freezing
wretch. Willemson paused; there was no one within sight or hearing save himself. Touched by the
peril of his pursuer, he recrossed and jeoparded his
own life to rescue that of a sinking brother. The
officer, on being fished out of the water, was about
to let his preserver go, when the burgomaster, who
had come suddenly upon the scene, cried sharply:
"Sir officer, fulfil your oath." Recollecting that
his own neck might pay for it if he let the prisoner
escape, the officer forced Willemson back to Asperen, where he was soon tried and sentenced to be
burned alive. He was led out to die on that side of

* Brandt, vol. 1, p. 278.   † Ibid.

the town of Asperen which is next to the village of Leerdam. When the fire was kindled, a strong east wind blew the flames away from the upper part of his figure, and caused him to suffer the excruciating agonies of a lingering death, insomuch that, as far off as Leerdam, towards which the wind sat, he was heard to cry over seventy times, "O my Lord and my God! O my Lord and my God!"*

Now, as always before when persecution became unusually harsh, multitudes left the states, and transported their effects and handicrafts to other shores—such multitudes that more than a hundred thousand houses were left tenantless.† The sight of so many empty dwellings frightened the merchants and traders of the Netherlands. Many of these were Romanists who had no sympathy with the reformed, and stood ready to treat the profession of Protestantism as an indictable offence. But as the publican was nearer the kingdom of heaven than the Pharisee, so the manufacturers of Ghent and Antwerp, of Brussels and Bruges, were drawn from fanaticism by their worldliness; they were willing to maintain holy church in all its dignity and honor, but relucted at Alva's method of procedure, and had no desire to ruin the country and themselves by the death or exile of the most skilful artificers in Christendom.‡

---

* Brandt, vol. 1, p. 281. † Ibid., p. 277.
‡ Froude, Hist of England, vol. 9, p. 314.
In 1603, when Sully visited England, two-thirds of the inhabitants of the town of Canterbury were Netherland refugees. "This

The governor-general was supremely indifferent to the opinions of the conservative Romanists of the provinces. It was Philip II. whose commission he bore; it was the pope who crowned him with honors. Self-interest, equally with fanaticism, impelled him to steer right on in a course known to square with the twin compasses of Madrid and the Vatican.

Accordingly, his measures proceeded from bad to worse. While the emigration was at the highest, those wives who went to visit their exiled husbands were declared to be themselves outlawed by that act.* All young men under twenty were forbidden peremptorily to study in any university outside of the dominions of Philip II., with the single exception of the schools at Rome.†

The press, too, always an ally of the Reformation, was, by a placard fulminated in May, 1569, put under strict censorship.‡ Nothing might be published without the *imprimatur* of Alva. Moreover, in order that it might be seen how books demeaned themselves, an ecclesiastical committee sat in Antwerp, with authority to judge all writings of all climes, and to place those which were objectionable to Rome in an *index expurgatorius*, in obedience to the mandate of the doctors of Trent.§

In civil affairs, usurpation kept pace with this

circumstance," remarks he, "accounts for the superior civilization and politeness of the denizens of that place." Memoirs, tom. 4, lib. 14, p. 217.

* Brandt, vol. 1, p. 277. Hoofd.   † Ibid.
‡ Brandt, *ubi sup.*, pp. 277, 287, 295.   § Ibid., p. 293.

ethical oppression. Commissioners, hounded on by
the blood-judges, prowled through the states to ferret out all who had maintained a correspondence
with the prince of Orange. The very arm of the
gibbet began to ache with incessant service. Rarely did the atrocious farces called trials awaken a
protest from the cowed provincial bar. Once, however, when the magistrates of Leyden were called
upon to execute an illegal sentence against several
of their fellow-townsmen, they refused unanimously
to play the executioner; nor would they recognize
the competence of the tribunal of blood to pronounce judgment within the limits of their municipality, alleging it to be against their charters, which
permitted only the schout—an officer appointed by
the sovereign or his deputy—and the supreme council of Leyden to bring the freemen of the town to
trial.* "Besides," said they, "we have an old custom which forbids that any man suffer death who
does not own his crime without torture or bands.
In any case, the culprit can no more than lose
life and be made to forfeit ten Flemish pounds.
Whence, then, these arrests and executions? and
whence these confiscations?"† A constitutionalist
would have been puzzled to reply; but as for Alva,
had not his echo, Vargas, said, " *Non curamus vestros privilegios?*"

This protest of the Leyden magistrates was not
answered by imprisonment and the block, only
because the governor-general was too much occu-

---

* Brandt, p. 277.   † Ibid.

pied at the time to heed it. The seizure of his
money-chests by the queen of England had crippled Alva, as Cecil meant it should. From day to
day his pecuniary embarrassments increased. The
civil list went unpaid. The men-at-arms became
vociferous in their demands for the arrears. To
those pledges had been doled out, and to these the
rhetoric of victory had been given; but creditors
only appreciate the eloquence of cash. Confiscations came in in driblets. The duke disliked to beg
again of Philip, since his most "catholic" majesty
had just ended a costly campaign against those
home-bred infidels the Moriscoes, and was even
now arming at great expense to battle with the
Sultan.*

Besides, had he not repeatedly assured the king
that his government in the Low Countries should
not only itself feed on gold, but also supply the
royal table at Madrid with ducat-viands? Were
not his enemies at court—Ruy Gomez, the fair
Anna de Mendoza, and the rest, filling Philip's ears
with sarcastic jests at his failure to keep that
promise?†

Under these circumstances, Alva concluded that
his exchequer, emptied by war and extravagance,
must be replenished in the provinces. For this
purpose he decided to substitute for the immemorial and chartered rights of the states to tax themselves, an irresponsible, wholly arbitrary system of

* Prescott, Philip II., vol. 3, p. 298.
† Vandervynckt, tom. 2, p. 118.

taxation by the crown.* Could this be done—and the haughty soldier did not doubt his ability to command success—the gain would be twofold; a perpetual fund would be at hand for future occasions, and the keystone would be knocked out of the arch of Netherland rights.

Then, as in the past, all legal applications for money were to be made to the states-general, composed of three orders—the nobles, the clergy, and the commons; and it was at their option to say Yes, or No, to the demand—the veto of any one of the branches being equivalent to the dissent of all.†

To the absolutist ideas of Alva, such a check on despotism was rebellion in a chronic form. Irritation, as well as the pecuniary pressure, urged him to assail it. Accordingly, on the 20th of March, 1569, he convened the states-general in Brussels,‡ their first meeting since the stormy farewell of Philip II. in the eventful summer of '59.

The duke was so confident that he did not deign to inaugurate the financial revolution by a measurably moderate demand in perpetuity, making the grant of this a precedent for greater exactions; with arrogant rapacity he claimed of the national representatives the cession to him of the right to impose three taxes, two of which were unprecedented. The first was an extraordinary tax of one per cent. upon all properties, real and personal, to be collected

* Bor., tom. 5, p. 279. Strada, tom. 2, p. 65.
† *Vide* Motley, vol. 1, Introduction. Bentivoglio, lib. 5, p. 82.
‡ Bor., tom. 5, p. 279. Bentivoglio, Vandervynckt, *et alii.*

immediately. The second was a perpetual tax of twenty per cent. upon every transfer of real estate. The third was a perpetual tax of ten per cent. upon personal property and all kinds of merchandise, payable by the vendor on every sale.*

This enormous demand, as suicidal as it was tyrannical, made the provincial deputies gasp for breath. No scientist was needed to demonstrate the bankruptcy; no economist was required to figure out the fact; the veriest financial tyro could read ruin in every syllable of the decrees.

The representatives ventured to remonstrate, maintaining unanswerably that the proposed taxes would strangle trade and exile commerce. "As for the hundredth penny," said they, "'t is exhorbitant, but it may be borne for once. But for the twentieth penny, that is insupportable. Such an assessment on the full value of real estate, made at every transfer, would soon eat up such property. An estate may be sold twenty times within a twelvemonth, in which case twenty per cent. means practical confiscation.†

"And for the tenth penny, that is still worse, since besides being a higher rate, it is imposed upon articles of merchandise, goods in rapid circulation. Many of these change hands a dozen times a week, so that ten per cent. paid by the vendor at each sale would be more than a hundred per cent. every seven days. Other commodities are trans-

* Bor., tom. 5, pp. 280, 281, et seq.
† Motley, vol. 2, p. 286.

ferred from one person to another, and by him to
a third, and so to a fourth, a fifth, a sixth, before
reaching the consumer. As each vendor paid the
tax, he would add ten per cent. to its original price
in order to reimburse himself, until a fictitious value
was reached which would be a prohibition upon
purchase.

"Then, too, most manufactured goods are made
up of many parts. Before cloth is woven and put
off the hands of the manufacturer, he must pay a
tenth part to the seller of wool, of thread, to the
weaver, to the dyer, until the payment of these
manifold tenths would run up the price of the completed cloth to a fabulous amount—placing it so far
above the means of ordinary consumers as to drive
them into foreign and more favored markets. Quick
transfers and unfettered movements being the nerves
and muscles of commerce, it would be impossible
for it long to survive the paralysis of such imposts."*

So spoke the deputies—strongly and with convincing logic. Viglius too lent his name and pen
to the opposition. The learned doctor was willing
to spend his eyesight in hunting up musty precedents for murder, but he would not quietly submit
to a tax which robbed his coffers of half their
wealth. "Remember, your highness," said he,
"that the Netherlands are situated in the heart of
Europe, with many enterprising nations bordering

* Bor., tom. 5, pp. 281, 282. Strada, tom. 2, p. 65. Motley,
ut antea.

on them; so that if trade be discouraged or oppressed, the merchants and manufacturers resident here can easily, and certainly will, transport themselves into adjacent lands—a consequence to be dreaded from much less burdensome taxation than this now proposed, which is such as was never before heard of in any commercial state."*

Alva was both astonished and provoked by this opposition in these halcyon days. Nor could he "upon the heat and flame of his distemper sprinkle cool patience." He was ignorant of the A B C of political economy, and he was obstinate in proportion as he was opposed—a man who would slap Reason in the face if she said nay to the idlest of his whims. "Know then," said he to the remonstrants, "that in my own town of Alva in Spain, a tax of ten per cent., analogous to this, is paid me without complaint, and yields an annual rental of some fifty thousand ducats. Let me hear no more, therefore, of your inability to pay it. Have it I must."†

" Yes, retorted Viglius, " but there is the widest difference between Spain and the Low Countries. We are a small nation, dependent upon provisions grown outside our limits—traders. Spain is complete within itself, shut out from want by a fertile soil. The people are devoted to agriculture, so that what goods are sold pass directly from the producer to the consumer with no intervention.

---

* Viglii Comm. dec. Deu., s. 7, p. 10.

† Meteren. Bentivoglio, *et alii.*

Ten per cent. on sales must be comparatively easy to pay in such a state."[*]

Viglius' advocacy of their cause emboldened the people at large to remonstrate. An avalanche of petitions rolled down upon the duke. One pamphlet informed him that if he acted Themistocles, and to raise money brought two goddesses, Persuasion and Violence, the states would play the Andrians, and to prevent payment, interpose as many and as potent goddesses, Poverty and Impossibility.[†]

" We will yield the hundredth penny," said the states-general.[‡] " I must have the tenth and twentieth also," persisted the duke. After a protracted struggle, the deputies were bullied into acquiescence, hinging their assent upon a condition precedent—that the veto of any one of the provinces should be held to invalidate the Amen of all the rest.[§]

Alva sat down and wrote Philip a jubilant letter, in which he announced the assent of the states to the taxes, and congratulated his majesty upon the gaining of the purse and the possession of an immense income in perpetuity.[‖]

Alas, before this assurance was in the mail-bag, word came that Utrecht had refused to ratify the decrees, offering instead a commutation, first of

---

[*] Viglii Comm. dec. Deu., *ut antea.*
[†] Strada, tom. 2, p. 67.
[‡] Bor., tom. 5, p. 286. Meteren, Hoofd, Campana.
[§] Bor., *ubi sup.* Brandt., vol. 1, p. 278.
[‖] Corresp. de Philippe II., tom. 2, p. 882.

seventy thousand florins, then of two hundred thousand florins.[*] This tender was rejected with disdain, and a renewed demand was made for the assent of the province to the imposts.[†] Utrecht again refused ; the clergy, one of the three branches of the stadtholderate, declaring that they could not agree to the taxes without incurring the censure of excommunication, denounced by the pope's bull " *in cœnâ Domini*" against those alike who imposed assessments upon the revenues of the church and those who paid them.[‡]

Alva resolved to try his " short method" with these cavillers. A regiment of Italian mercenaries was billeted upon the state. The intrepid burghers quietly put up with the soldiers, and still refused to indorse the decrees.[§] Other coercive measures were tried, with no better result. And finally the incensed duke declared the whole province guilty of treason and heresy, abrogated its charters, confiscated the public funds, took formal possession of the archives, and so far as words could do so, blotted Utrecht from the provincial map.[||]

In the mean time the whole question was reopened, the other states declaring that the refusal of Utrecht to ratify the taxes had annulled their assent.[¶] Alva coddled and threatened by turns. The burghers wheedled and juggled ; until the duke,

---

[*] Bor., *ubi sup.*, p. 287.   [†] Ibid.
[‡] Brandt, vol. 1, p. 279.   Hoofd, tom. 5. p. 195.
[§] Hoofd, *ubi sup.* Bor., tom. 5, p. 288.   [||] Ibid., Ibid.
[¶] Meteren, Campana.

now quite destitute of money, agreed to hold the taxes in abeyance for two years, accepting in lieu of them a payment of two millions of guilders at the end of each twelvemonth.* By this compromise the final struggle was postponed until August, 1571. "At the expiration of this time events may prevent any further attempt to collect the taxes," said the burghers. "Time will reconcile these shopkeepers to submission," thought the viceroy. Neither yet understood the other.

It was at this juncture that Philip's affianced bride, Anne of Austria, passed through the Netherlands *en route* to Spain.† The incestuous match had been legalized by Pius V., to the great offence of Protestant Europe.. The princess was, however, well received at Brussels, and Alva became an earnest suitor to the king for leave to escort her to Madrid.‡ For various reasons the duke desired to retire from the provinces. Of late his Spanish correspondence had teemed with hints that his favor at court was waning—Ruy Gomez required watching. Then too he felt that his work was about done in the Low Countries; armed treason had been crushed; the scaffold had been fed with victims; heresy had been sedulously racked and burned; confiscations had emptied the veins of plethoric and haughty traders; all the rest he esteemed certain to be heaviness and a weariness to the flesh.§ There were no

---

* Hoofd, *ubi sup.* Bor., *ubi sup., et seq.*
† Brandt, vol. 1, p. 209.   ‡ Strada, tom. 2, p. 68.
§ Corresp. de Philippe II., tom. 2, pp. 896, 908, 951, 970, etc.

more laurels to be gathered. But he pleaded in vain; Philip was not yet ready to sign a recall.[*]

For some time past the great wigs at Brussels and Madrid had been pondering the policy of an amnesty. Damon Viglius had urged Pythias Hopper to suggest it to "the master."[†] And Granvelle, convinced that the brutality of the governor-general was playing into the hands of Orange, had written from Rome to request his majesty to make at least a show of pardon.[‡] Now for many months the entire nation had been under the double ban of Philip and the Inquisition—all criminals, without a claim to fortune, family, or life.[§] A discriminating act of indemnity might conciliate the Netherlanders; it would surely tend to propitiate that public opinion which had arraigned Spain at the bar of Europe.

Influenced by these considerations, Philip drew up four different forms of pardon, towards the close of 1569, and despatched them to Alva, bidding him to select one, and be careful to destroy the rest.[‖]

Certainly the duke made no hasty choice, for it was not until the midsummer of 1570 that the amnesty was proclaimed[¶]—a protraction which would have lessened the favor of a much greater benefaction than this proved to be.[**]

[°] Strada, *ubi sup.*   [†] Epist. ad. Joach. Hopperus, pp. 82–110.
[‡] Corresp. de Philippe II., tom. 2, p. 815.
[§] *Vide* Chapter XXVII., p. 474.
[‖] Corresp. de Philippe II., tom. 2, p. 914.
[¶] Hoofd, tom. 5, p. 201.   Strada, tom. 2, p. 67.
[**] Strada, *ubi sup.*

The promulgation ceremonies were held in Antwerp on the 14th of July. All the world of the Netherlands had made a pilgrimage to the new Mecca to be at the festival. There was a pompous parade of gorgeously enrobed ecclesiastics, and this was succeeded by no end of *Te Deums*.[*] Alva commenced the day by listening to a sermon in Dutch— of which he could not understand a word—preached by the bishop of Antwerp. Then, richly habited and accompanied by his suite and a retinue of clergy, the duke marched to the cathedral of Our Lady, where a mass was intoned by the archbishop of Cambray. Towards the end of the service, the prelate read a papal letter of absolution, which removed the ban of the Inquisition from all good Romanists.[†] Taking this clement action as a text, the bishop of Arras began to harangue the attentive throng; but in the midst of his eulogium he was taken with a sudden qualm, and carried fainting from the pulpit—a *finale* which was not considered of auspicious omen.[‡]

Later in the day, Alva, crowned with his hallowed helmet and girt with his consecrated sword, entered the market-place with an illustrious following of lords and churchmen. Opposite the stadthouse stood a bedizened platform, erected for the occasion. Upon this the duke, together with his attendants, ranged themselves—Alva seating himself "high on a throne of royal state." Then the

[*] Bor., tom. 5, p. 319.   [†] Strada, *ubi sup.*, p. 68.
[‡] Ibid.

vast assembly was silenced, and a crier bawled out the amnesty, but in such a hoarse voice that few could understand him; "which was perhaps an accident," says Strada; "perhaps so ordered by his highness, who preferred that the auditors should measure the benefit by the pomp rather than by the text."[*]

However, contrary to the duke's expectation, the spectators did nothing but stare at the show. Not a huzza was heard in the afternoon, not a bonfire was kindled in the evening.[†] When the indemnity was read—as it was some days later in the printed copies which were thrown off by the government press—the feeling of the people, cool at the outset, went down to zero.

The act was in three parts—like most genteel comedies: a recitation of the sins of the Netherlanders, a statement of the terms of pardon, and a list of exceptions. What was done by the indemnity was undone by the exceptions, which excluded from benefit all reformed preachers, and all who had lodged them; the image-breakers; those who had subscribed the compromise; those who had countenanced the petitions of the nobles in Margaret's reign; those affiliated with the *gueux;* and all who had favored the opponents of the king under any circumstances, at whatever time.[‡]

Of course these exceptions included every class of offenders, and left only the innocent to be for-

---

[*] Strada, *ut antea.* [†] Ibid.
[‡] *Vide* the Ipsissima Verba in Bor., tom. 5, p. 320, *et seq.*

given ;* and equally, of course, the effect produced by such a juggle was the opposite of salutary. Very many Romanists denounced the act; for, connected by family ties with persons of the reformed belief, some of them had performed little offices of kindness, perhaps sheltered a hunted neighbor, in these hard times—deeds which an *amnesty* proclamation pronounced enormous crimes.† Jeers and execrations were heard on every side. The punsters transposed the letters of the word *pardona*, and rebaptised the new measure *Pandora*. The witticism was not without classical analogy. The amnesty, like the supposititious casket of the gods, on being opened, diffused curses instead of blessings.‡

On the 1st of November, 1570, the distress of the masses was increased by a calamity unparalleled since the ark landed on mount Ararat. An inundation, caused by a northwest storm, set the sea battling through two days with the dykes and sluices of the whole Netherland coast.§ The narrow peninsula of Holland was threatened with annihilation. The great cities of the north were transformed into islands in mid-ocean. The land became a watery waste. At every rising and falling of the sea—both tides alike merciless—household goods, merchandise, cattle, the broken ribs of ships, all were tossed hither and thither, presenting to the

---

* Motley, vol. 2, p. 298.
† Meteren, Bentivoglio, *et alii*.
‡ Motley, vol. 2, p. 300.
§ Hoofd, tom. 6, p. 205, *et seq.* Brandt, vol. 1, p. 289.

eye a model of the flood.* Nor was it property
alone that suffered shipwreck. In the single province of Friesland twenty thousand men, women,
and children were engulfed.† Others of the states
were proportionably afflicted. Everywhere the desolation was complete. Many of the Flemish towns
which were not on the coast-line, were invaded by
the rampant deluge.‡

In Friesland, hundreds climbed to the tops of
hills, and took refuge in church belfries, whence
they were taken by boats sent by the magistrates
to gather up the needy, and to fish out what property might be afloat. Upon the summit of one
mound, an infant, carried thither in its cradle, was
discovered fast asleep, in fear neither of shipwreck
nor the flood.§ When the waves retired, and the
burghers were at leisure to count up their losses,
they reckoned the property submerged to be incalculable, and put down the lives destroyed at one
hundred thousand.‖

In the millennium which Alva had reported, the
provinces were thus mangled between the upper and
nether millstones of human cruelty and elemental
wrath.

○ Strada, tom. 2, p. 69.   † Ibid. Brandt, *ubi sup.*
‡ Hoofd, *ubi sup.*   § Strada, *ut antea.*
‖ Meteren, Hoofd, *ut antea.*

CHAPTER XXXIII.

PENNIES AS REVOLUTIONISTS.

EUROPE three hundred years ago, almost as markedly as now-a-days, was a plural unit rather than a congeries of isolated states. Widely separated peoples were not then, as now, made neighbors—cosmopolized, by newspapers and the telegraph. The masses, in our modern sense, were indeed but just awakening from the sleep of ages, and stood drowsy-eyed. At present, it is not cabinets, but art, science, literature, opinion, fashion, commerce that are the motors of society, moulding national character and purpose. In the sixteenth century, government, the annals of half a dozen dynasties, the cabinets of Rome, Madrid, Paris, Brussels, London, covered the whole plane of human life—trade, letters, industry, religion; which explains why the old chronicles deal only with governmental doings—there was nothing else to record.[*]

Still, in the face of this fact, it is true that at the Reformation era the European states were more or less intimately allied, some by a union of interests, others by the bond of a common faith; so that it is impossible clearly to understand the story of any one of the foremost powers of that time without a comprehension of the foreign outlook.

[*] Wendell Phillips, Speeches, Lectures, and Letters, p. 306.

The connection between the Netherlands and England was especially close. Neighbors by position, cousins by blood, cradled in the same Saxon forests, the Dutchman and the Englishman had felt an immemorial affection for each other—an affection increased to the utmost cordiality when both struck off the spiritual shackles of the Vatican, and became worshippers at a freer altar.

The transition from the old creed to the gospel theology had been scarce more stormy in the Low Countries than in Great Britain; as the Lollards could tell, and as the still recent reign of "bloody Mary" avouched. The victory of the Reformation left Romanism large, imposing, puissant, and ill-satisfied to accept the result—prone, like Saul, to kick against the pricks.

During Alva's governor-generalship of the Netherlands, Elizabeth was on the English throne; a Protestant queen, but a half-Romanist woman, vacillating in action, marvellously overrated as a sovereign. Happily for the island, at this the most critical period of its history, its safety was in abler and more skilful hands than those of the daughter of Henry VIII. Cecil was at the helm,* and alert Protestantism stood beside him.

---

* "'Tell his majesty,' wrote Don Gueran, the Spanish ambassador at the court of St. James, to Cayas, 'that Cecil is a fox cunning as sin, and the mortal enemy of Spain. He moves in silence and falsehood, and what he will do against holy church is only limited by his power. The queen's opinion goes for little, and Leicester's for less; Cecil rules all, unopposed, with the pride of Lucifer.'" Froude, vol. 10, p. 258.

The Romanists, ousted at court, became plotters almost to a man—three-quarters of the peers and half the gentlemen of England.* Reactionist outbreaks were the order of the day; for churchmen, who on the Continent preached the divine right of kings, believed in Great Britain that obnoxious crowned heads might be lawfully deposed.† Nevertheless, the heretic princess retained the sceptre, and each baffled conspiracy weakened the papists and depleted their purses, while retaliatory legislation placed them under a harsh judicial ban.

In despair of unsupported success, they finally appealed to their natural leaders, the pope and the European princes, for guidance and aid. The *desideratum* was a grand crusade of the Romanist powers for the recovery of England. Ridolfi, a Florentine long resident in England, was the agent through whom the British papists communicated with their foreign sympathizers. The abduction or assassination of Elizabeth, the liberation of Mary of Scotland, then a prisoner in England, and the placing the beautiful adulteress upon the throne of Great Britain under Romish tutelage—such was the object of this the last combined effort of the English aristocracy to undo the Reformation.‡ In the service of this plot, Ridolfi, who gave his name to the conspiracy, plied incessantly between London and Rome, Brussels and Madrid.

---

* Froude, *ubi sup.*, p. 1.   † Ibid.
‡ Corresp. de Philippe II., tom. 2, p. 1038.   Froude, Hist. of England. vol. 10, p. 272.

In February, 1570, Pius V. licensed the proposed murder by excommunicating Elizabeth and absolving the lieges of the realm from their allegiance.* This bull—a weapon forged in the armory, not of heaven, but of the Vatican—elicited but a single response on the Continent, that of Philip II., the one crusader who survived in Europe. Maximilian was occupied in hunting up a market for his remaining daughters. France was busy in maturing the massacre of St. Bartholomew; besides, Catharine de' Medici was angling to catch the maiden-queen for one of the French princes. But it behooved Philip, the most orthodox of kings, and the Spanish nation, the most passionately Romanist in the world, to act. Was it not the duty of a monarch who was upholding the cross against the crescent in the Mediterranean, who was burning heresy in the Netherlands, to execute the behest of the vicar of God?

Philip set about the work with alacrity. Numberless interviews were held with Ridolfi;† the Spanish cabinet formally approved the plot;‡ and Chiappino Vitelli, who had travelled post from the Low Countries for the purpose, offered to strike the fatal blow.§

Alva was at once apprized of this resolution, and commanded to give the conspirators all the

<hr />

* Froude, *ubi sup.*, p. 10.   Camden, Annals of the Reign of Queen Elizabeth.   † Froude, *ubi sup.*, p. 250.

‡ Ibid., p. 251, *et seq.* MS., Simancas.

§ MS. Simancas.   Froude, *ubi sup.*, p. 256.

assistance in his power, acting secretly but with decision.*

Many letters had already passed between the duke and the king on this subject. The governor-general had long been looking for some "ford" by which to wade into England;† and, though he lacked confidence in Ridolfi,‡ he promised to stint nothing in the preparations against Elizabeth. Philip had written: "The end proposed is to kill or to capture Elizabeth, to free the queen of Scotland, and to set upon her head the crown of England. I hope that God, whose cause it is, will enlighten and assist us. Be ready to throw six thousand arquebusiers into England, two thousand into Scotland, and two thousand into Ireland the instant the blow is struck."§ To which the devout duke replied: "I highly applaud you for this plot, and cannot help rendering infinite thanks to God for having made me vassal to such a prince."‖

But, alas for ultramontanism, this murderous "practice" was not to prosper. In the autumn of 1571, Cecil, "who had his eyes everywhere," succeeded in unravelling the intricate web of the conspiracy.¶ "The affair is upset," said Alva, "and there's an end of it."** Nevertheless, Philip believed that it was not yet too late. "Angels," wrote

* Correspondance de Philippe II., *ut antea.*
† Froude, Hist. of England, vol. 10, p. 203.
‡ Correspondance de Philippe II., *ubi sup.,* p. 1035.
§ Ibid., p. 1038.   ‖ Ibid., p. 1041.
¶ Froude, *ubi sup.*, pp. 154, 301, *passim.* Burnet, Hume.
** Letter of Alva to Don Juan de Cuniga. MS., Simancas.

he, "will fight for the good cause."* But the astute duke desired to placate the queen whom he could not stab; therefore he favored leaving the angels to fight it out.† Eventually, the king decided to give over the attempt, though not until the failure of several assassins set to do the deed forced even his opaque intellect to see the madness of persistence.‡

While the king and the duke were incubating the plot against Elizabeth, and before their failure in England broke up the nest of the assassins, the prince of Orange was again in motion. William had spent upwards of a twelvemonth in France, doing the Huguenots yeomanly service at La Charité, Roche-de-la-Ville, and Poictiers.§ But though a volunteer in a foreign service, he had been no unconcerned spectator of passing events in the Netherlands. The persecution, the illegal taxes, the conspiracy to murder a neighbor sovereign, on the pretext of a spurious sanctity and the needs of despotism—he saw it all, and felt that duty as well as inclination bade him be at hand to checkmate, if possible, the royal game. The future was indeed but vacancy, but it was vacancy peopled with its million possibilities.

So, in the autumn of 1569, the prince left Count Louis to command the horsemen whom he had led

* Froude. *ubi sup.*, p. 302.
† Letter of Alva to Don Juan, etc., *ubi sup.*
‡ Corresp. de Philippe II., tom. 2, p. 1051.
§ Archives et Correspondance de la Maison d'Orange-Nassau, tom. 3, p. 316, *et seq.*

into France at the end of the disastrous campaign of '58, shook hands with Coligny, passed the pickets of Guise in a peasant's dress, and reached the castle of Dillenburg before the snow fell.*

But the beggar prince came back to no such reception as was wont to be given him when an annual income of two hundred thousand florins† built the portico of his philanthropy. Old friends fell off, and new ones were not easily made. His old debtors, the soldiers, too, began to trouble him.‡ The great ones insulted him with empty protestations of pity. All believed him to be a hopelessly ruined man.

William meant to live down this mistake. He was indeed forlornly broken in fortune; so much so, that he was compelled to give his personal attention to the homeliest details of a straitened domestic economy—he, the mate of emperors, the epicure whose dainty *cuisine* had been the envy of Europe.§ But what then ? His inheritance had been wasted, not in riotous living, as seemed its probable fate at one time, but in the service of the gospel and of liberty. Wasted? Nay, invested—laid up " where neither moth nor rust doth corrupt, and where thieves do not break through nor steal."

○ Archives et Correspondance de la Maison d'Orange-Nassau, tom. 3, p. 322. De Thou, tom. 5, p. 627.

† *Vide* Corresp. de Philippe II., tom. 2, p. 115. Even after the confiscation of his Netherland estates, his income was sixty thousand florins per annum. Wagenaer. Cited in Motley, vol. 2, p. 243, note.   ‡ Archives, etc., *ubi sup.*, p. 355, *et seq.*

§ Motley, vol. 2, p. 327.

All this William bore as a Christian should, without repining, with pious resignation, for he knew that God "doeth all things well." Nevertheless, he remembered the grand cause; and now that he was himself unable to support it unaided, he felt no hesitation in calling on all upon whom he had a claim, to contribute to its wants. This he did in the winter and spring of 1570,* in a series of able papers drawn up with a free pen, and used with great effect by those agents whom he employed in canvassing for funds.†

In one of these, styled the "Harangue," he made this forcible appeal to the reformed: "Our enemies spare neither money nor labor; will you be colder and duller than your foes? Let, then, each church, the feeblest congregation, set an example to others. We read that King Saul, when he would liberate the men of Jabesh from the hands of Nabash, the Ammonite, hewed a yoke of oxen in pieces, and sent them as tokens over all Israel, saying: 'Ye who will not follow Saul and Samuel, with them shall be dealt even as with these oxen. And the fear of the Lord came upon the people, and they came forth, and the men of Jabesh were delivered.' You have here the same warning; look to it, watch well, ye that despise it, lest the wrath of God, which the men of Israel by their speedy obedience escaped, descend upon your heads."‡

At the same time, the prince empowered the re-

* Brandt, vol. 1, p. 285.   Bor., tom. 6, p. 363, *et seq.*
† Ibid.   ‡ Cited in Bor., *ut antea.*

formed preachers of the provinces to make weekly
and monthly collections among their parishioners—
agents the most powerful and successful by reason
of their piety, eloquence, and thorough knowledge
of the disposition and sympathies of the masses.*
The pastors assured their hearers that all sums contributed should be used for the expulsion of Alva,
and the securing of the states in the possession
of their charters and of the evangelical religion.†
They acquitted themselves so zealously that those
who listened to their pleas not only made it a scruple of conscience not to give either nothing or
sparingly, but even esteemed themselves not good
Christians if they did not support the cause with
the most open-handed generosity ; though the richest were the slowest and most stinted in their contributions, and what was gotten came mostly from
the necessitous pockets of the lower and the middle
classes.‡

William made an especial appeal to the body
then called the Anabaptists, as being the most ill-
used of the mediæval sects. In response, one of
their pastors, Peter Boomgard—he deserves that
history should remember his name—collected at
the secret conventicles of his people ten hundred
and sixty guilders, a large sum for those days, and
placed the money in person in the prince's hands,
travelling many leagues at jeopard of his life to do
so. "Take in good part this trifling present from
your servants," said he ; "esteeming your favor to

* Brandt, vol. 1, p. 285.   † Ibid.   ‡ Ibid., p. 206.

be greater than the gift, we do not desire to be repaid, though we are poor withal." "What return,
then, can I make you?" queried William. "If God
bestows on you the government of the provinces,
give us recognition and the protection of the laws,"
was the reply. "That I will," said Orange; "you
and all men." Then he gave Boomgard a receipt
for the money, and also wrote out and signed an
obligation to bear the Anabaptists harmless in the
event of his success.*

By these and kindred means, the patriot exchequer was at least redeemed from bankruptcy. Best
of all, every guilder thus obtained was a prayer as
well as so much silver—a tool of action and a token
of the set determination of the people to be free.

William had wisely resolved to make the northern provinces his next scene of action.† In Holland, Zealand, Friesland, and the rest, the reformed
religion had made greater progress than in the
south; the inhabitants were more persistent; the
spirit of independence was higher. From the nature of the landscape, intersected by navigable
rivers, by canals, and by branches of the sea, men
dreaded less, and were less exposed to the power of
the Spaniard. It seemed a cluster of states fitted
by nature and by art to be the Thermopylæ of
Protestantism.

The prince was in active correspondence with
the chief men of the north. Paul Buys especially,

---

* Brandt, vol. 1, p. 295.
† Bor., tom. 5, p. 280, et seq. Watson, Life of Philip II., p. 165.

the shrewd and patriotic pensionary of Leyden,* sounded for him the current of events, and kept him carefully advised of the ebb and flow of opinion in the states.† Under the very eyes of the ubiquitous "sevenpenny men" of Alva, intrigues were set afoot, and plans were concerted between the exiled seigneur and his domestic allies; and all was so wisely contrived that not a rumor reached the governor-general's suspicious ears. From time to time, covert attempts were made to capture some one or another of the port towns of Holland—now Enchuyzen, and now Flushing; but when, from different causes, these proved abortive, they were quietly laid by till Heaven should be more propitious.

One of these attempts, however, had a different result. In the dusk of a December day in 1570, four men habited as monks of the order of mendicant Gray Friars, craved shelter for the night at the gate of the fortress of Löwenstein. The castle was situated quite on the verge of the isle of Bommel, a narrow but important jut of land shut in between the jaws of the rivers Meuse and Waal; and it commanded the junction of their waters, and also the adjacent cities of Sorcum and Dorcum.‡

Hospitality to the children of the church was always in order in the castles of King Philip, and

---

* A pensionary was the chief municipal officer of the towns of Holland and Zealand.

† Bor., *ubi sup.*, p. 289.

‡ Bentivoglio, lib. 5, p. 87. Cited in Motley, vol. 2, p. 317.

the mendicants were cheerfully admitted; but on being conducted into the presence of the castellan they proved beggars of an unexpected type. "For whom do you hold this fortress?" suddenly inquired one of the intruders, a giant named De Ruyter, and an enthusiastic partisan of William. "For his majesty King Philip, of course," replied the surprised commandant. De Ruyter's response was a pistol-shot. Within ten minutes the four supposed monks were in full possession of the castle.*

An additional number of men, twenty perhaps, were then admitted; and a large reinforcement was expected by De Ruyter, which, detained by an ice storm, failed to reach Löwenstein.† Meantime, the Spanish governor of Bois-le-Duc, apprized of the daring deed, despatched a company of veterans to retake the place. Presently it was escaladed; for how could such a garrison defend walls which hundreds should have manned? But De Ruyter had no idea of surrender. Inch by inch he fought with the stubborn valor of a Cœur-de-Leon; and finally, when pressed back by stress of numbers into the citadel, he stooped to the floor, touched a spark to a train of powder previously strewn over the apartment, and like Samson in the temple of the Philistines, brought the tower down in tumultuous ruin upon himself and his antagonists.‡

Upon deciding to gain a foothold in the north,

* Mendoza, tom. 5, p. 109.
† Ibid., p. 110. Motley, *ubi sup.*, p. 118.
‡ Ibid. Bor., tom. 6, p. 331.

Orange had also resolved, in compliance with the sage advice of the French admiral Coligny, given while the liberator was a sojourner among the Huguenots,[*] as much as might be to transfer hostilities from the land, where he was over-matched by Alva, to the sea, the natural element of the amphibious Hollanders, upon which the *gueux* would be invincible.

At this period the English channel swarmed with corsairs. The prettiest and the fleetest craft afloat were manned and officered by mariners who took the stars for their patrons and the tables of latitude and longitude for a liturgy. At the outset, the privateersmen sailed under letters of marque issued by Condé, with the Huguenot flag nailed to their masthead; and they regarded all papists as legitimate prey.[†] Not a Romish merchant in Europe or the Indies who "went down to the sea in ships," but came to grief. Alva rated the injury annually done by them to Spanish commerce at three hundred thousand ducats.[‡]

Since the advent of the duke, these rovers had been joined by scores of Netherland seamen. Every ruined trader, every outlawed seigneur scraped up the remnant of his fortune, invested it in a vessel, got a commission from Coligny or the queen of Navarre, drummed up a crew on the quays of the

<hr>

[*] Du Maurier, p. 43.

[†] Froude, Hist. Eng., vol. 10, p. 77, *et seq.*

[‡] Gueran de Espes to Philip, August 25, 1568. MS., Simancas.

provincial seaports, and took to privateering against Spain for the double purpose of amassing wealth and avenging wrongs.

In 1570, forty or fifty sail held the coast from the mouth of the Ems to the harbor of Rochelle.* Spanish galleons, freighted with the fragrant spices of the East, with the diamonds of Golconda, with the gold of either Ind, were seized at sight and sold openly in the favorite harbor of the corsairs at Dover.† Sometimes these "beggars of the sea," who asked their alms at the cannon's mouth, made descents upon the Spanish coast, sacking churches and convents, pilfering silver in such amounts that its price was depreciated in the European money-market, and at their wassails drinking success to privateering in wine tapped from monastic casks in the consecrated vessels.‡

For the threefold purpose of reducing the rovers to some degree of order—for, demoralized by the license of such a life, they were not always careful to discriminate between friend and foe in the exercise of their powers—of draining off some portion of their gains into the needy treasury of the good cause, and of employing them against the governor-general, the prince of Orange issued letters of marque to as many as were willing to receive them, and to come under the discipline established for his fleet.§

° Froude, *ubi sup.*, p. 78.   Vandervynckt.   † Ibid.
‡ Froude, vol. 10, p. 240.   MS., Simancas.
§ Bor., tom. 5, p. 289.   Brandt, vol. 1, p. 285.

This code prescribed the strict enforcement of the articles of war; the payment to the prince of a fifth part of all gains; the "providing a chaplain for every ship, so that the pure word of God might be preached to all the seamen;" and the reception of none save "folk of good name and fame,"* to serve as mariners.   Nevertheless, colossal abuses, impossible to be suppressed in an irregular service, hurt the reputation and hampered the usefulness of this infant navy†—the germ of those later puissant fleets which, under the conduct of Van Tromp, swept the sea with brooms lashed to their mast-heads, in token of the haughty supremacy of Holland.

In the utilizing the privateers, in the collection of friendly contributions, and in the maturing a comprehensive scheme of invasion, William spent the years 1570 and 1571.   Meanwhile, Philip's viceroy was proving the prince's unconscious but most efficient ally.   As the term for which he had arranged with the provincial deputies to hold the obnoxious taxes in abeyance verged towards its close, Alva prepared to resume his demand for the tenth and twentieth pennies.   Upon this subject there was incessant wrangling at the council-board, the duke affirming that the states had assented to the imposts, and Viglius, the new tribune of the people, or rather of the monied classes, begging to remind

* Brandt, *ubi sup.*, p. 290.   Bor., *ubi sup.*, p. 324, *et seq.*

† Archives de la Maison d'Orange-Nassau, tom. 4, p. 63.   MS., Simancas.

his highness that the assent had been nullified by the failure of the condition-precedent—the concurrence of all voices.*

This declaration of the learned Frisian always threw Alva into a towering rage, and on one occasion he threatened to chastise a repetition of the statement.† The menace was soon city gossip; every barber, every old woman in Brussels became its publisher.‡ But Viglius was firm for once— guilders were at stake. "I am convinced," said he to the governor-general, "that the king will not condemn me unheard; but at any rate, my gray hairs save me from fear of death."§

On the 31st of July, 1571, Alva decreed the summary collection of the taxes.‖ An unprecedented hubbub was the result. The estates of the respective provinces, the citizens of the great towns, met to protest and to avow their purpose to resist.¶ Holland refused to promulgate the edict.** And when the duke appointed collectors and receivers of the moneys, those designated refused to serve, nor would the magistrates compel them to perform the odious duty. At Amsterdam, the aldermen shifted the work on the burgomasters, and they again upon the aldermen; so that between the two the collection itself went begging.†† In consequence, the city was fined twenty-five thousand

---

* Viglii, Com. dec. Deu., secs. 45, 46.
† Ibid., sec. 28.   ‡ Ibid., sec. 50.   § Ibid., sec. 47.
‖ Ibid., sec. 38.   ¶ Bor., tom. 5, p. 345, *et seq.*
** Ibid. Brandt, vol. 1, p. 290.   †† Brandt, *ubi sup.*

guilders*—an exaction which increased, if possible, the popular rage, and set even the Franciscan monks to railing at Alva as an extortionate tyrant.† The estates of Holland ordered a fast to be observed, and had public prayers offered, "that God would vouchsafe to soften the hard and cruel heart of the duke, to the end that he might hearken to reason and equity."‡

On the 25th of September, 1571, Philip, in compliance with the reiterated requests of Alva—perhaps also because himself not quite pleased with the arrogance of the viceroy, commissioned the duke of Medina Cœli to succeed him.§ However, Alva was bidden to retain the government until the arrival of the new governor, who would not be ready for some months to sail for the provinces.‖

When a rumor of this news got abroad, the hostile spirit of the masses increased apace, and while the duke was yet in Brussels, even began in imagination to celebrate the outgoing of their oppressor.¶ The weak-knees of the councillors, Viglius, Barlaimont, Aerschot, were marvellously stiffened—for there is nothing so contemptible in the eyes of toadies as a falling courtier.

Presently, even Alva's haughty spirit was appalled by the tempestuous wrath of the people. He ordered the tax of ten per cent. to be remitted

---

* Brandt, *ubi sup.*   † Ibid.   ‡ Ibid.
§ Corresp. de Philippe II., tom. 2, p, 1055.
‖ Ibid., p. 1056.
¶ Strada, tom. 2, p. 69.

upon raw materials used in manufactures, and on
four staple articles—wine, beer, corn, and meat.*
But these immunities, which he regarded as crimi-
nally condescending, did not tend to reconcile the
provincials to his illegal and ruinous impost; on the
contrary, they construed the concession into proof
of the duke's inability to enforce the law.

Alva's correspondence with the king began to
teem with complaints—to hint the faults, and to
hesitate dislike of the councillors who had fallen
away from him at this critical moment ;† while the
opposition of the states to the tax was denounced
as being not in the interest of the fisheries, or of
trade, or of manufactures, but from a "fear that in
future they might not be able to dictate the law to
their sovereign."‡

The courtiers at Madrid openly scoffed at the
financial projects of the duke; and Philip felt that
his mission was the extirpation of heresy, not the
suppression of commerce; and he began to be
uneasy lest the trade of the Low Countries should
be hamstrung.§ This uneasiness was increased by
the reports which the Spanish ambassador at Paris
forwarded to him early in 1572, after a personal
visit to Brussels. "Sire," wrote he, "the duke is
the best hated man in Christendom. This whole
people are crying, 'Let him begone, let him begone.'
I do not think it possible to collect the tenth penny

° Bor., tom. 5, p. 345, *et seq.* Viglii, Com., etc.

† Corres. de Philippe II., tom. 2, pp. 1095, 1103, etc.

‡ Ibid., p. 1063.   § Motley, vol. 2, p. 340.

without ruining the states."[*]   Puzzled, undecided, half-hearted, Philip did not give his viceroy's method of finance the cordial support which would have been the stay of an *auto da fé* programme.

Though bereft of sympathy where he most expected it, Alva was far from the surrender of his pet imposts—feeling rather that his honor was staked upon success.   Thus far little or nothing had been harvested by the gleaners of the assessments.   Nettled, and in want of money, he decided, in the spring of 1572, to make a grand levy of the tenth penny in Brussels, convinced that his presence, backed by the men-at-arms in town, would insure the reaping of the tax in the capital, and give him a precedent.[†]

The citizens learned of the duke's intention, and unanimously resolved to cease all traffic.   Every counting-room was closed, every manufactory was locked, every shop was shut; the bakers forbore to bake, the brewers refused to brew, the tapsters would not tap, the butchers did not kill, the farmers' stalls were barred in the market-place, and even the innkeepers closed their doors against all custom.[‡]   Brussels looked plague-stricken.   Want was in every home.   Yet no one thought of submission.   It was a form of passive resistance against which cannon were powerless.

It may seem strange to some that these pennies

[*] Corresp. de Philippe II., *ubi sup.*, p. 1074.
[†] Bor., tom. 6, p. 361.   Brandt.
[‡] Ibid.   Strada, tom. 2, p. 70.   Brandt, vol. 1, p. 295.

should prove such potent revolutionists where martyr-piles and innumerable scaffolds had pleaded vainly. But it should be remembered that events are cumulative. The sufferings endured from the tyranny of Alva, the non-intercourse with England, and, finally, practical confiscation in the guise of taxation, had exasperated the provincials until they were prepared to adopt the most desperate retaliatory measures.

Besides, the most atrocious persecution assails but a class, extends but to a certain number of individuals. There are thousands whom it does not touch, and thousands more who sympathize with the most cruel bigotry. But the tax-gatherer knocks at all doors; imposts such as those of Alva mortgage the right hand of every man's labor; filching from all pockets and emptying all larders, they provoke all to rebel. Cobbett says that civilization comes through the stomach. Yes; but often, as in this instance, civilization gets no farther than the stomach, mistaking the half-way-house for the end of the journey.

When the burghers shut up their shops and warehouses, declaring that they had no goods to sell, and ought therefore to pay no taxes, the governor-general fell "to cursing like a very drab, a scullion." Such presumption, in the capital, under his very eyes, called for chastisement, public, immediate. Alva made out a list of eighteen principal citizens, and sent for Master Carl the hangman. "Here, sirrah," said he, handing his ghastly visitor the names, "see to 't that each and all of these stretch hemp at dawn to-morrow from their own sign-posts. *Cospetto!* I will carry justice to the doors of all."*

Master Carl bowed and withdrew to make ready for this impromptu execution. Don Frederic de Toledo hurried off to get Viglius to sign the death-warrants, arousing the reluctant doctor at midnight for that purpose. At dawn the soldiers were under arms, the hangman stood rope in hand; when suddenly a courier dashed into the city, and reported the capture of Brille, the key-town of the north, by the beggars of the sea—an announcement which untied the knot of the executioner, and postponed the duke's matutinal tragedy.†

* Bor., tom. 6, p. 261. Brandt, *ut antea.*

† Strada, tom. 2, p. 70. *Vide* Meteren, tom. 4, folio 70, and Hoofd, tom. 6, p. 216.

CHAPTER XXXIV.

THE RISING.

In the year 1572, William de Lumey, Count de la Marck, who, since the death of his pot companion Brederode, had been chief of the roysterers—an untamed, ferocious corsair, equally at home in the saddle and on the quarter-deck, according to an ancient Batavian custom wearing his hair and beard unshorn until the death of his cousin Egmont should be avenged*—held the rank of admiral in the outlaw navy of the prince of Orange.† Between the count, the two tenets of whose creed were the flaying of priests and the murder of Spaniards, and the prince, there could be little sympathy; but De la Marck was high in the favor of the privateers-men; and what is it that Gibbon says? "A thrifty statesmanship utilizes all."

The worst of it was, that the buccaneer admiral was not content to confine his depredations to Spanish commerce, but occasionally varied the monotony of such privateering by a pounce upon friendly or neutral vessels; a course which alienated foreign nations, and chilled the sympathy of the Netherlanders themselves, whose trade was impe-

---

° Strada, tom. 2, p. 58.   Meteren, tom. 5, folio 64.   Vander-vynckt, tom. 2, p. 127.

† Ibid.   Grotius, Ann., lib. 2. p. 49.

ded by these piracies.* Indeed, so much offended were the maritime powers, that even Sweden and Denmark returned a rude nay to William's request that his ships might be permitted to enter their ports to victual and repair.† England alone opened her harbors to the buccaneers.

Against this conduct of Great Britain, Alva had long protested. In the winter of 1572, he informed Elizabeth that her continued protection of the privateers would be construed by Philip II. into a declaration of war.‡ As the Netherland trade was of great importance to London, and as the money quarrel between herself and the duke was ripening to an agreement, the queen was desirous to avoid open hostilities with Spain. Accordingly, she issued an order for the expulsion of the corsairs from her ports.§

At this very time De la Marck lay in the straits of Dover with a fleet of twenty-six sail, manned by six hundred mariners.‖ Ejected from the last spot of land in Europe where he might set foot, he yet hoisted sail with seamanlike nonchalance, prepared to scud in whatsoever direction the wind should waft him.¶ On clearing the harbor, he descried a convoy of Spanish traders steering for Antwerp. This was fair game, and the privateers at once gave

* Bor., tom. 5, p. 289.
† Ibid., p. 334, *et seq.* Hoofd, tom. 6, p. 210.
‡ Froude, Hist. of England, vol. 10, p. 373, *et seq.*
§ Ibid., p. 374. Strada, tom. 2, p. 72.
‖ Brandt. vol. 1, p. 295. Compare Motley, vol. 2, p. 354.
¶ Froude. *ubi sup.*

chase, tacking and wearing ship, firing and hallooing up the channel. Two merchantmen were caught and robbed of sixty thousand crowns, the crews being drowned*—all in true corsair style.

After a few days' cruising, the squadron got short of water and provisions; whereupon De la Marck decided to trim his course for North Holland, land, and make a levy on the burghers. On the 1st of April, 1572, he dropped anchor in the mouth of the river Meuse, opposite and within easy eyesight of the town of Brille.† "Ah, ha! yonder are the beggars of the sea," exclaimed the ferryman who plied between Brille and the neighbor town of Maaslandsluis, on sighting the fleet.‡ After landing his passengers, he rowed boldly into the offing to speak the strangers, being himself a patriot. With little difficulty, the admiral prevailed upon this boatman to bear a message to the city magistrates demanding a conference. Rowing back to Brille, he elbowed aside the crowd of questioners who met him at the landing, and hastening to the Stadt-house, where the aldermen were gathered, informed them of the count's demand.§ "How many men do the privateers carry?" queried the city fathers. "Some five thousand in all," was the cool but lying answer.‖ In the face of such a force resistance was not to be thought of. But in order to gain time for flight, two envoys were sent to hold

º La Mothe Fénélon, April 14, 1572. *Dépêches*, vol. 4.

† Bor., tom. 6, p. 365, *et seq.* Hoofd, tom. 6, p. 216, *et seq.*

‡ Ibid.   § Hoofd, tom. 6, p. 218.   ‖ Ibid.

the *gueux* in parley. Meantime, the burghers gathered up their valuables and hurriedly departed.[*]

De la Marck was too impatient to be long cozened; and suspecting treachery, he landed the major part of his old salts, divided them into two parties, and advanced to the assault. The town was quickly taken—the admiral making a bonfire of one gate, and then beating down the charred portal with a battering-ram in the shape of an old mast.[†]

Thus extraordinarily was the first successful siege of the patriots conducted; so rude were the hands which laid the foundation-stone of the Dutch Republic—for this seemingly unimportant event was pregnant with just that result.

Strangest of all, it was an unintentional success. De la Marck meant merely to make a piratical foray upon Brille, revictual, plunder the churches, and ship the ecclesiastical furniture.[‡] It was due to the long-headed intelligence of the Seigneur de Treslong, that the town was definitively held for Orange, he pointing out to the admiral the importance of the place, its impregnability by land, and the advantages certain to accrue from its retention.[§]

But though concluding to remain in Brille, De la Marck was not to be stayed from an assault upon the churches of the place; which were speedily gutted, the images being broken, and the rich ecclesi-

---

[*] Hoofd, tom. 6, p. 218. Bor., tom. 6, p. 366.
[†] Ibid. Motley, vol. 2, p. 354.
[‡] Brandt, vol. 1, p. 295. Bor., *ubi sup.*   [§] Ibid.

astical vestments appropriated by the spoilers, while the murder of thirteen priests who had neglected to escape, crowned the *saturnalia.**

"*No es nada, no es nada*"—"'t is nothing, a mere nothing," said Alva, on hearing the news.† Nevertheless, he dismissed unharmed the butchers and grocers of Brussels, of whom he was about to make an example, and prepared to cope with the beggars of the sea. At heart the duke was uneasy. He knew the importance of the captured town—knew that its possession supplied the *gueux* with what they especially needed, a seaport citadel. He was especially chagrined because the disaster was largely his own fault, for he had drained off the seaboard garrisons, and stationed a host of men-at-arms in Utrecht, in order to dragonnade the burghers of that province into assenting to the taxes—a measure fraught with double mischief, though, to be sure, he had considered the corsairs to be fit only to war upon unarmed merchantmen.

However, it was the time for action, not for unavailing regret. "Brille must be retaken," cried the governor-general; and straightway Count Bossu, who had acted as stadtholder of Holland since William's resignation, was despatched to perform the work.‡ Probably Alva thought that, after all, it would merely be a second edition of the De Ruyter tragedy at the castle of Löwenstein.

° Meteren, tom. 4, folio 72.   Strada, tom. 2, p. 72.

† Motley, vol. 2, p. 356.

‡ Brandt, vol. 1, p. 295.   Bor., Hoofd.

At the head of ten companies of veterans gathered from Utrecht, Bossu made his appearance before Brille quite as soon as the privateersmen were ready to receive him.* Still, a daring defiance was returned to his summons to surrender; though De la Marck, uncertain of the citizens and greatly overmatched, determined to stand strictly on the defensive.†

Brille lay on the island of Voom, just on the southern lip of the mouth of the Meuse, whose navigation it commanded, and the Spaniards crossed to it from the mainland in boats. They were permitted to land unopposed; but scarcely had Bossu unlimbered his cannon, when an artisan of Brille swam, axe in hand, to the sluice of the Nieuland dyke, split it in pieces, and inundated the island.‡ At the same time, De Treslong and Captain Rabal fired and cut adrift the vessels in which their foemen had crossed the river.§

Appalled by the sight of their burning boats, and panic-struck by the rapid rise of the water, Bossu's veterans broke rank and fled wildly along the bank of the slippery canal, raked at every step by the merciless guns of the *gueux* vomiting fire and death from Brille. Many leaped into the turbid river and were drowned; others met death from the cannon-shot; hundreds were slain; and the survivors took their route, through streams and marshes, over New Beyerland to the city of Dordrecht, where

---

* Meteren, Hoofd, *et alii.*   † Meteren.
‡ Hoofd, tom. 6, p, 220. Bor., tom. 6, p. 367.   § Ibid.

they arrived wet, weary, and routed, only to be
denied admittance by the jubilant burghers.*

After the disappearance of the last of his assailants, the admiral repaired to the market-place of
Brille, assembled the townsfolk, most of whom had
returned on the subsidence of their first fear of the
beggars of the sea, by tap of drum, registered their
names, made all swear allegiance to the prince of
Orange as King Philip's legal stadtholder of Holland; and pledged all to defend the place against
Puppet Bossu, and against the duke of Alva, who
pulled the string which set others dancing.†

In the meantime, Bossu, shut out of Dordrecht,
hastened on to Rotterdam with his jaded cohorts.
Here, too, the citizens were reluctant to open their
gates, fearing lest their unwelcome guests should
make too long a tarry, or attempt to collect the
tenth and twentieth pennies, thus far unpaid.‡ But
Bossu's plight was so miserable, he pleaded so hard,
and promised so stoutly to march directly through
the city, that the magistrates gave a reluctant order
for the admission of his soldiers, a corporal's guard
at a time, with unloaded muskets; which terms
Bossu signed and sealed.§

His words, however, were "as false as dicers'
oaths;" for no sooner was the first detachment
within the gate, than assailing and mastering the

○ Brandt, vol. 1, p. 295. Strada, tom. 2, p. 72.

† Strada, tom. 2, pp. 72, 73. Hoofd and Bor., *ubi sup.*

‡ Bor., *ubi sup.*, p. 368. Brandt, *ubi sup.* Hoofd, Meteren.

§ Bor., tom. 6, p. 368.

burgher guard, they admitted the whole force. Led on by Bossu in person, the brutal soldiery at once spread through the town, robbing the traders, violating the women, massacring the burghers — four hundred of whom were quickly murdered.[*]

These events, the capture and successful defence of Brille, and the infamous treachery at Rotterdam, were like sparks dropped in a powder-magazine— the states, previously prepared, exploded with a detonation which shook Philip at Madrid. Treason was felt to be a lesser crime than inhumanity. Even in Brussels, the wits put treason into puns. The beggars of the sea had snatched Brille on All-Fools' day, and as Brille is the Flemish for *spectacles*, a popular couplet was at once struck off:

> "On April Fool's day,
> Duke Alva's spectacles were stolen away."[†]

The streets, too, were placarded with a caricature in which De la Marck was represented stealing the duke's spectacles from off his nose, he all the time muttering his habitual expression when any thing went wrong: "*No es nada, no es nada*"—'t is nothing, 't is nothing.[‡] The jest was made the keener by the fact that the Dutch had a jeering proverb, that when a man was overreached, he was spectacled and snaffled; so that the picture was supposed to signify that Alva's severity was now bridled.[§]

---

[*] Bor., tom. 6, p. 368. Hoofd, tom. 6, p. 220, *seq.* Meteren, tom. 6, folio 66.   [†] Vandervynckt, tom. 2, p. 142.

[‡] Ibid. Strada, tom. 2, p. 72.   [§] Strada, *ubi sup.*

At stormy crises, an after-dinner speech or an epigram will precipitate a revolution. Flushing, a wealthy, populous, and important town on the extreme south point of the island of Walcheren, in the Zealand archipelago, the bulwark of the sea, was the first to hoist the patriot colors.* The place was of vital consequence to Alva, since it commanded the navigation of the Scheldt, as Brille did that of the Meuse, two main arteries of trade. Charles V. had especially advised his son to see to its security; but the duke had drained off the garrison to reinforce the dragonnaders of Utrecht, leaving only eighty superannuated Walloons to guard the town.† These were quickly put *hors du combat* by the patriot burghers, who thereupon sent off to England, to France, to Orange, and to Brille for succor.‡

Ignorant of what had occurred, Alva too late bethought him to look to the safety of this key to the Scheldt. Ten companies of men-at-arms were embarked for Flushing, and Paciotti, the engineer, was sent post across the country to complete a citadel already in process of erection.§ Meantime, De Treslong had arrived with two hundred of the beggars of the sea, volunteers from other quarters had manned the walls, and the town grinned defiance as the belated Spaniards sailed into port. The fleet had hardly cast anchor when the artillery

* Strada, tom, 2, p. 72. Bor., tom. 6, p. 369, *et seq.*
† Watson, Life of Philip II., p. 170.
‡ Bor., *ubi sup.*, p. 370. Brandt, vol. 1, p. 396. Hoofd.
§ Hoofd, tom. 6, p. 222. Bor., *ubi sup.*, p. 369.

belched forth its warning. Surprised at their reception and ignorant of the number of the insurgents, the invaders were panic-struck, and slipping their cables, stood away in disorderly flight for Middleburg, the twin of Flushing.* A few days later, Paciotti, unaware of what had passed, and supposing the Spaniards to be in possession, entered the town. He was seized within an hour after his incoming, and hung by Treslong, who thus avenged his brother, beheaded by Alva in 1558, and secured the place to Orange by making the burghers participants in a deed which all knew the duke would never forgive.†

Thus passed the month of April, 1572. Early in May, Orange sent Jerome von 't Zeraerts to Flushing with a commission as lieutenant-governor of the island of Walcheren.‡ At the same time port after port throughout Holland, Zealand, Utrecht, and Overyssel rose, expelled, or slew the Spaniards, and declared for stadtholder William. On the 4th of May, the fishermen of Terveer, in Zealand, hung out De la Marck's banner§—a scarlet field crossed with ten gold pieces, symbolical of the hated tax.‖ Soon afterwards Enkhuyzen, a chief commercial port of Holland—the Spanish arsenal on the Zuyder Zee—placed its name on the bead-roll of revolted cities.¶

* Hoofd, tom. 6, p. 222. Bor., *ubi sup.*, p. 369.
† Strada, tom. 2, p. 72. Hoofd, tom. 6, p. 225. Bor., Mendoza, *et alii.*   ‡ Bor., *ubi sup.*, p. 371.
§ Ibid. Brandt, vol. 1, p. 296.
‖ Strada, *ubi sup.*, p. 71.
¶ Bor., *ubi sup.* Brandt, *ubi sup.*

Medenblik, Horn, Alkmaar, Oudenwater, Gouda, followed in the footsteps of Enkhuyzen.* When Gouda threw off its shackles, one of the burgomasters, long a satellite of the blood-judges, ran in a panic to the house of a patriot widow, and begged her to conceal him. He was huddled into a cupboard. "Am I safe here?" asked he. "Aye, truly, Master Burgomaster," replied the widow, "for my husband used often to hide in it from you, when you and others sought for him, and the keeper of the prison hath often stood there before him."†

The news of this rising in Holland made all Protestant Great Britain smile and rub its hands. The excitement in London was uncontrollable. A flood of money poured out of the reformed churches, and streamed across the Channel in the shape of powder and guns.‡ The resident exiles at once set out for home, accompanied by hundreds of English volunteers. In Parliament, the rising Puritans clamored for the expulsion of the Spaniards from the states, and their cry was echoed by the authoritative chorus of the bench of bishops, who called upon Elizabeth to declare war and complete the work.§

In the maiden flush of their triumph, the patriots reënacted some of the scenes of the iconomachy; for they esteemed popery to be to Alva what the atmosphere is to human lungs, the medium of

---

* Bor., *ubi sup.*, Brandt, *ubi sup.*, Mendoza, Cabrera.

† Brandt, *ubi sup.*   ‡ Froude, Hist. Eng., vol. 10, p. 376.

§ Froude, *ut antea.*

life. Images were once more demolished, altars were again defaced, monks were everywhere accounted a legitimate prey.* 'T is a sad and bloody chapter; but who set the example? Tyranny sours the oppressor more than the oppressed. Do what they would, not the harshest of the *gueux*, not De la Marck himself could match the atrocious cruelties of the blood-judges.

The burghers of Dort, on wheeling into the ranks of the revolt, made a stipulation honorable alike to their heads and their hearts, and especially remarkable at that passionate era. The agreement was, that they might observe their allegiance to Philip as count of Holland; that they might be secured in the possession of all rights and franchises; that all degrees and conditions of men, whether spiritual or temporal, all monks, nuns, magistrates, officials, should continue in the exercise of their functions free and unmolested; that all goods and estates of the ecclesiastical and civil spheres should be protected; and that the churches of all sects should be left unharmed.† But even in Dort the will was better than the deed; for the monastery of the Augustine friars was soon sacked, while the troopers stabled their horses in the nunnery of the Beguines.‡

In all the emancipated towns new municipal boards, in sympathy with the revolution, were chosen by popular vote, and sworn to obey Philip as

* Brandt, vol. 1, pp. 296, 297.
† Ibid., p. 297. ‡ Ibid.

27*

count or lord paramount, and Orange as his stadtholder—to protect the needy and to judge righteous
judgment.*   Thus the ballot supplemented and
finely guaranteed the rising—gave dignity to passion, and permanence to what might else have been
an ephemeral outbreak.

On the 2d of June, 1572, William's deputy, Diedrich Sonoy, entered Holland.† The prince, still
retaining the fiction of obedience to Philip, reas-
sumed his stadtholderate, and opposed to Alva's
authority that of his concurrent master, recreated
by construction into an ally of the beggars of the
sea; and this legal fable was stoutly held—formed,
indeed, the basis of the provisional government
until the provinces declared their independance at
a later day.‡

The tolerant wisdom of the liberator is most
clearly seen in the glass of his instructions to Sonoy.
"First of all," said he, "use your utmost power to
deliver the lieges of Holland from Spanish servitude, restoring always the ancient charters. Take
care, farther, that the word of God be freely preached within our lines, and that the religion conformable to that word be tolerated and published if so be
any, the meanest, would have it so. Yet by no
means suffer the Romanists to be prejudiced for
their faith's sake; secure them freely in their worship, nor withdraw your protection from them, unless the public safety warrants, and when so directed

---

° Bor., tom. 6, p. 375.   † Ibid.
‡ Motley, vol. 2, p. 368.

by me, with the consent of the local authorities."*
Such was Protestantism's initial policy.

Thus at last, on that bleak isthmus, the vivifying
light of freedom dawned, to stream for many years
upon struggling and yet half-expiring humanity in
Europe. The immediate cause of the beneficent
revolt seemed scarcely adequate to the result.
"Many times," says Strada, "did William cast the
dice in the hope to win a commonwealth, yet never
with success until the occasion of the tribute."†
And the bishop of Namur wrote Margaret of Parma:
"The tenth and twentieth pennies are the price with
which the prince of Orange hath purchased the
maritime provinces."‡ Neither the Jesuit nor the
prelate remembered that the taxes were but the
nurse of the infant commonwealth. Its mother was
the Reformation, its father, God.

---

* Bor., *ubi sup.*, *et seq.* Brandt, vol. 1, p. 298.
† Strada, tom. 2, p. 71. ‡ Ibid., p. 73.

CHAPTER XXXV.

TRIUMPHS ON THIS SIDE AND ON THAT.

At this hour, when the finger on the dial of the Netherland clock was pointing to the high noon of opportunity, the Nassaus were up and doing—William in Germany, focusing coalitions, collecting moneys, enrolling troops, manipulating the revolted states, dictator of the insurrection; Count Louis at the court of France, cementing a cordial alliance with Charles IX., as he fondly dreamed, but in reality the dupe of the masked plotters of St. Bartholomew.

Paris had become the puzzle of Europe. The politics of Catharine de' Medici were a hieroglyphic of which the astutest diplomats could make no sense, read it which way they would. The queen-mother seemed playing at political see-saw. At one moment "that devilish woman," as Walsingham, the English ambassador at Paris, styled her in his correspondence with Cecil,* courted the Guises and coquetted with Philip; at the next, she was caressing Coligny, and proclaiming the reëstablishment of the *entente cordiale.* We understand it all now, but it is wisdom after the event.

Since the dawn of the Reformation, the Protestants and the ultramontanists had been at deadly

* Froude, Hist. Eng., vol. 10, pp. 353, 354.

feud in France : those agonizing to obtain the right
legally to worship God ; these absolute in their determination to reclose the Bible and gag the Huguenots.* For fifty years success had oscillated
between the rival camps ; though when the Protestants had been triumphant, the perfidy of the court
had always robbed them of the fruits of victory.†
Recently, reform had seemed at its last gasp—quite
as death-stricken in France as in the Low Countries. Condé had fallen on the plains of Jarnac.‡
Coligny had been frightfully routed at Moncontour.
Nevertheless, the unconquerable soldier was again
in the saddle ere the lapse of half a twelvemonth—
in the saddle, and complete victor at Arnay-le-Duc.§
" 'T is hopeless," said Catharine ; " we must do by
artifice what it is impossible to achieve by means
of war."‖ A peace was negotiated—or what had
the look of a righteous and permanent peace ; for
an amnesty buried the past, religion was left free,
and both parties were declared equal before the law.¶

Christendom laughed at these terms. The *quid
nuncs* pronounced them a mere Medician makeshift, certain to be broken, like half-a-dozen previous treaties of a kindred scope, when they had
served Catharine's turn. And so the Huguenots
believed. In consequence, they avoided the capital—

---

* Hist. of the Huguenots, chap. 10, *et seq.*, *passim.* American
Tract Society, New York, 1866. † Ibid.

‡ Davila, liv. 4, p. 470. La Noné, p. 659.

§ De Thou, liv. 46, tom. 5, p. 638, *et seq.*

‖ Davila, liv. 5, p. 578.

¶ Vie de Coligny, p. 383. Hist. of the Huguenots, pp. 334, 335.

the queen of Navarre, the Bourbon princes, and Coligny making their headquarters within the stout walls of Rochelle.*

It was essential to the success of the court plan, that this suspicion should be disarmed, that these apprehensions should be laid asleep, that the victims should be coaxed to Paris. Little by little, man by man, by a series of master-strokes worthy of that diplomacy which declared that " the science of reigning was the science of lying," the crafty Florentine succeeded in petting, in cajoling, and in marrying the Huguenots into confidence.†

Indeed, Catharine schemed so cunningly that Europe at large was hoodwinked. A match was pending between Elizabeth and the duc d'Alençon, which Philip regarded as indicative of the dominance of the Protestant interest at the court of France.‡ Even the pope was duped; and the prospect of a marriage between an excommunicated heretic and a son of holy church set him entreating and threatening by turns; for in his eyes heresy was the only crime, the recognition of St. Peter's supremacy the single virtue. He offered to make Charles IX. " general of the holy league against the infidels" and "emperor of Constantinople," if he would break off the marital negotiations with Elizabeth; " in return for which," wrote Sir Thomas

---

* Vie de Coligny, p. 385. De Thou, liv. 47.

† Hist. of the Huguenots, chap. 24, p. 336, *passim.*

‡ Froude, vol. 10, pp. 208, 353, etc. *Vide* Cor. de Philippe II., tom. 2. Strada, tom. 2, p. 73.

Smith to Cecil, "Charles ought to make his holiness caliph of Bagdad—*summum pontificem Babyloniæ.*"[*]

In the meantime, the Huguenots were in high favor at Paris. In the spring of 1572, the Admiral, Jean d'Albrét, Henry of Navarre whose nuptials were to be the herald of the tragedy, and young Condé—the *élite* of the party, were in town, forming for happy Catharine that collection of enemies' heads on a single neck for which the Roman tyrant sighed, that he might strike off all at one blow.

Coligny seemed the special pet of the whole court. "There are no Egmonts in France," was the reply which the prudent chieftain had returned to an invitation to visit Paris a little back.[†] Now, however, even his caution had been cajoled, and he was the most frequent of visitors at the Louvre. But the great soldier had a purpose: he was bent upon the formation of an aggressive league between England, France, and the Protestant states of Germany against Philip II., and in aid of the prince of Orange and staggering reform upon the Continent.[‡]

Instigated by Catharine, Charles pretended to come into all these plans. "Philip," said he, "is the hereditary foeman of the Valois dynasty, the murderer of my sister Isabella; and as for Alva, 't is well to find employment for him and for the restless spirits in our own dominions at the same time, by sending an army into the Low Countries

[*] Froude, vol. 10, p. 355.   [†] Strada, tom. 2, p. 73.
[‡] De Thou, liv. 51, tom. 6, p. 342, *et seq.* Davila, Ranke, *et alii.*

to assist our cousin Orange: and you, admiral, shall lead our men-at-arms."[*]

Coligny at once began recruiting.[†] At the same time he introduced his friend and ally, Louis Nassau, to the king. Charles received him graciously, gave him repeated audiences, promised to furnish William with a subsidy of two hundred thousand crowns, granted Louis himself permission to make an unlimited levy of troops in France,[‡] and played his part to such perfection that *madame la mére* was all smiles and satisfaction.

Count Louis was in ecstasies; Coligny was sanguine; Elizabeth's envoy, Walsingham, did his utmost to forward the pending international marriage; and the sagacity of Orange was for once at fault, for he too believed implicitly in the good faith of the Valois alliance—why should he not, since his coreligionist, the admiral, and his own brother were at its head?

Both Coligny and Nassau considered the early possession of a fortified town in the frontier provinces essential to the success of the French invasion of the Netherlands; essential also to the welfare of the expedition which William was about to set afoot. Such a stronghold Count Louis undertook to capture; and Mons, the strong and populous capital of Hainault, was the place on which he fixed his eye.

---

[*] De Thou, liv. 51, tom. 6, p. 342, *et seq.* Davila, Ranke, *et alii.*
[†] Strada, tom. 2, p. 73.
[‡] De Thou, tom. 6, liv. 50, pp. 279, 280, *et seq.*

With the connivance of Charles IX., who promised him succor in case of need,[*] and assisted by La Noué, De Genlis, and others of the Huguenot chiefs, Nassau secretly but rapidly enrolled five hundred light dragoons and a thousand musketeers. Then, leaving his allies to recruit a larger force to follow him, he on the 23d of May, 1572, dashed across the confines of France with these few partisans, and arrived in the vicinity of Mons in the edge of the evening.[†] In a deep wood just at hand they bivouacked; while a dozen of the shrewdest and trustiest of the band pushed boldly into the town, disguised as wine merchants, for the purpose of communicating with those of the citizens who were patriots, and devising some plan for the opening of the city gates to their comrades. They entered the first hostelry they reached; ordered a good supper; opened a chat with their host; inquired the earliest hour at which the portcullis was lowered; learned that the port-warden might be bribed to unlock it at almost any time; informed the landlord, in explanation of the query, that they had some casks of wine without which they wished to bring into town bright and early; paid their reckoning; chucked the pretty barmaid under the chin, and went their way.[‡]

A few hours later, they went to the port-warden, repeated their story, persuaded him to let down the

---

[*] Hoofd, tom. 6, p. 251. Bor., tom. 6, p. 397.

[†] Meteren, folio 71. Hoofd, *ubi sup.*, p. 237.

[‡] Bentivoglio, lib. 6, p. 95, *et seq.* Mendoza, tom. 5, p. 121.

portcullis, and when this was done struck the poor wretch dead; while Count Louis, who had secreted fifty horsemen under the city walls in preparation for this event, galloped madly into Mons, shouting, "Liberty! The prince is coming! Down with Alva!"*

The gallant soldier wellnigh lost his prize ere it was secured. On quitting the bivouac with his fifty troopers, he had ordered the rest of the band to march Mons-ward with all speed; yet it was now sunrise, and not one of the partisans had come into town. Two or three score of men might surprise, but could not hold an unwilling city. Already the hum of angry opposition was heard. Fearful of disaster in the midst of success, Nassau rode furiously out in search of the missing men-at-arms. He found them wandering in the forests; but quickly conducted them out of the labyrinth, and again reached Mons, just as the burgher guard began to raise the drawbridge. A Huguenot cavalier, Guitoy de Chaumont, with ready gallantry, spurred his steed upon it, and brought it to the ground; whereupon the partisans rode into town with wild huzzas, and Mons was won.†

In the gray of the morning the astonished burghers were summoned to the market-place by the tolling of the great bell. Here they were addressed by De Genlis and by Count Louis. The Huguenot

---

* Bentivoglio, lib. 6, p. 95, *et seq.* Mendoza, tom. 5, p. 121. De Thou, tom. 6, liv. 51, p. 499.

† De Thou, Mendoza, Bentivoglio, *ut antea.*

assured his auditors that the French were present not as conquerors, but as allies of the prince.* Nassau proclaimed his intention to be to hold the town, not against Philip II., but in the interest of William of Orange, and to secure the defeat of Alva.†

The magistrates looked doubtful, for they feared the vengeance of the governor-general, and, after the custom of the world, held it better to be knaves and gain by it, than to be honest *gratis*. But the citizens were enthusiastic—many of the wealthiest of the manufacturers offering to raise and equip citizen-companies at their own expense for the defence of the place against the inevitable onset of the Spaniard.‡

Meantime, how went affairs at Brussels? Recent events had taken Alva completely by surprise. He had been petitioning for leave to retire from his government. According to late despatches from Madrid, his successor was already hastening to relieve him. He had believed rebellion buried in the graves of Horn and Egmont, smothered in the mud at Jemmingen, dead on those plains which had witnessed the discomfiture of Orange. In the citadel at Antwerp loomed the statue erected by himself to himself as the conqueror and pacificator of the Low Countries. And now the Netherlands were not conquered; the great marts of trade were nests of maddened hornets; the maritime provinces

* Motley, vol. 2, p. 371. *Vide* Bor., tom. 6, p. 377.
† Ibid.   ‡ Motley, *ubi sup.*

were in open revolt; the Huguenots, led by Louis Nassau—at that very moment playing at tennis in Paris,* according to his spies—were in a stronghold within half a day's jaunt of his capital. The news, too, came in successive shocks—that from the north but twenty-four hours earlier than that from the French border.† The taking of Brille had somewhat prepared him for the storm from the sea; but the land-wind from Mons was entirely unexpected.‡ "He tore his beard for spite," says one who saw and spoke to him at the time; "he seemed to despair that things would any more succeed as they had done."§ Against Catharine de' Medici the duke was especially bitter. "Aye, aye," muttered he, "this Florentine has played me false; but 't will not be long ere, instead of Tuscan lilies, she shall lie on Spanish thorns."‖

But it was not in Alva's nature long to despond. Now, after the first bewilderment, his courage rose with the occasion. War—what was it but his element? For some time, however, he could not decide whether to begin the reconquest of the states in Holland or in Hainault. Finally, he concluded to lay siege to Mons, and postpone the northern campaign, because Mons, held by the Huguenots, meant the key of the frontier in foreign hands. He saw, too, that the city might be easily

---

* Bentivoglio, Bor., Hoofd, et alii.
† Mendoza, tom. 5, p. 120; tom. 6, p. 122.
‡ Strada, tom. 2, p. 73.   § Vide Froude, vol. 10, p. 377.
‖ Meteren, folio 71, tom. 4.   Hoofd, tom. 6, p. 238.

furnished with supplies either by Charles IX., who seemed now actually bent on war with Spain, or by the prince of Orange. Delay here might insure the permanent planting of the foe in the heart of the states—Holland was but an extremity.[*]

In pursuance of this plan, he left the revolted towns to enjoy their freedom for a while, drew off the garrisons from Rotterdam and Delft-haven, and concentrated his scattered legions at several points contiguous to Mons, retaining his hold upon but two of the northern cities, both places of strategic importance—Amsterdam, the commercial capital of Holland, and Middleburg, on the island of Walcheren.[†]

On the 10th of June, 1572, while Alva was busy in these preparations for the siege of Mons, his successor, the duke of Medina Cœli, sailed into the mouth of the Scheldt.[‡] He brought with him a fleet of forty sail, twenty-five hundred fresh veterans, and countless chests of bullion.[§] When he embarked, the news of the revolt had not reached Spain; he was therefore wholly unsuspicious of the changed face of affairs. The squadron drifted gayly up the river, passing directly under the guns of Flushing, when, in an instant, a terrific broadside from the town sunk half the fleet.[||] Then, with a frightful yell, the beggars of the sea pounced on their vic-

* Watson, p. 182, *seq.*
† Brandt, vol. 1, p. 299. Bor., Hoofd.
‡ Meteren, tom. 4, folio 65. Mendoza, tom. 6, p. 127, *seq.*
§ Ibid. || Ibid.

tims, seized half a million crowns in gold and jewels, and took a thousand prisoners,[*] all of whom were drowned, in order to force Alva to a more humane mode of warfare, since he was wont to hang whatever patriots fell into his clutches.[†]

From this wholesale slaughter, Medina Cœli managed to escape; but he entered Brussels, a few days afterwards, with much less ceremony than he had expected.[‡] Of course, a transfer of the government at such an hour was not to be thought of, especially on the heels of this disaster. The new governor suspended his commission by his own act, and wrote to request Philip to sign his immediate recall, offering, meanwhile, to serve in any capacity under his highness of Alva. "Nay," retorted the duke, "you shall be treated like myself."[§] But this show of courtesy was all *ex officio.* 'T was not long before the two began to backbite and curse each other like a couple of pickpockets. And when, a few months later, the king gave Medina Cœli leave to retire, he left Brussels without so much as giving Alva an empty *good-night.*[∥]

Alva was just now so hard pressed that he held out the olive-branch to the insurgent provinces. On the 24th of June, 1572, he summoned the estates of Holland to meet on the 15th of July at the Hague, appending to the call a formal agreement to abol-

---

[*] Meteren, tom. 4, folio 65. Mendoza, tom. 6, p. 127, *seq.* Hoofd, tom. 6, p. 239, *seq.*   [†] Ibid.

[‡] Meteren, *ubi sup.*, folio 66. Archives de la Maison d'Orange-Nassau, tom. 3, p. 440.

[§] Meteren, tom. 4, folio 74. Bor., 6, p. 393.   [∥] Ibid.

ish the obnoxious pennies, provided the Netherlands would vote him an annual supply of two millions of florins.*

This was, in the duke, an act of extraordinary
complacence; but it came too late. The estates
did indeed assemble, but in obedience to a request
from Orange, not from Alva, and at Dort, not at
the Hague.† As the obedience and the place were
different, so also was the purpose of the deputies.
They met in the interest of William, and to declare
Alva the enemy of the common weal. The prince
was proclaimed stadtholder of Holland, Zealand,
and Friesland, legally appointed by Philip II. of
Spain, and count of Holland; and never removed
by any competent authority. The duke was denounced as a usurper in the states, as a traitor to
the king at Madrid.‡ And when William's representative, St. Aldegonde, appeared before the congress and appealed for funds, exclaiming, " Arouse
ye, awaken your own zeal and that of your sister
cities; seize Opportunity by the locks, for she never
looked fairer than she does to-day,"§ the enthusiasm was unbounded. Two hundred thousand guilders were voted on the instant to meet the expenses
of the pending contest, and five hundred thousand
more were granted to defray the cost of the prince's
projected expedition into the middle states.‖ "Truly," wrote Alva to the king, on hearing of this action,

---

* Bor., *ubi sup.*, p. 378, *et seq.* Hoofd, tom. 6, p. 242.
† Ibid. ‡ Ibid. § Hoofd, tom. 7, p. 248, *et seq.*
‖ Ibid., p. 350. Bor., tom. 6, p. 388.

" it drives me mad to see the difficulty with which
your majesty is furnished with supplies, and the liberality with which these folk place their fortunes,
yea, their lives, at the disposal of this rebel."*

"As to religion," said St. Aldegonde in one of
his speeches at the Dort congress, "the desire of
the prince is, that liberty of conscience be allowed
alike to the Romanists and to those of the evangelical faith; and that each party be permitted to
enjoy its churches and properties secure under an
equal law, provided no disaffection to the new *régime*
be shown."† And this too was freely voted by the
congress.‡

At the same time, De la Marck was confirmed
as admiral on appearing before the deputies and
exhibiting William's commission. But he was especially instructed " to protect the papists and their
clergy in future, and to guarantee them in the free
exercise of their worship, under pain of death to
their disturbers "§—instructions which he swore to
observe,‖ while meaning all the time to nullify them
in his own conduct, for which he was one day to be
drummed out of the Dutch service.

In all these doings the deputies were careful to
retain Philip's name, as if he were the inspiration
and the end of all—a necessary fiction until the
states grew to the stature of a declaration of independence.   The make-believe was like a baby

---

* Corresp. de Philippe II., tom. 2, p. 1198.
† Brandt, vol. 1, p. 298.   Bor., *ubi sup.*
‡ Ibid.   § Ibid.   ‖ Ibid.

creeping before it walks. Nevertheless, the estates clothed the prince with powers commensurate with those of a Roman dictator*—a pregnant fact behind the fable. The only agreement exacted from him was the mutual pledge that neither would treat with the king without the full assent and coöperation of the other.† Indeed, William himself esteemed his powers too large, and he imposed limits upon his own authority in an act supplementary to the proceedings of the congress of Dort‡—one of the few instances in history of a self-abnegating statesmanship.

Having thus taken counsel together and determined what to do, the deputies adjourned. The people received them with open arms. The moneys they had voted seemed about to be raised by spontaneous contributions. The clergy opened their purse-strings. The mechanic guilds voluntarily taxed themselves. The women stripped off their costliest jewels and sacrificed their daintiest luxuries. Old families melted down their plate. All appeared to be determined, rather than pay the tenth to Alva, to give William the whole.§

While these events were transpiring in the north, the duke was pressing the siege of Mons. Frederic de Toledo and Chiappino Vitelli, with five thousand men, had been sent some time before to begin the investment;‖ and Alva himself lingered but to col-

---

* Motley, vol. 2, p. 381.   † Ibid. Bor., tom. 6, p. 388.
‡ Motley, *ubi sup.*   § Grotius, Mem., tom. 2, p. 58.
‖ Meteren, tom. 4, folios 71, 72. Bor., *ubi sup.*, p. 384.

lect large reinforcements before following them to the camp.*

Count Louis was in excellent spirits. Within three days after the surprise of Mons, two thousand foot had joined him, and ere the end of May twenty-five hundred volunteers more were at his side;† led too by the famous Montgomery, whose stout lance had unhorsed and unwittingly slain King Henry II., some thirteen years before, at the Paris tournament. Farther reinforcements too were hastening up, and De Genlis had already posted off to Paris to conduct to Mons those confederates whom Charles IX. had promised, and Coligny was enlisting along the border.‡ As for funds, Nassau was in no pressing want, having seized and confiscated large quantities of plate and jewelry and precious trinkets, which the neighboring ecclesiastics had sent into town for safe-keeping in these troublous times, just previous to the incoming of the spoiler.§

Don Frederic, therefore, found no cowed opponent, no unknightly foe, on pitching his camp beneath the walls of Mons, the Huguenots conceiving it a punctilio of honor to give the Spaniards proof of their valor before permitting themselves to be cooped up within the beleagured works. Every thing the assailants got was paid for in the currency of good hard blows; nor did Don Frederic

---

○ Meteren, tom. 4, folios 71, 72. Bor., *ubi sup.*, p. 384.

† Hoofd, tom. 6, p. 238.

‡ Ibid., p. 251. Bor., tom. 6, p. 397. Strada, tom. 2. p. 79.

§ Bor., *ubi sup.*, p. 378. Mendoza, tom. 5, p. 120, *et seq.*, *et alii.*

succeed in planting his banner in the belfry of the Bethlehem cloister—a strategic point quite beneath the bastions of the city—until two assaults had given Count Louis a largess.[*]

Meantime, De Genlis, having made his levies with all haste, was on the march. Rumor gave him a force ten thousand strong; but fact, more prosaic, reduced the number to thirty-two hundred foot and a thousand horse.[†] Both Coligny and Nassau instructed him to use the utmost caution in his advance, and by no means to attempt to throw reinforcements into Mons until he had effected a junction with Orange, then about to cross the Rhine.[‡]

In the teeth of this warning, the vain and over-confident cavalier, impatient of delay, and jealous of a partner who must share, if he did not monopolize, the honor of delivering the besieged, determined to force an immediate passage through the Spanish ranks.[§] Toledo and Vitelli were nothing loath to fight—nay, they met De Genlis on a circular plain, girt with coppices and forests, and dotted with farm-houses, at some distance from the gates of Mons;[‖] and charging with fiery valor, surprised and routed the Huguenots almost as soon as their presence was discovered.[¶] In this dashing affair, the Spaniards lost but thirty men, the French

[*] Strada, *ubi sup.*, p. 74.   [†] De Thou, lib. 54, cap. 9.
[‡] Ibid. Bentivoglio, tom. 5, p. 102.
[§] Strada, tom. 2, p. 74. Bentivoglio and De Thou, *ut antea.*
[‖] Ibid. Motley, vol. 2, p. 383.
[¶] Strada, *ubi sup.* Bentivoglio, *ubi sup.* Hoofd, tom. 6, p. 251.

twelve hundred slain outright, besides as many more murdered by the unfriendly peasants of the vicinage.* De Genlis himself was taken, sent to the citadel of Antwerp, and, some months later, secretly strangled by the duke of Alva, who gave out that his victim died a natural death.†

Don Frederic, whose name grew famous from this field, returned to camp with flying colors, spent the day in warlike pomp, and gave public thanks to St. Leucadia, patroness of Alva's house.‡ The duke himself was as elated as his son; and, as haughty in ostentation as in action, he despatched a special courier to congratulate his majesty upon the victory, that both Philip's ears and Spain might be filled with the good news.§

On the 27th of August, a few days after De Genlis' rout, Alva arrived in the camp of the besiegers, bringing with him ten thousand five hundred cavalry and eleven new-raised regiments of German infantry‖—a formidable array. The wily soldier was well aware that Count Louis looked for succor both from Coligny and the prince. His first care, therefore, was so to fortify himself that his position should be equally impregnable against Nassau's sallies and exterior assailants; and this task he accomplished with admirable skill.¶ Then

* Strada, *ubi sup*. Bentivoglio, *ubi sup*. Hoofd, tom. 6, p. 251. Mendoza, tom. 6, p. 139.

† Corresp. de Philippe II. tom. 2, p. 1283.

‡ Strada, *ubi sup*.   § Ibid.

‖ Mendoza, Davies. Hist. of Holland, vol. 1, p. 588.

¶ Strada, tom. 2, p. 76. Mendoza.

he began to press the siege, erecting new batteries, mining, assaulting, harassing—putting in practice all the arts then known to war, in which he was the most thorough and pedantic professor since the days of Demetrius Poliarcetes, besieger of cities.

The defenders of Mons met these efforts with equal vigor and with answering prudence. Count Louis seemed endowed with prescience, and his indefatigable activity was ably seconded by La Noué, *bras de fer*, a brilliant Huguenot, who had won his fame in the civil wars of France.*

But what added tenfold energy to the defence was a rumor that the prince of Orange was advancing to the rescue. It was indeed so. William, after four years of weary and embarrassed waiting, had at last succeeded in recruiting another army, and he was now again to enter the arena for God and liberty.

Early in July, 1572, he passed the Rhine with fourteen thousand foot and seven thousand horse, Germans, and three thousand Netherlanders.† On the 23d of July, he stormed the city of Ruremonde; whereupon the mercenaries fell to plundering the citizens and murdering the monks.‡ William was incensed by this deed, but, unhappily, he was so deeply in debt to the army as to be unable sharply to curb the offenders. His poverty killed discipline. Nevertheless, he exhibited his wish by issuing a

* Mendoza, Watson, *et alii.*
† Bor., tom. 6, p. 398. Compare Strada, *ubi sup.*, p. 78.
‡ Hoofd, tom. 7, p. 259, *et seq.* Brandt, vol. 1, p. 299.

placard forbidding the ill-treatment of ecclesiastics and decreeing the toleration of all sects.*

Mark the contrast. The hirelings on both sides
were equally unprincipled, fought alike for what
they could get in the martial market—as foreigners
in an indifferent quarrel. Stabbers by trade, they
were always panting to cry havoc. Yet William
strained his authority to check license, protecting
even the arch-heresy of Rome; while Alva just as
sedulously strove to make his barbarians more barbarous, commanding them to call rape to the aid of
robbery, and murder to the aid of rape.†

It was at Ruremonde that the prince was intercepted by the deputies who brought him the supplies voted by the congress of Dort‡—very welcome
moneys, for the mercenaries were already demanding their pay, refusing to budge until they got it.§
It was late in August when William passed through
Ruremonde *en route* to Mons. He advanced with
jubilant step. Never had the horizon looked so
bright. Holland was in open revolt; England was
a *sub rosa* ally; the Belgic provinces were at least
not hostile, willing to side with the victor; France
had pronounced in his favor; Coligny only awaited
the consummation of Navarre's marriage with Margaret de Valois to take the field—in such a sky
who could see a cloud?

Alas, William, "some trust in chariots and some

---

* Hoofd, tom. 7, 259, *et seq.* Brandt, vol. 1, p. 299. Bor.,
tom. 6, p. 399.   † Motley, vol. 2, p. 385.

‡ Brandt, vol. 1, p. 299. Bor.   . § Motley, *ubi sup.*, p. 386.

in horses;" "now on whom dost thou trust?"* For a moment the statesman-soldier did not rely on God—God, more certain than Elizabeth, truer than false France.

As he trod on, the way seemed smooth. Nevelle, Diest, Sichem, Tillemont—town after town submitted to him, either out of fear or love.† Unfriendly Brussels shut him out, and Louvaine paid sixteen thousand crowns for an exemption from assault;‡ but Mechlin welcomed him with such cordial good-will that Alva laid up a day of wrath against the unhappy citizens.§

Making but brief halts, the prince pushed forward into Hainault. In the beginning of September, he came in sight of Mons,‖ the immediate objective point of his long march. But between him and Count Louis loomed Alva, and he marvelled at the cunning position of the beleaguerer, no less strong for keeping in and mastering the garrison, than impregnable to the assaults of those who should come to their relief.¶

One evening, while reconnoitring preparatory to an attack upon Alva's intrenchments, William beheld the Spanish camp all aglow with bonfires, while hilarious shouts, volleys of musketry, the rub-a-dub of drums, and the blare of trumpets made night hideous with blatant noise. Somewhat surprised at this uproar, which seemed like a resort to

---

* 2 Kings 18 : 20 ; Psa. 20 : 7. † Strada, tom. 2, p. 75.
‡ Ibid. § Corresp. de Philippe II., tom. 2, p. 1156.
‖ Strada, tom. 2, p. 76. Mendoza, Bor. ¶ Strada, ubi sup.

Chinese tactics, he sent out spies to learn the cause of the jubilation. The wild rejoicings of his foemen were not a masquerade; the prince's pickets brought him back news of the massacre of St. Bartholomew!*

The French court had at last thrown off the mask, so that the world could read the features of its policy. The victims had been collected in the shambles of the capital and petted into a feeling of security, and were awaiting slaughter. "*Que voulez-vous?*—What would you?" lisped the queen-mother; "after the blood-letting, a little water will wash the smeared pavements. All will pass as the last act of the civil war."†

So, on the eve of the saint's day, after long premeditation, the deed was done—in a panic, but thoroughly. The bars of hell's gates were broken, and the devils were loose. The mob of Paris lapped up Huguenot blood from every gutter. Throughout the realm, murder ran side by side with fanaticism, that striking where this said, "Stab." Coligny, Teligny, Rochefoucault, Lavardin, and seventy thousand more,‡ the bravest gentlemen, the best citizens of France, lay dead. The brain seemed to have been scooped out of the skull, the strong right hand appeared to have been lopped from the body of French Protestantism.§

---

* Strada, *ubi sup.*　† Martin, Histoire de France, vol. 9, *in loco.*

‡ The number slain has been variously computed at from 25,000 all the way up to 100,000. *Vide* De Thou, tom. 6, lib. 2, p. 430. Meteren, tom. 4, folio 74, *et alii.*

§ *Vide* Hist. of the Huguenots, chap. 25, *passim.*

At Rome, the unlooked-for good news was welcomed with unparalleled rejoicing. The cannon thundered from St. Angelo; honorary medals were struck to commemorate the deed; a day of public thanksgiving was set apart; the holy father went in person to render thanks to God, the just Avenger, in the great church of St. Louis; a bull was sent out which promised extraordinary indulgences to all who should pray heaven and the saints to bless Charles IX. and the devout butchers of his realm.*

But not in the circle of the saints itself could Philip's hilarity be matched. "Word reached us on the 7th of September of the doings on St. Bartholomew's day," wrote St. Goard, the French envoy at Madrid, to Charles IX. "The king, on receiving the intelligence, showed, contrary to his usual custom, so much gayety that he seemed more delighted than with all the good fortune he had ever known before. He called all his familiars about him, in order to assure them that your majesty was his good brother, and that no one else deserved the title of Most Christian. So, too, the next morning, when I came into his presence, he began to laugh."† Certainly, it was laughable. He had been regarding Charles as a covert foe, as an ally of the enemies of holy church; and he had turned out to be a brother butcher of heretics. Eager to aid the work of pious murder, and per-

---

○ Strada, tom. 2, p. 76. Esprit de la Ligne, vol. 2, p. 65.

† Van Prinst. Cited in Motley, vol. 2, p. 390.

haps a trifle jealous of the French king's laurels, Philip wrote Alva: "I desire that you kill every Huguenot you catch. The sooner these noxious plants are extirpated, the less fear is there of another crop."*

In Great Britain, the first shock of astonishment which the news caused was quickly succeeded by an outburst of indignation. Nothing but the presence of Cecil in London prevented the citizens from meting out "Paris justice" to every papist on whom they could lay hands.† The court went into mourning; and when the French ambassador, Le Mothe Fénélon, called upon the queen to present his master's letter of extenuation, Elizabeth received him in deep black, heard him with cold civility, and declared that the marital-alliance project was "off."‡

On the north side of the Tweed, the popular rage ran higher than it did in England. John Knox, no longer able to walk unsupported, but still Sunday after Sunday dragging his frail body to the church, and there with keen political sagacity interpreting out of the Bible the Scotland of his own day—Knox lifted up his voice, "like ten thousand trumpets," in denunciation of the "Paris matins."§

The apologists of the massacre affirmed that Coligny and his friends were plotting regicide—that they were slain by Charles in self-defence.‖ Con-

---

* Bulletins de l'Acad. Roy. de Belg.   Cited in Motley, *ut antea.*
† Froude, Hist. Eng., vol. 10, p. 414.
‡ Ibid., p. 619.   § Ibid., pp. 443, 444.
‖ *Vide* Strada, tom. 2, p. 76.   Hist. Huguenots, pp. 569, 570.

temporaneous Europe, though not in full possession
of the facts as we are, nevertheless forestalled posterity's denial of this charge.   " If the admiral and
the rest were guilty," pithily queried Sir Thomas
Smith, " why were they not apprehended and tried?
So is the journeyer slain by the robber, so is the
chicken by the fox, so the hind by the lion, and Abel
by Cain.   Grant that they at Paris were guilty—
that they dreamt treason in their sleep, what did
the innocent men, women, and children at Lyons?
What did the sucking babes and their mothers
at Rouen, at Caen, at Rochelle?   Will God
sleep?"*

But after the immediate sufferers, it was the
prince of Orange who was most fatally affected by
the treachery of the court of France.   The alliance
with Charles IX. was the pivot of his campaign.
Upon Coligny's coöperation he had absolutely depended.   Supplies from Paris were essential to the
holding together of his hirelings.   Of thrice ten
thousand gallant sons religion was now bereaved.
Of his own bright hopes, not one but this accursed
deed had taken from him.   His very heart was broken up.   " I am struck as with a sledge-hammer,"†
said he.   At another time he said: " So far from
being reprehensible that I did not suspect this
crime, I should rather be chargeable with malignity had I been capable of such a sinister suspicion.   'T is not an ordinary thing to conceal such

* Cited in Froude, vol. 10, p. 422, *seq.*
† Archives de la Maison d'Orange-Nassau, tom. 3, p. 501.

enormous deliberations under the plausible cover of a league and marriage festivals."*

Although convinced that the result of the campaign had been decided by the "Paris matins," William determined to do his utmost, and at least deserve success. The only hope for Mons was in the possibility that he might, ere the news came to the ears of his troops, provoke Alva into a pitched battle and come out the victor. Accordingly, he omitted nothing which could gall the haughty spirit of his opponent, and tempt him to the field.†

All in vain. The duke was much too cautious to march out of his impregnable entrenchments and fight a superfluous combat. He knew, as did the prince, that now, as in '68, he had but to remain inactive to insure his triumph. For were not the besieged already in despair? Was not Coligny dead? Was not Protestant France paralyzed? Were not the prince's mercenaries, enlisted but for three months, half-mutinous now, and certain to become unmanageable when they came to know that nothing was to be looked for from Paris?‡ So, despite the pleadings of the hot-heads, Alva sat still, and continued to batter the walls of Mons.§

Still unwilling to quit the vicinage of Mons without exhausting his means of raising the siege, William once and again hurled his massed forces against Alva's bastions, but only to be once and again re-

---

* Archives de la Maison d'Orange-Nassau, tom. 3, p. 501.
† Motley, vol. 2, p. 396.　　　　　　　　　　‡ Ibid., seq.
§ Strada, tom. 2, p. 76.　Mendoza.

pulsed.* Then, having contrived to convey to Count
Louis intelligence of his inability to do more, and
his wish that he should surrender on the best obtainable terms,† he decamped, retreating through
Mechlin across the Meuse and towards the Rhine.‡
On reaching Germany, he once more disbanded his
useless hirelings, not, however, without grave personal danger; for, maddened by his inability to pay
them except in the over-due securities of the northern cities, the brutal mercenaries would have given
him up to Alva, but for the intervention of their
officers.§

Late in the autumn of 1572—alone, defeated,
quite broken-hearted, his chivalrous brother perhaps a prisoner—William set out for Holland.
"There," wrote he to Count John of Nassau, "there
I will make my sepulchre."‖

On the 19th of September, Mons surrendered.¶
Robbed of all hope by the colossal crime of his
imagined ally and by the departure of the prince,
Count Louis had nevertheless held out until Alva
was glad to consent to the most liberal terms of
capitulation he had ever accorded—the garrison
being permitted to march out with the honors of
war, and their lives and estates being secured to the
burghers, though all Protestants were banished.**

○ Watson, p. 188.
† Meteren, tom. 4, folio 75.   Hoofd, tom. 7, p. 264.
‡ Ibid.   § Ibid. Bor., tom. 7, p. 408.
‖ Groen van Prinst., Archives, etc., tom. 4, p. 4.
¶ Mendoza, tom. 7, p. 158, *et seq.*
** Mendoza, *ut antea.*   Hoofd, tom. 7, p. 265.   Bor., Meteren.

Charles IX. had bidden his envoy at Brussels, M. Mondaucet, to urge Alva to execute the Huguenots who were shut up at Mons* with Count Louis—men whom he had himself despatched as allies across the border.   So, too, as we have seen, spoke Philip. Nevertheless, La Noué contrived to get his fellow-soldiers included in the articles of capitulation, and they all escaped the impending axe of the Spanish headsman.   Two motives were at the bottom of Alva's unwonted generosity—he was anxious to get possession of Mons, and he was willing to set off his liberality against the horrid background of St. Bartholomew.

Still, though Count Louis was left to pass into Germany and La Noué went unhung, Mons was not to escape scot-free.   Noircarmes, whose experience at Valenciennes some years back preëminently fitted him for such service—Noircarmes was empowered to create a Commission of Troubles, in imitation of the duke's Council of Blood at Brussels, and to drag before this tribunal whomsoever he would for examination and for punishment.†   The cruelty with which he performed this labor of love became traditional.   In after days nurses were wont to hush their charges by whispering his name.

As the keys of Valenciennes, in 1567, were said to have opened the gates of all the rebel cities in that initial outbreak, so now those of Mons were found to unlock the doors of the insurgent towns

---

* Corresp. de Mondaucet; cited in Motley, vol. 2, p. 394.

† Motley, *ubi sup.*, p. 403.

throughout the whole South Netherlands. What
places had embraced the patriot cause and minis-
tered to Orange, vied with each other in servile su-
ing for the despot's pardon. Most were graciously
permitted to redeem themselves from pillage and
the torch by the payment of large sums of money;*
others were reserved for punishment harsher than a
mulct in the coin of the realm.

Among these last was Mechlin. This beautiful
city was an archiepiscopal see—strongly, almost
unanimously Romanist.† Yet it had given William
a cordial greeting, though just before refusing to
receive a Spanish garrison.‡ This atrocious offence
might not be compounded. Alva wheeled his legions
from Mons straight to Mechlin. Then unloosing
the iron clasp of his discipline, he bade them indemnify themselves for the hardships of their recent life
in camp by the sack of the helpless citizens, at that
very moment suppliants at his feet.§

The soldiers, to whom heavy arrears were due,
received the order with a yell of delight; and while
a solemn procession was winding out of the city
gates, eager to make the *amende honorable*, while
the penitent psalms of attendant churchmen were
resounding, they threw themselves pell-mell into the
town, and carried thieving, dishonor, death, and the
torch to every home.‖ Inspired, not by fanaticism—

---

* Campana, tom. 3, p. 97. Bor., tom. 6, p. 409, *et seq.*
† Motley. vol. 2, pp. 408, 409.
‡ Bor., tom. 6, p. 409, *et seq.*
§ Ibid. Meteren, tom. 4, folio 76.   ‖ Ibid.

for here there were few of the reformed to fleece
and kill, and friend and foe alike were pillaged*—
but by a mere love of plunder, and attended by that
fearful triad, rapine, lust, and murder, these human
devils ransacked Mechlin for three days and nights,
respecting nothing, sparing nothing, leaving nothing.† These soldiers of the saints did not even
pause at sacrilege.   Convents were gutted as well
as mansions ; nuns were violated equally with matrons.‡   Over the outrage the Romanist historians
themselves hoot and cry, Shame.§

Alva justified every thing in an elaborate paper
to the king, and again in a public document.‖   The
effigy at Antwerp was not more brazen than its
original.   He had the effrontery to cover Mechlin
with the phrase, *Pro bono publico*.   Then, having
scourged Flanders and Brabant back to the shackles which they had so recently thrown off, he said :
"Now for a warlike bout i' the north," nothing
doubting that Holland too would soon be forced to
resume its fetters.

º Motley, *ubi sup.*   † Ibid.   ‡ Ibid.   Watson, p. 190.
§ *Vide* Motley, vol. 2, p. 608, note.
‖ Corresp. de Philippe II., tom. 2, p. 1185.   Bor., *ut antea.*

CHAPTER XXXVI.

SCENES OF HORROR.

From the town of Orsoy, where the mercenaries had been mustered out, the prince of Orange rode to Kempen, in Overyssel, scudding thence across the Zuyder Zee to Enkhuyzen.* Twice broken, hunted, and an outlaw, he brought with him only a few domestics and seventy dragoons.† Nevertheless, the cold lagoons of Holland echoed and re-echoed to the joyous shouts of welcome which the burghers gave him—cordial and admiring as they could have been had he come to them covered with laurels instead of cypress.

But neither in regrets nor pageants did William waste the time. Every moment was precious. The Spaniards were already facing to the north, and much still remained to be done ere they could be fitly met. Calm, resolute, prescient, he went to work. Chaotic masses of details were shaped into order by his plastic fingers. Drooping and half-hostile magistracies were moulded into patriotic organisms. Much space was given to advising with and visiting the towns. Indefatigable, the prince also made himself ubiquitous. Wherever he appeared, determination and enthusiasm followed in his footsteps and remained behind. All felt,

○ Hoofd, tom. 7, p. 265. Bor., tom. 6, p. 414.   † Ibid.

with him, that existence without liberty, life without religion to assuage its cares, would be valueless.[*]

Soon after his arrival in the province, Orange convened the estates at Haarlem.[†] Thither he went with them to mature the ways and means of resistance. With him also went up to the assembly the deputies of twelve cities, now added to the original six, which, with the nobles, had immemorially constituted the provincial legislature.[‡] This was a democratic innovation as gracious and popular as it was prudent and sagacious. It recognized the right of all to a voice in the decision of matters which were of general concern. It inspired the enfranchised towns to contribute with greater cheerfulness towards the public defence. It made the estates themselves more representative, bound the people in a more intimate and equitable union, and placed the province, like a pyramid, upon its broadest base.

Unlike some modern conventions, this at Haarlem met not to say, but to do. First, the prince was greeted; then, in secret session, William explained his plan of procedure; finally, several regulations—for the better ordering of the troops, for the forbidding any communication with the enemy, for the prohibiting the exportation of provisions,

---

[*] Watson, p. 195.

[†] Bor., *ubi sup.* Wagenaer, Vader. Hist., tom. 6, p. 396, *et seq.*

[‡] *Vide* Wagenaer, tom. 6, p. 377, *et seq.* Also Motley, vol. 2, p. 377.

for the confirming the impositions laid by the congress of Dort upon the masses—were made.* And since the existing members of the council of finance and of the supreme court of Holland, held under the Spaniard, and had retired to Utrecht on the revolt of the towns, these faithless stewards were declared to have forfeited their offices, which were refilled with patriots.† All these acts were done by the combined authority of William and the estates, without the usual reservation of the king's future approbation—without any appeal from Philip drunk to Philip sober: so that the exercise of these sovereign powers was, if not the formal, then the virtual enfranchisement of Holland.‡

After the fall of Mons, the faith of Orange had been momentarily eclipsed ; now it shone out the brighter for that dipping of its disk in clouds. Here at least were men trusty and resolute to be free. God too still reigned—Alva's tactics and St. Bartholomew had not deposed Him. "I trust ever," wrote the prince to John Nassau, "that the great God of battles is with me, and that he will fight in the midst of whatever forces I may gather withal."§

During all these months—indeed, since the revolt of Flushing, Zealand had been the scene of active hostilities. The island of Walcheren, especially, was a "debatable ground." On its south side stood Flushing, the rendezvous of "the beggars

---

* Bor., tom. 6, p. 409, *et seq.* Velius Hoorn, tom. 3, p. 200.
† Ibid. ‡ Ibid. Davies, Hist. of Holland, vol. 1, p. 391.
§ Archives et Corresp., etc., tom. 3, p. 461.

of the sea;" in the north lay Middleburg, held by
a Spanish garrison, who overawed the townsfolk,
honest patriots almost to a man.*

William's lieutenant, 'T Zeraerts, was anxious
to clutch the whole island for the prince.   The
Spaniards, aware of its vital importance to Alva,
were equally desirous to defend what portion they
already stood on.   Mutual defiances, assaults and
counter-assaults, single combats, and incessant
alarms—these, together with hatreds begotten of
religious differences and antipathies of race, transformed Walcheren into a miniature pandemonium.†

Early in the summer of 1572, 'T Zeraerts laid
close and skilful siege to Middleburg.   It was as
cleverly defended.   But the besieged were numer-
ically weak, and Alva wished, if possible, to relieve
them.   For this purpose, he fitted out two separate
fleets, both of which were gobbled up by " the beggars of the sea," who had complete command of the
waters of the archipelago.‡   Notwithstanding these
successes, the patriots were foiled in every effort to
take Middleburg; and 'T Zeraerts soon found that it
could not be starved into submission, until Tergoes,
a town upon the neighbor island of South Beveland,
whence a plentiful supply of provisions was obtained by the besieged, should be previously closed
as a Spanish *dépôt* of subsistence.§

---

* Watson, p. 172.   Bentivoglio.

† Meteren, tom. 4, folio 69.   Bor., tom. 6, p. 377, *et seq*.   Hoofd,
Wagenaer.   ‡ Ibid.   Watson, *ubi sup.*

§ Bor., tom. 6, p. 392.   Bentivoglio, Meteren.

Accordingly, he left his trenches before Middleburg, ferried his troops across the little belt of water
which separated the two islands, and with seven
thousand men, German, French, and English Protestants, volunteers, formally invested Tergoes.*

The governor-general knew that the taking of
Tergoes would insure the fall of Middleburg, which
would wrench Zealand from his hand.. Therefore
he ordered Sanchio D'Avila, who commanded at
Antwerp in his absence before Mons,† to make
every exertion to raise the siege.‡ D'Avila exhausted his ingenuity in the invention of plans
whereby to achieve this end, now essaying to relieve Tergoes by land, now by sea, but always to
no purpose.

One day—it was in late October—a Flemish mariner, Captain Plomaert, an ultra-loyalist, waited
upon D'Avila, and proposed an amphibious scheme
of relief, unique in the annals of war.

The river Scheldt, which divides the provinces
of Brabant and Flanders, throws open its arms, the
East Scheldt and the West Scheldt, ere reaching the
sea, and clasps the archipelago of Zealand—islands
half floating on, half submerged by the circumjacent waters.§ Of these islands, South Beveland, of
which Tergoes was the capital, was the largest.
Fifty years before, it had formed part of the mainland. But in 1532, one of those frightful storms

* Bor., tom. 6, p. 392. Bentivoglio, Meteren.
† Motley, vol. 2, p. 413.   ‡ Bor., Meteren, *et alii.*
§ Motley, *ubi sup.*, p. 414.

peculiar to those coasts, had torn it from the shore by drowning ten miles of the intervening territory—land which no skill had since been able to regain.[*] The space thus flooded could not be crossed in boats even at high-tide, on account of abounding flats and shallows; and at low-water it had always been esteemed unfordable because of the miry and treacherous bottom, which persons then alive remembered to have seen traversed by three deep streams before the overflow.[†]

Nevertheless, Plomaert thought it practicable for troops to cross this wilderness of water, where the average depth was five feet, and where the tide rose and fell at least ten feet—to pass from the shore, ten miles across, to the island.[‡] To satisfy himself of the possibility of doing so, he crossed and recrossed twice, with a couple of equally hardy comrades. Then he offered to lead over reinforcements to Tergoes.[§]

D'Avila, at his wits' end, listened to this proposition with delight; and after consultation with his companion in arms, Mondragone, he decided to make the venture. "I will officer the expedition," cried Mondragone.[||] Three thousand men were at once ordered to Bergen-op-Zoom.[¶] Thence Mondragone led them to Aggier, a village quite at the

---

[*] Mendoza, tom. 7, p. 166, *seq.* Bor., *ubi sup.* Hoofd.
[†] Bentivoglio, tom. 6, p. 110. Hoofd, tom. 7, p. 270, *et seq.*
[‡] Ibid. Meteren, tom. 4, folios 76, 77.
[§] Ibid.   [||] Ibid., Mendoza.
[¶] Bentivoglio, tom. 6, p. 112. Bor., tom. 6, p. 394.

entrance of the dangerous ford.* Here the veteran
informed the soldiers of the object of the venture,
pointed out the difficulty of the route, spoke of the
glory sure to result from success, distributed three
thousand knapsacks filled with biscuit, powder, and
matches, ordered the adventurers to keep close;
then at half ebb-tide, amid enthusiastic cheering,
in single file, and preceded by Plomaert and Mondragone, all plunged boldly, gayly in, and splashed
on, on, on towards the distant shore.

They entered the water at midnight, and for five
hours they pursued the watery war-path, through
the bottom of the sea, over the slimy quicksands.
Not a man of the three thousand, save Plomaert,
knew the face of the land before the inundation,
but all did know that if any unforeseen accident
should retard their passage, the incoming tide
would certainly engulf them. All were aware that
the patriots might massacre them man by man as
they essayed to land, numb and fatigued with the
dark and perilous march. Spite of all, they kept
cheerily on, and, strange to relate, reached the isl-
and in the gray of the morning with the loss of but
nine men†—certainly among the most brilliant feats
on any martial record.

Halting but an hour at the dyke of Yersichen,
some four miles from Tergoes, to breathe, and eat
a morsel, the Spaniards struck boldly for the camp

* Bor., *ubi sup.*

† Bentivoglio, tom. 6, p. 112. Mendoza, tom. 7, p. 167. Bor.,
tom. 6, p. 394.

of the besiegers, who, amazed and panic-struck at
their appearance, waited but to see their banners,
and then, despite 'T Zeraerts' pleadings, rushed
wildly to their boats, leaving their camp to be
plundered by the foe.*   Mondragone, after pursuing and routing the patriot rear-guard, entered
Tergoes amid the acclamations of the garrison,
strengthened its works, reinforced the stronghold,
left a good store of supplies, and returned to Brabant to rejoin Alva before Mons.†

When Orange came into the north, such was still
the political situation in Zealand—a war of races
and a war of creeds, fanatical, pitiless, demoniacal.
By his order, siege was again laid to Middleburg,
and a close blockade hermetically sealed the place.‡
At the same time, Zirickzee, and shortly afterwards
the whole island of Schouwen, expelled the Spaniard
and flung out the patriot banner.§

Meantime, Duke Alva, after scourging the recusant cities of Brabant and Flanders back to their
allegiance, retired to rest his weary and gout-
racked frame at Nimeguen, leaving his son, Don
Frederic de Toledo to conduct the army into the
maritime provinces, appointing Amsterdam as the
rendezvous in Holland, whither, after a few days'
repose, he meant himself to go.‖

Making a *détour* from Mechlin, Don Frederic

---

* Bentivoglio, tom. 6, p. 112.   Mendoza, tom. 7, p. 167.   Bor.,
tom. 6, p. 294.   † Ibid.

‡ Meteren, tom. 4, folio 87.   § Ibid.

‖ Mendoza, tom. 8, p. 172.   Meteren, tom. 4, folio 78.

marched into Guelderland, and thence, facing due
west, Holland-ward, through the province of Utrecht.
His object in this circuit was to desiccate the sore
of rebellion in the northeast ere attempting to medicine the yet more diseased seaboard. His advance
was a continued triumph.* Upon those towns
which just before had been enthusiastic for Orange,
the Spanish bugles acted as did the blowing of the
rams' horns under the walls of Jericho—they at
once succumbed.

One little town, however—Zutphen in Guelderland—had been garrisoned by William. It was
defended by a wall flanked with bastions and girt
by a deep ditch. The Yssel washed the fortifications on one side, the Berkel on another; while on
the two remaining sides the ground was a marshy
puddle, usually impassable.† But unhappily these
natural advantages were nullified at this juncture,
the frost having set in with uncommon severity a
night or two before the Spaniard demanded entrance. The garrison made but a show of resistance; then, convinced of the folly of inviting an
assault, fled, followed by those of the citizens who
had been prominently active against Alva.‡

Don Frederic, who was just ordering an escalade, was promptly informed of this fact by the
burghers, and implored to stay his hand and accept

* Mendoza, tom. 8, page 172.   Meteren, tom. 4, folio 78.
Strada, tom. 2, p. 77.
† Hoofd, Bor.   Watson, p. 191.
‡ Ibid.

a surrender at discretion.* Of this, the son of his
father, only too glad of a pretext for severity, would
not hear. Sword in hand, the army entered town;
and once in, platoon after platoon broke rank, each
soldier running off to his individual work of pillage,
lust, arson, murder. Scores of the unarmed citizens
were hung on the Zutphen trees; other scores were
killed in the streets; still others at their own
hearthstones. Finally, the assailants, dissatisfied
with such laggard slaughter, seized five hundred of
their victims, tied them two by two, and so plunged
them headlong into the Yssel.† Still worse fared
the women of the place, and when death came it was
mercy.‡ When neither chastity nor life remained,
the houses were fired, and what had been Zutphen
was a pile of charred corpses, a heap of ashes.§

The smouldering and fœtid ruins of Zutphen
affrighted the whole northeast into immediate submission.‖ Count Van den Burg, the brother-in-law
of Orange and his lieutenant in those parts, left his
post and his wife too, in ignominious flight for Germany.¶ Megen, the loyalist governor, was kept
busy receiving deputies from the repentant towns,
all of whom whimpered "Peccavi."**

So much achieved, Don Frederic started for
Amsterdam. Directly in his path stood the town

---

* Bor., tom. 6, p. 415. Watson, *ut antea,*
† Ibid. Meteren and Hoofd, *ut antea.*
‡ Ibid. Campana, p. 97.   § Ibid.
‖ Strada, tom. 2, p. 77.
¶ Cor. de Philippe II., tom. 2, p. 1186. Bor., Meteren, *ubi sup.*
** "I have sinned."

of Naarden, just on the border of Holland—according to Mendoza, "the first in that province in which heresy built its nest, whence it had taken flight to all the neighboring cities."* This "nest" these pious children of holy church were naturally desirous to clean out. Happily for them, Naarden had not sent in its submission, and yet more happily, when an *avant-courrier* summoned it to surrender, its burghers had replied, " By the help of God, we will keep our town, now as ever, to the service of the prince of Orange and King Philip."† This double crime of heresy and rebellion merited a twofold chastisement, which Don Frederic at once moved forward to bestow.

Meantime, the citizens, in want of arms, ammunition, a garrison—every warlike store—and therefore ill-prepared to repel an assault, immediately sent agents to purchase powder on the credit of the estates of Holland ; wrote to Sanoy, William's deputy, for aid ; and solicited Berthold Eutes, one of De la Marck's sea-beggars, then at Vianen, to throw his privateersmen into their citadel without delay.‡ In return, nothing was obtained but fair words§— very inefficient weapons with which to defend weak walls and unarmed bastions.

As the Spaniards were now close by, and as there was no prospect of succor, nothing remained for the inhabitants to do save to effect an honorable

* Mendoza, tom. 8, p. 173.
† Bor., tom. 6, p. 417.   Hoofd, tom. 7, p. 276.
‡ Ibid.   § Ibid.

capitulation, if that were still possible. Accordingly, on the 1st of December, 1572, they despatched two of the most influential of their number to Don Frederic's camp to surrender the place.* The messengers were refused admission to the tent of the commander, and ordered to return and expect his reply at the gates of Naarden.† Alarmed by this ominous answer, one of the deputies seized the first opportunity to leap from the sled in which both travelled, saying to his companion, "Adieu; I think I will not go back just now." The other, who could not so readily forsake his family and his fellow-citizens, returned alone.‡

At Bussem, a mile and a half from Naarden, the Spanish advance halted just at dark. Here they were met by another envoy, who was commanded to reënter the town, collect a deputation fully empowered to surrender the place, and return to confer with Don Frederic at daybreak. This he did, coming out bright and early the next morning with four other citizens, one of whom was Lambert Hortensius, a Roman priest, rector of a Latin school, a man eminent in mediæval letters.§ Before reaching camp, the Spanish captain, Julian Romero, met them, commissioned, as he said, by Don Frederic to settle the terms of capitulation. With him, therefore, the envoys agreed that Naarden should admit the Spaniards on the express condition that the

---

* Bor., tom. 6, p. 417.　Hoofd, tom. 7, p. 276.

† Bor., *ubi sup.*

‡ Bor., *ut antea.*　　　　　§ Hoofd, tom. 7, p. 278.

lives and properties of the inhabitants should be secure; that the burghers should take a new oath of allegiance to the king; and that one hundred soldiers should be permitted to take out of town so much spoil as they could carry—"in order," said Romero, "to satisfy the troops."[*]   The treaty was a verbal one; but it was confirmed by the customary form of joining hands, the ceremony by which the estates and William had recently promised fidelity to each other, and one deemed an ample security by these primitive and faithful men.[†]   Having thus plighted his word, Don Julian entered the city, followed by six hundred musketeers.[‡]

While the deputies were treating with Romero, the housewives were busy preparing a feast for their guests, to which all soon sat down, Don Julian being entertained with especial honor by a wealthy senator.[§]

On rising from the table, Don Julian ordered the great bell to ring a summons for the townsfolk to gather in the guild-hall to take the oath.   Five hundred of them obeyed the call; a few, seized with a vague suspicion went to secrete themselves.[‖]   Suddenly a priest, who had been pacing to and fro in front of the guild-hall, flung open the door and shouted to the crowded audience, "Prepare for instant death!"[¶]

[*] Hoofd, p. 277. Bor., *ubi sup.*
[†] Davies, Hist. of Holland, vol. 1, p. 593.
[‡] Bor., Hoofd, *ubi sup.*
[§] Hoofd, *ubi sup.* Motley, vol. 2, pp. 420, 421.
[‖] Hoofd, tom. 7, p. 278. Bor., tom. 7, p. 416, *et seq.*   [¶] Ibid.

These talismanic words conjured up unthought-of horrors. The musketeers, gorged with dainties, fired a volley into the midst of their defenceless entertainers, and then, with a frightful yell, sprang in upon them with sword and dagger. Before five minutes had elapsed the building was on fire and five hundred men were corpses.

"Inflamed, but not satiated," says the fullest historian of the massacre, "the Spaniards then rushed into the streets, thirsty for fresh horrors. The houses were rifled of their contents, and the citizens were forced to carry the booty to the camp, being then struck dead as their reward. The town too was fired in every direction that the skulkers might be singed from their hiding-places. As fast as they came forth they were put to death by their impatient foes. Some were pierced with rapiers; some were chopped to pieces with axes; some were surrounded in the burning streets by groups of laughing soldiers, intoxicated, not with wine but with blood, who tossed them to and fro with their lances and derived a wild amusement from their dying agonies. Those who attempted resistance were crimped alive like fishes, and left to gasp themselves to death in lingering torture. The soldiers becoming more and more insane as the foul work went on, opened the veins of their victims and drank their blood as if it had been wine. Some of the burghers were temporarily spared, that they might witness the violation of their wives and daughters, being then butchered in company with these still more unhappy sufferers. Miracles of brutality were accomplished. Neither church nor hearth was sacred. Men were slain, women were outraged at the altars, in the streets, in their blazing homes."*

In such a mass of horror, it seems superfluous to mention individual cases; the pen falters at its task. Nevertheless, where exaggeration is impossible, extenuation is base, reluctance crime. The life of Lambert Hortensius was spared, since he was a priest; but his son, organist of the chief church, was slain, his heart being torn out before his father's eyes.† A smith named Hubert Williamson,‡ snatching up a three-legged stool in one hand and wielding a sword in the other, bravely defended the entrance to his house for some time, killing a number of his assailants. At last, wounded and overpowered, he sank to the floor, dropping his rude shield; but he had sufficient strength left to grasp with his toil-hardened hands the blades of two swords pointed at his breast. The swords were drawn back, severing all his fingers; and the hero was then slain. At his side, through the whole scene, knelt his daughter, vainly begging for her

---

* Motley, vol. 2, p. 421, *et seq.*, after Hoofd and Bor.

† Hoofd, *ut antea.*

‡ "Those of the Hollanders who were not noble had at this time no surnames. Some were distinguished by the name of the trade they followed, or sometimes by personal or mental qualities, or by their birthplace; others added *son* to the Christian name of their fathers or ancestors. The nobles took their names from their estates." Davies, vol. 1, p. 396, note.

father's life. When he was dead, the soldiers flung her parent's yet quivering fingers in her face.

Of the entire population, not sixty remained alive.* And when all was over, Don Frederic, with impious barbarity—barbarity without a parallel in the annals of the most savage nations—forbade these few forlorn survivors to bury their dishonored dead. In the ruined streets, the corpses were left for three weeks to putrefy.†

Thus was Naarden dashed out of existence— quiet, happy Naarden, whose denizens for long years had been glad to carry into practice the counsel of the prophet to the Israelites: "Pray for the peace of the city in which you dwell; for in the peace thereof ye shall have peace."‡

Alva not only endorsed the massacre—he gloated over it. "The army cut the throats of all," wrote he to Philip, "not a mother's son was left alive. 'T was a permission of God that these people should have undertaken to defend a city so weak that only heretics would have attempted such a thing."§ Such was the pious comment of a man who believed that the more he burned on earth of that which holy church proscribed, the less would he himself burn in hell.

* Hoofd, ut antea. Meteren, tom. 4, folio 78.
† Ibid. Bor., tom. 7, p. 419.
‡ Jer. 29 : 7, French version.
§ Corresp. de Philippe II., tom. 2, p. 1186.

CHAPTER XXXVII.

HEROISM.

At Naarden Duke Alva overshot his mark. He meant here, as elsewhere to conquer by terror. But this massacre had an effect upon Holland and Zealand exactly the reverse of that produced by the sack of Mechlin upon Flanders and Brabant; of that consequent upon the slaughter at Zutphen, in Guelderland, Utrecht, Overyssel, Gröningen, and Friesland. The seaboard was never farther than now from all thought of yielding. In the glass of the past, all saw that submission was certain to undo them. Had not Mechlin surrendered? and Zutphen? and Naarden? Despair itself cried, Fight.*

But the outlook was gloomy. Holland and Zealand—sandbanks and floating islands—were absolutely without allies. Even England stood aloof; for what sane politician could believe that a few towns, half-a-dozen marshy isles, with a population to be counted by thousands, could resist successfully the first military power in Europe?†

Besides, these scant towns were not united. The most important of them and the wealthiest, Amsterdam, adhered to Spain; less, indeed, from inclination than from necessity, for the governor-general

* Strada, tom. 2, p. 78. Bor. and Hoofd, *ut antea.*
† Froude, Hist. of Eng., vol. 10, p. 427.

had taken the double precaution to keep ultra Romanists in the magistracy, and to billet a strong garrison upon the city.* Then, too, trade is proverbially selfish, and trade was the breath of this town's nostrils. At this very hour the fire of persecution was blazing furiously in the market-place; and, to use the fine words of Sir Thomas Brown, "saints were called to maintain their faith in the noble way of martyrdom, serving God in the flames."†

In the face of these manifold discouragements, the Hollanders continued their preparations for resistance. They meant, if possible, to make their position, strong by nature, impregnable. They intended that every ford of a canal should be a battle-ground, that every passage of a river should require an army to force it, that every siege should demand a campaign to finish it.

From the smoking ruins of Naarden Don Frederic led his butchers directly to Amsterdam.‡ Hither, after a little, came Alva from Nimeguen. The duke intended to make Amsterdam the base of his attempt to reconquer the northwest. It was upon the adjoining city of Haarlem that he decided next to swoop.

A combination of circumstances influenced this choice. Haarlem was the most important of the Holland towns next to Amsterdam. Its defences were weak. It was situated quite in the centre of the province. As Diedrich Sanoy, William's deputy,

---

° Watson, p. 194.   † *Vide* Brandt, vol. 1, p. 301.
‡ Bor., tom. 7, p. 420, *et seq.*

was at this time at Enkhuyzen, in the north, while
the prince himself was stationed at Delft, in the
south, its possession by the Spaniards would isolate these chiefs and cut the revolted states clean
in two.*

Alva began operations by ordering the magistrates of Amsterdam to send a deputation to the
menaced city, to inform the burghers of his purpose, exhort them promptly to submit, and pledge
their official word that mercy should be the guerdon of non-resistance.† The message threw Haarlem into consternation. Nine-tenths of the citizens
were stanchly patriotic, but they knew the weakness
of their walls—much less stout than their hearts;
they were aware that all warlike stores were lacking; and as they gazed on their wives and children,
they doubted. Taking advantage of the hesitation,
three of their magistrates went secretly to treat
with the duke.‡ In their absence, Wybant Ripperda, William's governor of the town, convened
the citizens in the market-place. In a few vivid,
eloquent phrases the dauntless soldier pictured the
necessity of resistance, affirmed that surrender would
but add Haarlem to the fatal list of dashed-out
towns, and cried: "Remember Mechlin, Zutphen,
Naarden. Accept no terms from men who have
shown themselves so cruelly perfidious. Much
more is to be dreaded from submission than from a

---

* Bor., tom. 7, p. 420, *et seq.*
† Davies, Hist. of Hol., vol. 1, p. 595.
‡ Bor., *ut antea.* Hooft, tom. 7, p. 282.

resolute defence. If we must die, let us at least fall sword in hand."*

These words were decisive. Reassured and quite won over, all shouted: "Yes, yes; no peace with the Spaniard. Our gates shall not swing open to the piping of the butcher-duke."† Two of the magistrates—one had been prudent enough to remain in Amsterdam—were arrested on their return from the enemy's camp, tried, convicted, and hung for treason. And when, a few days afterwards, a messenger came from Alva to urge a surrender at discretion, he too was put to death, as an emphatic announcement that the city would listen to no terms of agreement.‡

Orange, on being apprized of the heroic determination of Haarlem, promised the gallant burghers all possible assistance, left Delft, and fixed his residence at Sassenheim, on the south end of Haarlem lake, that he might be at hand, and despatched St. Aldegonde to put the municipality in possession of the patriots, and to substitute the reformed for the Romish creed—fresh evidence of the resolution of the populace.§

At this juncture an event occurred which the patriots construed into a favorable augury. Half-a-dozen ships, managed by "the beggars of the sea," had recently been frozen up off Amsterdam. Alva

* Bor., *ut untea.* Hoofd, tom. 7, p. 282. Meteren, tom. 4, folio 78.   † Hoofd, *ubi sup.* Bor., *ubi sup.*

‡ Hoofd, *ubi sup.*, p. 284.

§ Mendoza, tom. 7, p. 173. Brandt, vol. 1, p. 301.

sent out upon the ice a body of veteran musketeers
to capture the frost-bound intruders. The crews,
however, first cut a trench around their little fleet, and
then, scudding out upon the frozen sea on skates,
joined battle with the astonished foe. Trained from
infancy to such sports—for in that amphibious
land all were skaters—the assailed sped hither and
thither with winged feet, flew on the foe with drawn
sabres, and were away again ere the clumsy and
slipping Spaniards could take aim. In a brilliant
and unique skirmish, they completely routed the
duke's veterans, several hundred of whom were
stretched dead upon the ice. The survivors made
their way, chop-fallen and bleeding, back to Amsterdam.*

Within twenty-four hours a flood and a sudden
thaw released the patriot vessels, which spread sail
and made for Enkhuyzen, while a frost immediately
and strangely succeeding, put God's veto upon pursuit.† Alva was surprised at these novel manœuvres. "Sure," said he, "'t is a thing never heard
of before to-day: a body of arquebusiers thus fighting upon a frozen sea."‡ But the duke was an apt
scholar, even when the foe were his teachers. He
at once ordered seven thousand pairs of skates; and
soon his men-at-arms came to be quite at home
upon the ice.§

This slippery combat was the prelude of the
siege. On the 10th of December, 1572, Don Fred-

* Mendoza, *ut antea*.   † Motley, vol. 2, p. 428.
‡ Cited in Motley, *ubi sup.*   § Motley, *ubi sup.*

eric marched through Amsterdam gates with flying colors to "chastise" Haarlem.*

A glance at the map will give a clearer idea of the site of Haarlem than the most elaborate description. It lay just on the eastern edge of that narrow isthmus, scarcely five miles broad, which unites north and south Holland, and separates the waters of the Zuyder Zee from the German ocean. Due east, ten miles off, was Amsterdam, naturally divided from its sister city by an expanse of inland water, but connected with it by an artificial causeway.† Directly south, at about the same distance, lay Leyden, whose broad canal ran up to the walls of Haarlem, forming the commercial channel between the two.‡ The Haarlem meer too, an immense sheet of water covering seventy square miles of surface, stretched away from Haarlem almost to Leyden, with which it was connected by a little stream. 'T is important to note this topography because it is the hinge upon which the whole siege turned.

As for the city itself, it then contained about forty thousand inhabitants, and was moated and surrounded by a wall, old, tottering, and of such extent as to require a large force properly to defend it.§ It was a sightly place, with broad avenues embroidered with lofty trees; houses singularly picturesque, with sharply-pointed gables, such as

---

* Ibid., p. 431. Bor., Mendoza, *et al.*
† Meteren, Bentivoglio, Bor.   ‡ Ibid.
§ Bor., tom. 6, p. 422. Mendoza.

we are accustomed to see in old Flemish paintings; and in its centre loomed the ancient church of St. Bavon, a vast Gothic structure, with a prodigiously high square dome, visible over leagues of land and sea, and seeming to gather the whole town under its sacred and protective wings.*

Hither, through the December sleet, came the Spanish army, at least thirty thousand strong,† bent on plunder, thirsty for blood, and looking for an easy victory. To oppose this force, Haarlem had, at the outset, but a thousand men-at-arms, though to this number a reinforcement of five hundred and fifty Netherlanders was shortly added.‡ At no time during the siege could Wybant Ripperda count above four thousand effective soldiers.§

In passing from Amsterdam to Haarlem, Don Frederic crossed the causeway between the two cities, which ran along the top of a dyke and about midway was bridged over the channel which connected the V, an inlet of the Zuyder Zee, with the Haarlem meer. Here were situated sluices and gauge-posts for regulating the height of the water—sluices which, if opened, would inundate the adjacent territory. There was nothing like this highway in the world, save that in far-away America, at the ancient city of Mexico, through the lake of Teztuco, celebrated, like this, as the battle-ground of Spanish invaders.

○ Motley, vol. 2, p. 430. *Vide* also "A Tour in Holland," etc., by W. Chambers.

† Campana, Guer. di Fiand., lib. 3, p. 100. Motley, *ubi sup.*, p. 429.
‡ Davies, vol. 1, p, 596. § Hoofd, tom. 7, p. 285.

On the Haarlem side of this dyke stood the fort of Sparendam, in which Ripperda had stationed three hundred men, with orders to open the sluices and flood the country—a manœuvre which would have proved fatal to the besiegers by cutting off their connection with Amsterdam, their base of operations, whence came all their supplies; but, unhappily, the frost, by freezing up the sluices, rendered this attempt fruitless, and Don Frederic's advance escaladed the fort and took permanent possession of this vital point. Then, sweeping past Sparendam, the Spaniards soon reached Haarlem and completely encircled it.[*]

Don Frederic's initial labors were facilitated by a dense frozen fog which hung over the town, under whose cover he stationed his troops, dug his trenches, and arranged his artillery.[†] The besieged too, sheltered by the same icy curtain, sent out myriads of skaters and scores of sleds to bring up from Leyden provisions and warlike *matériel* against their time of need.[‡]

The Spaniard was hardly in position ere he learned that De la Marck, under orders from Orange, was advancing with three thousand men to reinforce the scant garrison of Haarlem. Romero, Noircarmes, and Bossu were detached with a strong *corps d'armée* to intercept his march. In the middle of December they met the famous sea beggar, cut his levies to pieces, and then hastened back to camp to press the siege.*

On the 18th of December, 1572, Don Frederic opened fire upon the cross-gate, the principal entrance of Haarlem, and continued the bombardment through three days. Sadly shattered were the rotten walls; but the whole populace rushed to repair the breaches, filling the holes made by the Spanish cannon with earth, stone, huge blocks of wood, and marble images torn from the Romish churches of the city.† When the besiegers saw the use to which these sculptured saints were put, they were filled with horror. Strange, that men should entertain so much more respect for breathless effigies of holy things than for the bodies of their fellows—living images of God.‡

Supposing that he had by this prolonged cannonade beaten a practicable breach, Don Frederic, on the morning of the 22d of December, gave orders for an assault. Through the previous night, the stir in camp had given to the burghers "dreadful note of preparation," and they were at their posts. Romero led the escaladers, who rushed impetuously forward, imagining the victory certain, and intent less on fighting than on pillage. They found no Mechlin, no Zutphen, no Naarden here. The dauntless citizens met them with an ardor equal to their own. While the great bell of St. Bavon clanged

* Hoofd, tom. 7, p. 286. Bor., tom. 6, p. 424.

† Bentivoglio, tom. 7, p. 121. Strada, tom. 2, p. 78

‡ Motley, vol. 2, p. 433, et seq.

the alarm to bring up succor, those already on the ramparts fiercely grappled with the over-confident foe, upon whose heads they hurled live coals, boiling oil, huge stones—any thing, every thing which could maim or kill.   Blind, staggering, decimated, the astonished Spaniards ere long turned back and fled, leaving four hundred of their number lifeless "i' the imminent, deadly breach."*   Twenty of their most gallant officers were slain, and Romero himself lost an eye.†

This rude reception of his "invincibles" convinced Don Frederic that his task was to be no halcyon gala.   He gave orders for a more regular investment of the place, began to mine and proceeded more circumspectly.‡

Meantime, the prince of Orange neglected no opportunity to assist and supply the wants of the besieged.   Immediately after this foiled assault, he collected some wagon-loads of munitions, seven field-pieces, and two thousand men, sending them forward under charge of Batenburg§ — an officer who had recently replaced De la Marck, dismissed and sent out of the province by William and the estates on account of his mutinous behavior and ferocity.‖

---

* Mendoza, tom. 9, p. 178, *et seq.*   Hoofd, *ubi sup.*, *et alii.*
  † Mendoza and Bor., *ut antea.*   ‡ Ibid.
  § Hoofd, tom. 7, p. 290.   Bor., tom. 6, p. 431.
  ‖ De la Marck was an able and enterprising partisan, and his loss was severely felt by Holland.   But his cruelties, committed chiefly on priests, had become so frequent and atrocious as to make him generally abhorred.   No honorable man could wink at

Batenburg was as unsuccessful as his predecessor. On nearing Haarlem, he lost himself in a
thick mist, led his men directly into the camp of
the enemy, and was entrapped by his own blunder.
Though he with a few score more escaped, his
force was massacred, his provisions stored in the
Spanish larder.*

Batenburg's lieutenant, De Koning, was among
those captured. Don Frederic struck off his head,
and shot it into Haarlem girt with these words:
"Accept the head of Philip Koning, for he came to
reinforce your city." The exasperated citizens replied by a jest equally cruel. Decapitating eleven
Spaniards, they put their heads into a cask, and at
night rolled it into the beleaguer's trenches, with
this direction: "The burghers of Haarlem send
these ten heads to Duke Alva in payment of the
ten-penny tax; and since they have been long in
his debt, add the eleventh head as interest."†

Varied by these ghastly pleasantries the siege
went on. In the Spanish pay were three thousand
miners from the bishopric of Liege, whose business
it was to sap the foundation of the walls of Haarlem.
"As fast, however, as Don Frederic mined," says

at his deeds—deeds which placed him beside Alva and Vargas.
Though often reproved by the estates, he would not mend his conduct, and at length he came to defy the authority of the estates
and of the prince himself to dictate his actions. Then he was imprisoned; but ultimately, at William's solicitation, permitted to
retire from Holland with his property. Some years later, he died
at Leyden of the bite of a mad dog. *Vide* Bor., tom. 6, p. 425,
et seq. Hoofd, tom. 7, pp. 288, 289. Brandt, vol. 1, pp. 300, 302.

  ° Hoofd, *ubi sup.*   † Ibid. Strada, tom. 2, p. 78.

the historian, "the citizens countermined. Spaniard and Netherlander met daily in deadly combat within the bowels of the earth. Frequent and desperate were the struggles within gangways so narrow that only daggers could be used, so obscure that the dim lanterns hardly lighted the deathstroke. They seemed the conflicts not of men, but of evil spirits. Nor were these hand-to-hand battles all. Often a shower of heads, limbs, mutilated trunks, the mangled remains of hundreds of human beings, spouted from the earth as from an invisible volcano. Still the Spaniards toiled on with undiminished zeal, and still the besieged, undismayed, delved below their works, and checked their advance by sword and spear and horrible explosions."*

Don Frederic especially directed his exertions against the Cross-gate, thinking that his securing it would open a pathway into the town. Aware of its weakness, and convinced of the impossibility of holding it, the citizens, secretly, but with great celerity, went to work constructing a ravelin of massive stone just behind it. All through the bitter winter nights men, women, even little children, labored at this task, until, unknown to the foe, a bastion was completed inside the menaced, crumbling portal of far greater strength than the Cross-gate itself.†

William was in constant communication with the

---

* Motley, vol. 2, p. 436 ; after the contemporaneous account of P. Sterlinex.

† Mendoza, tom. 4, p. 188. Bor., tom. 6, pp. 431, 432.

city. On the 28th of January, 1573, one hundred
and seventy sleds, laden with powder and bread—
that to destroy, and this to support life—glided
across the frozen surface of the meer into Haarlem,
under the convoy of four hundred volunteers.*

Three days later, Don Frederic, marking the
crippled state of the Cross-gate, determined to make
a grand assault. "This time," thought he, "success is certain to mount the walls· with me." At
midnight, on the 31st of January, a strong band of
escaladers threw themselves·with sudden fury upon
the half-ruined rampart. The sentinels, though
taken by surprise, were not dismayed. Toppling
over the scaling-ladders of their assailants, and at
the same time sounding the alarm, they held the
foe in play until the burghers came to the rescue.
After a hard struggle, in which the townsfolk dex-
terously encircled the necks of the Spaniards with
hoops smeared with pitch and set on fire, and
pelted them with stones, with clubs, with fire-
brands, defending themselves with musket and
sabre, the besieged pretended to give way, and
retired behind the new ravelin.† At dawn, Don
Frederic descried the Spanish banner floating
above the Cross-gate. Supposing that all was
over, he galloped up—when lo, the ravelin!‡

Chagrined and angered, he returned to camp,
and, after matins, ordered a general assault. On
came the veteran battalions with steady ranks and

* Bor., tom. 6, p. 432   † Hoofd, tom. 7. p. 293.
‡ Ibid., Mendoza.

loud huzzas. They had just scrambled to the summit of the Cross-gate, and were about to precipitate themselves upon the ravelin, when a frightful
explosion flung the deserted bastion, together with
what seemed a fourth part of Don Frederic's army,
into mid air.* The Cross-gate had been undermined by the citizens ere being abandoned, and
they had awaited this opportunity to blow it up.†
When the smoke rolled off, hundreds of mangled
wretches were seen stretched upon the plain, whence
came distressful groans and fierce imprecations.
Aghast at the unforeseen disaster, the survivors
beat a hasty retreat, seeking shelter behind their
outworks.‡

So greatly dismayed were many of the Spaniards by the destructive failure of these two elaborate assaults, that they began to clamor against the
continued prosecution of the siege. "Our miseries
are greater than those of the besieged," said they.
"On account of the difficulties of the communication with Amsterdam, we suffer from a perpetual
scarcity of provisions; and the severity of the season
slays more than the sword of these burghers. We
shall never take the town, or if we do, it will leave
us no army with which to reduce other places."§

Don Frederic himself took this view, sending
Mendoza to ask Alva to sign a recall.‖ The duke

* Mendoza, tom. 9, p. 184, *seq.* Bor., *ubi sup.*
† Bor., and Mendoza, *ut antea.*   ‡ Ibid.
§ Bentivoglio, tom. 7, p. 124, *et seq.* Mendoza, tom. 9, pp.
185, 186.   ‖ Mendoza, *ubi sup.*, p. 192.

was enraged. "I am sick and unable to go in person to the camp," wrote he in reply; "but if you do not hold on to success, consider yourself no longer son of mine. Should you fall, I will drag myself into the saddle; and when we have both perished, your mother the duchess shall come from Spain to carry on the siege."* This answer was decisive. Don Frederic spoke no more of a recall. Soon afterwards he was strongly reinforced, and giving up all hope of taking Haarlem by assault, he determined to starve it into submission.†

With the opening of spring the aspect of affairs changed. Alva had been busy all the winter building a fleet at Amsterdam. Towards the end of February, when the ice broke up, his admiral, Count Bossu, launched these vessels in the Haarlem meer, and sailing to the south, severed all communication with Leyden, whence the besieged drew all their supplies of men and stores.‡

In imitation of this manœuvre, the prince of Orange attempted, unsuccessfully, to cut asunder Amsterdam and Don Frederic's camp.§ Foiled in this, he next got a patriot flotilla on the meer, with which he hoped to chase off Bossu.|| After much preliminary skirmishing, the hostile fleets joined battle, and for the first and last time throughout the war,¶ "the beggars of the sea" were completely

---

Mendoza, *ubi sup.*, p. 192.　　　　　　　　† Ibid.

Bor., tom. 6, p. 436.

§ Hoofd, tom. 8, p. 300.　Bor., tom. 6, p. 437.

|| Bor., *ubi sup.*　Hoofd, *ubi sup.*, pp. 306, 307.

¶ Strada, tom. 2, p. 73.

defeated—themselves chased off by Bossu,* who thus became absolute master of the lake.

This untoward event reduced Haarlem to the verge of despair. Men, money, provisions began to fail. The inhabitants were put on short allowance—a pound of bread a day for each man, a malt cake for the women and children.† Yet they struggled on as vigorously and indefatigably as at the outset. Nor were they content merely to hold their walls. Sallies were of nightly occurrence. Once, a thousand of the besieged drove in the pickets of the beleaguerer, burned three hundred tents, took seven pieces of artillery, gutted the camp larder, slew eight hundred of the foe; and then, lighted home by the blaze of Don Frederic's fired outposts, returned to Haarlem with a loss of but four men, to erect on the ramparts a colossal funeral mound, on which was this inscription, writ in letters which might have been read from Amsterdam: "Haarlem is the graveyard of the Spaniards."‡

Even the women became soldiers. Kanan Hasselaar, a widow of rank and fortune and unspotted fame, organized a corps of three hundred matrons, who, retaining the dress of their sex, labored at all hours with spade and pickaxe in repairing breaches, with sword and matchlock in defending the walls, and figured too in most of the nocturnal sallies, no less to the encouragement of the burghers than to

---

* Bor., and Hoofd, *ubi sup.*   † Ibid.
‡ Hoofd, tom. 8, p. 302.

the admiration of the besiegers.* Knowing the fate
which awaited them should the city fall, they preferred death to dishonor—kindred in this to the
heroines of all ages. "These townsfolks," wrote
Don Frederic, "do as much as the best soldiers in
the world could do."† And Alva assured Philip,
"Never was a place defended with such skill and
bravery as Haarlem."‡

Meantime, famine, the Spaniard's most potent
ally, marched into town; starvation, which no heroism could push out, stood on the threshold of each
house.§ The burghers, powerless against this foe,
did their utmost to provoke assaults from the besiegers, hoping to forget the cravings of hunger in
incessant combats. But though they put their prisoners to death in sight of Don Frederic's camp,
appeared upon the walls decked out in the gor-
geous robes of the Romish church, and offered
every imaginable insult to the effigies of all the
saints in the calendar,‖ that wily soldier was not to
be tempted into another escalade. He knew his
advantage, knew from experience the fatality of
measuring swords with despair, knew that he had
but to maintain his position, and let starvation
conquer for his decimated army.

Under this policy, the sufferings of the citizens
became each day more terrible. As the month of

* Meteren, tom. 4, folio 79. Strada, tom. 2, p. 74.
† Corresp. de Philippe II., tom. 2, p. 1217.
‡ Ibid., p. 1198.
§ Hoofd, tom. 8, p. 309. Bor., tom. 6, p. 437.
‖ Strada, *ubi sup.*

June wore away, they were reduced to subsist upon rape and hemp seed; then upon the flesh of dogs, cats, and vermin, and finally the tanned hides of oxen and horses were greedily devoured.[*]

All this time Orange was doing what it was in his power to do. By means of carrier-pigeons he still encouraged the besieged to hold out, and communicated to them his various plans to relieve their wants. One day a couple of these winged posts, tired with flying, lighted upon a tent in Don Frederic's camp. A soldier, ignorant of the stratagem, shot one of them for sport, when the mystery of the letters was discovered. After this accident, no pigeon could fly over the beleaguerer without imminent danger of death, and thus many of William's projects became known at the wrong headquarters.[†]

Early in July, the prince, thinking that while there was any hope there was every hope, got afoot one more expedition. Troops there were none, but Delft, Rotterdam, Gouda—a host of friendly towns, volunteered to equip their train-bands for the purpose of relieving Haarlem.[‡] Orange announced his intention to head this essay in person.[§] The estates, however, would not permit it. "Your life is of more value than many cities," cried all; "if you fall, we are indeed undone."[||] With great reluctance William consented to intrust the conduct of

---

[*] Hoofd and Bor., *ubi sup.*   [†] Strada, tom. 2, p. 74.
[‡] Hoofd, tom. 8, p. 310. Bor., tom. 6, p. 439.
[§] Hoofd, *ubi sup.*, p. 311.   [||] Ibid. Bor., *ubi sup.*

the expedition to Batenberg, who soon after set
out with five thousand men—undisciplined and ill-
armed levies.* But alack, the whole Spanish army
fell upon him just beneath the Haarlem bastions,
and he himself, together with the major part of his
raw force made but a breakfast for Don Frederic,
all being slain.†

It was the beginning of the end. The prince's
resources were exhausted; those of the burghers
had long ago touched the saddest bottom. "Well,
then," said the citizens, "we can die but once. Let
us form ourselves into a square, place our wives and
children in the centre, fire the town, and sally forth
to cut our way through the Spanish camp, or perish in the attempt."‡

This heroic idea was of a piece with the defence;
and when Don Frederic was told of it, as he soon
was, he feared that the fruits of his victory would
escape him. Accordingly, he sent to offer terms to
the besieged, solemnly assuring them that ample
forgiveness should attend surrender.§ The burghers were incredulous—had they not memories? But
a large portion of the garrison, the Germans especially, favored submission.‖ On the 12th of July,
1573, after a resistance of above seven months, a
formal surrender was signed. Alva granted an amnesty to all but fifty-seven of the citizens, agreed to

---

* Bor., tom. 6, p. 440.
† Ibid. Meteren, tom. 4, folio 80, et alii.
‡ Bor., ubi sup. Mendoza, tom. 9, p. 204.
§ Bor., tom. 6, p. 413. Mendoza, ut antea, et al. ‖ Ibid.

dismiss the Germans unharmed, and commuted the plunder for two hundred and forty thousand guilders*—honorable terms had they been observed.

But the Spaniards had no sooner passed Haarlem gates than they again demonstrated the absurdity of reliance on their word. Pillage they did not, because the promised moneys were not in town; but murder was a safe pastime. Ripperda, Lancelot van Brederode—all the heroes of the long defence, were at once beheaded.† Within the space of eight days after the surrender, two thousand persons were butchered in cold blood.‡

Such was the fate of Haarlem. But the victory was not cheaply bought. Many of his ablest officers, and thirteen thousand of his choicest veterans§—this was the price which Alva paid for the stout old town.

* Bor., and Hoofd, *ubi sup.*, *et alii*.

† Ibid.   Brandt, vol. 1, pp. 303, 304.

‡ Campana, Guer. di Fiand., lib. 4, p. 112.   Hoofd, tom. 8, p. 315, *et seq.*, *et al.*

§ Hoofd, *ubi sup.*   Bor., tom. 6, p. 444.   Compare Mendoza, tom. 9, p. 206, and Cabrera, tom. 10, p. 759.   Strada, tom. 2, p. 70.

CHAPTER XXXVIII.

THE PATRIOT HORIZON BRIGHTENS.

THE capture of Haarlem caused little exultation
in the Spanish camp; all looked upon it as a Cad-
mean victory. Alva was a "pendulum betwixt a
smile and tear." He was inside the town; but at
what woeful cost of men and means and time! If
seven months, thirty thousand soldiers, and a dead-
list thirteen thousand long were requisite to the
taking the weakest place in Holland, how many
months, how many men, how many lives must be
sacrificed in reducing other and stouter cities? in
conquering the whole province? As the glum duke
essayed to make the calculation, these burghers, of
whom he had been wont to say, "I will smother
them in their own butter," rose many degrees in his
estimation. It now seemed as if Spain, and both
the Indies besides, would be beggared before half
these plebeian heads could be got inside the firkin.
Already twenty-five millions of florins had been sent
from Madrid to meet the expenses of the captain*
who had promised to make gold run in a current a
yard deep from, not to, the Netherlands—twenty-
five millions of florins in addition to what immense
sums had been dug from the mine of confiscation
and got from the imposition of gigantic taxes.†

---

* Motley, vol. 2, p. 456.   † Ibid.

Yet the lagoons still held out; and Alva, like the daughters of the horse-leech, was always crying, "Give, give."

Somewhat daunted by these facts, the duke determined to do by his pen what he had been unable to achieve by force of arms. On the 26th of July, 1573, he issued a monitory circular in the form of a royal address. "Notwithstanding your manifold crimes"—so ran the text of this appeal to these "men of butter"—"his majesty still seeks, like a hen calling her chickens, to gather you all under the maternal wing." But in the next line this billing and cooing is followed by an outburst of characteristic brutality: "If ye disregard this offer of mercy as heretofore, then understand that there is no rigor, no cruelty so great, but you may expect it. Waste, starvation, the sabre shall utterly depopulate the land, and cause it to be occupied again by strangers."*

But in this case the pen was *not* mightier than the sword. Threats and banishments were alike laughed to scorn by the incorrigible "men of butter."

While Alva still snarled under this failure, a mishap occurred which yoked alarm to his chagrin. The soldiery, disappointed in their expectation of pillaging Haarlem, sore from their recent losses, and exasperated by the non-payment of their long arrears, rose in sudden, furious mutiny.† Quarter-

* Bor., tom. 6, pp. 445, 446.
† Ibid., p. 444. Hoofd, tom. 8, p. 317.

ing themselves at will upon the wretched citizens of Haarlem, their license and greedy rage speedily completed the spoliation of the town.* Don Frederic, the duke himself, the most strict of disciplinarians, remonstrated, promised, threatened in vain. Indeed, in the teeth of their efforts, the insubordination spread from Holland into all the other states. Outlasting the entire month of August, the outbreak was only quelled in the end by the intercession of Chiappino Vitelli, the pet of the army, who, with much ado, prevailed upon the mutineers to accept thirty crowns apiece, and relapse into obedient automata.†

This mutiny was regarded by the Hollanders as a God-given opportunity. While Alva was occupied in composing domestic jars, they had space in which to recover from the half-despair into which they had been thrown by the successful leaguer of Haarlem. Orange had not lost his serenity. He had suffered, but he took that to be his lot. His faith nothing could shake. "I had hoped to send you better news," wrote he to Count Louis just after the capitulation; "nevertheless, since it has pleased the Allwise to order otherwise, we must conform ourselves to the Divine will; but I take God to witness that I did all within my power to succor the fallen city."‡ A few days afterwards he wrote again, to inform his brother that the Zealand-

* Bor., tom. 6, p. 444. Hoofd, tom. 8, p. 317.
† Corresp. de Philippe II., tom. 2, p. 1260.
‡ Groen v. Prinst., Archives, etc., tom. 4, p. 175.

ers had captured the castle of Rammekins, a famous
fortress on the island of Walcheren. "I hope,"
added he, "that this will reduce the pride of our
enemies, who, since the surrender of Haarlem, have
seemed to think that they were about to swallow us
alive."*

It was understood throughout the province that
Alckmaar, a town in North Holland, was to be Alva's
next point of attack. The inhabitants of that section were uneasy at the prospect of the unequal
combat, and Diedrich Sanoy, who was in command
there, wrote William that many were preparing to
fly. "Nothing," said he, "but a hope that your
princely grace has formed an alliance with some
powerful potentate stays the emigration. If this
be indeed so, I pray you let me know, that I may
publish it."†

"Be comforted," replied William, in a strain of
the grandest eloquence. "Though God hath permitted the town of Haarlem to suffer, men ought not
therefore to renounce or discredit his divine word.
Will any maintain from this that Jehovah's arm is
shortened? Are his church and people ruined by
the fall of one city? Charity excites pity for those
of Haarlem; but the blood of martyrs is the seed
of the church. Therefore the people of this state,
remembering the enemy's intention, and observing
that he trampleth on all laws human and divine,
should the more courageously and steadily appear

* Groen v. Prinst., Archives, etc., tom. 4, p. 171.
† Bor., tom. 6, p. 446, et seq.

in defence of this so righteous cause. You ask if I have concluded any alliance with other princes. Yea, and thrice yea. I have made a strict alliance with the Prince of princes—with Him who never forsakes those who trust in him. He will assuredly, at the last, confound both his and our opponents."*

By these words the godly prince touched that deep chord of enthusiasm which had lain unstrung till now, causing it to vibrate in "a seven-fold chorus of halleluias and harping symphonies." The voice of complaint was hushed. All sprang up to renew the struggle. Everywhere stores were collected, ammunition was heaped up, fortifications were repaired and strengthened. Orange "smote the rock of the national resources, and abundant streams of revenue gushed forth. He touched the corpse of public credit, and it sprang upon its feet." The seizure of ecclesiastical property, the sale of licenses and permits to trading-vessels—the most unpopular measures were acquiesced in without a murmur:† had not William affirmed that God himself demanded the sacrifice?

Meantime Don Frederic, having got his men once more in hand, moved forward, sixteen thousand strong, to the siege of Alckmaar. Having, by the capture of Haarlem, split Holland in two, it now remained to subjugate the north end of the province; then the conquest of the south would complete the work. On the 21st of August, 1573, the

* Bor., tom. 6, p. 447, *et seq*. Brandt, vol. 1, p. 304.
† Davies, vol. 1, p. 603.

place was formally invested—so closely girt that, in in Alva's phrase, "it was impossible for a sparrow to enter or go out of the city."[*] This time the duke meant to make clean work. Nettled by the contemptuous rejection of his pacific overtures, he wrote Philip: "If I take Alckmaar, I am resolved not to leave a single creature alive; the knife shall be put to every throat. Since the example of Haarlem has proved useless, perhaps an example of cruelty will bring the other cities to their senses."[†]

Alva felt certain of the speedy fall of the menaced town. Within its walls there was a garrison of but eight hundred men, supplemented by thirteen hundred raw and ill-armed burghers—twenty-one hundred in all, to oppose Don Frederic's sixteen thousand veterans.[‡]

Don Frederic, like his father, was bent on making short work of the siege. On the 18th of September he opened fire, continued the bombardment for twelve hours, knocked numberless holes in the walls, and then ordered a grand assault.[§] The escalade, gallantly attempted upon two sides at once, was as gallantly met. Here, as before at Haarlem, unslaked lime, molten lead, boiling water, tarred and burning hoops, were used to repel the foe; and as fast as any mounted the ramparts, they were faced by the unflinching garrison, and hurled bleeding, lifeless, back into the gaping moat. The

---

* Corresp. de Philippe II., tom. 2, p. 1264. † Ibid.
‡ Hoofd, tom. 8, p. 321. Wagenaer.
§ Hoofd, *ubi sup.*, p. 323. Mendoza, tom. 10, p. 217, *et seq.*

whole populace swarmed to the walls; women and little girls, never shrinking from the fight even where it was most deadly, passed to and fro, supplying their husbands, brothers, fathers with stones, and burning missiles, and loaded muskets, encouraging their defenders by the unceasing labors of devoted womanhood.* Once, twice, thrice was the attack repulsed; once, twice, thrice did the enraged assailants return to the assault, until, convinced that success was impossible, and disheartened by the fall of night, they fled back to their trenches, leaving a thousand of their dead to choke up the breaches.†

"As I looked down into the city," said one of the Spaniards who had mounted the ramparts for an instant, only to be plunged headlong from the battlements, "I saw neither helmet nor harness; only some plain-looking people dressed like fishermen."‡ Such were the men who had just foiled the elaborate assault of veterans trained to war in the school of the duke of Alva.§

After a rest of twelve or fifteen hours, Don Frederic reopened fire upon Alckmaar; after which he again ordered an assault. But the "invincibles" had had enough of it. When their officers shouted "form," when the bugles sounded the charge, not a soldier stirred. Numbers of them were sabred by their infuriated captains: in vain,

---

* Hoofd, p. 324.   † Ibid. Compare Mendoza, *ubi sup.*
‡ Hoofd; cited in Motley, vol. 2, p. 468.
§ Motley, *ubi sup.*

the rest were neither to be coaxed nor driven to the wall.*

The burghers soon heard of this, gleaning the full particulars from Jeronimo de Arcibu, a Spaniard whom they took in a sally. This prisoner made other disclosures on being promised his life—a promise which was not kept, to the displeasure of many, who were of the opinion that pledges given even to a foeman ought sacredly to be observed. On being led out to die, Arcibu begged hard for a reprieve. "Spare my life," cried he, "and I too will believe in the devil whom you worship."† A child of the mass, he really thought that all heretics made a god of Satan, every man of them crying, "Evil, be thou my good."

Disappointed in his hope of escalading Alck-maar, Don Frederic prepared to starve it into submission, esteeming the siege another Haarlem. But one day his pickets intercepted a letter from Orange to the besieged, in which the prince affirmed his purpose to succor the town by opening the sluices and laying the adjacent lands under water.‡ The harvests would be submerged, much property would be destroyed, many lives might be lost; but the Spaniard would be driven either to decamp or to go down before the deluge.

Don Frederic was startled by the imminence of the peril. For some weeks, the heavy autumnal

* Hoofd, tom. 8, p. 324.
† Brandt, vol. 1, p. 305. Hoofd, *ubi sup.*
‡ Hoofd, *ubi sup.*, p. 325. Mendoza, tom. 10, p. 219, *et seq.*

rains had been falling; his camp was already a
puddle; his legions were insubordinate; and now
he was menaced by a flood, certain to wash him
out of existence. Menaced? nay, the work had
been commenced. Driven by a strong northwest
wind, vast bodies of water were at that moment
pouring through the opened sluices, splashing
through and running over the surrounding net-
work of canals—hurried towards Alckmaar by
every breeze.*

Don Frederic waited no longer. Breaking up his
camp on the 8th of October, seven weeks after the
investment of the town, he fled rather than retreated to Amsterdam, rejoining his father, and putting
the troops, exhausted and demoralized, into winter
quarters.†

Nor did Alva, at this juncture, fare better at sea
than on the land. For some time, a patriot flotilla
had floated off the mouth of the river V, blockading Amsterdam, to revenge the assistance lent the
Spaniard by its burghers in the leaguer of Haarlem. So closely was the harbor watched, that the
smallest craft might not scud through the fleet into
or from the Zuyder Zee, whether inward or outward
bound.‡ The embargo created great discontent on
the Amsterdam quays, and was a sad blow at commerce, the life of a trading town.

The duke, provoked at the effrontery of the sea

* Hoofd and Mendoza, *ut antea.*
† Ibid. Cor. de Philippe II., tom. 2, p. 1280. Meteren.
‡ Bor., Hoofd.

beggars in blockading Amsterdam while he was himself in command, equipped a squadron with the utmost expedition, and sent Bossu to chase them off. On the 11th of October, 1573, the Spanish admiral bore down upon the patriot armada, cleared for action, his guns grinning through the open portholes. Dirkzoon, the Dutch commander, wanted no second invitation to engage, and a broadside from his galley commenced the action. The two fleets were about equal in number—twenty-five or thirty on each side;* but the Spanish vessels were the larger, and carried heavier cannon.† The engagement was sharp and prolonged, outlasting eight hours. For a while the scales of battle hung even; but at last the Hollanders closed with the foe, carried several of the royalist ships by the board, sank two of them, stranded three more, which were eventually taken, and dispersed the rest.‡

Bossu long disdained to yield, fighting his vessel—which, with some bravado, he styled "The Inquisition"—until every one of the thirty-two guns was dismounted, and the crew, three hundred strong at the outset, was reduced to fifteen men; then, conscious that he had done his utmost to redeem the day, he struck his colors and gave up his sword, being carried by the victorious *gueux* into Horn.§

º Motley, vol. 2, pp. 490, 491.
† Hoofd, tom. 8, p. 326, *et seq.* Bor., tom. 6, p. 455.
‡ Ibid., *et seq.*
§ Ibid. Mendoza, tom. 10, p. 214. Strada, tom. 2, p. 81.

This signal victory, coming, as it did, close upon the repulse of the Spaniard at Alckmaar, made Holland jubilant; and when, in the midst of the rejoicing, news came that William's partisans had surprised Gertruydenberg, which commanded the Meuse and gave the patriots a free entrance into Brabant,* it seemed as if the blessings invoked by the prince upon his country had been dropped from the pitying heavens. A feeling of deep, religious gratitude to God, who had, as in the days of the psalmist, "with his arm redeemed his people," succeeded the first outburst of gratulation. The estates, giving official voice to this emotion, hastened to appoint a day of solemn thanksgiving, which was duly observed in all the churches of the province.†

This succession of disasters visibly affected Alva. "Injuries," wrote Granvelle to a client who had complained to him of the neglect with which the king's best friends were treated at Brussels; "injuries, like pills, should be swallowed without chewing, that we may not taste their bitterness"‡— a noble maxim if the motive had been noble. But the duke was neither sufficiently Spartan nor sufficiently sycophantic to gulp down these reverses without making a wry face. He had been about to sit down to the siege of Leyden, which he meant to preface by the execution of St. Aldegonde—that

* Watson, p. 211. Brandt, vol. 1, p. 305.

† Watson, ubi sup.

‡ Lavesque. Mem. de Granvelle, tom. 2, p. 96.

eminent personage, master of the deepest mysteries of state, having been taken recently by his forces at Maeslandsluis*—when this news came to postpone the siege, and also to stop the proposed murder; William sending the duke word that whatever measure was dealt out to St. Aldegonde, should be requited to Bossu.†

While the patriot arms were thus crowned with unwonted triumph, the prince's pen was also active. Alva, unable to obtain any farther remittances from Spain, and equally unable to exact the twentieth and tenth pennies, was driven at this crisis to the irksome and now hazardous measure of convening the states-general of the provinces, in order to obtain from them the vote of a subsidy with which to carry on the war.‡ The national deputies assembled in Brussels early in September, 1573;§ whereupon Orange, in his own name and in that of the estates of Holland and Zealand, drew up and despatched to them an earnest exhortatory manifesto. "The Spaniards came," said he, " to reduce us, our wives, our children, into vassalage. Worst of all, they expect us to be accountable to them for our souls and consciences, over which they wish to tyrannize at pleasure; though some among them hardly know that there is a God in heaven, and have scarce ever heard of the Son of God, our only

---

° Cor. de Philippe II., tom. 2, p. 1283. Meteren, tom. 4, fol. 85.
† Hoofd, tom. 8, p. 331.
‡ Bor., tom. 6, p. 459.   Brandt, vol. 1, p. 305.
§ Ibid.

Saviour. Yet these pagans assume to object to our faith and practice, seeking, under that pretence, to enslave us to their Inquisition, used in Spain against Moors, Jews, and apostate Christians. Now, because we will not bow the knee to Baal, Alva endeavors to persuade you that we are rebels; hoping thereby to separate you from us your brothers, and to make you the tools of his insolence, the executioners of his cruelty, the defenders of his impious desires. But, fellow-countrymen, do you rather unite with and assist us in opposing this bad steward of the king. 'T is only by the Netherlands that the Netherlands can be subdued. Whence hath the duke the power of which he boasts, but from yourselves? Whence his ships, supplies, moneys, weapons, soldiers? From the Netherland cities. Why has poor Netherland become degenerate and bastard? Wist ye not that our forefathers never brooked the tyranny of foreign nations, nor suffered aliens even to hold office within our borders? If this little strip of land called Holland, if a marshy archipelago like Zealand, can thus hold at bay the power of Spain, what could not all the Netherlands accomplish? As for ourselves, we intend to perish one town after another, man by man, rather than submit to Alva's tyranny over the soul and over the body."*

These ringing words were prodigiously effective; and though the states-general were not prepared to make common cause with Orange, they did refuse

* Bor., tom. 5, p. 459, *et seq.* Brandt, vol. 1, p. 305.

to advance a penny to refill the empty exchequer of the viceroy,* and the object of the manifesto was so far gained.

Encouraged by this success, William next indited an "epistle" to the king—not so much with the hope of touching Philip, as for the purpose of placing his cause before the world. "We contend, sire," wrote he, "for nothing less than our ancient franchises and freedom of conscience. We do not desire to shake off our allegiance to your majesty; but only that our consciences may be preserved free before the Lord our God, that we may be permitted to hear his holy word, and walk in his commandments, so that we may be able to give an account of our souls to the Supreme Judge at the last day. This, Alva denies us in your name; therefore have we taken up arms, therefore do we strive to free ourselves from his bloodthirsty hands. If he prove too strong for us, we can at least die honorably, leaving a praiseworthy name and an unconquered fatherland. Herein are all our cities pledged to each other and to God, to stand every siege, to dare the utmost, to endure all imaginable miseries; yea, rather to set fire to our homes and give back these toil-won lands to the sea, than ever to submit our souls to a Satanic yoke."†

Soon after the publication of this letter, the dauntless advocate of Luther's axiom, that "thought is toll-free," publicly united with the Reformed

* Bor., Hoofd.

† Bor., tom. 6, p. 469, *et seq.* Brandt, *ut antea.*

Dutch church at Dort, in order that his testimony and his life might be of a piece.[*]

Meantime, galled by his losses, aware that the towns of Holland had been delivered from immediate peril, and convinced that his continued residence at Amsterdam would be a practical imprisonment, since the *gueux*, surrounding the city on all sides, effectually barred communication with the southern provinces,[†] Alva determined to leave the lagunes and return to Brussels. But so much had he suffered in *prestige*, so bitterly was he hated, and above all, so ruinously had he run in debt to the burghers, that he feared an insurrection might stay an open departure. Accordingly, he resorted to stratagem. One day in November, he gave notice by sound of trumpet, that all to whom he was indebted should attend him the next morning to receive their dues; then this free-liver on the money of other men, who was prodigal *not* within the compass of a guinea, this hero of a hundred battles, cheated his creditors by skulking out of Amsterdam under cover of the night[‡]—certainly not a dignified proceeding on the part of his highness, the governor-general of the Low Countries.

Since Medina Cœli had peeped into the country, and then, observing the chaos, slipped out, leaving the burden of affairs on the shoulders of him whom he had come to relieve, the duke had

[*] Archives de la Maison d'Orange-Nassau, tom. 4, p. 226.

[†] Velius Hoorn, book 3, bl. 221, *et seq.*

[‡] Hoofd, tom. 8, pp. 329, 330. Brandt, vol. 1, p. 305.

never ceased importuning the king for leave to retire
from the vice-regal throne. Now Philip, marking
the general shipwreck of his interests in the Netherlands, again acceded, commissioning on this occasion, as Alva's successor, Don Luis de Requesens,
grand commander of the order of St. Iago.[*]

The new governor arrived at Brussels on the
17th of November, 1573;[†] upon which event, Alva
wrote to "kiss his majesty's feet;" preparing
meantime to follow the salute with all speed. On
the 18th of December, he left the states never to
return, amid the smothered curses of all classes;[‡]
though, as the Romans said of Augustus Cæsar,
that he should either not have been born or not
have died, the ultra-loyalists affirmed that the duke
ought either not to have entered the provinces, or
not to have departed at that time, in eclipse, when
the patriot horizon was all ablaze with success.[§]

[*] Hoofd, tom. 8, p. 331. Bor., tom. 6, p. 474.   [†] Ibid.

[‡] Corresp. de Philippe II., tom. 2, p. 1291. Brandt, vol. 1, p.
306.

[§] Strada, tom. 2, p. 81. On reaching Madrid, Alva was well
received by the king, residing at court until Don Frederic brought
both himself and his father into disgrace. Having betrayed one of
the queen's maids of honor, he suddenly married his cousin, to
avoid that reparation by espousal which was claimed; whereupon
Philip banished and imprisoned Don Frederic, and Alva also because he had advised the baseness. Some years later, when he
undertook the conquest of Portugal, the king required the old soldier's sword once more, and he was intrusted with the chief command of the Spanish army; which caused Alva to wonder that, for
the conquest of a kingdom, his majesty should have use of a fettered general. He managed the war with his accustomed skill,
subdued the Portuguese, and annexed their land to Spain. But
having overtoiled himself in this campaigning, he soon after fell

He went out, taking with him his ferocious son, Don Frederic de Toledo, and jackal Vargas, and "Egypt was glad when they departed." On the homeward journey, Alva boasted that during his five years' rule eighteen thousand six hundred citizens had been done to death by the headsman;[*] and this in addition to the myriads of both sexes, of all ages, who had perished in battle and siege, by famine, by massacre; and at the stake, put to death in the wantonness of impunity—a phantom host whose number may not be computed. Yet, though perfectly familiar with the details of this dead-list—who knew it better?—Vargas complained pathetically that over-clemency was the rock upon which the administration of the duke was wrecked.[†] Alva himself seemed to think so, for he wrote the king: "Err no more in that direction, sire; burn to the ground every city in the Low Countries except here and there one, which can be permanently garrisoned."[‡]

But thoroughly brutal as he was, absolutely lost to all compassion, 't is certain that the butcher duke did not exceed his instructions[§]—never ran without his message, even though he returned without his answer. As the image of the murderer is said to

ill at Lisbon, and died on the 12th of December, 1582. *Vide* Strada, tom. 2, p. 81, *et seq.*   Vie du Duc d'Albe, *in loco.*

  [*] Hoofd, tom. 8, p. 332.   Brandt, vol. 1, p. 306.   Bor., tom. 6, p. 474.

  [†] Meteren, tom. 4, folio 86.   Brandt, *ut antea.*

  [‡] Corresp. de Philippe II., tom. 2, p. 1276.

  [§] Strada, tom. 2, p. 82.

be stamped upon and reflected by the retina of the
victim's eye, so in the denouncing orbs of these cruelties Philip's face glints into sight, cold, pitiless,
approving.

Of Alva's character it were superfluous to speak;
he had none. His acts are before us, and they tell
the story. His merits may be summed up with
judicial fairness in the words—a consummate soldier. Yet despite his military skill, he took the
provinces from the duchess of Parma in seeming
repose, and left them in open and successful revolt.
All his victories were defeats; every patriot defeat
a victory; for liberty is vital in every part, and cannot die but by annihilation.

As a statesman, he was despicable; as a financier, crazy. Unlike Granvelle, he did not even
understand the politics of despotism. Finding his
party strong, he left it broken in utter shameless-
ness. Succeeding to a treasure-house measurably
full, he left it defeated, in hopeless bankruptcy.
His whims replaced the ancient charters of the
Netherlands; his confiscations replaced legitimate
finance.

Alva knew only to destroy. His last act was, to
roast alive, over a slow fire, Uitenhaave, a Protestant gentleman of Ghent. His whole rule was a
hunt for plunder. Even the soldiery were accustomed to take, without a "by your leave," whatever
they fancied from the burghers upon whom they
were billeted; for had they not been taught to think
that the Netherlanders had forfeited all rights by

their rebellion against that brace of divinities, Philip and the pope? The duke had won fame elsewhere; here, only infamy. The blood of martyrs blighted his laurels. When he departed, humanity thanked God that it had one enemy the less.

CHAPTER XXXIX.

THE GRAND COMMANDER OF ST. IAGO.

In awarding Alva's relinquished sceptre to Requesens, his majesty of Spain gave evidence of an altered policy, but not of a changed purpose. Having, now for above five years, moved bishops, knights, and castles across the chess-board of the provinces with no definite result, he meant to use this viceroy as a counter in a new game for the same stake.

Requesens was a man of engaging manners, but of mediocre parts. He brought with him into the Netherlands an established reputation. As governor of Milan, he was esteemed by Philip to have been alike firm and prudent—a kind of military Machiavelli.* In the Levant, in manifold fightings with the Turk, and especially at the battle of Lepanto—a splendid victory, but barren as the waves on which the conquering galleys rode—he had won some fame. And though, like his predecessor, a soldier, he was, unlike the duke, at least human and accessible.

His reception at Brussels was cordial. Wearied of the brutal monotony of Alva's rule, the people felt that any change must bring relief.† Still, it

* Strada, tom. 3, p. 1.
† Bor., tom. 7, p. 477. Strada, *ubi sup.*

was whispered that this smiling stranger knew how to be cruel, and the suspicion was strengthened by mutterings which swept seaward from Milan, and by the recollection of his crucifixions of the Moriscoes in Grenada.* Besides, since the sovereignty of the house of Austria began over the Netherlands, had it not been customary to seat a prince of the blood as governor-general in the capital? Yet the new-comer was but a "gentleman of cloak and sword."†

As for Requesens, it was his cue to court popularity and to play the part of a conciliator. Not that he really felt kindly towards the states; he distinctly averred that, at heart, he approved of Alva's severities.‡ He only assumed the part because the king, unsuccessful in the field, had determined, if possible, to resort once more to guile.§

He began his administration by punishing the insolencies of several mutinous bands of men-at-arms, living at free-commons upon the provinces, as was their wont. The citizens applauded. Next he hurled Duke Alva's statue from its pedestal in Antwerp citadel. The burghers shouted themselves hoarse.‖

Elated and self-confident, Requesens imagined from these demonstrations that the people might be

* Prescott, Hist. of Philip II., vol. 3, *in loco.* Watson, Life of Philip II.

† Corresp. de Mondoucet et Charles IX. Cited in Motley, vol. 2, p. 512.   ‡ Corresp. de Philippe II., tom. 2, p. 1291.

§ Strada, tom. 3, p. 1. Motley, vol. 2, pp. 514, 519.

‖ Strada, *ubi sup.*

made clay in his hands, to be fashioned after any pattern which he might select. "Sire," wrote he to Philip at this juncture, "religion has naught to do with this struggle. 'T is but a trumped-up fulcrum for demagogues to rest their levers on in their attempt to overthrow your majesty's authority. Grant me to pardon penitent heretics, and to reconcile them to holy church, permit me to send into perpetual exile a few of the obstinate, with some small portion of their estates; and we shall have peace."[*]

Such was the new governor-general's diagnosis of the Netherland disease; a diagnosis based upon a huzza and a few *vivas*—symptoms occasioned, too, by the curbing the free lances and the toppling over a hated effigy; a diagnosis which at once stamped the viceroy as a quack in politics. Alva, Philip himself, could have told him better.

However, as the war was as yet in mid-career, Requesens wished, before applying his panacea, to signalize his advent by some exploit which should at once sustain his fame and advance him in the estimation of the king. He thought that an amnesty would attract more attention if set off against the background of a victory.

An opportunity to "sound the clarion, fill the fife," was not lacking. For twenty-four months past, the patriots had been besieging Middleburg, grimly persistent to clutch it for Orange. With as stern determination, stout old Mondragone held it for the king. Various attempts made by Alva to

---

[*] Corresp. de Philippe II., *ubi sup.*, p. 1293.

succor the town—the last in the archipelago which floated the Spanish banner—had been thwarted by the Dutch fleet. Now, reduced to famine-rations, Mondragone sent word to Brussels that, unless relieved at once, he must surrender.*

Such an announcement, from such a soldier, meant all it said. Requesens had essayed to persuade the besiegers to raise the leaguer, promising in that event to purge their treason with the hyssop of a royal pardon. Deaf to this offer, the Zealanders only drew their lines more closely about the starving city.†

The governor-general hastened to Antwerp, rigged out a flotilla, freighted it with provisions, crowded it with soldiers, gave the command of seventy-five vessels to his admiral, De Glimes, and to Romero, intrusted thirty ships to Sanchio D'Avila, ordered those to sail towards Middleburg by one passage, these by another, and then passed on to the village of Schakerloo, in order to witness from its quays the triumphant raising of the siege.‡

The patriots, apprized betimes of the expedition, prepared to defeat it. Orange himself came over from Holland to officer " the beggars of the sea."§ He, like Requesens, divided his armada, upwards of a hundred ships, into two squadrons, retained the command of one, and gave the chieftainship of the

* Bor., tom. 7, p. 479. Strada, tom. 3, p. 1.

† Strada, *ubi sup.*

‡ Meteren, tom. 5, folio 88. Hoofd, tom. 9, p. 335. Mendoza, tom. 9, p. 225. § Ibid.

other to Boisot, the skilful admiral of Zealand, whom he ordered to grapple with De Glimes and Romero, remaining off Middleburg in person to deal with D'Avila.*

On the 27th of January, 1574, De Glimes and Romero hove in sight, and Boisot lifted anchor and bore down to meet them† with forty men-of-war. Both fleets cleared for action, and broadsides given and returned commenced the engagement. It was short, decisive. For a time the enveloping smoke hid all. When this rolled up, ten of the Spanish vessels were seen to have been sunk.‡ A little later the Zealanders, pursuing their favorite tactics, carried what ships still contended by the board, killed De Glimes, slew twelve hundred of the enemy's marines, took Romero's galley, forced that veteran to swim ashore for his life, and in sight of watching Requesens, scattered the remainder of his armada in wild flight.§

The prince did not go into action; for D'Avila, informed of the utter route of the companion-fleet, wore ship, and put back to Antwerp, chased almost into port by the victorious *gueux*.‖

The mortified viceroy at once returned to Brussels, and Middleburg surrendered. William granted terms of remarkable liberality, as a merited recognition of the stubborn gallantry of the defence,

---

* Bor., book 7, p. 479.
† Ibid. Hoofd, book 9, p. 335, *et seq.*
‡ Ibid. Mendoza, tom. 11, p. 226, *seq.*
§ Bor., Hoofd, *ubi sup.* Meteren, book 5, folio 89. ‖ Ibid.

permitting the garrison to march out with arms and baggage, the priests to pass over to the mainland; granting a pardon to the citizens, on condition that they took the oath to him as stadtholder, and paid a subsidy of three hundred thousand florins, two-thirds of which he afterwards remitted; and freeing Mondragone on a parole which required him, within two months, either to secure the release of St. Alde-gonde or to return himself as a prisoner-of-war.*

By the acquisition of Middleburg, the patriots gained the island of Walcheren, freed all Zealand, and swept the whole seaboard clear of foes. So much was achieved, too, by a volunteer navy. The siege and the repeated attempts to raise it, had cost the king seven millions of florins, in addition to the pay of the men-at-arms;† and if such were the footing up of one item in the budget of expense, is it strange that the aggregate should mortgage the gold-mines of Peru and Mexico and empty the home-treasury?

Contrarywise, the *gueux* had no regular fund from which to draw. Fighting for God and the fatherland, they scorned to put their hands into the necessitous pockets of the state—the unselfish "beggars of the sea" left that for the mercenaries whom Orange was forced from time to time to recruit. Usually they subsisted upon the free-will offerings of their fellow-citizens of the towns off which they chanced to anchor. When this resource failed, they gave chase to any Spanish merchantman which

---

* Mendoza, tom. 9, p. 229.   Hoofd, tom. 9, p. 338.   Bor., *et al.*
† Davies, vol. 2, p. 3.

might cross their watery path, wringing their support at the sword's point from the enemy. When their lookouts could descry no Spaniard, and their larder was at low ebb, men and officers alike were content to live for weeks at a time upon the salt-herring, a staple export of their country. Nor were they more terrified by death than by privation and hunger. If menaced by capture, they always preferred to blow up their ships rather than strike their flag to the hated foreigner.* What had such men to fear? What human power could reduce such combatants to vassalage?

Requesens himself soon came to understand this. "Before my arrival," wrote he to Philip, "I could not comprehend how the impoverished rebels could maintain such considerable fleets, while your majesty could hardly support a single squadron. It appears, however, that men who are fighting for their lives, their firesides, their properties, their false religion, for their own cause, in a word, are content to receive rations only, without asking for pay."†

But this nation of mariners, unconquerable at sea, were unable to cope with their oppressor on the land. Patient to suffer, dauntless in defence, they yet lacked the experience and the discipline essential to success in offensive warfare. Consequently the prince was driven to enroll armies outside of his own boundary lines. This was the vulnerable spot in the heel of that Achilles; for

* Davies, vol. 2, p. 3. Meteren, book 5, folio 99.
† Corresp. de Philippe II., tom. 2, p. 1291.

men who spill their blood for hire estimate a cause by the value of its gold-setting.

But in war armies are essential, and William was at this time doing his utmost to raise one. He had applied for aid to Elizabeth, though vainly at the moment; for her majesty had but recently re-opened commercial intercourse with Spain,* and she feared that long interrupted trade would balk at any fresh quarrel.†

Some time since diplomatic relations, broken off by the massacre of St. Bartholomew, had been renewed with France. It was not without grave doubt that Orange permitted himself again to clasp in amity hands red with the blood of the slaughtered Huguenots.‡ But of late Charles IX. had professed bitterly to lament that crime, and he had humbly courted a reconciliation not only with the prince, but with the Protestant powers of Europe.§ Of course the motive which inspired this move was patent. Everybody knew that the queen-mother still wished to obtain the marital alliance with England, and that she was equally anxious to see Anjou elected king of Poland.‖ As Orange was thought to be influential in both these quarters, his coöperation was a *desideratum*.¶ William was aware that private griefs ought not to be allowed

* On the 1st of May, 1573.
† Hume, Hist. of Eng. Bor.   ‡ Motley, vol. 2, p. 476.
§ Archives de la Maison d'Orange-Nassau, tom. 4, par. 2. De Thou, *et alii*.
‖ De Thou, Davila. Hist. of Huguenots.
¶ Motley, *ubi sup.*, p. 483.

to stand in the way of public necessities; and finally he consented to trade help for help.

Between Gaspar de Schömberg, the keen but honorable agent of the French court in Germany, and Count Louis, a treaty was negotiated and signed. Under this instrument, Charles IX. bound himself to guarantee toleration to the Huguenots—without which the prince refused to act—to permit Count Louis to levy a thousand horse and seven thousand foot in France for service in the provinces, and to contribute to the patriot exchequer a hundred thousand crowns, money in hand, and an equal sum quarterly.* In return, William promised, in the name of the estates, to place under the protection of the French throne whatever towns might be taken outside of Holland and Zealand, to reimburse his royal ally for the sums advanced, and if possible to obtain the hand of Elizabeth for D'Alençon, and for Anjou the crown of the Jagellons.†

With this treaty and the French moneys in his pocket, Count Louis began to recruit in Germany, the customary chattel-soldier market. Three thousand riders and six thousand arquebusiers were soon enrolled.‡ Late in February, 1574, Count Louis, at the head of this force, and accompanied by his brother Henry, a boy of twenty-four, and by Prince Chris-

---

* Archives de la Maison d'Orange-Nassau, tom. 4, p. 116, et seq.
† Ibid.
‡ Meteren, tom. 5, folio 90. Compare Strada, tom. 3, p. 3; Mendoza, tom. 9, p. 231.

topher, son of the elector palatin, a leal friend of
the good cause, passed the Rhine and opened the
campaign.*   Count Louis' plan was, first, to pounce
upon the important town of Maestricht; or, that
failing, to cross the Meuse at the fords of Stochem,
push thence directly into Holland, form a junction
with William at Delft, and then throw their united
armies as a barrier between the revolted states and
any invasion from the south.†

Requesens, listening through the ears of his spies,
soon heard the din of Count Louis' preparations.
Acting promptly, he too began to make a levy in
the lesser German states.‡   Nor did he neglect to
put his house in order by reinforcing the garrisons
of Valenciennes, of Ghent, of Antwerp, and especially of Maestricht—in all which the prince had
many partisans.§   The greater part of his troops
had gone into winter quarters, sore from recent defeat, sulky because unpaid.   By liberal promises of
spoil and the speedy payment of their arrears, they
were finally prevailed on to take the field; and as
the viceroy had decided to remain at Antwerp with
Chiappino Vitelli, to watch and thwart a rumored
outbreak in favor of Orange, Sanchio D'Avila was
ordered to take the saddle and beat off the invasion.‖

Count Louis, moving with alacrity, pitched his

* Bor., book 7, pp. 489, 490.
† Archives, etc., *ubi sup.*, p. 246, *et seq.*
‡ Bentivoglio, De Thou.   § Mendoza, tom. 9, p. 230.
‖ Ibid. Bor., tom. 7, p. 488.

camp on the banks of the Meuse, opposite Maestricht, in the early days of April, only to find his purposed "pounce" forestalled by the presence of the Spaniard.* Then, in pursuance of the preconcerted plan, he folded his tents and started to meet the prince, who, meantime, had massed six thousand men, and was now advancing to expedite the junction.†

Anxious to foil this union, D'Avila moved down the left bank of the Meuse with extraordinary rapidity, crossed the river at Mook-heath, a hamlet on the confines of the duchy of Cleves, and finding that he had been successful in outmarching his opponent, flung his army across Count Louis' pathway, calmly awaiting his upcoming.‡

On the 13th of April, 1574, Count Louis came upon the scene. He saw at a glance that a battle was inevitable—a battle not of his own seeking, for which he was ill-prepared. .His forces did, indeed, somewhat outnumber those of the Spaniard; but D'Avila was being reinforced from hour to hour, and Mendoza, Braccamonte, Mondragone were already with him; while the patriot ranks, weakened by desertion, were, as usual on the eve of an engagement, broken by a mutiny of the hirelings, clamorous for their wages.§ Under these circumstances, a postponement of the struggle could only make bad worse; and Nassau saw that it would be impos-

---

* Mendoza, *ubi sup.*, p. 233.   † Bor., Hoofd.
‡ Mendoza, *ubi sup.*, p. 239.   Bor., tom. 7, p. 490.
§ Meteren, book 5, folio 91.

sible to give his wary foeman the slip—knew that no herring drawn across the scent could throw him off.

Therefore he spent the night in strengthening his position by girting the camp with a deep trench. In the morning he formed in line of battle, and braced himself to bear the shock.* D'Avila, bright and early, massed his columns and moved to the attack. In a moment the Spaniards leaped the trench, and each singling out his antagonist, pushed the fight with resolute purpose. For a little, all was enraged confusion—glittering casques, clanging swords, blood-smeared faces; then the scene changed, and the hireling infantry of Count Louis was descried quite trampled down and dashed in pieces.†

Count Louis, charging at the head of his riders, momentarily turned the tide; but the Spaniard, regathering his scattered cavaliers, and freshly reinforced, thundered down upon the exhausted patriot horsemen, and hopelessly routed them. Nassau, disdaining to fly, called his young brother to his side, was joined by Duke Christopher, and the dauntless companions-in-arms plunged anew into the fight—plunged in never to come out; never more was either of them seen; nor, though all bore witness to their gallantry, could any tell the precise manner of their fall.‡ It was only known that

---

* Bentivoglio, tom. 8, p. 142, *et seq.*   Mendoza, tom. 9, p. 239.
† Meteren and Mendoza, *ubi sup., et seq.*   Hoofd, book 9, p. 350.
‡ Bentivoglio, Hoofd, Mendoza, *ubi sup.*   Strada, tom. 3, p. 3, *et alii.*

somewhere on the battle-field, strewed with four thousand corpses, lay the intrepid trio, the noblest spoils of D'Avila's victory.

Of itself, the defeat at Mook-heath was a disaster to the patriots; these deaths made it the saddest of calamities. In Count Louis, preëminently, the states lost the stanchest of champions; and William was bereaved at once of the most devoted of brothers and of the trustiest of assistants. The others were lamented; he was missed.

Count Louis was one of those men who inspire friendship and compel respect. He did not possess extraordinary parts, but he was greatly good. Prompt, incisive, fertile in resources, self-reliant, enterprising—he was all this, and more. As a soldier, his chief defect was a lack of prudence. He seemed always to think that nothing could be more indiscreet than discretion. 'T is this trait, perhaps, which explains his frequent failures in the tented field. Nevertheless, his military skill was highly rated by contemporaries, and he had measured swords with some of the foremost warriors of that age.

As a politician too, he was esteemed; and at that time, when Machiavelli was thought to be the model of a diplomat, he was an honest negotiator, and successful withal, though never stooping to a lie for help, and never angling with dissimulation as with a hook. A Christian soldier, he had learned his divinity at Calvin's feet; a steadfast reformer, he understood the why and the wherefore of the war. With such a character, and so equipped, all generous souls might well bemoan his untimely taking-off.

Young Henry Nassau was but just entering upon the stage of action—now cut off in the May of life, as his brother in the mellow ripeness of near middle age. Sadly grieved must have been their widowed mother, who still lived in Germany: called, some years back, to mourn for her son Adolphus, and now weeping over the unknown graves of two more of her children. Happily, she knew where to look for consolation in this bitter hour, and had learned to say, " Father, not my will, but thine be done."

As for Duke Christopher, his father, who was a Christian of the John Knox type, felt proud that he had died in the bed of honor, contending for Jehovah's cause. " 'T were better thus," said he, " than for the boy to have passed his time in idleness, which is the devil's pillow."*

Immediately upon the reception of the melancholy news from Mook-heath, the prince of Orange faced about and marched back to Holland, knowing his inability to keep the field against the victorious Spaniard.† He looked for an eager pursuit. Such was D'Avila's purpose, but an unexpected occurrence held him back: his troops, to whom thirty-six months' arrears were due, mutinied on the battle-field. " Pay us in full," cried

---

* Archives et Cor., tom. 4, p. 367.
† Meteren, book 5, folio 91. De Thou, Bentivoglio.

they, "or we will not advance a step."* Though
lavish of promises before the fight, now that the
day was won, Don Sancho was unable to comply
with the demand. The furious soldiers drove him
out of camp, elected another commander from the
ranks, and started for Antwerp, intending to live at
free commons upon the burghers of that wealthy
city until paid. On the 26th of April they entered
the metropolis, and halted in the great square.
Requesens attempted to harangue them. "Dollars,
not speeches," shouted the armed mob.† As he, like
D'Avila, was flush of promises but scant of funds, the
troops left him haranguing vacancy and proceeded
to quarter themselves upon the town, seeking the
most famous kitchens and the most sumptuous apartments; seating themselves at the tables of bishop
and burgomaster, margrave and merchant, eager,
like Offellius Bibulus, to gluttonize and to guzzle.‡

Some weeks passed ere the viceroy succeeded
in reducing his insubordinate followers again to
order; nor did he master the mutineers until they
had mastered him by obliging him to mulct the
townsfolk in the sum of four hundred thousand
crowns in gold and as much more in merchandise,
with which to settle the king's debt, linking there-
with a full pardon.§

As Requesens rejected all the measures which
Champigny, governor of Antwerp in the absence of

---

* Meteren, *ubi sup.* Bor., book 7, p. 494. Strada, tom. 3, p. 4.
† Ibid.   ‡ Ibid.
§ Bor., *ubi sup.* Bentivoglio, tom. 8, p. 149.

D'Avila, had proposed for the security of the city, forcing him, in compliance with the demand of the mutineers, to quit the citadel with his Walloons, he was, perhaps not unjustly, accused of conniving at the outbreak for the purpose of extorting a contribution from the Brabanters.*

The governor-general was persuaded that the Hollanders could only be met with success upon their chosen element, the water. Recently, he had equipped a flotilla to take the place of that sunk off Middleburg. When the insubordinate troops arrived, these ships lay moored at Antwerp quays. Fearing that they might be seized as security by the soldiers, he ordered their commander, Adolphus Hanstede, to sail down the Scheldt and cast anchor below the town. But in clearing Scylla he ran into Charybdis. The patriot admiral Boisot, learning of the change of station, slipped unsuspected into the river, assailed the Spaniard, sunk fourteen of his vessels, captured Hanstede, and put the surprised crews to the sword.† In several of the galleys vast amounts of plate and valuables had been stowed, to rescue the treasure from the pillage of the mutineers; and this too was transferred to the prince's exchequer.‡ It was a brilliant victory, crippling to Requesens, who intended shortly to employ this armada in the recovery of Zealand; and thus it proved a set-off to the misery of Mook-heath.

° Strada, tom. 3, p. 6. Bor., Hoofd, *et alii*.

† Hoofd, book 9, p. 359, *et seq*. Bentivoglio, tom. 8, p. 149.

‡ Bor., book 7, p. 513.

At the very moment that Boisot was making this havoc in the Scheldt, Philip, thinking with Requeseus that it was essential to his cause to gain a foothold on the sea, was fitting out a flotilla with which he meant to coöperate with his viceroy's squadron and annihilate the privateersmen.* Every dockyard in Spain was kept busy in building vessels. And still farther to increase his fleet, his piratical majesty not only seized what merchant vessels from the Netherlands were in his ports, but likewise pressed into his service traders belonging to Embden and the Hanse towns. In this way, a large force was collected—three hundred ships, laden with fifteen thousand soldiers.†

The *gueux* on being apprized of the impending expedition, prepared, with their wonted energy, to defend themselves. The archipelago was on the *qui vive*. In all the chiefer ports, watch was kept day and night; the wealthier inhabitants voluntarily subscribed loans for the equipment of twenty additional men-of-war; along the whole stormy coastline the buoys and beacons were carefully removed, and the fishermen were forbidden to go out in a west wind, lest, haply, they might be seized by the Spaniard, and compelled to conduct his fleet through the intricate and dangerous channels, impossible to pass without experienced guides.‡

* Bor., book 7, p. 524, *et seq.*
† Bor., *ut antea.*
‡ Ibid. Davies, Hist. of Holland, vol. 2, p. 7.

In anticipation of this difficulty, Philip had imported fifty skilful native pilots ; but they all took the first opportunity to desert, as did thirty-seven of the pressed merchant ships, whose business it was to turn an honest penny, not to meddle with edged tools.*

Just as the armament was about to sail from the bay of Biscay, a frightful plague, which no Aaron standing between the living and the dead was found to stay, broke out among the crews and carried to the grave ten thousand men—among the rest, Don Pedro di Menendez, the valiant and able admiral of the king. Unable to recruit another force to fill this gap, unable also to find another captain of sufficient skill and experience to carry out what remained of the stricken armada, and informed of the destruction of Requesens' auxiliaries by Boisot, Philip was compelled at the last moment to abandon the enterprise,† which, to the devout, seemed a special interposition of Providence in behalf of menaced Holland.

In the meantime, the viceroy, having appeased his mutinous followers, thought it now expedient to proclaim an amnesty, the measure which he esteemed a certain cure-all. All offenders, except a few score clergymen who were named, were informed one bright day in the summer of 1574 that they were pardoned, but on condition that within sixty days, they should go to confession and receive abso-

* Davies, Hist. of Holland, vol. 2, p. 7.
† Bor., Davies, *ut antea*.

lution from a priest.* Gregory XIII. confirmed the act by a special bull for the benefit of the penitents.†

Nevertheless, the Netherlanders, thinking themselves more sinned against than sinning; convinced, moreover, that to accept the pardon was to concede the victory by giving up the very point at issue—their right to worship God at the altar of the Reformation—and readier to go to the grave than to mass, united to scout the amnesty. But two men were found willing to bow the knee to Baal.‡ Had the masses been anxious to enter the Roman fold they would have distrusted the sheep-dog, whose life thus far had been spent in worrying the lambs, and whose fangs were not yet cleaned of wool.

° Meteren, book 5, folio 93. Hoofd, book 9, p. 368. Published June 6th, 1574.

† Brandt, vol. 1, p. 310. Bor., book 7, p. 510.

‡ Bor., *ubi sup.*, p. 516.

CHAPTER XL. .

"FAITHFUL UNTO DEATH."

LEYDEN, one of the most elegant and airy of me-diæval cities, was, in 1574, a thrifty, well-to-do town of forty thousand souls. Lying in the fat bottom-lands of Lower Holland, as in a cradle, it had Delft, Gouda, and the Hague but a few hours' walk away, while Rotterdam upon the left, Haarlem on the right, were within easy reach.

The whole neighboring country was a labyrinth of canals and rivulets—the garden of the state ; and the good burghers were justly proud of these pas-tures, which their persistent skill had reclaimed from the sea and fattened into fertile beauty. Through the centre of the town the old Rhine poured sluggishly towards its sandy death-bed on the coast; for though once the main channel of that classic stream, it had been depleted by the distribution of its waters into innumerable artificial currents, created to irrigate all Rhynland. These canals divided the site of Leyden into a multitude of little islands, tied together by a hundred and forty-five bridges of hammered stone, which were equally subservient to the picturesqueness of the place and to the convenience of the citizens. The *coup d'œil* was not unlike that

"Where Venice sate in state, throned on her hundred isles."

Leyden was an important town, from its position and on its own account, and the Spaniards had long coveted the prize. Alva, on running away from defeat and his creditors at Amsterdam, had left behind him Francesco di Valdez, with orders to invest the place;[*] which that obedient soldier was doing when Count Louis' invasion obliged the duke's successor to summon him off to defend the frontier.[†] Now, having hacked Nassau to pieces and gotten the reins again upon the neck of the army, Requesens decided to resume the leaguer.

On the 26th of May, 1574, Valdez, with eight thousand companion vultures, once more swooped to batten upon Leyden.[‡] Mindful of Haarlem and of Alckmaar, and informed that the townsfolk were ill-provisioned—had not above three months' supplies within their walls—the Spaniard resolved to forego escalades, to jeopard nothing by precipitation, but to isolate the place, and then faminize it into giving him a welcome.[§] In pursuance of this plan, all avenues of communication with the outer world were blocked up, the neighbor towns of Maeslandsluis, Vlaardingen, and the Hague were seized and transformed into Spanish citadels, and Leyden itself was shut in by a circular chain of sixty-two redoubts which ran quite round the city.[‖] This done, the self-satisfied beleaguerer smiled grimly,

* Bor., book 6, p. 472.
† Hoofd, book 9, p. 344.   Mendoza, tom. 9, p. 232, seq.
‡ Bor., book 7, p. 504.   § Ibid.   Mendoza, et alii.
‖ Bentivoglio, tom. 8, p. 152.   Bor., Hoofd.

pattered an *ave maria*, and quietly sat down to see his victims starve.

The town was poorly enough prepared to outlive a siege. Orange had once and again urged the burghers to employ the interim between the departure and return of Valdez in strengthening the garrison and crowding in supplies; "for," added he sagaciously, "the Spaniard will soon reappear."[*] But the easy-going townsfolk doubted the prophecy, refused to look beyond the pleasant now, and heeded not the warning. The consequence was, that on the second coming of Valdez Leyden was only ordinarily provisioned, and stood absolutely ungarrisoned. Its sole reliance, under God, was upon its own train-bands and the coöperating efforts of stadtholder William.[†]

Nevertheless, the citizens, wasting no time in regretting carelessness after the event, made haste to organize a manful resistance. What provisions there were the authorities purchased, and began to husband betimes, placing all upon a strict allowance—a pound of meat and half a pound of bread per day to a full-grown man, and to the rest a *pro rata* amount.[‡] John Van der Does, seigneur de Nordwyck, was appointed military commandant.[§] A consummate scholar, he was equally renowned as a soldier, poet, and historian.[||] He was of gentle birth

[*] Bor., *ubi sup.*, p. 502.

[†] Ibid., p. 505. Hoofd, *ubi sup.*, p. 362.

[‡] Meteren, book 5, folio 94. Hoofd, Bor.

[§] Bor., book 7, p. 505. Mendoza, tom. 12, p. 254. Hoofd, book 9, p. 362.   [||] Ibid.

withal; though, stamped with nature's signet, he would have been noble in despite of blood, had each of his fellows agreed to say with Sir Philip Sidney, "I am no herald to inquire into men's pedigrees; it sufficeth me if I know their virtues."

Valdez had hardly gotten into position, when several royalist Netherlanders in his camp opened a correspondence with their rebellious friends within the city, whom they urged to give up the keys to the Spaniard, and trust to his mercy. Valdez himself invited the besieged to yield, and take shelter under the *ægis* of his majesty's amnesty. To all which the scholarly commandant replied by sending back a letter, in which he cited a single pat line from the Latin poet:

 'Fistula dulcé canit, volucrem dum decipit auceps."*

Orange, by means of carrier-pigeons, constantly flitting to and fro, sent frequent messages to the citizens, encouraging them to hold steadfast in the defence, and assuring them of his intention to exhaust the resources of the province in effecting their deliverance. "Reflect," said he, "that you contend not for yourselves alone, but for us all."† The zeal of the besieged was greatly inflamed by these missives. Not content to stand idly on the ramparts, they made desperate sorties from time to time, carrying consternation and death into the ranks of the beleaguer. Eventually, however, the cautious com-

---

º "The fowler plays sweet notes upon his pipe, while he spreads his net for the bird." Hoofd, book 10, p. 364. Meteren, *ubi sup.*   † Bor., book 7, p. 505.

mandant forbade his followers to pass the gates, because these conflicts would, little by little, weaken the defenders, already too few to man the walls.[*] After this, the days passed without either sortie or assault; no animating sound of war, no martial strife serving to beguile the weary time. For Valdez, true to his policy, closely hugged his trenches, and declined attack.[†]

By the middle of August, notwithstanding the careful husbanding of the provisions, want began to make itself felt in Leyden. The meat and bread were eaten up; nothing remained but a slender stock of malt-cake. "If not soon assisted," wrote the citizens to the prince, "human strength can do no more. The malt-cake will last four days; after that, starvation stares us in the face."[‡]

William replied encouragingly, "Expect succor hourly, until it comes."[§] All the time he had been busy. At the outset he labored to recruit a force equal to the task of raising the leaguer. Foiled in this, he determined to reënact the scene at Alckmaar, and invoke the ocean against the beleaguerer. By flooding Rhynland, the Spaniard would probably be driven to decamp; at all events, a patriot fleet might be floated into Leyden with a plentiful store of rations and men.[‖] It was a desperate project, but Orange was a desperate man.

---

[*] Hoofd, book 9, p. 366. Bor., book 7, p. 552.
[†] Mendoza, Bentivoglio.
[‡] Jan Frugliers; cited in Motley, vol. 2, p. 560.
[§] Ibid.　　[‖] Hoofd, *ubi sup.* Meteren, book 5, folio 94.

He convened the states at Delft, and laid his plan before them. The deputies were in doubt. Nothing could be more alien to the feelings of the Hollanders than such an act. To drain their lands, to filch fresh territories from the sea, to preserve the dykes—these were objects to the Dutch of constant attention, of immense expense; and now it was proposed to inundate the very garden of the province, to wash seven hundred thousand guilders out of existence; for the damage certain to be done was estimated at that sum.* But at length the luminous eloquence of the prince convinced the doubters of the necessity of the spoliation. "Better a drowned land than a slavish land," was the unanimous cry.† A fund was formally subscribed for the accomplishment of the work; the men, the ladies, the children of the devoted state freely contributed their plate, their jewels, their toys; all classes applied themselves to the demolition of barriers upon which the national existence depended; laboring with an ardent industry equal to that employed in the annual repair of the self-same bulwarks.‡

In the midst of these exertions, commenced early in July, Orange was stricken down by fever.§ Quite worn out by anxiety, by the recent loss of his brothers at Mook-heath, and by over-exertion—for it was a trait of his always to mix his work with his brains—

---

* Strada, tom. 3, p. 7.
† Hoofd, *ut antea.* Meteren, *ut antea.*
‡ Ibid.   § Motley, vol. 2, pp. 560–563.

he lay for some weeks tossing in delirium, with death
for a bed-fellow. His sickness paralyzed the exertions of the estates; all Holland seemed to hold its
breath. Towards the end of August, the fever left
the illustrious patient, and he improved the first
hour of his convalescence to resume the interrupted
preparations for the relief of Leyden.* The physicians protested, but to no purpose. "I fear not,"
wrote he to John Nassau; "God will ordain for me
all which is necessary for my good and my salvation. He will load me with no more afflictions than
the fragility of nature can sustain."†

The waters of the Yssel and the Meuse, which
bounded two sides of the alluvial quadrangle which
it was proposed to flood, had already begun to pour
through the opened sluices and to tumble over the
demolished dykes. Soon the whole basin between
Rotterdam, Delft, Gouda, and Leyden was filled.‡
In the beginning of September, two hundred flatboats, built for the occasion, were launched, armed,
laden with provisions, and manned by eight hundred Zealanders—ferocious, battle-scarred warriors,
wearing a crescent embroidered on their hats, with
the motto, "Rather the Turk than the Pope"§—
whom Boisot, the leader of the fleet, had brought
with him from the Archipelago.‖

With ringing cheers, the strange flotilla pushed

* Motley, vol. 2, pp. 560–563.
† Archives et Corresp., tom. 5, p. 53.
‡ Bor., book 7, p. 552. Hoofd, book 9, p. 375.
§ Hoofd, book 9, p. 374. Bor., book 7, p. 552. ‖ Ibid.

out upon the extemporized lake, and made for Leyden.   Once, twice was its progress stayed by intervening dykes, from which the enemy, in full possession, were gallantly dislodged by Boisot's beggars.*
But, alas, when but a few miles distant from the
starving town, the entire fleet, which drew but two
feet of water, grounded.   The waves, diffusing themselves over a broad expanse, sufficed only to make
a few puddles ahead of Boisot.   Nothing more could
be done until the tide should rise.†   Worst of all,
this could not happen until the wind, then blowing
steadily from the northeast, and thereby holding
the waters of the Meuse and the Zaetermeer—a
little lake about midway between that river and the
city—in their beds, veered to another point of the
compass.‡   Ere that occurred, the town might be
taken or be driven to surrender, which would render the vast sacrifice utterly unavailing.

Meantime, with . succor within easy eyesight,
Leyden was a prey to the worst horrors of famine.
The larder had long been empty of all wholesome
edibles.   Now there was no food so odious that it
was not esteemed a dainty.   Some ate vine-leaves
mixed with salt and starch; others boiled the foliage
of trees, devoured roots and chaff, and chopped the
skins of animals in a little milk; women veiled their
faces, that their misery might not be seen, and seating themselves on heaps of refuse, searched eagerly
for bones, dried fish-skins, and the vilest offal;

º Bor., *ubi sup.*, p. 554.   Hoofd, *ubi sup.*, p. 376, *seq.*
† Ibid., pp. 552, 554.   Ibid., p. 375.   ‡ Ibid., Ibid., *et seq.*

young girls ate the lap-dogs with which they had
been wont to play.* The plague, famine's hench-
man, was at hand, making many a merry meal on
the skeleton victims—eating up eight thousand of
the inhabitants. Those who survived could barely
drag their attenuated limbs to the ramparts; and
often, on returning from their watch, they came
back to find their wives and children dead, their
homes desolate.†

Hardest of all to bear were the taunts of those
few citizens who sided with the foe: "Ah ha! where
now are your relievers? where linger these beggars
of whom ye wist?"‡ Once the burgomaster, Van
der Werf, was surrounded in the street by a starving
mob, clamorous for food or a capitulation. Mounting the steps of the church of St. Pancreas, the
magistrate, whose tall, haggard, but imposing figure and unquailing eye commanded instant attention, shouted: "What would ye, friends? Why do
ye murmur that we do not break our vows and surrender?—a fate more horrible than the agony we
now endure. I tell you I have made an oath to
hold the town; and may God give me strength to
keep my oath. I can die but once, whether by
your hands, or the enemy's, or by the stroke of my
Maker. My own fate is indifferent to me; not so
that of the city intrusted to my care. I know that
we shall starve, unless soon relieved; but starvation
is preferable to the dishonorable death which seems

° Bor., book 7, p. 556.   † Ibid., *ut antea.*
‡ Ibid., p. 551. Hoofd, book 9, p. 374.

the sole alternative. If my death can serve you, take it. Here is my sword: cut my body into morsels, and divide it amongst you."[*]

These words kindled new enthusiasm in all hearts. The murmurs ceased. All exchanged fresh vows; consecrated themselves anew to the defence; and the feeblest women cried: "Yes, yes, death by starvation before submission."[†] At that very moment Valdez, who had never ceased to urge capitulation, sent a fresh summons into town. In reply, all rushed to the ramparts, and shouted back: "Ye call us rat-eaters and dog-eaters, and 't is true. So long, then, as ye hear a dog bark or a cat mew within our walls, know that Leyden still holds out. Nay, when all save ourselves have perished, we will devour our own left arms, leaving our right to defend our wives, our liberty, and our religion. Should God, in his justice, doom us to destruction, hope not even then to take the town; for when the last hour comes, we will fire our houses and die together—any thing, every thing, before submission to tyranny and antichrist."[‡]

Before such a spirit, the Spaniard himself began to feel uneasy. Moreover, the water was rising in the camp. Nothing but the repeated assurances of those natives who stood beside him that the expected deluge was a miracle beyond the prince's power to work, kept Valdez at his post.[§]

---

* Meteren, book 5, folio 94.   Hoofd, *ubi sup.*, p, 379, *et seq.*
† Ibid.   ‡ Meteren and Hoofd, *ut antea.*
§ Bor., book 7, p. 551.

The end was nearer thán any knew. On the 29th of September, the long obstinate wind changed, and getting into the right quarter, blew the refluent waters forward. A few hours later, the dry land was swallowed by the sea, and the stranded patriot armada was once more afloat and sailing on.* So eager were the wild Zealanders to get at the city, that when shallows were to be passed, they dashed into the water, and by sheer strength shouldered their vessels through. Soon the girdling redoubts of the Spaniard were reached, and one after another captured;† for though the forces of Valdez outnumbered Boisot's seamen ten to one, both wind and water fought with these, while those were appalled by the fierce onset of the ocean.

By the 1st of October, but two of the enemy's forts remained untaken, those of Zaeterwoude and of Lammen; these, however, were the most important and the strongest of the chain.‡ At midnight, in the soughing of the equinoctial gale, Boisot again slipped cable, and scudded out to assail these barriers. Midway, he met a fleet equipped by Valdez to stay his farther progress. In the height of the storm, in the inky darkness, the foes joined battle, the flash of the Zealanders' cannon lighting up the black waste of waters at frequent intervals, and showing that the sentinel vessels of the Spaniard were being steadily pushed back. At last the patriot artillery roared out a triumph; but day

* Bor., book 7, p. 557.   † Ibid.
‡ Hoofd, Bor., Mendoza.

peeped above the horizon ere the admiral could moor his ships broadside to the Zaeterwoude redoubt.[*]

The Spaniards, however, had no appetite for the breakfast prepared for them. Without waiting to fire a gun, they rushed from the citadel, and poured in a dense mass across the fast-crumbling dyke which stretched away towards the Hague. Boisot's cannon belched forth rapid death as the frightened fugitives hastened past, while the wild Zealanders sprang after them with boat-hook and dagger, and transfixed many with harpoons, hurled with accuracy acquired in polar chases after far different prey. Upwards of twelve hundred of them fell in this frightful passage of the dyke; the rest reached the Hague.[†]

But one fort now separated the flotilla from Leyden gates—Lammen—and towards that the jubilant seamen scudded. This too, on being reached, was found to have been evacuated in the night. Valdez himself had taken to flight, and his favorite fortress was left with a garrison of one little boy and a white flag.[‡]

The armada at once headed for the city, floating through groves, among the branches of quiet orchards, over submerged villages, quite up to the walls where stood the spent and dying, but rejoicing heroes of the siege. Five minutes more, and

[*] Hoofd, *ubi sup.*, p. 383. Mendoza, tom. 12, p. 264.
[†] Ibid. Bor., *ubi sup.*, p. 558.
[‡] Ibid. Motley, vol. 2, p. 573.

the town was saved—plenty again reigned in Leyden.*

Boisot entered the place on the morning of the 3d of October, 1574, four months after the beginning of the siege.† The stout admiral's first act on stepping from his galley was, to head a solemn procession to the great church of Leyden, where all bent in devout gratitude before Him who had so marvellously snatched the city from the jaws of death. After thanks had been rendered "to that God who had made them a sea upon the dry land," ten thousand voices joined in a thanksgiving psalm, broken ere the close by sobs and halleluias.‡

Then the vast audience adjourned, to make provision for the sick, and to distribute the supplies; of which some ate so greedily as to find in the midst of plenty, that death spared them by famine.§ A note was speedily sent to the prince, informing him that Leyden was succored. William received it while at church in Delft, and rising, with tearful eyes read the good news aloud.‖

Soon afterwards he crossed over to the town, though still very weak from his recent illness, that he might in person thank the citizens for their extraordinary courage and fortitude. Not contenting himself with empty words, he sent boats and wagons throughout the province to collect charitable contributions for the impoverished townsfolk. All

---

* Bor., Hoofd, Meteren, *et alii*.   † Ibid.

‡ Meteren, book 5, folio 95. Hoofd, book 9, p. 386. Bor., book 7, p. 560.   § Ibid.   ‖ Ibid.

connected with the defence and succor were suitably rewarded, and Boisot was presented with a medal suspended from a massive chain of gold.* Even the carrier-doves, those faithful posts, were gratefully remembered, being kept with great care while they lived, embalmed after death, and placed in the stadthouse, where they still repose.†

Two incidents which marked the siege were esteemed by the burghers as special interpositions of Providence in their favor. On the very night Valdez retreated, twenty roods of the wall of Leyden suddenly fell—which, two days before, would have been fatal to the town, but served now only to accelerate the flight of the Spaniard, who imagined the crash to indicate a desperate sortie of the citizen train-bands. And the day after the town was relieved, the wind, returning to the northeast, drove back the rampant waters of the Meuse and the Yssel into their wonted channels, thereby enabling the burghers to repair the dykes, reclose the sluices, and again reclaim their fertile pastures.‡

Still farther to mark his appreciation of the heroism of Leyden, the prince of Orange proposed to the burghers either to found a university within their walls, or to grant them permission to hold an annual fair without taxation. With honorable preference, the academy was chosen; but the estates, judging that the traders and the illiterate had shown

* Bor., *ubi sup.*
† *Vide* Chambers, Tour in Holland, etc., art. Leyden.
‡ Davies, vol. 2, p. 14.

themselves no less strenuous than the wealthy and the educated in the defence of their fatherland, decreed both.

Such was the origin of the famous University of Leyden, the Oxford of Holland, *alma mater* of the grandest bead-roll of *alumni* in the world, where Grotius studied, where Scaliger raised letters to the stars, where Boerhaave revolutionized the theory of medicine, and where John Robinson, the venerable pastor of our pilgrim fathers, won wide fame in disputation with Episcopius.

CHAPTER XLI.

DIPLOMATIC "PRACTICE."

WHILE the siege of Leyden was yet pending, but more perceptibly after its miraculous close, a secret fencing-match was going on between the diplomats. Orange was as closely besieged by letter-writers as the town by the Spaniard's men-at-arms, and with much the same result.

Requesens was still anxious to end the revolt by a pen-stroke. All through these months his quill was as busy as his sword, and active for the same purpose. He yet believed, notwithstanding the contemptuous rejection of the royal amnesty, in the possibility of getting the states to bite at the hook, and that too without baiting it with any measure which should concede, on the angler's side, the points at issue.

Early in 1574, St. Aldegonde had emerged from his dungeon on parole and repaired to Delft, armed by the viceroy with power to negotiate what was called a peace ; but he had been carefully instructed that two questions were to be omitted from discussion—his majesty's prerogative, and freedom of worship.* As these were precisely the questions in conflict, a parley which commenced by the declination of one of the parties to consider them was

* Cor. de Guillaume le Taciturne, tom. 3, p. 400, *et seq.* Bor., book 7, p. 534.

death-marked from the outset. However, the distinguished envoy performed his mission, held interviews with Orange and the estates, and was, of course, unsuccessful; whereupon he returned to Brussels and reëntered prison, whence he did not again emerge till autumn, when events struck off his shackles.* He took back with him an elaborate paper, drawn up in the name of the acting government of the revolted provinces, and addressed to the king of Spain, in which three conditions-precedent to a pacification were announced: his majesty's recall of the exiles, the reëstablishment of the ancient charters, and the proclaiming an equality between religious creeds, each free from each.† This document was offensive both to Requesens and to Philip, though it was merely the counter-statement of earnest men, made in reply to an absurd proposal—to have been expected, like the kicking of an overloaded gun.

Champagny, the viceroy's confidential agent, wrote Junius de Jonge, a learned and astute representative of William the Silent, that the king could not be expected to give ear to such idle words. "Indeed, quotha!" was the retort; "if he does prove deaf to our petitions, we will tell him, as the old Roman matron told the emperor Adrian, 'The potentate who has no time to attend to the interests of his subjects, has not the leisure to be a sovereign.' "‡

* Cor. de Guillaume, etc., *ubi sup.*
† Bor., book 7, p. 535, *et seq.*   ‡ Ibid., p. 536, *seq.*

But the grand commander would not take No for an answer. Some months later, he deputed a batch of new negotiators to seek out the prince and treat secretly with him upon the matter of his pardon and reconciliation with his majesty.* Orange was wont to say, "A friend is cheaply bought by a bow;"† and therefore he received these tempters, one after another, with grave courtesy. He was, however, somewhat plain-spoken in these encounters of wit. "I cannot treat without the coöperation of the estates," said he; "and if I could, I should require no pardon, for I have done nothing which demands forgiveness. Besides, we can give no credit to the words which come to us from Madrid, we have been too often cheated. There are the provincial deputies, speak to them. You remind me that the king is powerful, and that I am weak. Yes, I know that his majesty is very mighty; but there is a sovereign yet more resistless, even God the Creator, who, as I humbly hope, is on my side.‡

The discomfited diplomats next waited upon the estates. "You attempt to reap where you have not sown," said the deputies, "when you talk of pardon without prefacing it by the recall of the troops, the convening the states-general, and a guaranty of the toleration of the reformed faith."§

* Bor., book 7, p. 585. Cor. de Guillaume le Taciturne, tom. 3, p. 403, *et seq.*   † Du Maurier, p. 167.

‡ Cor. de Guillaume, etc., *ubi sup.*, pp. 378–380.

§ Bor., book 7, p. 565, *et seq.* Gachard, Cor., etc., tom. 3, p. 403, *seq.*

William and his friends of the revolutionary junta were sincerely anxious to "beat their swords into ploughshares and their spears into pruning-hooks;" but they craved an honorable peace, which should not renounce the most precious objects of the war, make every dollar spent a swindle, and render every life lost a public murder. Across all the Spanish plans of accommodation thus far opened the word dishonor was most plainly written. The pet policy of Requesens, which looked to reconciling the provinces by forcing the Protestants into exile, was peculiarly obnoxious. In a letter to John Nassau, the prince wrote, "There are no papists left in Holland, except a few ecclesiastics, so much has the number of the reformed been augmented through the singular grace of God. 'T is therefore out of the question to suppose that a measure dooming all who are not Romanists to exile can be entertained. We cannot desert our altars; nor will we consent voluntarily to abandon for ever property, friends, and fatherland. Such a peace would be poor and pitiable indeed."*

As for the king, he was weary of the war, which was a constantly-increasing drain upon his exchequer; for the viceroy found it impossible either to coax or to coerce the Netherlands into granting any adequate fund for the support of the struggle, and so was forced to get his dishonored drafts cashed in Madrid.† Nevertheless Philip, whose mind bigotry strait-laced, was as far as ever from a willingness

* Archives et Corresp., tom. 5, p. 73.   † Ibid., pp. 28–32.

to "remove violence and spoil, and execute judgment and justice."[*]

Thus, though both Orange and the king desired peace, one could not and the other would not make the requisite concessions. At this juncture, the emperor Maximilian once more stirred himself to accommodate the quarrel; this time with an earnest wish to succeed, for he feared, unless a pacification could be negotiated, that the German electors would depart from the house of Austria and openly take the field for their Protestant cousins in the states.[†]

Having received authority from Philip to mediate, he transferred his powers to Count Schwartzburg, William's brother-in-law, and despatched him post to Dort to confer with his illustrious kinsman.[‡] The prince received him graciously, and out of respect to the emperor consented to empower a number of his friends to treat with the royal negotiators.[§] At the same time, he was too sagacious to expect much from this convention; and he hastened to remind the estates of Holland and Zealand, then in session, that peace, though desirable, might be more dangerous than war. "Therefore," added he, "let us stand to arms, push all warlike preparations with vigor, and sign no treaty inconsistent with our charters and with the claims of God."[||]

On the 3d of March, 1575, the peace congress

---

[*] Motley, vol. 3, pp. 11, 12.   [†] Archives et Cor., tom. 5, p. 81.
[‡] Bor., Wagenaer, Hoofd, *et al.*   [§] Ibid.
[||] Bor., book 8, p. 595, *seq.*

met at Breda—St. Aldegonde, Boisot, Junius de Jonge, and Paul Buys being present for the states; while four ultramontane diplomats appeared for Philip. The patriot quartette opened the proceedings by demanding the withdrawal of the foreign troops; the convocation of the states-general; the legal recognition of the reformed religion as then established; leave for William and the estates to place garrisons wherever they might think necessary; the restoration of their estates and titles to those who had suffered during the war; the removal of the new bishops; the expulsion of the Jesuits from the Low Countries, as "a pestilent race, desirous of tumult;" an acknowledgment of the right of the estates to meet at will, and on the death of Orange to appoint another stadtholder by their own act over Holland and Zealand; and security for the fulfilment of these terms.*

The royal envoys took up and scanned this programme, drew their pens across those clauses which touched upon religion, and replied, "Mayhap all else might be arranged, but we insist on the supremacy of the mother church, conceding permission to those who cannot conform thereto to retire from the Netherlands any time within six months; and we likewise claim the surrender to his majesty of all warlike _matériel_, and require the placing six of your chiefest towns in his hands as pledges of good faith."†

---

* _Vide_ Bor., book 8, p. 598, _et seq._ Meteren, book 5, folios 108, 109. Bentivoglio, tom. 9.

† Bentivoglio, liv. 9, _ab initio._ Meteren, Bor., _ut antea._

This response was, of course, unsatisfactory; for religion was the main point at issue. Of what use, then, would be the restoration of the ancient franchises if the whole population of the states were to be expatriated? However, anxious to step to the verge of honor, St. Aldegonde said, "We will refer the question of toleration to the states-general, if you wish it; but more we cannot do. Nor will we disarm, nor yet give up our towns, for that would be like the silly sheep in the fable, who gave up their watchdogs to the wolves."*

These differences of opinion proved fatal to an accommodation—the patriot delegates would not desert their faith, the ultramontanists would not concede toleration; and though they continued to harangue each other for nine months, referring this claim and that exception, now to the estates, and now to Madrid, in the fall of 1575 they separated with increased bitterness, these charging those, those these, with the whole fault of failure.†

To the prince, this negotiation was not so fruitless as it might seem. It had, at least, the effect of justifying his cause at the bar of Europe;‡ it served also to conciliate the favor of the southern provinces, to whom the proposal of referring the question of toleration to the states-general appeared both judicious and equitable; while they were equally pleased by that clause in the patriot demand which called for the departure of the Spanish

* Bor., *ubi sup.*   † Ibid., p. 612.
‡ Davies, vol. 2, p. 18.

hirelings.* Besides, like all discussions of first principles, the conference opened to the masses the closed book of communal rights. John Nassau had been fearful that the plausible mean-nothings of the king's advocates might cheat the Hollanders into assenting to some proposition which should lead them unwittingly to "lay bare their own backs to the rod, and bring fagots for their own funeral piles."† On the contrary, the people, enlightened from Breda, became more resolute than ever never to submit. "Spanish faith" they held to be a synonyme for "Punic faith." All saw that swords were in King Philip's lips, and that it was in his programme to reclose the Bible, "pervert the prophets and purloin the psalms," and crucify Christ anew in the persons of his elect.

On the 4th of June, 1575, some weeks before the final adjournment of the diplomats, an act of union between Holland and Zealand was solemnized.‡ It was a germ destined to bud soon in the important confederacy of seven provinces at Utrecht, and to flower eventually in the Dutch Republic. By the articles of this initial union, the prince of Orange was intrusted with the supreme direction of affairs, charged with the regulation of the state expenses, and especially directed to maintain the reformed evangelical religion, and to suppress Romanism.§

º Davies, *ut antea*.
† Archives, etc., tom. 5, p. 131, *et seq.*
‡ Wagenaer, book 7, p. 19. Brandt, vol. 1, p. 313. § Ibid.

Against this last enactment the prince at first
protested; and through his efforts, the word Romanism was replaced by the phrase, "religion
at variance with the gospel," which left the door
open for a toleration.[*]   Still popery was for a time
prohibited, though the interdict was not meant
to be definitive, but was done under martial law,
and made lasting while the war continued, or so
long as the general safety should warrant.   "For,"
explained William, in speaking of this act at a later
day, "they who at first judged it for the best of all
that one creed equally with another should be tolerated, were afterwards obliged, by the bold attempts,
cunning devices, and treacheries of the papists who
had insinuated themselves into place and power,
and then striven to undo the state, to suspend the
Romish worship; more especially since those who
practised it, the priests particularly, had sworn allegiance to an outside power, the pope, laying greater
stress upon their oaths to him than on others taken
to our polity.   And it was a manifest injustice for
these folk to enjoy our privileges, and then take
advantage of them to reduce the land into a spiritual thraldom hateful to the commonwealth."[†]

Surely such a measure, so necessitated and with
such limitations, was radically different from the
truculent bigotry which, in time of profound peace,
with no martial law to justify it, assumed to ransack
non-conforming consciences by means of thumb-

* Wagenaer, *ubi sup.*, p. 22.   Archives, etc., tom. 5, p. 272.
† Apology of Orange, cited in Brandt, vol. 1, pp. 307, 308.

screws and *autos-da-fé*. Besides, in this case, though expelled the churches, the papists were permitted to hear mass in their own homes; nor were those magistrates who were Romanists ejected from their offices, unless, indeed, the ballots of their adversaries ousted them in the elections. Some, however, remained in office until death released them.[*]

This prohibition was but once washed in blood. William's deputy in North Holland, Diedrich Sanoy, discovered, or thought he discovered, a plot of papists to fire several of the towns under his care, in aid of an impending invasion of the Spaniards; whereupon, in imitation of the Blood-council at Brussels, he set up an extraordinary court, before which he dragged the accused, and endeavored to rack from their tortured lips what was styled a confession, in true inquisitorial fashion.[†] Before these imitators of Juan Vargas had committed many murders, the prince learned of the mischief, and at once broke the tribunal, and liberated several of the victims.[‡] This prompt action brought him honor in all men's eyes, and it was a general saying that "the prince embraced all the good of whatsoever persuasion, with fatherly tenderness and impartial justice."[§]

The recent angry ending of the peace-congress, and now the union of Holland and Zealand, laid the

[*] Brandt, *ubi sup.*, p. 108.

[†] Ibid., p. 315. Bor., tom. 8, p. 623, *seq.* Hoofd, book 10, p. 412.   [‡] Ibid.

[§] Brandt, vol. 1, p. 316.

last ghost of hope that any reconciliation was to be looked for with Spain.   Under these circumstances, and considering the vast disparity between these little provinces and the mighty, many-sided power which Philip wielded, William and the estates felt justified in offering the sovereignty which his majesty had forfeited, and which they at this time represented, to some potentate who should promise to defend and to guarantee the national liberties. Some time before, Orange, in one of his interviews with the "Artful Dodgers" sent by Requesens to overreach him, had hinted at the possibility of this action, saying: "The land is a beautiful damsel, who certainly will not be found to lack suitors able and willing to champion her against the world."[*]

The "damsel" had now come of marriageable age—ceased to be a *femme covert*—and it was time to assert her independence of the whilom guardian. The first week in October, 1575, the estates met at Delft, and voted, formally and unanimously, to depose Philip II., drop from all public papers the long-retained fiction of allegiance, and lodge in William's hands the power of selecting the successor of the cast-off monarch.[†]

Here was a " new thing under the sun"—a national diet made up of plain burghers and a few small nobles, representatives of a little land half bogs and the rest marshes, solemnly assembling to vote their sovereign, monarch of half the world, off

[*] Corresp. de Guillaume le Tacit., tom. 3, p. 387.
[†] Wagenaer, book 7, p. 81.   Bor., book 8, p. 651.

the throne, for good and sufficient reasons—blasting the dogma of regal divinity with the lightning of democratic ballots.

The question now was, To whom shall the sovereignty be transferred? The prince leaned personally towards France. He had been recently divorced from the crazy and profligate Anne of Saxony, whereupon he had espoused an escaped nun, Charlotte de Bourbon, a daughter of the royal house of France, and a lady of piety and talent, who drew him towards her fatherland.* But to this alliance there were grave objections. The treaty cemented by poor Count Louis with Charles IX. was " off" since that monarch's death, some months back. The accession of Henry III. had reconvulsed the kingdom, and it was thought that but little real protection could be expected from a power torn by internecine broils.

As for Germany, it was a mere congeries of independent principalities—a purely nominal state, whose emperor was doubly related to the deposed king. An excellent market to buy soldiers in, a good powder-magazine, Germany was neither able nor inclined to defend the provinces.

Upon the whole, a union with England seemed most feasible. Such a connection might be bottomed upon mutual advantages, the best bonds of a definitive connection. Great Britain claimed to be a bulwark of Protestantism. Between the states and her there was an essential uniformity of faith.

* Bor., book 8, p. 660, *seq.* Hume, Camden.

The genius of both peoples was maritime; while the reciprocal conveniences of trade, the mastery which would thus be acquired at sea, and the readiness with which Denmark and the Hanse towns would enter into an alliance with the united nations gave promise of puissance not to be gainsaid.

Late in December, 1575, Orange despatched a trio of envoys to negotiate with Elizabeth. The maiden queen received them cordially, but feared equally to accept or to refuse their offer. Acceptance would embroil her with Philip, and expose her to danger from the side of Scotland; refusal might drive the provinces into the arms of France, and thereby strengthen the Gaul at the Briton's expense. It was a dilemma whose either horn was full of danger. Therefore her majesty temporized—a species of political coquetry in which she was an adept. After a dalliance of many months at the court of St. James, the envoys of the prince returned home to report the substantial failure of their mission.*

Meantime Requesens was pressing the war with renewed vigor. He was, indeed, much hampered by a want of funds, and by the sharp denials and prolix remonstrances with which the obedient provinces invariably met his requests for money.† The troops, too, ill-paid as usual, frequently frustrated his favorite schemes by untimely insubordination. And once those soldiers whom the deluge had driv-

---

* Camden, Hist. of Queen Elizabeth, book 2, pp, 207–210. Bor,, book 8, p. 662; book 9, p. 667. Meteren, book 5, folio 101.

† Bor., book 7, pp. 562, 576, 577, 583.

en from the walls of Leyden broke into such savage mutiny, that the viceroy was obliged to grant to the inhabitants of the region which they undertook to lay under contribution leave to wear arms in their own defence—a somewhat dangerous precedent.* Nevertheless, aided by the skilful swords of Hierges and Vitelli, the Spaniard met with no mean success in the work of conquest, smiting into submission town after town on the confines of Holland.†

But while these triumphs crowned the efforts of Requesens, a parallel success attended the patriots at sea, the *gueux* seizing and burning twelve ships built at Antwerp for coastwise warfare, and shortly afterwards, falling upon and sinking another royalist fleet—part of that equipped for conquest by the king, but stayed in the Bay of Biscay by the plague,‡ as the crews were trimming sail for Dunkirk harbor.§

Nettled by these losses, stirred to action by the complaints of the Antwerp merchants that their commerce was clogged by the forays of the patriot Zealanders, and more than ever convinced of the absolute necessity of opening the closed jaws of the Scheldt, the grand commander determined to make one more effort to reannex the Archipelago.

His objective point was Zierickzee, the capital of the island of Schouwen. The island lay between

* Bor., book 7, p. 584. Campana, lib. 5, p. 156.
† Hoofd, book 10, p. 424, *seq.* Bor., book 8, p. 646
‡ Chap. XXXIX., pp. 736, *seq.*
§ Bor., Davies, vol 2, p. 23.

Zealand and Holland, and the town looked out upon
the ocean; its possession by the Spaniard would
at once provide him with what he lacked in this
outer territory—a safe harbor—and enable him to
sever the easiest avenue of intercommunication between the revolted provinces.*

Having decided where to strike, the how was
the next thing to be determined. The grand commander knew not how to solve this problem, for the
estuaries and lagoons swarmed with the flatboats of
"the beggars of the sea." Finally, a party of rene-
gade Zealanders volunteered to point out a path.†

Three islands—Tholen, Duiveland, and Schouwen—formed the northern barrier of the archipelago. Tholen, which adjoins the mainland, already
held for Spain. Between this island and its neighbor, Duiveland, stretched a shallow bay, eight
miles wide; and Duiveland again was separated
from Schouwen by a frith about half as broad. In
imitation of the feat of Mondragone in relieving
Turgoes three years before, it was proposed to
wade across to Zierickzee—the renegades vouching
for the fordability of the intermediate waters at
ebb tide.‡

After some little hesitation, Requesens resolved
to make the venture, although this expedition was
much more desperate than that of Mondragone,
more daring than Cæsar's fording of the Thames

* Bor., Hoofd, Strada.
† Mendoza, tom. 14, p. 282. Bentivoglio, tom. 9, p. 165.
‡ Ibid.

many ages earlier; for in those no obstacle but the waves was to be surmounted, whereas here, Orange, apprehending some such essay, had crowded the waters with his most audacious seamen, and placed upon the islands themselves strong bands to beat back the invaders, should they make the passage through his fleet.*

Nevertheless, the Spaniards, who loved nothing better than to cope with what seemed impossibilities, received the proposal to face these manifold dangers with enthusiastic cheers. On the 27th of September, 1575, the force, eight or ten thousand strong, weighed anchor from Antwerp and sailed down the Scheldt to Bergen-op-Zoom. Disembarking, they were ferried thence to the island of Tholen; whence three thousand men, headed by a picked corps of two hundred pioneers, crossed in boats to Philipsland, a half-submerged and desert islet hard by Tholen.†

Here the peril began; here the water was to be entered. At midnight, at neap tide, the adventurers stripped off their clothes, retaining naught but their shoes and trousers, slung their knapsacks around their necks, shouldered their pikes and muskets, and after a brief harangue from Requesens, plunged into the ford.‡ Those who looked on commiserated them as devoted to assured death, ex-

* Mendoza, tom. 14, p. 282. Bentivoglio, tom. 9, p. 165. Strada, tom. 3, p. 12.

† Mendoza, Bentivoglio, ut antea. Bor., book 8, p. 650.

‡ Hoofd, book 10, p. 428. Bentivoglio, ubi sup.

posed as they were, first to the cruel waters, then to the guns of the rebel fleet, with no other gabions to defend them than their bodies, and at last, to the arquebuses of the waiting garrison upon the island.[*]

At the outset, the sky was overcast; but suddenly the darksome night was lit up by burning meteors until the blind heavens blazed again—a prodigy repeated at intervals until dawn.[†] The Spaniards hailed the display as an auspicious omen. "See, fellow-soldiers," shouted Osorio di Alloa, captain of the advance, " the army of the sky joins forces with us, leading us to victory and boding revenge upon our foes."[‡] Animated by this hope of celestial aid, all splashed on over the narrow ridge of submerged sand, marching three abreast, with the hissing waters at their throats.

About midway, they came upon the patriot fleet stranded purposely across the ford. A mad, weird fight at once began, though the combatants could hardly see each other, save when, for a moment, the northern lights kindled the heavens, or the cannon spat fitful fire from their mouths. The Zealanders, not content to do battle from their ships, dashed into the waves to grapple with their antagonists, whom they transfixed with their harpoons, or dragged from the sea-road with boathooks, or brained with flails.[§] Several hundred of the royalists perished in these fights, either done to

---

[*] Strada, tom. 3, p. 10, seq.
[†] Ibid., p. 11. Mendoza, tom. 14.
[‡] Strada, ubi sup.   § Mendoza, tom. 14, p. 285.

death by the fury of the *gueux* or sucked into the surrounding whirl-pits.* The rearguard, affrighted by the onset of the beggars, and observing that the tide was rising, faced about and waded back ;† but the van pushed resolutely on, slipping by their assailants in the darkness, or fighting their way past the wooden rocks and through the human tempest to the shore of Duiveland, up which they scrambled just at dawn.‡

Here they were met by ten companies of French, English, and Scotch auxiliaries, upon whom the "sea monsters" dashed, although numb and giddy with six hours' prior conflict with the water. They had no alternative but to win a victory or perish ; so they won a victory, routing the allies, and killing their commander, Charles Boisot, brother of the valiant admiral of Zealand§—from which it should seem that the best weapon to conquer by is the necessity of conquering.

Presently the patriot flotilla, imagining that the whole Spanish force had passed the ford, made sail for Zierickzee to warn its citizens of the impending siege—a blunder of which Requesens hastened to take advantage by ferrying the rest of his troops across the deserted estuary to Duiveland, where mutual congratulations were exchanged.‖

Without further adventure, the army, led this

* Strada, tom. 3, p. 12.
† Mendoza, *ubi sup.* Hoofd, book 10, p. 429.
‡ Ibid. Strada, *ubi sup.*, p. 13.
§ Bor., book 8, p. 649. Bentivoglio, tom. 10, p. 168.
‖ Strada, *ubi sup.*

time by Mondragone, passed the frith from Duive-land to Schouwen; and pausing but to reduce two intermediate villages—one of which, Benunenede, detained them by a gallant resistance of three weeks*—pressed forward to lay siege to Zierickzee. By the end of October the place was formally invested;† but since the burghers were well supplied with stores and resolute withal, the beleaguerers saw that success was only to be won by a recourse to the tedious and ruinous expedient of blockading, and that Zierickzee was to be another Haarlem.

Orange was inexpressibly grieved by this unexpected chapter of events. The toils seemed tightening about the good cause. Holland and Zealand were now separated. No foreign power could be enlisted to give needed aid: England, France, Germany were alike deaf to the pleading voices of self-interest and of humanity. The prince himself momentarily despaired. It was at this time that he announced the desperate but sublime resolution to freight what vessels he could collect with the citizens and the moveable property of the lost provinces, burn the windmills, pierce the dykes, open the sluices, give back brave Holland to the sea, and seek with his dauntless colonists a new home in some virgin land where Madrid and the Vatican were names unknown.‡

* Meteren, book 5, folio 103. Meursii Auriacus, p. 147.

† Bor., book 8, p. 652. Mendoza, tom. 14, p. 293, seq. Bentivoglio, et alii.

‡ Bor., ubi sup., p. 664. Hoofd, book 10, p. 443. Wagenaer, book 7, p. 88, seq.

Happily for mankind, the sacrifice was not demanded. When all human helpers failed, God descended on the scene. In February, 1576, Vitelli, the ablest and most dreaded of the Spanish captains, fell from his litter and was killed.* On the 5th of March, in the same year, Requesens also sickened of a fever in the trenches before Zierickzee, and died.† His decease radically changed the aspect of affairs. The dawn of a brighter day rose from his grave among the marshes.

---

* Strada, tom. 3, p. 13, *et seq.*

† Ibid., p. 15. Hoofd, *ubi sup.*, p. 436, *et seq.* Bor., *ubi sup.*, pp. 663–665.

CHAPTER XLII.

THE GHENT PACIFICATION.

INTRINSICALLY, the demise of Requesens, great merely by position, was of little consequence; for "pigmies are pigmies still, though perched on Alps." But adventitious circumstances imparted unlooked-for importance to the event. Dying suddenly, the grand commander had been thereby prevented from naming a successor, which letters-patent in his possession empowered him to do. Therefore, as the custom was at such junctures, the council of state seated itself in the vacant executive chair, to await his majesty's nomination of another viceroy.

Such nomination the king, doubtful upon whom to bestow the honor, and constitutionally predisposed to procrastinate, was as yet unwilling to make. Therefore he sent the counsellors full authority to rule *ad interim.** Aerschot, Barlaimont, and Viglius composed the regnant junta; but presently several others were taken in, among the rest, Jerome di Rhoda, one of the blood-judges, added by royal diploma as a kind of overseer of his fellows.†

The arrangement was a fatal blunder, a makeshift of Hopper's advising; for Philip had taken counsel with the paltering and time-serving keeper of the seals. "'T is a devout man, that poor Mas-

---

* Meteren, book 5, folio 104. Bor., book 9, p. 663,   † Ibid.

ter Hopper," observed Granvelle, " but rather fitted
for Platonic researches than for affairs of state."*
The interests of the king demanded that his representative at Brussels should focus regal divinity;
instead of which, this many-headed administration
was the most opaque of bodies. At this critical
hour, the welfare of absolutism called for the presence in the Netherlands of a viceroy able either to
command or to conciliate esteem; instead of which,
the state council was a stench in all men's nostrils;
in those of the seigneurs, because they despised to
be ruled by a committee of their peers; of the burghers, because bigoted Aerschot, "Hispaniolized"
Barlaimont, and octogenarian Viglius were generally supposed to be politically dead and buried.
Nothing could have been more inopportune for despotism than such a graveyard government; nor
more opportune, as the sequel showed, for liberty.

For a time, however, all went smoothly. The
counsellors vigorously prosecuted the plan of operations which Requesens had sketched out, pressing especially the siege of Zierickzee. The change
occurred in March, 1576, and until midsummer the
island-city was the pivot of affairs. In the trenches
before its walls were stationed the major part of the
Spanish forces—all save those absent in the garrisons of the larger cities of the provinces. Orange,
too, hovered near, organizing to relieve the town.†
His efforts were fruitless, or worse; for in one of

* Archives et Corresp., tom. 5, p. 374.
† Archives de la Maison d'Orange-Nassau, tom. 5, p. 365.

them Boisot, hero of the raising of the siege of Leyden, and of a score of sea-fights besides, was drowned.*

Finally the prince, his means exhausted, instructed the gallant citizens to surrender, if they could do so upon honorable terms. They at once opened a parley with Mondragone, who commanded the besiegers; and he, in turn, sent off to Brussels, to inform the counsellors of their offer, and to request instructions. The coterie were at first unwilling to permit him to accept the proposed terms, as they feared his troops would mutiny for their pay promised them when they should have taken Zierickzee. But Mondragone painted in such vivid colors the want and discontent in camp, that he was given *carte blanche* in the matter.†

On the 21st of June, after a resistance of above eight months, the city struck its flag, the garrison being permitted to march out with the honors of war, the burghers redeeming themselves from pillage by the payment of two hundred thousand guilders.‡

The fall of Zierickzee was followed by the precise consequences which the counsellors had dreaded. The veterans, enraged by the non-payment of their arrears, chagrined at the escape of Zierickzee from sack, incensed against the impecunious government, determined, as aforetime, to take the law

---

° Archives de la Maison d'Orange-Nassau, tom. 5, p. 365. Hoofd, book 10, p. 440.

† Bor., book 9, p. 678. Hoofd, *ubi sup.*   ‡ Ibid. Meteren.

into their own hands. King Philip owed them moneys, but the provinces belonged to him, therefore they were a legitimate prey. Such was the syllogism by which the mutineers justified themselves.

Assembling, they deposed Mondragone, chose a captain, swore mutual fidelity over the sacred host, left a few of their companions to hold their hard-won conquest, and then, abandoning the island, marched tumultuously into Brabant, eating the land bare as they advanced—a swarm of human locusts.*

The frightened counsellors despatched Count Mansfeld to treat with the mutineers, arming him for the encounter with all but the one thing needful—gold. He was met with jeers. "What is it you say about tarnishing our glory?" shouted the armed mob. "We have had enough of it. Glory can't be put into our pockets, nor will it fill our stomachs."† Other mediators fared no better, being met with the *ultimatum*, "Money, or a city as security."‡ Not receiving either satisfaction, they swarmed off again, menacing first Mechlin, then Brussels, and finally swooping upon Alost, in Flanders, a rich old town about equidistant from Antwerp and from the capital.§

Thus far the Spanish officers—Romero, D'Avila, Mondragone—had frowned upon the mutiny, which they were, nevertheless, thought by the populace

---

° Bor., book 9, p. 679, *et seq.* Mendoza, tom. 15, p. 300.
† Mendoza, *ubi sup.*   ‡ Ibid. Por., *ubi sup.*, p. 692.
§ Ibid. Bentivoglio, tom. 9, p. 173.

to favor in their secret hearts.   In one of Chrysostom's homilies, the mind upon which first impressions have been made is compared to a palimpsest parchment, in which, however carefully reprepared, the old lines and characters are sure to appear peeping through the new writing.   So in the *tabula rasa* of the captains, the Netherlanders imagined they could see beneath the denunciation of the mutiny the letters of a substantial sympathy with the brigands.   In ever-present danger from the exasperated masses, hated strangers in a foreign land, and drawn towards the soldiery by the double magnet of *esprit du corps*, and a common peril, they at last gave in their adherence to the outbreak, which thus became general throughout the provinces.*   This accession gave the mutineers prestige, and at the same time placed in their hands the citadels of Antwerp, Ghent, Valenciennes, and Utrecht†—fortresses which, like the gigantic helmet in the fiction, hung suspended in mid-air, as if ready to crush the dwarfed towns below.

Meantime the excitement was on the increase. The masses, of all sects and parties, began to arm, impelled by a common hatred of the mutineers. On the 26th of July, the council of state formally banned the soldiery—made it legal for any man to slay them at sight;‡ and this was followed, on the 2d of August, by a yet more stringent edict.§   Next

---

* Mendoza, tom. 15, p. 301. Bor., Hoofd, *ut antea.*
† Ibid. Cabrera, tom. 11, p. 864, *seq.*   ‡ Bor., book 11, p. 693.
§ Ibid. Hoofd, book 10, p. 445.

the counsellors commenced enrolling troops. "They say," wrote the Spaniard Verdugo to a friend, "that 't is to put down the mutiny, but I assure you 't is to attack us all."* Between the patriot levies and roving bands of the brigands the bloodiest collisions were of daily occurrence.† The whole land seemed a camp. Anticipation, spendthrift of the future, could imagine nothing sadder; memory, miser of the past, could find in the heaps of its recollections nothing worse than the existing situation.

On getting news of this commotion in the hitherto obedient provinces, the prince of Orange had travelled post to Middleburg, that he might be near the scene of action, ready to reap the harvest of this wild sowing.‡ He left Holland in comparative repose, the inhabitants occupied in repairing the ravages of war; for, physically, the provinces sat desolate—seemed quite undone. The dykes were down, the cattle swept away, the land half-submerged; the country called for recreation.§ But no one despaired, and all went to work—reaping more from sterility than tyrants could from the fattest valleys. Politically, there were changes for the better. The union recently cemented between Holland and Zealand, whose tenure was from six months to six months, had been renewed and made closer in the spring of 1576, and republicanized

* Cited in Motley, vol. 3, p. 79.
† Hoofd, *ubi sup.*, p. 450. Strada, tom. 3, p. 18, *seq.*
‡ Bor., *ubi sup.*, p. 694.
§ Wagenaer, book 7, p. 158, *et seq.*

withal; for the confederacy was a group of virtually independent cities and nobles, represented in
the diet by deputies of their own electing.* William ruled as stadtholder, and possessed large powers of peace and war, joint control with the estates
of the magistracies and courts of justice, and absolute supremacy over the army and the fleets.†

The little commonwealth was poor; for years
of single-handed warfare with the mightiest captains of the foremost military power of Europe had
decimated population and half ruined trade. Nevertheless, here probity supplied the place of wealth.
The word of these men was held to be as good as
their bond, and either was never known to be protested. Within the borders of Holland and Zealand,
patriot mutinies, scenes analogous to those which the
prince was watching from the walls of Middleburg,
were quite unknown. At Haarlem, at Alckmaar, at
Leyden, at Zierickzee, when specie had failed the
citizens in the long sieges, they issued promissory
notes or coined money of tin, which the foreign soldiers, in their pay, received without complaint; nor
was such traffic as remained embarrassed by want
of confidence in a circulating medium wholly destitute of intrinsic value. Behind every piece of paper currency, in every tin coin, the holder saw the
pledged faith of the commonwealth, and knew that
no plea of distress, no complaint of extortion, no
claim of usury would be interposed to bar eventual
redemption—there stood the promise, certain to be

* *Vide* Articles of Union, in Bor., book 9, p. 620.   † Ibid.

fulfilled, unless William and the estates went down.*
It was this integrity and the boundless confidence
which it inspired, that enabled this impoverished
nook of land to protract the contest with Spain to
the ultimate exhaustion of the Crœsus at Madrid.
Philip conducted his exchequer upon opposite principles.   On one occasion he had incurred a debt of
some fifteen millions of ducats to Spanish and German merchants.   He paid his creditors by obtaining from the pope a dispensation which permitted
him to revoke his engagements, "lest," said he, "I
should be ruined by usury while combating heresy."†   Is it strange that the soldiers of the royal
repudiator should demand their wages, not in promises, but in current coin of the realm?

When they could not get this, they mutinied—
as they were now doing in Flanders and Brabant.
But while these provinces suffered from the mutiny,
Holland, happily out of reach of the marauders,
gained by it; for the garrisons of those towns
within its borders of which the Spaniard had possessed himself now deserted their posts and hurried south to join their insurgent comrades.‡   Thus
by the *laches* of the conqueror, Haarlem, Naarden,
Sparrendam, and the Hague reverted to the state,
never again to bow in vassalage to a foreign power.
Amsterdam, however, still adhered to the royalists,
which caused the patriots infinite vexation, and

° Davies, Hist. of Holland, vol. 2, p. 32, *seq.*
† Meteren, book 5, folio 116.
‡ Brandt, vol. 1, p. 325. Bor., Hoofd, *et alii.*

crippled the union.* But upon the whole, liberty and religion were regnant in the confederacy.

It was William's purpose to evoke a similar order from the southern chaos. He aspired to unite the seventeen provinces in one great political brotherhood. Hitherto the presence in Brussels, first of Alva, then of Requesens, and fatal differences of religion—Holland and Zealand unanimously Protestant, the sister-states at least half Romanist†—had prevented this "consummation devoutly to be wished." The latter impediment still existed; but the prevailing disorders had already drawn all into closer relations with each other, tiding over, at least for the moment, the quarrel of creeds. Men of all parties were now clamoring for the expulsion of the foreign brigands; and as the provinces had been akin in their whilom constitutions, so at this hour all seemed inclined to use the crisis in effecting a restoration of the ancient government.‡

These were the rocks of William's hope. Putting himself in active communication with the malcontents at Brussels, at Antwerp, at Ghent, he began to labor with a swift subtlety which no ken of common intelligence could follow, precipitating and moulding events months before his agency was suspected by the uninitiated. In multitudinous appeals to the respective estates and to influential individuals, he touched the chords of national

* Motley, vol. 3, p. 56, *seq.*   † De Thou, liv. 62.
‡ Motley, vol. 3, pp. 56, 83, 84.

feeling with skilful fingers, drawing forth a stormy, revolutionary chorus.* In the autumn of 1576, the result became manifest. The southern provinces appointed delegates to confer with the representatives of Holland and Zealand in a grand interprovincial congress summoned to meet in Ghent.†

Meantime the burghers of Brussels, convinced that several members of the council of state were secretly encouraging the mutineers, determined upon a *coup d'état*. On the 5th of September, 1576, a revolutionary committee burst in upon the counsellors in full session, and placed that antiquated gathering under arrest—laid them up among other fossils in the museum of history.‡ At the same time the Blood Council, which even since the retirement of Alva had been spasmodically active, was suspended, and that too became an antique.§ A few days afterwards, Aerschot and two or three others of the counsellors, who had of late assumed the Phrygian cap, were liberated and permitted to resume their nominal functions under surveillance;|| the existence of the council of state, in some shape, being essential, since it alone was competent to sprinkle executive action with the rose-water of legality. Some weeks previous to this scene, one of

---

* *Vide* the letters in Bor., book 9, pp. 695, 696, 702, *seq.*

† Bor., *ubi sup.*, pp. 703, 718, *seq.*

‡ Ibid., p. 712. Meteren, book 5, folio 197. Archives de la Maison d'Orange-Nassau, etc., tom. 5, p. 408.

§ Archives et Corresp., tom. 5, p. 406.

|| Motley, *ubi sup.*, p. 92. Davies, vol. 2, p. 34. Meteren, book 6, folios 120, 121.

the counsellors, Jerome di Rhoda, scenting danger, had escaped to Antwerp. Now, claiming that his companions were in duress, he set up his person as all that remained of the outraged majesty of Spain, counterfeited the royal seal, and gave to the mutineers the sanction of the law.* Thus, as in a former century, there had been two popes—one at Rome, the other at Avignon, both claiming to be the undoubted successor of St. Peter—so now in the Netherlands there were two representatives of his majesty, and men were privileged to take their choice.

On the 19th of October, 1576, the interprovincial congress held its opening session at Ghent.† The citadel, built to curb, not to protect the town, was held by the mutineers, somewhat to the alarm of the delegates, whose first act was to solicit aid from William for its reduction.‡ He willingly responded by sending twenty-eight companies of foot; who, assisted by the burgher train-bands, at once besieged the castle, which was ably commanded by the amazonian wife of Mondragone, in that veteran's absence.§ Thus the congress commenced its deliberations to the warlike music of a cannonade.

While these events were afoot, the brigands were astir. On the 20th of October, the opulent town of Maestricht was escaladed and sacked—

---

* Hoofd, book 30, p. 449. Bor., book 9, p. 705.

† Bor., *ubi sup.*, p. 719, *seq.* Meteren, book 6, folio 3.

‡ Meteren, book 6, folio 108. Bor., *ubi sup.*, p. 716.

§ Meteren, *ubi sup.*

stabbing, drowning, burning, and ravishing filling
up the measure of its woe.*   About two weeks later,
what is called the "Spanish fury" occurred at Antwerp.   The citadel which commanded that magnificent city was held by Don Sanchio D'Avila, in the
interest of the mutineers.   For some time past the
citizens, supported by what levies they had been able
to mass, had held the garrison in close confinement.
Don Sanchio managed to send word to Alost, the
headquarters of the mutineers, of his precarious con-
tion.   "March to my relief," wrote he, "else we
must lose our hold on the riches of these smug and
gold-footed burghers."†   The message was effectual.   Alost was speedily emptied of the pirate horde;
all swarmed off to succor their imperilled comrade.
The citizens, apprized of their coming, rushed to
the city-gates, resolute to defend their plethoric
warehouses and their hearths.   A furious fight ensued.   But the undisciplined valor of the multitude
proved no match for the trained skill of the mutineers.   At dusk the assailants, aided by a desperate sortie of D'Avila from the citadel and by the
treason of the German troops in the pay of the
townsfolk, forced their way through the well-defend-
ed portals, and early evening saw them in full possession of the commercial metropolis of Europe.‡

   Humanity shudders at the rest.   Antwerp was
fired in a hundred different quarters; and, lighted by

   ° Meteren, *ubi sup.*, folio 109. Strada, tom. 3, p. 21.
   † Meteren, book 7, folio 110. Hoofd, Bor., *et alii.*
   ‡ Mendoza, tom. 15, p. 315. Meteren, *ubi sup.*

these frightful torches, the brigands spread throughout the town, intent equally on robbery, rape, and
murder.   Raging up and down like devils loosed,
they spared neither crippled age nor blooming
youth; neither the feeble matron, the helpless
maid, nor the wailing babe.   Houses and churches
vomited blood.   Not shrieks, nor sobs, nor prayers
could move the pity of the pitiless.*   Every mansion, every warehouse was ransacked from garret
to cellar.   The houses of the foreign merchants, of
the clergy, of the patricians, of the mechanics were
alike gutted in the fierce democracy of the sack.†

Details need not soil these pages.   It shall suffice to note that, with a loss to themselves of less
than two hundred men, the Spaniards slew upwards
of eight thousand of the burghers, burned five hundred of the costliest buildings in the world, pocketed six millions of dollars in gold, and destroyed
property to twice that value.‡   Afterwards, being
thus handsomely in funds, and become desirous of
aping the despised and plundered merchants, they
sauntered daily into the exchange, like men accustomed to affairs, wasting their gains in gambling at
the Bourse, or melting their blood-spotted gold into
coats-of-mail.§

Such was the holiday of the soldiers of the saints
in Antwerp.   The image of Him who said, "Love

* Bor., book 9, p. 731.
† Campana, lib. 5, p. 165.   De Thou,, Bor., Hoofd, *et multi alii.*
‡ Hoofd, book 9, p. 463.   Bor., *ubi sup.*   Strada, tom 3.
§ Motley, vol. 3, p. 117.

your enemies" and the gentle face of the Madonna were supposed to smile from heaven upon deeds which might cause a shudder in the depths of hell.* Di Rhoda stood forth as the apologist of the infamy. "I wish your majesty much good of the victory," wrote he to Philip; "'t is a very great one, and the damage to the city is enormous."† What the king thought is not known; but if silence gives consent, he too may be ranked among the pious cynics who rejoiced.

The "Spanish fury" had one good result—it decided the action of the congress at Ghent. On the 8th of November, 1576, four days after the massacre, St. Aldegonde, with eight others, commissioners for Holland and Zealand, and the deputies of the southern and middle provinces, put their hands and seals to a paper by which it was unanimously agreed:

That all should pardon the past offences of all.

That, for the future, the Netherlands should constitute an offensive and defensive alliance—in all else, each state to retain its individuality.

That the Spaniards should be expelled without delay.

That all edicts against heresy and all acts of inquisition should be suspended.

That in the Romanist provinces the prevailing creed should suffer no injury by word or deed.

That in Holland and Zealand the established faith should be guaranteed.

° Motley, vol. 3, p. 106.   † Cited in Bor., book 9, p. 737, *seq*

That every vexed question arising under the .compact should be subject to the decision of the states-general.*

Such, in rough outline, was the famous " Pacification of Ghent;" and these were the chief of the twenty-five articles which it contained, other clauses bearing in the main upon individual interests. By it, the Low Countries were united, somewhat loosely indeed, but still united, and pledged to drive out the brigands. The Reformation was recognized in the states in which it was dominant, and in the fifteen ultramontane provinces it was tacitly acquiesced in, since the inquisitorial decrees were abrogated. With the return of the exiled Protestants, the gospel theology might haply become regnant in the south, as it was already in the north. As the pigeons, in their journeyings, carry in their crops precious cargoes of undigested seed—as the swallows pack the interstices of their feathers with tiny, close-pressed bales of insects, blessing with their visits islands far distant from any mainland, where they drop their freight, and thus become the scatterers of myriad generations of insect life, planters of mighty forests—so the reformers hoped that here the seed with which their lives were freighted might fall into good ground, and bring forth a thousand fold.

While the deputies were in the act of signing the treaty, they were informed that the castle of

* _Vide_ the articles in Bor., book 9, p. 738, _et seq._ Meteren, book 6, folio 112, _et al._

Ghent had surrendered at discretion;* and shortly afterwards word was brought that the city of Zierickzee, with the whole island of Schouwen, had again shaken off the recently-imposed yoke of Spain, and rehoisted the patriot banner.† Thus closed this memorable day, amid universal gratulation, the cheering of all parties save the mutineers, and both creeds,‡ and the peal of jubilant, merry-making bells.

In the midst of the excitement attending these occurrences, Don John of Austria, whom Philip had at length selected as governor-general of the Low Countries, arrived at Luxemburg.§ Disguised as a Moorish slave in the train of a Castilian grandee, he had travelled with all speed to reach his post—only at last to arrive too late, as was the common fortune of Spanish haste.‖ This was the *Odyssey*, as the Pacification was the *Iliad*, of the epoch.

* Bor., *ubi sup.*, p. 727.   Mendoza, tom. 16, p. 326.

† Bor., *ubi sup.*   Hoofd, book 11, p. 470.

‡ Strada, tom. 3, p. 21.

§ Hoofd, *ut antea*, p. 472.   Bor., *ut antea.*

‖ Strada, tom. 3, p. 19.

CHAPTER XLIII.

PRAISE GOD.

In deputing Don John of Austria to govern the
provinces, Philip had for once deferred to the prejudice of the Netherlanders against foreign rulers;
for though their new viceroy bore a Spanish brand,
he was not a Spaniard. His romantic story was
known of all men. Like Margaret of Parma, the
offspring of one of the many illicit loves of Charles
V., his reputed mother was Dame Barbara Blam-
berg, who, before the emperor honored by dishon-
oring her, had been a washerwoman of Ratisbon.*
Recognized as a son by Charles and as a brother
by Philip, the imperial bastard had been liberally
educated; and now, at thirty-one, stood haloed
with fame won at Lepanto, and in campaigns against
both Ottoman and Moriscoe.

Elegant and graceful in person and deportment,
lively, facetious, affable, Don John was the curled
darling of chivalry. Events were soon to show that
he lacked prudence, patience, self-command, and
dexterity in managing the passions and prejudices
of men—the precise qualities which the times and
his *rôle* demanded in the states. From his advent
great results were looked for both at Madrid and
at the Vatican. He himself dreamed of a glory
surpassing that of Lepanto and the Alpuxarras;

* Strada, tom. 5, p. 16, *et seq.*

for his appointment had a double meaning.   After
subduing the Netherlands, the pope had stipulated
with Philip that the conqueror should pass into
England and liberate and wed the captive queen of
Scots, with Great Britain for her dowry, which
would be a plausible title for the house of Austria
to base a war upon for the dethroning of Elizabeth.*
The hero meant, therefore, to placate the provinces
in a summary and ostentatious fashion; then to
plume his wings for a flight at the higher quarry.

· Unhappily for the impatient and passionate
dreamer, he had first to encounter the prince of
Orange—an antipodal character, untimely aged at
forty-three, who knew not *seems*, but inquired for
the *is;* spare of figure, plain in apparel, benignant
but haggard of countenance, with temples bared by
thought as much as by the helmet, earnest, devout
in manner, in his own phrase " *Calvus et Calvin-
ista.*"† What chance of success had the knight
errant in his impending joust with the foremost
statesman of the age?

Don John's instructions were brief but pregnant: "You will bring about a pacification, if possible," said the king; "always maintaining, however, the absolute authority of the crown and the
exclusive exercise of the Roman faith."‡ How the
paradox of conciliation without concession was to
be accomplished, his majesty did not deign to say;

---

* Strada, tom. 3, p. 18.   † Motley, vol. 3, p. 146.
‡ Instruccion Secreta, MS.   Cited in Motley, *ubi sup.*, pp.
146, 147.

but the viceroy seems not to have noticed the omis
sion.

On reaching Luxemburg, Don John's first act
was formally to apprize the states-general, then in
session at Brussels under call of the recent congress
at Ghent, and what remained of the council of state,
of his arrival. "I shall not go on to the capital,"
added he, "until I receive hostages for your peaceable behavior, a guard for my own security, and
the command of the army and navy. I am inclined
to peace; but if you fail in these respects, you will
find me no less prepared for war."*

This message, made up of an announcement, a
demand, and a threat, perplexed the patriot government; and embarrassment soon became foreboding, for intercepted letters showed that both
Philip and Don John were in active correspondence
with the mutineers, whose conduct was approved,
whose faithfulness was applauded.†

Upon ascertaining this fact, the states-general
applied to Orange for advice. It was readily given.
In a letter, varying through every key in which
human wisdom could be sung, the prince exhorted
the national representatives to be firm, cautious,
incisive. "Above all," wrote he, "make no treaty
with Don John; take no step towards his reception
without swearing him to the observance of these
conditions-precedent: the maintenance of the Ghent
pacification in its entirety, the recall of the Span-

* *Vide* his letter in Bor., book 10, p. 761.
† Davies, vol. 2, p. 40.

ish troops, no fresh battalions to be recruited without the consent of the states-general, the demolition of the citadels, the recognition of the charters, the assembly of the states-general at pleasure."[*]

The deputies promptly determined to heed this counsel, remembering that they who prorogue the honesty of to-day till to-morrow, will probably prorogue to-morrow to eternity. Towards the end of November, 1576, a committee waited upon his highness at Luxemburg to present the programme which Orange had sketched as a *sine quâ non.*[†] Tedious and indecisive negotiations ensued. Each looked askance at the other, the Netherland diplomats stoutly adhering to their *ultimatum,* Don John offering to guarantee any thing except the essential points—eager, in Burke's phrase, to " mortgage his injustice as a pawn for his fidelity."

Meantime, the states-general were preparing for the worst issue. The sieur de Sweveghem was accredited to England, and other envoys passed into France and into Germany to solicit aid or to cement alliances. At all these courts they were graciously received, Elizabeth especially acting with unwonted frankness and alacrity. She advanced one hundred thousand pounds in negotiable paper, hinging the loan upon the fair conditions that the pacification should be adhered to, and that no treaty should be made with Don John without her assent.[‡]

---

[*] *Vide* Bor., book 10, p. 747, *et seq.*
[†] Ibid., p. 762, *seq.* Wagenaer, Vandervynckt, *et alii.*
[‡] Camden, book 2, p. 215. Meteren, book 6, folio 128, *seq.*

Nor were the patriots less active at home. On the 5th of January, 1577, the "Union of Brussels" was formed.* This pact covered the same ground as the pacification; but whereas that was a diplomatic convention, subscribed by the deputies of the contracting parties the states, this was a popular agreement, signed by the people at large—nobles, ecclesiastics, citizens, peasants, convened for the purpose of giving to the demands put forth at Ghent the broad authority of democratic sanction.†

At the same time the states-general, as evidence of the sincerity of their desire for peace and the *statu quo*, got the council of state to declare that there was nothing in the text of the pacification hostile to the prerogative of his majesty, and procured from the pedant doctors of Louvain an elaborate opinion that the treaty did not conflict with the supremacy of holy church.‡ These papers, plentifully garnished with exclamation points—the crutches upon which lame rhetoric habitually hobbles—were forwarded to the viceroy, whose scruples they were expected to satisfy.§

Thus supported, and assisted by mediators sent by the new German emperor Rudolph, who now succeeded his father, the trimmer Maximilian, recently deceased,‖ the patriots resumed negotiations with Don John. For some weeks the interviews

---

* Bor., book 10, p. 769.   † Ibid. Meteren, book 6, folio 116.
‡ Bor., *ubi sup.*, pp. 766, 768.
§ Ibid. Hoofd, book 11, p. 478.
‖ He died on the 12th of October, 1576.

were bickering and stormy; but in the end, convinced that only so could he hope for success, and fearful that longer delay might cause the voyage into England to slip out of his hands, Don John decided to accede to the *ultimatum* of the obstinate provinces, thinking that, once recognized, it would be easy for him to find or invent some clause in the agreement through which he could drive the coach and six of absolutism.* Still with an eye to Great Britain, however, he insisted upon a proviso that the troops should depart by sea.† In the first flush of triumph, the states-general conceded so much; but suspecting, on reflection, that some unknown danger lurked under a stipulation so strenuously urged, they withdrew their assent, pleading the expense and delay which the providing ships for ten thousand men would necessitate.‡ Protracted and heated negotiations resulted; but finally, the patriots again carried their point. Don John agreed to the exit of the army by land, and with a secret sigh, deferred the darling and romantic project which had lured him to the Netherlands.§

On the 17th of February, 1577, the provinces were officially apprized of the successful close of the conferences by the "perpetual edict," which pledged Don John to the maintenance of the pacification of Ghent,‖ and which, a few weeks later, his

---

* Bor., book 10, p. 775.   † Ibid.
‡ Davies, vol. 2, p. 43.   § Bor., book 10, p. 486.
‖ Ibid.   Meteren, book 6, folios 117, 118.

majesty formally approved in a decree fulminated from Madrid.*

Nevertheless, Orange viewed the treaty and its royal endorsement with absolute disdain. Why? Because he saw the trickery by which both were inspired. "Call him wise," says Lavater, "whose actions are a clear *because* to a clear *why*." In a solemn manifesto he warned the states-general of the insidious danger that threatened the new policy. "New men come out of Spain, not new purposes; for in that shop intents are always cast in the same mould," wrote he. "Be not cajoled by empty protestations and blotted parchments. Vigilance and determination—these are alone trustworthy; palladiums these."† He refused to sign the "perpetual edict," as did also the maritime provinces; nor did he remit his warlike preparations.‡ Some better bulwark against the returning tide of tyranny was needed than the hollow promise of a necessitous viceroy, the solemn saws of a timid council of state, and the quiddities from Louvain.§ Events were soon to prove the accuracy of his prophetic ken.

At the outset, however, affairs tripped smoothly along. In the last days of June, the Spanish battalions departed, marching through the crowds of jubilant spectators who lined the way to see them off with sulky, half-mutinous mien, and comforted

---

* Vandervynckt, book 2, p. 232. Strada, tom. 4, p. 30.

† Strada, *ubi sup.*, p. 33. Compare the letter in Bor., *ubi sup.*, p. 790.   ‡ Bor., Hoofd, Vandervynckt, *et alii.*

§ Motley, vol. 3, p. 167, *seq.*

by the reflection that the war, now raked up in embers, would ere long burst forth in fresh flame, when they would be recalled to extinguish it.* They went out laden with the spoils of ten years' rapine, boasting that within six months they had slain thirty thousand Netherlanders, with a loss to themselves which was not perceptible by the light of their camp-fires.† The popular rejoicings were dampened by the memory of this slaughter, by the fear that their exit was but a feint, and by the fact that ten thousand German mercenaries, whose arrears the states-general had not been able to pay, still held the provincial strongholds for the king.‡

On the 1st of May, Don John made his official entry into Brussels, amid the extravagant plaudits of the populace, never so happy as on a show-day, and only less excitable and volatile than the giddy Parisians. It was, as Dryden sang of the Restoration,

> "A very merry, dancing, drinking,
>   Laughing, quaffing, and unthinking time."

In the midst of the revelry, Viglius "shuffled off this mortal coil"§—dying not much regretted by any faction. A man of prodigious acquisitions, learned in both laws, the adroitest of politicians, he was an egotist who lived for himself alone; he was left therefore to be the chief mourner at his own funeral. He had been prominent in public affairs now for forty years, yet had never allowed

---

* Strada, tom. 4, p. 32.   † Grotius, Ann., lib. 7, p. 70.
‡ Hoofd, book 11. Bor., book 10.
§ He died May 8, 1577.

himself to be betrayed into an honest act. He had doubtless been honest once, and he was for ever trading on that fact; but some one has said that the worst of all knaves are those who can mimic their former honesty. Like Martial's lawyer—*Iras et verba locant*—he was in the habit of hiring out his words and anger, proportioning both to the amount of the fee. He was accustomed to say, "A good lawyer is a bad Christian," and his own life did not give the lie to the device.

In Holland and Zealand, the citizens took advantage of the present hour of sunshine to reconstruct their dykes, and generally to rehabilitate the land. In obedience to the popular invitation, the prince, accompanied by his wife, Charlotte de Bourbon, made a tour through these little states at this juncture, for the purpose of marking the progress of internal improvement, making suggestions, promoting a closer union between the towns, conciliating jarring interests, and strengthening the resolution of the masses to sustain, if need were, a renewal of the war. He was everywhere received with tears of gladness and shouts of welcome. And as he passed from village to village, there was one continued cry of, "Father William has come! Father William has come!"* This crown of a nation's gratitude was the only one which the liberator cared to place upon his brow.

At the request of the burgomaster of Utrecht, he visited that ancient Episcopal see, reëstablishing

* Hoofd, book 12, p. 520. Bor., book 10, p. 830

thereby the *entente cordiale* which ere long impelled that province to adhere to the seaboard confederacy.*

Meanwhile affairs at Brussels were drifting towards that imbroglio which the astute prince had predicted. Don John, galled by the limitations imposed upon his authority, was making resolute efforts to break through the meshes. He had already tampered with the German hirelings,† and he had even gone so far as to make overtures to Orange—overtures which, it is needless to add, were received with merited contempt.‡ The states-general, apprized of these machinations, viewed the governor-general with daily increasing suspicion. "These people," said he, "are beginning to abhor me, and I abhor them already."§ At length, feeling sure of the mercenaries, he determined to bring matters to a crisis. Repairing to Namûr on pretence of welcoming Marguerite de Valois, the fair and frail wife of Henry of Navarre, who was passing through that town *en route* to the baths of Spa, he made a sudden attack upon the citadel of that city, and took it, exclaiming, "This is the first day of my regency."‖

Thence he despatched a letter to the states-

* Hoofd, book 12, p. 520. Bor., book 10, p. 830. Wagenaer, book 7.   † Ibid.

‡ *Vide* Corresp. de Guillaume le Taciturne, vol. 3, preface, p. liv., *seq.*

§ Cartas del S. Don Juan, MS., cited in Motley, vol. 3, p. 192. Strada, tom. 4.

‖ Meteren, book 7, folio 122. Bentivoglio, tom. 10, p. 194, *seq.*

general, alleging, in apology for this action, the existence of a plot to seize his person. "I will return to the capital," wrote he, "when you agree to reëstablish me in the rights of the governor-generalship, abolish the Pacification of Ghent, and declare war against Orange and his nests of heresy in Holland and Zealand."*

This truculent epistle reconvulsed the provinces. For a while, indeed, the states-general were irresolute and inclined to temporize. They deprecated the return of war—trade was white-lipped at the thought. They were without an army. The Germans were in Don John's pay, and they held the citadels from Valenciennes to Breda. These considerations made them half-minded to concede every thing except warfare with the prince; and a profuse interchange of protocols, of propositions and counter-propositions, of crimination and recrimination, was the result†—a parchment babel.

Before any thing decisive had come out of this confusion of tongues, a discovery was made which necessitated war. Just prior to his instalment at Brussels, Don John and his confidential secretary, Escovedo, had written in cipher to Philip, requesting moneys and a fresh supply of troops against the time when the farce of reconciliation should end, and the tragedy of force, the only cure-all, should begin; "for," added they, "whatever we may *seem* to think, our *real opinion* is that the diseased part

○ Bor., book 11, p. 835, *seq.* Meteren, *ubi sup.*
† *Vide* Motley, vol. 3, pp. 244-275, *passim*

of the Netherlands must be cut off." As it fell out, the courier lost this packet *in transitu*, and it was picked up on the heath of Bordeaux, and handed to Henry of Navarre, who sent it to Orange. The prince had the letters deciphered, and then he despatched them to the states-general.* Perceiving, therefore, the slight security which any contract with Don John would afford, the national representatives at once suspended negotiations, and began to prepare for war.

The first thing to be done was, to expel the Germans. As the patriots were without troops, they determined to fight with gold—to bribe the hirelings from the land. At Antwerp, whose citadel was Don John's pillow, the first essay was made. After much running to and fro, the burghers finally prevailed upon the mercenaries to evacuate the town in consideration of a hundred and fifty thousand guilders, cash in hand. The parties were about to close the bargain, the last parley was being held, the merchants stood by with large purses full of gold to pay the price, when suddenly a patriot flotilla sailed up the Scheldt, and fired three broadsides among the barricades of the soldiers. With a shout of, "The *gueux!* the *gueux!*" the Germans scattered and fled pell-mell, leaving their baggage and the fat purses behind. Within five minutes, Antwerp was free from a garrison which had vexed and pillaged it for twelve weary years.†

* Hoofd, book 12, p. 516. De Thou, lib. 64, cap. 7.
† Bor., book 11, p. 855. Hoofd, *ubi sup.*, p. 522.

The work thus auspiciously commenced was thriftily pursued, and by the autumn of 1577, the provinces were swept clean of the Germans by the bloodless broom of burgher coin.* As a measure of security for the future, the liberated towns determined to destroy those "nests of tyranny," the citadels. Antwerp set the example. While occupied in the demolition, the citizens found, lying in an obscure crypt, the statue of Alva, which Requesens had thrown down. The hated effigy was first dragged through the streets for general inspection and outrage, and then dashed in pieces by a thousand sturdy sledge-hammers.† Soon afterwards Ghent, Valenciennes, Utrecht took a similar holiday, razing the castles amid hoarse *vivas*.‡

In September, 1577, Orange was urgently invited by the states-general to visit the capital, and give them the aid of his personal presence.§ Alone, and against the advice of his more timorous friends, he immediately started on what John Nassau styled "the gallows-journey to Brussels."‖ On the 23d of the month he entered the town, whose pavement had been so long unfamiliar to his feet, where Vargas had proscribed him, hailed by the mercurial and boisterous populace as friend and deliverer.¶

He found three parties in the state—the adhe-

---

* Meteren. Hoofd, Bor.   † Strada, tom. 4, p. 909.
‡ Meteren, book 7, folio 125. Hoofd, book 12, p. 524.
§ Ibid. Bor., 11, p. 871.
‖ Archives et Corresp., tom. 6, p. 215.
¶ Hoofd, *ubi sup.*, p. 528. Meteren, book 7, folio 126. Bor., *ubi sup.*, p. 873.

rents of Don John, commonly called the "Johanists;" the nobles, led by Aerschot, whom events had taught to hate the Spaniard, but who were even more jealous of the prince, who stood aloof from the people, and were intent upon harvesting from the troubles a crop of self-aggrandizement, careless of the commonweal; and the patriots, his partisans, the great middle class, embracing the wealth and the political capacity of the Belgic provinces—the controlling power when Pilate and Herod were not at agreement.*

As a counterpoise to the preponderating influence of William, Aerschot and his compeers resolved to set up a new governor-general, who should be their creature, whose hands might be the hands of Esau, but whose voice should be the voice of Jacob. Secretly, without consultation with the states-general, they opened a correspondence with the archduke Matthias, brother of the German emperor, a mild and pliant boy of twenty.† His April blood was fired by the thought of the proposed honor, and eagerly closing with the offer, he set out in disguise at midnight from Vienna, without Cæsar's knowledge, travelling post to Maestricht, where he arrived at the end of October, 1577.‡

When the states-general got news of his advent they were both surprised and angered; indeed they were about summarily to eject the youthful

---

* Motley, vol. 3, p. 219.

† Bor., book 11, p. 898, *seq.* Campana, lib. 6, p. 191.

‡ Ibid. Hoofd, book 12, p. 530.

interloper.   The keen good sense of Orange averted
the impending blow.   This stumbling-block which
the jealousy of his opponents had rolled into his path,
he meant to transform into an additional stepping-
stone towards his goal.   On his genius alone, as
Ariadne on her clue, had he to rely in threading the
doubtful and dubious mazes of this labyrinth; but
his genius was equal to the emergency.

He foresaw the advantages which might arise
from the rivalship into which Matthias had entered
with his kinsman, Don John.   He thought it possible that armed men might spring from the dragon's
teeth of enmity thus sown between the German and
Spanish offshoots of the house of Austria.   He esteemed it well too that the Romanist grandees had,
by taking the initiative in this scheme, for ever
alienated the ousted viceroy.

William, therefore, fell cordially into the plot,
persuaded the states-general into voting Aerschot's
supposed puppet into the governor-generalship,
after reducing his authority to a nullity by checks
and balances, and by this magnificent management,
took Matthias wholly into his own possession, gaining one piece more in the great game which he was
playing against his antagonist of the Escurial.*

At this juncture, Aerschot having got a hoist
with his own petard, was appointed stadtholder of
Flanders, with his headquarters at Ghent, whither,
on the 20th of October, 1577, he repaired.†   Here,

---

* Motley, vol. 3, pp. 276, 277, 281, *seq.*
† Vandervynckt, book 2, p. 276.   Meteren, book 7, folio 126.

in the very stronghold of his power, a fresh mortification awaited him. He found two demagogues,
Ryhave and Hembyse, omnipotent in the town, one
holding the civil, the other the military sword, while
twenty thousand resolute and well-armed men formed the bodyguard of the oligarchs.* Protestantism
too was in full possession of the churches. Aerschot was an ultra aristocrat and a bigoted Romanist, and he speedily assumed the task of righting
this double wrong. A bitter conflict of authority
ensued. " I will have these anarchs hanged," exclaimed the enraged stadtholder ; " yes, even though
Orange himself were at their back."

These words caused an immediate outbreak.
That same night, Ryhave summoned the captains
of his bands, and quickly assembling the burghers,
proverbially prone to rioting, marched to the hotel
of his excellency, dragged him from his bed, gave
him scant time to dress, carried him through the
midnight streets now ablaze with torches, and
plunged him into prison, whither he was soon followed by his trembling retinue.†

William, on being told the story, hurried off to
Ghent, quieted the tumult, and persuaded the incensed Ghentese to liberate their captive.‡ But
the indignity annihilated Aerschot's political importance.

On returning to Brussels, the prince found that

* Vandervynckt, *ubi sup.*, *et seq.* Bor., *et al.*
† Hoofd, book 12, p. 535. Meteren, *ubi sup.*
‡ Bor., book 11, pp. 905–916.

he had been, in his absence, nominated "ruward" of Brabant, an office which had long been in disuse—the governor-general being stadtholder of that province *ex officio*—but which carried with it dictatorial powers. The first use which he made of this augmented authority was to promote what the old chroniclers style the "nearer union of Brussels," under which the notables again pledged themselves to mutual support, and which rewelded such links of the Ghent pacification as recent events had broken.*

At the same time,† the states-general formally deposed Don John of Austria, banned him as a public enemy, ordered him to quit the provinces without delay, and branded as traitors all who should acknowledge his forfeited authority.‡ A solemn justification of this act was written in seven different languages, and presented at all the courts of Europe.§

This decisive step was followed by an embassy to solicit the alliance of England. Elizabeth, always jealous of Netherland negotiations with any other court, had been somewhat estranged by the treaty with Matthias. The envoys related to her the circumstances of his incoming; but she would do nothing until she received a pledge that Orange should be installed as lieutenant-governor of the states.‖ This being readily accorded, she, for the

---

* Motley, vol. 3, p. 299.   † December 7, 1577.
‡ Bor., book 11, p. 916. Meteren.   § Bor., *ubi sup.*, p. 881.
‖ Ibid., p. 903. Camden, book 2, p. 221.

first time, entered into a coalition with the Low Countries as an independent power, engaging to send over fifteen thousand men-at-arms and a hundred thousand pounds, but on condition that the states-general should not make peace without her consent, and should agree to give her, if need were, similar assistance.* It was a thrifty bargain; but it openly compromised the coy political coquette.

On the 18th of January, 1578, Matthias made his formal entry into the capital, receiving an ovation.† He was at once placed at the prow of the ship of state as figure-head, while William, as lieutenant-governor, took the helm.

Meantime, Don John was at Namûr watching these proceedings with grim complacency, for he saw that at last the pen was to be superseded by the sword, and he was thoroughly at home in the saddle. "Now, sire," wrote he to the king, "nothing will do but to pick up the gauntlet." Philip reluctantly assented, for he had been anxious to carry his point by artifice; and Christendom once more rang with warlike preparations. But suspecting that the brilliant bastard had ulterior designs upon the Spanish crown—his ambassador at Paris had recently discovered a secret league between Don John and the duke of Guise, whereby they pledged themselves to "protect" France and Castile, which meant the reducing their sovereigns to a state of tutelage‡—he had resolved never to en-

---

* Camden, book 2, p. 221.　　† Meteren, Bor., Hoofd.
‡ De Thou, lib. 64, cap. 8.

trust an army to the sole command of Lepanto's hero. Therefore he now appointed Alexander Farnese, one of the ablest soldiers of any age, generalissimo of the royal levies, and sent him to lead back from Italy those veterans over whose sulky outward march the provinces had rejoiced.*

Farnese effected a junction with Don John at Namûr. Their united muster was twenty thousand strong — seasoned campaigners, officered under themselves by Mendoza, Mondragone, Mansfeld.† For the purpose of affrighting the consciences of those Romanists who were in the patriot service, the pope had blessed this host, and fulminated a bull analogous to those which had stirred the crusades in the bygone time.‡ Don John's banner bore a crucifix with the inscription, "By this sign I have conquered the Turks, and by this sign I will conquer the heretics."§ Philip, not to be outdone by his holiness, accompanied the bull with a decree, which prorogued the states-general, annulled the pacification of Ghent, and cashiered the Netherland magnates.‖

The states had put into the field a force approximating the Spanish in numbers, but in all else immeasurably inferior; "made up," as John Nassau expressed it, "of very few patriots, but plenty

---

° Strada, tom. 4, p. 41. Both the original Latin editions of Strada, and an English translation—London, 1650—have been used as convenience dictated; which will explain diversities in the citations.   † Ibid., *et seq.*

‡ Meteren, book 8, folio 148.   Brandt, vol. 1, p. 333.

§ Ibid.   ‖ Bor., book 12, p. 939, *et seq.*

of priests, with no lack of inexperienced lads ; some looking for distinction, the rest for pelf."*

On the 31st of January, 1578, these so different arrays fell upon each other at Gemblours, on the confines of Brabant.† Farnese's dash decided the day within fifty minutes. Conjecturing from the sway of the crossed and tangled pikes of the raw patriot levies that their line of battle was disordered, he caught a lance from his captain of horse, and turning to an aid, said, " Go tell Don John that Farnese, remembering the Roman, has plunged into the gulf, hoping to bring thence a certain and glorious victory."‡ Then, followed by a train of gallant cavaliers, he launched himself upon the quaking battalions of the states. With a loss to himself of twelve men, to the provinces of six thousand, he sent his pasteboard foemen whirling in utter rout through Gemblours quite up to the walls of the panic-stricken capital§—another proof of the invincibility of disciplined enthusiasm.

Thinking that the Spaniard would next assail Brussels, the prince put Matthias in his pocket and retired to Antwerp, with the states-general for a retinue.‖ Don John was desirous of doing so ; but, fearful of dulling the alacrity of the soldiery by a long siege, he decided to postpone that pleasure. Therefore, giving the insurgent capital the go-by,

---

* Archives de la Maison d'Orange, etc., tom. 6, p. 227.
† Strada, tom. 4, p. 50. ‡ Ibid., p. 51.
§ Ibid. Hoofd, book. 13, p. 459. Cabrera, tom. 12, p. 968, *seq.*
‖ Strada, *ubi sup.* Meteren.

he marched hither and thither, stringing Neville, and Louvain, and Mechlin, "that sweet city with the dreaming spires," to his saddle-bow.*

These reverses were severely felt by the patriots; but they were more than counter-balanced by the accession of the wealthy and influential city of Amsterdam to the good cause, which at this eleventh hour came into the vineyard, a welcome laborer.† Encouraged by this occurrence, Orange pushed recruiting with fresh vigor, re-collected the troops dispersed by Farnese's prowess, and placed affairs upon a broad war footing.‡

The remodelled army was inferior, even in numbers, to the force of the Spaniard. Its commander, Count Bossu—who, like Aerschot and Havre and Lelain, had recently passed over to the states—was therefore ordered to remain on the defensive and await reinforcements now looked for from England and from Germany.§ Don John, anxious to crush this muster before the incoming of the expected auxiliaries, presently moved up to attack Bossu, entrenched at Rymenant. The assault was bloodily repulsed, chiefly by the valor of a regiment of bonnie Scots; whereupon the royalists retired to Namûr, fortified their camp, and, like Cimon, fell to whistling for want of thought.‖

William seized this opportunity to settle the disordered internal affairs of the provinces. The sole

---

* Strada, *ubi sup.* Meteren. † Bor., book 12, p, 926.
‡ Hoofd, book 13, p. 581. § Bor., book 12, p. 942, *seq.*
‖ Ibid., p. 987. Hoofd, book 13, p. 584.

point of union was a hatred of the Spaniard; in all else the heterogeneous masses were at odds; city ranged against city, sect raving against sect, anarchy everywhere rampant. The religious quarrel was especially pronounced. Where the Romanists were a majority, they meted and peeled those of the Protestant faith; where the reformed were all-powerful, they barred the papists from their churches and razed convents.

As a panacea for these ills, the prince got the states-general to proclaim "a religious peace," whereby toleration was made the law of the land.* This measure, meant to promote harmony, merely stirred a wilder chaos; for parchment law is worse than useless, unless supported by public opinion. There was at this time no party in the states sufficiently enlightened to observe the golden rule of agreement in disagreement; William alone had mounted to that Christian height. Even St. Aldegonde favored disfranchising the papists, and also the Anabaptists, whom Orange had admitted to citizenship in Holland.† "To all my dissenting arrows," wrote that able diplomat, "the prince opposed this shield of tolerance."‡ Peter Dathenus, one of the foremost of the reformed divines, on this very account denounced William as a godless man, shrieking from the pulpit, "The prince cares nothing for religion."§ And now John Nassau, though favoring a religious peace in the papist

---

* Meteren, book 8, folio 142. Bor., *ubi sup.*, p. 974, *seq.*
† Brandt, vol. 1, p. 330, *seq.*   ‡ Ibid. p. 332.   § Ibid., vol 1.

provinces, could see no reason for extending it into the Protestant states. The reformers everywhere were much of this opinion, scouting the new law, and in its very face expelling swarms of priests and monks from Ghent, Bruges, Ypres, and Antwerp.*
The Romanists were even more violent in their opposition to the toleration, going so far as to withhold their contributions from the necessitous military chest.†

At this juncture Prince John Casimir, an ardent German Protestant, entered the Netherlands at the head of seven thousand horse and eight thousand foot, Elizabeth's promised contingent.‡ His presence added fresh fuel to the flame. The Walloon regiments in the patriot service broke into open mutiny, assuming the name of "Malcontents;" and as a foil to the count palatine, the states of Hainault, Artois, and French Flanders, unanimously papist, formally invited their co-religionist, the duke d'Alençon, to come to their assistance.§ The states-general, hoping thereby to placate the Walloons, sanctioned this action, invested D'Alençon with the sounding title of "Protector of the liberties of the Low Countries," and welcomed the force, twelve thousand strong, which he led in, with assumed cordiality.‖

* Meteren, book 8, folio 152. Bor., De Thou, et al.
† De Thou, lib. 57, cap. 15. Strada, tom. 4.
‡ Meteren, ubi sup., folio 155. Hoofd, book 13, p. 584.
§ De Thou, ubi sup. Vandervynckt.
‖ De Thou, ubi sup. Vandervynckt. Compare Motley, vol. 3, pp. 337, 341.

Casimir, jealous of D'Alençon, fell back on Ghent, and ignoring the Spaniard, made common cause with the turbulent Ghentese against the Walloons. D'Alençon halted in Hainault and rested on his arms, afraid to move. This then was the situation—an army of forty thousand men, ill-paid and disorganized, commanded by three generals of equal authority, of different nations, and of clashing interests: Casimir, idle in Ghent; D'Alençon, at a stand-still on the southern frontier; Bossu, entrenched at Rymenant; the Spaniard watchful at Namûr; distrust and dissension in all the camps, and worse still, rampant among the masses.*

This poise of affairs was too abnormal to last. On the 1st of October, 1578, Don John of Austria, after a week's sickness, died at Namûr,† from mortification at his loss of *prestige*,‡ as some said, but according to others, poisoned by Philip's order, who thus rid himself of a brother who stood too near the throne.§ A little later in the autumn, D'Alençon disbanded his levies, and returned in disgust to Paris.‖ Soon afterwards Casimir too, after marching up the hill, marched down again, like the French king in the nursery-ballad, and repaired to England to explain his conduct to the maiden queen.¶

These events were the signal for new complica-

---

* Davies, vol. 2, p. 70, *seq:* Bor., Meteren.
† Strada, tom. 5, p. 16.   ‡ Bor., Hoofd, Meteren.
§ Bentivoglio, Herrera, Cabrera, *et alii.*
‖ Bor., book 12, p. 12.   ¶ Ibid., book 13, p. 13, *seq.*

tions.　The Walloon provinces—French Flanders, Hainault, Artois, Arras, Lisle, Douay—deserted by D'Alençon, and now wholly alienated by differences of faith from the patriot cause, formed a confederacy with each other, pledging themselves to stand by the king, to adhere to holy church, and to resist the religious peace.*　Farnese, who had succeeded Don John in the nominal governor-generalship of the Netherlands, hastened to take advantage of the schism.　As Philip of Macedon had refuted the wisdom of Athens with golden syllogisms, thereby confounding her statesmen, striking her orators dumb, and finally arguing the " fierce democracie" out of their liberty, so the wily Italian ere long effected a reconciliation between these backsliders and Madrid, with ducat-reasons.†　For what is it that Addison says?　" A man who is furnished with arguments from the mint will convince his antagonists much sooner than one who draws them from philosophy."

This defection rang the death-knell of the *entente cordiale*.　What human wit could do, William had done, to mould irreconcilable elements into concord. The moderation, the prudence, the skill, the self-abnegation of his rule—not even Romanist telescopes could discern a spot on the disc of the record.　But the odds were too great.　A love of the fatherland was the single point of adhesion between the congeries of states.　In all else, not the waves of the sea were more inconstant, not Euripus was

---

* Bor., book 13, p. 10.　　　† Motley, vol. 3, p. 396, *seq.*

more uncertain. Upon this *point d'appui* the prince
had seized, hoping that the sentiment of nationality
might be potent enough to charm down discord,
subordinate the quarrel of creeds, and transform
the dependencies of a distant despotism into self-
governing republics. For a space, William was
successful. Under the stimulus of passionate resentment, the provinces seemed drawn irresistibly
towards union—as we are told that bystanders were
drawn by the contagion of passion to join in the
wild dances of the Grecian Mænads. But it was
impossible that permanent crystallization should
take place where so strong a dissolvent as Romanism existed. In the end, bigotry proved stronger
than patriotism, and now nothing remained of the
various attempts at union save the memory and a
few despised statutes—the ghost of pacification
walking after the death of the body.

As an offset to this Belgic secession, William
turned to the north, and began to spin the web of a
new confederacy. It had long been a favorite project of his to unify the states of Holland, Zealand,
Friesland, Gröningen, Overyssel, Utrecht, and Guelderland—seven provinces substantially homogene-
ous, similar in race, language, customs, habits, interest, preëxisting incitements to brotherhood. The
old alliance between Holland and Zealand supplied
a nucleus. The imperilled pacification of Ghent
formed a pretext. So the prince put the diplomats
to work. They hunted up a musty pact between
Holland and Utrecht, which bore the date of 1534,

cleaned it of cobwebs, and declared it still binding.*
Then Guelderland was taken in hand. As this province commanded the entrance of four of the chiefest
of the Netherland rivers—the Rhine, the Waal, the
Meuse, the Yssel—and formed a frontier to the projected commonwealth, its securing was of vital importance ;† otherwise, Friesland, Gröningen, and
Overyssel might reluct. After some manœuvring, this
was achieved. Then, on the 23d of January, 1579,
the deputies of the respective states met at Utrecht,
and solemnly cemented the immortal union, which
bore the name of that famous town, basing it upon
these four broad principles : the perpetual alliance
of the seven provinces—one state against all foes,
but each in its internal government independent of
the rest; the common expense to be met by taxes
laid upon the common purse; local disputes to be
adjudicated by the ordinary tribunals, interprovincial quarrels by the states-general; and toleration
in religious differences, Protestant and Romanist
alike free to worship God each at his chosen altar.‡
    Such, briefly sketched, was the union of Utrecht.
Into its nice checks and balances we need not go.
Suffice it to say that, whether we consider the critical juncture at which it was effected, or the results
with which it was pregnant, it may be regarded as
a masterpiece of enlightened and successful statesmanship. By it, a moiety of the Netherlands rescued their existence from impending death. By it,

---

* Bor., book 10, p. 893, *seq.*   † Davies, vol. 2, p. 74.
‡ See the Articles of Union in Bor., book 13, pp. 26–30.

the Dutch Republic came into being—a union closer
than the Swiss confederacy, less democratic than
the Achaian league; like the United States, a plural unit.

Above all, this act thenceforth guaranteed the
Reformation in the United Provinces; made it an
accomplished fact; provided the hunted Bible with
an asylum in continental Europe; bade it, like the
angel in the apocalypse, go forth with bow and
crown, conquering and to conquer.

By the union of Utrecht, Philip II. received
notice that even his nominal sovereignty was abolished in the maritime provinces. Furious thereat,
he commanded Farnese to take the field and press
the war with all possible rigor. The consummate
soldier hastened to obey; and fighting simultaneously with a sword of gold and a sword of steel—
both alike sharp in his hands—he made brave progress. Maestricht was escaladed and sacked; Mechlin and Bois-le-Duc bowed anew to take the Spanish yoke.

In March, 1579, a new attempt was made to
effect a reconciliation between the provinces and
his majesty. The diplomats met at Cologne, and
held a prolonged council, which resulted in nothing save an immense bill of expenses. The king
was resolute in demanding the extirpation of Protestantism; the states were determined in requiring
toleration. Late in the year, the conference broke
up amid mutual curses.

The new year was inaugurated by the renunciation of the sovereignty of Spain by the states-general of the Netherlands.   The archduke Mathius was politely sent back to Germany, and the duke D'Alençon was voted into the sovereignty, but on such terms as guaranteed the virtual independence of the land.   D'Alençon's rule was neither long nor prosperous.   Disgusted by the narrow boundaries set to his authority, he early began to scheme for an absolute sceptre.   On the ceremony of his installation, Orange had placed the ducal mantle upon his shoulders.   "Fasten it well, prince," said the Frenchman, in a stage *aside*, "so that they can't take it off again."   He was soon to learn that he asked an impossibility.   After an attempt to capture Antwerp in the interest of his idea, which failed, he was compelled to retire into France, where he shortly died.   The provinces at once resumed their sovereignty, and in 1583, decided to vest the supreme power in the prince of Orange.

Some years before, Philip had formally banned William, set a price upon his head, and invoked the stiletto of the bravo to abridge his life.   Orange replied by publishing his famous "apology"—a paper which recites the story of his contest with Spain, and forms one of the grandest vindications ever penned.   Nevertheless the royal act of outlawry was to bear bitter fruit.   Already repeated attempts had been made to assassinate the illustrious offender, one of which wellnigh proved fatal.   On the 10th of July, 1584, the sands in his glass of

life ran out—not naturally, but by the breaking of
the glass. A wretch named Balthazar Gerard, who
had taken service with him for that purpose, shot
the liberator as he left the dining-room of his palace at Delft. Falling into the arms of an attendant, he cried faintly in French, "God pity me! I
am sadly wounded. God have mercy on my soul,
and on this unhappy nation." Soon after he expired, and "flights of angels sang him to his rest."

It were superfluous to pronounce the eulogy of
such a man—his whole life was a panegyric. Certainly history presents no better specimen of disin-
terested and entire manhood. Humanity is richer
for his living: the world is heir to the inheritance
of his example.

With the fall of Orange, a new epoch opened
for the Netherlands. The animation of the drama
seems suspended, for the central hero dies out of it.
A new generation appear upon the stage; and, as
Grattan has it, "the stirring impulse of slavery
breaking its chains yields to the colder inspiration
of independence maintaining its rights."

But the war ceased not. Farnese fought now
with fresh enthusiasm; and the people, greater
than any individual, rallied to defend what had
been thus far achieved. Prince Maurice of Nassau,
a boy of eighteen, was inducted into the stadtholderate just vacated by his father's death; and this
was the commencement of his long, stirring, and
successful career.

It was Farnese's plan to separate those provin-

ces tied together by the union of Utrecht from the
Belgic states; and in this he was slowly succeeding.
Ypres, Termonde, Ghent, Brussels, succumbed, one
after another, ere William had been in the grave a
twelvemonth; and when, in 1585, Antwerp was
taken by the Spaniard after one of the most famous
sieges in military history, the desired separation
was substantially secured—the Belgic and the
Dutch were to be thenceforth alien and often inim-
ical nationalities.

Leaving the reconquered states of southern
Netherlands, forlorn beyond description, the genius
of independence retired to the nascent republic in
the north; and preferring destruction rather than
submission, continued to resist, bulwarked by the
Dutch morasses, bucklered by the unconquerable
will of a people set "never to submit nor yield."

From the year 1585 onward to the close of the
sixteenth century, the history of the Low Countries
is a stirring record of battle and siege and diplomatic *ruse*, in which success inclined now to one
side, now to the other, though the united provinces
made perceptible progress towards independence
and the position of a first-rate power. On the sea
they were without a rival; in Europe alone they
had twelve hundred merchant ships, manned by
seventy thousand sailors, constantly employed. Two
thousand vessels were annually built; and in the
year 1598, eighty ships sailed from their ports for
America and the Indies. They carried on an active
trade on the coast of Guinea, whence large quanti-

ties of gold-dust were brought; and, indeed, all quarters of the globe yielded them the reward of their commercial industry, skill, and daring. At this time, too, England was the close ally of the Dutch, making common cause against the Spaniard; while Maurice of Nassau led the trained cohorts of the republic from victory to victory.

In September, 1598, Philip II. died, bequeathing to his successor the legacy of the Dutch war. But upon his demise, Belgium was erected into an independent sovereignty, under Philip's daughter, the infanta Isabella, and her husband, Albert of Austria. In 1609 a truce for twelve years was signed between Spain and the republic at Antwerp, and the Dutch made use of this interval of peace to recuperate their resources, renew their alliances with foreign powers, and spread the expanding interests of their commercial enterprise. It was at this time that the famous East India Company was organized—a company which carried the name and fame of the republic to the remotest corners of the earth, and annexed continents as coffers wherein to garner honest gains. It was at this time too that the synod of Dort was held, which settled the ecclesiastical affairs of Holland; that the Pilgrim Fathers of New England were domesticated at Leyden; and that the internal religious dissensions began which were one day to work the ruin of the commonwealth.

In 1621 war with Spain was renewed; and just before the thirty years' war in Germany began, so

that the whole continent was now ablaze. A dance
of death which lasted a quarter of a century ensued.
And ere peace came in continental Europe, England
was rent by the civil war of the Roundheads and
the Cavaliers.

It was not until 1648 that peace was declared
between Spain and Holland; but at that date, after
a conflict of eighty years, the Spaniard acknowledged the independence of the Dutch, and by the
treaty of Munster definitively yielded all claim upon
the sovereignty of the republic. A few months
later the peace of Westphalia was signed, and Europe at large was pacified.

A brilliant epoch succeeded for Holland. In
wealth, in commerce, in navigation, in letters, in
painting, the Dutch were preëminent. Their trading companies outranked all rivals—were alike
puissant in the orient and in the occident. Their
navy, officered by Van Tromp and De Ruyter,
maintained the dominion of the sea; and headed
by William of Orange, afterwards William III. of
England, the republic actually humbled the haughty
power of Louis XIV.

But after a hundred years of such supremacy,
internal religious conflicts began to undermine this
prosperity—a commonwealth impregnable to outward attack, consolidated in war, born of battle,
gradually crumbled away self-consumed. Calvinists on one side, Arminians on the other, contended
to their mutual undoing; and when, in 1793, the
republican army of France swept into the Nether-

lands, the ancient liberties of the country fell prostrate before the invasion. The Batavian republic was formed by foreign dictation; and from this time till the banishment of Napoleon to Elba, Holland was dragged an unwilling victim in French chains. For, to quote the striking language of Lafayette, "the tyranny of 1793 was no more a republic than the massacre of St. Bartholomew was a religion."

After the battle of Waterloo, the Netherlands were reconstructed by the allies, Belgium and Holland being united in one kingdom. It was, perhaps, a well-meant arrangement, but it was short-sighted; for the Dutch and the Belgians, now widely separated in the lapse of time, dissimilar in language, customs, and religion, soon quarrelled; and, in 1830, the heterogeneous kingdom fell apart, Holland becoming a constitutional monarchy, as it is in our day.

And now, familiar with the facts, with our eyes upon the record, shall we marvel that Holland, cradled in the morasses—bred up between two grave and holy nurses, the doctrine and discipline of the gospel—went on from success to success, invincible alike on land and sea, belting the globe with its dependencies, and reaping a hundred-fold even in material fields, in return for the precious seeds of its losses? That blessing which God breathed over the tents of Jacob through the reluctant lips of the old prophet, descended also upon this Israel: "Blessed is he that blesseth thee, and cursed is he that curseth thee."

BIBLE HELPS.

PUBLISHED BY THE AMERICAN TRACT SOCIETY,

150 NASSAU-STREET, NEW YORK.

QUARTO BIBLE. A new edition of the FAMILY BIBLE, with Notes, Instructions, References, Maps, Tables, and Family Record; on fine paper, and substantially bound; an elegant volume for the household, and unsurpassed in value for general use. Sheep, $12; sheep gilt, $14; morocco antique, $20; morocco extra, $21.

FAMILY BIBLE WITH NOTES, ETC. As above, super-royal octavo. One volume sheep, $6; gilt, $7 50; gilt sides, $8; morocco gilt, $11; antique, $12. In a set of three volumes, cloth, $6; gilt, $7 50; sheep, $8; morocco, $13.

THE POCKET BIBLE. With Notes. etc., as above, large 18mo. In a set of 3 volumes, cloth, $3; sheep, $4 75. The OLD TESTAMENT in 2 volumes; cloth, $2 25; sheep, $3 50.

NEW TESTAMENT AND PSALMS. Notes, Maps, etc., super-royal octavo. A handsome volume; cloth, $1 75; gt., $2 25.

POCKET TESTAMENT. As above, in a large 18mo form, for the use of young people, Sabbath-schools, travellers, etc.; cloth, 90 cts.; gilt, $1 20; sheep, $1 30.

DICTIONARY OF THE HOLY BIBLE. The most popular and excellent book of the kind, invaluable for general use in the study of the Scriptures. 250 engravings, 5 maps, and chronological and other tables. Large 12mo. Price, $1 50 cloth; $2 gilt; $2 sheep; $2 50 half bound morocco, red edges; $3 50 morocco.

BIBLE ATLAS AND GAZETTEER. Super-royal octavo. Of great value to the Bible student. $1.

CRUDEN'S CONDENSED CONCORDANCE. Valuable for ministers, teachers, and families, 8vo. $1 50; sheep, $2.

LOCKE'S COMMONPLACE BOOK TO THE HOLY BIBLE. For the study table, and the Christian library, 8vo. $1 25.

COMPANION TO THE BIBLE. By Rev. E. P. Barrows, D. D. Part I. The Evidences of Revealed Religion. Large 12mo; paper, 40 cts.

BIBLE TEXT-BOOK. With colored Maps, Index, and Tables. 40 cts.

THE BIBLE READER'S HELP. Very helpful for Sabbath-schools. 35 cts.

YOUTH'S BIBLE STUDIES. Complete in six parts. 175 engravings. In a set, with case. $2 50.

GALLAUDET'S YOUTH'S SCRIPTURE BIOGRAPHY. Finely illustrated. Eleven volumes in a case. $4 50.

AMERICAN TRACT SOCIETY, 150 Nassau-street, NEW YORK; 28 and 40 Cornhill, BOSTON; and in other principal cities and towns.

CPSIA information can be obtained
at www.ICGtesting.com
Printed in the USA
BVOW06*1047011117
499253BV00010B/237/P